# The Book of the Warships

*(The Western Region D600/D800/D833 Class 41/42/43 diesel-hydraulics)*

**By John Jennison**

**In association with Mark Alden and Martin Street of the Diesel Traction Group**

**Irwell Press Ltd.**

Copyright IRWELL PRESS LIMITED
ISBN 978-1-906919-11-5

# ACKNOWLEDGEMENTS

In the second issue of *British Railways Illustrated*, published in December 1991, the first article in the *Diesel Dawn* series observed 'No group of diesels perhaps caught the imagination like the hydraulics; they were Swindon inspired for a start, they were wreathed in that *if only* mystique and they looked very fine, to boot'. Not a bad summary to introduce this, the second Irwell Press book devoted to a class of diesel locomotives, and plenty to live up to.

As with the *Book of the Deltics* we are hoping to produce a *Photographic Accompaniment* entirely in colour, to utilise some of the excellent new colour material we have unearthed.

I have tried to avoid, as far as possible, repetition to no good effect of what has previously been written. I have, however, quoted extensively from the railway and professional press of the 1950s and 1960s because this provides a contemporary picture of the battle to build the hydraulics as well as an insight into their first few years of operation. I have been fortunate to obtain the views of some of the men who were involved in the operation of the fleet in the workshops and depots, and their recollections provide another perspective on the Warship story. My thanks here go to Alan Wild, John Savage, Jeremy Clarke and Alec Morrison for digging deep into their memory banks.

The main sources I have drawn on are BR and NBL brochures, training guides and drivers' manuals, the locomotive maintenance files, material held in the National Railway Museum and the National Archives, and technical papers published by the Institution of Locomotive Engineers. Where appropriate, I have included extracts from these documents so the reader can read what was written in the sometimes formal, but authentic language of the time.

As ever, good photographs are essential to tell the story and again I have tried to use as many previously unpublished, quality photographs as I could beg, borrow or otherwise scrounge to accompany the text. I would record my thanks especially to Paul Chancellor, Peter Groom, Michael Mensing, Norman Preedy, Rail-Online and The Transport Treasury for the use of their excellent pictures.

Finally, and in this case it is definitely last but not least, I could not have produced this book without the help of Mark Alden and Martin Street of the *Diesel Traction Group*, which owns one of the two preserved Warships. Between them, these two gentlemen have probably unearthed and analysed everything which will ever be found about the operation, workings and details of the Class. I can only hope that the results presented here do justice to their many years of dedicated study.

First published in the United Kingdom in 2009
by Irwell Press Limited, 59A, High Street, Clophill,
Bedfordshire MK45 4BE
Printed by Konway Press

# Contents



# References

As with any book of this nature reference has been made to other published works. I have found the following particularly useful:


| Name | Details |
|---|---|
| *Diesel-Hydraulic Locomotives of the Western Region* | Brian Webb; David & Charles, 1975 (ISBN 0-7153-6769-2) |
| *The Great Western Railway Gas Turbines - A Myth Exposed* | Kevin Robertson; Sutton Publishing, 1989 (ISBN 0-86299-541-8) |
| *The Western's Hydraulics* | J Lewis, Book Law Publications, 2006 (ISBN 1-901945-54-5) |
| *The Swindon-built Diesel-hydraulic Locomotive* | GE Scholes - paper to The Institution of Locomotive Engineers 17/11/59 |
| *Dieselisation - Problems, Prospects and Progress* | RA Smeddle - BR (WR) London Lecture and Debating Society, 19/02/59 |
| *Dieselisation - Planning and Progress* | FD Pattisson - BR (WR) London Lecture and Debating Society, 02/03/61 |
| *Some Design Problems of Diesel Locomotives* | SO Ell - paper to The Institution of Locomotive Engineers, 12/12/66 |
| *Works Maintenance of Mechanical and hydraulic transmission* | AAW Loveday - paper to Locomotive & Allied Manufacturers' Association of Great Britain 1970 Diesel Motive Power Course |
| *The Decline and Fall of the North British Locomotive Company, 1940-62: Technological and Financial Mismanagement or Institutional Failure?* | AIM Fleming, S McKinstry, K Wallace, January 2000 |


I have also consulted magazines including *The Railway Gazette, Diesel Railway Traction, The Railway Magazine, Railway World, Trains Illustrated, Modern Railways, SLS Journal, The Railway Observer, Traction* and the *Western Region Diesel-hydraulic Locomotives* website (www.WRDHL.co.uk*). The Diesel Traction Group* is to be found at www.westernchampion.co.uk.

# THE DIESEL-HYDRAULIC TRANSMISSION

**The booklet which was produced for the launch of the D600s provides a good introduction to the subject:**

*A special feature of the main line diesel traction scheme in the Western Region is the decision to employ diesel-hydraulic transmission. Although the diesel engine is very efficient, its characteristics (which are not unlike those of a motor-car engine) do not make it suitable for direct drive from the crankshaft to the driving-axle. It is therefore necessary to interpose an intermediate transmission which will convert the high-speed low-torque characteristics of the diesel engine into effective power at the axle. In the smaller forms of diesel locomotives, such as shunting units of up to about 200-300 h.p., it is usual to employ purely mechanical transmission involving an orthodox gearbox with power-operated change and some form of clutch—although even in this restricted field there is now a definite tendency towards a more flexible type of transmission. In the higher power-ranges, the purely mechanical form of transmission is not so suitable because of the heavy loads involved when starting a train, and the alternatives are either to use the diesel engines to generate electricity for driving the axles, or to employ a special form of flexible transmission. To derive full advantage from the diesel engine such form of transmission must be capable (as is electric traction) of affording infinitely variable conversion and effective control over the whole range of power output. In the diesel-hydraulic locomotive, the transmission consists of an oil-filled torque converter interposed between the crankshaft of the diesel engine and the gearbox (if fitted), or, alternatively, two or more converters are used instead of a gearbox. The torque converter comprises three basic parts: the centrifugal pump, or impeller, driven by the engine; the turbine or output member, fixed to the output shaft which drives the wheels through gearing; and the fixed guide wheel or stator; all mounted co-axially, and contained in an oil-filled casing.*

*The input (engine) shaft turns the impeller whose blades force the oil (by centrifugal force) on to the blades of the turbine (fixed to the output-shaft) imparting a torque which makes it rotate. The oil then passes to the vanes of the fixed guide wheel which divert it back to the impeller blades. The oil is continually circulating while the torque converter is in use. The converter is so designed that the torque transmitted to the turbine rises as the turbine speed drops. Hence the torque converter is ideally suited to the well-known locomotive requirement that the lower the speed the greater must be the pulling power. It also provides over the whole range of engine power a smooth, shock-free drive between the engine and the locomotive wheels.*

**Two different types of transmission were used in the Warships: those built by North British employed the Voith system whereas Swindon used the Mekydro type. The D600s had the L306r model and the D833s an upgraded version, the LT306r, both of which used three converters in conjunction with gear ratios to drive the output shaft. They had no fluid couplings and the change in speed was automatic through the filling and emptying of each oil circuit according to the relative speeds of the diesel engine and the locomotive. The emptying and filling was concurrent which meant that during the change there was only an insignificant drop in tractive effort lasting only a fraction of a second.**

**The Mekydro used only a single converter with four speed-change gears. The control gave automatic change whenever conditions of track speed required. At each change the converter, which remained full, was momentarily disengaged axially. The practical operation was due to the Maybach over-running claw clutch with automatic change, which had been invented in the 1920s for use in automobiles, and was developed significantly during World War II to absorb 1000hp. Unlike the Voith system, there was a complete break in tractive effort at each gear change, though normally this only lasted for a fraction of a second.**

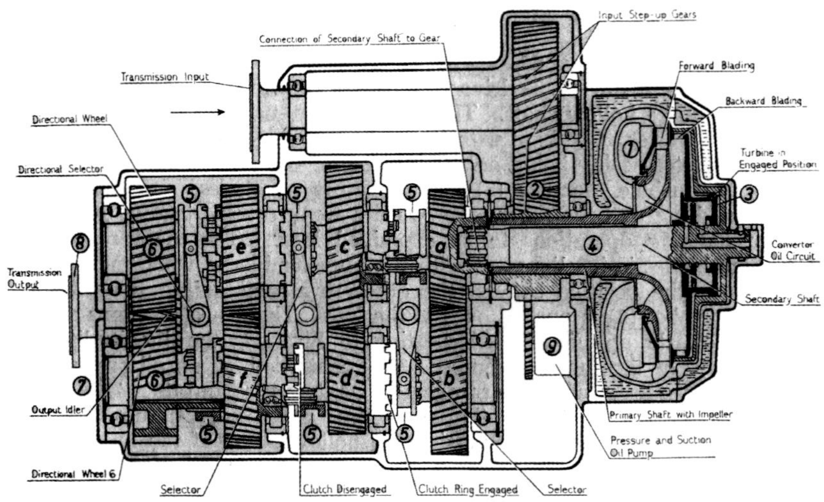


DIAGRAM OF MEKYDRO TRANSMISSION

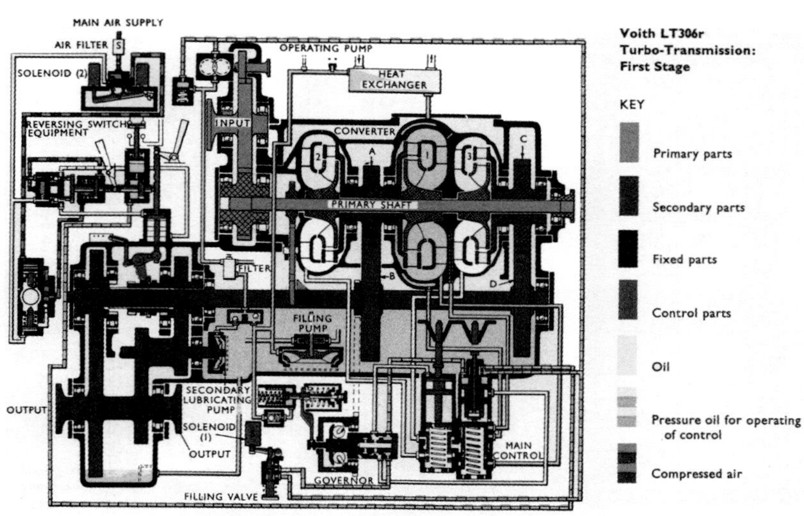


*Top.* The Mekydro transmission.

*Above.* Voith LT306r transmission in the first stage of operation.

# Chapter 1
# WHY HYDRAULICS?

R A Smeddle, the WR Chief Mechanical & Electrical Engineer, explained to the BR (WR) London Lecture and Debating Society in February 1959: *Whilst in the early days of modernisation the tendency generally on British Railways was to develop designs for Diesel-Electric Locomotives, the Western Region Management was considering the possible advantage of the hydraulic transmission, and it was decided, with the concurrence of the British Transport Commission, that this Region should, in fact, take the initiative in exploring the possibilities in this field.*

Why did the Western Region build diesels with hydraulic transmissions when the rest of British Railways opted for diesel-electrics for their first locomotives built under the 1955 BR Modernisation Plan? The answer probably lies somewhere between the urban myths of GWR independence continuing post-1948, the rational case put forward by the WR management and the loose control exerted from BTC headquarters in the early years of BR. What is certain is that the choice was heavily influenced by developments in Germany in the early 1950s, building on the work started there in the 1930s.

**The legacy of the GWR**

Shortly after the end of the Second World War the GWR started looking at alternatives to the steam locomotive for main line operation. Unlike the LMS and SR who ordered medium speed diesel-electric prototypes, it decided to investigate the possibility of using gas turbine propulsion. As early as February 1946 it had reached a verbal agreement with Metropolitan Vickers to share the costs of developing a prototype locomotive. The initiative was announced at the shareholder's AGM in March and the *Swindon Evening Advertiser* reported it under the headline 'Swindon to build Jet Propelled Locos'.

In June 1946 FW Hawksworth, the Chief Mechanical Engineer, went to Switzerland to the International Railway Congress meeting and whilst there saw the first gas turbine application in rail use, which had been operating for the previous six years. Shortly afterwards a gas turbine was ordered by the GWR from Brown-Boveri, the Swiss firm who had developed this prototype, at a cost of £99,000. By September terms had also been finalised with Metropolitan Vickers to design and construct a British gas turbine, with the construction costs borne equally between the two companies.

The Brown-Boveri locomotive, numbered 18000, which had a continuously rated tractive effort of 12,400lb and produced 2,500hp, arrived in England in February 1950. The British-built locomotive, numbered 18100, more powerful at 3,000hp with a continuously rated tractive effort of 30,000lb, was not delivered to Swindon until December 1951 and was officially unveiled at the end of January 1952.

Christian Barman, later to become BTC Chief Publicity Officer and executive member of the BR Design Panel, produced a publicity booklet for the GWR in 1947, *'Next Station - a railway plans for the future'*, which shows what the GWR management was intending: *The Great Western is determined to press forward the completion of these locomotives because it sees the possibility of a brilliant future for the new method of propulsion. One reason for this belief is that the output of power, both in relation to the weight of the engine and in relation to the fuel consumed, compares very favourably with that of the traditional piston engine.*

Yet a further reason for the Railway's preoccupation is a more interesting one:

*The Great Western intends to maintain its position of leadership in the application of new forms of energy to railway traction. In a long view, it is possible that the gas turbine locomotives may prove to have been chiefly significant as the forerunner of even greater and more exciting Great Western locomotives to come.*

Sadly the optimism proved unfounded: 18100 was an unmitigated disaster and was returned to Metropolitan Vickers in December 1953 with BR's 50% share having cost it over £170,000. In the eighteen months from its hand-over to the Motive Power Department in April 1952 to November 1953 it was in use for only 232 days and covered approximately 102,000 miles. Among the many problems were cracks in the bogie main frame plates, electrical flash-overs, turbine failures and excessive fuel consumption.

18000 fared better, covering 85,000 miles at an average availability of 58% between May 1950 and April 1952. Although it was out of use for the first half of 1953 and for the whole of 1956, it ran around 350,000 miles before its eventual withdrawal in September 1959 (compared with a likely mileage of 480,000 miles for a 'Castle' 4-6-0 over the same time). By this time, events had overtaken it with full-scale dieselisation well under way, although its overall performance was creditable for a very experimental prototype machine.

It may be, however, that the biggest legacy from the two prototypes was their influence in the decision by WR management to choose diesel-hydraulic locomotives with their high power-to-weight ratio in preference to diesel-electrics when implementing the 1955 Modernisation Plan.

**Pre-war development of the diesel-hydraulic**

Pre-war Germany led the way in the development of hydraulic transmissions, based on the pre-1914 inventions of the German engineer Hermann Föttinger, coupled with quick-running diesel engines. In 1930 Maybach produced its first quick-running engine, a 12-cylinder V lightweight, and engines of a similar type rated at 410bhp were used in the Flying Hamburger streamlined diesel sets. Two other German manufacturers, Daimler-Benz and M.A.N., followed suit in the next few years with their own quick-running engines which were installed in railcars, Maybach retaining their lead in engines above 300bhp. Initially the railcars had mechanical transmission but from 1935 onwards Voith hydraulic drive was employed. Another advance was the development of the 'Reichsbahn boxer motor' which was produced by four different manufacturers yet was fully interchangeable because of the mountings and connecting pipes, a principle which would be used in the 1950s.

By 1938 Maybach had achieved 650bhp by the use of pressure charging in a batch of three car diesel-electric sets. The development work was not confined to railcars and in 1935 Krauss-Maffei built a 1-C-1 diesel-hydraulic with a M.A.N. 1400bhp slow-speed engine driving through a Voith transmission – this drive remained for over 20 years the highest output hydraulic transmission in railway use. A year later another diesel-hydraulic, latter classified as the V36, appeared in the form of a 42 ton three axle jackshaft drive shunter with a Deutz four-stroke 360bhp engine and Voith L.37 drive. By the outbreak of war around thirty of these were in service, and many more were built during the war years.

The final pre-war development was the Mekydro transmission which evolved because Maybach wanted to proceed with a dis-engageable, permanently-filled converter and Voith, who they had been collaborating with on transmissions, did not wish to depart from the Föttinger emptying-and-filling principle.

**Brown-Boveri gas turbine 18000 arrives at Paddington on 5 July 1955. The GWR chose to build its two gas turbine prototypes instead of opting for diesel-electrics – perhaps a sign of things to come? (www.rail-online.co.uk)**

**Post-war Germany**

During the war German locomotive production was almost entirely steam, with the exception of the V36s and small *kleinlokomotiven* of around 110bhp, although a prototype four-axle development of the V36 producing 550bhp was built. Unsurprisingly, the first few peacetime years saw little development, which was restricted to the re-engining of pre-war railcars and the introduction of a series of lightweight railbuses. It was 1952 before there was a significant new diesel; this took the form of a three car diesel-hydraulic streamlined train, the VF.08, powered by Maybach 800bhp MD engines, but interchangeable with M.A.N. and Daimler-Benz engines, and employing both Voith and Mekydro transmissions. This marked the first implementation of the German decision to stop using electric transmission for all new construction.

Further diesel-hydraulic sets appeared over the following years but the Deutsche Bundesbahn ended its concentration on these *schnelltriebwagen* for main line passenger traffic in April 1952 when the V80 800bhp B-B was introduced. These locomotives were prototypes to test various design ideas which had matured in the years 1949-50, principally around the pivotless bogie and full cardan shaft drive from one transmission to four axles and the desire to achieve high power-to-weight ratios. Only ten were built and although they naturally suffered from inevitable teething problems, these were overcome within 2-3 years and they settled down to intensive use, mainly on push-pull trains averaging around 75,000 miles a year despite a reasonably high proportion of heavy shunting work.

**The V200s**

The V80 was the forerunner of the twin-engine, 2000bhp V200 B-B, the first of which was completed in May 1953. Five units were built by Krauss-Maffei for evaluation purposes and they were designed to use any of three engine types, from Maybach, Daimler-Benz and M.A.N. and two transmission types, Voith and Mekydro. These were all fully inter-changeable and it was not unknown for a locomotive to be running with two different makes of engine and two different transmissions.

The V200s entered service from February 1954 onwards and up to August 1955 the five locomotives had already accumulated almost 800,000 miles. They were followed by a production series of fifty delivered between late-1956 and mid-1957. These used either two Maybach or two Daimler-Benz engines set to produce 1,100bhp, thereby maintaining the original power-weight ratio of the prototypes which were six to ten tons lighter, depending on which engine/gearbox combination was installed. A further 31 locomotives were built by Krauss-Maffei in 1959, and a 2,700bhp version, the V200.1 appeared in 1962 – a batch of fifty using Daimler-Benz engines with Mekydro transmissions.

**The 1955 Modernisation Plan and Dieselisation**

In January 1955 the BTC published its report titled *Modernisation and Re-equipment of British Railways* (colloquially known as the Modernisation Plan). It had four objectives, the second of which was 'steam must be replaced as a form of motive power, electric or diesel traction being rapidly introduced' and the fourth was 'Continuous brakes will be fitted to all freight wagons' It aimed to achieve 'as soon as possible a complete changeover from steam to diesel in specified areas. By this means the maximum economies will be obtained ...and it will also be possible to obtain experience of the operating costs of diesel units without mixed working involving two forms of traction'. The Plan said 'on the Western Region it is intended to eliminate all steam working beyond Newton Abbot and also to employ diesel units based in that area for hauling a large proportion of the passenger and freight trains from the West to London and Bristol and back'.

Experience with main line diesel traction in Britain up to this date was extremely limited. Although diesel powered shunting locomotives, first developed by the LMS in the 1930s and followed by the other companies after the war, were beginning to proliferate there were only seven main line diesel locomotives running on British Railways. Of these, only the LMS designed 10000/1 and the SR's 10201-3 could be viewed as having any relevance to the future, the other two being the complicated and unsuccessful 10100, the Fell multiple-engined diesel mechanical experiment and 10800, the LMS 800bhp Bo-Bo prototype built by the North British Locomotive Company which was intended for secondary and branch line services.

Four of the five used the Mark 1 version of the 16 cylinder turbocharged English Electric '16SVT' four-stroke engine which was a direct descendant of the 'K' series used in the diesel shunters. This ran at 750rpm and produced 1,600bhp on 10000/1, increased to 1,750bhp on 10201/2, and powered six nose-suspended, axle hung traction motors. 10203 was delivered in March 1954 and therefore represented the 'state of the diesel-electric art' at the date of the Modernisation Plan; it used the '16SVT' tweaked in its Mark II form to produce 2,000bhp. 10000/1 were Co-Co units weighing over 127 tons; 10201-3 were even heavier than the LMS pair at 135 tons and to carry the additional weight had articulated pony trucks in a 1Co-Co1 wheel arrangement to reduce the axle loading.

**A rational case?**

Much has been written about the Western Region's reluctance to adopt diesel-electrics for main line use; it has even been traced as far back as a January 1946 GWR report rejecting diesel-electrics in favour of gas turbines. Even though the latter were very much early prototypes, they compared favourably with the five diesel-electrics in use up to 1955 and it isn't difficult to see why the hydraulic developments in Germany were of great interest since they exhibited several of the characteristics which had attracted the GWR to the gas turbines. The WR faced an immense task to convince the BTC that they should be allowed to use German technology for the locomotives to be ordered under the Pilot Scheme. This was intended to evaluate diesels before large-scale orders were placed to implement the Modernisation Plan, and the Commission's central mechanical engineers favoured diesel-electrics.

Brian Reed's book *Diesel-Hydraulic Locomotives of the Western Region* describes how the case for the hydraulics was developed by HH Philips, the WR Assistant General Manager, who believed the aims of the Modernisation Plan could only be realised fully by working from fundamental principles, with the fitting of continuous brakes to freight stock accompanying locomotives with high power: weight ratios. He was supported by the WR senior management in the persons of KWC Grand, the Regional General Manager, and RF Hanks, the Regional Chairman, who embraced the principle which said it was much more logical to build a 2,000hp locomotive weighing less than 80 tons using hydraulic transmission rather than a diesel-electric of over 130 tons. They also believed hydraulic transmission was more suited to the haulage of heavy loads on steeply graded lines such as those on its South Devon main line. A further consideration was the lack of depot facilities and workshop skills on the WR to deal with electric transmissions.

In May 1955 the BTC announced the Pilot Scheme for main line diesels. Its purpose, 'before final decisions are taken as to the types required for bulk delivery' was that 'extensive trials' could be made '...on all types of train', and this included eleven diesel-hydraulics. Interestingly, the internal debate at the BTC leaked (it was probably done deliberately) into the public domain as a small-scale outbreak of fighting took place between the hydraulic and the electric 'supporters' in the contemporary railway press. An unnamed 'correspondent' in the August 1955 *Diesel Railway Traction* set out the benefits of the hydraulics under various headings including much high power per ton, better fuel economy and increased reliability. He went much further than this and with a clear dig at the diesel-electric establishment said it was necessary 'to raise the limited outlook and training of departmental and supra-departmental executives to a wider outlook trained in the fundamentals of railway operation and management as a whole, and one not bound up in knowledge and social life, wittingly or unwittingly, with one technical method or another. In other words, men of completely sound and independent judgement on wider problems are needed'. He went on with words which were, with hindsight, quite prophetic: 'In view of (such) experiences, and they are by no means isolated, is it not really diesel-electric locomotive manufacturers who should be on trial, and who should produce evidence, rather than manufacturers or users of something evolved to get over the bad performance of an older drive?' (Think about the Metrovick Co-Bos, the Baby Deltics, and the NBL Types 1 and 2 for starters!)

Having described the characteristics of the German V200s he had no doubts that 'this motive power is an altogether superior traffic machine than the most modern existing British diesel-electric'. He concluded, again with unerring foresight, that: 'Unless there is adoption of the most modern forms of motive power viewing the locomotive as a traffic machine and as an integral part of a railway, and sound judgement applied to the wider questions of operation, Great Britain may find itself saddled with a most expensive main line dieselisation programme for effects which could be obtained without any change at all'.

In the October 1955 *Diesel Railway Traction* the case for the opposition was put forward by H Howard with equal vigour: 'To summarise, the hydraulic transmission may in some cases have an advantage in weight, although this is nothing like as great as an efficient publicity campaign would lead one to believe. In efficiency and in its ability to provide power at the wheel-tread at all speeds, the electrical transmission is, on the whole, markedly superior. As far as reliability is concerned, there is insufficient evidence to draw a conclusion, but on the more complex wheel arrangements hydraulic transmissions appear still to be in the experimental stage, whereas electric transmissions have proved satisfactory on several thousands of locomotives ...the only group of railways which has had extensive experience of both electric and hydraulic transmission appears to have decided that hydraulic or electrical transmissions are suitable for rigid frame locomotives and for simple bogie locomotives of low power and axle load, and that electric transmission is best for powerful locomotives of the bogie type necessary for main line operation'.

**The decision is made**

The Western had fought its corner sufficiently well so that when BR announced the firm orders at the end of 1955 for its diesel Pilot Scheme, based on 171 locomotives in 13 types from six manufacturers, the eleven to be built for it by the North British Locomotive Company (NBL) were to employ hydraulic transmission. However, it had been touch and go: Brian Reed (*op cit*) noted that 'BTC approval of the diesel-hydraulic *idea* was held up until a formal offer had been submitted by NBL'. In fact NBL's licence for Voith transmissions was the only politically acceptable way in which the German technology could be used. NBL had also taken out a licence in 1954 to build M.A.N. engines and these were to be used in the WR locomotives. The WR did though lose out to the BTC central staff engineers who, for the Type 'C' (later Type 4), rejected the lightweight four-axle V200 design which the region wanted and insisted on a six-axle 117 ton locomotive of conventional design.

Behind the scenes the WR had not given up and were determined to get the machine they really wanted. In the summer of 1955 they went directly to Maybach in Friedrichshafen who had supplied both engines and transmissions for the V200, and to Krauss-Maffei who were responsible for the mechanical portions and erected the locomotives, and who held patents for the stressed-skin construction and bogies.

Not surprisingly, the Germans made the right impression on their visitors,

A V200 under construction showing the intricate stressed skin construction which contributed significantly to the low overall weight.

indicating that a scaled-down version of the V200 was practical, and moreover the system of standard, inter-changeable engines and transmissions would enable the WR to apply the hydraulic principle across its whole range of diesel requirements. However there was still the political problem of a foreign supplier to overcome and the Germans proposed a solution whereby Maybach would supply six sets of engine-transmission-cardan shaft-axle drive-control groups for three 2,000bhp locomotives and, if these proved satisfactory, would find a British licensee to manufacture them. Krauss-Maffei was also willing to grant a licence for manufacture to the BTC and provide drawings and the initial expert advice and collaboration.

The door had been opened and three locomotives were added to the Pilot Scheme in January 1956, to be built at Swindon utilising the six Maybach power-transmission-control sets. It was to be opened even wider when the Modernisation Plan was accelerated in 1957, as the Pilot Scheme was overturned and large-scale orders were placed for locomotive types that were still on the drawing board. As part of this, in February 1957 another thirty diesel-hydraulics were ordered from Swindon similar to the three under construction. In view of the urgency the power-transmission-control equipment sets were to be supplied by Maybach.

The publicity department, as always, put its spin on events and in the booklet prepared for the official launch of the five NBL 2,000hp D600s proclaimed:

*A new chapter in the British Railways Modernisation Plan begins with the introduction of the first diesel-hydraulic main line locomotive for service in the Western Region.*

*In pursuance of the British Transport Commission's policy of progressively introducing the latest forms of motive power, giving greater speed, economy and cleanliness, the Western Region are embarking upon an extensive scheme for the complete replacement of steam by diesel traction on the whole of the W.R. lines between Newton Abbot and Penzance, including all freight and passenger services, and, initially, on many of the through trains between Paddington and Bristol and the West of England. This programme involves the replacement of over 200 steam locomotives by about 130 diesel-hydraulic main line locomotives, comprising:-*

*5 of 2,000 h.p. from the North British Locomotive Company.*

*58 of 1,000 h.p. from the North British Locomotive Company.*

*33 of 2,000 h.p. from Swindon Works.*

*34 of 2,000 h.p. for which orders have still to be placed.*

*This is the first application of the diesel-hydraulic principle to main line traction in this country, but locomotives of this type are giving satisfactory service on the German Federal Railways.*

**The first Krauss-Maffei V200 on show at Munich in June 1953 a few weeks after completion.**

*These locomotives are being designed and constructed to the general requirements of the British Transport Commission under the overall direction of Mr. R. C. Bond, Chief Mechanical Engineer, British Railways Central Staff, British Transport Commission. Mr. R. A. Smeddle, Chief Mechanical and Electrical Engineer, Western Region, is responsible for the detailed design and construction of the locomotives to be built at Swindon, and for collaboration with the manufacturers and for inspection of the contract-built units.*

In the best tradition of the GWR, the Western Region had scooped the Eastern Region: D600 was the first type 4 diesel delivered to British Railways, antedating by over two months the first English Electric D200 diesel-electric, which was not officially inspected until 9 April 1958.

# NBL HISTORY

The North British Locomotive Co Ltd (NBL) was formed in 1903 by the amalgamation of Neilson Reid & Co with its principal Glasgow competitors, Sharp, Stewart & Co Ltd, (founded 1828 in Manchester but moved to the works of Clyde Locomotive Co, Springburn, Glasgow, in 1888) and Dubs & Co, founded in 1864.

NBL retained the premises of each of the amalgamated companies, maintaining Neilson, Reid's Hyde Park works and the Atlas works of Sharp, Stewart, both in Springburn, and the Queen's Park works at Polmadie, Glasgow, established by Dubs. It was the biggest locomotive builder in Europe at the time, with 60 acres of works and nearly 8,000 employees and at its peak, production was averaging 447 completed locomotives per year. During the First World War the company produced shells of all sizes, shell forgings, portable pill boxes and sea mines. It also manufactured aeroplanes, trench Howitzer carriages, tanks, military bridges, artificial limbs and machine tools as well as continuing to produce locomotives.

The firm was typical of British capital goods businesses: profiting from economic booms across the pre-World War I years, enduring lower profits in the 1909-14 period, prospering during World War I and slumping after the post-war boom years of 1921-22. It was a victim of the depression years of the 1920s and 1930s, and made losses from 1928 to 1935, although these were reversed from 1936 to 1939.

Up to this point, however, the firm was still regarded as one of the premier locomotive manufacturers in the world and had sold 9,015 locomotives, 1,783 in the UK to all four companies, although its greatest strength was in the export market, and in particular India and South Africa. During World War II NBL produced light tanks and other munitions, and large numbers of locomotives for the Ministry of Supply. Unfortunately for NBL the post-war market for railway locomotives was much more volatile than the one it faced in 1939. This was caused by technological changes associated with the move away from steam traction and, more directly, political changes including the granting of independence to India, which resulted in increasing indigenous manufacture of locomotives.

Once the post-war pent-up demand had been fulfilled, a buyer's market prevailed after about 1951 and overseas NBL found itself tendering against major competitors such as ALCO, LIMA and Baldwin of the USA (especially in India), in South Africa against Henschel of Germany, and with UK rivals such as Beyer Peacock and the Vulcan Foundry, in both South Africa and India. In the home market, NBL's biggest orders were for a total of 290 LNER B1 4-6-0s – but these were to be the company's final major steam orders from the UK, and the last large orders from India and South Africa had been received by the end of 1951.

The company's first significant non-steam order was in 1948 for a batch of 40 electric locomotives for South Africa, with the tractive machinery being supplied by GEC. Delivered in 1952, they gave problems in operation and NBL had to pay compensation to the customer. Thus, when further orders for electrics came up in the middle and late 1950s, they went to Vulcan Foundry, which supplied 160 locomotives with English Electric equipment between 1955 and 1958.

By 1951 NBL was fitting Voith hydraulic transmissions to several ranges of shunters and small mine locomotives it had started to develop from 1946 onwards. The transmissions were manufactured under licence in NBL's Queen's Park works, and the locomotives were powered by bought-in Paxman diesel engines. Most were sold to UK mines and industrial concerns, with a few going overseas.

Orders were also gained for eight main-line diesel-electrics for Ceylon in 1953, with Paxman engines and GEC electrical equipment, and in the same year twenty similar locomotives driven by Paxman engines through Voith transmissions. The prototype for these was the 800hp Bo-Bo diesel-electric with Paxman engine and GEC electrics, numbered 10800, which had been ordered by the LMS in 1947 and delivered in 1950.

In 1954 NBL took out a licence to manufacture the German designed M.A.N. oil engines of medium speed and quick running types from 100 to 2000bhp, but it was the BR Modernisation Plan which was to have the greatest impact on the company. NBL was one of a number of British locomotive builders to gain a share of the Pilot Scheme diesel orders in 1955 and the follow-ons placed in 1957, even before any of the first orders had been delivered. BR placed a final order for 33 further 2200hp diesel-hydraulics in July 1958, but these were to be of the Swindon design, albeit with M.A.N. engines and Voith transmissions used in place of the Maybach/Mekydro combination in the BR-built locomotives.

| No. | Type | Engine/transmission | First loco due to be completed | Actual date into stock | Follow-on orders |
|---|---|---|---|---|---|
| 5 | C | M.A.N. 2000hp hydraulic | Feb 1957 | Jan 1958 | - |
| 6 | B | M.A.N. 1000hp hydraulic | May 1957 | Jan 1959 | 52 |
| 10 | B | M.A.N. 1000hp electric | Nov 1957 | Dec 1958 | 48 |
| 10 | A | Paxman 800hp electric | Aug 1957 | May 1958 | - |

The BTC orders were for power increases of 25 per cent in engine-transmission groups and 250 per cent in locomotive output over anything NBL had built up to that date; moreover NBL had not yet installed any of the M.A.N. engines in its locomotives. It was hardly surprising that delays in delivery occurred, although BR must take some share of the blame for late design and specification changes.

The problems did not stop there: several of the first-built locomotives failed their acceptance tests and had to be returned to NBL; the worst offender was the Paxman Type A D8400 which eventually went into traffic nearly three months after being added to stock. Even when finally put into service they were still causing problems; the diesel-electric Type B D6100s were particularly bad, with many being placed into store for extended periods and later nearly half were re-built with Paxman 'Ventura' engines in an attempt to cure the problems with their M.A.N. engines.

The hydraulics were less spectacular failures and the 2200hp D833 Warships worked alongside their Swindon-built counterparts for almost ten years, before succumbing to the rationalisation of diesel classes under the 1965 Traction Plan. The D600 and D6300 Pilot Scheme locomotives were the first to go in 1967/68 and were quickly followed by the remainder. The last D833 Warships were withdrawn by early October 1971 and both the diesel-electric and diesel-hydraulic Type 2 classes became extinct in 1972.

The main problems undoubtedly arose from the M.A.N. engines and Voith transmissions, and the relationship between NBL and the BTC 'quickly turned sour ... The files are full of internal qualms about inflated prices, late deliveries and technical defects'. Although NBL did not, in the initial stages, have the precision machining skills required for diesel manufacture it appears that some of the problems may have originated with the German designs. In his memoirs, Hugh Fulton, who in 1957 took directorial charge of the diesel facility at Atlas Works, recalled that the M.A.N. engine design was not fully developed for the rating at which it was to run in British Railways service, which resulted in numerous embarrassing modifications at a time when production was building up. Also, for almost two years, M.A.N. refused to accept that there was any design problem with the engine, attributing all the faults to manufacture at NBL, where a lack of experience of working to aircraft-level tolerances and having to make do with old machinery caused poor quality and endless delays in manufacture. Ironically, Fulton had difficulty at first in convincing his fellow NBL directors that the prestigious German company could possibly be at fault, and he also described similar problems with the Voith transmissions.

Losses mounted during 1958 and 1959 due to the massive expenditure on the design of the new locomotives for the BTC, not yet compensated for by deliveries. Rumours were already circulating about NBL's financial difficulties: the April 1959 *Trains Illustrated* reported that it had been forced to raise £3.75 million by borrowing from a combination of the Government, two banks and General Electric Co. One of the main problems was the additional working capital needed to finance an order for diesel compared to steam locomotives, compounded by BR ceasing to make interim payments for work in progress. NBL estimated that on an order for 50 locomotives the funding requirement increased from £150,000 to £1.4 million.

In June 1958 NBL made proposals for more Type 2 diesel-electrics which were 'as far as possible, exact repeats of the 38 locomotives we are presently supplying to the Eastern Region' and also for quantities of Type 1 (750/1000hp), Type 2 (1000/1250hp), Type 3 (1500/1750hp) and Type 4 (2000/2500hp) locomotives. The following July they quoted for 59 2700hp C-C diesel-hydraulics , in three alternative designs, all with Maybach MD655 engines and Voith L308qr transmissions, and in July 1960 for Type 1 Paxman-engined 900hp twin 6ZHXL or 1000hp 16YHXL single engined diesel-electrics.

The BTC was not attracted by any of these proposals and by 1960 NBL's problems were compounded by penalties for late delivery and rectification costs. As the situation deteriorated the firm made 50 staff redundant in May, with the prospect of many more to follow if new orders were not obtained. NBL lobbied the BTC and the Government to place an order for an additional 20 Type 2 hydraulics with them as an interim measure before tenders for the 1962 diesel programme were sent out. This was turned down in July and was soon followed by the news that NBL's prices for the Type 1 and Type 4 locomotives in the programme were well above those of the successful tenderer. Their quoted delivery dates were also worse and the BTC was clearly extremely wary of their ability to meet these based on their current experience. In desperation, NBL slashed its prices in January 1961 but to no avail, and in April 1962 the lack of new orders, either from BR or overseas, left the directors with no choice but to put the company into voluntary liquidation. Its goodwill was later acquired by Andrew Barclay, Sons & Co Ltd of Kilmarnock and in mid-1966, the liquidator paid out the final dividend to creditors which resulted in them receiving 17 shillings in the pound – a high return from a business which was perceived to be in such a dire state.

## Chapter 2
# THE NORTH BRITISH A1A-A1A D600s

**Preliminaries**
In January 1955 NBL were given an intimation that the British Transport Commission would place an order with them to design and build the 2,000hp and 1,000hp diesel-hydraulic locomotives for the WR. Both types were to be of orthodox construction and were to use M.A.N. engines and Voith transmissions. NBL submitted their Specification for the 2,000hp design on 22 February 1955. It was an A1A-A1A powered by two M.A.N. L12V17.5/21BmA 12-cylinder four-stroke supercharged engines rated at 1,000hp at 1,500rpm and using Voith L36r transmissions. The water tanks carried 1,600 gallons and had square covers, slightly curved at the top to blend into the body. The bogie had 3ft 9in driving and 3ft 0in carrying wheels which resulted in a maximum continuous tractive effort of 42,500lb.

The overall outline was not dissimilar to that which finally emerged but there were several interesting features which were left behind. The most noticeable visual difference was the broad band running the length of the body side which ended in sweeping chevrons, reminiscent of the DELTIC prototype, on the high bulbous nose ends. There was no tumblehome and the cab had small front windows with single sliding side windows and a round topped door. The body side had three sets of double doors but only one large radiator bank at each end set behind the cab doors.

The stripes were quickly discarded and the nose end was remodelled as the detailed design evolved over the year before a firm order was finally placed on 16 November 1955 under BTC contract No.PRE/A/725/2; the NBL contract number was L76. NBL's programme dated 13 February 1956 set out the timetable for the

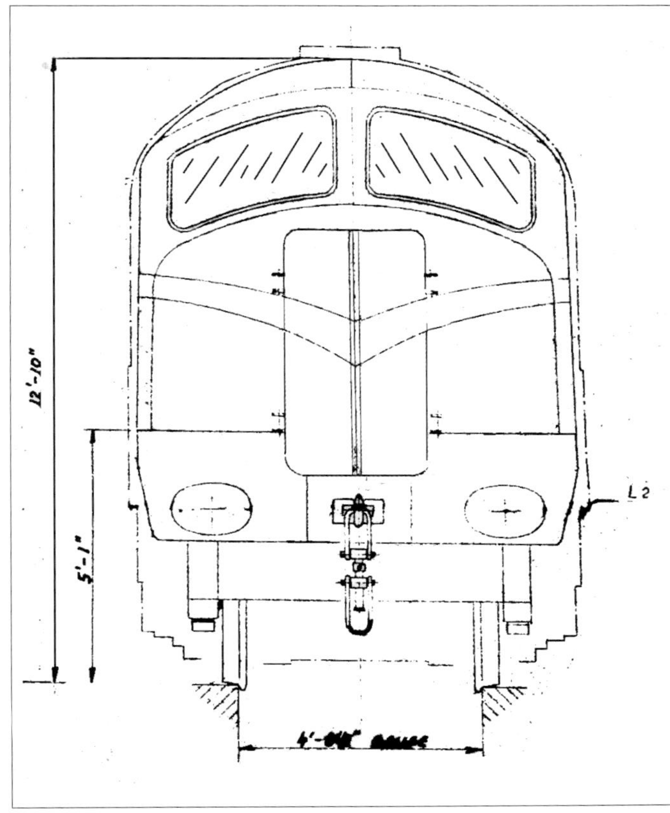


**DELTIC-style chevrons on the original NBL outline design submitted with the tender in February 1955. The windows were enlarged on the finished locomotive.**

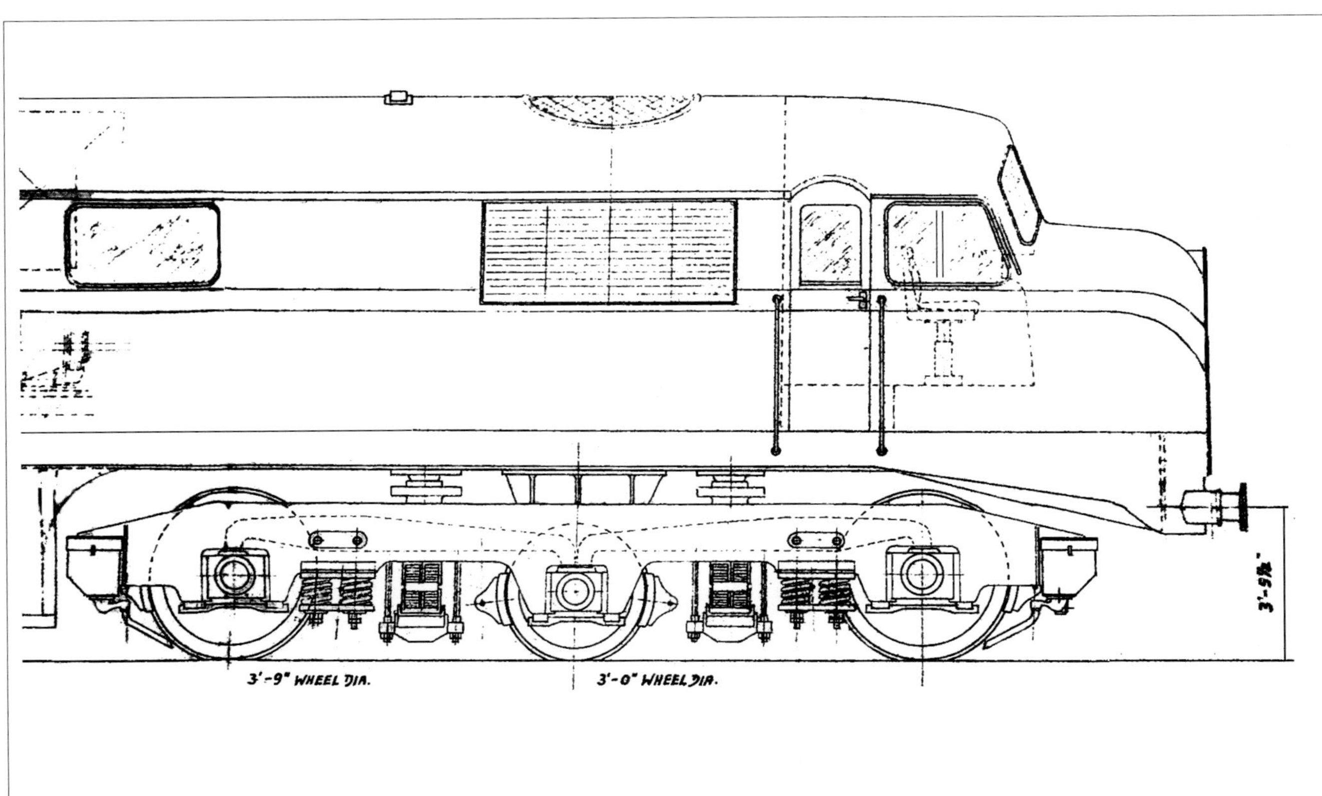


**Side view from the February 1955 design showing the bodyside stripe, hooded door and longer wheelbase bogie.**

**One of several livery styling schemes produced – this was the one closest to the final version, with the white lining band changed to grey. Another had a wider grey band higher up the body and a third included white cab window surrounds and a full length lining band finishing under the side windows.**

'2000hp Diesel-hydraulic for Swindon' as:
*March 1956: Main shapes finalised*
*July 1956: Details finalised*
*February 1957: First locomotive completed*

**External design**

The design was well advanced by the time BR began to consider the external appearance of its forthcoming diesels: RC Bond, the BTC Chief Mechanical Engineer, had been instructed by the Secretary General in September 1955 'to obtain expert advice regarding the aesthetic design of the main line diesel locomotives.' Bond wrote to RA Smeddle, the Chief Mechanical & Electrical Engineer at Swindon, in

**The final plywood cab mock-up. In the days long before computers and CAD JP McCrum, the designer working for NBL on the D600s, used sketches and produced clay and wooden models to demonstrate his initial ideas.**

**Building by numbers: the nose-ends, built up from aluminium castings to form a complete sub-assembly, were delivered to NBL from the sub-contractor.**

December that 'the North British designs for the diesel-hydraulics are now so far advanced that only a minimum of structural change could be agreed' and that a discussion with Christian Barman, then the BR Publicity Officer, showed the latter was 'still of the opinion that some benefit to the appearance would result from some relatively minor changes'. There was a sense of urgency because he had arranged a meeting with NBL just five days later, after which Barman wrote to McCrum with a list of comments and proposed changes:

*Skirt – lacks character and the front-end termination is terrible.*

*The 6 pairs of side windows should be treated as one horizontal unit with each pair to be framed with rubber and with four rounded corners.*

*The side walls of the cab and nose became vertical at the rear of the cab door and need some good profiling to tie up with the main body profile.*

*The side and front cab windows must be linked together somehow into a single coherent design by reducing the arching of the front windows, making the corner pillars as thin as possible, profiling down the front end of the cab roof and bringing the roof forward over the front windows to form a hood.*

*The channels behind the grip handles at the side of the cab doors should be eliminated.*

*The whole of the nose needs sensitive profiling. We have to get rid of the impression of a square box with an arched top.*

*They did not care for the horizontal (lining) band at floor level but thought running a line along the bottom of the windows and ventilator panels would be better.*

Barman concluded 'The BTC from the Chairman downwards, are determined to achieve the highest possible standard of appearance design in the new railway locomotives (which) they will be building under the £1,200m plan of modernisation, and it is clear that the North British Locomotive Company want to do their utmost to co-operate with the Commission in following this policy'.

In his reply on 20 December McCrum said that 'another crisis has arisen with the locomotive'. BR had asked for a larger compressor which would not fit into the existing space in the nose. BR would not agree to a longer nose and therefore it would have to be fitted in elsewhere. However, he thought that 'this may allow some of the squareness at the buffers to be taken away'. He was 'determined to make a good job of this' but it was difficult dealing 'with two sets of engineers to please, and the Scots tendency always to say "Ye canna dae that" when confronted with something new'. He was looking for support from Barman.

McCrum beavered away over Hogmanay and by 2 January 1956 had sketched out some possible changes to the cab doors and windows. By the 27th Barman was becoming annoyed and wrote to A Hood, the Chief Draughtsman of NBL, that he was 'seriously concerned about the delay in getting to grips with the appearance design ...which we discussed ...on 13 December'. Hood replied on 1 February that there had been some misunderstanding with McCrum about the compressor and that it was 'vitally important that appearance design details be finalised in the Drawing Office by the end of this month'. Bond weighed in to the discussion and kept Barman in his place by 'asking' him to meet this deadline, adding that 'Mr Smeddle and myself will wish to have a sight of these proposals before the right away is finally given to the firm.'

Barman needed support and invited Misha Black, one of the partners from Design Research Unit, the design consultancy which was to be used extensively by the BTC Design Panel over the next few years, to the next meeting with NBL. Black reported back that by the end 'we had considerably improved and refined the design' and 'most of the modifications you suggested have now been incorporated.' He continued: 'The problem of the nose, the skirt and the cabin windows are all now sensibly resolved but the coupling still retains its primitive arrangement, and the overall appearance would be greatly improved if it were possible to build-in at least some of the identification lights and markers. Detailing will need careful watching particularly as far as the door furniture, window trim, etc are concerned. In this respect McCrum is at a slight disadvantage being commissioned by North British who do not feel obligated to take more notice than they care to of his recommendations'. (McCrum was subsequently employed directly by the BTC on other diesel projects).

Events moved forward quickly and on 20 March Bond was able to write to Smeddle at Swindon to record that he had approved the design which 'offered a considerable improvement on the appearance of the full-size mock-up which we have both seen in Glasgow'.

The NBL Drawing Office got on with implementing the proposals but on 25 April Barman wrote to McCrum expressing concern 'with the finish of the nose' as presented in a pencil perspective drawing the latter had prepared. The Chairman and General Manager of the Western Region were 'extremely allergic to the idea of an extreme 'sheer line' treatment of the kind associated with the Triumph car'.

McCrum was more than defensive, saying 'I don't care for the Triumph car either' and pointing out that the sketch was intended only for internal discussion and not for the eyes of the WR top brass. He said he still had concerns about the sharp edges at the corners of the cab windows. He had resolved the issues by mid-May when he sent a model of the nose section to Barman, having 'radiused the edges and given a slight camber of one inch to the profile on centre section. I could not give more, on account of housing the corridor framing, and I wished too to avoid overmuch projection on the top hinge'.

A full-size wooden mock-up of the cab and nose was produced for inspection by all parties at the end of August, with Black writing to Barman: 'In general I am quite pleased with it, although there are still some slightly uncomfortable shapes which I was assured could easily be corrected when the patterns for the aluminium castings are made.' He was however less happy about the painting 'in a rather unpleasant green and, as the window trim is painted black, the effect at the moment is slightly depressing.' However his attempts to introduce 'cool grey tones' and green or dark blue seats in the cab interior were quickly rebuked by NBL, the firm citing a directive from the WR CME specifying cream and green with brown upholstery. Barman politely pointed out that cab interiors did not fall within his terms of reference.

Not one to let an issue drop, Black wrote to Barman on 17 January 1957 that 'both McCrum and I still remain distressed at the present colour scheme for the cab interior'. Progress had been made with the aluminium castings for the cab and nose due for delivery by mid-February, albeit that was the original planned delivery date for the whole locomotive.

Black was still grumbling in April when he reported back to Barman following a visit to NBL at the end of March – this time observing that NBL had produced 'a rather slipshod' model to show to Bond and his Assistant ES Cox which was adorned with a 'sickly orange/yellow line on it, drooping at the nose into the now "traditional" chevron'. After his visit a few days later, Bond was impressed with the alloy cab but he agreed with Black about the orange/yellow line although he thought 'it is in other respects a very good model and gives an excellent idea what the locomotives will look like'.

At the BTC meeting on 26 April 1956 the Commission had approved the adoption of the standard locomotive green livery with lining-out. Barman wrote to Cox on 3 May 1957 telling him that he had asked Black to instruct NBL to use the blue-grey colour for lining which was agreed by the Design Panel. A few days later Cox replied saying it was unclear where the lining was to be applied and 'Having regard to Mr Grand's very personal interest in what is to be adopted for his three Maybach locomotives, I do feel it will be courting trouble if some form of lining is applied to the North British locomotives without reference to him'.

By 28 May Black had produced the final painting scheme:

*Standard locomotive green – BODY throughout including cab roof to forward line of cab door*

*Black – BOGIES, UNDERGEAR DETAILS, DRAWHOOK GUIDE*

*Mid-grey – ROOF (excluding forward section of cab roofs), TOP OF OUTSIDE FOOTPLATING*

*Red – BUFFER STOCKS*

*LINING – a 2½ inch light grey line on the skirt equidistant between base of cab doors and bottom of skirt; this line to stop at inward edge of cab doors.*

*Bright metal – WINDOW FRAMES TO CAB*

The numerals and prefix were to be white in the new standard format, designed by Black, with a small crest on the centre line of the side windows, on a clear panel towards the centre line of the locomotive.

Finally, on 25 November 1957, the BTC issued a press release announcing the completion that day of D600, 'Britain's First Diesel-Hydraulic Locomotive for Main Line Service'. It was in plain green and unlined, with temporary oil lamps for testing.

Messrs Grand and Smeddle journeyed north to inspect it at the end of December and decided that the buffer housings should be red instead of green and the nameplate should be fixed to the body in the space below the crest, and then looked to Barman and Black to decide its form and lettering. This was becoming urgent because the locomotive was due to be delivered to Swindon on 14 January. Black quickly turned round a drawing incorporating the GWR-style 'Fat Face' lettering in polished aluminium on a bright red background, to be lined up with the locomotive number.

So all was set for the official inaugural run on 17 February 1958 from Paddington to Bristol. True to form, Black produced afterwards an eight point list of unsatisfactory style and finishing items, and he was still unhappy about the colour of the cab interior, to which he now added the termination of the grab handles and the NBL makers plate. A few weeks later he wrote to George Williams, the BTC Design Officer, 'Do you think it is possible to do anything about the named train board used for the D600 class?' Williams explained that the headboard was designed for steam locomotives and since there were so few diesels the WR hadn't devised a special headboard for them.

**Technical Description**

The BR publicity people produced a booklet describing their new diesels which summarised the construction and

**The lightweight cast aluminium cab in place on the heavy mild steel girder framework. The white objects on stilts under which the dynostarters will sit are the fuel tanks, either side of the Spanner train heating boiler.**

**An overhead view with the engines in place; the circular train heating boiler is flanked by the fuel tanks.**

| | |
|---|---|
| Length over buffers | 65 ft. 0 in. |
| Weight in working order | 117tons 8cwt. |
| Fuel capacity | 800 gallons |
| Water capacity | 1,000 gallons |
| Max. speed | 90 m.p.h. |
| Maximum Tractive Effort (30% Adh.) and continuous rating | 50,000 lbs. |
| Driving Wheel dia. | 3 ft. 7 in. |
| Carrying Wheel dia. | 3 ft. 3½ in. |
| Bogie Wheelbase | 15 ft. 0 in. |

equipment. It is quoted here in full, with comments where appropriate.

*The locomotives, which are classified as type '4', are for express working and have an A-1-A, A-1-A wheel arrangement. They are designed for operation in multiple with each other. The main frame of the locomotive is constructed from mild steel plates and sections; the main longitudinal members are built up to form an 'I' section and braced by suitable cross-stretchers. Plates and channels complete the framework on top of which the platform is built to form a continuous floor. Standard side buffers and drawgear are fitted at each end of the locomotive together with connections for carriage warming and vacuum train pipe. Jumper sockets are provided at each end to allow multiple-unit operation and remote control.*

[The cab was constructed from aluminium alloy castings, in the form of a complete sub-assembly, including the side doors and roof carlines, delivered to NBL by Lightalloys Limited. The assembly was broken down into units for casting; they were $^5/_{32}$ inch thick and were flanged and bolted together, seal welded and then finished by hand using rotary sanders. The use of aluminium produced a light but rigid assembly and avoided the skilled metalwork otherwise needed with a complex curved shape. Insulation and noise reduction was provided by blown glass fibre behind melamine lining panels.]

*The six-wheel bogies are of double-plate design with sub-assemblies which are welded, stress relieved. Traction, braking and transverse forces are taken by an inner and outer centring ring. The inner part of the ring is attached to the underframe, the outer part is integral with the bolster.*

*The total weight of the main frame and superstructure is taken by four widely spaced bearing pads which rest on a double swing link bolster. The bolster in turn rests on the transverse laminated springs supported from the bogie frames by spring link planks and swing links. From the bogie frame the load is transferred to the grease-lubricated Timken roller-bearing axleboxes by a system of beams and coil springs. There are manganese steel liners on axlebox and hornface guides.*

[The bogie was based on the Ivatt design for the LMS 10000/1 Co-Cos, reduced in length from a wheelbase of 8ft 0in+7ft 8in to 7ft 6in+7ft 6in. Ironically, the LMS locomotives were originally going to have only the outer axles powered but this was changed to drive all three; NBL were unable to arrange for all the axles on D600 to be driven, thereby producing an A1A arrangement. The wheels were spoked with 43 inches diameter drivers but the carrying wheels were smaller at 39½ inches. By all accounts the bogie was one of the best features of the design: several sources have commented on its excellent riding qualities.]

***Engine***

*The two N.B.L. - M.A.N. L12V 18/21S 12-cylinder-type engines are each pressure charged by Napier exhaust gas turbo blowers. The engines are mounted on bedplates which are flexibly mounted to the*

BRITISH TRANSPORT COMMISSION 255/57

Telephone: AMB... ...sador 7711 ...ion 47

Press Offic,
222, Marylebone Road,
LONDON, N.W.1.

FOR PRESS INFORMATION

November 25th, 1957

BRITAIN'S FIRST DIESEL-HYDRAULIC LOCOMOTIVE FOR MAIN LINE SERVICE

COMPLETED AT GLASGOW TODAY:

WILL RUN TRIALS ON B.R. SOON

Britain's first main line diesel locomotive to employ hydraulic transmission was completed today at the Queens Park Works of the North British Locomotive Company. Running-in trials on British Railways local lines in the Glasgow area will precede the transfer to the Western Region, in which it will go into regular service in due course.

Locomotive No. D600 - it has yet to receive a name - is of 2,000 H.P. and it weighs 116 tons. It is the first unit in this high-power range to be completed out of the initial programme of 174 main line diesels ordered under the Railway Modernisation Plan.

The diesel-hydraulic transmission principle has been used with success in B.R. shunting locomotives, but this is its first application in this country to a type of locomotive designed for main line duty, and its performance under British conditions will be watched with particular interest in view of its successful application abroad. No. D600 embodies the N.B.L./Voith design of hydraulic transmission and N.B.L./M.A.N. engines which are being manufactured by the North British Locomotive Company in Glasgow under licence, and the British Transport Commission have so far placed orders with the North British Locomotive Company for 63 such locomotives - five of 2,000 H.P., and 58 of 1,000 H.P. (This total of 63 locomotives includes 52 of 1,000 H.P., for which the placing of a contract was announced on Thursday last, November 21st). All will be employed in the Western Region.

**BTC press release of 25 November 1957 announcing the completion of D600.**

*underframe. Connection of the engine shaft to its transmission is through Hardy Spicer cardanshaft. The cylinder banks are at 60 deg. with the cylinders staggered to allow for side-by-side connecting rods on each crank. The wet-type cylinder liners are of cast iron, located in place by individual cast iron cylinder heads, and are free to expand downwards, being fitted with rubber sealing rings at the lower end. The crankcase is of a fabricated steel construction incorporating seven cast steel bulkheads carrying the main bearing housings. The two cylinder blocks are welded to the main crankcase frame and are constructed from formed steel plates. The banks are joined at the top by a steel platform which carries the monobloc fuel pumps and governor. To relieve the stresses set up in the cylinder blocks, tie bolts are fitted and extend from the top of the blocks into the cast steel bulkheads. The crankshaft is made from an alloy steel forging hardened and ground, the crank webs being drilled to allow an oil flow from the main bearings to the crankpin bearings. Individual cylinder heads are fitted each with two inlet and two exhaust valves, a fuel injector and a pre-combustion chamber.*

*The valves on each bank are operated by a camshaft situated between the two banks, the camshaft being positively driven by spur gear wheel. The gear drive to the tandem fuel pumps is taken from the free end of the camshaft. The connecting rods are one-piece forgings of alloy steel with a copper/lead steel-backed bearing at the large end and a phosphor-bronze bush at the small end. Oil is carried from the big end to the small end by a centrally drilled oil hole.*

*Exhaust manifolds from the engine connect with the Napier pressure charger inlet, and the output from the pressure charger is ducted through the roof. The hydraulic-boosted governor is gear driven from the crankshaft and electro-pneumatic remote control gear gives seven speed steps from idling to full load. Engine lubrication is primed from a pump driven by an electric motor which cuts out when the engine starts as the oil pressure switch closes and operates the dynostarter motor contactor.*

***Transmission***

*Two Voith-North British type L306r hydraulic transmissions are fitted, each connected through a Hardy Spicer cardanshaft to its appropriate diesel engine. The transmission contains three torque converters. Infinitely variable torque multiplication is inherent in the design of each hydraulic torque converter, but one is designed to be the most efficient at starting and low speeds, the next for intermediate speeds and the third for high speeds. One converter is filled as another is emptied and the change is made without interruption to the transmission of torque to the wheels. This is the distinctive Voith principle. Transmission oil is cooled in a heat exchanger where the heat is transferred to the engine cooling water. This method ensures rapid warming up to the best operating temperature and prevents excessive temperature rise even under severe overloads. Reverse gears are built into the transmissions, the direction of change being controlled by electro-pneumatic valves. An incorporated safety device will not allow the driver to reverse the locomotive while it is still in motion.*

***Final Drive***

*The drive from each hydraulic transmission to the axle-mounted gearboxes on the outer axles of each bogie is through Hardy Spicer cardanshafts fitted with needle-bearing universal joints. The gearboxes on each bogie have spiral bevel reduction gears and the*

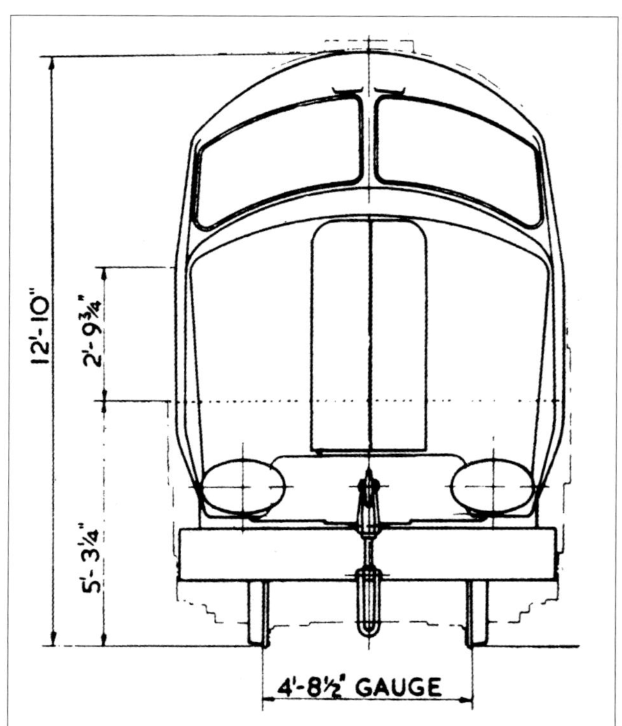

D600, on trial in late 1957 in Scotland, is still to receive its numbers and lining. It carries the oil lamps which Misha Black hoped were for the test period only.

*Below*. D600 general arrangement. *Below left*. D600 nose end.

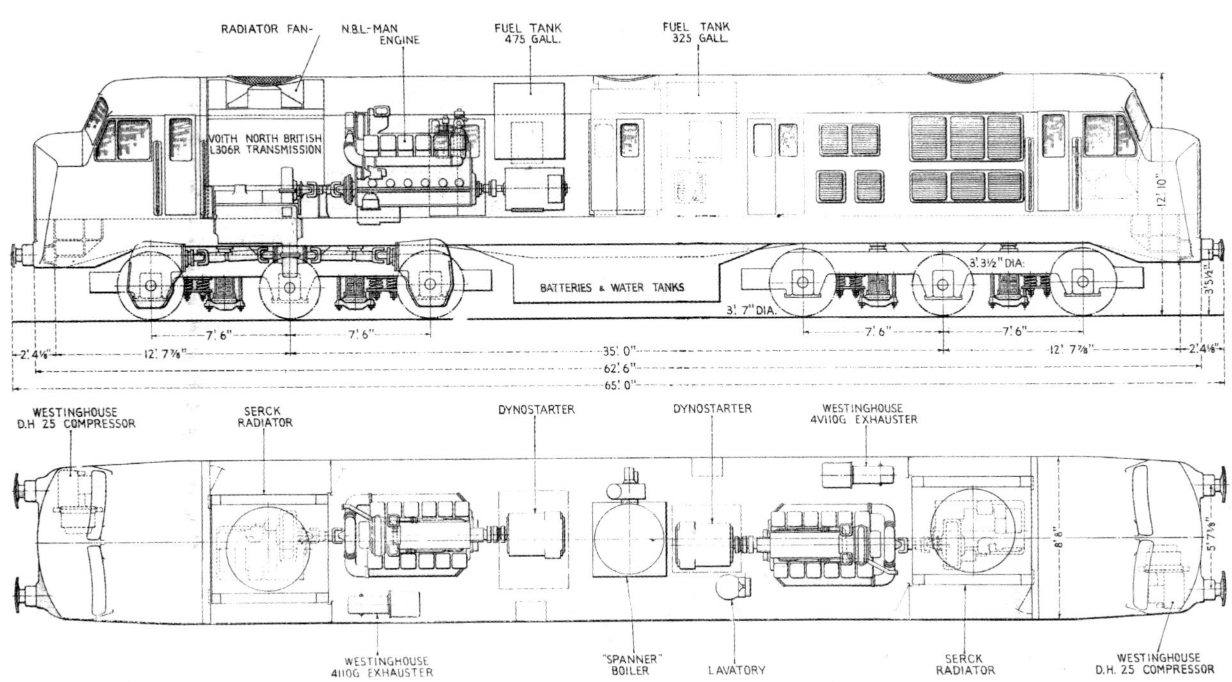


| | | | | | | | | | |
|---|---|---|---|---|---|---|---|---|---|
| Wheel arrangement .. | A1A-A1A | Starting tractive effort | 50,000 lb. | Engines .. | Two, N.B.L./M.A.N. | Transmission .. | Hydraulic | Train-heating | Spanner Swirlyflo boiler, 2,000 lb. per hr. |
| Wheel dia. .. .. | 40 in. | Continuous rated t.e. | 39,600 lb. | Engine model no. | L12V 18/21S | Transmission make | N.B.L./Voith | Braking .. | Westinghouse straight Eight 10 in. by 8 in. cylinders. Braking power 88 tons |
| Service weight .. .. | 117½ tons | Corresponding speed | 12·6 m.p.h. | Top engine output .. | 1,100 b.h.p. | Transm. model | L.306r | | |
| Adhesion weight (full tanks) | 80 tons | Top speed .. .. | 90 m.p.h. | Top engine speed .. | 1,500 r.p.m. | Drive .. .. | Cardan shaft, divided | | |
| Max. axle load .. .. | 20 tons | Approx. converter speed changes .. | 27 and 53 m.p.h. | Approx. engine dry weight | 8,750 lb. | Axle drive .. | David Brown, bevel & helical double reduc. | | |

D600 ACTIVE – the official portrait with the early non-serif 'D' which was also used on D601 and D602 and D800. Note the rather quaint spoked wheels; the carrying wheels, which were of smaller diameter than the powered wheels, were forced upon the designers by the BTC central engineers.

*reaction torque from each gearbox is taken through torque arms and rubber bushes to the bogie frame. Each engine and transmission unit is independent of the other and can be cut out if required.*

### *Dynostarter*

*The dynostarter on each engine is driven directly from the engine crankshaft and when acting as a generator provides a pressure of 110 volts for supplying the electrical load and charging the battery. The voltage is automatically held within fine limits irrespective of the generator speed. When acting as a starter, the starting current is drawn from a 48-cell lead acid battery of ample capacity.*

### *Cooling System*

*The radiator cooling fan motor for each engine is controlled by the water outlet temperature from the engine. When the water temperature reaches 180°F (max.) the fan is automatically switched on; engine water temperature is then controlled by Drayton regulator. When the water temperature drops to 170°F the fan is switched off.*

### *Brake Equipment*

*A Westinghouse vacuum-controlled straight air brake is fitted; the driver's vacuum brake valve applies the train brake and makes a proportional application of the locomotive air brakes. The air brake handle does not affect the train, but makes a straight air application on the locomotive, or on all locomotives in multiple. In the unoccupied cabs the air brake handle is in the 'release' position and the vacuum brake handle in the 'running' position. When hauling an unbraked or partially braked train the brake application on the locomotive must be controlled by the three-chamber reservoir unit. The operation of the vacuum emergency valve must be delayed until that application is completed. This is accomplished by introducing into the supply pipe to the vacuum emergency valve a 'Train braked/Train unbraked' changeover cock and a timing reservoir.*

*A flyhandle on the driver's air brake cuts out the proportional application and allows the locomotive to be moved even if the train pipe vacuum is broken. There are four brake cylinders on each bogie, operating clasp brakes on each wheel. Slack adjusters are provided to take up slackness due to brake wear. Exhausters and compressor are each electrically driven from individual motors.*

*A deadman's pedal is provided in each cab and when released after a time delay, the locomotive brakes are applied and the engine reduced to idling. A deadman's pushbutton is provided for manoeuvring purposes.*

*Compressed air is also used in the control system, sanding and operation of windscreen wipers.*

### *Electrical*

*The internal lighting is all at a pressure of 110 volts and may be connected to an external supply of 230 volts A.C. through a changeover switch and a step-down transformer. The marker lights work at a pressure of 24 volts.*

### *Controls*

*The controls are grouped together in each cab. At the first step of the power handle the engine idles but no power is transmitted since the filling valve of each transmission is in the closed position, allowing no oil to the first torque converter. At the next step the transmission filling valve of each transmission opens and power is transmitted to the wheels. The remaining steps give progressively greater engine speeds and greater power to the wheels up to the maximum. When the master reversing handle is at the 'off' position in the driving and driverless cab, all controls are dead. This master handle is locked in the 'off'*

**The cab layout, tidy and well laid out; the two tone green paintwork was used despite Misha Black's best endeavours. The instrument panel on the left had the driver's main gauges (speedometer, engine rev-counter and air, vacuum and brake cylinder pressure) and that on the right, for the fireman, the lighting and train-heating boiler controls. Brakes for both locomotive and train were operated from a small desk to the driver's left. The pedestal to his right contained various warning lights, the engine starting controls and the power and reversing levers for the main control system.**

*position when the master key is removed. In this way unoccupied cabs are made safe in multiple working. Interlocks prevent incorrect operation of the reverse gears and the application of power unless the gears in all transmissions are home in the correct direction.*

*Gauges, instruments, light switches and warning lights are grouped in each cab. Separate start and stop buttons allow either engine to be cut in or out at will.*

*Automatic safeguards protect the engines and transmissions against excessive oil temperatures, and the engines against loss of oil pressure, loss of water or excessive overspeed. Warning lights are provided at each engine position and a general warning light shows the driver if a fault has developed. Remote-reading tachometers indicate to the driver the engine speeds of any engine, even when in multiple. On the control pedestal, lights indicate the functioning of the reverse gears. Failure of air pressure or vacuum prevents the engine being used to drive the locomotive. When in multiple the control between the locomotives is through jumper cables, air and vacuum hoses.*

[Provision was made for the multiple working of locomotives with another D600 or up to two D6300s, with one driver controlling the working of all locomotives coupled in multiple from the leading cab.]

***Train Heating Boiler***
*The Spanner boiler is situated at the centre of the locomotive and is automatic after the initial lighting up. The boiler working pressure is 80 p.s.i. and the water level of the boiler is maintained by a regulator at the correct working level.*

***Automatic Train Control***
*Automatic train control apparatus is fitted indicating to the driver whether the distant signal is at 'Clear' or 'Caution.' At the 'Caution' signal, the brakes are applied unless the driver acknowledges the receipt of the warning by re-setting the apparatus.*

**Delivery**
D600 finally arrived at Swindon on 14 January 1958, almost a year late, and spent the next few days in the works where it was fitted with WR ATC and named ACTIVE. It was released on 24 January for crew training and familiarisation before it was officially launched to the world on 17 February. It took a nine-coach special, conveying distinguished guests including the Minister of Transport and the BTC Chairman, from Paddington to Bristol and 'was understood' to have reached speeds of over 90mph. Unfortunately, one engine failed near Badminton on the return journey and it had to limp back on the remaining engine, arriving 19 minutes late. However this did prove the usefulness of the ability to isolate one engine/transmission and continue working on the other. D601 also disgraced itself when it failed en route

| ***DIESEL ENGINES*** *( 2 per loco.)* | *N.B.L.-M.A.N. L12V 18/21S Vee-type Turbo Pressure Charged.* |
|---|---|
| *Rated Output* | *1,000 b.h.p. @ 1,445 r.p.m. or 1,100 b.h.p. @ 1,500 r.p.m.* |
| *Cycle* | *Four stroke.* |
| *Cylinder number* | *12* |
| *Bore* | *180 mm (7.087 in.)* |
| *Piston stroke* | *210 mm (8.268 in.)* |
| *Valves per cylinder* | *2 inlet; 2 exhaust* |
| *Pistons:* | |
| *Pressure rings* | *4 (top ring chrome plated)* |
| *Scraper rings* | *2* |
| *Cylinder liners* | *Wet type, cast iron* |
| *Supercharger* | *Napier* |
| *Main and big end bearings* | *Copper/lead-lined steel shells* |
| *Fuel injection equipment* | *C.A.V* |
| *Weight of engine* | *9,520 lbs.* |
| | |
| ***TRANSMISSION*** *(2 per loco.)* | *Voith-North British type L306r.* |
| *Maximum rating* | *925 h.p. @ 1,445 r.p.m. input; 1,036 h.p. @ 1,500 r.p.m. input* |
| *Number of circuits* | *3 converters* |
| | |
| ***FINAL DRIVE*** | *David Brown & Sons (Huddersfield) Ltd.* |
| | |
| ***DYNOSTARTER*** *(1 per engine)* | *Electric Construction Co. Ltd.* |
| *Continuous Rating* | *110 volts-50 k.w.* |
| | |
| ***COOLING SYSTEM*** | |
| *Radiator Unit (2 per loco.)* | *Serck Radiators Ltd.* |
| *Fan Motor (2 per loco.)* | *British Thomson-Houston Ltd.* |
| *Temperature Control (4 per loco.)* | *Drayton Regulator & Instrument Co. Ltd.* |
| | |
| ***BRAKE EQUIPMENT*** | *Westinghouse Brake & Signal Co. Ltd.* |
| *Type* | *Westinghouse Vacuum Controlled Straight Air Brake* |
| *Air Compressor (2 per loco.)* | *Westinghouse type DH.25* |
| *Vacuum Exhauster (2 per loco.)* | *Westinghouse type 4V110G* |
| *Exhauster Motors* | *Electric Construction Co. Ltd.* |

from Glasgow and spent a week at Wolverhampton Stafford Road before finally arriving at Swindon on 24 March.

The next two did not appear until November and were finally followed by D604 at the end of January 1959. These three had NBL-built engines and transmissions; the former were suffixed 'S' rather than 'A' on the four Augsburg M.A.N. manufactured engines. The ancillary equipment was also sourced in the UK to remove the dependency on overseas suppliers for future spares.

**Cheap at the price?**

NBL quoted £86,000 per locomotive, with the usual labour and material variation clauses, and by the time the last of the five was completed the authorised additions and alterations had increased the price above £87,500. The additional £1,500 covered dynamic balancing of the wheel sets, the supply of special deadman apparatus, extra tachometer equipment, cab heaters, fire detection apparatus, fitting of end footsteps and storage number boards, and the fitting and wiring of WR ATC equipment.

However, NBL had absorbed significant overheads such as drawing office costs in the hope of gaining repeat orders from the BTC to compensate for the falling volume of steam traction work. Although to reduce costs they had based much of the structural design and the bogies on the already proven LMS 10000/1, they were forced to cut corners wherever possible in the workshops during construction. The Western Region would soon suffer the consequences.

The WR management now had a hydraulic but nothing like the one they wanted...

**[The table at left is representative of D602-D604 which had Glasgow-built engines and equipment from British sub-contractors; D600-D601 were fitted with engines and ancillaries supplied from Germany.]**

**D603 CONQUEST. The lettering was designed by Misha Black but the positioning below the BR crest was decided upon by the WR management. The spacing of the letters was slightly wider on D603 and D604 than on the first three.**

**A D600 in summer 1961 at Reading with South station in background. Despite the efforts of Misha Black and JP McCrum the nose-end was less than elegant. The D600s were taken off all workings east of Newton Abbot from July 1962. (J Savage)**

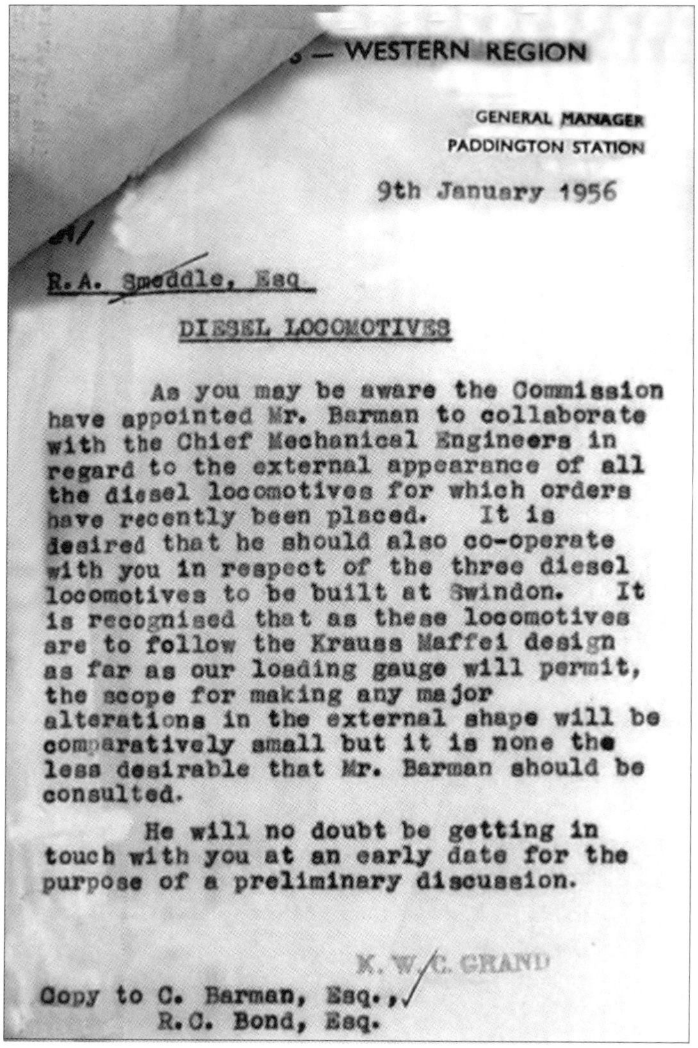
— WESTERN REGION

GENERAL MANAGER
PADDINGTON STATION

9th January 1956

R.A. Smeddle, Esq

DIESEL LOCOMOTIVES

As you may be aware the Commission have appointed Mr. Barman to collaborate with the Chief Mechanical Engineers in regard to the external appearance of all the diesel locomotives for which orders have recently been placed. It is desired that he should also co-operate with you in respect of the three diesel locomotives to be built at Swindon. It is recognised that as these locomotives are to follow the Krauss Maffei design as far as our loading gauge will permit, the scope for making any major alterations in the external shape will be comparatively small but it is none the less desirable that Mr. Barman should be consulted.

He will no doubt be getting in touch with you at an early date for the purpose of a preliminary discussion.

K. W. C. GRAND

Copy to C. Barman, Esq.,
R.C. Bond, Esq.

*Left.* The letter from KWC Grand to his CME in January 1956 was unequivocal that the design must follow the German Krauss Maffei V200 as far as possible.

*Below.* The model produced by Misha Black which was turned down by Grand. Elements of the styling were to re-appear on the Westerns in 1961.

# Chapter 3
# THE D800 AND D833 B-B WARSHIPS

On 9 January 1956 KWC Grand, the WR General Manager, wrote to RA Smeddle, his Chief Mechanical & Electrical Engineer: *As you may be aware the Commission have appointed Mr Barman to collaborate with the Chief Mechanical Engineers in regard to the external appearance of all the diesel locomotives for which orders have recently been placed. It is desired that he should also co-operate with you in respect of the three diesel locomotives to be built at Swindon. It is recognised that as these locomotives are to follow the Krauss Maffei design as far as our loading gauge will permit, the scope for making any major alterations in the external shape will be comparatively small.*

**From Munich to Swindon**

Smeddle summarised the events of the following three years when he presented a paper entitled *Dieselisation – Problems, Prospects and Progress* to the BR (WR) London Lecture and Debating Society at a meeting in February 1959 chaired by Grand who introduced him as someone who 'for the last few years ...has been intimately concerned with the development of our diesel locomotives and the problems associated with them'. In his introduction, Smeddle told his audience that many problems had been encountered both in the design and building of the new locomotives. He went on to describe briefly all three WR Pilot Scheme hydraulic classes, but his main subject was the D800 Warship: *The Swindon locomotive was to be based on the German V200 locomotive designed by Krauss-Maffei of Munich as this was considered by this Region's Management to be of outstanding merit, particularly as its weight was less than 80 tons for a horse-power of 2,000.*

*The major problem was to accommodate all the equipment, or its equivalent, of the German V200 in a locomotive 10 inches lower and 16 inches narrower, to come within the restrictions imposed by the BR loading gauge.*

*Once the licensing agreement had been concluded with Krauss-Maffei, which allowed British Railways to use its principles of light-weight design, despatch of the V200 drawings began in the spring of 1956. The Swindon Drawing Office Staff were faced with the tedious task of translating all notes from German into English and all measurements from Metric into British. This accomplished, they then had to re-design the whole of the under-frame and superstructure to come within the restricted dimensions of the BR gauge, and this involved learning and applying the aforementioned design technique evolved by Krauss-Maffei.*

*The whole of the equipment had to be arranged on the drawing board into the new framework. The engines, transmissions and bogies were exactly as on the German locomotive, and it was decided to use similar engine control and compressed air brake equipment. Most of the rest of the installation, including carriage warming boiler, cooling equipment, vacuum exhausters, windows, etc., was to be of British manufacture and this involved consultations, often protracted, with the suppliers.*

*However, in due course, the drawings began to take shape and material was ordered. And then came the turn of the works. A manufacturing technique entirely new to locomotive builders in the Country, had to be learned and applied.*

The wooden mock-up of the cab.

He included illustrations; these showed: *the appearance of the underframe, body and bogie in course of construction and it will be realised that instead of dealing with plates up to 1¼ ins. thick, bolted or riveted together, as for an orthodox steam locomotive, the whole of the construction here is of plate of wafer-like thinness, all welded together, the backbone of the structure being two steel tubes 6½ ins, outside diameter each running in one length from one end of the locomotive to the other.*

*Such a construction obviously presented many difficulties to our Shops at Swindon, both as regards equipment and type of labour available. Sheet Metal Workers and Welders were at a premium and none of the Supervisory Staff had had any experience of the sort of work they were now to undertake.*

*However, several visits were made to Germany and with the ready assistance of Krauss-Maffei, the first locomotive began to take shape, slowly and tediously, with a new lesson learned every day.*

There was a very steep learning curve; Brown-Boveri personnel installed

# D800 CONSTRUCTION METHODS

Brian Reed (op cit) described the construction methods for the D800s at Swindon in some detail: *The D800 frame was begun by welding up several honeycomb sub-assemblies and threading them along the two 6½in diameter tubes. First the large centre honeycomb section was welded to the tubes and the wrapped-round floor plate of the section welded on. Working outwards from this section at each end, the intermediate, over-bogie, and end honeycomb sections were welded in sequence to the tubes and the floor skin extended as the frame grew. The completed frame was levelled by twisting and heating, marked off, and cambered in by pulling down the ends about 2in and applying heat. Then the large floor apertures were cut, the bogie rubbing faces accurately fixed, and the cab inner bulkheads and side frame members welded in position. The roof framing, in two sections, was applied next, followed by the cab top nose framework and then the bottom nose framework. Many of the plates of the honeycomb were machined on the edges to keep the assemblies square and flat, and to control contraction on welding, for unless gaps were uniform the weld would pull more in one place than another.*

**The Warships were built at Swindon alongside steam locomotives undergoing repairs – not exactly ideal conditions for the assembly of a sophisticated piece of machinery. The two 6½in diameter mild steel tubes which run the whole length of the locomotive are clearly visible.**

***Left.*** **The stressed skin construction used 0.80in thick steel plate on a framework of 0.104in steel sections. No wonder the exterior buckled!**

***Below.*** **Underframe during construction.**

**Fabricating the bogie frame.**

*Before erection on to the whole frame, the outer side skin was pieced together by welding until each side from cab door to cab door was in one piece, and had straps welded to the ends so that the skin could be given some pulling up on the body frame-sections before welding. After this was complete the side apertures for cooling block, windows, etc, were cut out. At this stage the side wall was still rather slack and flabby, and was tensioned by thousands of spot heatings about 1in apart, done by a small welding torch. The end nose skins were added, but in view of the curved shape little tensioning could be applied or flat areas would appear. Finally the insulation pads were put up and the inner perforated light alloy skin fixed to hold them in position.*

*Many jigs were used, and were made in the shops, simply and without frills; many were on trunnions so that the fixture could be turned over and every possible weld made in the fixture. Some fixtures for bodyside and roof framing were of light construction reinforced with tubes so that the whole could be swung by hand between end pivots when turning upside down, for access from top and bottom was essential for easy welding. Woodworkers' clamps were found best for holding light sections, and hundreds were employed.*

*Only electric welding was used and there was no spot welding. About 2000 man-hours were spent on a D800 in welding superstructure and attachments. Over a score of AC Murex welding sets were acquired, and had the wide current range of 15 to 330A to suit the wide variety of sheet and plate thicknesses. Few welds in the superstructure were examined by X-ray and fabrications were not relieved of stress. One problem associated with the numerous thin sheets was storage, for it had to be under cover in a dry atmosphere. The steel sheets came to the works pickled and oiled, and the oil had to be removed by sawdust before being worked.*

*An Eckold machine was used to form the nose ends. It could shrink or stretch the plates, and was used also for angle bending and similar jobs. A Pullmax Major machine cut out curved shapes in plates up to ⅜in thick, and its high speed nibbler could cut apertures of any shape in the centre of a sheet or cutting in from the edge. An 8ft press brake produced many of the light folded sections used in the framework after first attempts with a hydraulic press; some curved box sections were bent hot on a hand bender.*

*Most of the superstructure sub-assemblies were produced in one of the old smiths' shops of steam days. Large surface tables about 7in above floor level were used when fabricating the honeycomb frame; they were made up of cast iron blocks about 10ft long and 4ft wide, placed end to end on level runners to get the equivalent of a 60ft by 10ft table. Adjustable height staging was used in the assembly so that the whole superstructure could be encircled and every part reached; in the later stages of locomotive erection when all equipment could be put in and secured there could be too many men for comfort on the job at once, and custom was to take out again the two diesel engines after they had been lined up and pipe connections adjusted, to give more room. They were re-installed finally only near the end.*

*Bogie frame welding required a different technique, for the plates were thicker and many of the pads, brackets, and gussets welded in needed machining and squareness to close tolerances. Bogie side frames were assembled and tack welded on a jig, they were then fully welded up in two stages on manipulators which could provide 360° of rotary movement and 50° of tilt. Only after all brackets and pads were on did the frame go for marking off and machining. For the latter a number of combined shaper-driller-miller machines were employed to do several operations at one setting and help to observe exact centre distances.*

**Black's livery scheme for D800, which was approved by the WR General Manager on 12 July 1957, had the numbers behind the cab doors at the ends of a 6½in lining band. He also wanted to put the nameplates below the cab windows. D801 was to have stainless steels numerals and (thinner) lining band.**

all of the 2½ miles of wiring in D800 as the Swindon electricians watched. In effect, much of D800 was hand-built, creating the jigs for use on the later locomotives after they had completed the stressed steel superstructure for the first of the class. This was a difficult enough task in its own right but they also had to keep a watchful eye on its overall appearance with the help, or otherwise, of the Design Panel and its consultants.

**What did the 'stylists' achieve?**

Although the WR General Manager had written to him on 9 January 1956 to tell him to co-operate with the Design Panel, Smeddle clearly had a lot on his plate and did not want to be bothered with 'stylists'. His 'other' boss, the BR CME RC Bond, told Barman on 24 February 'he is not yet in a position to discuss questions of styling' and 'There is a great deal of development work to be done first in adapting the German method of construction to British conditions'.

Two months passed before a meeting was arranged with GE Scholes, then the Chief Draughtsman at Swindon, and Barman informed him, in confidence without telling Bond and his assistant ES Cox (who Scholes was due to meet a few days before), that he would have Misha Black working as his associate designer on the project. In the same letter Barman offered a little praise: 'Whilst writing, may I just say how very much I admire the excellent treatment you have given to the side walls of the locomotive, and the way you have solved the difficult problem of the various apertures. I know you will give Black all possible co-operation in his attempt to deal with the somewhat tricky matters arising in connection with the cab windows and the treatment of the ends'. He also mentioned a difficulty with 'the little triangular shelf which is formed at the edge of the four corners where the body is set back from the underframe' and that 'they will want a small door in the nose similar to the one you see in the German locomotive'.

Black duly visited Swindon on 9 May and promised to produce some preliminary drawings for discussion and a model was quickly made to support his proposals. However Grand stuck to his guns and Smeddle wrote to Barman on 13 June: 'I have this morning heard from my General Manager to the effect that the design we prepared ...is the one preferred.'

Black was not yet ready to give up and told Barman on 15 June: 'It seems to me that there are now only two courses of action open to us. Either you could try to persuade Smeddle that our design is the better of (the two), alternatively for us to try and improve the original model while keeping generally to its present form'. Barman had accepted the inevitable and told Smeddle on 25 June: 'I am very pleased to find that you have got a clear lead from your General Manager as to the main forms of your diesel-hydraulic locomotive'. When he wrote to Smeddle on 11 July after a meeting at Swindon he said: 'We are being very careful to confine ourselves to a further study of detail treatments (mainly around the cab windows) within the general shape approved by Mr Grand last month'.

Cox's observations of the meeting to Smeddle are interesting: 'We were in some difficulty in proceeding because it was not known how literally Grand's preference for the styling shown by your original Swindon model was to be taken. If his decision was absolute, then of course there was nothing further for Barman to do. On the other hand it was the opinion of all present that accepting the shape of nose of the original model some improvement in the relationship between the front and side windows was desirable. They concluded that Barman and his associate will alter one end of their model to indicate how far an improvement in window layout might be possible, which incidentally should have the effect of bringing the front end appearance rather more into line with that of the actual German V200 locomotives'.

The model was quickly amended and Black's revised treatment was accepted by Smeddle on 25 July. He and his colleagues might have been tiring of the designer's input when Scholes wrote to Black on 7 August: 'As far as we can see at the moment you have complied with our various requests and it remains for us to produce our drawing of the cab structure and to show thereon the position of the various fitments. Some little time must elapse before this part of the work is completed but I will communicate with you again as soon as we are ready'. Black chased up Scholes for a meeting at the end of September but was put off until 19 November when he was asked to produce a 'fairly finished' model, but was still waiting for drawings from Swindon on 17 January 1957 before he could start work on this. J Beresford-Evans then went to a meeting on Black's behalf in Swindon on 7 February from which he produced a list of nine points on 15 February: *It was agreed that, the cab windows being in polished aluminium frames with very narrow separating columns, there should be no attempt to give* ***special treatment to the face of the columns. At the point where the nose curvature runs into the flat side plating, near the base of the window column, JBE suggested that a more generous curve be provided.***

***Cab Door***
*The radius of the top corners should be reduced to about 1 inch. The door handle should be inset slightly to make it flush with the face of the door. The grab rail troughs should align at the bottom with the locker doors immediately forward.*

***Side Windows***
*These should be frameless. The middle window, being odd sized, should preferably be omitted.*

***Lockers***
*The recessed bar handles, as shown, are satisfactory but they should be dropped to be as close as is practical to the base of the door.*

***Sand Boxes***
*These are framed so as to project beyond the casing at the point where this turns under. It was agreed that the hinge should be bent inwards, so that the drip channel hugs the curvature of the casing at this point.*

***Cab Steps***
*One inset foothold should be cut out in the skirt, with possibly another one in the casing beneath the door. Two further steps are carried in a stirrup beneath the skirt.*

***Nose Door***
*With a projecting handle and latches, this is still rather untidy and it is hoped that this may be considered again at the next meeting.*

***Front skirt***
*It is not possible to contrive a recessed or defined area in which to group the jumpers, air lines, etc. There is, however, a protection plate for the coupling which could be painted red if necessary. Two mounting steps must be provided beneath and out-board of the buffers. The placing of these and the associated grab rails has not been decided and requires careful consideration in relation to appearance.*

In his covering letter to Scholes enclosing the meeting notes he asked when he could visit Swindon to see the full-size mock-up of the cab. By July the new model was complete and Black turned his attention to the livery and the train reporting numbers which it was intended to display using an illuminated box on the cab front. Black and Barman met Grand and George Williams at Paddington on 12 July where these were discussed: *Mr Grand said that the first of these locomotives should be painted with the light grey lining as shown on the model. The second locomotive to be built should have an applied stainless steel band in approximately the same position as the grey band on the model. The stainless steel band would probably be narrower than the painted one and the numerals should also be stainless steel in that instance. When the first two locomotives are completed a decision will be reached as to which form of lining should be adopted in the future.*

*The problem of amending the nose of the locomotive to accommodate an illuminated number box was considered. Mr Grand's view was that this could be satisfactorily positioned in the door in the nose of the locomotive.*

Williams told Smeddle on 2 August that Grand had confirmed the 'train classification/route indicator box' will 'incorporate four 9 inch numbers, each contained on separate blinds'. A few days later Black sent the detailed colour specification to Williams:
The scheme for D800 was essentially the same as for the D600s except for the lining and the numbers; the lining was over twice the thickness and the numbers were positioned at the two ends of the lining band. The more radical

**Lowering in the 4½ ton MD-650 engine. The framework for the stressed steel construction of the locomotive under construction in the adjacent bay can clearly be seen.**

**The Mekydro transmission in a Swindon D800. Although the WR wanted full compatibility of engines and transmissions with the NBL D833s this proved impossible to achieve because of differences in the transmission blocks. (www.rail-online.co.uk)**

| | | |
|---|---|---|
| 1. | *BODY throughout including louvres and fixed roof areas* | *Standard locomotive green* |
| 2. | *ROOF panels: the seven removable panels including ventilators, ring bolts, etc* | *Mid-Grey* |
| 3. | *BOGIES* | *Black: but tyres and hubs bright polished* |
| 4. | *BUFFER STOCKS, ETC* | *Red* |
| 5. | *DRAWHOOK, BUFFER STEP, STIRRUP, ETC* | *Black* |
| 6. | *APPLIED LINE AT WAIST OF LOCOMOTIVE, AND NUMERALS* | *No. D 800*<br>*Light Grey Line 6¼", numerals 6½", all between cab doors*<br>*No. D 801*<br>*Stainless steel Line 3" between cab doors, numerals 6½", forward of cab doors, aligning at front.* |
| 7. | *CREST* | *Centred between ventilators.* |
| 8. | *GRAB RAILS AND HANDLES* | *Stainless steel* |
| 9. | *WINDOWS* | *Cab windows framed or trimmed stainless steel. Other windows frameless or frames painted body colour.* |

treatment proposed for D801 included stainless steel numbers to match the lining band.

Black visited Swindon on 22 October to see the progress and came away unhappy with the bracket welded to the nose to carry the train reporting number frames. He wrote to Williams: 'I have been worried about the gadget they have fixed to the nose to carry the train number frame. You will remember that this appears to have been taken straight off the smoke box of a steam locomotive and looks absurdly out of place on the carefully shaped nose of the diesel. I wonder if you would feel inclined to have a word with Scholes about this? If it is essential to hang the numbers on the nose – at least for an interim period – surely a better fixing method could be devised'.

Williams took this up with Bond who was having none of it, declaring it 'the least obtrusive kind of fitting which can be designed to support the existing train identification indicator. I am quite satisfied that there is no alternative but to make use of such a bracket until such time as schemes for an agreed indicator box may have been finalised. In any case this will be too late for incorporation in the three locomotives now under construction'. (In fact it was also too late for the first ten locomotives of the next batch; D813 was the first of the class built with route indicator panels).

In December Black suggested a radical treatment of the nameplates. The name, he thought, 'should be in a cast panel with raised letters and border. The recessed ground would be colour filled. The panel of cast stainless steel is 6½ inches in height and of an appropriate length for the name. It is placed in front of the cab door to align and correspond with the engine number'. Grand was not happy with this but Black pleaded with Scholes to try out the idea when he wrote to him on 13 January 1958: 'I would prefer not to place the names either below or above the crest as the two tongues of the locomotive badge would be unsatisfactorily related to the shape of the name panel. If the name is placed on the lining band, that band will then be so sub-divided as largely to destroy its effectiveness. That would be particularly the case on the second locomotive where we are experimenting with a stainless steel

**Krauss-Maffei's patented pivotless bogie which was to give so much trouble in the first few years of operation.**

band. In fact, I feel that if the name must be placed centrally on the locomotive, then we should completely reconsider the whole question of lining. I appreciate our present proposal, in which the name-plate is positioned on the near side of each cab only, may seem unusual – but I still think that it would relate satisfactorily to the lining and numbers which have previously been agreed'.

Barman wrote to Williams the following day '...if Mr Grand has expressed a definite opinion it is quite useless for Misha to write to Scholes ...however, we had better see what happens next'. As with the overall V200 shape, the General Manager's view prevailed.

By March Black was still considering how to fix the stainless steel numbers and lining and told Scholes he was happy to agree with Swindon's own proposal, although he did recommend minor changes to the layout, moving the '8' nearer to the '0' to 'improve the spacing between the numbers and separate them a little from the index letter'. On 18 March he wrote to Scholes about the nameplates for SIR BRIAN ROBERTSON: *You will see that we have had to contrive a special condensed letter to accommodate this long name within the available space while not appearing to be overcrowded. This could become a standard letter form for any other names of similar length.*

*We have now shown the words 'Warship Class' in an expanded type which I think is preferable to the lettering we earlier proposed for 'Active'. If you approve, this type of lettering could be standard for all following locomotives in this class.*

*We have retained the simple rectilinear shape for the plate as I think this suits the general form of the locomotive body. I suggest that it should be positioned on the centre line 5 inches above the top of the grey band. The crest will then need very careful positioning above this name-plate but the top of it should, in any case, not be higher than the commencement of the curvature of the body side.*

*I think we agreed that the lettering and rim would look well in polished brass, and I hope you can agree to having the background in bright red. I think that spot of colour would help to liven up what is otherwise a rather monochrome colour scheme.*

*I shall be sending you within the next few days a proposed layout for 'Vangaurd' which will be in your standard GWR lettering, although I have amended one or two of the letters which I think are rather weak in their present form. That lettering can then be standard for all following locomotives, with the present 'Sir Brian Robertson' letters being used only when a long name is required.*

*I suggest, however, that you follow the style used on 'Active' for the remainder of those locomotives built by North British to differentiate them slightly from those which are being built to your Swindon design.*

Black copied the letter to Williams who noted: 'there has been some criticism of the bright red colour (and) you may care to consider whether this should be in the alternative black which I believe you mentioned. I thought I would let you know there have been some comments on this rather large splash of bright colour on an otherwise subdued livery'.

Discussion had returned to the detailing by the end of the month. Black was now happy with 'the position and detail of the horn grilles' but wanted the coupling protection plate extended and the profile of the buffer beam casing plate changed. He was 'much more concerned with the proposed grille for the cab heater filter box' which although it had been 'detailed very well, its position on the nose ...presents a visual interruption which I very much hope can still be avoided.'

The next correspondence, on 16 June, was about the handrails on the nose. Swindon had changed these so that they met on the centre line parallel to the windscreen and Black agreed with this. They had also been able to reduce their size to ¾ inch OD but Black was 'anxious that these should be as inconspicuous as is practicable' and hoped the diameter of the bosses to which they were attached could also be reduced.

Black and Beresford-Evans went with Barman to Swindon on 11 July, for a final check on D800 before its official unveiling on 14 July. Having apologised for choosing 'so inconvenient a day for our visit' they told Scholes they were 'very impressed by its general appearance' but 'there were, however, some points of detail where we thought further improvements could be made'. They were especially concerned about the problem of the louvres as some of these were already bent and out of true at the naming ceremony. A memorandum of 12 points was produced for Barman and Black said 'I share your anxiety about the louvres. We have had some trouble with Swindon about these as they wanted to reduce their weight to a minimum, while I stressed the necessity of their being sufficiently rigid to remain absolutely true. They are, in fact, of a curved section which was supposed to ensure their remaining straight'. Black was also not impressed with the cab interior but appreciated that it was a delicate matter, for Scholes has 'personally accepted responsibility for the design and colour of the instrument casing'.

*Memorandum of points arising from a visit to inspect locomotive D800 (Sir Brian Robertson) at Swindon on 11th July, 1958.*
*Grab handles*
*The bow handles on the nose were 1in diameter and were thought to appear heavy. It is suggested that these handles should be ¾in or ⅞in at the most in diameter. The flanges upon which they were set also seemed rather massive, and a $^{3}/_{16}$ x 1¼in washer is proposed, with chamfered edges.*
*Nose Door*
*The louvres in this door appear coarse. When this door is redesigned to accommodate the Route Indicator box, special attention could be given to incorporating means of air intake with the framing or recession of the box.*
*Air Port in Nose*
*This opening, which is ducted to a motor with a 4in diameter flexible pipe, seems to be placed as well as it can be, but the form of the opening might be improved. The present form is a semi-circular top and bottom with straight sides. A rectangular form, of approximately the same area, could be considered as an alternative with large radii on the corners so that the top and bottom edges have about 1½in of flat.*

*The present grille consists of an internal fine gauge expanded metal, covered with a coarse gauge expanded metal on the skin level. It is proposed that a visible grille of ⅞in pitch louvres (or even of rectangular perforations) to preserve the visual continuity of the skin might be an improvement.*
*Buffer Beam*
*The trapezium shaped protecting plate – in way of the swinging draw-bar gear – has been finished in red as originally agreed. This, however, does not look well now that the buffer beam has also been painted red and it should preferably be painted body colour, or black.*

*A red band, the width of the buffer flanges, has been carried across the beam from buffer to buffer. This should be stopped at each end 1in short of the flanges (just clear of the weld line).*

*The whole question of 'vision painting' may need further consideration when the Route Indicator Box is incorporated in the nose.*
*Named Trains*
*Swindon will let us have a full list of named trains that are likely to be served by the Warship class, so that suitable boards and fixing details may be designed.*
*Engine Names*
*The placing of 'Sir Brian Robertson' was thought to be slightly higher than desirable. (No 'Warship Class' is used on this locomotive, and this might affect the placing of following name plates)*

*The fixing of this name board was by large shallow mushroom-headed bolts. Alternative methods of fixing with flush heads and spigots welded to the back of the name plate might be explored.*
*Kicking Plate*
*It had been found that the skin beneath the cab door was being scarred, and a green rubber panel had been added. It is effective but the method of fixing needs to be further considered.*
*Fire Extinguisher Handle*
*The glass panel covering this handle has been set with a somewhat wide frame which could usefully be reduced in size.*
*Grey Banding*
*This was 3" wide, not 6" as had been suggested. The narrow band was considered an improvement on the original proposal.*
*Engine Number*
*The D is not sufficiently differentiated from the ciphers that follow. It is proposed that the D should have small Egyptian serifs.*
*Panel Joints*
*The wide joint line of the door on the battery box area was thought to avoid many of the difficulties associated with close joints. It is proposed that the lockers at the sides of the cab should have the doors so reduced in size as to leave a clear gap of ⅞in all round between door and skin, and that all similar joints should be carefully considered with particular relation to their appearance after panels have been removed for maintenance and then replaced. This edge problem also applies to the removable roof panels.*
*Louvres*
*Some of these were already out of true and the profile of the louvres and the detail of the louvre openings require urgent consideration.*

Black and Beresford-Evans took another trip to Swindon on 22 October to inspect D801 and D802, and to discuss with Scholes and his colleagues the points raised at the July meeting and review their application to the production series from D803 onwards:

*Grab Handles*
*It was noted that the reduction in diameter of these handles to ¾in (and the reduction in size of the flanges) is being adopted on the production run.*
*Nose Door*
*If the new standard 4 figure route indicator box is to be incorporated this will necessitate the redesign of the nose door, as the space required is somewhat larger than the present door width. Swindon will keep in touch with Doncaster so that they have up to date information on the development work for the route indicator in connection with the 25kV electric locomotives. Mr Black said that he would be interested to see the proposed method of incorporating the route indicator box as this would be a major new element in the design of the nose.*
*Air Port in Nose*
*It was agreed that DRU should supply samples of suggested materials for use as grilles.*
*Named Trains*
*DRU is preparing suggestions for layout of named train boards and shall shortly be submitting them for consideration.*
*Engine Names*
*It was agreed that the placing of these named boards, including the words 'Warship Class' was generally satisfactory but that they should be lowered by 2in. It was emphasised that the fixing of these boards by large mushroom-headed bolts gave undue prominence to the bolt heads. Swindon agreed to consider the use of flush countersunk bolt heads in lieu of these projections.*
*Kicking Plate*
*Mr Black pointed out that though the green rubber panel was effective, the method of securing or protecting the edges made it appear as an after-thought. Suggestions for a lighter form of trim were discussed.*
*Cab Door Step*
*The foot step immediately below the cab door was observed to be wider than absolutely necessary for safety. Furthermore, it was placed at the lower edge of the belt line where it not only disturbed the free flow of this line but was functionally limited because of the restricted toe room. Mr Black asked that it should, if possible, be lowered by 2in, shortened in width by 3in, and that the tread, which is now 6in from front to back, should be reduced to 4in so as to allow a clear gap between the foot step and side plate.*
*Engine Number*
*Whilst the 3in painted grey banding was generally liked, it was felt that the engine numbers in stainless steel could add dignity. As a set of these numbers was in existence, Mr Black asked if they could be fitted to the next locomotive to be painted for the Chief Mechanical Engineer's approval.*
*Louvres*
*It was agreed that the present form of louvre as appearing on the first few locomotives was not visually satisfactory as they so easily became bent. Swindon said that they proposed to insert additional vertical stiffening members and that the monsoon type of louvre was under consideration. Mr Black would not mind if the edge of the louvres was thereby increased. He felt that it was one of the most important visual details that these louvres should remain absolutely true throughout service.*
*Plating*
*It was noted that the finish being achieved in general plating work was steadily improving with successive locomotives, and shape in that of the cab roof curvature was much better. Mr Black asked that further consideration might be given to the finish of the roof line at the top of the quarter column.*

Black told Barman afterwards 'In general they are making most of the amendments which we suggested but ...it is a fairly slow process as

**D800 in the very early stages of construction on 15 September 1957 with just the basic body shell completed. It was almost hand-built, with the jigs for its classmates created as it was constructed. The nose end demonstrates the thinness of the stressed steel with the supporting framework showing through. It also has a V200-style chevron chalked on! (www.rail-online.co.uk)**

modifications are being scheduled for two locomotives or more ahead in the production series. Nevertheless the D 803 is an improvement on D 800 and I hope they will get better as the series progresses'. He also took the opportunity to offer his services on the forthcoming 2,700hp diesel-hydraulic design: 'It would of course, give me greatest pleasure if you should decide that it would be useful for me to work with Swindon on this new and exciting locomotive.' (To be continued in *The Book of the Westerns*).

Black next turned his attention to the train headboards and put forward a proposal for a cast aluminium oval incorporating a coat of arms but Williams told him: 'we are not very enamoured of the train board design'. His final contribution to the Warships was in March 1959, to agree the shape of the Train Classification Indicator which Swindon had, by then, managed to fit into the double access doors on the nose. But never one to give up on an opportunity, with Barman and Williams' help, he tried unsuccessfully to get involved with the batch to be built by North British. Cox may well have taken some pleasure in putting the stop on this: 'There is no occasion for the collaboration on which you suggest because the locomotives which the North British Loco Co are to build are to be to the identical design of the Swindon built locomotives as far as styling is concerned. There is no wish on anybody's part that this should be modified in the further series of these locomotives which N.B.L. are to build'.

**Swindon and the 'Stylists'**

Swindon's views on the 'styling' process may be imagined by reading between the lines of Scholes' paper to the Institution of Locomotive Engineers in November 1959: *The external shape and decoration of a diesel locomotive seem to give rise to more argument and divergence of views than do any other elements of the design. Locomotive Drawing Offices are apt to be a little impatient over this matter, considering that, if left alone, they could probably do as well as anybody else! In this, however, they are perhaps mistaken. There is a growing tendency today to leave the styling to specialists in this field, and, in the case of the D.800 Class, the Design Research Unit of 37 Duke Street, London, W.1, was asked by the Design Panel of the British Transport Commission to undertake this part of the work.*

*Scope for originality in this direction is, of course, severely restricted by exigencies of technical design, itself largely influenced by the limitations imposed by the loading gauge. However, very substantial differences in appearance can be achieved by the shaping of the ends of the locomotive and the cab windows and by the surface treatment of the exterior.*

*Close co-operation between the Design Research Unit and the Swindon Staff at first resulted in the building of a ½ in. to the foot model embodying proposals which were promptly rejected by the management. Further efforts, based on directives given after the first proposals had been studied, resulted in a second model which was declared to be of outstanding merit and was therefore acceptable!*

*There was no room for the usual prominent nose, which, in the opinion of many people, was fortunate, but by careful attention to the contours and by causing the front and side cab windows to appear as a unified shape, an end of some distinction, it is considered, has been achieved.*

*The body side was continued downward as a skirt wrapped under at a belt line which is naturally created at 3ft 6in above rail level by the shape of the loading gauge.*

*The final touches were the form and position of the locomotive name and numbers, the latter having been regarded as punctuating the painted-on horizontal line, and the separation of the roof area in grey paintwork in contrast to the standard green of the body.*

*No effort was made to over-dramatise the locomotive with streamline decorations, nose-ends of irrelevant shape, or startling colour schemes, but rather was it the intention of both technical and styling designers so to simplify the shape and the surface treatment that the whole mass could be appreciated for its own sake as a dignified and powerful machine.*

### The PR Department's view

As with the D600s, a publicity booklet was produced for the D800s and it began with this statement: 'The design, which embodies many interesting features comparatively new to railway practice in this country, is based upon that of the V200 locomotives of the German Federal Railways, which have proved very successful in service. *The experience gained in running these locomotives in Germany has been made available to the Western Region and should prove valuable in eliminating many of the initial troubles usually experienced'* (author's emphasis).

The booklet went on to reiterate some of the points in the WR management's original case for its hydraulics, before providing a detailed description of the new locomotives: *A high power-to-weight ratio has been achieved by the use of stressed skin construction, by means of which the superstructure bears a considerable portion of the weight of the locomotive. The weight saved by this form of construction, compared with that of the weight of a more conventional design of locomotive of the same power, is between 30 and 40 tons, equivalent to the weight of one coach. One advantage of the low weight is that the locomotive, although having a nominal horsepower of 2,200, can be carried on two four-wheeled bogies without the axle load exceeding 20 tons. The bogie design is one of the features of unusual interest and is described under its appropriate section. Welded construction is used practically throughout the locomotive.*

*LOCO. D800*
*TECHNICAL DESCRIPTION*

*The locomotives, which are included in the B.R. Classification as Type 4, are designed for operation in multiple with each other. They have a BB wheel arrangement, which means that each locomotive has two bogies having two axles each both of which are driven. Following are some brief particulars:-*

| Length over buffers | 60 ft. |
|---|---|
| Weight in working order | 78 tons |
| Fuel capacity | 800 galls. |
| Water capacity | 1,000 galls. |
| Maximum service speed | 90 m.p.h. |
| Maximum tractive effort at 30% adhesion | 52,400 lb. |
| Driving wheel diameter | 3 ft. 3½ ins. |

***Framing***

*For descriptive purposes, the framing may be divided into two main parts, namely the underframe and superstructure, although the two are welded together to form one load-carrying unit. The material used for the whole of this framing is mild steel. Two tubular members 6½in o.d. running the whole length of the locomotive from one buffer beam to the other, form the basis of the underframe. Their centres coincide approximately with the buffer centre lines and, therefore, transmit the buffing forces directly. Deep longitudinal plate members provide strength from the bending point of view and for the tractive forces, these members and the tubes being connected by transverse plate members, the whole being welded together. The resulting structure is then covered on the top and sides by sheet steel plate, which is welded to it. Suitable holes in the decking are provided for the transmission and engine sump. Most of the steel sheeting for the underframe is $^{5}/_{32}$in thick.*

*The superstructure consists of framing of angle, 'Z' and other sections folded from steel plate of 12 S.W.G. (.104in) thickness at Swindon Works, and covered by steel sheeting 14 S.W.G. (.078in) thick. The main components of the framing are four cant rails with horizontal and vertical members connecting these to the underframe. The steel skin covering the framing is welded to it and to the underframe, forming a boxlike construction. For rigidity, two bulk-heads are provided which are welded to the sides and underframe and which separate the cabs from the engine room. These bulkheads also incorporate transverse roof members, more of which are provided at intervals along the length of the locomotive, dividing the roof into seven sections. Five of these sections are covered by removable roof panels through which the transmissions, engines and carriage warming boiler can be lifted. The framing of the roof panels is of aluminium welded construction.*

***Bogies***

*The bogie frames are also of all-welded*

**D800, not yet fully dressed, on trial near Swindon on 4 June 1958.**

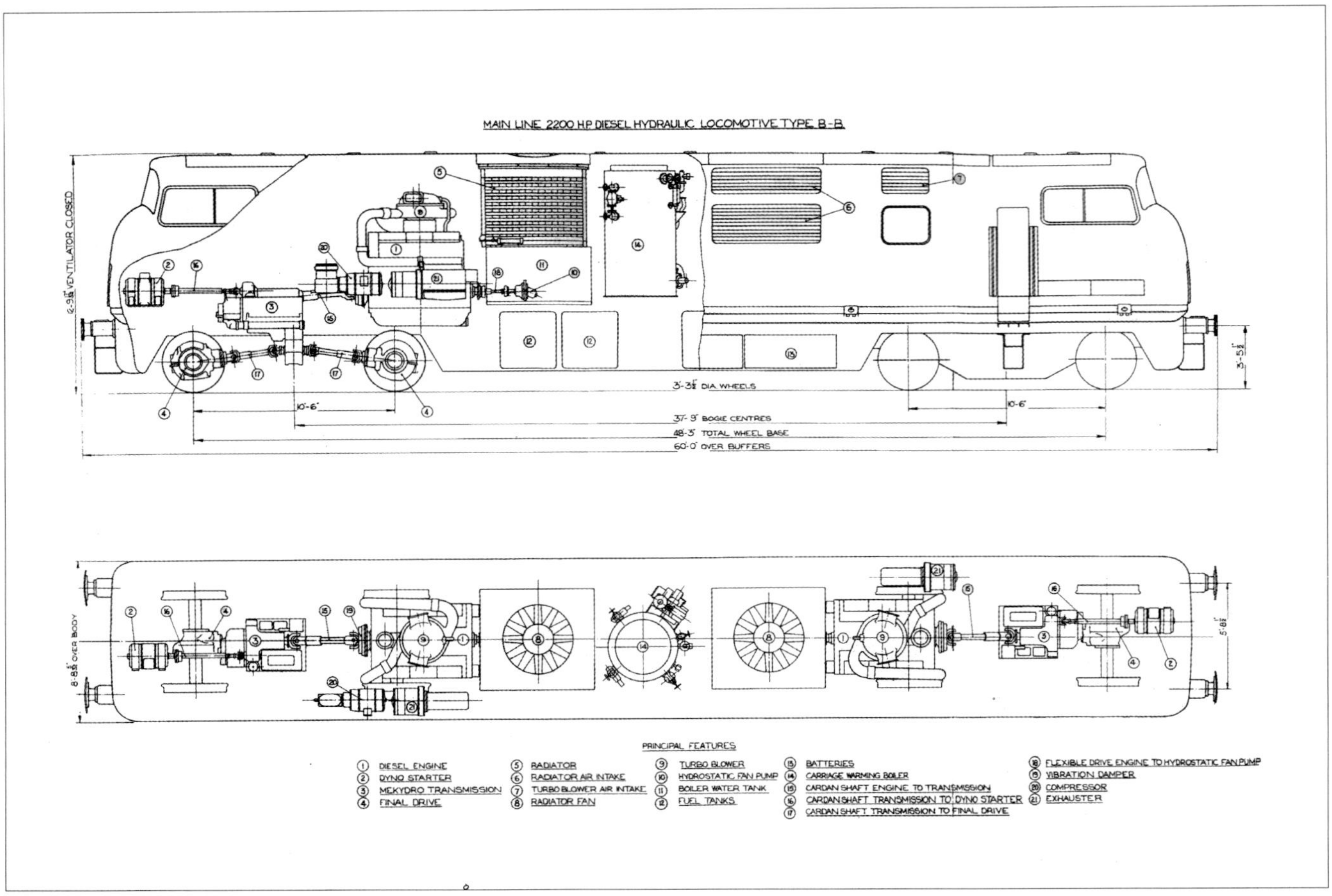


**D800 General Arrangement.**

*construction, composed of mild steel plate, mainly $^5/_{16}$in or $^3/_8$in thick. The centre of the bogie is a hollow rectangle into which projects a part of the underframe and the lower part of the transmission containing the output shaft and flanges. The traction and braking forces are transmitted between bogie and under-frame by means of curved manganese steel rubbing plates. Transverse forces are transmitted by a linkage system connecting bogie to underframe, which allows the former to turn relative to the latter about a geometrical centre. The ends of the links are provided with flexible rubber bearings which thus need no lubrication.*

*The body weight is transmitted to each bogie by means of brackets connected by pin-joints to the buckles of two large laminated springs. From these springs the weight is transferred through coil springs to the bogie frame, and thence by means of laminated springs to the top of the roller bearing casings and finally to the axle. The S.K.F. roller bearings are of the self-aligning type of ample capacity. No axleboxes and horns of the conventional type are used, but each bearing is contained in a casing forming an arm which is connected to the bogie frame by means of large pins with flexible rubber bearings.*

### *Engine*

*The two Maybach MD 650 type 'tunnel' engines are pressure charged by single-stage exhaust gas turbo-chargers of Maybach make. These engines have 12 cylinders divided into two banks in 'V' formation. The basis of the engine is the one-piece cast iron crankcase accommodating the disc-webbed crankshaft. The roller main bearings are mounted on the crankwebs, the outer races being mounted in the annular walls of the crankcase. The crankshaft with the roller bearings is introduced into the crankcase from the front end of the engine; hence the designation 'Tunnel' engine. The pistons have detachable heads and are cooled by pressure oil, supplied through telescopic pipes mounted on spherical joints. A continuous flow of oil is circulated through the cavity between piston skirt and crown, resulting in intensive cooling of the piston ring lands. A special heat exchanger is provided for cooling the piston oil. This feature contributes to the very low cylinder wear rate of these engines. The piston rings are contained in the detachable head, which has the advantage that, when inspecting or changing the rings, it is only necessary to remove the piston head after removing the cylinder head. It is, therefore, not necessary to dismantle the piston and connecting rod. The piston liners are interchangeable and are of the 'wet' type.*

*The individual cylinder heads each have three inlet and three exhaust valves. The two cam shafts for each bank of cylinders are housed in a common cylinder head top which may be lifted as an integral unit. All the rocker arms have an automatic hydraulic adjustment, which ensures at all times that no 'backlash' is present in the valve motion. The injectors combine the pump and injection valve in a single unit, and were developed jointly by Messrs. L'Orange and Messrs. Maybach.*

*Engine lubrication is by means of a mechanically driven pump situated in the sump; but to ensure adequate lubrication at starting, an electrically operated priming pump is provided, which is started as soon as the engine starting switch is operated, and only when the oil pressure in the engine has reached a pre-determined amount is the dynostarter brought into action.*

*The engine speed control is electrical and six speed notches are provided, the actual speeds being readily adjustable if required.*

### *Transmission*

*Two Maybach Mekydro type K 104 hydraulic transmissions are fitted, each connected through a cardan shaft to its appropriate diesel engine. The cardan shaft is similar to that used on the V 200 locomotives. The K 104 transmission has four speeds and consists essentially of a single torque converter permanently filled with oil, together with mechanical change gears in permanent mesh. The actual gear changing is accomplished by means of special overrunning dog clutches, which are so designed that engagement is effected with little noise or wear. The necessary torque relief while gear changing is obtained by withdrawing the turbine blades of the converter in an axial direction. This is done automatically by hydraulic pressure. The control mechanism for gear changing is oil pressure operated, and initiates the change fully automatically in relation to the locomotive and engine speeds. The reverse gears are contained within the transmission casing, the direction of change being controlled by electro-hydraulic means. If the reversing handle in the cab is operated while moving, no forward/reverse gear change is made until the locomotive comes to rest.*

### *Final Drive*

*The drive from each hydraulic transmission to the axle-mounted gearboxes is through two cardan shafts each having two universal joints. These cardan shafts are also similar to those used on the V 200 locomotives. The final drive gearboxes, type C33, are of Maybach design and construction. They are simple and compact and have been designed with a view to complete reliability and durability. The drive casing is of cast steel, and the bevel wheels are spiral-toothed, the driving pinion being supported on both sides. A gear-type twin pump is provided, situated within the base of the casing, for lubrication of the gear wheels and roller bearings in both directions of running. The reaction torque is taken through torque arms and rubber blocks to the bogie frame.*

### *Dynostarter*

*A dynostarter situated in each nose of the locomotive is provided for each engine, and is driven through a Hardy-Spicer cardan shaft incorporating a Layrub flexible coupling from an auxiliary driving flange on the transmission. When acting as a generator, the dynostarter supplies current at a maximum voltage of 135 at no load down to approximately 120 volts at maximum load on the first three locomotives; but this will be changed to a constant voltage of 110 for future locomotives. The current is used for engine speed control, supplying the various auxiliaries and charging the battery. When acting as starter, the starting current is drawn from a 56-cell lead acid battery.*

### *Cooling System*

*The radiator, cooling fan and motor, header tank and associated pipes are supplied by Messrs. Serck as a complete unit for each engine. The unit is placed into position in the locomotive through one of the holes in the roof, and is carried on a rubber mounting strip which completely surrounds the unit at header tank level. The fan drive, cooling water temperature control and shutter actuating device are of particular interest, being the first of their type on a main line locomotive in this country. The fan is driven by hydraulic motor using oil at a pressure of 1,500lb. per sq. in. The pressure is supplied by means of a hydraulic pump which is an exact replica of the motor, and which is driven directly from the free end of the diesel engine through two Layrub flexible couplings. The pressure of oil to the motor and hence the speed of the fan is controlled by means of a thermostatic valve situated in the cooling water system. In addition, movable shutters are provided on the outside of the radiator units, controlling the flow of air through the units. The shutters are actuated by means of hydraulic cylinders, the pressure of oil in the cylinders being controlled by the thermostatic valve controlling the fan motor speed. The normal cooling water temperature is approximately 170°F. The cooling water circuit includes the engine, lubricating oil and piston cooling oil heat exchangers, also the transmission torque converter and torque converter oil heat exchanger.*

*Means for heating the cooling water is provided, and normally the engines cannot be started until the water temperature has reached 130°F. This is done to reduce cylinder wear.*

### *Brake Equipment*

*A Laycock-Knorr vacuum-controlled straight air brake system is fitted, in which the driver's vacuum brake valve applies the train brake and makes a proportional application of the locomotive air brake. By means of the driver's air brake valve the locomotive brake only can be applied. A 'Passenger/Goods' cock is provided in each cab, by means of which, when placed in the 'Goods' position, the normal proportional brake application is slowed down. This is for use when hauling an unbraked or partially braked train, and prevents the unbraked stock from running into the locomotive or braked portion of the train with violence.*

*A deadman's system of brake application is also included, by means of which the locomotive and train brakes are applied if the driver does not press down a foot pedal or the main control handle. On release of either of these, a brake application is made after a delay of about 5 seconds. The application is in two stages, between which a delay occurs, allowing 'bunching' of the train before the brake is fully applied. When a deadman's brake application is made, the engines are automatically reduced to idling speed.*

*Compressed air is also used for sanding and operation of the windscreen wipers.*

### *Automatic Train Control and Passenger Communication*

*The Western Region system of Automatic Train Control is fitted. In this system a steel shoe on the locomotive makes mechanical*

**The second and third locomotives, substantially complete on 7 September 1958. The stainless steel lining band planned for D801 appears to have found its way onto D802, although it had been removed by the time it entered service. (P Kingston)**

**The driver's view, taken after the resetting of the vacuum brake system to operate at standard 21in of vacuum rather than the GWR 25in, which dates it to post-1960. The driver's controller showing notches 0 to 7 controls electrically the engine speed (rpm); directly above the controller are the A and B end engine starting switches which were rotated clockwise to start each engine. Above the driver's brake valve, left, are two air gauges, the left reading loco air pressure, the right A and B end bogie brake cylinder pressures. Above those is the loco straight air brake. The lever to the left was part of the ATC system. When operating in tandem with another locomotive the driver was expected to hold down the lever in order to 'cut out' the ATC and allow the leading loco to create a train vacuum brake. Notice the amendment to the locomotive's maximum speed SPEED NOT TO EXCEED 80 MPH below the speedometer, a temporary reduction enforced due to rough riding at speeds in excess of 80 mph. The switches above the horn valve, as originally fitted, operated (left to right top): power, compressor, exhausters, fire alarm bell, passenger/goods switch (fitted from D818 onwards; D800 to D817 had a cock), blanked out, instrument lights. Left to right bottom are: sanding, cab lights, cab heaters, window demister, train heating emergency stop (D803 onwards) and ATC in use/not in use. The four warning lights left of the speedometer showed 'D' for deadman, 'R' for engine speed regulator, 'T' for transmission and 'E' for engine stopped or reverted to idle due to overheating engine or transmission. (www.rail-online.co.uk)**

*contact with a fixed ramp associated with the distant signal. If the signal is at 'clear' the bell sounds in the cab; if at 'caution' the siren warning is given to the driver and the brakes are partially applied. If the driver acknowledges the warning by resetting the apparatus in the cab, the partial brake application is cancelled. But if for any reason this is not done within a certain time the brake application is completed by the Emergency Automatic Brake Valve (the action of which cannot be cancelled by the driver) in a manner which brings the train to rest as quickly and safely as possible according to the type of train being hauled. By means of the locomotive's brake equipment the air brake is proportionally applied on the locomotive and power is cut off automatically – when the train pipe vacuum falls to a pre-determined value.*

*The selection and application of the emergency braking appropriate to each type of train is fully automatic as the Emergency Automatic Brake Valve (which was developed recently at Swindon) functions in parallel with any partial brake application which is not initiated by the driver. It responds also to the opening of a Passenger Communication Valve in any part of the train when it brings the train to rest in a manner similar to that initiated by an unacknowledged A.T.C. warning.*

### *Electrical*

*The internal lighting can be supplied either from the battery or the dynostarter and may also be connected to an external supply of 200-250 volts A.C. through a change-over switch and a stepdown transformer. The code lights work at a pressure of 24 volts. Handlamp points are provided for inspection purposes.*

### *Controls*

*A comprehensive system of electrical controls and warning devices is fitted. The main controls, warning lamps, gauges and brake handles are grouped conveniently together in the driver's desk, while other gauges and warning lamps not necessary for driving purposes are situated on the other side of the cab. The main controller or power handle is the only one used by the driver, apart from the brake handle, for controlling the speed of the locomotive, as all gear changing is done automatically. The reversing handle, which is removable in the neutral position, is used as a master switch, and when in this position all controls are 'dead'. The engines are started up with the reversing handle in either the forward or reverse position, and the power handle may then be used for controlling the speed of the engines, but no power is transmitted to the road wheels until the power switch is operated. Only one reversing handle is used, even when locomotives are working in multiple, and in this way unoccupied cabs are made safe. Automatic safeguards protect the engines and transmissions against excessive oil temperatures, and the engine against loss of oil pressure, loss or excessive temperature of cooling water, and overspeeding. Two general warning lights, one for the engines and one for the transmissions, indicate to the driver if a fault has developed in any of these units, whether working singly or in multiple. The actual engine or transmission at fault is indicated by warning lights on the right-hand side of the cab, each cab containing the warning lights for the engine and transmission nearest to it. Instruments on the driver's desk indicate locomotive speed, degree of vacuum and air pressure. Others indicate the engine lubricating and transmission oil temperatures, cooling water temperature and engine speed of the particular engine and transmission situated nearest the cab in which the instruments are placed. Failure of air pressure or vacuum brings the speed of all engines to idling. When working in multiple the control between the locomotives is through electric jumper cables and air and vacuum hoses.*

***Train Heating Boiler***

*The locomotive is fitted with a Spanner boiler situated in the centre compartment. After the initial lighting up the boiler is completely automatic and adequate safeguards are provided. The working pressure is 80lb. per sq.in. The same fuel is used as for the diesel engine, and, in fact, is carried in the same tanks.*

***Fire Equipment***

*Comprehensive fire fighting apparatus is provided for both automatic and hand operation. The equipment for each engine consists of a spring-loaded discontinuous wire connected to a shut-off valve in the fuel line. Joining the wire and situated immediately above the engine is a fusible metallic strip which melts on the application of sufficient heat, shutting the fuel valve and ringing the electric warning bell situated in the cab. The wire may also be actuated manually from the cab by means of a handle. To give warning of fire in the boiler room, a Sunvic detector is used which also rings the bell in the cab. For the actual fire fighting, three 50lb. cylinders containing liquid CO2 are provided, connected to spray nozzles situated in suitable positions. The CO2 can be released by means of handles situated in either cab and in two glass-fronted boxes accessible from outside the locomotive. In addition, two hand-type CO2 extinguishers and one C.T.C. extinguisher are carried in each cab.*

***Water and Fuel Tanks***

*The water for the train heating boilers is carried in two tanks of equal capacity situated in the body of the locomotive under the cooling units. The fuel for the engines and boiler is carried in four tanks of equal capacity below the deckplate between the inner axles of the bogies, in spaces formed by the plates of the underframe. All these tanks are formed of mild steel plate and are of all-welded construction.*

## TECHNICAL DATA

| | |
|---|---|
| *Diesel Engines (2 per loco.)* | *Maybach MD 650 Vee-type turbo-pressure charged* |
| *Rated Output per engine* | *1056 b.h.p. at 1400 r.p.m. (First three locos.)*<br>*1152 b.h.p. at 1530 r.p.m. (Subsequent locos.)* |
| *Cycle* | *Four-stroke* |
| *Number of Cylinders per engine* | *12* |
| *Cylinder Bore* | *185 mm. (7.283 in.)* |
| *Piston Stroke* | *200 mm. (7.874 in.)* |
| *Valves per Cylinder* | *3 inlet 3 exhaust* |
| *Supercharger* | *Maybach* |
| *Injectors* | *L'Orange* |
| *Main Bearings* | *Roller* |
| *Big End Bearings* | *Plain* |
| *Fuel Consumption (Approx.)* | *.375 lb./b.h.p.hr.* |
| *Lubricating Oil Consumption* | *1.5 - 2 gr./b.h.p.hr.* |
| *Weight per engine* | *10,250 lb.* |
| *Transmissions (2 per loco.)* | *Mekydro Type K 104* |
| *Maximum Rating of each* | *966 h.p. at 1400 r.p.m. input*<br>*1035 h.p. at 1530 r.p.m. input* |
| *Number of Gears (forward and reverse)* | *4* |
| *Final Drive* | *Maybach type C. 33* |
| *Electrical Control System* | *Brown Boveri* |
| *Cooling System* | |
| *Radiator Unit* | *Serck Radiators Ltd.* |
| *Hydraulic Fan Drive* | *Serck-Behr.* |
| *Brake Equipment* | *Laycock Ltd.* |
| *Type* | *Laycock-Knorr vacuum controlled straight air brake* |
| *Air Compressor* | *Knorr type W 100/100* |
| *Vacuum Exhauster (2 per loco.)* | *Westinghouse type 4V110* |
| *Train Heating Boiler* | *Spanner type of 2000 lb. /hr. capacity* |

**Production Batches**

The thirty locomotives ordered in 1957, over a year before D800 had first turned a wheel, incorporated a number of modifications from the first three locomotives. Some of these arose as a result of improvements made by Maybach in the light of the German experience, and which it was wisely decided to leave out when converting the original V200 design to avoid additional complications in the Swindon drawing office. The two most important changes were a redesigned torque converter housing that replaced the original light alloy by cast iron, and with other modifications increased the input capacity which allowed the engines to be uprated by around 10%, and a revised Brown-Boveri control system with seven power notches instead of the earlier six notch version. This made the control system incompatible with D800-D802 which could only work in multiple among themselves; the later locomotives could work with Type 2s D6306-D6357 as well as with each other.

D802-D812 had the same Spanner Swirlyflo Mark 1A vertical fire-tube pattern train heating boiler as D800-D802, but BR then had a policy change in favour of the Stone-Vapor steam generator, a fundamentally different type in which steam is generated in a very long continuous coil of copper pipe. D813-D832 were equipped with the

**D800 in August 1958 waits at Reading General platform 5. The uneven bodywork shows that Swindon was still mastering the tricky techniques of stressed steel construction. The driver's cardholder is clearly in use although after the first few days of service this rather nice touch fell into disuse. (J Savage)**

Stone-Vapor O.K. 4616 type (as were the NBL D833-D865), but D866-D870 reverted back to the Spanner Swirlyflo, using the Mark 1B boiler. In June 1961 D818 was fitted with a horizontal barrel Spanner Swirlyflo Mark 3B train heating boiler 'to obtain experience with and to assess the potentialities of this type of boiler before being installed in the new 2,700 H.P. D H locomotives'. It retained this pattern of boiler until withdrawn.

Externally, the most noticeable difference was the fitting from D813 onwards of four-character route indicators, set in the front cab doors, in place of the steam-style train number panels. Also beginning with D813, the two screwed traps on each cab side below the floor level were replaced by pairs of hinged doors to improve access for transmission maintenance.

There is some mystery surrounding the numbers of locomotives to be built: the PR booklet of 1958 stated 67, of which 33 were to be from Swindon, but in the event an order for five more Maybach-Mekydros, numbered D866-70, was placed under a separate Lot Number in April 1959. D870 was to be the subject of a trial fitting of electric train heating, which would involve increasing the level of turbo-charging by using intercoolers to produce the additional power needed. The experiment was aborted whilst D870 was still under construction, leaving as the only visible sign the Desilux air horns which were moved to a fibreglass cowling at the front edge of the cab roof to make space for the ETH jumper cables below the buffer beam.

### Paxman Engines

There was only one departure from the parent German engines which arose when Paxmans of Colchester persuaded BR to try out two of its 12YJXL engines with a view to installing these in future hydraulic orders. These were fitted from new to D830 MAJESTIC in January 1961 and used the standard Mekydro transmission. The only outward difference from the rest of the batch was the oval offset exhaust ports and boiler room ventilating louvres above the cantrail. D830 is covered in more detail later, in the *On the Record* section.

### The North British D833s

The remaining 34 Type 4 hydraulics still to be ordered when D600 was unveiled were quoted for by NBL in January 1958, in lieu of the BTC apparently relinquishing an option for a further 33 D600s. The deal was finalised for 33 Swindon-design locomotives, numbered D833-D865 and placed on Order P.R.E/A/725/20 dated 3 July 1958; the NBL contract number was L100 and all were to be built at the Hyde Park Works, Springburn.

The major difference was that these locomotives, like their D600 predecessors, were to have British-built M.A.N. engines and Voith transmissions and, to allow the use of the Krauss-Maffei stressed steel construction, a limited licence for NBL to use the technology on locomotives of 2,000 bhp and upwards had been granted in late-1957. The L12V18/21B engines were a modified version of the type used in the D600s and were set to produce an additional 100 bhp each which matched the production series Maybach MD650s. The transmissions were also of a revised type, the LT306r, which was more compact and had a higher input capacity than the L306r of the earlier locomotives.

As the contract began, regular meetings took place between the Swindon drawing office staff and NBL to transfer the knowledge and expertise accumulated there to Glasgow. As might be expected in a project of this type, and given the relative inexperience of both parties involved in building a completely new type of locomotive, difficulties began to emerge, not least because of the need to accommodate the different engine/transmission layout into a design which had already been compressed significantly from the V200. The minutes of these meetings show a certain amount of tension between customer and supplier building up as the contract progressed.

One of the first issues emerged at a meeting on 17 October 1958 attended by Scholes and Sly with ES Cox in attendance: 'Engine interchangeability – WR confirmed that work was proceeding on this aspect and that all necessary information had been received from NBL regarding main dimensions. They mentioned that they were experiencing considerable difficulty in accommodating the M.A.N. engine and Voith Transmission in a frame structure which had been designed to suit a Maybach and Mekydro combination'. Further problems arose because although the mountings on the engines themselves were inter-changeable, the transmission blocks were different and their layout prevented the cardan shafts from being inter-changeable. The Maybach-Mekydro cardan shaft sloped down from the engine to the transmission and the dynostarter cardan was horizontal whereas both sloped upwards in the M.A.N.-Voith arrangement.

Perhaps NBL were getting their own back when they met at Swindon on 21 January 1959, the minutes recording 'NBL again stressed the importance of receiving the remainder of the drawings in order to complete the locomotives within the specified time. Of the estimated total of 350 drawings NBL have only received 183. The latest estimate from Swindon shows that the drawings will not be completed until July 1959, but every endeavour will be made to improve on this date'.

Unsurprisingly, much of the discussion related to costs and more particularly additional items which NBL attempted to charge for. A letter in October 1959 listed seven headings where NBL were seeking to recharge additional drawing office costs. These varied from 32 hours each for outline drawings on eight items concerning electrics, fuel and water equipment changes to the 64 hours for drawing office work on breakfast cookers for each loco to replace the driver's hotplates in the original contract – because the design was 'entirely different'. Perhaps they couldn't be blamed for trying it on, having entered a fixed price contract with the BTC.

The debate on the drawings continued and Smeddle complained to NBL in February 1960 about the cab floor arrangements: 'I am most disturbed to discover that the arrangement of the cab floor shown on your (drawing) bears little resemblance to that now under construction at Swindon for the last ten of the D.800 class locomotives', Next he chided the firm that: 'There have been in your possession for at least eight months tracings of Swindon produced drawings'.

By March 1960 the first locomotive was nearing completion and when NBL asked Swindon for Test and Acceptance Schedules, the reply was: 'Whilst we have established adequate tests and inspection during the final stages of construction on the locomotives of similar type which we are building, we have not hitherto produced any schedules covering the requirements. However, we are proceeding to compile outline notes regarding our procedures'. Smeddle suggested that 'one or two of your people' should come to Swindon for two to three weeks so they could follow through the final stages of testing and inspection. NBL replied that in the meantime it would use its own standard schedules suitably adapted.

D833 was ready two months later and when it was inspected in the first week of May, the Swindon Mechanical Inspector reported that fumes from the engine crankcase breathers escape directly into the engine room, and that it was understood that on the M.A.N. engines there was no provision for connecting a pipe to carry these fumes away. Unfortunately, this was a foretaste of things to come.

When D833 arrived at Swindon it was subjected to an extensive examination and the inspectors listed 49 points which required attention or discussion covering both mechanical and electrical items. Generally of a minor nature, they included:

Modifications on brake gear and ATC fitting
Incorrect fuel oil filters
Rubber Head Protection Pads over Doors and on Lavatory Cistern
Repositioning of Fire Extinguishers
NBL arranging to adopt the (painting) technique advised by BR specialist
Nose air intake drains not fitted
Reversing knobs required on Headcode Indicator
Problems with fitting of ashtrays both on the drivers and co-drivers sides
Rubber covering to be fitted on the cab floor
Front cab roof ventilator to be reversed as early as possible
Additional drain cocks to be fitted on Main Tank Inspection Covers
Increase aperture in side apron for fuel gauge
Drivers desk extension to be stone enamelled instead of painted in gold colour

As part of the political desire to use British components wherever possible, the cardan shafts were to be supplied by Hardy-Spicer. This caused further problems and NBL told Smeddle on 7 June 1960 that modifications were

**SIR BRIAN posing for the official portrait. Note the step on the front skirt on the driver's side fixed to the right hand buffer - some publications state these were not fitted to the first locomotives but this is clearly incorrect.**

required to the bogies and frames to accommodate the British cardan shafts; D833 had been delivered with German-made shafts loaned from Swindon because the modifications would have caused a 'considerable hold up in delivery'.

### Costings

It is clear that a considerable effort went into the design and building of the scaled-down V200s. When George Scholes answered questions arising from his paper to the Institution of Locomotive Engineers on the D800s in November 1959 he said approximately 75,000 man-hours of drawing office were needed to produce the drawings for the first locomotive. The total cost of D800-D802 was £430,000 which worked out at £24,000 each more than D803-D832, which did not bear the drawing office and tooling charges applied to the first three.

The quoted price for the NBL batch was £115,000 including the bought-in Stone-Vapor train heating boiler and Brown-Boveri control system, which was around £4,000 less than the Swindon charges for D803-D832; D866-D870 were even more expensive at £122,000 each. The complex contract with NBL was on an actual ascertained cost plus basis, with a penalty for delay in completion at the rate of ½% per week up to a maximum of 15% of the contract price for each locomotive. Delays built up, not always through the fault of NBL but often with its suppliers such as Hardy-Spicer who delivered the cardan shafts late, and by the time D865 went into traffic in June 1962 the potential claim amounted to over £300,000.

The WR now had around £9 million worth of hydraulics: was it money well spent?

**Key to Numbers —**

1 ENGINE OIL FILLER CAP
2 VALVE COVER.
3 CYLINDER HEAD WATER JACKET
4 WATER JACKET COVER PLATE
5 WATER CONNECTING PIPE.
6 SNUBBER PLATE MOUNTING
7 CYLINDER HEAD
8 EXHAUST MANIFOLD
9 AIR INTAKE PIPE
10 RESTRAINING LINK BRACKET
11 ENGINE CASING.
12 FLYWHEEL LOCATING DOWEL
13 ENGINE CASING EXTENSION
14 SUMP
15 COVER PLATE
16 OIL DRAIN PLUG
17 OIL FILTER
18 OIL DELIVERY PIPE FROM SCAVENGE PUMP
19 OIL DELIVERY PIPE TO MAIN BEAR INGS
20 OIL PRESSURE PUMP SUCTION PIPE.
21 OIL SUCTION PIPE TO SCAVENGE PUMP
22 OIL PRESSURE PUMP.
23. OIL SCAVENGE PUMP
24. BELT TENSIONER.
25 OIL PUMP DRIVE IDLER WHEEL.
26. FUEL-INJECTION PUMP DRIVE BEVEL GEAR HOUSING.
27 RESILIENT MOUNTING.
28 FUEL-INJECTION PUMP.
29 INLET VALVE
30 EXHAUST VALVE

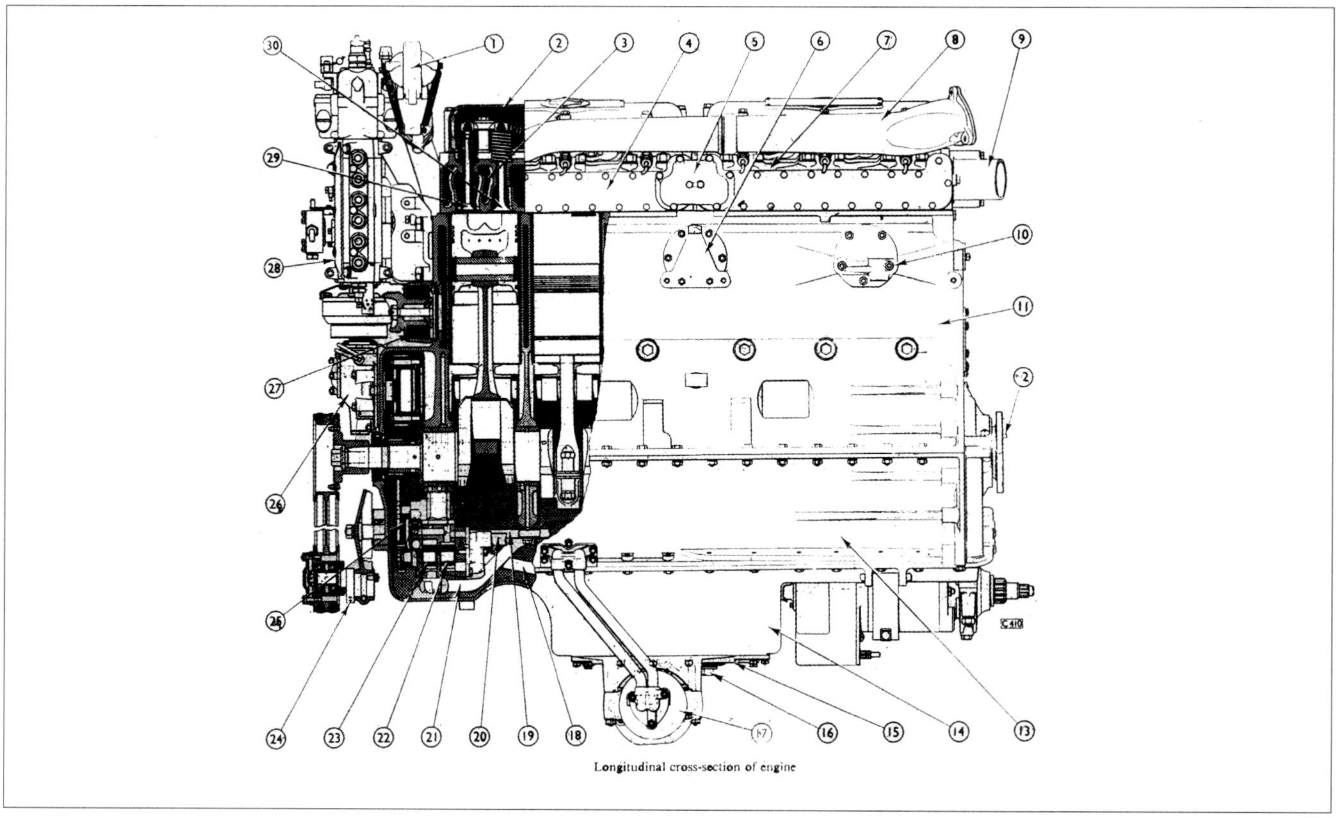


**The MAN L12V18/21B engine which proved inferior to the Maybach in the Swindon-built locomotives.**

Though still cluttered by the steam-age lamp holders above the electric lights, the nose end was considerably cleaned up by the addition of the route indicator box. A posed D837 RAMILLIES on 28 March 1961 has an 82A Bristol Bath Road shedplate (no Warships were allocated there) being fixed into position on the pad by the left-hand buffer – a clear indication that this is a NBL machine.

Crowds gather to inspect D600 ACTIVE at Paddington prior to departure on its first official run hauling a nine-coach special to Bristol on 17 February 1958. The WR pipped the Eastern Region to the post with the first Type 4 into BR service, but things almost backfired when one of D600's engines failed on the return journey. (www.rail-online.co.uk)

On 19 March 1958 D600 ACTIVE made its first visit to Plymouth and is pictured with a 10-coach test train on Rattery Bank.

## Chapter 4
# OPERATION

In this chapter I have tried to present new material wherever possible, including recollections from some of those with first-hand experience of the Warships. The published works by Brian Webb and JK Lewis provide much additional detail on the depots, workshops and organisational background of the Western Region.

**D600s – the first tentative steps**

After its almost disastrous official debut in mid-February D600 continued with crew training and testing from Swindon; ACTIVE made its first run to Plymouth on March 19 1958 with a 10-coach test train. The following week it worked the 8.50am Swindon-Paddington, with a layover and refuelling at Old Oak Common before taking the 12.45pm Old Oak-Neyland fish as far as Gloucester, returning to Swindon on the 7.12pm Gloucester-Swindon. On 19 April it worked a special to Newton Abbot and then made its first visit to Penzance two days later on empty stock. In early May it was regularly working between Plymouth and Penzance including the up *Cornish Riviera Express* (*CRE*) and the up Postal.

D601 visited Oxford on April 23 during its trial running with a 10 coach train, and again on 5 May; it was in Swindon on May 18 after a test run to Plymouth and back on 15 May with the GWR dynamometer car as part of a 440 ton train. Two runs were made between Newton Abbot and Plymouth, the first pair non-stop and the second pair with stops at selected points on the banks at Dainton, Rattery and Hemerdon to check its ability to restart. In each case ARK ROYAL proved unable to shift its heavy load without putting sand on the rails, slipping so much that it damaged the rails at Dainton. Later in the month it began work on the down *CRE* returning on the 9.30pm sleeper from Penzance.

D601 made a series of runs on 11 June with a 12 coach train and the dynamometer car between Newton Abbot and Plymouth to assess the capacity of steam plus diesel double heading to handle the heavy summer Saturday loads over the South Devon hills. It piloted Castle No.7000 and Manor No.7815 and was piloted by Hall No.4905.

The fuel capacity of the D600s allowed a round trip between London and Plymouth without refuelling, even when using the train heating boiler. On 16 June ARK ROYAL began what was planned to be a regular working between Paddington and Plymouth on the down *CRE*, returning on a night train. The *CRE* was the first diesel-hauled non-stop between London and Plymouth and once again the WR had stolen a march on its peers: the Eastern Region English Electric Type 4 diesel-electrics did not start working the *Flying Scotsman* until nearly a week later. Unfortunately, its triumph was short-lived, and after two failures in four days D601 was taken off this duty and put back onto the up and down *CRE* between Plymouth and Penzance.

During July both D600 and D601 were at work in Cornwall with occasional duties east of Plymouth. Their Monday-Friday rosters were:

(1) 6.50am Plymouth-Penzance
11.0am Penzance-Plymouth
4.30pm Plymouth-Penzance
8.45pm Penzance-Plymouth

(2) 4.50am Plymouth-Penzance
11.0am Penzance-Plymouth
2.35pm Plymouth-Penzance
8.45pm Penzance-Plymouth

They did not work on Sundays, but on Saturday 19 July D601 was piloted by Manor No.7816 on the 10.35am ex-Paddington from Plymouth to Penzance. On August 9 D600 was piloted by King No.6012 on the Saturday 10.30am from Paddington; the King had the old *Cornish Riviera Limited* headboard but D600's was the new *Cornish Riviera Express* introduced with the diesels in April 1958.

They began to venture further afield again and, on weekdays in early August, D600 regularly worked the 9.30pm Penzance-Paddington and the following day returned on the down *CRE*, while D601 worked the up *CRE* from Plymouth to Paddington, the 6.30pm Paddington-Bristol and the 2.55pm ex-Manchester from Bristol to Plymouth.

CJ Allen reported in the December 1958 *Trains Illustrated* a footplate trip on D601 from Paddington to Plymouth with 11 coaches, reduced by slip to ten from Heywood Road, which covered the 225½ miles in 235 minutes, 15 minutes ahead of schedule and reaching a maximum speed of 92mph at Curry Rivel. The novelty of the new diesels was evident: 'The smooth riding of the locomotive at high speed was most impressive' and the soundproofing of the cab was 'just as notable'. CJA was unsurprisingly much taken with 'the magnificent view through the big windows ahead'.

D602 BULLDOG finally appeared at the beginning of October and spent most of the month running in from Swindon. By this time the first two had begun to settle down: D600 was on the 9.30pm Penzance-Paddington and the down *CRE*; D601 was on the 7.15am Plymouth-Paddington and down *Royal Duchy*. D603 CONQUEST arrived in November and in the first week of the month D602 worked the 7.50am Taunton-Paddington and a down afternoon parcels. On December 8/9 D601 worked special speed trials between Didcot and Bristol, via both Bath and Badminton routes, reportedly in connection with the acceleration of the *Bristolian*.

**Problems begin to emerge**

Although the Component Change and/or Exchange records summarised in the *On the Record* section contain details of the works visits and depot repairs, they do not tell the full story of the problems in the first few years, not least because they did not record the return visits of the locomotives to NBL in Glasgow. The latter were reported in the operating statistics included in the minutes of the BR Motive Power Committee which show how bad the position became; for long periods in 1959-62 two and sometimes three of the five locomotives were out of service.

**D600-4 Statistics from the minutes of the BR Motive Power Committee**

| Period ended | % avail. (1) | Daily mileage (2) | 4 weeks ended | % avail. (1) | Daily mileage (2) | 4 weeks ended | % avail. (1) | Daily mileage (2) |
|---|---|---|---|---|---|---|---|---|
| 08/08/59 | 71.0 | 471 | 13/08/60 | 70.0 | 464 | 12/08/61 | 45.0 | 472 |
| 05/09/59 | 68.5 | 493 | 10/09/60 | 50.0 | 577 | 09/09/61 | 50.0 | 462 |
| 03/10/59 | 73.3 | 433 | 08/10/60 | 55.0 | 468 | 07/10/61 | 65.0 | 415 |
| 31/10/59 | 32.5 | 467 | 05/11/60 | 50.0 | 364 | 04/11/61 | 60.0 | 404 |
| 28/11/59 | 37.5 | 536 | 03/12/60 | 35.0 | 272 | 02/12/61 | 55.0 | 396 |
| 26/12/59 | 36.5 | 415 | 31/12/60 | 45.0 | 332 | 30/12/61 | 60.0 | 408 |
| 30/01/60 | 45.8 | 500 | 28/01/61 | 40.0 | 472 | 27/01/62 | 60.0 | 417 |
| 27/02/60 | 50.8 | 531 | 25/02/61 | 40.0 | 482 | 24/02/62 | 20.0 | 333 |
| 26/03/60 | 48.3 | 485 | 25/03/61 | 45.0 | 415 | 24/03/62 | 20.0 | 496 |
| 23/04/60 | 21.8 | 585 | 22/04/61 | 40.0 | 401 | 21/04/62 | 60.0 | 447 |
| 21/05/60 | 43.5 | 285 | 20/05/61 | 60.0 | 409 | 19/05/62 | 80.0 | 206 |
| 18/06/60 | 57.3 | 406 | 17/06/61 | 45.0 | 498 | 16/06/62 | 80.0 | 317 |
| 16/07/60 | 45.0 | 484 | 15/07/61 | 35.0 | 540 | 14/07/62 | 80.0 | 189 |
| | | | | | | | | |
| Average | 48.6 | 468 | Average | 46.9 | 438 | Average | 56.5 | 382 |

(1) % availability for the whole 24 hours (2) Miles per locomotive per weekday - in use

| D600 ACTIVE | |
|---|---|
| Sun 7th - Mon 8th | Laira - M/R (*Battery charging, W/M resistances since 26 June*) |
| Tue 9th | Laira - M/R (*Battery charging and waiting materials; Resistances; Off A.M.*) / 5B57 8.05am Tavistock Junction - Penzance to Truro / 5B77 11.45am Truro - Tavistock Junction / 5B81 3.50pm Tavistock Junction - Truro / 5B78 5.0pm Penzance - Bristol West Depot > 8.07pm from Truro to Tavistock Junction / Laira. |

| D601 ARK ROYAL | |
|---|---|
| Sun 7th | **Truro** |
| Mon 8th | **Truro / 0Z36 12.50am Truro - Laira / Laira / 4C07 3.42am Tavistock Junction - Penzance to Truro / 5B77 7.25am Truro - Tavistock Junction / 5B81 12.05pm Tavistock Junction - Truro / Truro / 5A17 2.50pm Penzance - Paddington > 6.15pm from Truro to Tavistock Junction / 5B81 9.20pm Tavistock Junction - Truro / Truro.** |
| Tue 9th | **Truro / 5C05 12.50am Truro - Tavistock Junction / Laira / 4C07 8.30pm Paddington - Penzance > 3.42am starting from Tavistock Junction to Truro / 5B77 7.25am Truro - Tavistock Junction / 5B81 12.05pm Tavistock Junction - Truro / Truro / 5A17 2.50pm Penzance - Paddington > 6.15pm from Truro to Tavistock Junction / 5B81 9.20pm Tavistock Junction - Truro / Truro.** |

| D602 BULLDOG | |
|---|---|
| Sun 7th – Tue 9th | **Laira - M/R (*exhaust manifold cracked and 375 hour exam since 6 July*)** |

| D603 CONQUEST | |
|---|---|
| Sun 7th | **St. Blazey** |
| Mon 8th | **St. Blazey / 5B28 6.45am St. Blazey - Fowey / 5C13 8.10am St Blazey - Burngullow / 5B77 9.40am Burngullow - St Blazey / 5B28 10.35am St. Blazey - Fowey / 5B77 11.10am Fowey - St Blazey / 5B28 11.55am St Blazey - Fowey / 5B77 12.30pm Fowey - St Blazey / 5B78 1.30pm St. Blazey - Tavistock Junction / 5B70 7.30pm Tavistock Junction - St. Blazey / St. Blazey.** |
| Tue 9th | **St. Blazey / 5B28 6.45am St. Blazey - Fowey / 5C13 8.10am St Blazey - Burngullow / 5B77 9.40am Burngullow - St Blazey / 5B28 10.35am St. Blazey - Fowey / 5B77 11.10am Fowey - St Blazey / 5B28 11.55am St Blazey - Fowey / 5B77 12.30pm Fowey - St Blazey / 5B78 1.30pm St. Blazey - Tavistock Junction / 5B70 7.30pm Tavistock Junction - St. Blazey / St. Blazey.** |

| D604 COSSACK | |
|---|---|
| Sat 6th | **Penzance / 3C74 10.20pm Penzance - Plymouth ECS.** |
| Sun 7th | **.....3C74 to Plymouth / Laira / 1C08 10.30pm Paddington - Penzance *'Sleeper'* > 5.25am from Plymouth / Penzance / 1A81 9.55am Penzance - Paddington *'Cornish Riviera Express'* to Plymouth / Laira.** |
| Mon 8th | **Laira / 3C08 2.20am Plymouth - Penzance *'Mails & Milk empties'* / Penzance / 2C74 8.0am Penzance - Plymouth / 3C15 1.55am Swindon - Penzance *'Parcels'* > 11.30am from Plymouth / Penzance / 1M78 4.50pm Penzance - Manchester to Plymouth / Laira.** |
| Tue 9th | **Laira / 3C08 2.20am Plymouth - Penzance *'Mails & Milk empties'* / Penzance / 2C74 8.0am Penzance - Plymouth / 3C15 10.40pm Paddington - Penzance *'Parcels'* > 11.30am from Plymouth / Penzance / 1M78 4.50pm Penzance - Manchester to Plymouth / Laira.** |

On 13 February 1959 D603 and D604 were returned to Glasgow for rectification just a few weeks after delivery and D604 was still in Scotland in early April. D600 was out of traffic for two months from April until early July with the records noting that it underwent modifications by NBL engineers.

After a brief upturn, the rot set in during the autumn: in October availability plummeted with D601, D603 and D604 in works; two locomotives were there for the whole month and another for three weeks. One was having the engine rebuilt, one had transmission defects and the other had its engines modified. The rebuilding continued into November when an engine defect resulted in another being taken out of traffic, and in the final week of the month one was sent back to NBL. December saw the engine rebuild still continuing and D602 was in works for a month after collision damage when it was hit by Castle No.5028 at Devonport Junction on 15 December.

NBL still hosted one D600 and in the second week of January 1960 it was joined by another of the class. By the end of February they were both still in Glasgow, although one was returned to the WR in early March. Later in the month one went to Swindon after an engine seizure and was joined the following week by another for modification to its bogies, by NBL engineers. April saw the locomotive at NBL remain there (it stayed until the end of June) and in week ending 16 April the availability reached its nadir of *ten per cent* as two were now in Swindon with defective engines and a third for cylinder head modifications and transmission defects.

Two more of the class were sent to Glasgow for short stays in July: one for attention to its transmissions and a bogie repair and the other for examination of its engines. In August D600 went into Swindon for a Light Casual repair which took more than three months and no sooner had it returned to traffic then it was stopped at Laira for two weeks waiting for materials from Swindon. All told, it was stopped for 143 days during 1960, and D601 and D602 were not far behind.

1961 was even worse with each locomotive in the class stopped for over

**D600 ACTIVE in the classic sea wall pose at Teignmouth with the up 'Cornish Riviera Limited' on 2 September 1958. The 'Limited' headboards were used from 1956 until it became the 'Cornish Riviera Express' in April 1958. Perhaps they couldn't find the new headboards at Laira on this day. (KI Cook)**

100 days, and D601 and D604 for more than 200 days. The problems continued into the following year even though from the final period in July 1962 they were no longer used east of Newton Abbot: hence the sharp decrease in daily mileage. Things declined even more by period ending 6/10/62, when the figure reached a low point of just 94 daily miles per locomotive in use, with 40% availability.

Typical duties in the later years are illustrated by their workings during the three days from Sunday 7 to Tuesday 9 July 1963 when one was under repair for the whole time, three were wholly on freight and only D604 was on passenger duties (*see table page 42*)

Although their already limited use on top duty passenger work continued to decline as the Westerns took over most of the West of England work from 1964, the D600s still occasionally worked the prestige duties, right up to their demise. For example, D600 and D604 were seen on the Western turn covering the down *CRE* from Plymouth returning on the up 'Postal' from Penzance on 11 and 27 July 1967 respectively.

**Statistically speaking**

The D600s were certainly damned by their availability statistics, although in fairness their stopped time was due as much to their low number and their non-standard components, which for engines and transmissions were only inter-changeable with the six Pilot Scheme D6300s.

**Days stopped by year – as recorded in the maintenance files**

| Year | D600 | D601 | D602 | D603 | D604 |
|---|---|---|---|---|---|
| 1958 | 26 | 26 | 0 | 23 | 0 |
| 1959 | 96 | 66 | 57 | 137 | 43 |
| 1960 | 140 | 93 | 124 | 28 | 74 |
| 1961 | 119 | 234 | 167 | 99 | 208 |
| 1962 | 159 | 19 | 120 | 93 | 109 |
| 1963 | 52 | 36 | 10 | 38 | 100 |
| 1964 | 73 | 26 | 232 | 98 | 107 |
| 1965 | 37 | 145 | 1 | 289 | 12 |
| 1966 | 76 | ? | 118 | 5 | 206 |
| 1967 | 133 | ? | 43 | 30 | 22 |
| **Total** | 911 | 645 | 872 | 840 | 881 |
| **%** | 25.1% | 18.2% | 26.1% | 25.2% | 27.0% |
| **Mileages** | | | | | |
| Total | 637,000 | 587,000 | 500,000 | 512,000 | 480,000 |
| Annual Average | 64,086 | 60,032 | 54,559 | 56,171 | 53,627 |

Note – the information for D601 is incomplete from 1964 onwards and the visits to NBL in 1959/60 for rectification work are not included

Although other writers have stated that the three locomotives with Glasgow-built engines and transmissions were significantly inferior to the first two German equipped locomotives, both the lifetime mileage and stoppage figures show there was little to choose between them, even before allowing for the later entry into service and shorter time on the longer-distance work. The regular changing of these main components in fact meant that, over time, they were shared across the whole class as well as with D6300-D6305.

Many of the problems on the Glasgow-built L12V18/21S units arose from sub-standard components in their initial construction, though when NBL-supplied spare parts were used on the original L12V18/21A engines, their failure rates increased too. Lewis in *The Western's Hydraulics* says that some senior BR officers later admitted that NBL might have done better to have sourced all the M.A.N. engines required direct from Augsburg, but the political climate at the time made this impossible.

It is certain that poor reliability of the engine/transmission units had a significant effect on both usage and availability, especially after the demise of NBL when engine parts had to be ordered direct from M.A.N. in Germany. The M.A.N. engines suffered from excessive crankshaft vibration, and there was much experimentation before the correct specification of joints in the cardans linking engine and transmission was arrived at, but not before a series of premature transmission bearing failures.

The problems were amplified when difficulties also emerged with the D833s, which began to overload maintenance facilities at Swindon Works and also at the running depots. The limited applicability and restricted parts compatibility of the D600s often gave them a very low priority for the

**D602 BULLDOG trundles through Hayes with an express freight on 4 May 1959. D600s were more often found on front line passenger services at this time but as the years went by the ratio of freight to passenger increased greatly.**

completion of routine maintenance and overhaul work, which in turn caused higher failure rates and longer periods out of service. In later years many of the faults which kept the locomotives out of traffic were concerned with the supporting auxiliaries rather than the major units. As they aged, the David Brown final drive units were a regular service problem, as were parts of the electrical system and the electrical machines, such as dynostarters and cooling fan drives, which often resulted in damage to the locomotives' mechanical parts or electrical systems.

### Unwanted, unloved, withdrawn

The decision not to build any more D600s after the initial Pilot Scheme batch left them as a non-standard class and they naturally took second place after the introduction of the 71 D800/D833s. By the mid-1960s BR was in a position to take stock of the benefits and shortcomings of its hastily assembled diesel fleet. In the National Traction Plan published in February 1965 it was observed that overall WR diesel-hydraulic availability fluctuated considerably over the nine months to December 1964, with the report noting that although this standard of availability was unsatisfactory there was no evidence it would exceed 70% 'for some time'. (This was against an 80% benchmark – which was also missed by all the diesel-electric classes). However the figures for the D600s varied between 20% and 60%, by far the worst availability figures for any Type 4 on BR, and they were singled out as having 'frequent defects'. The actual figures shown by the accompanying graph show a wider variation – perhaps the 100% in the first couple of weeks was a statistical blip.

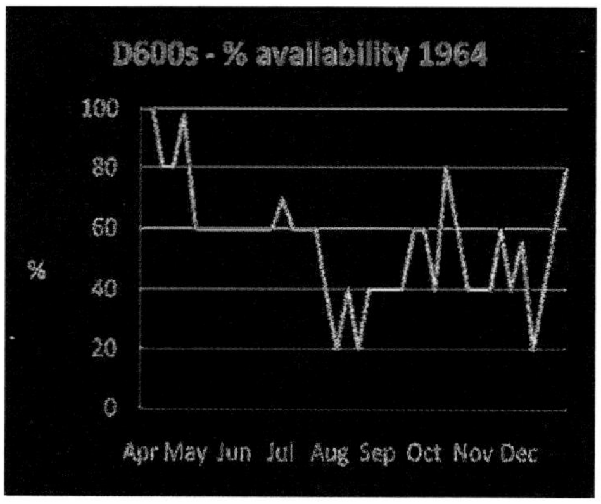


The plan showed WR Type 4 requirements had been reassessed from 347 to 231 between December 1963 and December 1964; the actual stock was 274 at 26 December 1964. The 231 included 23 Contingency and 46 Maintenance Spares. The writing was on the wall for the D600s but it was to be a further two years before the Plan was implemented by eliminating types which had given trouble, had excessive maintenance costs, or which were non-standard. Incredibly, four of the class received Intermediate overhauls in 1965/66.

Apart from the early acceptance trials and testing of D600 and D601 in 1958 working from Swindon, all five were allocated to Plymouth Laira, where their idiosyncrasies were well-known to maintenance staff. They were away only for a few weeks in late-1967 when three of them had a brief sojourn in South Wales. D602 moved to Llandore on 4 August; D601 followed a fortnight later on 21st, double-headed with D1017 to Newport as part of the transfer working; D604 joined them on 18 September, working the same train as D601, this time in tandem with D1057. They were sent to work mineral trains in place of English Electric Type 3 diesel-electrics transferred to the Eastern Region, and it was hoped to take advantage of their weight and braking capacity. They were based at Landore, and worked out of there and Pantyffynnon on mineral trains in the Swansea and Llanelly areas as well as on general goods traffic over the southern end of the Central Wales line.; they were observed on two occasions on trip workings from Llandeilo Junction up the Central Wales line as far north as Llandrindod Wells.

Their Welsh excursion did not last long and on 22 November D601 piloted by D602 returned to Laira, and D604 followed light engine two days later. They rejoined D600 and D603 on their regular Cornish duties and these continued right up to the day before withdrawal on 31 December, with D602 BULLDOG recorded on the 12 noon Penzance-Paddington as late as 28 December 1967.

After they were switched off for the last time, all five remained at Laira for several months, but finally on 22 July 1968 D600 and D601 were towed by

D7055 to Woodham's scrapyard at Barry. A week later D1006 took D602-D604 to Cashmores at Newport where they were scrapped by the end of November. D600 was cut-up in 1970 but D601 lingered on until 1980.

**D600s - the last word**

The D600s had their supporters on the Western Region and the case for the defence was summarised by BL Wilson, Traction Controller at Paddington, in a letter to the RCTS *Railway Observer* in 1968: *These locomotives like most other diesel types (particularly hydraulics) gave a fair amount of trouble when new and for some time afterwards in this case. I agree that some in particular have spent longer spells than usual in Works. However, of those in service at Plymouth (generally 4 or 5 per day through most of last summer and autumn until the transfers took place), their performance was no worse and no better than other locomotives over the same route. They were allocated with discretion when it came to the heavier trains but the down 'Limited' was quite often entrusted to them.*

*The Laira and Penzance men became very conversant with them and they presented no undue obstacles apart from route availability in some of the sidings in Cornwall. Route availability was in fact the main reason for their return from South Wales to Plymouth, not their unreliability or the fancies of the Landore drivers. I am not convinced that Landore men handled them anyway, they were usually with Margam or Pantyffynnon men and suitable instructors.*

*With regard to the withdrawal of these locomotives the fleet was being reduced and the elimination of a non standard class with the associated savings in stores etc., was considerable.*

**Into battle with the D800s**

The official unveiling of D800 was on 14 July when it ran light from Swindon to Paddington to be named SIR BRIAN ROBERTSON by the WR General Manager KWC Grand. Afterwards it worked a four-coach special conveying high ranking WR employees and the press on a run to Reading and back – the WR were clearly taking no chances after D600's debacle earlier in the year! D800 carried a headboard which proclaimed it to be FIRST 2,200 H.P. DIESEL-HYDRAULIC LOCOMOTIVE BUILT IN BRITISH RAILWAYS WORKSHOPS - SWINDON 1958 (the actual rating was 2,100hp – D803 was the first at 2200hp).

After an overnight stay at Old Oak Common D800 worked its first passenger train, No.416 the 10.30am Paddington to Penzance *Cornish Riviera Limited*, through to Plymouth North Road where it had been intended to hand over to D601 ARK ROYAL. Unfortunately D601 was failed whilst leaving Laira on its way to North Road and instead a Hall 4-6-0 No.6907 was turned out to relieve D800. The following day D800 returned to London at the head of the 1.20pm Penzance-Paddington, leaving Plymouth at 4.10pm. This train ran to Newton Abbot loaded to nine vehicles weighing 312 tons, where a further four vehicles were attached bringing the load up to 448 tons. Despite a 15 minute delay at Taunton D800 still managed to bring its train into Paddington 10 minutes early. The special headboard remained on the locomotive until it returned to the safe confines of Swindon on the 17th.

The next passenger working for D800 was on Saturday 26 July, a rugby special from Paddington to Swansea. Conveying guests in the Pullman coaches of the *South Wales Pullman* D800 departed from Paddington at 08.55 am, returning later that same day. D800 re-entered Swindon Works on 27 July for final acceptance testing and was officially taken into traffic from 11 August, allocated to 82C Swindon until the following month when it moved to Laira.

D801 VANGUARD did not enter traffic until early November because during October it took part in Traction Performance and Fuel Consumption Tests on the Controlled Road Testing System to establish the characteristics for the class. These tests were made over the main routes between Didcot and Bristol, down via Bath and up via Badminton. George Scholes summarised the results of the tests in his paper to the Institution of Mechanical Engineers in November 1959: *The locomotive was tested in all notches from 0 to 6, except for notch 1, each with the load which enabled the speed range to be covered. In notch 6 the maximum speed from which test data was obtained was 103 m.p.h.*

**D602 BULLDOG passes under Westbourne Bridge as it leaves Paddington on 6 August 1960 with the 1C30 10.30 Paddington-Penzance 'Cornish Riviera Express'. The chalked C45 train reporting code, just visible under the headboard, relates to a previous working on the 1C45 5.30pm Paddington-Plymouth 'Mayflower'. (RC Riley, www.transporttreasury.co.uk)**

**D601 ARK ROYAL departs from Exeter on 1 February 1962 with the down 'Cornish Riviera Express'. From the beginning of the summer 1962 service the D600s were restricted to operating west of Newton Abbot. The 'CRE' headboard was often worn right of centre – not surprisingly given the crude fixing. (R Shutter)**

*Fuel consumptions were measured and recorded by precision fuel meters and compared with consumptions relative to b.h.p. obtained for the same engines on the test bed. The mileage run between the two types of tests was very small.*

*The overall mechanical efficiency of transmission and final drive reaches 82½ per cent between the gear changes, a figure only marginally lower than the overall efficiency of the electric transmission of Southern Region Diesel-electric Locomotive No. 10203 previously tested by the Western Region. A noteworthy feature of the arrangements in the D.800 series is that high overall transmission efficiency is associated with the highest operating speeds.*

*The maximum test load was 15 coaches and the minimum three coaches. All trains were started on a rising gradient of 1 in 74 in the appropriate notch positions without any difficulty whatsoever although rail conditions varied between moist and dry. Nevertheless, separate tests on steeply graded routes in the West of England demonstrated that starting from signals on track graded steeper than 1 in 100 proved difficult when a Rail Tractive Effort greater than 0.276 times the nominal adhesive weight was required to start the load on a dry rail. Since conditions such as occur with hill-fog and sea-mist are not exceptional, Rail Tractive Effort no greater than 0.24 times the nominal adhesive weight should be used for determining practical maximum loads in such situations.*

*The notch spacings provided, therefore, appear to be too coarse for obtaining that fine balance which is desirable between starting Rail Tractive Effort and Adhesion over the practical range of adhesion conditions. In view of this arrangements have since been made to add one more notch to future D.800 Class control equipment, the maximum addition possible without making radical modifications to the apparatus.*

*During the tests of D.801, test periods under extreme conditions were endured without overheating.*

*To conclude this section of the Paper, it should be stated that the performance on test of Locomotive D.801 was almost exactly that predicted for it from a consideration of the characteristics originally furnished by the engine and transmission manufacturers.*

By the end of October 1958 D800 was working a diagram comprising the up *CRE* from Plymouth to London, returning with the 6.30pm Paddington-Bristol and 9.5pm Bristol-Plymouth. The next month D801 followed suit and was quickly joined by D802 FORMIDABLE which went into service on 16 December.

On February 16 1959 the *Bristolian* was worked by a diesel for the first time when D801 powered both down and up services. This was a prelude to the summer service beginning on 15 June, when the schedule for the seven-coach train was cut by five minutes to 100 minutes, the first 70mph schedules since before World War Two. Meanwhile, deliveries of the production batch began in March with D803 and continued at roughly one each month until D812 appeared in November. Next off the line was D804 AVENGER which became the first main line diesel to be stationed at Bristol; based at Marsh Junction from 11 May it worked a diagram consisting of 6.25am Bristol-Plymouth, 10.30am Plymouth-Bristol, 6.26pm Bristol-Paddington, 11.50pm Paddington-Bristol.

As would be expected the Western Region made sure that their accelerated *Bristolian* made the headlines. On 15 June, the first day of the new timetable, the load for D805 BENBOW on the down service was 8 coaches, the usual Monday 'extra' having been added. It reached Bristol in a net time of 91 minutes; this was nine minutes better than the accelerated schedule and was almost certainly the fastest run yet made from Paddington to Bristol, with a maximum speed of 95mph. The return with D804 AVENGER was even more spectacular and arrived at Paddington in a net time of 87 minutes, albeit with seven coaches, and after maxima of 102mph at Little Somerford and Wantage Road. To emphasise that the first day was no fluke, during the first week of diesel operation the *Bristolian* was between 2 and 7½ minutes early into Bristol. The *Bristolian* duty was part of a roster comprising:

7.00pm Penzance-Paddington 'Postal' from Plymouth
8.45am Paddington-Bristol *Bristolian*
12.00pm Bristol-Paddington
4.15pm Paddington-Bristol-Plymouth
The reverse diagram was:
11.08am Plymouth-Bristol
4.30pm Paddington-Bristol *Bristolian*
8.05pm Paddington-Bristol
6.25am Bristol-Plymouth

The WR Civil Engineers were not happy with this high speed operation on their tracks and quickly imposed a 90mph ceiling on all lines. The Derby Research Department was brought in to supervise high speed tests, using D800 and D602 between Maidenhead and Twyford, investigating cases of damage to rail ends by diesels; D800 was reported to have reached 105mph. But worse was to come.

**That K-M bogie**

The WR's glory came to an abrupt halt before the end of the year as the *Bristolian* was decelerated back to its former 105 minute schedule and an 80mph maximum speed limit was imposed on the Warships, with a temporary speed notice to that effect fitted in their cabs. The problem lay with Krauss-Maffei's patent bogie; Sam Ell, Head of the Experimental Section at Swindon, gave a comprehensive account in a paper to The Institution of Locomotive Engineers in 1966 of the 'serious troubles' of 'diesel-hydraulic locomotives as a result of a fundamental error in bogie design': *The D.800 B-B Diesel-hydraulic Type '4' locomotive is the British version of the two-engine German V.200 Class of Krauss-Maffei design. As built, the bogie embodied a novel feature identical in each class. Because the space normally occupied by the bogie centre pin was required by the drive system a virtual centre was provided by a link and bell crank system without, however, making provision for the lateral freedom which is apparently required by first principles and which is, moreover, traditionally provided. This engendered the misgivings felt when the design was acquired by British Railways, in spite of the good repute gained by the V.200 Class on the German State Railways reinforced by the proving trials carried out on modern conventional lines between Aalen and Hamm in Germany.*

*These misgivings did not long remain unjustified, for it was found (a) when negotiating isolated and groups of lateral and cross-level track irregularities, high lateral accelerations of the body were experienced, occasionally, irrespective of tyre condition, (b) sustained high-frequency lateral oscillation of the body was experienced in high-speed running when the tyre mileage exceeded 30,000. Condition (a) gave rise to concern as to the extent of the margin remaining against instability whilst (b) was extremely uncomfortable, the frequency being 2-3 c.p.s. and the amplitude in space, measured in the cab, as much as plus or minus 1.1 ins., the maximum acceleration then being 0.58g: recordings from the same locomotive taken at the same places at the same speeds on successive occasions exhibited not only the same pattern but were identical, oscillation for oscillation, with amplitude increasing with tyre wear.*

*The problem emerged as one of track and vehicle interaction involving the lateral stiffness of the connection between body and bogie. Pending a solution of the problem a speed limit of 80 m.p.h. was imposed on the locomotives and the tyre mileage limited to 50,000.*

*Meanwhile the same design of bogie, extended to the C-C arrangement, was appearing on the Type '4' D.1000 Class, providing an experience which was exactly a repetition of that of the D.800 Class.*

[The body was carried on integral central pillars which transmitted the weight to the centre of the inverted laminated springs, via rubber blocks originally. Subsequently they were replaced by metal blocks faced with non-ferrous plates to take the 'twist']

*From the ends of the laminated springs, swing links and rocking plates transfer the load to the bogie frame via guided helical springs in pairs. As stated previously the primary/secondary deflection ratio is 20/80 ...and the centring linkage, in elevation, lies on the axle horizontal centre line. The fulcrums of the bell cranks are attached to the bogie frame. The arms of the two cranks that normally lie parallel to the longitudinal centre line are connected by links to two points on a downward extension of the body. The other arms of the cranks, normally at right angles to this centre line, are connected by another link. All pins are in*

**D603 CONQUEST at Plymouth in August 1964 – the D600s were almost ignored by photographers by this time with the D800s and Westerns prevalent. This was not helped by D602 and D603 each spending almost a year in Swindon Works during 1964/5. (www.rail-online.co.uk)**

**D603 CONQUEST with a long train of china clay at Saltash on 4 April 1967. Freight duties in Cornwall were the staple work for the class in its final years. (Alec Swain, www.transporttreasury.co.uk)**

*rubber bushes with a combined compression characteristic of 0.068 ins. under a load of 8 tons. The linkage forms a virtual centre pin, allowing relative rotation and also the transference of lateral load between body and bogie frame, movement being limited to the small amount permitted by the rubber bushes. Traction and braking forces are taken on pads placed between the body extension and the bogie, fore and aft the virtual centre.*

*From measurements of the displacements of the links during transverse body oscillation it was established that the centre of oscillation of the body in the horizontal plane was at a point on its centre line 3 ft. forward of the central position between bogie centres and that then the bogie lateral displacement was parallel to the track centre line and mean centre line of body transverse movement. The lateral stiffness between body and axles amounted to 25 tons per inch, part of which was accounted for by the rubbers in the radius arms which carry the outer and inner axleboxes.*

*Reduction of this stiffness (was) effected by removing the Krauss-Maffei link and crank gear altogether, leaving control over the lateral and rotational movements to the swing links, which function then as in the Dean bogie that, in its time and for several decades, was a highly successful carriage bogie on the former Great Western Railway. Stops limiting the lateral movement to ¾in. each way were fitted and, as a precautionary measure, adopted only after extensive proving trials without them, a pair of hydraulic dampers are now fitted per bogie, each with a resistance varying from 400 Ib. at 1.9 ft./min. to 2000 Ib. at 14.6 ft./min. Traction and braking forces continue to be taken on the original pads, slightly modified.*

*The proving trials were made over a long length of track in both directions in order to obtain a fully representative range of track and vehicle interaction. On each run 155 miles of frost-affected track were covered at 85 m.p.h. and above and 91 miles at 90 m.p.h. and over. The incidence of lateral acceleration of 0.3g was extremely rare.. Frequency of lateral oscillation was found to have fallen (and) all discomfort at high speeds to have disappeared. The tyre mileage then was 64,500 and the tests were followed up at intervals until the mileage reached 150,000 without the riding qualities being adversely affected.*

*All bogies of the D.800 and D.1000 Classes were then modified and with the modification the speed restriction was removed.*

*When the bad riding of the D.800 Class as built was first investigated the conclusions reached by British Railways that it stemmed from the restriction on lateral movement imposed by the centring gear was resisted by Krauss-Maffei engineers who considered it originated in the transverse sinusoidal movement of the wheels and suggested that the tyre profiles be changed from the standard B.R. to the Heumann-Lotter, which had been adopted as standard by the German Federal Railway in 1953. The claims made for this profile are (a) the 70° flank is capable of taking higher side forces, (b) reduced flange and tread wear – a shape fitting more closely into the rail head so that wear is more evenly distributed, and (c) the form of root absorbs the sinusoidal movements on straight track instead of the flange. In the circumstances as they then were, with high lateral forces and mileage between reprofiling down to 50,000 this recommendation was accepted and the standard German profile was adopted for the Krauss-Maffei bogies, but with the flange depth increased to provide additional protection. This profile became known as the 'Composite.'*

*Before the effect of the composite profile on the original riding condition could be assessed, the centring gear was removed and the riding position, as previously stated, became satisfactory at all stages of tyre wear. The question then arose as to the extent, if any, of the contribution made by the composite profile. A number of locomotives of this Class were therefore given the standard B.R. profile with the 1 in 20 slope. Comparative riding tests were then made at various tyre mileages, which proved that the riding of the modified bogies with the B.R. profile was comparable in every respect to that with the composite and also remained unimpaired by tyre wear. The ultimate wear is less for the composite for the mileage attained but the difference is more marked at relatively low mileages. In both classes the worn profiles from each axle are very similar and tread and not flange wear is the criterion for returning.*

*The original profile has not therefore played a significant part in the improvement in the riding and from this standpoint the retention of the Heumann-Lotter profile cannot be justified.*

Four locomotives, D815-D818, were involved in the first experiment ('W/SW/L/167') using the German tyre profile which began in December 1959. On 8 March 1960 D804 was used in experiment 'W/SW/L/174' when both bogies were given a modified side control linkage incorporating rubber pad springs and modified thrust bearings to reduce lateral accelerations of the bogie by permitting increased movement between body and bogies. Initial trials showed an improvement in riding qualities but some undesirable resonances remained and further modifications were made in an effort to reduce them. Following further trials the locomotive remained in service with a maximum permitted speed of 80 mph until shelling necessitated tyre turning. Examination of the linkage found one side control link broken and three badly worn, which necessitated the re-design of the link. Softer rubbers were fitted at the same time.

Trials with the softer springs, used in conjunction with hydraulic dampers and tyres turned to the German composite profile were first carried out at a maximum of 80 mph, and finally this was raised to 90 mph. The riding was considered very satisfactory and it was decided that the locomotive should go into traffic for a trial period. When inspected after 77,530 miles the modified rubber springs were found to be in reasonably good condition and were re-fitted for further service.

The final solution was not reached until almost two years after the problems first emerged, when D813 was fitted with hydraulic dampers as a centring device instead of its original bogie side control linkage under experiment 'W/SW/L/204' on 31 August 1962. It had an approximate tyre mileage since last turning of between 55,000 and 60,000 miles. Initial trials were carried out in three stages at speeds of up to 90 mph:

1) A controlled test run under the supervision of the Research Department with both hydraulic dampers in position on one bogie with none on the other bogie.
2) As stage 1, but with one hydraulic damper in position on each bogie.
3) As stage 1, but with both hydraulic dampers in position on each bogie.

The riding of the locomotive was satisfactory during all three tests and it was returned to traffic with the two hydraulic dampers in position on each bogie. Due to the initial success of the experiment approval was granted in October by the WR General Manager for the conversion of a further twelve locomotives. Results continued to prove satisfactory and the modification was applied to the remainder of the class.

The final experiment 'W/SW/L/212' was applied from May 1963 to D819 which had the bogie side control linkage removed and hydraulic dampers connected directly from bogie to body, with tyres to the BR Standard Profile. This was extended in late-1964 to D815, D832 and D849. The bogies from D819 were subsequently fitted to D811 and D806. Comparison of these records against those for locomotives with the composite profiles, at similar tyre mileages and on similar routes, showed that the profile made little difference to the riding qualities. Regular examination of the tyres showed the tread wear to be slightly heavier than with the composite profile, but the difference was considered to be insufficient as far as tyre life was concerned. To aid standardisation of the tyre profiles therefore, the BR Profile 'A' was adopted for the D800, D833 and D1000 class locomotives. Ell, having recently retired from BR, concluded his paper: *...the support of the body in the original design is made through a deep rubber block. Preceptors of old advised us what happens to houses built on sand, and on rock, but, because the material had not then been invented, they could not advise us what happens to a house which is built on rubber stilts. This momentous discovery was left to British Railways. Hence the replacement of the rubber with a metal block and the end of the troubles with Krauss-Maffei bogies due to 'under-design.'*

So the WR's embarrassment which was due to mechanical and not hydraulic problems was over; the 80mph restriction was lifted once the bogies had been modified, although the Warships had to wait in the queue behind the Westerns because the latter were needed for the accelerated South Wales services in the winter 1963/64 timetable.

**Proliferation**

D813 DIADEM, the first of the second Swindon production batch, emerged in December 1959. Although D814 entered traffic on the first day of 1960 the locomotive's records state that 'for statistical purposes' the construction date should be considered as 1959 and therefore it carried a 1959 works plate. It was followed by D815-D829 at the rate of one every three weeks or so. This allowed the class to extend its sphere of operation to regular freight workings such as those in Laira's diagrams which included the 9.45pm Bristol-Penzance and 1.20am Tavistock Junction-Crewe D

**D602 BULLDOG waits at Truro with the 1V33 07.02 Bradford-Penzance 'Cornishman' on 2 August 1967, shortly before its transfer to Landore. It was repainted in the early version of blue with single double arrow and small warning panel during its final works visit in late-1966. (Alec Swain, www.transporttreasury.co.uk)**

**D602 BULLDOG on 24 November 1967 at Bristol with D601 ARK ROYAL en route to Laira after their brief stay in South Wales. BULLDOG is in an early version of rail blue with small yellow warning panels, single centrally placed double arrow, serif numbers and black background to the nameplate. (TW Nicholls)**

class freights. Deliveries were soon to accelerate as the D800s were joined by their sisters from Scotland.

RA Smeddle wrote to JJ Finlayson, the CM&EE of the Scottish Region, on 28 April 1960 asking for permission to run trials on 4 May and D833 was noted on a test train from South Side to Kilmarnock on 5 May. A few days later, on 16 May, D833 was to leave the Hyde Park Works at 8.0 am and take twelve coaches from there to Dumfries Goods, run light to Gretna Green and back, and then take the twelve coaches on a round trip to Gretna Green arriving back in Dumfries at 4.3pm. On the next day it was to take the same load on two return trips from Dumfries to Gretna before taking the test train back to Glasgow; these trials continued through early June before it arrived at Swindon on 17 June. NBL delivered another eight locomotives by the end of the year and despite its financial troubles kept up the rate of at least one per month from December 1960 until D865 ZEALOUS in June 1962.

Full scale dieselisation was now well underway in the South West and the winter timetable brought substantial accelerations in Cornwall, such as a 20 minutes saving on the *Royal Duchy* between Plymouth and Penzance. D815 DRUID may have been first of the class to work on the Southern Region when it was seen at Yeovil Pen Mill on 28 October with an up sleeping car express which had come from Exeter via the ex-LSWR line. More were observed in December when heavy flooding hit the south west with trains from Exeter diverted via the SR rejoining the WR at Castle Cary.

Initially, all the Warships except the Paxman-engined D830 MAJESTIC were allocated to Laira but from early 1961 a number were transferred to Newton Abbot to join D830, beginning in January and February with D823-D829.They were followed by D831-D838 between July and November, with D839-D852 and then D822-D823 joining them during 1962. The mathematical precision was somewhat spoiled when D820 rather than D821 was reallocated in March 1963. (There was a further rearrangement in May/June 1965 when ten D800s were transferred from Newton Abbot to Laira with the same number of D833s moving in the opposite direction).

Double heading was not usual in ordinary service at this time except for operational reasons to facilitate unbalanced workings such as the 12.00 midnight sleeper from Penzance which was a regular double header as far as Newton Abbot. Similarly on Fridays the up *CRE* was regularly powered by two Warships from Exeter to Paddington to provide a locomotive for the Friday 6.19pm Paddington-Paignton, although they did not work in multiple. Summer Saturdays also saw much double heading over the South Devon hills on the heavy excursion trains, usually with D6300s.

Even at this early date the class was not confined to main line duties as shown by D812 ROYAL NAVAL RESERVE 1859-1959 which spent the day on 22 April 1961 working china clay empties from Fowey to St Blazey in the morning and then in the afternoon worked two-coach trains on the Par-Newquay line. They also deputised for D6300s – for example on 22 December D870 was provided for the 2.35pm Plymouth-Okehampton-Exeter Central and D815 followed suit the next day.

**Spreading their wings**

As 1962 began the vestiges of steam era diagramming were still evident: most turns from Laira and Newton Abbot involved out and home work both to Paddington and Bristol, and locomotives were still changed at Plymouth on many through workings to Cornwall. A sign of the new era was the handing over from 5 March of the celebrated Castle working from Plymouth to Shrewsbury, the 9.10am Liverpool Lime St-Plymouth and the 8.00am in reverse. The Warship had a fill-in turn between Shrewsbury and Crewe on the 5.10pm ex-Cardiff, returning with the 9.50pm York-Swansea Victoria.

This was a sign of things to come: D860 VICTORIOUS was loaned to Crewe North in April for training to allow through working into Crewe from Bristol/Cardiff, eliminating locomotive changing at Shrewsbury. The 1962 summer timetable which started on 18 June saw the North West-South West services accelerated by up to sixty minutes with the introduction of the Warships on all class A trains and rearrangements to avoid the previous complicated marshalling of through portions for both Liverpool and Manchester. (The Warships' reign on these services was short-lived: they succumbed to the tide of Brush Type 4s delivered to the WR in early 1964 and we have found no photographs of them in regular service on this route after July 1964).

An interesting aside was the decision to employ Warships as substitutes for failed Westerns on the Paddington-Wolverhampton accelerated services. D817 was seen on the usual Western crew training diagram from Wolverhampton to Chester and back on 22 August 1962. Both FOXHOUND and D819 were used during the month on the 9.00am Wolverhampton-Paddington and the 1.10pm return. When not on passenger duty, the locomotives were used by Oxley on one of its daily freight diagrams – the 4.25pm Penzance-Crewe and 3.55pm Crewe-Stoke Gifford, where D817 was recorded in the first week of the winter service. D824 was another Western substitute on 15 September; D827 KELLY managed two return trips to London on most days during October, giving rise to comments from Oxley that it was more reliable than any of its Westerns!

**Workings in July 1963**

With the final delivery of D865 ZEALOUS in June 1962 the last Warship was in service. In Appendix 1 Mark Alden has assembled a wonderful record of the workings of the whole class over five days in July 1963, which was their last summer as the primary motive power on both the Paddington-Bristol-West Country and the South West-North West services.

The D800s and D833s were regarded as interchangeable at this date and shared the more onerous workings equally. Four were in Swindon Works and around twenty were under examination or repair – a total of about 30% were therefore not available each day, and the figures were slightly worse for the NBL machines compared to the Swindon-built locomotives. Around 20% of their time was on freight with a similar amount on parcels, perishables and milk, but their principal duties were on Class 1 work. These accounted for around 50% of the total with an average of eight on South West-North West services, ten on Bristol turns, and thirteen working between London and the West Country. There were none on the Cotswold line and no visits to South Wales in the period; they did not work on either route regularly at this time.

The Warships worked the Western Region's premier named trains – *Royal Duchy, Mayflower, Cornish Riviera Express, Torbay Express, Bristolian* plus the Postal from London to Penzance. One of the more exacting duties featured D800 SIR BRIAN ROBERTSON on Monday 8th and on the next day D835 PEGASUS. It began at Truro with the 6.45am Truro-Paddington *Mayflower* to Plymouth (handing over to another Warship), then the *'Cornish Riviera Express'* to Paddington departing at 12.30pm from Plymouth (with D1057 off on both days). After a layover at Old Oak Common the Warship returned to Plymouth on the 10.20pm Paddington-Penzance 'Postal'. There were still many locomotive changes at Plymouth but there were now regular through workings between Paddington and Cornwall:-

| | Saturday 6th | Sunday 7th |
|---|---|---|
| 8.55pm Penzance - Paddington 'Sleeper' | D815 DRUID | D852 TENACIOUS |
| 1.30pm Paddington – Penzance | D825 INTREPID | D841 ROEBUCK |
| 7.30am Paddington – Penzance | D844 SPARTAN | - |
| 2.30pm Paddington – Penzance | D846 STEADFAST | - |
| 9.30pm Penzance - Paddington 'Sleeper' | D847 STRONGBOW | - |
| 8.30pm Penzance – Paddington | D860 VICTORIOUS | |
| 10.20pm Paddington - Penzance 'Postal' | - | D815 DRUID |
| 11.50am Penzance - Paddington 'Perishables' | - | D825 INTREPID |
| | | |
| | Monday 8th | Tuesday 9th |
| 2.30pm Paddington – Penzance | D812 ROYAL NAVAL RESERVE | D844 (failed at Newton Abbot) |
| 2.40pm Penzance – Paddington Goods 'Perishables' | D815 DRUID | D824 HIGHFLYER |
| 9.30pm Penzance - Paddington 'Sleeper' | D822 HERCULES | D802 FORMIDABLE |
| 7.0pm Penzance - Paddington 'Postal' | D845 SPRIGHTLY | D827 KELLY |
| 4.30pm Paddington - Truro *Mayflower* | D849 SUPERB | D814 DRAGON |
| 12.45pm St. Erth - Wood Lane 'Milk' | D854 TIGER | D853 THRUSTER |
| 8.30am Paddington - Penzance *Royal Duchy* | D865 ZEALOUS | D827 KELLY |
| 10.30pm Paddington - Penzance 'Sleeper' | D848 (failed at Bristol) | D815 DRUID |
| 10.20pm Paddington - Penzance 'Postal' | D800 SIR BRIAN ROBERTSON | D835 (to Plymouth) |

Other duties show the range of work undertaken by the Warships. On Monday 8th D816 ECLIPSE went light from Old Oak Common to Acton to take the 5B17 2.55am Acton-Bristol Kingsland Road. It was then at Bristol Bath Road on stand-by before it hauled the 2B96 11.00am Bristol-Weston-super-Mare. At Weston-super-Mare it was to 'shunt as required' before returning to Bristol with 2B96, the 5.15pm Weston-super-Mare-Bristol. Another light trip to Avonmouth saw it end the day on 4C25, the 7.50pm Avonmouth-Tavistock Junction.

D808 CENTUAR on Monday 8th and D805 BENBOW on Tuesday 9th both worked 1C80, the 11.45 Paddington-Taunton, returning with 1A33, the 16.47 Taunton-Paddington, as far as Swindon. They were then sent on 2B79, the 19.55 Swindon-Purton, returning as the 3B79 20.30 Purton-Swindon before taking over the 3A27 15.50 Whitland-Kensington 'Milk', departing 22.05 from Swindon. The logic behind taking a locomotive off the Taunton-Paddington just to work a local four miles up the line to Purton and then send it on its way again to London with the Whitland Milk remains unclear.

On Tuesday 9th D831 MONARCH, having worked into Crewe the previous evening on the 8.0pm from Plymouth, took the 9.05am Liverpool-Plymouth departing from Crewe at 10.07am, and in multiple from Shrewsbury to Newton Abbot with D838 RAPID. After visiting Laira depot it took over the 3A42 6.0pm Penzance-Kensington Olympia milk train from D1039 at 10.0pm from Plymouth to Southall. On the same day D866 ZEBRA relieved D856 TROJAN at Plymouth on the 3C09 7.45pm Kensington Olympia-Penzance 'Milk empties & Parcels', departing at 3.10am.

**D800 at Paddington on 14 July 1958 waiting to be officially named by KWC Grand and Sir Brian Robertson. It then worked a four coach 'Chocolate and Cream' special to Reading and back conveying Mr. Grand, Sir Brian Robertson and numerous invited guests. (www.rail-online.co.uk)**

It worked back east with the 11.30am Penzance-Paddington *Royal Duchy* as far as Plymouth where it handed over to D848 SULTAN. ZEBRA visited Laira before returning to Cornwall with 2C70, the 3.46pm Plymouth-Penzance, followed by the 8.55pm Penzance-Paddington sleeper to Plymouth, handing over to D1039 before retiring to Laira. Before working the *Royal Duchy* SULTAN had run light from Bristol Bath Road to Stoke Gifford Yard to take over 5C14, the 9.10pm Oxley-Tavistock Junction, departing at 4.15am, and then on to Laira. After arrival at Paddington with the *Royal Duchy* it had a brief rest at Ranelagh Bridge before working 3C12, the 10.0pm Paddington-Penzance 'Parcels', to Plymouth.

**The Warships meet their Waterloo**

In early 1964 the WR announced that the D1000s were to be moved onto the Paddington-Bristol and Paddington-Plymouth services, displacing Warships which would release them for other duties including dieselisation of the Southern Region Exeter-Salisbury-Waterloo route and Bristol-Plymouth freight workings. Anticipating the change in regional boundaries which brought the Waterloo-Exeter line west of Salisbury under WR control from September 7 1964, trials and crew training began on 10 March 1964 with D827 KELLY and a 12-coach rake of empty stock which worked up from Exeter at 08.35 and back from Salisbury in the afternoon.

D829 MAGPIE arrived at Salisbury for crew training at the beginning of June and was replaced after a week by D819. Three return trips each day were made to Basingstoke using a train of 13 condemned coaches. The roster included a twice-weekly trip to Westbury for refuelling and servicing. D829 made test runs to Waterloo on 9 August prior to the full introduction of the class from 17 August. From that date two more Warships were based at Exmouth Junction for duties through to Waterloo allowing coverage of three return diagrams departing Exeter at 07.30, 12.30 and 17.54, and returning from Waterloo at 13.00, 19.00 and 01.15 (newspapers). During the first week D815, D824 and D827 were amongst those used. While at Waterloo the locomotives were stabled in the Windsor line carriage sidings beyond platform 21.

The WR introduced a regular interval pattern of semi-fasts between Waterloo and Exeter to replace the express service hauled by the Bulleid Pacifics. Trains ran on the hour at 9,11,13,15,17,18 and 19.00 from Waterloo to Exeter, except for the 11.00 (the former *Atlantic Coast Express*) which terminated at Salisbury, and a similar service operated in the up direction. Stops were made at Woking, Basingstoke, Andover Junction, Salisbury, Gillingham, Templecombe, Sherborne, Yeovil Junction, Axminster and Sidmouth Junction. The diesels' rapid acceleration from stops allowed sharp point to point timings to be scheduled but the best time to Exeter was still 3hr 35mins down compared with 2hrs 58mins (for the *ACE*) and 3hrs 38mins against 2hrs 59mins up. However, the average times were slightly faster to Exeter and only one minute slower to Salisbury.

In the first few weeks there were several diesel failures, which in some cases caused severe delays of over an hour. It did not take long before the SR railwaymen began to put the blame on the WR for giving them worn-out examples of the class, despite the fact that none of them were over five years old at the time. Matters did not improve and the December 1964 *Railway Observer* did not pull any punches: 'It is depressing to record little or no improvement in timekeeping on West of England services to and from Waterloo. Failures of the Warship diesels are all too frequent, and the number of times that steam has replaced diesel traction are too frequent to record. This service is indeed a poor advertisement for modernisation'.

On 9 October the sidings at Waterloo contained four Warships: D813 and D828 intended for the 09.00 and 11.00, D805 which had failed before taking the previous day's 13.00 and D824 which had failed on the 01.15. The next day D823 and D831 were there serviceable but non-runner D824 hadn't moved and had been joined by D813 which had also failed on the 01.15. During November and December 1964 the performance of the WR diesels showed some improvement but steam substitutions were still commonplace.

After that things went quiet for a couple of years until the WR started to take the axe to its inherited territory. Exmouth Junction shed was closed on 5 March 1967, replaced by an Exeter shed partially rehabilitated with track alterations but remaining roofless. On 2 April it took the first step in singling the Exeter-Salisbury line with the Wilton-Templecombe section, leaving crossing facilities only at Gillingham. Work was completed on 10/11 June with the Chard-Pinhoe section. Inevitably there were soon reports of excessive delays due to failure of Warships in the single line section and the *Observer* started firing again in September: 'Loco availability has improved little – one has only to look at the Waterloo-Exeter service to see what the Maybachs are like, more than one has been collected from Waterloo and taken to Old Oak Common in July. On at least one occasion the 15.00 Waterloo-Exeter changed engines at Gillingham, a D65XX working to that point and changing with a Warship sent from Exeter – now a difficult proposition over so much single line'.

Poor timekeeping continued: August 10 was particularly bad – D806 on the 15.00 from Waterloo failed at Brookwood and was replaced by D6535 which reached Exeter two hours late. D866 on the 17.00 failed before it started and was replaced by D6551 as far as Salisbury where D7005 took over only to fail at Yeovil where it was replaced by D805 off the 19.30 Exeter-Clapham perishables. To cap it all, the 19.00 from Waterloo was worked by D829 on one engine only from Clapham Junction which caused it to reach Exeter late into the night; passengers for points west were catered for by putting platform seats into the van conveyed on the 18.55 Kensington-Plymouth milk empties.

Punctuality problems continued into September and a head of steam was building up. On 16 October the Acting Divisional Manager from Bristol attended an Open Forum at St Georges Hall, Exeter during which it was stated that the punctuality on the Exeter-Salisbury line was improving. At the end of the meeting a visit to St David's unfortunately found the 17.00 from Waterloo running 45 minutes late behind an ailing D816! The railway press continued regularly to report failures and delays until the SR finally achieved their goal: Warship operation into Waterloo was scheduled to finish with the service handed over to Class 33s on 4 October 1971. The latter had been deputising for them on this route for some time, with failures due to broken springs a common problem. These had reached a peak in the spring of 1971 with Class 47s and Hymeks also substituting.

On Sunday 3 October, the last day of Warship operation, D817 FOXHOUND was the busiest, taking the 01.35 Waterloo-Yeovil Junction 'News', returning with the 07.40 Yeovil Junction-Waterloo and ending with the 17.08 Waterloo-Exeter. 811 DARING hauled the 09.08 to Exeter and returned to Waterloo with the 16.55; D822 HERCULES brought in the 10.15 Exeter-Waterloo and took the final train from Waterloo, the 19.08 to Exeter. 812 and 823 also worked up to Waterloo that day from Exeter on the 16.00 and 18.20 respectively. For D817, D822 and 823 these were their final workings and they were withdrawn on the same day.

The D800s had a virtual monopoly of the Exeter-Waterloo trains in order to simplify maintenance procedures and crew-training; Salisbury drivers were the only ones with Class 43 training. The Class 43s were very infrequent substitutes and usually only when there was a failure at the London end. In that case the replacement locomotive came from the 8O68 03.40 Jersey Marine Colliery (Neath) to Wimbledon coal train which Class 43s normally worked. It departed from Westbury at 09.45 and arrived at Wimbledon at 13.32, returning as 7V08 to the colliery. Sometimes it would return with a Class 42 on one engine limping back to the WR, the Class 43 having gone to Waterloo. Those recorded included D855 TRIUMPH in May 1966 and D836 and D850 in December 1969.

**To the West Midlands**

Like itinerant travellers, the Warships were moved on again in 1967 when this time it was the turn of the NBL examples to be transferred. The newly-electrified LMR London-Birmingham-

**D800 SIR BRIAN ROBERTSON on 18 October 1958 at Plymouth North Road with the 'Cornish Riviera'. By the end of October D800 was working a diagram comprising the up 'CRE' from Plymouth to London and a return with the 6.30pm Paddington-Bristol and 9.5pm Bristol-Plymouth. (SV Blencowe)**

**D805 BENBOW waits to depart from Paddington on 15 June 1959 with the inaugural run of the accelerated 'Bristolian'. The schedule for the seven-coach train was cut by five minutes to 100 minutes, the first 70mph schedules since 1939, but unfortunately was to last for only a few months before bogie troubles beset the Warships.**

Wolverhampton line had taken over the through traffic to the West Midlands, leaving the Paddington-Bicester-Birmingham route handling only intermediate traffic which was served by six light-weight semi-fast trains each way daily, with four on Sundays. Brush Type 4s, which had displaced the Westerns on the WR route, were no longer needed and were to be replaced by the Warships, which would release the diesel-electrics for use on the LMR to ease a motive power shortage.

The D833s were to work freight and passenger services on the Paddington-Birmingham line, and freight services in and out of Bescot. They were to be allocated to and maintained at Old Oak, but Tyseley and Bescot would carry out examinations and minor repairs. Conversion courses for around 80 drivers were to be held at Wolverhampton, Bescot, Tyseley and Banbury. Six diesel fitters from Bescot went to Newton Abbot for a training course. In June D833 and D846 were reallocated to Old Oak Common before going to Bescot and Tyseley, respectively, for crew training. They were followed by four more which were temporarily allocated to Midlands' depots: D834 to Wolverhampton on 31 July, D835 to Bescot (7 August), D836 to Banbury (14 August) and D837 to Tyseley (21 August).

Training took place on various duties between Coventry and Leamington, on former LNWR lines between Birmingham and Wolverhampton to and from Bescot yard, and on eight-coach empty trains from Oxley sidings to Chester. It continued throughout September over the ex-GWR lines and in addition D833 and D836 made regular appearances at Coventry on freight workings from Bescot, including the mid-morning freight, in place of the usual Type 2.

The Warships were scheduled to take over the Paddington-New Street passenger services from 2 October. Although twenty-one D833s were transferred to Old Oak Common between July and October, it was only on 11/12 October that the full service was Warship-hauled for the first time. Two interesting diagrams north of Wolverhampton were also introduced:

(1) 21.00 Kensington Olympia-Dorrington milk empties, 07.25 Shrewsbury-Wolverhampton, 09.18 SX Bescot-Coton Hill and the 20.15 SX Shrewsbury-Kensington Olympia milk train.

(2) 18.52 Wolverhampton-Shrewsbury, with the return Euston through coaches, 22.50 SX Shrewsbury-Didcot parcels and 20.15 SO Shrewsbury-Kensington Olympia milk train.

The re-signalling work at Paddington saw Warships appear at Marylebone for the first time when the Birmingham services were diverted there from 15 October to 19 November; D836, D838, D840, D841, D846, D847, D848 and D850 were recorded during this period. The authorities must have assumed they had plenty of power in hand because no alterations were made to the timings for the eight coach trains of 275 tons.

By late October six Warships were lined up at Bescot having failed. Their unreliability forced the decision to restore Brush Type 4s to the Paddington-Birmingham services from 20 November. They remained on freight workings in the area, and crew training continued between Bescot and Banbury, via Stechford and the Berkswell loop. A regular trip was the daily Leamington to Nuneaton parcels previously worked by a Tyseley Type 2 out-stationed at Leamington; D850 SWIFT was the usual locomotive during December.

They still appeared occasionally on passenger duties, such as on 1 December when D848 took a Southampton-Birmingham New Street train north from Banbury, replacing a failed Brush Type 4. A Swindon-built example, D828 MAGNIFICENT, also substituted for a failed Brush on 5 December when it hauled the 19.13 Paddington-New Street.

Although the Warships had regular workings into Crewe on parcels trains, for example the 20.40 Wellington-Crewe parcels, they went into new LMR territory on 2nd and 3rd February 1968 when D853 and D837 headed freights from Bescot to Stoke, returning light to Bescot. However, the LMR swiftly deemed the class unsuitable for working into the Stoke area. Another first came on 18 May when D835 PEGASUS hauled an Andover-Liverpool Riverside troop special through to Crewe via Bescot and Stafford – probably the only instance of a Warship working a passenger service on the LMR electrified lines between Stafford and Crewe.

Now that they had been removed from the Birmingham passenger services, Old Oak needed to find a use for its large fleet of NBL-built machines. They were not exactly worn-out as most were only around six years old. Throughout 1968 the D833s continued on freight duties over the ex-GWR routes in the Midlands from Bescot and Banbury, where they had taken over most of the English Electric Type 4 duties, and the through train from Wolverhampton to Shrewsbury, which remained their only passenger duty in the area.

### On to the Cotswolds

At the same time as the plan to displace Brush Type 4s from the Birmingham passenger services, it was also intended to use the D833s to release more of the diesel-electrics on the London-Cheltenham/Worcester/Hereford services from the start of 1968. This would require eight locomotives and crew training was scheduled to commence during October 1967. D851 TEMERAIRE was observed at Cheltenham Spa Lansdown on 8 October in charge of the 19.40 Cheltenham to Paddington. During November and December D855 and D864 were used to train Worcester men, running between Bristol and Gloucester, and D839 was also seen several times at Worcester in December. By the end of the year a number of the Worcester-Paddington services were Warship-hauled, but the planned take-over on 1 January did not fully materialise until a few months later. Newton Abbot transferred two more of its NBL allocation to Old Oak during the month.

The rosters from Old Oak Common included freight as well as passenger services: for example one of the duties was the 23.40SX Paddington-Worcester freight before taking up its passenger work during the day and then returning to its home depot with the 21.10SX freight to Temple Mills. The locomotive on this diagram stabled at Worcester over weekends. The full Warship operation was in place by the start of the new timetable in May. At Worcester on 10 May D842, D851, D854 and D865 were recorded on Paddington services and D844 on the evening freight to Temple Mills.

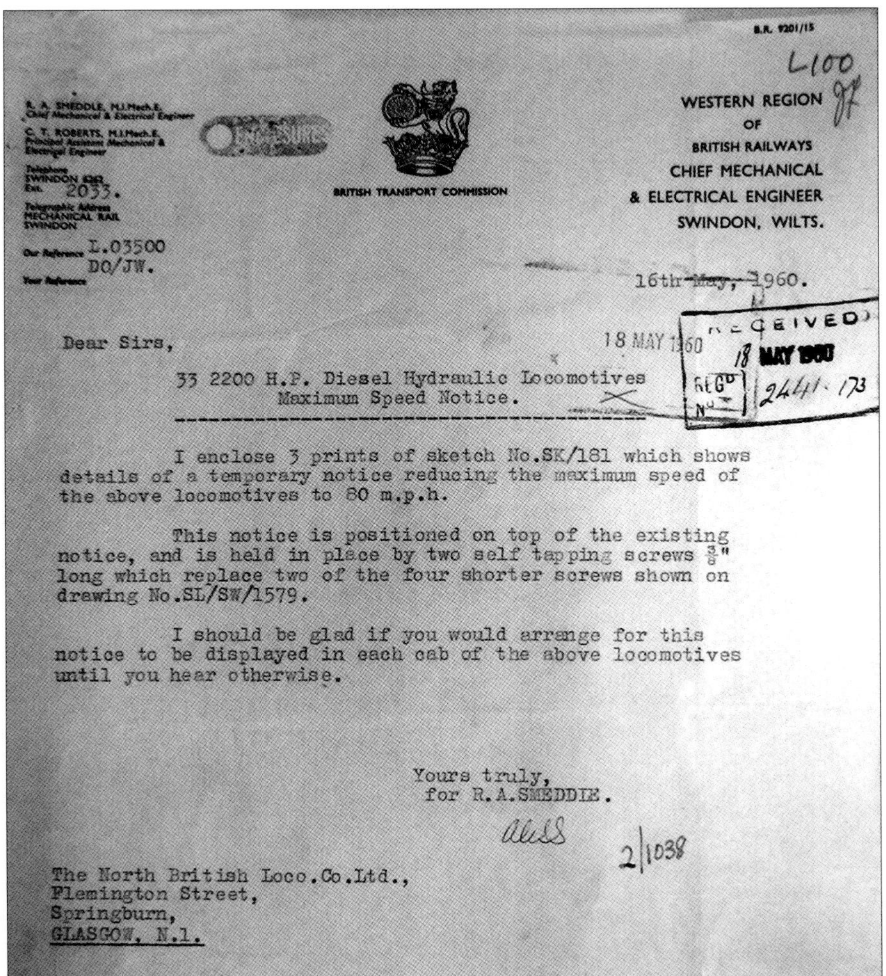
B.R. 9201/15

L100

R. A. SMEDDLE, M.I.Mech.E., Chief Mechanical & Electrical Engineer
C. T. ROBERTS, M.I.Mech.E., Principal Assistant Mechanical & Electrical Engineer
Telephone SWINDON Ext. 2033.
Telegraphic Address MECHANICAL RAIL SWINDON

BRITISH TRANSPORT COMMISSION

WESTERN REGION OF BRITISH RAILWAYS
CHIEF MECHANICAL & ELECTRICAL ENGINEER
SWINDON, WILTS.

Our Reference L.03500 DO/JW.
Your Reference

16th May, 1960.

RECEIVED 18 MAY 1960

Dear Sirs,

33 2200 H.P. Diesel Hydraulic Locomotives
Maximum Speed Notice.

I enclose 3 prints of sketch No.SK/181 which shows details of a temporary notice reducing the maximum speed of the above locomotives to 80 m.p.h.

This notice is positioned on top of the existing notice, and is held in place by two self tapping screws ⅜" long which replace two of the four shorter screws shown on drawing No.SL/SW/1579.

I should be glad if you would arrange for this notice to be displayed in each cab of the above locomotives until you hear otherwise.

Yours truly,
for R.A.SMEDDLE.

The North British Loco.Co.Ltd.,
Flemington Street,
Springburn,
GLASGOW, N.1.

**The Warships were restricted to a maximum speed of 80mph because of the ride problems which were eventually attributed to a basic design fault in the original Krauss-Maffei bogie. RA Smeddle wrote to NBL in May 1960 to tell them to fit notices to this effect in the cabs of the locomotives they were building.**

### Doubling-up

Meanwhile, the Swindon-built members of the class were about to enjoy an Indian summer when the WR decided to employ them in pairs on the principal West of England services when it introduced an accelerated timetable in May 1968. The *Cornish Riviera Express* with a limited load of eleven coaches covered the 225.7 miles between London and Plymouth in 3¾ hours at an average of 60mph, inclusive of stops at Taunton and Exeter. The twin Warships could also maintain any schedule permitted by the track alignment and the line limit of 90mph with other heavier trains such as the 14.30 Paddington to Penzance, which could load up to 14 or 15 vehicles weighing 450 to 500 tons as far as Newton Abbot.

During March/April 1968 trials were conducted with the first pair refitted with multiple working equipment, D824 and D825, in preparation for the new timetable. They worked the 08.30 Plymouth-Paddington and the 16.30 return, and several other pairings were recorded on the same duties including D827/D829 on 11 and 18 March, D832/D823 on 1/2 April and D822/D831 from 3rd to 7th, D822/D828 8th to 10th and D827/D831 on 11th and D869/D866 on 20 April. The official launch was on 6 May when D831 MONARCH and D819 GOLIATH took the first six hour *CRE* as far as Plymouth where they handed over to a Western for the final leg to Penzance. Four pairs of D800s were needed to cover the accelerated services, working between London and Plymouth, with only one exception each day when they went through to Penzance. Maintenance costs were high because each pair was fitter- and electrician-assisted and there was a significant effect on brake blocks, engines and transmissions; the locomotives were refuelled at the end of each leg of the diagram.

From 5 May 1969 the WR introduced radical changes to its West of England services: all had strictly limited eight or nine coach formations with separate trains for Torbay and Plymouth. These were within the capacity of a single Western, although the accelerated nine coach *CRE* remained double headed for the next twelve months until May 1970; two of the four Warship pairings therefore ended with the new timetable.

On its inaugural run the accelerated *CRE* hauled by D819 and D808 reached Exeter nearly 8 minutes early in 131½ minutes, 128 net, for the 173.5 miles; on the first up run D822 and D827 took 136½ minutes, 129½ net, compared with the scheduled 142 minutes. One welcome side effect of the reduced formations was the occasional return of single Warships of both varieties to the West of England trains – for example on 10 June 1969 at Paddington D864 was on the 12.25 arrival, D838 on the 13.25 arrival and D859 on the 13.30 departure.

**Warship multiple working diagrams 1968**

| Day of week | 2 x D800 (A) | 2 x D800 (B) | 2 x D800 (C) | 2 x D800 (D) |
|---|---|---|---|---|
| Monday | Laira<br>1A65 21.00 Penz - Padd<br>Old Oak Common<br>1C45 10.30 Padd - Penz<br>Laira<br>1A79 15.05 Penz - Padd<br>Old Oak Common | Old Oak Common<br>1C10 00.55 Padd – Penz<br>Penzance<br>1A48 10.15 Penz - Padd<br>Ranelagh Bridge<br>1C72 18.30 Padd - Ply<br>Laira | Old Oak Common<br>1C30 08.30 Padd - Penz<br>Laira<br>1A59 14.30 Ply - Padd<br>Old Oak Common | Old Oak Common<br>1C08 00.40 Padd - Penz<br>Laira<br>1A30 07.10 Pen - Padd<br>Ranelagh Bridge<br>1C60 14.30 Padd – Penz<br>Laira<br>3A97 19.20 Ply – Padd<br>Old Oak Common |
| Tuesday | Old Oak Common<br>1C08 00.40 Padd - Penz<br>Laira<br>1A30 07.10 Pen - Padd<br>Ranelagh Bridge<br>1C60 14.30 Padd – Penz<br>Laira<br>3A97 19.20 Ply – Padd<br>Old Oak Common | Laira<br>1A65 21.00 Penz - Padd<br>Old Oak Common<br>1C45 10.30 Padd - Penz<br>Laira<br>1A79 15.05 Penz - Padd<br>Old Oak Common | Old Oak Common<br>1C10 00.55 Padd – Penz<br>Penzance<br>1A48 10.15 Penz - Padd<br>Ranelagh Bridge<br>1C72 18.30 Padd - Ply<br>Laira | Old Oak Common<br>1C30 08.30 Padd - Penz<br>Laira<br>1A59 14.30 Ply - Padd<br>Old Oak Common |
| Wednesday | Old Oak Common<br>1C30 08.30 Padd - Penz<br>Laira<br>1A59 14.30 Ply - Padd<br>Old Oak Common | Old Oak Common<br>1C08 00.40 Padd - Penz<br>Laira<br>1A30 07.10 Pen - Padd<br>Ranelagh Bridge<br>1C60 14.30 Padd – Penz<br>Laira<br>3A97 19.20 Ply – Padd<br>Old Oak Common | Laira<br>1A65 21.00 Penz - Padd<br>Old Oak Common<br>1C45 10.30 Padd - Penz<br>Laira<br>1A79 15.05 Penz - Padd<br>Old Oak Common | Old Oak Common<br>1C10 00.55 Padd – Penz<br>Penzance<br>1A48 10.15 Penz - Padd<br>Ranelagh Bridge<br>1C72 18.30 Padd - Ply<br>Laira |
| Thursday | Old Oak Common<br>1C10 00.55 Padd – Penz<br>Penzance<br>1A48 10.15 Penz - Padd<br>Ranelagh Bridge<br>1C72 18.30 Padd - Ply<br>Laira | Old Oak Common<br>1C30 08.30 Padd - Penz<br>Laira<br>1A59 14.30 Ply - Padd<br>Old Oak Common | Old Oak Common<br>1C08 00.40 Padd - Penz<br>Laira<br>1A30 07.10 Pen - Padd<br>Ranelagh Bridge<br>1C60 14.30 Padd – Penz<br>Laira<br>3A97 19.20 Ply – Padd<br>Old Oak Common | Laira<br>1A65 21.00 Penz - Padd<br>Old Oak Common<br>1C45 10.30 Padd - Penz<br>Laira<br>1A79 15.05 Penz - Padd<br>Old Oak Common |
| Friday | Laira<br>1A65 21.00 Penz - Padd<br>Old Oak Common<br>1C45 10.30 Padd - Penz<br>Laira<br>1A79 15.05 Penz - Padd<br>Old Oak Common | Old Oak Common<br>1C10 00.55 Padd – Penz<br>Penzance<br>1A48 10.15 Penz - Padd<br>Ranelagh Bridge<br>1C72 18.30 Padd - Ply<br>Laira | Old Oak Common<br>1C30 08.30 Padd - Penz<br>Laira<br>1A59 14.30 Ply - Padd<br>Old Oak Common | Old Oak Common<br>1C08 00.40 Padd - Penz<br>Laira<br>1A30 07.10 Pen - Padd<br>Ranelagh Bridge<br>1C60 14.30 Padd – Penz<br>Laira<br>3A97 19.20 Ply – Padd<br>Old Oak Common |

### Workings in 1971

By 1971 the workings of the fleet were less wide-ranging than in their heyday but there was still plenty to interest the Warship fans. Appendix 2 contains details provided by Mark Alden of the Class 42- and 43-only Turns from Newton Abbot and Laira operating from 3 May 1971. There were also Turns that operated from Severn Tunnel Junction, Old Oak Common and St. Blazey. Laira had seventeen Turns for Class 42, Newton Abbot had eight for Class 42 and eleven for Class 43. Of the 34 Class 42s available in May four were in 'Works (803, 820,821 and 827), with 818 stopped awaiting Works leaving 29 available in traffic. Of the 25 Class 43s available nine were in store leaving sixteen in traffic.

Appendix 3 has a diary for the month of August 1971 and detailed workings, again from the research of Mark Alden, for each locomotive from the 13th to 18th. This was the last summer when almost all of the Class 42s were still operational and less than two months before the final Class 43s were withdrawn. The range of duties was still wide although there was a noticeable difference between the classes: almost half of the sixteen remaining NBL locomotives were stopped with faults during the period, and those that were working were employed mainly on local freight duties.

The most interesting and longest workings in the period were freights hauled by 854 TIGER. On Friday 13th it took 7V68, the 00.05 Eastleigh-Severn Tunnel Junction, returning on the 8O09 07.50 Severn Tunnel Junction-Hither Green, then back to Eastleigh with 7Y71, the 19.33 Hither Green-Eastleigh, before running light to Basingstoke at 23.25 from Eastleigh. The next day it left early with 4V14, the 00.30 Basingstoke-Reading, then took the 8C00 03.30 Reading West Junction-Severn Tunnel Junction, the 8C67 13.45 Severn Tunnel Junction-Ebbw Vale, and ended with the 8C67 16.35 Ebbw Vale-Severn Tunnel Junction and stayed there on Sunday.

On Monday 16th TIGER worked 7C20, the 08.10 Severn Tunnel Junction-Barry Docks , and then 8E69, the 13.10 Barry Docks-Temple Mills. The next day it took over 6V59, the 20.20 Norwich Thorpe-Bristol Kingsland Road, leaving Temple Mills at 00.43, then ran light from Bristol Bath Road to Avonmouth to pick up the 7C22 07.05 Avonmouth-Radyr. It returned to Bristol on 8B41, the 10.20 Radyr-Filton C.C.D, ran light to Bristol Bath Road and took the 7E12 19.38 Bristol Kingsland Road-Temple Mills to Swindon Cocklebury Yard and was stopped for attention with low lubricating oil pressure. This was only a temporary break before it took over the 7E18 20.32 Worcester-Temple Mills, departing at 23.50 from Swindon Cocklebury Yard to West Ealing from where it went light to Old Oak Common in the early hours of Wednesday. After visiting the depot it ran light again, this time to Acton to work 7C14, the 04.30 Acton-East Usk. Another light trip to Bristol Bath Road and finally back to Temple Mills with the 7E12 19.38 Bristol Kingsland Road-Temple Mills.

Another Class 43 visitor to Wales was 845 SPRIGHTLY. On Monday 16th it began the day on 6Z68, the 08.00 Newton Abbot Hackney Yard-Paignton 'Engineers duty', before taking the 6C13 17.50 Newton Abbot-Waterston 'oil empties' to Severn Tunnel Junction. On Tuesday 17th it left South Wales with the 8A09 00.55 Severn Tunnel Junction-Taplow and worked light to Old Oak Common in preparation for the 1B45 09.30 Paddington-Paignton. From Paignton it took 1A35, the 13.55 Paignton-Paddington to Newton Abbot, where it failed with a fault on the A engine speed regulator and was replaced by D857.

Two more NBL Warships went into the Principality on Wednesday 18th: 857 UNDAUNTED left Laira with the 0F73 05.40 Laira-Swindon Works hauling D1001 and D1057, then went light from Swindon to Severn Tunnel Junction to pick up 8A43, the 16.10 Severn Tunnel Junction-Acton. 858 VALOROUS worked the 7C26 08.45 Plymouth Friary-Severn Tunnel Junction and then penetrated deeper into Wales as the 0O67 21.50 Severn Tunnel Junction-Jersey Marine.

The Class 1 workings for the diminishing band of NBLs were mainly between Plymouth and Penzance, except for 842 ROYAL OAK which worked on the Cotswold line every day, assisted by 834 PATHFINDER on Friday 13th. 857 went further afield on Tuesday 17th; after repairs for a final drive cardan shaft defect at Newton Abbot it replaced the failed D845 on the 1A35 13.55 Paignton-Paddington, departing at 14.16 from Newton Abbot. It returned west with 1B25, the 19.30 Paddington-Plymouth. 858 VALOROUS visited Acton, Park Royal and West Ruislip on the 'milk turn' where it picked up 8A69, the 12.15 West Ruislip-West Ealing milk empties, which became the 6M15 13.35 West Ealing-Kensington Olympia before it headed west as the 6V05 15.00 Kensington Olympia-Plymouth. (834 PATHFINDER had covered the same duties on the previous day). On Tuesday 17th 844 SPARTAN went into the West Midlands after running light as the 0F74 00.01 Newton Abbot-Bristol Bath Road to take up 5B73, the 10.30 Malago Vale C.S-Worcester. From there it went on the 6M20 18.00 Worcester-Birmingham before returning to the WR on 4V03, the 21.30 Birmingham Curzon Street-Bristol.

The Class 42s were, unsurprisingly, more gainfully occupied, although four were in works and one was stored for the whole period, and the number on shed for scheduled and unscheduled repairs averaged eight each day. The Exeter-Waterloo services used eight or nine each day with SR freight work included in their diagrams, as is shown by 812 ROYAL NAVAL RESERVE 1859-1959 on Friday 13th. It worked 6K21, the 04.05 Waterloo-Clapham Junction 'vans' via Kensington, then light back to Waterloo for the 1V04 06.38 Waterloo-Exeter. From there it went as 0O55 13.30 Exeter-Tiverton Junction before picking up 6O55 14.48 Tiverton Junction-Fawley 'oil tank empties', returning with the full tanks on 6V78 21.40 Fawley-Tiverton Junction.

WR freight work accounted for around a third of the duties and Class 1 passenger work was restricted to four or five per day, except for the Saturday when twelve were in action. Although most of these were in Cornwall with the occasional foray to Bristol there were plenty of exceptions. Friday 13th saw 817 FOXHOUND working the 1A54 06.40 Westbury-Paddington, and the 1B84 17.46 Paddington-Westbury before returning on freight with the 7A42 21.00 Westbury-Acton. 868 ZEPHYR took over 1A61, the 19.00 Penzance-Paddington 'postal' at Bristol from D853, leaving at 00.57 before a very long day working 1B45, the 09.30 Paddington-Paignton, the 1A35 13.55 Paignton-Paddington and finally the 1B25 19.30 Paddington-Penzance to Plymouth. 808 CENTUAR 1A61 worked right though with the 19.00 Penzance-Paddington 'postal', returning on Saturday 14th with 1B05 12.10 Paddington-Paignton, then the 1B86 17.55 Paignton-Bristol, ending with 1B28, the 21.15 Bristol-Plymouth.

815 DRUID worked to London on Monday 16th with the 1A61 19.00 Penzance-Paddington 'postal', in preparation for the next day when it hauled 1Z15, the 08.13 Paddington-Buckfastleigh 'Ian Allan Charter', as far as Totnes, running light Totnes-Newton Abbot and back before returning to Paddington with the charter departing

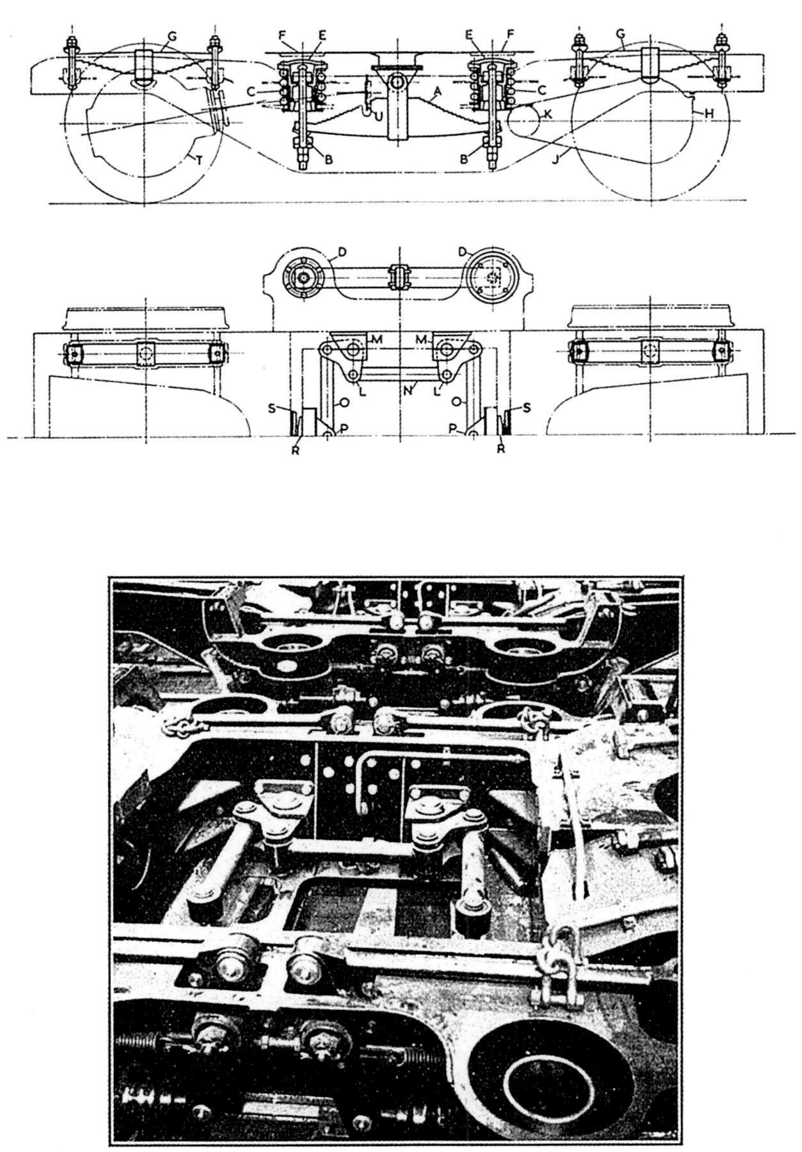

**The weight of the superstructure was carried by the buckles of the laminated springs (A) through which it was transferred to the bogie frame by way of spring hangers (B), coil springs (C) and frame brackets (D). The pads (E) resting on the tops of the coil springs were immediately beneath pads (F) affixed to the superstructure, but were separated therefrom by a little under an inch. The bogie frame was carried on four laminated springs (G) which in turn transferred the weight to the four axlebox housings (H) and thence through self-aligning Skefko roller bearings to the axles. The housings (H) were integral with arms (J) which were pivoted at their inner ends to the main frame by long rubber-bushed bearings at (K) thus eliminating the need for axlebox liners and horns and thereby avoiding the wear normally associated with such parts. The bogie frame was constrained to pivot about its geometrical centre by the Krauss-Maffei patent linkage consisting of two bell-cranks (L) carried in brackets (M) on the bogie frame, a link (M) connected the laterally disposed arms of the bellcranks and two links (O) connected the longitudinal arms to brackets (P) secured to the superstructure. Each of the eight pins in this linkage was carried in substantial rubber bearing bushes. Traction and braking forces were transmitted from the bogie to the superstructure by way of thrust pads (S) on the bogie and (R) on the superstructure, the surface of each pad (S) being part of a cylinder and that of each pad (R) part of a sphere. These pads were of manganese steel.**

at 17.30 from Totnes. Other long distance workings on Monday included 823 HERMES on the 1Z15 12.20 Paddington-Penzance 'relief' to Plymouth and 827 KELLY with the 1B95 11.30 Paddington-Paignton. 827 then took 1A55, the 15.55 Paignton-Paddington, returning west with 6B31, the 22.20 Paddington Goods-Plymouth Friary 'sundries'.

Two similar duties the following day saw 816 ECLIPSE begin with the 8B45 09.29 Westbury-Yeovil Pen Mill and the 7B47 12.30 Yeovil Pen Mill-Westbury before taking over from D1008 the 1A65 06.35 Penzance-Paddington. After refuelling at Ranelagh Bridge it hauled the 1B35 14.30 Paddington-Penzance to Plymouth and then assisted D1048 with 6A17, the 15.05 Penzance-Paddington 'perishables and milk' from Plymouth to Exeter. 825 INTREPID worked the 1A54 06.40 Westbury-Paddington, and after taking the 5A06 09.16 Paddington-Old Oak Common C.S. it returned to Westbury with 1B84, the 17.46 Paddington-Westbury.

Wednesday 18th saw 831 MONARCH on 1B95, the 11.30 Paddington-Paignton, returning with the 1A55 15.55 Paignton-Paddington. After visiting Old Oak it worked 6B31, the 22.20 Paddington Goods-Plymouth Friary 'sundries'.

Some of the freight workings during the period were:-

| Friday 13th | |
|---|---|
| 810 COCKADE | 4B05 05.15 Paddington - Bristol, 6A27 11.00 Malago Vale C.S. - Old Oak Common C.S. at 11.20 from Bristol; 0B24 23.00 Old Oak Common - Acton; 7B24 23.35 Acton - Exeter Riverside Yard to Bristol. |
| 823 HERMES | 6B38 01.40 Southall - Exeter City Basin; 6B23 08.20 Exeter City Basin - Westbury; 8B45 14.59 Westbury - Swindon Cocklebury Yard; 7B00 19.25 Swindon Cocklebury Yard - Stoke Gifford Yard. |
| 829 MAGPIE | 4O10 05.05 Bristol - Salisbury, 7V76 08.20 Salisbury - Meldon Quarry 'Ballast empties', 6O81 19.00 Meldon Quarry - Salisbury 'Ballast' to Exeter Riverside Yard. |
| 867 ZENITH | 7V70 09.40 Hither Green - Severn Tunnel Junction; 4B45 20.30 Severn Tunnel Junction - Plymouth Friary. |
| Monday 16th | |
| 867 ZENITH | 03.35 from Plymouth on 6V07 19.00 Kensington Olympia - Penzance 'Milk empties'; 6B13 08.40 Penzance - Dolcoath 'Milk empties'; 0B29 09.50 Dolcoath - Drump Lane; 7B29 10.40 Drump Lane - Roskear; 0B26 LD Roskear - St. Erth; 6B26 11.35 St. Erth - Penzance; 6A17 15.05 Penzance - Paddington 'Perishables and milk'. |
| 869 ZEST | 7A08 19.10 St. Blazey - Paddington Goods. |
| Tuesday 17th | |
| 822 HERCULES | 7V70 09.40 Hither Green - Severn Tunnel Junction; 8O30 22.20 Severn Tunnel Junction - Hither Green. |
| 869 ZEST | 7C41 10.35 Acton - Severn Tunnel Junction; 7B14 23.24 Severn Tunnel Junction - Totnes. |
| Wednesday 18th | |
| 815 DRUID | 4B05 05.15 Paddington - Bristol; 4B15 12.50 Bristol - Yeovil Pen Mill; 4B16 16.10 Yeovil Pen Mill - Bristol; 1O69 21.05 Bristol - Eastleigh to Salisbury. |
| 817 FOXHOUND | 7C41 10.35 Acton - Severn Tunnel Junction; LD Severn Tunnel Junction - Llanwern; 6Zxx 21.25 from Llanwern as far as Worcester; 0F82 LD Worcester - Severn Tunnel Junction. |
| 825 INTREPID | 6V76 01.00 Northam Yard - Westbury A.P.C.M. 'Prestflo empties' to Westbury Yard; 8A04 00.45 Westbury - Theale; 7B01 03.25 Theale - Westbury; 8B43 09.29 Westbury - Yeovil Pen Mill; 7B47 12.30 Yeovil Pen Mill - Westbury; 8B45 14.59 Westbury - Swindon Cocklebury Yard; 7B00 19.25 Swindon Cocklebury Yard - Stoke Gifford Yard. |
| 826 JUPITER | 6V07 19.00 Kensington Olympia - Penzance 'Milk empties' at 03.35 from Plymouth; 6B13 08.40 Penzance - Dolcoath 'Milk empties'; 0B29 09.50 Dolcoath - Drump Lane; 7B29 10.40 Drump Lane - Roskear; 0B26 LD Roskear - St. Erth; 6B26 11.35 St. Erth - Penzance; 6A17 15.05 Penzance - Paddington 'Perishables and milk'. |

From Sunday 8th August locomotive workings were recorded on Job Cards. These 'T' shaped cards (see pages 272-3) were colour coded according to the locomotives' home depot and recorded the duties performed by that locomotive, including the date, departure time, from and to and also the locomotive diagram. An example of this taken from the card for 803:

$^{9}/_{8}$ 01.35 Exeter - Ponsandane
(NA153)
14.50 Pons - Exeter
(83A153)

$^{10}/_{8}$ 00.15 Exe - Pons
(LA29)
14.50 Pons - Exeter
Off Plymouth

$^{10}/_{8}$ 22.55 Plymouth - Par
(LA153)

$^{11}/_{8}$ 02.05 Par - Truro
05.50 Truro - Drump Lane
06.40 Drump Lane - St. Blazey

04.51 St. Blazey trips

$^{14}/_{8}$ 06.15 Par - Newquay

From the card for 803, on the 10th, the actual train was 7B34 20.03 Bristol Temple Meads Goods to Ponsandane which 803 worked forward from Riverside (depending on the person the diagram was written either as NA or 83A for Newton Abbot.) On the 11th the next part of the diagram wasn't worked by 803, which instead was taken for China clay trips to Drinnick Mill. It is presumed that the continuation from 02.05 was worked by another loco type or perhaps even cancelled.

**Into the sunset**

From 1964 the class was relegated to second-line power behind the Westerns on the Bristol and West of England services, as the D1000s were themselves displaced from other duties by Brush Type 4s. Although they were the principal traction on the Exeter-Waterloo and Paddington-Worcester trains, much of their time was spent on freight work throughout the WR, in the south west, the south east into SR territory and the Midlands onto the LMR, and on local passenger work in the south west. They remained the staple power for the NE/SW trains, generally taking over from diesel-electrics at Bristol; the up and down *Devonian* was a Warship turn for many years. An interesting piece appeared in the February 1969 issue of *Modern Railways*. The WR was to retain the Swindon-built Warship diesel-hydraulics in service it announced: 'Previously they were slated for withdrawal and the NBL Warships were to survive, because the latter are more suitable for use under the LMR's 25kV catenary. But because of the steady rise in the NBL version's maintenance costs and its deteriorating performance the plan has been reversed. The Swindon-built units will not be able to work LMR-bound inter-Regional freights further than Banbury, so that several rosters will require revision'.

The National Traction Plan, having seen off the D600s, turned its attention to the D800/D833s (now described as Class 42s and 43s) and at the start of 1969 its latest update, which foresaw the withdrawal of the Class 43s with the Class 42s to follow, confirmed the position. The three Pilot Scheme D800s, however, had already succumbed by this time: D801 VANGUARD was the first withdrawal in August 1968 and D800 and D802 followed two months later. Unsurprisingly, the non-standard, Paxman-engined D830 MAJESTIC was next; after going into store in February 1969 it was withdrawn in March.

From 3 March the Class 43s lost many of their booked workings when their duties were taken over by diesel-electric traction. This resulted in a surplus of the NBL locomotives and so several were stored pending further use, whilst others continued working on the LMR from Bescot. In February 848 SULTAN was stored at Old Oak Common and a further fifteen (D833, D839, D840, D841, D842, D845, D850, D852, D854, D855, D857, D858, D861, D863 and D865) had joined it by the end of May. The first two Class 43s to be withdrawn, 848 and 863 WARRIOR, were officially condemned in March, and 840's resistance, as it were, ended in April, but the others were reinstated later in the year because of delays in transferring diesel-electrics from the LMR. By November 1970 all of them had been transferred back to Newton Abbot from Old Oak but their reprieve came to an end in May 1971 when fourteen (836, 837, 838, 843, 846, 847, 849, 850, 851, 856, 859, 860, 864 and 866) were taken out of service.

The first two of the production Class 42s were the next to go in August 1971 when 828 and 870 were withdrawn, the former after a serious fire the previous month and the latter with damage from a collision at Laira Junction on 8 June. The take-over of the Waterloo-Exeter service by Class 33s on 4 October marked the beginning of the end for the D800s. They had also been displaced from many of their remaining passenger turns in the previous year by the eventual transfer of Class 46s to the WR from the LM and Eastern Regions, and spent much of their time on freight workings between Plymouth and Bristol.

The Class 43s continued to work the Worcester/Hereford services until the end of the summer timetable when twenty-nine locomotives from both classes were taken out of service in the first week of October 1971. This rendered the NBL locomotives extinct; the last recorded D833 passenger working was 857 UNDAUNTED on the 1B48 23.25 Paddington-Newton Abbot 'news' on 2 October. The final working of all was 857 which hauled a track recovery train on the Heathfield branch on Sunday 3 October. It then returned to Hackney Yard and to Newton Abbot depot where it was withdrawn. On the same day 853 THRUSTER had worked the 06.00 Westbury to Taunton Engineers' duty where on arrival it was failed and withdrawn, and 858 VALOROUS worked light diesel from Exeter at 11.45 to Newton Abbot where it too was withdrawn. There was as usual a twist in the tale: several weeks after withdrawal 844 SPARTAN travelled from store at Bristol St Phillips Marsh to Worcester in late October for carriage heating duties. When these were finished the locomotive returned light to Swindon for scrapping on 26 November.

Only nineteen Class 42s remained in service at the end of December 1971 after nine more were withdrawn, although three of these, 814, 825 and 829, were reinstated in March 1972 because the WR had a motive power shortage, partly due to increased stone traffic from the Mendip quarries. They ran without nameplates and 825 and 829 were finally withdrawn from service in August. This was the start of the final decline, with withdrawals in each successive month until at the end of November there were just five left in stock.

On 1 December only three of these were operational: 812 ROYAL NAVAL RESERVE 1859-1959 was stopped at Laira with B transmission faults and 832 ONSLAUGHT was in store at Laira, and had been since 7 November. (It was not officially withdrawn until 16 December). Of the working trio, 810 COCKADE was on South Wales freight duties before ending the day at Old Oak Common, 824 HIGHFLYER was on local trips between Plymouth Friary and the Dockyards and 821 GREYHOUND was available at Westbury. 821 worked 8B18, the 06.10 Westbury Yard to Yeovil Pen Mill, returning on 7B46 at 11.50 before taking 8B45, the 15.06 trip freight to Swindon Cocklebury Yard. From there, after a brief rest on shed, 821 headed west again on 7B18, the 20.40 Reading West Junction to Exeter Riverside Yard from the Transfer Yard. Although expected to work through to Exeter, 821 was failed at Bristol and sent to Bath Road depot.

The following day 821 was sent to work 1Z00, the 04.00 Bristol to Reading breakdown van special to rescue D1029 which had become de-railed all wheels in the loop line between platforms 8 and 9 at the General station during the early hours. Afterwards 821 returned its train to Bristol whilst D1029 was hauled over to Reading shed by the local pilot locomotive. Not long after GREYHOUND had left Reading, COCKADE passed through Reading on its final working, 6B09, the 15.55 Acton

**D816 ECLIPSE on china clay duty in Fowey Yard on 22 July 1960. Although in their early years most of their work was on express passenger duties the diagrams did also include many freight workings. (RC Riley , www.transporttreasury.co.uk)**

**A Warship at Carlisle – brand new D853 makes its way south from North British in Glasgow on 17 August 1961. It is already fitted with its THRUSTER nameplates. D853 entered service on 30 August after the normal inspection and acceptance process which often resulted in rectification work before the locomotive was passed to the Running Department. (www.rail-online.co.uk)**

to Plymouth milk empties; this was the only other Warship at work on that date.

Early on Sunday 3 December all the remaining Warships were at Laira, except one. Engineers' duty Z07 was a trip working from Bristol East Depot to Stoke Gifford and 821, at Bath Road, was the ideal candidate. After performing this undemanding task, 821 returned to the shed before making the final working of a Warship class locomotive over British Railways owned metals. The train was 6Z10, the 15.30 Bristol to Plymouth special vans, operated to convey extra postal traffic leading up to the Christmas period. Slipping quietly into Plymouth North Road station in the late evening GREYHOUND left its load behind and returned light, as 0F77, to Laira. Fifteen years of Warship history was over.

### Keeping them running

In October 1965 *Modern Railways* described in detail the *Control and Maintenance of Diesel Traction on the WR*: *All WR-based diesel locomotives are allocated for maintenance purposes to one of the Region's six maintenance depots: Plymouth Laira; Newton Abbot; Bristol Bath Road; Cardiff Canton; Landore or Old Oak Common, London. Each maintenance depot has a separate servicing point and servicing depots have been or are being established at Margam, Reading, Penzance, Newport (Ebbw Junction), Swindon, Westbury, St. Blazey, Gloucester and Severn Tunnel Junction.*

*Each depot is classified according to the type of work it undertakes. "Heavy" maintenance, which requires facilities to lift diesel-hydraulic engines and transmissions, and train-heating boilers, is carried out at Laira, Canton and Bath Road. Although lifting apparatus will be provided at Old Oak Common, heavy maintenance here will normally be confined to the smaller types allocated to the London area. Bath Road depot cannot undertake bogie changes or tyre-turning and locomotives needing attention to bogies or wheels are sent to Laira or Canton. All six depots undertake general scheduled maintenance, which involves the periodical inspection, changing, dismantling and cleaning of specified components.*

*Servicing points do not normally undertake maintenance, except in some cases where it would be inconvenient for diesel shunters operating near a servicing depot to run to and from a maintenance depot. A servicing depot caters for such day-to-day locomotive upkeep as refuelling, topping up radiator water, checking fuel and lubricating oil purity and general examination of running gear.*

*In addition, each diesel locomotive class is allocated to a specific main locomotive works for general repair and overhaul. At present, all WR diesel-hydraulic locomotives and all WR-based shunters, regardless of transmission type, are put through the shops at Swindon.*

*The design and layout of a diesel-hydraulic locomotive is entirely different from that of a diesel-electric locomotive, particularly in the weight and bulk of the principal components. The high-speed engines of WR diesel-hydraulic locomotives are comparatively light and can be removed from a locomotive at a principal depot.*

*Because of the less cumbersome nature of the main components, diesel-hydraulic locomotive maintenance is readily adaptable to the unit replacement system, in which individual components needing attention are replaced with ones freshly overhauled, so that the locomotive can be returned to traffic promptly. Essential to such a system, however, are precise records of the hours in traffic of each part of the locomotive, since engine or transmission components will not necessarily reach the same maintenance stage together. To compile such records, details of every duty performed by a locomotive must be filed. Hence the WR has established a control system by which the whereabouts of every locomotive and the duty it is performing are known and recorded daily.*

### *Traction control section*

*The nerve centres of the WR diesel locomotive control system are four traction control offices, one in each division at Plymouth, Bristol, Cardiff and Paddington, plus the headquarters shopping control office, which is also located at Paddington. The function of traction control is to allocate locomotives to diagrams that will fully utilise the motive power, but which take account of day-to-day maintenance requirements, and to schedule maintenance for each locomotive at times appropriate to the hours it has been in traffic. Traction controllers are responsible for recording details of the work performed by each locomotive which, from the scheduled times for each train, are converted into "hours in service"; these figures form the basis for assessment of maintenance needs.*

*The three records from which maintenance is chiefly controlled are the daily movements list, the record of hours in service, and the Roneodex visible records card, which is the heart of the recording system. The movement lists, showing each train working in and out of a Division, which are prepared for the duration of the timetable by the Divisional Office, are completed from hour to hour by the duty traction controller of the Division. The traction controller first records the locomotive number against the train which it is working away from his Division, then phones the details to the traction controller of the receiving Division. The "home" controller can assume that, unless anything unforeseen occurs, that locomotive will automatically work the next leg of its diagram and he therefore pencils its number against its scheduled working back to his Division (though, in the cyclic nature of some of today's diagramming, this will not necessarily be the locomotive's next duty).*

*The traction controllers maintain close contact with the foremen at the maintenance depots for their division. When a locomotive is returned to traffic after a break for servicing or maintenance, or if a locomotive has no diagrammed working after arrival at a depot, the traction controller will allocate it a duty in consultation with the depot foreman.*

***Record card for each locomotive***

*From the movements list the "hours in service" of each locomotive, calculated from each train working, are transferred to a "record of locomotive working" form. This lists all locomotives allocated to the division in numerical order and against each unit are entered the trains it has worked and its hours in service from day to day. At the end of each week the hours in service of every locomotive are totalled and this information is transferred to the Roneodex visible records cards.*

*In the Roneodex system each locomotive has a record card and the cards, segregated by locomotive class, are kept in flat trays. The visible edge of each card has headings to indicate the availability of the locomotive – whether it is in traffic, in maintenance depot, in works, stopped for repair and so on – together with a scale of hours in service. The traction controller keeps the actual state of each locomotive easily identifiable by sliding coloured tabs to the appropriate heading of its card. Thus the controller can quickly scan the tray of cards for a particular class and verify at a glance the locomotives in traffic, those under repair, and the hours in service each has amassed. Supplementary sheets show details of repairs and failures. It is from these Roneodex cards that the traction controller learns which locomotives are nearing their next scheduled "hours" examination and maintenance and plans their next duties and the maintenance programme accordingly.*

*Three times a day, at 4.00, 12.00 and 20.00, each traction controller compiles an availability return listing every locomotive allocated to the division and whether it is in service, available but not in use, in depot, in works or awaiting repair. This return is circulated to the other divisions in the WR. Also prepared from the movement lists are various other statistical returns of diesel locomotive availability, which are without the scope of this article.*

*Proposed dates for locomotive maintenance are submitted by the traction controller to the maintenance depot for approval, or revision in the light of the work capacity of the depot. Ideally the WR aims to have maintenance work planned about a week in advance. Unhappily this is rarely achieved in practice, for while recording and planning on the lines described function satisfactorily, unscheduled maintenance and repairs to locomotives which have failed in traffic are still sufficiently frequent to affect most depots' capacity for scheduled maintenance. A pattern of failures can lead to design modification, perhaps minor, but nevertheless necessitating special attention to every locomotive in a class. Other suspected faults - for example, axle flaws, which had been detected in several locomotives (last summer) have required an entire class to be examined specially at short notice. All this has a disruptive effect on scheduled maintenance.*

***Procedure for locomotive failures***

*Individual locomotive failures are dealt with in one of two ways. A failure at the depot can be covered by the traction controller, who uses a spare locomotive not yet rostered or, if a spare locomotive is not available, transfers a locomotive from another roster starting later in the day. This in turn may lead to several alterations to rosters until a spare locomotive can be found to fill the gap.*

*A failure in traffic, however, may entail a traffic controller "borrowing" a locomotive from another train, perhaps transferring a locomotive from a freight to a passenger train. There is not always time to advise the traction controller immediately of such*

**D811 DARING in July 1962 at West Drayton with a train of vanfits. (www.rail-online.co.uk)**

**D819 GOLIATH paired up with D839 RELENTLESS on 16 August 1962 at Newton Abbot with the 1V86 12.45am Manchester-Plymouth. Note the uneven placement of the overhead livewire flashes on the nose of D819. (Paul Chancellor Collection)**

*an improvisation, but obviously he must be informed as soon as possible. In any case, he will eventually be notified of the altered working when his depot foreman reports the arrival of an unexpected locomotive.*

*The traction controller must then make arrangements for the delinquent to be sent to a depot for examination and repair, and for the substitute to be restored either to its previous diagram or to one which will ensure that its next scheduled maintenance is not unduly delayed. The substitute locomotive may, for example, have been working a train to Bristol in order to undergo maintenance on arrival. But it may have been removed from the train, at say, Swindon to take over an up express for Paddington on a diagram that will keep it away from Bristol for several days. This could intolerably delay its next maintenance period and the traction controller must negotiate with his colleague in the receiving division to regain the missing locomotive on time.*

*The maintenance of WR diesel locomotives, whether they have hydraulic or electric transmission, is based on predetermined hourly periods in service at 125hr, 750hr, 1,500hr, 3,000hr, 6,000hr, and 12,000hr. Schedules specify the type of maintenance at each period; the shorter period maintenance is repeated at each interval; for example, a locomotive will receive five 125hr maintenance sessions between each 750hr examination. Many of the general maintenance jobs apply equally to diesel-electric and diesel-hydraulic locomotives, but from about 6,000hr upwards maintenance of the engines and transmissions of the two types differ completely.*

***Engine replacement routine***

*On diesel-hydraulic locomotives, the high-speed engines need a complete overhaul at about 6,000hr. This entails the removal of the engine from the locomotive and its despatch to Swindon works for attention. Meanwhile, another engine fresh from overhaul is fitted to the locomotive, which is then returned to traffic.*

*In the case of a diesel-hydraulic locomotive, the engine is changed at about 6,000hr and the transmission at 12,000hr; both are jobs that can be tackled by maintenance depots. As a result, a diesel-hydraulic locomotive needs to visit a main works only for a body repair or overhaul.*

***Headquarters shopping control***

*The decision whether a locomotive is to undergo heavy repair at a maintenance depot or at a main works is taken by Headquarters Shopping Control at Paddington. Such repair at a depot invariably means repair by replacement and this is the course taken whenever practicable for diesel-hydraulics. A diesel-hydraulic in need of repair may not necessarily be dealt with at its own base, but may be sent to one of the other heavy repair depots according to the capacity of work that they can undertake. Here again, Headquarters Shopping Control decides the depot to which a locomotive will be sent.*

*Components are readily changeable at depots, although this in itself can introduce fresh problems. Care must be taken, for example, to ensure that when a Hymek Type 3 undergoes a bogie change it emerges with all its wheels of the same diameter.*

*Repairs to major components come under four classifications: unscheduled; light attention; intermediate; and general. Light attention covers such items normally undertaken at depots as the fitting of a new turbo-charger to the engine, or tyre turning on a ground lathe without removing the bogies from the locomotive. Intermediate repairs apply primarily to bodies, bogies and power units (engines and transmission), which are normally dealt with at main works.*

*An unscheduled repair, as its name implies, is the consequence of a failure. In some instances an unscheduled repair may become a scheduled repair if, for example, a component has almost reached the time for its next scheduled repair. Train-heating boilers and transmissions, on the other hand, normally have unscheduled or general repairs. After all types of scheduled repair a component starts its hours in service/mileage at zero, but after an unscheduled repair it resumes work at its existing hours/mileage/months.*

*A locomotive is considered for repair in one of three ways:*

*(a) as in service but in need of scheduled repair at main works;*

*(b) as in service but due for a scheduled change of components at depot;*

*(c) as about to be stopped with defects or damage.*

*The Headquarters Shopping Control initiates action in the first two cases when its records show that components have reached or are about to reach their specific total of miles/ hours/months in service between overhauls. In the third case, the locomotive may already have been taken out of service by accident or failure, in which case the depot to which it is taken will advise headquarters control of the details by telegram. Shopping Control will then initiate a shopping proposal form, if it is decided to deal with the locomotive in works, or a component change advice, if it is decided to change components at a maintenance depot.*

*The shopping proposal form raised by Headquarters Shopping Control details each component of the locomotive with its miles/ hours/months in service. A copy of the form is sent to the depot to which the locomotive is allocated (or where it has failed), requiring the locomotive to be examined physically and the condition of the components entered on the form. On receipt of the completed proposal form Shopping Control can (a) order the locomotive to works immediately, (b) agree that a works repair is needed, but that the condition of the locomotive and/or the works capacity will allow a deferment up to a normal maximum of two months; or (c) allow a deferment of more than two months, in which case a further shopping proposal will be initiated at the end of an agreed period.*

***Separate component records***

*The advice for a locomotive to receive a scheduled change of components at a depot is also initiated by Headquarters Shopping Control. In cases where replacement components are fitted either at works or depot the repair details of the component concerned are advised by Headquarters Shopping Control to the owning depot so that the aggregate mileage/ hours/months in service are known for future day-to-day maintenance plans. A depot may carry a stock of certain components so that a particular part sent from Swindon to the depot may not be the one actually fitted to the locomotive in question. It is essential, therefore, for the details of the component actually fitted and the replacement component sent from Swindon to be carefully documented and advised to all concerned.*

*Here again the Roneodex visible records system is in use at Headquarters Shopping Control. In this case each major component has its own card, on which are entered details of mileage/hours and overhauls, dates and the locomotive to which it is fitted. A quick reference coloured tab shows the accumulated mileage or hours in service. Although each locomotive has a master Roneodex card, this applies only to the locomotive body and auxiliaries; each of the major removable components on a particular locomotive has its own card grouped with the other components of that locomotive. As a component is changed, its card is removed from that locomotive's group until it is returned to service in another locomotive.*

*The WR diesel-hydraulic types have been by no means trouble-free in their first few years. This is one of the results of rushing into production with untried designs. Clearly the effects of the failures would have been far more widespread but for the close control of components and records, the liaison between shopping control, works, depots and traction control and, above all, the flexibility of the control system as a whole.*

**Workshop Overhaul Schedules**

The Workshop Overhaul Schedules laid down in great detail, from pre-stripping through to post-assembly testing, the workshop maintenance procedures. Those for the Warships are summarised thus: *All work to be done to a locomotive when shopped will be authorised through the medium of the Shopping Proposal Form. The Shopping Proposal Form will indicate the classification of repair for each of the major components of the locomotive. For the purpose of shopping, the locomotive will be divided into five major components as follows:-*

*ENGINE*
*TRANSMISSION*
*BODY*
*BOGIE*
*BOILER/STEAM GENERATOR*

*The Schedules for each type of locomotive will be issued in six separate sections as follows:-*

*PRE-STRIPPING AND POST ASSEMBLY PROCEDURE*
*ENGINE*
*TRANSMISSION*
*BOGIE*
*BODY*
*BOILER/STEAM GENERATOR*

*A locomotive may be agreed for Workshops attention to any one or more of the major components. The classification of repair may be different for each component but it is essential that all components agreed for classified repairs are repaired to a standard which will enable the component to run the full scheduled period before it requires to be shopped for the next classified repair.*

**A rare appearance north of Wolverhampton for D817 FOXHOUND hauling the 2.10pm Paddington-Birkenhead near Wellington on 27 August 1962. This was one of several Warships employed as substitutes for Westerns on the Paddington-Wolverhampton-Birkenhead services in the second half of 1962. (M Mensing)**

***Classification of Repairs:-***

| *CLASSIFIED* | *INTERMEDIATE* |
|---|---|
| | *GENERAL* |
| *Classified repairs are those which are carried out on a regular basis with the object of enabling the component to remain in service for a pre-determined number of engine hours until the next classified repair.* | |
| *UNCLASSIFIED* | |
| *Unclassified repairs are those which arise In consequence of a collision or accident, or failure for any reason of a component which necessitates shopping the locomotive to rectify the defect.* | |
| *NOTE The changing of major components requiring classified repairs shown in this Schedule may be carried out at Maintenance Depots.* | |

*The periodicity of Workshops repair will vary, depending on various factors. Basically, however, shopping will be a function of the condition of the locomotive and the responsibility for deciding the periodicity of shopping should rest with the Regional C.M & E.E. The following table is offered as a guide only to assist in the fixing of periods between Workshop repairs for this type of locomotive.*

The Component Change Records show that some D800s had components which lasted far beyond their normal expected 'service' life between repairs, such as:

D805 (new 13/05/59) had its first A transmission change at Laira on 18/10/63, transmission 10475 having completed 15,000 hours (53 months) without failure. It was removed for a general repair.

D818 (new 30/03/60) had its first B transmission change at Laira on 14/01/65, transmission 10493 having completed 12,656 (57 months) hours without failure. It was removed due to metal in filters.

D821 (new 25/05/60) had its first B transmission change at Laira on 15/11/64, transmission 10508 having completed 10,120 hours (54 months). It was removed due to being unable to select direction. Records show that some components seemed to go on forever whilst others could fall apart in no time!

| PERIOD | ENGINES | TRANSMISSIONS | BODY | BOGIES | FINAL DRIVES | BOILER/STEAM-GENERATOR |
|---|---|---|---|---|---|---|
| Engine Hours | | | | | | |
| 6,000 | INTERMEDIATE | - | - | - | - | - |
| 12,000 | GENERAL | GENERAL | - | - | - | - |
| 18,000 | INTERMEDIATE | - | - | - | - | - |
| 24,000 | GENERAL | GENERAL | - | - | - | - |
| | | | | | | |
| 2 Years | - | - | - | INTERMEDIATE | INTERMEDIATE | GENERAL |
| 4 Years | - | - | INTERMEDIATE | GENERAL | INTERMEDIATE | GENERAL |
| 6 Years | - | - | - | INTERMEDIATE | INTERMEDIATE | GENERAL |
| 8 Years | - | - | GENERAL | GENERAL | GENERAL | GENERAL |

***For Workshop planning purposes, these periodicities should be converted into calendar months dependent on utilisation.***

**Looking at the numbers**

George Scholes in his paper to the Institution of Locomotive Engineers in 1959 set out the yardstick for the new diesels: *The first cost of diesel locomotives, irrespective of the type of transmission, is very much greater than that of steam locomotives of corresponding power. If such a high first cost is to be justified, the new form of motive power must have a much higher availability than the old and, of equal importance, advantage must be taken of such high availability. Whilst experience with the D.800 Class is as yet insufficient to enable a firm assessment to be made, trends are encouraging, as the following statistics for the first five months of 1959 will show: -* *(See page 65).*

*Care has been taken to make this comparison as reliable as possible. Because the D.800 Class locomotives were new or nearly new and therefore spent no time under or awaiting factory repair, the same was assumed to be true for the steam locomotives, the average miles and hours per locomotive per day being calculated from the four-weekly returns by dividing the total miles and hours in service on week-days by the number of locomotives multiplied by 24 in the case of the D.800 Class and by the same figure less the locomotive-days under or awaiting factory repair in the case of the steam locomotives. Time for servicing and maintenance at depots is not reliably recorded and it is for this reason that average miles and hours per day, ignoring servicing and maintenance, have been given for comparison, the figures indicating clearly the improvements in these respects afforded by the diesel locomotives. There are at present no very reliable means of assessing whether or not the new locomotives are being used up to the limit of their availability, but the fact that they are doing about twice the daily mileage achieved by steam locomotives of corresponding power is of great significance. It is impossible to say how these figures will be affected as the locomotives grow older because on the one hand availability may tend to fall as the time for a general overhaul approaches, whilst on the other hand it should tend to rise as initial teething troubles, inseparable from any new design, are overcome. Also, there is perhaps a tendency to put these first diesels to more intensive use than may be possible when they become available in large numbers, but this simply stresses the need to re-cast the timetables to ensure the best possible utilisation of the new form of motive power and to take the greatest care in diagramming the locomotive services.*

*A fairly careful record of teething troubles has been kept and an analysis of these is of some interest. Considering the first 29 weeks of 1959, during which time the number of D.800 Class locomotives in service increased from four to nine, the reported defects can be divided broadly as opposite: -*

*Analysis emphasises the importance of using only the very best electrical equipment and of paying great attention to the installation of the wiring, although it could be argued that, in view of the complexity of the circuitry, anything short of perfection must lead to a good deal of trouble.*

*The only engine defects of any note have been a few cracked turbo-charger casings, the occasional production of black smoke and erratic performances now and again. The turbo-charger defects have been ascribed to faults in manufacture, whilst the engine performance troubles are thought to be due to air leakage into the suction line. Investigations are proceeding.*

*The few transmission troubles, mainly concerned with damage to claw-clutches and control operating mechanisms, are ascribed either to intermittent electrical faults or to very occasional mishandling by insufficiently experienced staff and an endeavour is being made to render the apparatus automatically immune from such occurrences.*

*Failures of brake adjusters and valves were due to small defects in design, which have since been rectified, whilst flexible connections, of course, always leave something to be desired.*

*The remaining miscellaneous defects are of the type which might be expected to develop from time to time on any locomotive.*

The statistics from the minutes of the

| Class | | 4 W.E. | Stock | Average Miles per Day per Locomotive | Average Hours in Service per Day per Locomotive |
|---|---|---|---|---|---|
| STEAM | King 4-6-0 | 24 Jan. | 30 | 165 | 5.3 |
| | | 21 Feb. | 30 | 169 | 5.7 |
| | | 21 Mar. | 30 | 165 | 5.6 |
| | | 18 Apr. | 30 | 159 | 5.9 |
| | | 16 May | 30 | 159 | 5.4 |
| | Castle 4-6-0 | 24 Jan. | 165 | 158 | 7.3 |
| | | 21 Feb. | 163 | 153 | 7.6 |
| | | 21 Mar. | 163 | 152 | 7.3 |
| | | 18 Apr. | 163 | 149 | 7.4 |
| | | 16 May | 163 | 152 | 7.2 |
| | Britannia 4-6-2 | 24 Jan. | 12 | 143 | 6.3 |
| | | 21 Feb. | 12 | 179 | 7.6 |
| | | 21 Mar. | 12 | 176 | 7.9 |
| | | 18 Apr. | 12 | 179 | 8.1 |
| | | 16 May | 12 | 183 | 8.2 |
| DIESEL | D.800 BB | 24 Jan. | 3 | 385 | 9.8 |
| | | 21 Feb. | 3 | 458 | 13.0 |
| | | 21 Mar. | 4 | 340 | 11.0 |
| | | 18 Apr. | 4 | 357 | 11.0 |
| | | 16 May | 6 | 369 | 12.2 |

BR Motive Power Committee show the average mileages of the D800s improved through to the end of 1960 as the fleet increased, before falling back over the next two years; although the D833s never achieved the higher levels. In both cases this probably reflects the more varied nature of their duties as more locomotives came into service – there was after all only a finite number of long-distance high mileage turns each day.(*see table overleaf*).

To put these into context, the figures for the Warships compared favourably with their diesel-electric Type 4 peers on the other regions. Over the three years the D800s were better on both availability and mileage than the English Electrics and far ahead of the woeful performance of the Peaks.

In August 1963 the BR Chief Mechanical Engineer reported to the British Railways Board on 'Diesel Train Locomotive Performance' in which he referred extensively to the poor performance of the flagship Type 4s in the new diesel fleet and explained what was being done to rectify the situation:

*MAJOR DIFFICULTIES AND MODIFICATIONS*

*Towards the end of 1962, availability deteriorated due largely to the following causes:*

*Western Region type 4 diesel-hydraulic locomotive engine and transmission failures.*

*London Midland Region type 4 (2300 and 2500 h.p.) Sulzer/B.R. failures due to excessive liner corrosion, high crankcase pressure, and a number of modifications required with these locomotives.*

*London Midland Region type 4 (2000 h.p.) English Electric traction motor and generator flashovers.*

The report went on to discuss each of these three problem children, albeit with confusing (some may say deliberate) mixing of the different engines and transmissions of the two B-B hydraulic classes.

***Western Region Type 4 diesel-hydraulic locomotives***

*One of the main difficulties in coping with this situation as it arose was the shortage of spare parts caused by the failure of the North British Locomotive Company.*

*Some twelve months after the failure of this company there was formed "Voith Engineering" who took over the North British Locomotive Company's responsibilities to us for the supply of transmissions, engines and spare parts. From the formation of this company the supply of spare parts improved and was put on a sound basis. Latterly, however, the supply position is getting acute again generally because the quantities held in stock at the main workshops are inadequate. The matter is, however, being dealt with by the General Manager, Workshops in conjunction with the Chief Mechanical & Electrical Engineer, Western Region.*

*These locomotives are fitted with German high-speed Maybach engines manufactured by the Hawker Siddeley organisation in this country. Technical design failures in the German designed engines have been largely dealt with by the Hawker Siddeley Research & Development organisation who have now built up a considerable technical "know-how". There remain however, some problems affecting life of parts, which it has been agreed this Research & Development organisation shall continue to deal with on our behalf.*

*If at any time the position worsens with regard to the Maybach engines, there is available a substitute English built engine, the Paxman "Ventura", two of which been running in our main line service for some four years now with much satisfaction.*

*Many technical difficulties have been experienced with Voith hydraulic transmissions of 1100 h.p. capacity. These transmission troubles can now be said to have been cleared up to a reasonable stage.*

*The hydro-mechanical transmissions (Mekydro) used on some of the type 4 locomotives when rated at 1100 h.p. have been reasonably satisfactory, although here again modifications are still being carried out to the transmissions as they pass through the shops to prevent recurring failures.*

Despite this, and even with the inclusion of the D600s and the early

| *Type of Defect* | *Number of Incidents* |
|---|---|
| Electrical Apparatus or Wiring Faults | 50 |
| Engine troubles, partly due to faults elsewhere | 14 |
| Pipes and Joints | 10 |
| Transmissions | 8 |
| Brake Adjusters and Valves | 8 |
| Spring Gear | 6 |
| Vapor Watchman Heaters | 5 |
| Heat Exchangers | 4 |
| Flexible Hoses | 4 |
| Dynostarter Cardan Shaft Couplings | 3 |
| Boilers | 3 |
| A.T.C. Shoe Switches | 2 |
| Exhausters | 1 |

D800s

| No. | Period ended | % avail. | Daily mileage | No. | 4 weeks ended | % avail. | Daily mileage | No. | 4 weeks ended | % avail. | Daily mileage |
|---|---|---|---|---|---|---|---|---|---|---|---|
| 9 | 08/08/59 | 76.8 | 446 | 25 | 13/08/60 | 78.8 | 442 | 37 | 12/08/61 | 80.4 | 365 |
| 10 | 05/09/59 | 73.5 | 475 | 27 | 10/09/60 | 80.7 | 432 | 37 | 09/09/61 | 69.0 | 386 |
| 11 | 03/10/59 | 82.5 | 466 | 28 | 08/10/60 | 88.1 | 399 | 37 | 07/10/61 | 69.6 | 350 |
| 12 | 31/10/59 | 74.3 | 477 | 29 | 05/11/60 | 82.6 | 391 | 38 | 04/11/61 | 79.3 | 343 |
| 13 | 28/11/59 | 79.5 | 483 | 30 | 03/12/60 | 80.4 | 408 | 38 | 02/12/61 | 75.0 | 325 |
| 14 | 26/12/59 | 89.3 | 438 | 30 | 31/12/60 | 81.7 | 385 | 38 | 30/12/61 | 78.3 | 329 |
| 17 | 30/01/60 | 81.9 | 443 | 32 | 28/01/61 | 72.0 | 376 | 38 | 27/01/62 | 68.4 | 305 |
| 17 | 27/02/60 | 75.3 | 491 | 33 | 25/02/61 | 70.2 | 338 | 38 | 24/02/62 | 86.8 | 364 |
| 18 | 26/03/60 | 78.3 | 511 | 34 | 25/03/61 | 72.2 | 375 | 38 | 24/03/62 | 78.9 | 374 |
| 19 | 23/04/60 | 75.0 | 516 | 34 | 22/04/61 | 63.3 | 403 | 38 | 21/04/62 | 76.3 | 361 |
| 21 | 21/05/60 | 76.1 | 509 | 36 | 20/05/61 | 73.7 | 357 | 38 | 19/05/62 | 78.9 | 359 |
| 23 | 18/06/60 | 81.3 | 505 | 36 | 17/06/61 | 72.9 | 374 | 38 | 16/06/62 | 84.2 | 356 |
| 24 | 16/07/60 | 88.4 | 459 | 37 | 15/07/61 | 78.6 | 375 | 38 | 14/07/62 | 78.9 | 426 |
| | | | | | | | | | | | |
| | Average | 79.4 | 478 | | Average | 76.5 | 389 | | Average | 77.2 | 357 |

D833s

| | | | | No. | 4 weeks ended | % avail. | Daily mileage | No. | 4 weeks ended | % avail. | Daily mileage |
|---|---|---|---|---|---|---|---|---|---|---|---|
| | | | | 3 | 13/08/60 | 100.0 | 121 | 20 | 12/08/61 | 80.9 | 348 |
| | | | | 3 | 10/09/60 | 83.3 | 330 | 21 | 09/09/61 | 75.6 | 342 |
| | | | | 5 | 08/10/60 | 87.5 | 188 | 22 | 07/10/61 | 78.0 | 344 |
| | | | | 5 | 05/11/60 | 75.0 | 398 | 23 | 04/11/61 | 74.3 | 322 |
| | | | | 7 | 03/12/60 | 64.3 | 359 | 24 | 02/12/61 | 80.1 | 349 |
| | | | | 9 | 31/12/60 | 85.4 | 264 | 26 | 30/12/61 | 75.5 | 308 |
| | | | | 10 | 28/01/61 | 77.5 | 307 | 28 | 27/01/62 | 82.1 | 302 |
| | | | | 11 | 25/02/61 | 88.6 | 278 | 29 | 24/02/62 | 75.9 | 320 |
| | | | | 12 | 25/03/61 | 86.8 | 332 | 30 | 24/03/62 | 73.3 | 340 |
| | | | | 15 | 22/04/61 | 68.8 | 354 | 31 | 21/04/62 | 80.6 | 357 |
| | | | | 16 | 20/05/61 | 70.3 | 316 | 32 | 19/05/62 | 78.1 | 377 |
| | | | | 18 | 17/06/61 | 64.0 | 322 | 32 | 16/06/62 | 78.1 | 336 |
| | | | | 19 | 15/07/61 | 83.5 | 349 | 33 | 14/07/62 | 69.7 | 384 |
| | | | | | | | | | | | |
| | | | | | Average | 79.6 | 301 | | Average | 77.1 | 341 |

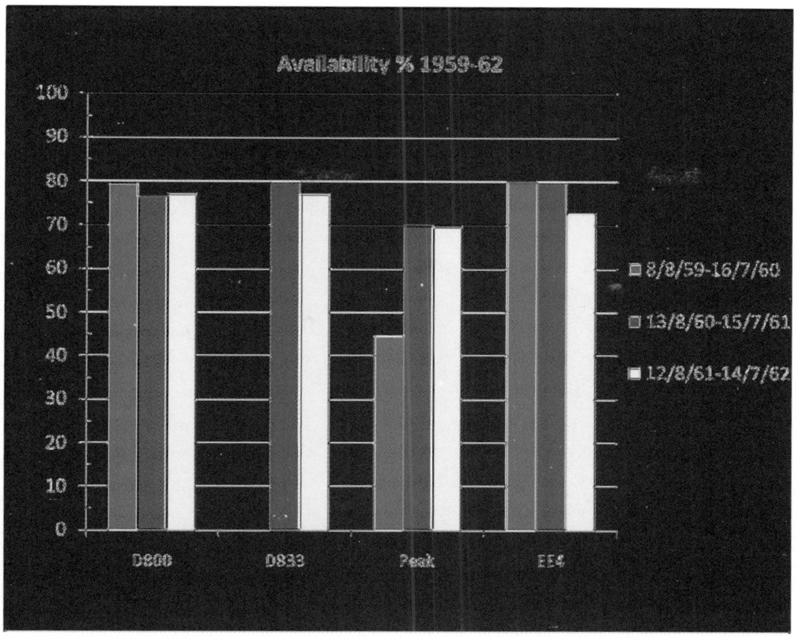


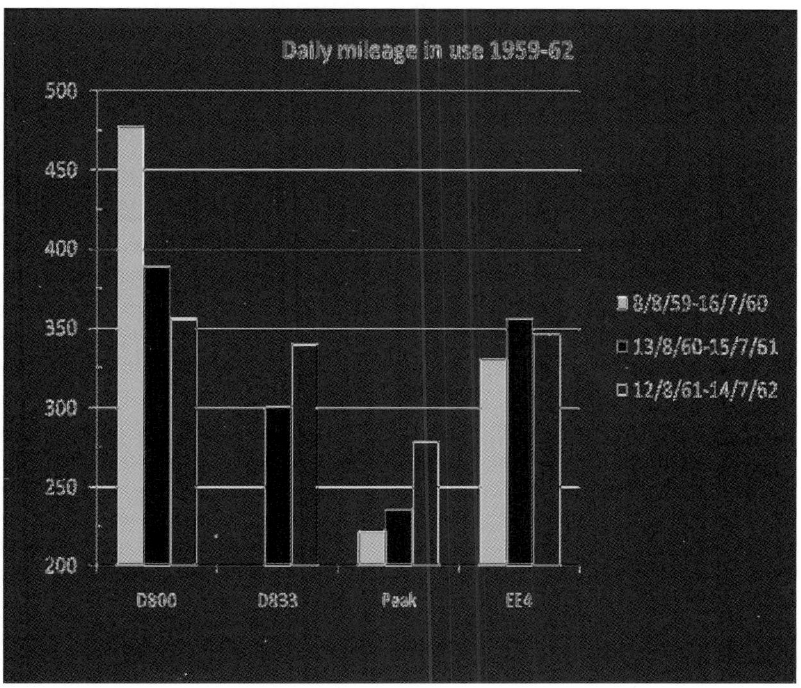


| *Availability - Average daily position during week ended* | *3 Nov 1962* | | *15 June 1963* | |
|---|---|---|---|---|
| | No. | % | No. | % |
| WR type 4 hydraulic | 97 | 76% | 128 | 83% |
| | | | | |
| BR Sulzer type 4 | | | | |
| LMR | 134 | 70% | 135 | 56% |
| ER | 1 | 100% | 25 | 84% |
| NE | 39 | 67% | 48 | 77% |
| WR | 10 | 70% | 10 | 60% |
| | 184 | 69% | 218 | 64% |
| E.E. Type 4 | | | | |
| LMR | 105 | 76% | 105 | 74% |
| ER | 10 | 60% | 10 | 60% |
| NE | 66 | 77% | 66 | 86% |
| ScR | 19 | 95% | 19 | 84% |
| | 200 | 77% | 200 | 78% |

Westerns in the statistics, the hydraulics' record was still better than that of the diesel-electrics. Moreover, the comments on the two diesel-electric classes did not exactly inspire confidence that their shortcomings had been rectified:

***LMR Type 4 (2300 and 2500 h.p. Sulzer/ BR locomotives***

*During 1961 and 1962 as these locomotives went into service they were satisfactory until it was noted that excessive liner wear was taking place and high crankcase pressures were building up. During this time modifications had been required to turbo blower blades and to water tanks. The excessive liner wear stemmed from lack of engine coolant water treatment which had not been applied by the LMR. Other regions had however carried out the necessary treatment. This had effect, of course, in the excessive liner pitting. Standard treatment is now coming into force on the LMR and this trouble should not, therefore, be experienced in the future.*

*The high crankcase pressures were caused largely through the extended use of lubricating oils beyond the specified periods and because we were using the BR specification oil which was not entirely satisfactory to these particular locomotives which have now been placed on Shell "Tacona" 945. Further investigations into the general use of BR specification fuel and lubricating oils are now taking place between engine manufacturers, oil companies and ourselves.*

*Early in March the LMR arranged to diagram only 50% of their Type 4 Sulzer locomotives until such time as each one of the 136 in their stock had been passed through the main works for a special top overhaul to rectify the liners and pistons affected by causes mentioned above, at the same time having all other modifications carried out.*

***LMR Type 4 English Electric - flashovers***

*Flashovers on the above locomotives which occur regularly on the London Midland but not so seriously on other Regions, have been a continuous problem, the causes of which have not yet been clearly understood. The Chief Electrical Engineer and I discussed this with Lord Nelson with a view to his setting up, within his organisation at Rugby, a full research programme to simulate such flashovers, determine the cause, and effect a permanent cure. Much evidence is being accumulated, but this is undoubtedly a long term research exercise, and it may be some time before a satisfactory solution has been achieved. In the meantime the availability of these engines is materially affected by this difficulty.*

Unsurprisingly, the position was not much different by the end of 1964 based on the figures for the last nine months of the year included in the 1965 National Traction Plan. The Swindon-built Warships had an average 75% availability compared with 67% for the NBL locomotives.

**A battered D804 AVENGER under the wires at Crewe on 26 October 1962. Warships took over the services to the North West from the start of the 1962 summer timetable until replaced by Brush Type 4s in 1964. (Paul Chancellor Collection)**

The Peaks continued to perform badly with average availabilities in the range 57% to 65.5% with the highest proportion, the LMR fleet, still failing to achieve 60%. The two main allocations of English Electric Type 4s continued their downward trend with the LMR falling by a further 1% to 73% and the previous star, the NER, by 6% to 80%; the only improvements were the ten locomotives on the ER which rose by 6% and the nineteen on the ScR which increased by 1% to 85%. Thus over their first five years in service the D800s returned the best overall availability and mileage figures of any of the Type 4s on British Railways, and even the D833s were far from being the worst performers.

**Tales from the workshops and depots**

So much for the official statistics, now for the view from some of the men at the sharp end of the battle to keep the fleet running. Memories of the D600s have almost disappeared but Alan Wild and Alec Morrison have dug deep into the past for these snippets. Firstly Alan: 'My only direct involvement was as an apprentice in the AE Shop when a small modification to some control air piping and a valve up at cantrail level was required in 1959/60. The fitter I was assisting was Bill Elford and we had D602, if memory serves me right. We had difficulty in tracing the pipe run and asked a fitter who had just done the same work on another alongside how he had tackled the job. He came across and looked at 'our' loco and said: "Blowed if I know, this one's quite different."

'Eventually we saw what he had done and realised that NBL had altered the layout of a lot of the ancillary equipment on succeeding locos. They were generally detested by the Swindon workmen because of the variations between them and the sometimes not very good workmanship. Their only saving grace was that because of these problems you could often claim some piecework price enhancements and overtime!'

Alec Morrison was originally a fitter at Laira in 1958/9, then a Head Office Diesel Inspector at Swindon in 1960 for a year before moving to Paddington where he spent two years travelling around the WR 'mending' locomotives. His first job at Laira was to fit a pair of fuel pumps to a D600 which had been standing for a week waiting for an NBL service engineer to arrive. He

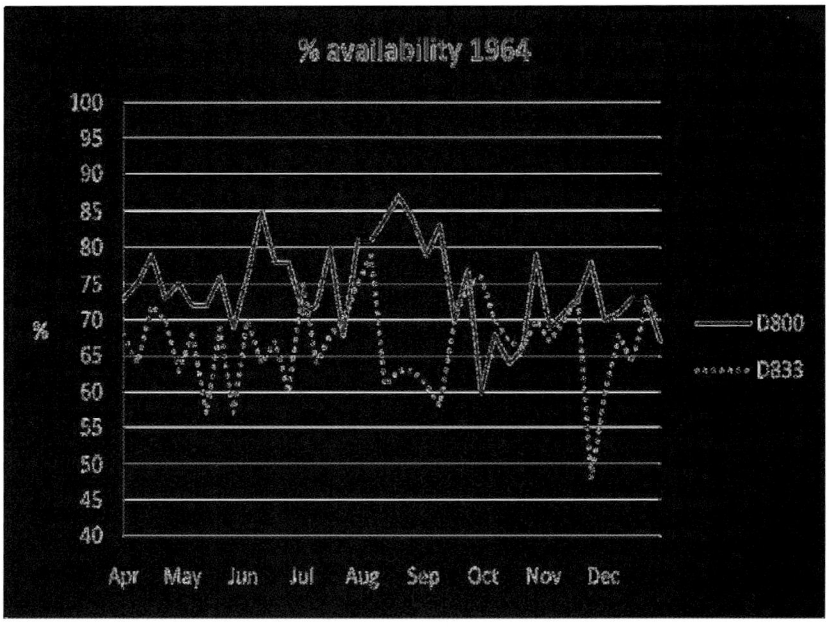

remembers 'that we had a lot of trouble with the cooling system, the electric fan was controlled by a Drayton regulator which was forever malfunctioning. This device consisted of a bimetal rod and a tube, which was in contact with the cooling water, and contained oil under pressure. As the rod heated up it expanded and opened a valve allowing oil to escape with a resultant drop in pressure. This drop was detected by a series of switches which controlled the fan motor. The regulator was clearly unsuitable for the purpose; it apparently performed well in a stationary mode but could not contend with the vibration, and was subsequently replaced by a series of temperature probes which proved satisfactory'.

Alec also recalls that there were many problems with the engine; seized pistons were not unknown for instance. Another problem was 'the governor of the Voith transmission: its central stem was controlled by three rollers engaging with the convex unit which rotated. These rollers were not positively driven but relied on friction, and they would slip and cause "flats" on the rollers causing malfunction of the change points with consequent loss of traction. The engine speed was controlled by the governor which had three solenoids actuating a triangular plate giving a combination of six steps. Unfortunately any attempt to increase revs was usually via notch 6 with the consequent over-fuelling exacerbated by the inverted helices (to advance the injection point) of the pump elements. I have seen these surges in pressure cause combustion gases to escape from beneath the cylinder heads!'

Turning his attention to the D800s and D833s, Alec recalls that 'the Swindon built locos were far superior to the NBL build in every way. The body finish (of the latter) was poor and great lumps of filler often dropped off. The first few locos from Glasgow were out of service for some time due to coolant leaks. The pipework was not up to Swindon standards, and many pipes fractured because no allowance was made for the flexible engine mounting! The gearbox switches were a constant source of trouble as were cardan shaft failures'.

Alan Wild had plenty to say about the D800s and D833s: 'My involvement was initially as an Engineering/Student Apprentice in the Loco Works (1959-63) and later on the Works Technical Section (1963-71). The latter's role was to disseminate information received from equipment suppliers to the shop-floor supervisors and artisan staff who were involved in overhauling the kit. We recorded data requested by the Design Office on the condition of equipment received for attention from both the Erecting Shop and Regional Maintenance Depots. Monitoring the status in Works of official Experiments and Modifications was also our responsibility. This was done in conjunction with representatives of the M&E Engineer (Design) in Swindon Drawing Office. This section was the principal point of contact between the suppliers and BR as far as technical matters were concerned.

'During a short stint in Swindon Running Shed stint during my apprenticeship I did get a couple of trips on these locos. In both cases it meant boarding a 'sickly' loco at Swindon station and trying to cure it during the journey: in one case to Paddington and in the other to Weston-super-Mare. In the first instance the obvious problem was a leak on the Serck cooling fan drive pipe system. This was simply cured by my climbing inside the cooler unit and tightening a loose joint, taking care to avoid de-capitation by the fan – nowadays such action would be outlawed! Although this repair was carried out with the train running at normal speed there was some other problem, which I cannot now remember, but it was deemed advisable to get the loco back to Swindon Works for examination.

My first trip behind one on a fast schedule was shortly before the 80mph speed limit was imposed, on the Bristol-Paddington train which was allowed 36 minutes from Swindon to Reading start-to-stop. By my reckoning we attained 94mph at Steventon and again after Maidenhead; this was with a D800. During the "limited" period I never recorded more than 81mph with either

**D833 PANTHER at Shrewsbury on 31 August 1963 with the 1M12 07.40 Leamington-Birkenhead. This was more usually a Western turn at this time; a Warship would have been far more common on one of the SW/NW trains via the Marches. (AW Battson, www.transporttreasury.co.uk)**

**D827 KELLY, piloted by D6332, approaches Laira Junction on Friday 5 July 1963 with a down express. The smaller NBL Type 2s were regularly used as pilot engines for heavy expresses over the South Devon Banks, especially on summer Saturdays. (RC Riley, www.transporttreasury.co.uk)**

type but after the modifications cruising at 90 or slightly over became common. A colleague once clocked a D833 at 97mph on the level near Goring working an Up Worcester train shortly before the loco was withdrawn.'

On the D800s Alan remembers 'The MD650 engine was the least troublesome of the Maybach series, mainly because of its low specific rating and absence of charge-air cooling. The cast iron crankcase gave much less trouble than the fabrications of the higher-powered engines but it was, of course, heavier, When flaws did appear they were more difficult to repair but one particular welder, Les Johns, became a past master of the technique. Even the Germans thought the task impractical and were very impressed by his results.

'Crankcase damage largely arose from erosion caused by use of BSM cooling water inhibitor. This was far worse on the fabricated crankcases and afflicted all quick-running engines. This was one of the most expensive mistakes made by BR in relation to diesel engine operation. All Maybach, M.A.N. and Paxman engines (and many others used by BR) were designed to use a soluble-oil coolant inhibitor. Its purpose was to prevent corrosion in the engine, cooler group and all associated pipework. Unfortunately a large number of LM Region Depots lacked waste water trapping systems and discharge of oil-inhibited water to local sewerage systems caused many complaints and a lot of compensation claims. The LMR solved the problem by operating their slow-running engines with raw water. This solved the discharge problem but it fairly quickly gave rise to corrosion in the locomotive systems and the BRB Scientific fraternity came up with borax sodium metasilicate (BSM) as an inhibitor. It also contained sodium nitrite, which I believe was a later addition. This additive solved the problem of drainage as it was easily neutralised in the sewerage systems and, as far as I am aware, it did what it was required to do in the slower-running engines.

'The BRB issued an edict that all diesel engines must use the BSM inhibitor and the Western Region dutifully did as it was told. The result was the rapid development of erosion on wet cylinder liners and a little later on the crankcases themselves and to some extent on cylinder heads as well. Corrosion was negligible but that was no help when erosion instead caused failure after a few thousand hours service. Once the true extent of the damage became apparent the WR appealed to the BRB to be allowed to revert to soluble-oil inhibitor; the drainage was not a problem as all WR Depots had proper water treatment systems – not that they always did their job properly! The Board was adamant so the premature failure of components in contact with the coolant had to be lived with until the last diesel-hydraulic was withdrawn. I don't think anybody actually determined the cost of this decision, but it was probably several millions of pounds. Only after the diesel hydraulics had gone did the WR discover that the Southern had never switched to BSM treatment. They carried on using soluble-oil and kept quiet: it was only when the class 33s started wandering all over the system and were occasionally serviced away from Eastleigh and Hither Green that trouble arose, and by then it was too late for anyone to bother!

'Without recourse to records I cannot be sure of the actual rate of erosion but I know that in some cases cylinder liners had to be changed after only a few months in service. Of course the water discharge into the crankcase caused damage to virtually all internal components to a greater or lesser extent. Naturally the MD650 suffered more slowly than the higher-rated engines but the BSM episode still added enormously to their maintenance costs.

'Cylinder heads and turbocharger lower casings (cast iron) also suffered to some extent from the change of inhibitor but in their case it was probably more a question of minor erosion exacerbating the high temperature stresses which affected these components. Cracked Maybach cylinder heads became endemic (again mainly MD655 and MD870) and a 'Berlin Wall' of many hundreds accumulated in the BD Shop whilst repair techniques were being developed.

'Another problem which affected all Maybach engines was self-inflicted by the Western Region. The sump of a 12 cylinder engine carried over 30 gallons of lubricant and it was supposed to be changed at a set interval (I cannot remember the actual number of engine hours). This was a tedious and messy job in the confines of a locomotive built to BR loading gauge and someone had the bright idea of burning off the oil at a controlled rate so that drainage was unnecessary. The regular topping-up with fresh lubricant would keep the oil reasonably clean and drainage could await removal of the engine for periodic attention at Works (6,000hrs). In order to burn off the oil the piston ring 'pack' needed altering to allow oil to find its way past the rings into the combustion area. As I recall one scraper ring was omitted and one of the upper rings was altered. The result was embarrassing. After a very short period complaints arose that topping-up was necessary far too frequently: it became necessary for oil bowsers to be available at Taunton to refill sumps on locos working Paddington to Plymouth trains due to low oil level after 150 miles since leaving the depot! It was necessary to pay extra-special attention to the oil sampling procedure as, when the engine ran for long periods without draining, any wear particles which would normally be obvious at oil changing might go undetected until disaster struck.

The next three years were spent trying to rectify this problem – without complete success. It was expected that reversion to the original ring pack would do the trick, but it certainly did not. All engines were, of course, tested before despatch to the Erecting Shop or to Depots and it was decided to extend the running-in period prior to the full-load test with an additive in the lubricant which should promote bedding-in of the piston rings. It worked to a degree but was never entirely satisfactory and the extra few hours on the test bed all added to the cost of the engine overhaul. Different ring packs were tried experimentally but the original Maybach set was as good as any, though no longer ideal – one of life's imponderables!

'Turbocharger bottom casings, which were subject to very high temperatures, cracked when the wall was thinned by coolant erosion. Some MD650 blowers were afflicted but far fewer than on MD655 and 870 types. Bearing failures also occurred, but again the MD650 was least affected.

'The K104 hydraulic transmission was not particularly troublesome, although it did require very careful attention when assembling and fitting the command block. There were odd occasions when topping-up with oil had been neglected and roller bearings failed as a result; gear and dog-clutch teeth could also suffer badly from this cause. It was not unknown for a transmission to arrive from a depot with perfectly clean oil but disintegrated bearings. It seemed rather pointless to try and disguise the cause of failure in this way. A classic was a seized transmission which was found to contain pieces of chopped up rubber - the filler hose having been inserted too far and getting trapped between gear teeth whilst the input shaft was still rotating!

'The C33 final drives suffered from a degree of gear wear due to the geometry of the drive system and associated torque reaction arms. As the locomotives rolled along track which was not to the high standard found on German main lines the axles rose and fell in relation to the torque arm pivots on the bogie frame. This superimposed a fluctuating torsional twist on the final drive casing relative to the axle. The effect was not regarded as particularly serious on the D800 class but it did accelerate wear on the spiral gear teeth. Most serious problems were caused by lubrication failure – leakage due to ballast or debris being thrown up from the track and cracking the casing, leaking oil seals or lack of topping up at appropriate intervals.

'Eventually the axles themselves did suffer serious failure due to a

**D824 HIGHFLYER on 17 August 1964 after arrival at Waterloo with the 07.00 from Exeter – the first Warship-hauled service train into Waterloo after they took over from the Bulleid Pacifics on that day. (JC Haydon)**

**D870 ZULU at Semley Station on 6 March 1966 with the 1086 10.40 Plymouth-Brighton. (M Mensing)**

manufacturing defect. This applied to all axles machined at Swindon on the D800 (and D1000) classes, until such time as an actual failure occurred and the fault was exposed. The NBL axles for D833s and any from Crewe on D1000s were unaffected. The complex geometry of the axles was dictated by the number of components which were mounted using an interference fit, i.e. wheels, axlebox and final drive casing bearings. To avoid cyclical stress reversal with every revolution of the wheels 'stress relieving grooves' were incorporated either side of each of the fitments – which of necessity had to be of slightly different diameters, largest in the middle and smallest at the wheelseats.

'At Swindon the axles were machined on special copying lathes built by Georg Fischer & Co. of Switzerland. A flat steel template with the profile of the axle machined along it (in the Toolroom) was mounted on the lathe and a probe followed the template which actuated the tool feed mechanism to reproduce the profile on the axle. Naturally the toolpost traversed the workpiece longitudinally in only one direction. This was fine if the changes of profile were no sharper than the angle at which the tool could be set. Unfortunately one groove on either side of the central portion of the axles in question was too deep and narrow for the tool to exactly reproduce the complete smooth transition radius. As a result half of the affected groove was perfectly formed but the other half finished up with a straight angled section. In many cases the transition from radius to angle was quite sharp and in time a fatigue flaw could commence at this junction.

'The first failure (as far as I can remember) occurred on a D1000. The frequency of ultrasonic detection of axles was increased across the entire diesel-hydraulic fleet and several flaws were discovered. Because of the wheelset configuration, with axleboxes between the final drive and wheels, it was possible for an axle to break in service without it being immediately obvious. At least one locomotive worked its way to Swindon and the wheelset only collapsed once the bogie frame was lifted from the wheelsets! Once the cause was revealed it was clear that all affected axles would have to be renewed in short order. That no D800 had failed prior to the D1000, despite having been in service longer, was purely fortuitous. The new axles were manufactured in the same fashion as before but they had to be remounted in a centre-lathe to finish the critical grooves to a perfectly smooth profile. (I believe that neither NBL nor Crewe used the same type of copying lathe as Swindon so their processes were different.) Some axles remained in service, with increased frequency of ultrasonic testing, until the flaws were seen to be extending whereupon they were immediately stopped and the bogies sent to Swindon for renewal. Not every original Swindon axle actually suffered flaws but all were eventually renewed as a precautionary measure.

'The GWB cardan shafts gave relatively little trouble on the D800s. In time wear occurred on the splines of the sliding sections and this was reclaimed by 'Tescolising' (a proprietary nickel deposition process) and re-machining to original dimensions. The cross-piece bearings were renewed at overhauls and gave relatively little trouble in service.

'The Serck cooling system (as on all locomotives) suffered from leaks due to vibration of the pipework. This arose from track induced shocks and engine/transmission system as well as pressure fluctuations in the Serck system itself. The compression joints had to be perfectly formed to minimise the problem but the cramped location of many joints made this difficult to achieve. The pumps and motors themselves gave little trouble. The radiators suffered from mechanical damage to the fragile fins – a lot of it induced when trying to clear debris which had been sucked into the matrix. The relatively flimsy design of the radiators made maintaining water-tightness difficult in a locomotive subject to shock loading from points and crossings and "heavy shunts".

'The Spanner Mk.1 boiler could be a fearsome beast to light at times. If everything was not set up just right it could be over-fuelled before igniting, the resulting flash of flame from around the base being scary to say the least. From the Works viewpoint the worst feature was the water feed pump. The pistons of this item wore at a surprisingly rapid rate and its efficiency dropped accordingly.

'Control Equipment was not my field, but I do recall that the "flag switches" on the driver's desk and back panel had a habit of tripping whenever a dipped rail joint was encountered and it was the secondman's job to reset them PDQ. The Brown Boveri instruments were marvels of ingenuity but likewise were easily upset by jolts. As time went by almost all the 'monitoring' instruments, i.e. those whose job was to advise whether a major component was functioning correctly, were isolated and eventually removed. Far more failures were due to the instruments themselves than to the kit they were monitoring; this seems to be a universal rule in engineering!'

Moving onto the D833s Alan confirms Alec's recollection of the poor bodywork: 'The North British built locos had a different external appearance from those built at Swindon due to the painting regime. The thin skin welded to the light framing of the bodyshell had to be 'shrunk' to ensure that it was uniformly stressed. This was done by spot-heating the skin with a welding torch and quenching the spots with cold water applied with a sponge. With practice the shrinkage was reasonably even over each "panel" but there were always slight ripples in the finished product. The skin was then given a coat of primer and at Swindon a layer of "Prestolith" was spread over the whole surface on the D800s. This was applied quite thickly (about 1/8" - 3/16" if memory serves) and rubbed down to give as uniform a surface as possible. The under and top paint coats were then applied, the latter at least was a chlorinated rubber type, I'm not sure whether the undercoat was as well, but I doubt it. This gave a rather "flat" (dull) finish. I believe that NBL did not apply "Prestolith" but used a different filler, which being a thinner coat was less able to hide the unevenness of the stressed skin. The top coat was probably an enamel type paint which gave a glossier finish than Swindon's. The down side was that the wrinkles in the bodyshell were more apparent.

'It was quite common to see class members with huge blisters on the side where water had got under the filler, and this would cause huge patches of filler to simply break off. As early as February 1963 D838 RAPID, then just over two years old, was photographed with two huge patches on the side where the filler had fallen off. To try and protect the metal body side it had been painted green and this shot has been shown in magazines with the caption of 'fire damage' which it certainly was not.

'The M.A.N. L12V18/21 engine was an uprated version of that in the D600s and although a less complicated engine than the Maybach there were several weak points, the most niggling being coolant leakage from crankcase to cylinder head joints and lubricating oil leakage into the 'air-box' in the Vee of the engine. The latter distributed charge air from the Napier turbo-charger to the cylinder heads. The exhaust manifolds were also prone to leakage. When the hot gas en route to the blower turbine reached the accumulated oil in the air-box the resulting conflagration caused damage to surrounding equipment.

'Another problem due to the oil leakage was carbon build-up in the turbine casing which led to bearing failures and sometimes complete seizure. It became the practice at depots to periodically inject paraffin into the turbocharger and rev up the engine to ignite it. The resulting explosion loosened accumulated carbon – the filthy emission from the exhaust pipe showering everything in the vicinity!

'The exhaust manifolds were fabricated in sections, each section having a twisted guide vane welded within the tube portion. These welds were difficult to execute in the confined space and the use of mild steel by NBL in place of the stainless used by the German manufacturer led to frequent failure. The broken vanes, needless to say, found their way into the turbocharger with catastrophic results. An experimental assembly was tried, using stainless vanes mounted in channels welded within the tubes. The theory was that by allowing differential expansion to occur – the vane always being hotter than the tube – failure was less likely. It was an expensive proposition and came too late in the day to be widely applied. I cannot remember how many engines were so equipped: I do recall that the stainless steel components were supplied by Cross Manufacturing in Bath. Their processes were really ingenious and they could manipulate materials which defeated most other engineering firms, but obviously this expertise came at a price which the M.A.N. engine didn't justify.

**D803 ALBION on 17 June 1967 ready for departure from Bournemouth Central with the 1V12 13.12 Poole-Swansea. Warships were extremely rare at Bournemouth and this particular summer Saturday turn lasted for just one year. (Paul Chancellor Collection)**

**Maroon liveried D806 waits to depart from Ilfracombe in the summer of 1968. It faces a climb up the 1 in 36 gradient from the standing start but with only four coaches this should not trouble CAMBRIAN. (www.rail-online.co.uk)**

'The connecting rod/cap joints were prone to fretting corrosion. The resulting loosening of the fit on the bearing shells exacerbated the wear of these items. I cannot recall any particular problems with the Voith L306 transmission until quite late in the life of the D833 class. The hydraulic oil was supplied by Esso and was quite satisfactory for several years but there came a time when 'foaming' became endemic in the Voith transmissions. The D1000s were the main cause of concern but the smaller transmissions also suffered. Once foaming occurred the pressure in the transmission built up until the dipstick was blown out of its tube and the pressure relieved. This, needless to say, caused oil to spray everywhere! The foaming also reduced the ability of the oil to lubricate the interior of the 'box' with resulting damage to bearings, etc. The Swindon Area Scientist could find no difference in analysis between 'good' oil and 'bad'. Esso scientists observed the tests and claimed they were equally at a loss to explain the cause of the problem. The Area Scientist then opined that the blending process must have been changed. Within weeks of this view being conveyed to Esso HQ the problem disappeared! It had been a costly matter though, but nothing could be proved'.

Jeremy Clarke, who worked as a Traction Inspector at Paddington in the early 1960s, commented on the propensity of the NBL locomotives to catch fire: 'one serious problem with the D833s related to the M.A.N. engine. The exhaust manifolds ran along the side of the engine below the level of the cylinder heads, and any leakage from the high pressure fuel pipes in the Vee of the engine would often result in an engine room fire. Underframe fires could also be a problem on both the D800 and D833 classes if the underframes were not kept reasonably clean. The main frame tubes, particularly above the inner wheelsets, would collect a lot of brake block dust, and if there was a bad oil leak from the engine which run out into this brake block dust and saturated it a fire would occur after a spell of heavy braking'.

John Savage, who was a trainee on the WR between 1966 and 1971 based at Swindon Works, Reading and Old Oak Common, provides a vivid description of the automatic gear change in the Mekydro transmissions using as an example the change from first to second gear (second to third and third to fourth were similar). 'Believe me, the command block is devilishly clever, all little pistons and oil pressure, and the ratchetting noise is unforgettable:

1. The dual governor moves to the upchange position
2. The gear selector moves from 1st to 2nd gear
3. The torque converter engaging (forward blading) pressure stops
4. The torque converter disengaging pressure starts. (Clutches are now relieved of load)
5. The clutches disengage
6. The new dog clutch ratchets. (Decelerating ratchetting pressure holds the converter disengaged with the backwards blading engaged, which slows the input gearwheels down to enable the new dog clutch to engage)
7. The new dog clutch engages
8. The torque converter engaging pressure starts again
9. The torque converter disengaging pressure stops
10. The transmission is now in 2nd gear

Think how many gear changes occur every trip! A down change going up a hill is even more exiting!' Jeremy Clarke explained the effect of this in the workshops: 'The Mekydro transmissions fitted to the D800s were quite complex pieces of machinery when it came to fault finding, much more complex than the Voith transmissions fitted to the D833s. So very few could sort out the more difficult problems on these transmissions. In the early days there were some service personnel around, both British and German, from the locomotive suppliers, some of whom (the British ones) later joined BR (in the Traction Inspectors' department that I was originally in) when the service contracts ran out. These men proved to be very useful in helping to sort out the more complex problems, both in their original roles and when they were later employed by BR.

'Both the D800s and D833s had an array of electrically operated protection devices, known as 'moment contactors', mounted on the desk in the cab in front of the second man's position. These provided protection for a number of different systems, but often caused more problems than the systems themselves due to incorrect operation, sometimes because they became overheated when in direct sunlight for some time. So eventually a rationalisation process resulted in some of these being eliminated, where it was known that the systems themselves caused very few problems.

'Some serious failures of cardan shafts occurred due to unbalance, as it was not appreciated immediately how important it was to keep the two sections correctly assembled in relation to one another, after the splined sections had been split. Correct, regular lubrication of the several lubrication points on these was not always followed in these early days, with disastrous results! In some of the drive systems torsional vibrations were experienced which caused heavy wear in the joints and splined sections of the shafts. Various types of anti-vibration couplings were tried in these systems, but the most effective of such couplings did not appear until various trials had taken place on the D1000s.

'Exhaust connections into the base of the Maybach turbochargers was always a problem as it was difficult to get a long lasting seal, and turbochargers themselves would occasionally crack because of the high temperatures.

'Transmission heat exchangers on the D800s caused a problem due to overheating, resulting in melting of the solder holding the exchanger tubes in position, and therefore the cooling water and oil mixing together. Then you were faced with the problem of cleaning the systems out, and in particular the oil out of the cooling system. This problem was eventually solved on these locomotives and the D1000s by the use of a much higher melting point solder to solder the tubes to the tube plate.

'The Maybach engined locomotives were fitted with preheaters to preheat the cooling water system up to 110°F before the engine could be started, as the Maybach engines ran very roughly when they were cold. These preheaters were very unreliable, and were in constant need of attention. One problem was caused by carbon deposits building up in the burner unit quite quickly if combustion was not perfect, and various methods were tried to remove these deposits without having to strip the whole unit down, usually resulting in the surrounding area being covered in soot along with the operator who was trying to clean the preheater!'

'On the D833s the M.A.N. engine used to pass loads of oil into the exhaust pipes when idling, and when setting off from Paddington it all had to burn off, completely filling the engine room with thick smoke. I remember being told not to attempt going into the engine room till after Slough'.

An unnamed West Midlands driver similarly commented on the propensity of the NBL locomotives to produce smoke where it was least wanted. 'These locomotives may have been very versatile, but I should say most drivers and secondmen will be glad to see them go to the scrap heap. My recollections as an ex-fireman and secondman on Warships are of dislike for them. When there was a shortage of Brush Type 4s in the Wolverhampton area to work the Londons the locos that replaced them were Warships from Newton Abbot. To be sure, we did not get the pick of the crop, but even so I consider the Warships as the most unhealthy and least reliable locos that I have ever been on.

'We would leave Birmingham, and before Leamington the hydraulic transmission would begin to overheat and the cab would fill with blue smoke and fumes from the burning oil in the transmission under the floor. The noise level was sometimes unbearable and the cab was cold through having all the doors and windows open to let the fumes out. It was not unusual to travel miles on one engine while the other engine was cooling down after overheating.

'On booking on one morning my driver was told that the locomotive for our job had failed and he had to collect one from the shed that had come off the first London. Before we could leave

**Maroon-liveried D829 MAGPIE and blue D827 KELLY speed through Newbury with the 16.30 Paddington-Plymouth on 18 March 1968. This was one of the trains used for trials with Warships working in multiple before they were introduced at the start of the summer timetable in May. (DE Canning)**

**D831 MONARCH ready to leave Paddington on 6 May 1968 with 'The First Six Hour Run' to Penzance of the 'Cornish Riviera Express' in multiple with D819 GOLIATH. The Warships worked to Plymouth with a Western taking over for the final run into Cornwall.**

we had to have 17 gallons of oil in the front transmission and 14 gallons in the rear, replacing what the locomotive had burned on the run down from London and back in the early morning'.

[This tale seems to have gone awry slightly in its telling: transmissions didn't normally burn oil unless there was a serious fault, e.g. overheating bearings. Just topping up the oil wouldn't have saved the component from failure; normally they only lost it through leaks etc. Almost certainly it was the engines that burnt this huge quantity of oil and the fumes were dragged through. It is quite likely that enginemen didn't really understand hydraulic principles and only really understood that it 'slooshed' oil, so if you could smell hot oil it must be from the transmission... Also, the transmission only held about 90 gallons and so losing that amount would seriously impede the ability of the locomotive to move).

**Experiments and modifications**

Inevitably with a new and untried form of traction there was much experimentation in response to problems, both major and minor, which arose in the first few years of service, and some of these have been described above. The extensive work to cure the problems with the Krauss-Maffei bogie has already been discussed and Appendix 4 contains the surviving details of the other experiments.

When experiments were completed those which were deemed successful were applied as modifications to the class. Although urgent modifications were applied as quickly as possible, many of the less important ones were left until Intermediate overhauls, mainly in the period 1964-67. As with the experiments, many details have not survived; Appendix 4 summarises those which have.

**Interchangeability**

From new, D800-D802 were fitted with two Maybach MD 650 power units rated at 1,050bhp at 1,500 rpm, each coupled to a Mekydro K104 series transmission. Train heating was provided by a Spanner Mk. 1 boiler. Only the bogies and boiler were interchangeable with other class members; however by 1962 modifications enabled any MD 650 type engine from the series D803-D829, D831-D832, D866-D870 to be fitted. This effectively increased the output of the first three from 2,100bhp to 2,270bhp in line with the remaining D800s. Throughout the life of D800-D802 only the transmissions remained unique to these three locomotives.

Originally it was intended that Swindon and North British built locomotives would have interchangeable engine and transmissions as well as bogies (the same system that operated on the Deutsche Bundesbahn). However, tests showed that Swindon built locomotives D803-D822 had cab floors which were too low to accept a Voith transmission and to correct this, D823-D832 and D866-D870 were built with higher cab floors. Also the North British locomotives were not fitted with engine preheaters (to reduce construction costs) and so would have to have been retro-fitted by Swindon to allow Maybachs to be fitted. This meant that out of a class of 71 locomotives only the final fifteen built could be fully inter-changeable.

Thus a major 'selling point' of the class was never achieved and the D800s retained Maybach engines and Mekydro transmissions and the D833s retained their M.A.N. engines and Voith transmissions throughout their careers; only the bogies were interchanged. However, engines and transmissions *were* exchanged between the NBL-built locomotives. In general engines were interchanged between D600s and D6300s and between D600s, D833s and D6306s. Examples include engine number 141 which was new with D603 and then went to D6303, D6327, D6345, D6318 and D6356 up to withdrawal, and engine 146, new on D604, which moved to D600, D603, D840, D861, D852, D857 and finally D835 until withdrawn. The Voith transmissions on the D600s and D6300-D6305 were inter-changed only between themselves, and the remainder only between D833-D865 and D6306-D6357.

The D800s also exchanged engines across the class, for example D800-D802 received engines from the D803-D832 series in 1961/62. However they were still rated at 2,000bhp rather than 2,200bhp because the power output of the locomotive was restricted by the capacity of the transmission and not the engine output.

**Doomed from the beginning?**

The Pilot Scheme D600s and D800s were ordered in 1955/56 well before the

Deutsche Bundesbahn had gained large-scale experience with their V200s. In fact, when the further thirty D800s were authorised in February 1957, the main production batch V200s were only just entering service. However, by any stretch of the imagination, BR experience of main line diesel-electric traction to this date could hardly be described as extensive, and so there was no overwhelming evidence on either side of the hydraulic/electric divide.

RA Smeddle, the WR Chief Mechanical and Electrical Engineer, described the headlong rush into dieselisation on his Region in a paper read to the WR London Lecture and Debating Society in February 1959: *Dynamometer Car tests of D.801 and D.600 show that they are capable of the performances which were expected of them and they have been putting up an excellent show in service. This latter statement needs qualifying to the extent that, as is only to be expected with any new design, a number of teething troubles has been experienced, but these are being systematically combed out and, while it is too early to say with complete confidence that the promise of the hydraulic transmission will be fulfilled on British Railways, results so far are very encouraging, and it is hoped that we shall ultimately have in service a fleet of reliable Diesel-hydraulic Locomotives capable of meeting all the demands made upon them. In this connection it should be noted that, because of the urgent need to press forward with the Dieselisation programme, we were not given the opportunity of trying out prototypes before placing large orders and this in itself, of course, has presented us with the difficulty of having to make alterations on a considerable number of locomotives instead of on one, as we go along.*

As we have already seen there was a considerable anti-hydraulic faction in British Railways throughout the period during which the Modernisation Plan was being implemented. The departure of three of the main protagonists, HH Philips (retired in 1956), KWC Grand (promoted to the BTC in 1959) and R Hanks (retired in 1962) was severely detrimental to the hydraulic cause. The change in BTC Chief Mechanical Engineer from RC Bond to JF Harrison in 1958 did not help: almost from the date of his appointment Harrison was determined to produce a standard high power diesel-electric to fulfil national requirements. This manifested itself as early as January 1963 when *Modern Railways* reported, in what was virtually a press release from the BTC CME's Department, the effective death-knell for the Warships and their hydraulic sisters: *The recent order of English Electric diesel-electric Type 3 locomotives for the Western Region signals the end of British Railways' employment of hydraulic transmissions in mainline locomotives. Now it has been announced officially by British Railways that some of the new Sulzer-engined 2,750 h.p. Hawker-Siddeley diesel-electric Type 4s are to be built for the Western Region in the near future. The units still to be delivered from existing orders for Beyer Peacock (Hymek) Type 3 and Swindon "Western" class Type 4 diesel-hydraulics will be the last of their kind. What has persuaded B.R. to conclude this protracted evaluation of both types of transmission? Were they justified in conducting it?*

*In the light of data available when the 1955 Modernisation Plan was formulated – and in view of some of that Plan's proposals – the B.T.C.'s assent to the Western Region's keen desire to employ hydraulic transmissions could not be faulted. There was substantiated evidence to support German claims for the operational performance, reduced maintenance needs and lower first costs of their combination of high-speed diesel engines and hydraulic transmissions. The early anxieties of the B.R. Civil Engineers at the effect diesel locomotives would have on the track led them to make stringent stipulations limiting wheel diameter in relation to axleload – to such an extent that, taking account of the bulky medium-speed engines and electrical plant then available, the first diesel-electric Type 4 units had to be unreasonably heavy 1Co-Co1s. In these conditions, there was a great deal to be said for the strikingly lighter, four-axle Type 4s which the much more compact high-speed engine and hydraulic transmission alliance made possible. Estimates showed that a diesel-hydraulic would cost less; and, by virtue of its own much lower weight, it would have a haulage capacity of some two coaches more per train by comparison with the first series of diesel-electric Type 4s of similar power.*

*For three years after the general introduction of the first W.R. diesel-hydraulic type, the "Warship" Type 4, no difficulties were experienced that materially swayed debate on the major issues of engines*

**Blue-liveried D819 GOLIATH paired with maroon D823 HERMES at Exeter St David's on 5 September 1968 with the 1C60 14.30 Paddington-Penzance. (www.rail-online.co.uk)**

**D849 SUPERB at Paddington ready to depart with the 13.15 to Hereford on 28 March 1970. The NBL locomotives were used on the Worcester/Hereford line from early 1968 until October 1971.**

*and transmissions. But from then on troubles proliferated. Oddly, it was only then that the German Federal Railway began to encounter them as well, although it had been employing the same pattern of equipment for some three years prior to its introduction in the B.R. "Warships". The discrepancy in time that elapsed before these difficulties came to light is attributed by the B.T.C. to the fact that the Germans reserved their V200 type diesels to consistently heavy express passenger work, whereas the British locomotives were used on a wider range of duties.*

*So far as one pattern of German-designed high-speed engine* [the Maybach] *is concerned, its British licensees have done a great deal to overcome the problems and in many ways have markedly improved on the original concept, at considerable expense. But a basic difficulty cannot be surmounted; the engine, although a clever work of design, is an extremely complex piece of machinery that makes many repair operations far more lengthy than on other types of engine. Another brand of German-designed engine* [the M.A.N.] *has been frankly disappointing; a notorious failing is its tendency to leak oil, which has resulted in a number of locomotive fires.*

*However, it is a credit to British industry that it has conceived a range of British-designed high-speed engines which, so far as B.R. experience goes, has given entire satisfaction. This is the Paxman Ventura - "extraordinarily reliable, rugged and simple to maintain" is a testimony I have heard in high places. Two such engines have now been running for some time in "Warship" No. D830.*

*There is thus a very promising range of high-speed engines available if B.R. had no other reason than their setbacks with earlier types for abandoning the associated hydraulic transmissions. But the policy decisions that have been taken on future B.R. dieselisation do not result solely from experience with high-speed engines. The hydraulic transmissions themselves, after a British debut that was initially satisfactory, are increasingly susceptible to defect, for a variety of reasons. On what was, I gather, a typical day in November, almost a third of the Western Region's total diesel-hydraulic main-line locomotive stock was stopped for attention – and only a quarter of the units idle were inactive for scheduled examination; a good proportion of the failed units was crippled by transmission troubles.*

*While the diesel-hydraulic system has been failing to live up to its early promise, development in other directions has negated some of the advantages which prompted its trial. The Modernisation Plan of 1955 forecast the brake-fitting of all goods wagons; but the majority of mineral wagons remain loose-coupled and un-braked and a four-axle locomotive of Type 3 or 4 power is, therefore, unsuitable for heavy mineral work – without a fitted "head" on the train – because of inadequate braking power. So far as Britain is concerned, the cramming of 2,000-2,400 h.p. into a four-axle, 78-ton locomotive like the "Warship" has lost a good deal of its original point.*

*At the same time, civil engineering restrictions have been relaxed, to the extent that a Co-Co diesel-electric of greatly enhanced output, with all axles powered, is now permissible. The possibilities have been further improved by development work both in the electric traction equipment industry, resulting in lighter traction motors, and by medium-speed engine manufacturers, who are steadily increasing the power that can be offered per ton and cubic foot of engine. Thus, in the diesel-electric Type 4 range, B.R. have progressed from the early 2,000-2,300 h.p. 1Co-Co1s of 130-140 tons to the latest Brush/Sulzer 2,750 h.p. Co-Co of about 114 tons weight.*

*The outcome of these trends in diesel-electric traction is that the original power/weight ratio advantages offered by the diesel-hydraulic system have been cancelled out in the 2,750 h.p. or higher class of locomotives B.R. now require for their Type 4s. Moreover, prices of Type 4 diesel-electric locomotives and their component diesel and electric traction equipment have tended to fall, whereas there is an opposite tendency in diesel-hydraulics. A six-axle diesel-electric Type 4 is now cheaper than a six-axle diesel-hydraulic of comparable power; this was not the case five years ago.*

*These are the chief reasons that have led B.R. to discard diesel-hydraulic locomotives in the medium- and high-power ranges. All in all, the evidence of British experience overwhelmingly justifies the decision to standardise electric transmissions in B.R. main-line locomotives.*

A reader replied anonymously to the 'article', pointing out amongst other things the problems on the BR/Sulzer Type 4s already discussed; if only he had known what was to happen with the Brush Type 4s within a few years! With hindsight, it is clear that the story was 'fed' to the magazine by the proponents of the new standard Type 4, and with scant regard to what was actually happening on the ground. The lesson from the Pilot Scheme debacle that bulk orders should not be placed without extensive testing was cheerfully ignored.

Given the decision had already been made by 1963 it is not clear why the Department of Chief Engineer (Traction and Rolling Stock) took over two years, until August 1965, to produce a *Report on Diesel-electric & Diesel-hydraulic Locomotives on British Railways* which set out 'the accumulated experience over the past eight years with fleets of main line diesel locomotives now attaining 2,315 units with electric transmission and 358 with hydraulic transmission'. Its conclusion was predictable: 'British Railways having regard to all their experience, consider that the balance of advantage is now and will remain in favour of electric transmission, at any rate so far as our own operating conditions are concerned. They have decided that all current and future orders are or will be diesel-electric'.

**Back to the V200s**

Although by 1972 the Warships had all been withdrawn after less than fifteen years in service the DB V200s were still in main line use. They had consistently achieved availability figures of around 90% with average annual mileages a third more than their English cousins, albeit the average distance for their duties was higher than on the WR. One of the primary reasons for this apparent superiority was that the German locomotives were originally treated much more gently than the Warships as a well-known story clearly explained. A driver from Germany was in the UK to help the WR drivers get the best from their charges and when he was in the cab of a Warship, he was just going through a list of do's and don'ts when they got the green light. As usual, the Warship was opened to full throttle from standing and it took off in customary fashion with the normal rapid acceleration. This took the German driver completely by surprise, and he made it clear that "we do not give full power" until at least 60mph (at the time the V200s were limited to 75 mph). Exit one very impressed German driver.

The V200s experienced only two transmission failures in the period 1956-59 but in 1960 their loadings were increased in response to traffic demands and speed restrictions eased to allow greater mileages at the maximum 87.5mph. Very quickly transmission wear of the same kind as on the Warships was discovered and quickly deteriorated to 33 failures in the first quarter of 1961. In both countries the failures were traced to inefficient lubrication. The transmission manufacturers said the oil grade originally recommended would have been satisfactory if the WR units had been rostered for the same kind of work as the V200s. But they were put on duties with consistently higher power demands – a German engineer said that they must have been "hammered". Extensive tests led to a different grade of oil being used on the Voith transmissions on the WR which appeared to cure the problem.

On the V200s the second-stage converter of the transmission was not getting enough oil when working hard so that the oil overheated and thus did not lubricate properly. Once this was modified the transmission failures were almost eliminated, even though the V200s' workload had risen to the extent that it was some 30% higher than the original design specification. In 1962 the class averaged 145,000 miles pa and about 85% of their road time was now on full power with average loads of 420 tons.

The second reason for the higher availability was the quality of the components in the German engines and transmissions. These not only lasted much longer but were more reliable in service. There was a noticeable difference in quality between the engines and transmissions supplied from Germany compared to the UK-built counterparts with a consequential effect on the reliability figures for the WR locomotives. The comparison was worsened by the troubles experienced with the M.A.N. engines in the UK; the Germans had quickly dismissed the L12V18/21B as unreliable and in fact only five were supplied from new in the V200s, with Maybach and Daimler-Benz units in almost the whole fleet. The

**856 TROJAN passes Copper Mill Junction south of Tottenham on 5 June 1970 with a mixed freight from Acton to Temple Mills which would have come round the North London line. (PH Groom)**

**821 GREYHOUND at Kensington Olympia in the winter of 1970-71 with milk tanks from Cornwall. (www.rail-online.co.uk)**

V200s remained in front line service until the late-1970s before they were moved on to less demanding duties before their final withdrawal in the mid-1980s. Properly built and well maintained, the German hydraulics showed what might have been in the UK.

**In conclusion**

*No group of diesels perhaps caught the imagination like the hydraulics; they were Swindon inspired for a start, they were wreathed in that 'if only' mystique and they looked very fine, to boot.* (*British Railways Illustrated* December 1991.) Like Brunel's broad gauge GWR, the Western Region hydraulics never really had a chance because they were effectively non-standard from the start. The Technical Development and Research Committee had stated quite clearly on 13 December 1957 under the heading *Effect of Different Transmissions on Inter-Regional running*, 'No difficulties due to different types of transmission (electric and hydraulic) are anticipated by the General Managers; maintenance will normally be undertaken by the home Region only'. These were fine words but within five years the good intentions had been swept away.

The Warships were the first hydraulics into service and inevitably became early victims of the flood of so-called standard diesel-electric types. The quality problems and consequent poor reliability of many of their components made in the UK, and especially the M.A.N. engines, were exacerbated by the demise of North British in 1962. Given this and the prevailing views of BTC management it was not surprising that the decision was taken in late-1962, before many of the hydraulics were even in service, to build no more of them, and this was reinforced by the 1965 National Traction Plan. It hardly mattered that in fact the Warships' performance was better, at least for the Swindon-built locomotives, than that of their diesel-electric peers. Although Warship devotees can take some satisfaction from the disastrous events which overtook Harrison's standard high-powered lightweight (Brush Type 4) they really had no chance in the wider scheme of things. Sam Ell, who was one of the finest practical engineers of the day, confirmed this in the Introduction to his 1966 paper *Some Design Problems of Diesel Locomotives*: *In the "Report on Diesel-electric and Diesel-hydraulic Locomotives on British Railways" issued by the Department of Chief Engineer (Traction and Rolling Stock) in May 1965 occurs the evocative statement: "The prime cause of hydraulic transmission failure on British Railways has .... been under-design". This Paper takes neither side on the main issue and does not question the facts of the Report as they then were. But it does challenge the clear implications that the design problems of the diesel-hydraulics are so intractable as to proscribe their progress and are by nature so different that they make no useful contribution to the common stock-pot of knowledge and experience.*

Conceived by Swindon, nurtured by Swindon, by the end many of the Western men even took them to their hearts after their beloved Kings and Castles were taken away. If only they had been given a fair chance...

807 CARADOC on 22 January 1972 at Radipole having just left Weymouth with the 2V55 09.50 Weymouth-Westbury. The Warships remaining at this date were confined mainly to secondary passenger and freight services.

810 COCKADE on 6 June 1972 at Merstham with stone for the M25 construction, from Westbury and the Mendip quarries. 810 was on the Westbury stone turns for several days but on the 8th it was called on to relieve failed D1004 on the 1A05 11.55 Paignton-Paddington. It returned to Westbury on the 1B88 17.46 Paddington-Westbury and resumed its stone carrying duties. (CS Heaps)

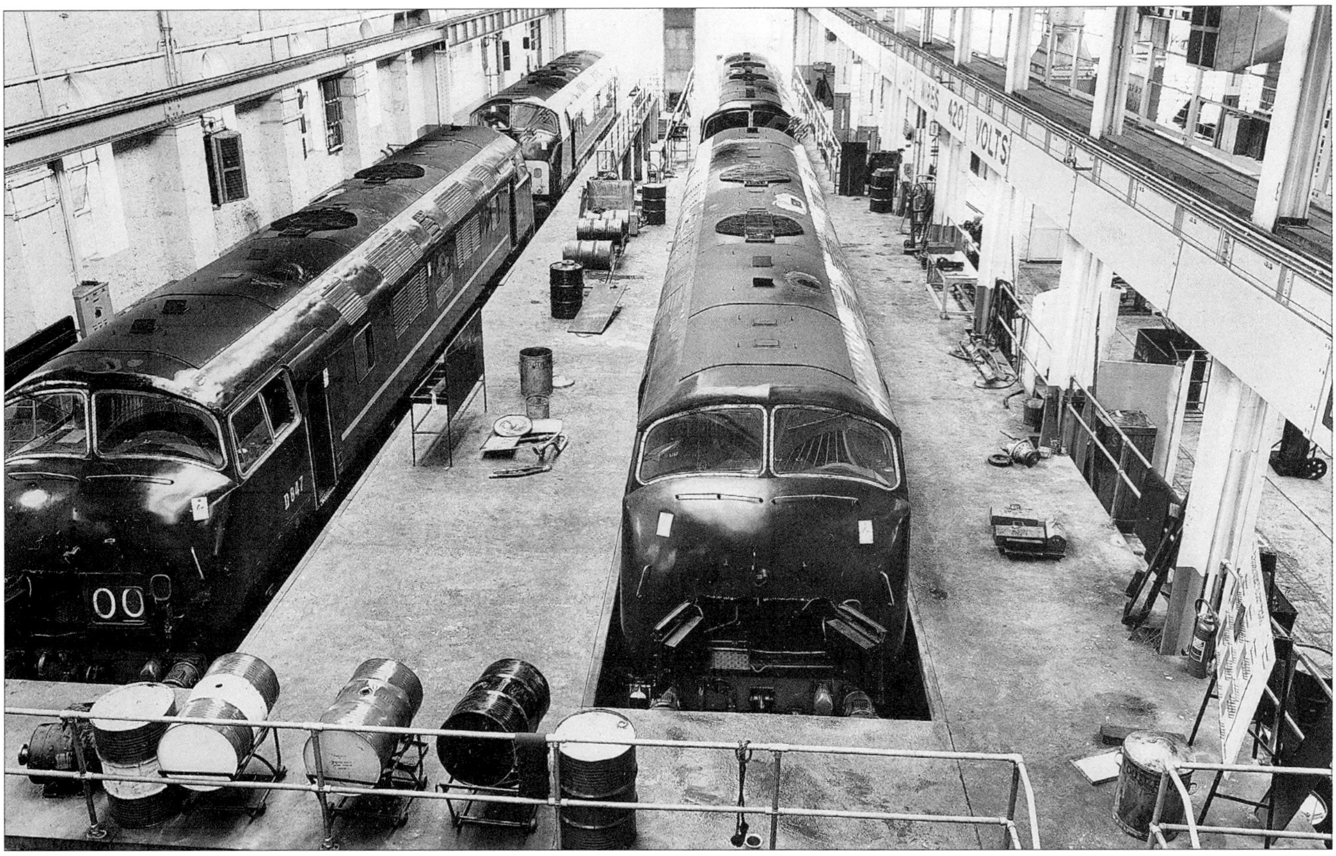


*Above.* Newton Abbot was the first WR diesel depot and was adapted from the existing steam motive power depot. D847 and another three NBL Warships in the maintenance shed on 16 May 1962. The loco behind STRONGBOW is D861 VIGILANT, identified by having one NBL and one BR radiator fan cover. The shot clearly shows the offset exhaust ports; the Swindon Warships had these in line, down the centre of the loco.

*Top right.* A WR DENFLAT.E wagon used for transporting engines and components between Swindon Works and the depots at Laira and Newton Abbot. This example worked to and from Laira. The instructions on the side read: DIESEL LOCOMOTIVE ENGINES AND ACCESSORIES ONLY and on the raised platform ACCESSORIES TO BE BOLTED TO THIS BEDPLATE.

*Right.* Opened partially in 1960 and completed in 1961, Laira was the principal diesel depot for WR Conversion Scheme No.1 A large new structure was erected on wasteland adjacent to the existing steam shed; it carried out all three levels of maintenance on the diesel-hydraulics, as originally envisaged by the WR planners. The buildings were reinforced concrete with extensive glazing on the side walls to provide maximum daylight. This view taken on 1 February 1962 shows eight hydraulics resting during the middle of the day – two D600s , two D800s and four D6300s.

DW 39676
DENFLAT.E
PLYMOUTH (LAIRA)
TO SWINDON ONLY
XP

The 'untidiness' at the front end of the D600s is clearly demonstrated in this 1958 photograph of D601 at Paddington. From the 'eyebrows' above the windows to the jumble of pipes and fittings below the bufferbeam with the discs and their ugly fittings – and it still has to get those horrible footsteps and the headboard fixings. ARK ROYAL has the short-lived brackets which were used to fix the headboards in place before the reporting numbers were displayed.

# Chapter 5
# THE DEVIL IN THE DETAIL

The five D600s exhibited only a small number of mostly minor visual changes during their lives, and therefore are dealt with in full in the first section; the remainder of the variants relate solely to the D800s and D833s. For simplicity in this section, references to left and right are when looking at the locomotive from the side.

**D600s**

Apart from the application of yellow warning panels in 1962, three of the class retained their original green livery throughout. In 1960/61 overhead line warning flashes were added, two near the top of each nose front and three on each side slightly below the cantrail, above the outer cab door handrails and towards the centre of the bodyside. The original yellow warning panels had rounded top corners and sloped slightly upwards to meet in the centre; when route indicators were fitted the panels were shallower with flat tops and less rounded corners and the warning flashes were moved to several different positions, either above or to the side of the indicator boxes.

In 1962 two small orange squares were supposed to have been painted on each buffer beam to denote the type of multiple working equipment fitted, but this has not been verified against photographs. The equipment was compatible only between the D600s and the six Pilot Scheme Type 2s, D6300-D6305, and was later removed because it was not used and was liable to cause electrical failures.

When built, the standard 'D'-prefixed numbers in white Grotesque No.9 font designed by Misha Black were applied under the cab windows at both ends. In August 1958 Black modified the 'D' by adding serifs at the top and bottom because it was realised that the 'D' could be mistaken for the number '0'. D600, D601 and D602 were the only locomotives to have the early 'D' and came into line when repainted, D603 and D604 having the later pattern from new.

None of the five was given maroon livery and the two that received Rail Blue very late in their lives managed to carry different patterns of the new garb. D602 BULLDOG kept its small yellow warning panels and had a single double arrow symbol above each nameplate when repainted in early-1967, but D600

**D601 ARK ROYAL at Laira in December 1967 showing the diamond-shaped NBL makers plate, the red route disc and the holder for the driver's name badge. (P Rae, www.transporttreasury.co.uk)**

received the prescribed Corporate Identity version. When ACTIVE was released from Swindon in May 1967 it had double arrow symbols on each cabside and full yellow ends enthusiastically extended over halfway across the bonnet and also onto the buffer housings. In both cases the D-prefixed numbers were the old serif rather than the new Rail Alphabet type.

The stainless steel nameplates were 12⁷/₈in high with rounded corners and a thin beading, and were positioned directly below the BR crest with the top of the plate in line with the top of the lower bank of louvres and thus lined up with the top of the locomotive number. The background was red and the polished lettering was 3¾in high for the individual name and 2¹/₈in high for the class name. The style of lettering for the individual name was devised by the Design Research Unit based on the GWR 'Fat Face' or, to give it the correct title, 'Standard Letters for Engine Name-Plates - 1937' with slight modification to the letters G, J, O,R and S; the class name was in sans serif letters below it. The spacing of the lettering was increased slightly on D603 and D604 and the red background was changed to black on D600 and D602 when they were painted blue.

There were four diamond-shaped NBL maker's plates, fixed on the cabsides below the numbers with the red WR route discs below. When D600 was repainted in blue the plates had to be moved to accommodate the double arrow symbols and two were transferred to the centre of the bodyside just above the solebars.

In late 1960/1961 the horizontal louvres in the upper row of bodyside radiator grilles were replaced by vertical louvres to increase the air flow over the elements and thereby the cooling capacity.

The nose-ends were an untidy mess from start to finish – immediately above the two windows were two short vents which gave the impression of eyebrows, and below were the tall connecting doors. Even when first delivered D600 and D601 had a confusion of five marker lights topped by four lamp irons and two short horizontal handrails. To make matters worse, the two central lights and lamp irons had to be placed off-centre to the left, giving a lop-sided appearance from the outset. It was no better below, where in the centre between the carefully flared buffer housings was the coupling backed by a large 'bang-plate', the multiple control sockets, the AWS shoes and a collection of hoses and pipework. Underneath the oval buffers on D602-D604 were protruding open steps supported by large triangular brackets, and these were soon added to D600 and D601.

White circular train classification discs, held up when in use by large clips mounted at an angle, were fitted over the marker lights for daytime operation; when not required these folded down revealing more metalwork in the form of an 'A'-shaped supporting frame.

Crude metal brackets to hold the train headboards were fitted slightly below halfway down the connecting doors of D600 and D601 for a short time during 1958. When reporting numbers were introduced from late-1958 the headboards had to be moved higher up and suspended from the upper lamp iron to clear them. Often the reporting code was simply chalked on the front but an arrangement was soon cobbled together to allow the numbers to be displayed in GWR-style frames precariously attached to the lower central lamp iron.

By 1960/61 the headboard fixing was reinforced by two angle irons fixed on by clips either side of the upper lamp iron inboard of the two horizontal grab rails; if not in use these metal angles just dangled down from their clips. When a headboard was carried it was off-centre because of the offset position of the central lamp iron, adding to the already lop-sided appearance of the nose end caused by the irregular positioning of the white classification discs.

As with the other early hydraulics built before route indicators were fitted, the headcode discs on the D600s were subsequently removed and replaced by two enormous indicator boxes on each nose end, one either side of the gangway. The first to be modified was

*Above.* D848 SULTAN on 5 March 1966 at Dawlish in green with coaching stock roundel and no lining. This would appear to have been a temporary stop-gap, due to the poor external condition of the loco, until a full Swindon repaint into maroon could be completed in June 1966.

*Left.* D811 DARING in original green livery without yellow warning panel or overhead warning flashes, at Ranelagh Bridge in 1960/61. Adorned with the grey lining band, red-backed nameplate and oval brass worksplates and red route availability discs on the cab access panels. The fuel tank filler access is covered whereas from D813 onwards it was open.

D829 MAGPIE at Exeter Central about 1967-68 in the maroon livery applied in January 1966. It has the coaching stock roundel and the repositioned red route availability disc while the lining band is absent. Other points to note are the positions of the overhead line warning flashes and the additional horizontal grill above the nameplate. (www.rail-online.co.uk)

D864 ZAMBESI in May 1967 showing Swindon's first attempt at corporate blue – including full yellow ends and the dark brown underframe and bogies prescribed in the original specification for the livery.

D602 in December 1964 and the final one D600 was not done until May 1967.

Physically, there were comparatively few alterations to the type, one of the first being the fitment of additional heating units after crews complained of the cabs' tendency to become unduly cold during the winter months. Demisting of the cab windows proved similarly poor, and in October 1959 oil-damaged heater hoses beneath D604's cab floor were replaced by units of an up-rated specification, a modification which was progressively applied to the other members of the class.

Under the TOPS system introduced in 1968 the D600s would have become Class 41 but their early withdrawal meant that none was renumbered or had the TOPS data panels.

**Liveries**

The Warships, along with the Class 52 Westerns, were the only BR diesel classes to appear in green, maroon and blue liveries. The liveries evolved over time from green through maroon to blue in accordance with prevailing BR policy and despite their relatively short service life they went through many minor variations.

The original Swindon Painting, Lining and Letter spacing diagram, SL/SW/1342, was modified several times, although it was not re-issued for the maroon livery. In version A dated 25 June 1958, as used on D800 and D801, the nameplate, numbers and route discs were repositioned, and the lining band reduced from 6¼in to 3in. Later in the year, following Misha Black's inspection of D800, in July there were minor changes which were applied from D802 onwards: issue B on 2 September added serifs to the letter 'D', and was quickly followed by C on 13 November when the nameplate was lowered from 6ˆ!in below the louvres to 8ˆ!in, the draw hook protector plate altered from red to black and the length of the red buffer beam was stopped 1in from buffer flanges.

From mid-1961 plates for overhead live wire warning flashes began to be fitted when locomotives went through the works. The first was D805 BENBOW in July; D854-D865 and D870 were the only ones to have them from new. The plates were fitted two on the nose ends just below the outer end of the horizontal handrails, and three on each side, one at the top right hand side of the left-hand radiator grill and one above each inner cab door handrail. The exceptions were D801 and D828 which had the flashes to the left of the right-hand grill on one side.

The next change was the repainting into the same maroon livery as the Westerns in autumn 1965; the painting diagram was not amended, presumably because the only change was in the paint colour and the omission of the lining band. D857 UNDAUNTED was the first following an Intermediate overhaul; it returned to traffic on 22 September and was unique in having its numbers in the same position as in the green livery, level with where the lining band was positioned. It was quickly followed by D858 and D863 before the first D800, D811 DARING on 5 November. In all these subsequent repaints the serif running numbers were repositioned centrally below the cab windows and higher than on D857 which allowed the red RA discs to be moved up under the number and off the cab access flaps. These flaps were originally secured top and bottom with 'budget' locks which often seized and led to them not being properly secured; hence they often fell out with the vibration/movement.

All of the repaints were carried out at Intermediate overhauls when there was a full bodywork repair. A total of 32 Warships eventually carried the maroon livery, and the last repaints were D815 and D840, outshopped on 17 and 20 October 1966 respectively.

It is an unconfirmed story but D838 RAPID, following the instructions for the new blue repaints, was said to have (uniquely) received four emblems. There was one on each cab side with the numbers (similar to D831 when it first emerged in blue) under the bodyside windows. If true, it would have been a straightforward error, a misinterpretation of instructions to place the emblems on the cab sides and which was corrected before it left the Works. The same locomotive was, again with no obvious explanation, repainted in

**D831 MONARCH was the second repaint into blue, in November 1966 with double arrows on the cab and the numbers repositioned below the body side windows. Unfortunately it failed on two counts to meet the full 'corporate' specification, with its small yellow warning panels and old-pattern serif numbers.**

D819 GOLIATH at Exeter on 2 February 1967 with the 1V32 08.35 Nottingham-Paignton wearing one of the early incarnations of rail blue. It has serif numbers with small double arrows below and the red route availability disc above the access panel.

852 TENACIOUS at Old Oak Common on 3 May 1970 in the final version of the blue livery with 'rail alphabet' numbers without the 'D'-prefix and single double arrow symbol. It has a TOPS panel below the number and both a cast 81A shedplate on the front skirt and a stencilled version behind the cab door. The nose doors have the circular ventilation grills below the route indicator panels applied by Old Oak Common to its Class 43s in an attempt to improve the cab ventilation. (www.rail-online.co.uk)

maroon in August 1968; more than a year after blue had been in use for all repaints.

In late-1965 proposals were drafted to introduce the BR 'Corporate Blue' identity: the locomotive body would be unlined rail blue with yellow visual warning panel, dark grey roof and dark brown running gear, bogies, etc. and the BR symbol below the driver's window. The new livery would be applied using airless spray painting and it was envisaged that there would be a 'complete strip and re-paint every 9 or 12 years and a single coat every 3 years'.

The proposals were finally approved by the BR Board on 9 June 1966 and a directive was issued on 10 June 1966. The Warship was one of five locomotive types selected in July for an early example application to allow evaluation of the new style.

Unfortunately the workshops were not clear how to interpret this and the Chief Engineer (Traction & Rolling Stock) wrote to the BRB Director of Industrial Design on 18 July that 'no clear directive has been issued by the Board stating that the locomotive body shall be Rail Blue and under frame, bogies and brake gear, "brake dust" brown, and it is felt (that) a general directive of this sort is required. It should include mention of the fact that a larger yellow warning panel individually designed for each type will also be part of the finished locomotive'.

The confusion was addressed in the supplementary notes issued on 13 September that amended the scheme in several areas:

***Paintwork***

*Diesel and electric main line locomotives will be painted as follows:-*
*Roof and bodysides - BR Rail Blue*
*Buffer beams, undergear, bogies - Black*
*Body ends - Yellow*
*The yellow area will extend from the top of the buffer beam up to the roof gutter. On locomotive bodies where the front is blended into the side by a curved panel the yellow will be extended to the flat vertical section of the side.*

***Lining***

*No lining of any kind is incorporated in the new livery.*

The first locomotive to emerge from Swindon in the new attire was D864 ZAMBESI on 31 October and it followed the original specification to the letter, complete with full yellow ends and dark brown underframe and bogies. However, within a few days, D831 MONARCH appeared on 18 November with Swindon following the amended instruction as far as the black underframe was concerned, but for some reason ignoring the part relating to the full yellow ends and reverting back to the small yellow panels. It may have been because P.W. Staff were reported to have complained that the full yellow ends merged with the background in bright light, and a return to the small yellow panel was requested because the difference between the blue and yellow highlighted the front better.

Confusion reigned for the next few months as we shall see when we look at numbers and insignia but, perhaps fortunately, only two more locomotives were repainted during this time. The next attempt was on D830 MAJESTIC which returned to traffic on 29 December, again with a small warning panel, but the full yellow ends came to stay beginning with D847 STRONGBOW on 24 February 1967.

It has been suggested that the first three repaints were in a slightly different blue which was more matt, but there is no firm evidence to support this. Possible explanations are the contrast with the small yellow panels, or the use of spray painting which gave a different finish/sheen than hand painting.

Issue D of the painting diagram dated 6 April finally gave clear instructions to the paintshop: 'Livery of body changed from Green to Rail Blue, yellow warning nose ends, BR small crest altered to a 2'6" white symbol and prefix and numerals to locomotive number to use the new Rail Alphabet.'

Six of the class kept their green livery beyond the end of 1968: D824, D833, D852 and D854 were repainted blue in 1969, but D845 SPRIGHTLY did not receive blue until February 1970 and D810 COCKADE was the last in May of that year. D800, withdrawn in October 1968, was the only one to retain green livery to the end but seven, D801, D809, D815, D817, D838, D840 and D848, remained in maroon until taken out of traffic. D864 retained its brown undergear after collision damage repairs in May 1967 and until its withdrawal.

All of the repaints were done at Swindon with two exceptions; by mid-1971 the paintwork of two locomotives was in such an appalling state that they were repainted at Laira. When 826

**868 ZEPHYR at Exeter on 10 July 1971 showing the reseults of the repaint carried out at Laira the previous month because the paintwork was in such appalling condition. The double arrow sybols were hand-painted and the serif numbers without D-prefixes are not level.**

One of Misha Black's 1958 sketches, produced during the design changes for the route indicator panels, may have been the blueprint for the first experimental panels applied to D845 in August 1961.

D845 SPRIGHTLY lays over at Crewe North in 1963. It had the experimental yellow warning panel and white roof from August 1961 until February 1964. (www.rail-online.co.uk)

JUPITER was stopped for engine and transmission changes in June/July its paintwork was so bad that the original lining band from its days in green was showing through. 868 ZEPHYR was also at Laira in June 1971 and John Savage recalls 'I did get the job of organising a repaint of 868 in 1971, which was in an appalling paint state. Unfortunately I was only allowed the shed labourer to sand down the filler on the body sides and he left loads of marks, which showed badly after the paint was applied. However the locomotive ran like that till withdrawal'. Photographs show the outline where the BR symbols were removed from the cab which suggests 868 had the bodysides painted but not the cab sides, or that the symbols were painted over rather than removed.

**Yellow panels and front ends**

In August 1958 Misha Black produced four sketches showing alternative visual colouring for the D800s when fitted with route indicator boxes. He hoped that the box itself would provide sufficient colour variation but he produced three alternatives with small, bright yellow panels around the boxes.

There was considerable debate about the track safety of the new diesels and electrics over the next two years and experiments included a flashing light on the first Deltic. Finally a decision was made in April 1961 to paint a bright yellow warning panel on the front-ends of the new traction. Swindon as ever was ahead of the game and when D845 SPRIGHTLY was returned to traffic at the end of August 1961 it had a yellow panel applied to the route indicator box, which bore a striking resemblance to one of Black's sketches. At the same time D845 was also given thin white crescents at the front of the cab roofs and it retained these and the small panels until October 1963, emerging from Swindon four months later with the standard version.

Final authorisation came through on 4 September including the comments: 'The dimensions of the panel are not critical. Where circular white disc indicators exist, a ¾in wide black edging is to be painted round the circumference, in order that they may show up sufficiently against the yellow background.' The Design Office set out further guidance on 8 September: 'The yellow panel to extend from above the buffers to above the indicator box. The top corners only have a 2½in radius and in the case of the D.800 class the top of the panel is curved slightly in sympathy with the curved shape of the top of the nose.'

The first locomotive to enter traffic from new with the standard panel was D859 which was delivered from NBL in January 1962, followed by D860-D865. The rest received the panels during works visits under Modifications 'W/SW/L 2949' for the disc headcode locomotives and 'W/SW/L/2950' for the remainder. The first to be treated at Swindon were D834 and D822 on 16 and 26 January 1962; D856 was the last one modified, in May 1965. D803 ALBION was the only disc-fitted locomotive to retain all-over green until it was fitted with route indicators during a works visit from 10 November 1964 to 1 February 1965.

One anomaly was D858 VALOROUS which photographs show had yellow doors at one end in July 1962 but these had disappeared within a few weeks; it seems that D858 required a change of headcode box doors and as a temporary measure these were taken from a locomotive with warning panels which was probably out of service with more serious problems. As soon as convenient the yellow doors were either painted, or more likely, swapped back.

The tops of the warning panels varied over the years and between locomotives. There was a much more pronounced 'point' on most of those without route indicators, but of course with D801, D806

**D814 DRAGON on 24 November 1961 at Paddington showing the electrification warning flashes, the route availability disc on the access panels, multiple working fittings and the route indicator panel.**

and D808 the exceptions to prove the rule. (D803 received its route indicators at the same time as its warning panels). Otherwise, panels with almost flat tops were the norm, this time with a larger number of non-conformists and interpretations of 'curved in sympathy'.

Other than this minor variation in shape, things settled down until the blue repaints started and D864 received full yellow ends in accordance with the June 1966 BRB Directive. However the next two repaints, D831 in November and D830 in December 1966, reverted to small yellow panels. On 22 February 1967 the Chief Engineer (Traction & Rolling Stock) stated that 'there is considerable pressure (for) the earliest and widest adoption of the enlarged yellow treatment, and in view of the important safety aspect I should be obliged if you would arrange to apply this to locomotives being repainted or extensively touched up, in advance of the adoption of the new livery, and receipt of the latest painting diagrams'. It is not clear whether this had filtered down to the paintshop by accident or design but when the next two repaints emerged, D846 STEADFAST in January and D847 STRONGBOW in February, they both had full yellow ends. All subsequent blue repaints included the yellow ends and these were also applied to two green-liveried locomotives, D808 in December 1967 and D810 the following month. Sixteen of those remaining in maroon also received the treatment beginning with D811 DARING in August 1967.

**Numbers and insignia**

When built, D800 had the same non-serif 'D'-prefixed numbers as the first three D600s but gained the standard serif pattern in December 1961; all were positioned below the inner (fixed) side window. The green Warships had a single standard transfer version of the small BR locomotive crest on the bodyside immediately above the nameplate. On those repainted in maroon this was replaced in the same position by the circular BR coaching stock insignia, as on the Westerns.

Inevitably there was one exception and there is a photograph dated March 1966 of D848 in green but with a carriage type roundel. The best explanation for this is that its green paint was so bad it was quickly touched up until it could receive full works attention. The whole side would have received a coat of green paint covering the lining band and the BR crest, the latter then being replaced with the current roundel used on maroon locos.

The final change came with the introduction of the Corporate Blue livery and the double arrow symbol. The BR Management Committee approved on 27 October 1965 the proposal that all locomotives should have the BR symbol as a transfer, during normal repainting, located 'one at each end on each side'. (They rejected Barman's original proposal of a cast aluminium symbol). Unlike many other diesel classes none of the Warships received the new symbol before repainting in blue.

The fun began with the first repaints which were also supposed to have 6in 'D'-prefixed numbers in the new Rail Alphabet immediately behind the cab door as well as double arrow symbols on the cab sides. On the first two, D864 ZAMBESI and D831 MONARCH in October and November 1966, Swindon got the positioning correct but used old pattern serif numbers underneath the bodyside windows in line with the double arrow symbols on each cab.

The third into blue, D830 MAJESTIC in December, was completely different: it had a smaller double arrow above each nameplate and the serif numbers went back under the cab windows with the RA disc below as for the maroon livery. As if to justify this, the CM&EE wrote to the Chief Engineer and the Director of Industrial Design on 3 January 1967 declaring that he did not favour the positioning of the numbers to the rear of the cab doors. This, he noted, raised an operational problem as the further the numbers were placed from the nose of the locomotive the more difficult it was to identify them 'when standing on parallel tracks or round a turntable'.

The reply came on 16 January: 'it is thought that, when all types of locomotive used throughout BR are considered, the front end detail varies to such an extent that to find a standard position for the number would not be possible'. Meanwhile, D846 STEADFAST appeared during the month with the same style and positioning as D830.

Matters were clearly still fluid because on 21 February the Director wrote to a member of the Design Panel: 'there seem to be blockages in the flow of information down to shop floor level with the consequence that locomotives are appearing in peculiar non-authorised liveries which do not correspond either to our directions or to the old liveries.' Proof came three days later in the shape of D847 STRONGBOW, returning to service with its numbers positioned below the inner sliding cab windows and not centrally as on D830 and D846. Swindon of course got its own way in the end; on 16 March 1967 the Director of Design relented: 'for the NBL Type 4 and Type 2, I note that it is now proposed to show both symbol and Locomotive number on the cab side. It has been agreed with WR representatives that this method would also be suitable for adoption on the D.800 Class Locomotives as well, thus ensuring that the locomotive number can easily be read'.

In May and June came the next variant when D819 and D857 appeared with small double arrows squeezed in between the numbers on the cab sides and red RA discs above the access panels. It is possible that these were hand painted rather than transfers.

At last, from June onwards, came a period of stability – the red discs were moved below the access panels which enabled the correct larger double arrow symbols to be placed on the cab sides. Intriguingly, the original blue repaint, D864 ZAMBESI, was the first following collision damage repairs after it ran into the wreckage of a train at St Annes near Bristol in January. It was quickly followed by D859 and D818. But it couldn't possibly last... Although Issue D of the painting diagram had specified in April 1967 the use of Rail Alphabet transfers, it was not until January 1968 that these found their way onto a Warship. Whether Swindon was simply using up its existing transfer stocks or was deliberately ignoring the instruction is of course a matter for conjecture!

D863 and D868 were repainted in December 1967 with serif numbers and then the following month D821 GREYHOUND and D826 JUPITER were returned to traffic with Rail Alphabet sans serif 'D'-prefixed numbers, the double arrows remaining in the same position below. A total of fifteen locomotives were turned out in this style before the next change: following the end of steam on BR the 'D'-prefix was omitted in October 1968 on 856 TROJAN and in November on 825 INTREPID.

Version E of the painting diagram was issued on 18 December showing the BR symbol and loco number repositioned and with a TOPS data panel in place of the red RA disc. 803 ALBION was the only one to have this combination with the data panel fixed to the right of the double arrow symbol, before the final change on version F (dated 28 January 1969) which moved the symbol and data panels. 816 ECLIPSE duly emerged from Swindon in February with a single double arrow below the nameplate which allowed the data panel to be positioned below the number and above the access panel.

Although the 'D'-prefix was painted out on many WR locomotives with metal numbers before they were painted blue, only one Warship, 852 TENACIOUS, had this done whilst in green livery, around October 1968. There is also no evidence that any maroon or serif numbered blue locomotive was similarly dealt with at this time. However when 826, which had previously had Rail Alphabet numbers and D-prefix, and 868, with serif numbers and D-prefix, were repainted at Laira in 1971, they both received serif numbers without D-prefixes. Their double arrows below the numbers were also replaced by single hand-painted symbols under the nameplates; and to cap it all, the numbers on 826 were not even level when applied!

None of the class received TOPS numbers in view of their imminent

When in green, the Warship nameplates had red backgrounds, as here on D846 STEADFAST; the background was changed to black on maroon and blue locomotives. (www.rail-online.co.uk)

The letters on D800 SIR BRIAN ROBERTSON were narrower to minimise the length of the nameplate. It was fitted using eight mushroom headed bolts, which Misha Black took exception to, and were replaced by flush bolts on subsequent locomotives. (P Kingston)

**D812, which was originally to have been named DISPATCH, became ROYAL NAVAL RESERVE 1859-1959 – the other one without the WARSHIP CLASS wording. Look at the state of the paintwork!**

withdrawal by the time these were introduced.

**Names and nameplates**

The BTC set up an ad-hoc committee with ES Cox and DSM Barrie of the BTC and George Dow for the LMR and CJ Rider for the WR to deal with the names to be used on their new traction. Their report in March 1957 set out:

***Principles Governing Selection***

*Names should be euphonious. Their meaning should be readily intelligible to the public and staff, and should not be of merely transient topicality. Duplication between regional names, or between the new locomotives and existing steam locomotives, should be avoided.*

***Nameplates***

*Names should not be painted on, but should be exhibited on plates. It is suggested that one nameplate on each side of the locomotive, as near the centre as external features permit, is sufficient.*

***Recommendations as to Names***

*The first main-line diesel locomotives to be introduced under the Modernisation Plan will be 3 Swindon/Maybach Diesel-Hydraulic Type "C" and 5 N.B. Loco. Co Diesel-Hydraulic Type "C". The Western Region, with the approval of their Area Board, propose to name these locomotives after fighting ships. This Committee supports this recommendation, but suggests that the first locomotive of the W.R. series should be named DUKE OF EDINBURGH, for the following reasons:-*

*(i) H.R.H The Duke of Edinburgh is one of the few members of the Royal Family after whom British Railways or their predecessors have not already named a locomotive.*

*(ii) Not only does the Duke himself hold high Naval rank, but there was a cruiser, HMS "Duke of Edinburgh", which was launched at Pembroke (in GWR territory) in 1904, took part in the Battle of Jutland, and was finally broken up in 1920.*

*(iii) H.R.H The Duke of Edinburgh has closely identified himself with progress in science and engineering, and for this reason the use of his name (subject to Royal permission) would symbolise the Modernisation Plan in its first locomotive, and would therefore be of great publicity value.*

*The Committee recommend that the rest of the present series of W.R. diesel-hydraulic locomotives, and subsequent units for that region... should employ suitable names of fighting ships, provided that they do not conflict with the large number of names already in use.....* (notably on the LMR Jubilees.)

They then listed 25 possible names, all of which were actually used on either the D600s or the D800s. The BTC approved the recommendations on 25 July with a few caveats, including the requirement that 'naming should not take place prior to reference to Commission headquarters where an approved list of names would be maintained'. In the case of fighting ships, it was ordered, approval of the Admiralty should be obtained. Matters were more delicate so far as HRH The Duke of Edinburgh was concerned; the use of names of members of the Royal Family required 'special consideration.'

A list produced by the WR in September 1959 of the names allocated to D803-D865 included D812 as DISPATCH and had ZEST and ZULU as spares, because D800 had been named SIR BRIAN ROBERTSON, after the Chairman of the British Transport Commission, and the NBL contract was now for 33 instead of 34 locomotives. The spelling for D812 is interesting since there were several ships named *HMS Dispatch* in the 18th century and five ships also carried the name *HMS Despatch* between 1691 and 1946. However it did not carry the allotted name and became ROYAL NAVAL RESERVE 1859-1959 instead. D864 was originally to become ZEALOUS and D865 ZENITH but, when the additional five locomotives were ordered from Swindon, D864 became ZAMBESI and D865 ZEALOUS with ZEBRA (D866) and ZEPHYR (D868) added to the original list and D869/D870 taking up the two spares.

Thus the Western Region followed the GWR tradition of a class naming theme for its new diesels and so they became Warships, with the explanation

WARSHIP CLASS below the name on all except D800 and D812. D800 received its plates on 14 July 1958 at a Paddington ceremony attended by Sir Brian himself; all the others were fitted at Swindon Works without ceremony, except for D812 which received its name at Paddington on 13 November 1959.

The aluminium alloy plates, except for D800 and D812, were 11⅛in high with a ⅜in beading and 3½ in high lettering for the individual name and 1½ in high for the class name. The letters on D800/D812 were smaller to accommodate the longer names; D800 had a single line name but D812 needed two lines. Eight fixing bolts were used on these two and six on the remainder; after Misha Black noticed the raised bolt-heads when he inspected the new D800 all of the subsequent plates had flush bolt-heads.

The plates were positioned directly below the BR crest with the top of the plate slightly above the bottom of the ventilating louvres. On D800 and D801 they were 2in lower with the top in line with lower bottom ventilator slat rather than next slat upwards as on D802 onwards.

On 29 October 1965 D823 was presented by the crew of HMS Hermes with commemorative plaques, fixed on the driver's cabside in place of the driver's name badges. The plaques were positioned above the numbers while in green livery and behind the numbers in maroon and blue, the numbers being moved forward to accommodate them.

The nameplate background was changed from red to black when locomotives were repainted into maroon and blue – the one exception was 818 in blue which reverted to red in September 1972 for an open day at Laira.

### Classification and Route Availability

BR originally designated the Warships as Type 'C', amended to Type 4 by the time D800 came into service. Under the original Diesel Classification scheme D800-D802 were D22/1, D803-D832 and D866-70 D20/1 and D833-D865 D22/2; the D was dropped in 1962.

The WR gave both classes red route availability – the same as a GWR Castle – indicating an axle loading between 17tons 12cwt and 20tons. As with the steam locomotives, a 4½in red disc was applied to the cab sides, at both ends positioned directly below the numbers on the access panels. When repainted in maroon, the discs were repositioned just below the numbers to avoid the problem which occurred when the access panels occasionally fell off. The discs continued in use as the first blue repaints emerged and they remained below the numbers as these were variously repositioned during 1966/7.

When the BR TOPS scheme was introduced in 1968 D800-D832 and D866-D870 became Class 42 and D833-D865 Class 43. The data panel mentioned earlier was applied below the number from early 1969, using a 10in x 6in self-adhesive 'Scotchcal' plastic sticker with white letters on a Rail Blue background which showed the Class, Weight (79 tons), Brake force (35 tons), Route Availability (6) and the Maximum Speed (90 mph). These were applied to three green and fifteen maroon locos, not just those repainted in blue. As ever, the three green examples were different: on D854 the panel was above the number at the left-hand end, on D845 it was below the left-hand number on the access panel in place of the red RA disc, but on D810 it was slightly higher above the access panel, again in lieu of the red disc. On the maroon locomotives they replaced the red disc at the left-hand end; D842, D858 and D861 ran in maroon without the panels until repainted in blue.

On the early blue liveried locomotives with double arrows on the cabsides the position of the TOPS panel differed as already partly described in the 'Numbers and Insignia' section. On the D833s all except one, D835 PEGASUS, had the TOPS panel below the access panel replacing the red RA disc; on D835 it was placed to the right of the double arrow with the red disc remaining in place. The BR-built locomotives all had the same placing as D835 except for D808 which had the TOPS panel to the left of the double arrow on the right-hand end of the locomotive during 1969, and D866, which had it below the access panel.

Finally, the fog cleared. On the repaints with a single centrally positioned double arrow the RA discs were dropped and the TOPS panels

**866 ZEBRA was one of the 'extra' names added to the original list when the last five locomotives were ordered. (www.rail-online.co.uk)**

This late-1960s view of a D800 shows it with refitted multiple working equipment and the corresponding white diamonds on the bufferbeam. Also clearly visible are the horns below the buffers and the headboard clips, with the angle brackets dangling down.

placed below the number. Consistency was spoilt by the 1971 Laira repaints of 826 and 871 when the TOPS panels were omitted on the former and on the latter found their way to a brand new position almost against the cab handrails. 857 UNDAUNTED was photographed in April 1970 with panels proclaiming it to be a Class 42; well, they looked pretty similar to most people!

**Worksplates and shedplates**

The Swindon-built Warships had oval brass worksplates, with a light grey background and red letters and numbers, fixed on the centre line of the side skirt immediately above the tanks. When painted maroon or blue, the background was changed to black with polished letters. The NBL locomotives had that company's traditional black diamond with polished letters and numbers throughout, positioned as the Swindon locomotives.

Steam-style cast shedplates were fitted, but their positioning differed according to builder. Most had a black background with white characters but a few had polished letters on a red background. Swindon put them on the side skirt at the left-hand end just back from the bufferbeam, but issued an instruction to NBL on 8 January 1960 to include a 'pad' for the fixing of depot identification plates: 'the actual plates will be fitted at the respective MPDs.' The pads were positioned on the left-hand side of the bufferbeam to the right of the multiple working fitting. In spite of this most of the D833s managed to acquire plates on the side skirts at various times when the depots ignored the pads. Over time the plates often disappeared and were not always replaced, but the pads on the NBL locomotives remained even after the plates had gone.

From late-1967 the cast plates were replaced by stencilled shedcodes applied to the right of the driver's cab door in line with the numbers on maroon and blue liveried locomotives. On those still in green, the stencil was positioned between the ends of the lining band and the cab doors. Inevitably there were more variations with some locomotives having the code on alternate ends and others at both ends. The codes disappeared on repaints from around 1970.

**Train reporting numbers, headboards and route indicators**

D800-D812 originally had GWR-style frames built into the nose doors to carry the train reporting numbers. Although this was an improvement on the D600s they still had the reversible white train classification discs: the three lower ones below the level of the lamp brackets and the upper central one protruding at the top of the nose above the lamp bracket.

Several of the WR trains which the Warships started operating in 1958/59 had names and all the D800s/D833s were delivered with clips either side of the upper lamp bracket on each nose end to hold the steam-style headboards with brown letters on cream backgrounds. Unlike the D600s the angled brackets attached to the clips were not normally left on.

From D813 onwards, the nose doors had four digit route indicator panels and the earlier locomotives were gradually brought into line at Intermediate overhauls beginning with D810 and D804 in September 1963; D803 and D807 were the last to be dealt with, in February 1965. During the fitting of the panels both A and B nose ends had the central marker light removed. The centre lamp bracket and headboard clips were removed and not replaced on D800, D802, D803, D805, D807, D808, D810 and D811, but these were retained on D801 and D804. Just to keep things simple, D806, D809 and D812 lost the headboard clips but kept the lamp brackets.

Finally, a hybrid. When D846 STEADFAST suffered severe collision damage at one end in October 1966, the rebuilt cab at that end had neither lamp bracket or headboard clips, but these remained on the undamaged end.

**Multiple working fittings**

D800-D802 had only six power notches and therefore could only be coupled in multiple between themselves, whereas D803-D870 with seven notch control gear could also be coupled with NBL Type 2s D6306-D6357. The three early locomotives had an exposed arrangement of fittings with the jumper cables on the left-hand side of the bufferbeam to the right of the buffer stock and the sockets below to the left of the right-hand buffer. These were the same pattern as the German V200 type, locked into place by pushing the cover over the jumper plug, thus securing it.

At the end of 1961 D803-D870 were given the coding of two white diamonds under the new BR system but, with the exception of D834 and D862 in 1962, these do not appear to have been painted on the bufferbeam until early 1968. They had a much neater arrangement of cables and sockets with the cable plug held when not in use in a receptacle to the outside of the left-hand buffer; the cable was clearly visible as it looped below the buffer and the socket was under a cover inboard of the right hand buffer. The control system, which was supplied by Brown Boveri, used 30 of the 36 pairs of contacts in the jumper connections to allow multiple control of two locomotives with four engine/transmissions units.

The fittings fell into disuse by the mid-1960s and were eventually removed because they were prone to electrical faults through dampness; rectangular blanking plates were fitted on the bufferbeams over the hole left behind (Modification 414/72). The maintenance files recorded the dates of removal for some of the class and, with the exception of D837 in October 1964, were mainly done in 1966 with a couple in

**D823 HERMES carried a plaque presented by the crew of HMS Hermes on 29 October 1965. The driver's name badge holder was removed to allow the plaque to be fitted. The 10in x 6in TOPS data panel below the number was applied in 1969. The numbers were below the plaque when it was in green livery and in front of them when maroon and blue.**

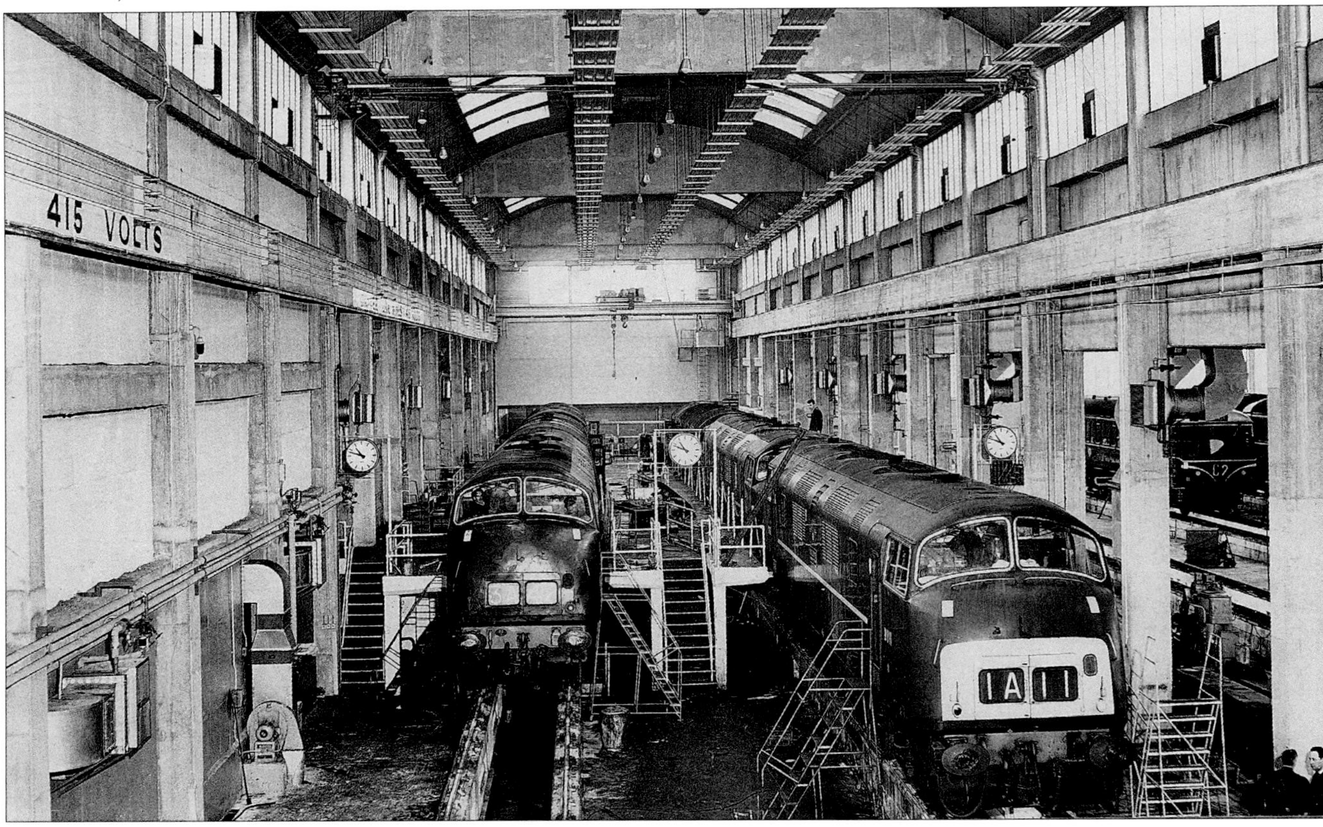


**D816 ECLIPSE alongside an NBL D833 at Laira on 22 March 1962. A useful exercise perhaps in 'engine picking' – how many detail differences can you spot? The most entertaining and illuminating account (to reach the publisher by March 2010) might well warrant a modest prize...**

1967. Although the fittings were removed on the whole class three of the D833s regained them: D857 in April 1967, D862 by August 1969 but taken off again by September 1970, and D864 by June 1967. These are not recorded in the files and there is no obvious explanation for the work.

As often happened, the equipment was soon needed again and this was the case when pairs of D800s were required for the accelerated West of England services in May 1968. The equipment was restored to twenty-two locomotives: D803, D804, D807, D808, D814, D816, D819, D822-D829, D831, D832 and D866-D870, and it would appear that the work was done at the depots rather than in Swindon Works, except for D816 which was modified during a works visit in January/February 1969. Two white diamonds were painted on the bufferbeam, one either side of the coupling. By May 1971 the fittings on one end of both D866 and D870 had been taken off again; all others retained them until withdrawn.

### Dual AWS

The class was built with WR Automatic Train Control (ATC) though the Warship Maintenance files refer to it as AWS (Automatic Warning System). D818 was the first to be dual fitted with BR AWS during a works visit ending on 8 June 1967, although D819 was the first released to traffic, in late May, because of fitting problems with D818. The equipment was mounted on the transverse bulkhead at the back of the driving cabs, with a conduit running down through the floor just behind the cab doors. The dual fitting was confined to the batch D803-D821 which were also fitted with short circuit bars for operating over Southern Region electrified lines between Basingstoke and Waterloo. The last to be modified was D812 in April 1968.

### On the nose

The nose ends of the D800s, with the front skirting and without the connecting doors, were a significant improvement over the D600s, and when the route indicator boxes were introduced this allowed the appearance to be tidied up further.

D800-D802 originally had short curved handrails, which had the appearance of two large staples, below the front windows; these were replaced by the longer type used on D803-D870 when route indicator panels were fitted. For some reason, D859 VANQUISHER uniquely always had longer vertical grab rails on the nose. Some writers have said that the early locomotives did not have the front footstep attached to the skirting on each side, but there is no photographic evidence for this.

Marker lights were positioned over each buffer with a lamp bracket above and a third bracket centrally about half-way up the nose. D800-D812 had an additional central red light below the upper lamp bracket until they were fitted with route indicator panels. Swindon placed the brackets directly above the lights but on the D833s they were offset outwards. The NBL lights also differed slightly – they were more prominent. D819 GOLIATH had the NBL configuration at the 'A' end following collision damage in 1964 when it also lost its headboard clips at that end.

Both Swindon and NBL locomotives had a small oval shaped grill located just outside top right of the reporting numbers. This was an air intake (not the horn as often stated) that went back to the V200 design.

The demisters were heated from the engine cooling water via pipework off the transmission from new but were still ineffective, hence the change to electric demisters in 1965/66. The modification can be identified because the grill mesh was replaced with a blanking plate.

803 ALBION suffered severe damage following a derailment at Uffington in March 1971 and when it emerged from Swindon on 3 June it had been repaired – apparently by fitting the nose end from withdrawn D830 – resulting in the re-appearance at the B end of the headboard clips removed in 1965. Another hybrid to match D846 mentioned earlier.

In early 1968 an attempt was made by Old Oak Common to try and improve the cab ventilation on the D833s allocated there by cutting two circular ventilation holes below the Route Indicator panels. The locomotives modified were D833-D835, D839-D848, D850 and D852-D855; inevitably there were minor differences in positioning with those on D848 and at least one end of D841 under the centre of each pair of

indicators, whereas on the remainder they were below the outer corners although in slightly varying positions. The centred holes were covered by mesh grills on D841 until late 1969; while in store it donated a set of headcode box doors to 803 which were used when it received its replacement B end nose in June 1971 so the latter, uniquely among the D800s, had the small outer holes in the doors. When D841 was reinstated in 1970 it had new, more centrally cut, holes in the one end. The other variant was D839 which had rectangular ventilation holes in the headcode panels.

**Up on the roof**

The exhaust ports on the Swindon locomotives, with the exception of D830, were on the roof centre line whereas those on the NBL ones were diagonally opposed; D830 had oval offset exhaust ports due to its Paxman engines.

A characteristic of both classes was the five pairs of ventilator flaps on the centre line which can often be seen raised in the open position in photographs. These flaps were individually hand worked and locked into position. They were pushed up/ pulled down using a ring welded to the lid. They were held up on a short arm mechanism which often seized in the open position so the ones over the engine rooms were probably left often because they were forced and then inevitably the mechanism snapped leaving a 'floppy' flap!

Those locomotives with Stone-Vapor steam generators, D813-D865, had boiler room air intake and ventilating louvres cut horizontally into the curve of the roof above the cantrail on one side only, centrally above the nameplate.

D800-D802 had two circular radiator fan housings with mesh grill covering almost flush with the cab roof, whilst rectangular walkways were added across the housings on the production series, D803-D831. However, photographic evidence suggests that D832 was built with raised NBL-style fan housings.

D833 had the Swindon pattern from new but on D834-D865 the housings had rims raised to the same height as the walkway and with the circular mesh grill across both the housing and the walkway. D861 would appear to have started life with one Swindon and one NBL fan housing but emerged from a works visit in December 1963 with two Swindon ones which it retained until withdrawn. D834 retained one NBL housing, but received a Swindon one at the other end, almost certainly during a works visit in late-1963, and ran in this hybrid condition until withdrawn.

Just to complete the confusion, it appears that D866 and D867 were both built with the NBL raised type, but D868-D870 had the flat Swindon style, albeit with the fan housing stiffened with a low rim. These cooler groups were interchangeable between locomotives and therefore it is possible that other changes went unrecorded.

**More minutiae**

D800-D812 exhibited a few minor differences to the later locomotives: the bodyside grills had a single vertical dividing bar on the early locomotives and two bars on D813-D870. Also, two pairs of hinged doors below cab floor level allowed better access than the screwed traps on D800-D812. The fuel filler access was covered on D800-D812 but on the subsequent locomotives there was a single central cut-out on one side, and one large and one small offset to the left on the other side.

D800and D801 did not have preheaters and originally used the train heating boiler to preheat the engines as on the DB V200s; preheaters were fitted around 1965/66. It appears that D802 had them from new as did all subsequent locomotives.

D800-D802 had rubber kicking pads below the cab doors which wore easily and were quickly superseded by aluminium plates with vertical ribs; these were retro-fitted to the first three locomotives after 1960. Their door hand rails were also different, curved at the top and bottom, whereas all the others were straight.

In addition to the variations between the Swindon and NBL locomotives already discussed, there were inevitably a host of less noticeable differences. For instance, while in green livery the D833s had the grey lining band and numbers 2in to 3in lower than the D800s – Swindon used the lowest point of the nose end corner handrails for the bottom of the stripe whereas NBL used the top point for theirs. After a Swindon repaint the grey band on the D833s was moved up as for the Swindon-built locomotives. The D800s had the 'A' and 'B' end designations stencilled below the handle on the cab door whereas the D833s had these below the cab footsteps. The holders for the driver's name card, which were rarely if ever used, were flush with the bottom of the window on the Swindon-built locomotives but slightly lower on the NBLs, except for D833-D835.

The overhead line warning flashes on the nose ends were positioned slightly differently: they were straight vertically on the D800s compared with slightly sloping on the NBLs roughly in a line between the top of the vertical handrail and the outer edge of the horizontal handrails. Over time, not surprisingly, these sometimes changed both position and orientation, e.g. D827 KELLY had no flashes on the bodyside from July 1967 but in 1968 both it and D856 TROJAN had them placed in front of the door rather than behind. The plates were fixed to the locomotives with self tapping screws and if the holes rusted and there was no bodywork to hold the screw, they were just moved to a new position where there was solid metal to drill.

**D826 JUPITER in Swindon Works on 17 August 1964 showing the effects of collision damage. The fuel tank filler access was covered on D800-D812 but open on D813 onwards. The oval brass worksplates, with a light grey background and red letters and numbers, are clearly visible.**

A hydraulic gathering at Swindon in the late-1970s with the Diesel Traction Group's D821 and Hymek D7029 joined by 818 which had somehow survived since withdrawal in November 1972. (www.rail-online.co.uk)

D821 GREYHOUND at Swindon Works alongside a withdrawn Western about 1979. The Works provided a safe haven where restoration could be carried out and D821 remained there until 1981 when it moved to the North Yorkshire Moors Railway. (www.rail-online.co.uk)

# Chapter 6
# POSTSCRIPT - PRESERVATION

Two of the D800s escaped the cutter's torch and have been preserved, although neither is certified for main line operation. None of the NBL-built locomotives survived although D600 and D601 did linger for some time at Woodham's scrapyard at Barry. All except the D600s and the pioneer D800 were cut up at Swindon.

Didcot Railway Centre was not keen to have diesel locomotives on its site and as a result D821 had to move. On 9 February 1974 it was hauled to Reading Gas Works where it was returned to maroon livery. This was not the best location for restoration because it was outside with no power supply, water came from the nearby River Thames and use until it was purchased by a group in April 1979 and moved to Derby for safe storage in June 1979. It appeared at the Open day at Derby three months later before moving to Horwich in June 1980 for another Open Day. It finally reached the East Lancashire Railway in February 1981 where it has been based ever since, and was restored to working

## The DIESEL TRACTION GROUP

The Diesel Traction Group was formed in 1977 from a group of six enthusiasts led by Chris Reid and Colin Massingham. Colin came up with the idea of preserving a diesel locomotive in 1971 which eventually led to the purchase of Warship D821 GREYHOUND in 1973, after losing their original choice of NBL type 2 D6319..

By 1975 Colin and Co. had been joined by enthusiasts Paul Koch, Chris Broadhurst and Chris Hatton who maintained D821 and helped save Hymek D7029 from Old Oak Common. Paul Koch and Chris Hatton were Swindon apprentices and gained much experience with the diesel-hydraulics enabling them to restore and operate the Warship and Hymek.

When the Brush prototype FALCON was withdrawn by BR during the autumn of 1975, the group attempted to save it but despite offering a reasonable sum, the DTG's plan was unsuccessful because of an unusual clause in the contract that was drawn up when FALCON was purchased from Brush by BR in 1971. Brush believed that no-one else should profit from their prototype so, as a condition of the sale, they insisted that when BR had no further use for the locomotive it was to be cut up, and could not be sold into preservation.

With the loss of FALCON the group turned its sights to purchasing a Western and looked at several candidates, including D1001, D1005, D1009, D1022, and D1071. Eventually, in a last-ditch operation it secured D1015 WESTERN CHAMPION in January 1980 after almost losing it to the cutting torch in late-1979. Paul Koch was the driving force behind the many years of restoration work that amounted to complete rebuilding, and which allowed D1015 to return to the main line in January 2002; the locomotive is now in regular use on charter trains and excursions.

The fledgling group also helped secure the Class 28 Co-Bo locomotive. This was bought by Colin Massingham with the obvious intention of restoring D5705 to running order. As ever, time and money were never in the group's favour and the loco was passed on to another group for eventual restoration.

Membership of the DTG is by purchasing shares, when they become available, in a locomotive. This means there is a very low turnover of members, which has led to it often being referred to as the 'Masons of Preservation'. However with the advent of main line running the group is taking on new blood to ensure that the preservation of its locomotives is secured for the future.

The group regularly offer assistance and advice to other locomotive owning groups and have helped maintain class 27 No 5410 at the Severn Valley Railway on behalf of Dudley Council. They have even been called in to repair Maybach engine fitted boats on behalf of the Chilean Navy!

Today the DTG has around two dozen active team members and seventy-five shareholders. The DTG owes its success to its team of highly skilled mechanical and electrical engineers who constantly strive to improve the performance of the group's locomotives. Many of the remaining members of the team come from a professional railway background, from both fitting and operational services.

**D821 GREYHOUND**

In late 1972 two enthusiasts, Chris Reid and Colin Massingham, attempted to buy NBL Type 2 D6319, which had recently been through Swindon where it had been completely rewired. Unfortunately, through an internal mix-up between Swindon and Derby, it was cut-up while their offer was being processed. They kicked up a fuss and were offered a Warship instead, and were given a choice from a handful of survivors awaiting disposal at Laira. They chose D821, which had been in store since its withdrawal in December 1972, because it was in the best condition.

Staff at Laira ran the locomotive's engines to ensure all was in order and on 23 May 1973 GREYHOUND was delivered, running light under its own power, to the Railway Centre at Didcot. This was the first main line diesel locomotive to be preserved by a private group and the second privately owned diesel locomotive to operate under its own power on the main line.

the locomotive was subject to attention from local youths on numerous occasions. Eventually in February 1977, with the hydraulic era on British Railways drawing to a close, it was moved along with Hymek D7029, which had also been purchased by the Diesel Traction Group, to Swindon Works for secure accommodation where restoration to a higher standard could begin. They were subsequently moved to the North Yorkshire Moors Railway on 16 April 1981 which hosted D821 for ten years. In the 1990s GREYHOUND did the round of Open Days before eventually ending up at the Severn Valley Railway in late-1994, where it is still based today.

**D832 ONSLAUGHT**

After withdrawal at Laira in December 1972 D832 was moved to Derby Railway Technical Centre in January 1973. It was transferred to the Old Dalby test track for use as a dead load in October 1974 and then moved to Eggington Junction in September 1976 where it lay out of order. Today, it regularly visits other preserved lines for diesel gala appearances.

**D818 - the one which almost escaped**

D818 GLORY, which was one of the last to be withdrawn, in November 1972, was retained at Swindon Works until October 1985 when it was cut up following the announcement that the Works was to be closed in 1986. It had been kept as a source of spares for D832 at Derby (D821 also benefited) and although cosmetically restored, it had gradually become little more than a shell.

*Above.* After withdrawal 832 ONSLAUGHT was moved to Derby Railway Technical Centre in January 1973 where it is pictured on 9 October. It was transferred in 1974 to the Old Dalby test track for use as a 'dead load.'

*Top right.* D832 ONSLAUGHT was moved from Old Dalby to Eggington Junction in September 1976 where it lay out of use until purchased by a preservation group in April 1979. Over the next few years it was restored to working order on the East Lancashire Railway where it was photographed at Bury along with the DTG's D1015 WESTERN CHAMPION on 7 July 2006. (Author)

*Right.* D818 GLORY flattering to deceive on 17 February 1981 at Swindon Works. It had been kept as a source of spares for D832 and, although cosmetically restored, it gradually became little more than a shell and was finally cut up in October 1985. (www.rail-online.co.uk)

D832
1B 55

D818
5K 55

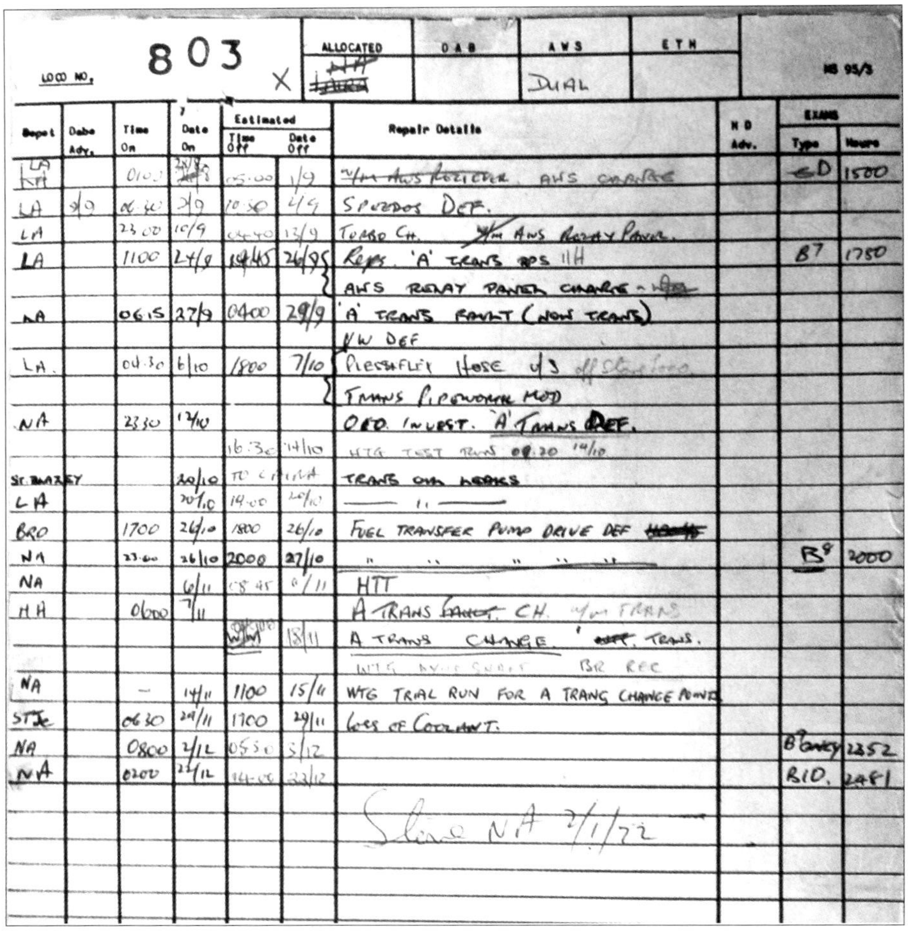

LOCO No. 803

ALLOCATED | OAB | AWS: DUAL | ETH | HS 95/3

| Depot | Date Adv. | Time On | Date On | Estimated Time Off | Estimated Date Off | Repair Details | ND Adv. | Exams Type | Exams Hours |
|---|---|---|---|---|---|---|---|---|---|
| LA | | 0100 | 28/8 | 05.00 | 1/9 | AWS CHANGE | | ED | 1500 |
| LA | 1/9 | 06.40 | 1/9 | 10.50 | 2/9 | SPEEDOS DEF. | | | |
| LA | | 23.00 | 10/9 | 04.40 | 13/9 | TURBO CH. AWS RELAY PANEL | | | |
| LA | | 1100 | 24/9 | 19.45 | 26/9 | REPS. 'A' TRANS | | B7 | 1750 |
| | | | | | | AWS RELAY PANEL CHANGE | | | |
| NA | | 06.15 | 27/9 | 0400 | 29/9 | 'A' TRANS FAULT (NON TRANS) | | | |
| | | | | | | NW DEF | | | |
| LA | | 04.30 | 6/10 | 1800 | 7/10 | FLEXIBLE HOSE | | | |
| | | | | | | TRANS PIPEWORK MOD | | | |
| NA | | 23.30 | 12/10 | | | OCO. INVEST. 'A' TRANS DEF. | | | |
| | | | | 16.30 | 14/10 | WTG TEST RUN 09.20 14/10 | | | |
| ST. BLAZEY | | | 20/10 | TO LAIRA | | TRANS ON REPAIRS | | | |
| LA | | | 20/10 | 14.00 | 20/10 | — " — | | | |
| BRO | | 1700 | 26/10 | 1800 | 26/10 | FUEL TRANSFER PUMP DRIVE DEF | | | |
| NA | | 23.00 | 26/10 | 2000 | 27/10 | " " " " " | | B8 | 2000 |
| NA | | | 6/11 | 08.45 | 6/11 | HTT | | | |
| NA | | 0600 | 7/11 | | | A TRANS CH. | | | |
| | | | | | 18/11 | A TRANS CHANGE TRANS. | | | |
| | | | | | | BR REC | | | |
| NA | | — | 14/11 | 1100 | 15/11 | WTG TRIAL RUN FOR A TRANS CHANGE | | | |
| STJ | | 0630 | 29/11 | 1700 | 29/11 | LOSS OF COOLANT. | | | |
| NA | | 0800 | 2/12 | 05.50 | 3/12 | | | B | 2352 |
| NA | | 0200 | 22/12 | 14.00 | 23/12 | | | R10. | 2481 |

Stored NA 2/1/72

**The Repair card for 803 for its last few months in service from 28 August 1971 until stored on 2 January 1972.**

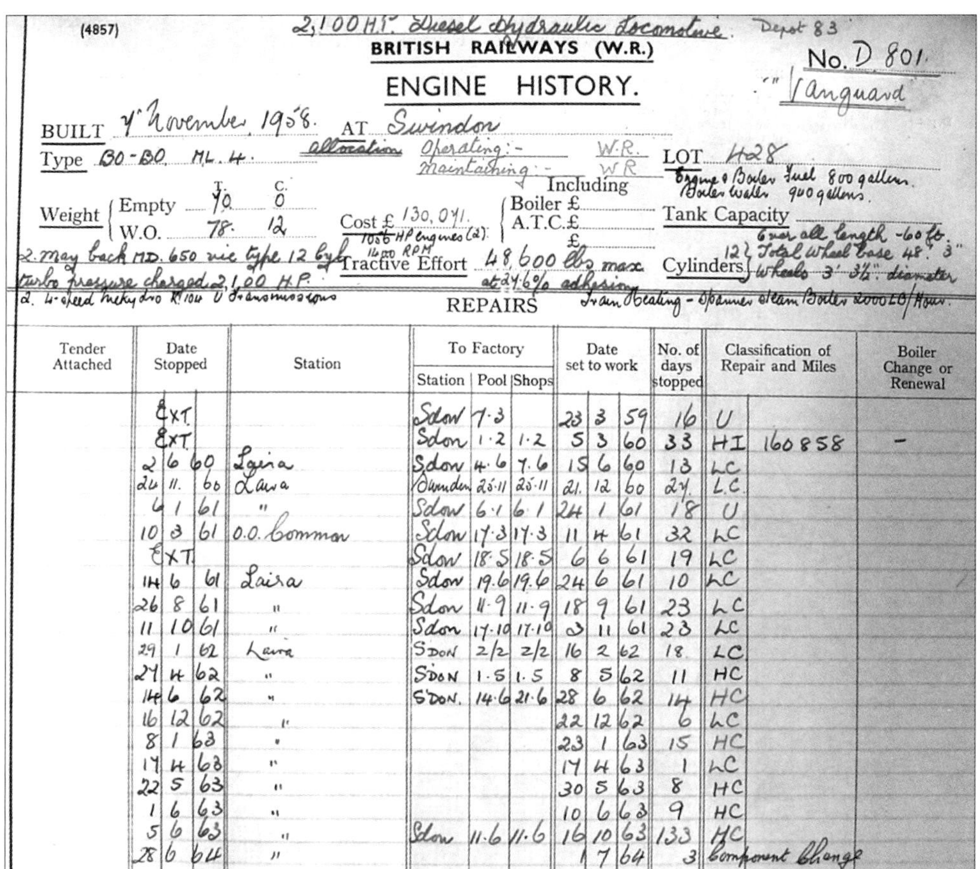

(4857) 2,100 H.P. Diesel Hydraulic Locomotive. Depot 83

BRITISH RAILWAYS (W.R.)

No. D 801

ENGINE HISTORY.

"Vanguard"

BUILT 4th November 1958. AT Swindon

Type BO-BO. ML. 4. Allocation Operating: W.R. Maintaining: W.R. LOT 428

Weight: Empty 70 T. 0 C.; W.O. 78 T. 12 C.

Cost £130,041. 1056 HP engines (2) 1600 RPM

Including Boiler £ A.T.C. £ £

Engine & Boiler fuel 800 gallons. Boiler water 900 gallons. Tank Capacity

2. Maybach MD. 650 vee type 12 cyl turbo pressure charged 2,100 HP.

Tractive Effort 48,600 lbs max. at 24.6% adhesion

Cylinders 12; Over all length 60 ft. Total wheel base 48' 3" Wheels 3' 3½" diameter

2. 4-speed Mekydro K104 U transmissions. Train Heating – Spanner steam boiler 2000 LB/Hour.

REPAIRS

| Tender Attached | Date Stopped | Station | To Factory Station | Pool | Shops | Date set to work | No. of days stopped | Classification of Repair and Miles | | Boiler Change or Renewal |
|---|---|---|---|---|---|---|---|---|---|---|
| | EXT | | Sdon | 7.3 | | 23 3 59 | 16 | U | | |
| | EXT | | Sdon | 1.2 | 1.2 | 5 3 60 | 33 | HI | 160858 | – |
| | 2 6 60 | Laira | Sdon | 4.6 | 7.6 | 15 6 60 | 13 | LC | | |
| | 24 11 60 | Laira | Swindon | 25.11 | 25.11 | 21 12 60 | 24 | LC | | |
| | 4 1 61 | " | Sdon | 6.1 | 6.1 | 24 1 61 | 18 | U | | |
| | 10 3 61 | O.O. Common | Sdon | 17.3 | 17.3 | 11 4 61 | 32 | LC | | |
| | EXT | | Sdon | 18.5 | 18.5 | 6 6 61 | 19 | LC | | |
| | 14 6 61 | Laira | Sdon | 19.6 | 19.6 | 24 6 61 | 10 | LC | | |
| | 26 8 61 | " | Sdon | 11.9 | 11.9 | 18 9 61 | 23 | LC | | |
| | 11 10 61 | " | Sdon | 17.10 | 17.10 | 3 11 61 | 23 | LC | | |
| | 29 1 62 | Laira | SDON | 2/2 | 2/2 | 16 2 62 | 18 | LC | | |
| | 27 4 62 | " | SDON | 1.5 | 1.5 | 8 5 62 | 11 | HC | | |
| | 14 6 62 | " | SDON. | 14.6 | 21.6 | 28 6 62 | 14 | HC | | |
| | 16 12 62 | " | | | | 22 12 62 | 6 | LC | | |
| | 8 1 63 | " | | | | 23 1 63 | 15 | HC | | |
| | 17 4 63 | " | | | | 17 4 63 | 1 | LC | | |
| | 22 5 63 | " | | | | 30 5 63 | 8 | HC | | |
| | 1 6 63 | " | | | | 10 6 63 | 9 | HC | | |
| | 5 6 63 | " | Sdon | 11.6 | 11.6 | 16 10 63 | 133 | HC | | |
| | 28 6 64 | " | | | | 1 7 64 | 3 | Component Change | | |

**D600 ACTIVE was stopped many times in its early years with periods of around 100 days in each of 1959, 1960 and 1962.**

# Chapter 7
# ON THE RECORD

GWR-style Engine History sheets were set-up for all the diesel-hydraulics but were only maintained until around mid-1964. They contain no detail of the work carried out at each date, only the type of overhaul. All the other information in the individual locomotive histories in this section has been prepared by Mark Alden from the 'Component Change and/or Exchange Advice' records, cross checked against other surviving material such as the Job Cards used from mid-1971.

Unfortunately, for some locomotives the information available is less complete than for others, particularly between 1965 and 1970. (This applies especially to D601 and D819, D830, D838, D839, D853, D869 and D870). In presenting this information the policy has been to include a summary of the work carried out during the period stopped, even where there is only minimal information such as a turboblower change, because this still provides useful information about the individual locomotive. In the case of modifications, such as the removal and later re-instatement of Multiple Working equipment, only those recorded at specific works or depot visits are listed.

**Abbreviations used**

Inevitably abbreviations have had to be used to try to cram as much information as possible into the smallest space; throughout '?' signifies not recorded. Depot allocations are shown without brackets; brackets indicate location, eg where stored.

| Depots/works | |
|---|---|
| Ex-T | Ex-traffic |
| BS | Bristol Bath Road |
| LA | Laira |
| NA | Newton Abbot |
| OOC | Old Oak Common |
| SB | St.Blazey |
| SHR | Shrewsbury |
| SO | Southall |
| SW | Swindon |
| TYS | Tyseley |
| WES | Westbury |
| WOR | Worcester |

| | |
|---|---|
| Class | Classified |
| Int | Intermediate |
| L/C | Light casual |
| H/C | Heavy casual |
| H/I | Heavy intermediate |
| H/G | Heavy general |
| Uncl | Unclassified |
| Unsch | Unscheduled |
| D/A | Delivery or acceptance |

The Overhaul Schedule in Chapter 4 set out the full extent of the work which was carried out at each type of overhaul. To minimise the information in each table, 'normal' repairs and component changes due to mileage/hours run are included with the notation 'changed' (where it is known that a different component was re-fitted) or 'removed' (where it is not recorded whether the same or a different item was replaced). Explanations in brackets are given for out of course failures and problems where available.

There is insufficient space to detail the individual application of the Modifications listed in Appendix 4; where the 'Work carried out' includes reference to these they were generally applied at a major overhaul and would normally include all those required up to the date of the works visit which had not previously been applied.

**Availability and mileages**

Although the Engine History sheets do not give detail of the work carried out they do provide a reasonably but not totally complete overview of the first few years up to mid-1964 for each locomotive. In particular, they show how much stoppage time occurred with the first few locomotives from each works visit, with the first D833s being particularly poor. The two locomotives with the worst records were D801 VANGUARD which was stopped for over 450 days during 1960-3 and D834 PATHFINDER which was out of traffic for one year over the four years 1961-4. The tables below show that 1961-2 were disastrous years for availability with many locomotives 'stopped' for over 100 days, especially those from NBL which was partly as a result of that company's demise.

The mileages achieved over the lifetime of the class reflect the short lives

**Days 'stopped' for Swindon-built Warships 1958-64**

| | Into service | 1958 | 1959 | 1960 | 1961 | 1962 | 1963 | 1964 |
|---|---|---|---|---|---|---|---|---|
| D800 | 11/8/58 | 10 | 33 | 93 | 93 | 18 | 87 | 69 |
| D801 | 7/11/58 | - | 28 | 103 | 135 | 52 | 166 | 21 |
| D802 | 16/12/58 | - | 16 | 85 | 49 | 107 | 29 | 65 |
| D803 | 16/3/59 | - | 13 | 56 | 28 | 33 | 11 | 87 |
| D804 | 23/4/59 | - | 45 | 9 | 128 | 74 | 61 | 3 |
| D805 | 13/5/59 | - | 10 | 62 | 54 | 17 | 37 | 59 |
| D806 | 3/6/59 | - | 11 | 70 | 60 | 23 | 58 | 83 |
| D807 | 24/6/59 | - | 29 | 50 | 72 | 37 | 65 | 79 |
| D808 | 8/7/59 | - | 15 | 31 | 81 | 20 | 74 | 3 |
| D809 | 19/8/59 | - | 13 | 59 | 57 | 7 | 41 | 46 |
| D810 | 16/9/59 | - | 0 | 24 | 38 | 59 | 61 | 0 |
| D811 | 14/10/59 | - | 11 | 47 | 57 | 45 | 55 | 85 |
| D812 | 12/11/59 | - | 0 | 53 | 32 | 45 | 56 | 55 |
| D813 | 9/12/59 | - | 0 | 0 | 78 | 39 | 114 | 1 |
| D814 | 1/1/60 | - | - | 37 | 84 | 17 | 59 | n/a |
| D815 | 20/1/60 | - | - | 22 | 94 | 37 | 25 | 54 |
| D816 | 17/2/60 | - | - | 29 | 50 | 37 | 30 | 70 |
| D817 | 9/3/60 | - | - | 20 | 110 | 9 | 21 | 39 |
| D818 | 30/3/60 | - | - | 15 | 112 | 39 | 27 | 29 |
| D819 | 25/4/60 | - | - | 0 | 56 | 30 | 27 | 52 |
| D820 | 4/5/60 | - | - | 5 | 96 | 34 | 17 | 38 |
| D821 | 25/5/60 | - | - | 25 | 67 | 18 | 20 | 39 |
| D822 | 15/6/60 | - | - | 25 | 68 | 101 | 50 | 42 |
| D823 | 6/7/60 | - | - | 0 | 51 | 23 | 38 | 26 |
| D824 | 27/7/60 | - | - | 0 | 56 | 29 | 39 | 72 |
| D825 | 24/8/60 | - | - | 0 | 161 | 23 | 110 | 2 |
| D826 | 7/9/60 | - | - | 0 | 36 | 38 | 27 | 72 |
| D827 | 4/10/60 | - | - | 0 | 47 | 41 | 16 | 96 |
| D828 | 19/10/60 | - | - | 0 | 44 | 77 | 38 | 63 |
| D829 | 23/11/60 | - | - | 0 | 68 | 15 | 60 | 24 |
| D830 | 19/1/61 | - | - | - | 30 | 37 | 70 | 135 |
| D831 | 11/1/61 | - | - | - | 67 | 15 | 45 | 58 |
| D832 | 8/2/61 | - | - | - | 25 | 19 | 55 | 16 |
| D866 | 24/3/61 | - | - | - | 27 | 19 | 81 | 14 |
| D867 | 26/4/61 | - | - | - | 27 | 41 | 43 | 1 |
| D868 | 18/5/61 | - | - | - | 3 | 58 | 28 | 3 |
| D869 | 12/7/61 | - | - | - | - | 37 | 30 | 25 |
| D870 | 25/10/61 | - | - | - | - | 2 | 43 | 1 |

## Days 'stopped' for NBL-built Warships 1960-64

| | Into service | 1960 | 1961 | 1962 | 1963 | 1964 |
|---|---|---|---|---|---|---|
| D833 | 6/7/60 | 27 | 100 | 47 | 71 | 33 |
| D834 | 26/7/60 | 1 | 47 | 123 | 118 | 76 |
| D835 | 5/8/60 | - | 35 | 87 | 51 | 38 |
| D836 | 13/9/60 | - | 125 | 53 | 18 | 56 |
| D837 | 8/11/60 | - | 31 | 36 | 56 | 163 |
| D838 | 3/10/60 | - | 39 | 135 | 57 | 29 |
| D839 | 12/11/60 | - | 31 | 64 | 4 | 53 |
| D840 | 3/2/61 | - | 57 | 81 | 130 | n/a |
| D841 | 14/12/60 | - | 51 | 63 | 37 | 32 |
| D842 | 20/12/60 | - | 22 | 36 | 38 | 57 |
| D843 | 2/1/61 | - | 56 | 36 | 35 | 140 |
| D844 | 16/3/61 | - | 42 | 74 | 63 | n/a |
| D845 | 7/4/61 | - | 29 | 158 | 58 | n/a |
| D846 | 12/4/61 | - | 0 | 57 | 7 | 108 |
| D847 | 22/4/61 | - | 31 | 69 | 107 | 63 |
| D848 | 27/4/61 | - | 23 | 106 | 75 | 21 |
| D849 | 29/5/61 | - | 0 | 44 | 55 | 139 |
| D850 | 8/6/61 | - | 0 | 40 | 103 | 161 |
| D851 | 10/7/61 | - | 32 | 82 | 23 | 69 |
| D852 | 24/7/61 | - | 14 | 15 | 46 | 8 |
| D853 | 30/8/61 | - | 21 | 24 | 29 | 1 |
| D854 | 26/9/61 | - | 0 | 88 | 22 | 39 |
| D855 | 16/10/61 | - | 7 | 46 | 13 | 33 |
| D856 | 16/11/61 | - | 1 | 22 | 53 | n/a |
| D857 | 11/12/61 | - | 0 | 12 | 56 | 8 |
| D858 | 15/12/61 | - | 0 | 28 | 79 | 24 |
| D859 | 9/1/62 | - | - | 26 | 11 | 19 |
| D860 | 22/1/62 | - | - | 43 | 72 | 3 |
| D861 | 14/2/62 | - | - | 0 | 189 | 29 |
| D862 | 13/3/62 | - | - | 25 | 34 | 17 |
| D863 | 7/4/62 | - | - | 0 | 17 | 6 |
| D864 | 10/5/62 | - | - | 9 | 4 | 5 |
| D865 | 28/6/62 | - | - | 23 | 14 | 45 |

of many of the locomotives with the D800s, except for the Paxman engined-D830, were the highest ranging from 922,000 to 1,317,000 with the D833s trailing well behind at 537,000 to 801,000.

In January 1959 Davey Paxman & Co. Ltd. of Colchester announced their new 'YJ' or 'Ventura' range of quick-running engines, which were intended to compete with European manufacturers such as Maybach, Daimler and M.A.N. The 'Ventura' was designed for outputs of up to 1,500hp from 12 cylinders, and the 12YJXL variant was roughly the same weight and outline as the Maybach MD650 engine.

Finally there was a British engine which was a suitable alternative for the German designs used in the diesel-hydraulics. BR arranged with Paxman to fit two of these new engines, coupled to standard Mekydro K104U transmissions, into one of the Swindon-built Warships which were still under construction. D830 was put into traffic on 19 January 1961, and allocated to Newton Abbot where it remained throughout its career.

Alan Wild picks up the story and sheds more light on MAJESTIC's brief career: 'This one loco was fitted with Paxman engines. In order to be interchangeable with both the M.A.N. and Maybach engines the chosen 'Ventura' model had to be shortened to fit the locomotive. This involved reducing the bearing journal lengths slightly, amongst other changes. As a result many of the components were non-standard in the Paxman range, and hence more expensive. For a number of years the locomotive was always accompanied by a Paxman service engineer when in traffic, one of whom was David Coverdale. The locomotive earned a reputation for its reliability as, with three people on board at any time, any incipient faults could be identified before they became problematic. After a few years the firm's representative was withdrawn and the loco left to normal WR supervision.

With two engines installed there was one complete spare engine plus a spare crankshaft and range of smaller components held in reserve. Because of the non-standard design of crankshaft (and the more arduous nature of the work demanded compared with normal 'Ventura' operation) the risk of crankshaft failure always loomed and one failed in service (at Truro in February 1964). The spare engine was fitted at Swindon, the failed engine overhauled and fitted with the spare crankshaft. A year or so later the other original engine suffered a crankshaft failure so the repaired engine was exchanged for it. There was now no spare crankshaft available at Swindon. In October 1968 another crankshaft broke and it fell to me to enquire of Paxman whether a replacement could be supplied. I can still remember David Coverdale's anguished tone: "Oh No! Has MAJESTIC failed again?" when I telephoned! The price to produce a new crankshaft was quoted as over £4,000. On relaying this news to the CM&EE the answer came back almost straight away - D830 would be withdrawn. At that time a new Maybach crankshaft (supplied by Bristol-Siddeley Engines Ltd.) was priced at £1,600. It would have been feasible to re-engine D830 but as the fleet was beginning to be run-down the cost of conversion would have been unjustifiable'.

So the experiment ended abruptly and D830 was officially withdrawn on 26 March 1969. It remained for several months at Newton Abbot before it was moved to Laira by June 1969, and then on to Exeter in October. After component removal it was towed to Swindon in July 1970 and had been cut up by October 1971. It had run only 447,000 miles which was less than half the class average, but still a creditable performance for a 'one-off' with all the issues associated with this.

The 'Ventura' was also fitted as a replacement for the M.A.N. engines in twenty of the NBL diesel-electric Type 2s in Scotland. The six-cylinder version was used in the D9500 diesel-hydraulics and the E6100 series Class 74 electro-diesel conversions, neither of which could be classed as successful. However Paxman did eventually achieve a break-through with its 'Valenta' engines in the large fleet of High Speed Diesel Trains which were developed from the 'Ventura' range and ran millions of miles over thirty years from 1975.

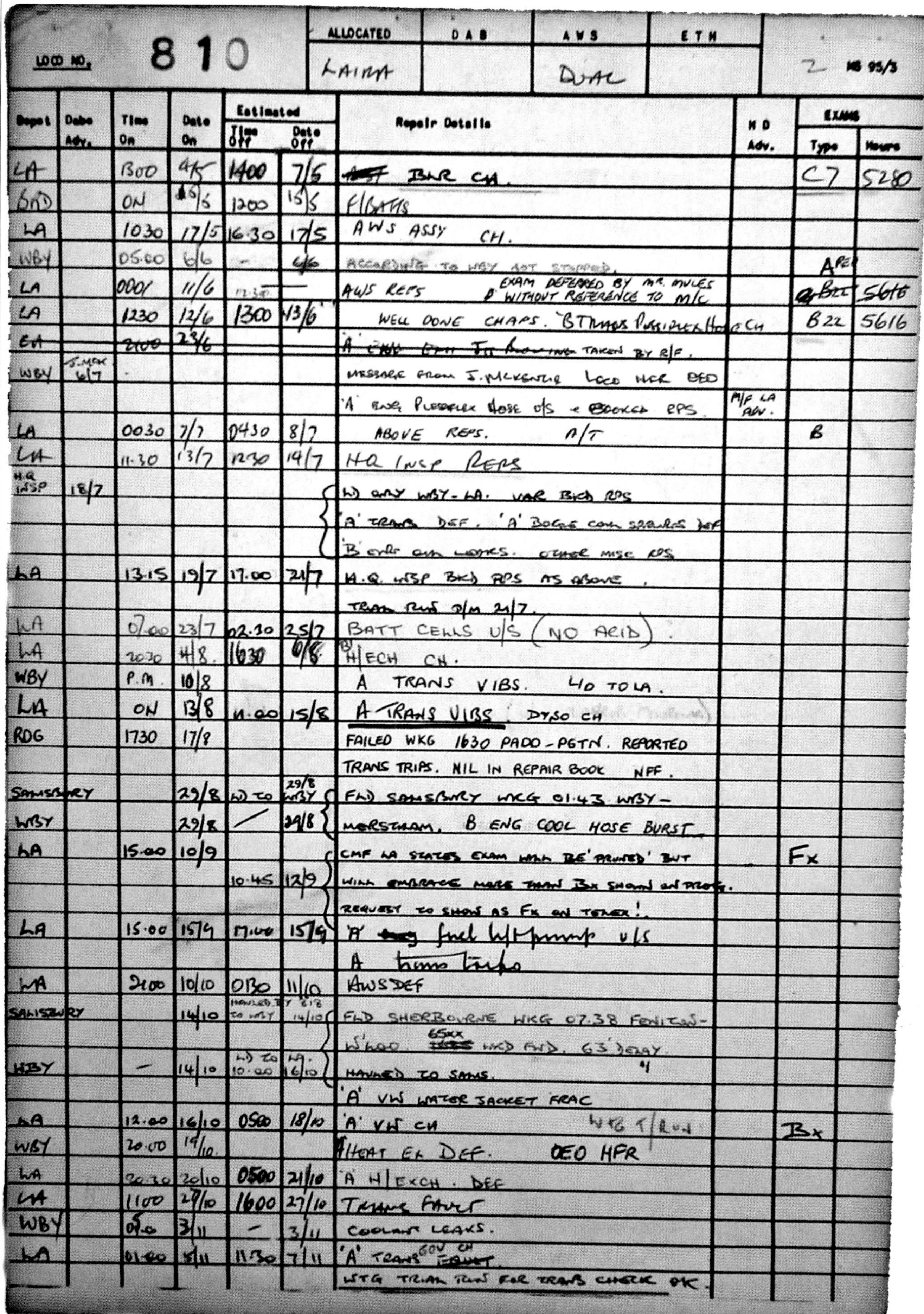

| LOCO NO. 810 | ALLOCATED | DAB | AWS | ETH | 2 MS 95/3 |
|---|---|---|---|---|---|
| | LAIRA | | DUAL | | |

| Depot | Date Adv. | Time On | Date On | Estimated Time Off | Date Off | Repair Details | HQ Adv. | Exams Type | Hours |
|---|---|---|---|---|---|---|---|---|---|
| LA | | 1300 | 4/5 | 1400 | 7/5 | BKR CH. | | C7 | 5280 |
| BRD | | ON | 10/6 | 1200 | 15/5 | F/BATTS | | | |
| LA | | 1030 | 17/5 | 16.30 | 17/5 | AWS ASSY CH. | | | |
| WBY | | 05.00 | 6/6 | – | 6/6 | RECORDING TO WBY NOT STOPPED. | | A | |
| LA | | 0001 | 11/6 | 12.30 | | AWS REPS / EXAM DEFERRED BY MR MYLES WITHOUT REFERENCE TO M/C | | BCC | 5616 |
| LA | | 1230 | 12/6 | 1300 | 13/6 | WELL DONE CHAPS. 'B' TRANS PLESSIFLEX HOSE CH | | B22 | 5616 |
| EA | | 2100 | 23/6 | | | 'A' ENG ... TAKEN BY R/F. | | | |
| WBY | J. MCK 6/7 | | | | | MESSAGE FROM J. MCKENZIE LOCO HFR OEO | | | |
| | | | | | | 'A' ENG PLESSIFLEX HOSE O/S & BOOKED RPS | M/F LA ADV. | | |
| LA | | 0030 | 7/7 | 0430 | 8/7 | ABOVE REPS. A/T | | B | |
| LA | | 11.30 | 13/7 | 1230 | 14/7 | HQ INSP REPS | | | |
| HQ INSP | 18/7 | | | | | W) ANY WBY-LA. VAR BKD RPS | | | |
| | | | | | | 'A' TRANS DEF. 'A' BOGIE COIL SPRINGS DEF | | | |
| | | | | | | 'B' ENG ON WORKS. OTHER MISC RPS | | | |
| LA | | 13.15 | 19/7 | 17.00 | 21/7 | H.Q. INSP BKD RPS AS ABOVE. | | | |
| | | | | | | TRAIN RUN D/M 21/7. | | | |
| LA | | 07.00 | 23/7 | 12.30 | 25/7 | BATT CELLS U/S (NO ACID). | | | |
| LA | | 2030 | 4/8 | 1630 | 6/8 | B H/ECH CH. | | | |
| WBY | | P.M. | 10/8 | | | A TRANS VIBS. LO TO LA. | | | |
| LA | | ON | 13/8 | 11.00 | 15/8 | A TRANS VIBS. DYSO CH | | | |
| RDG | | 1730 | 17/8 | | | FAILED WKG 1630 PADD-PGTN. REPORTED | | | |
| | | | | | | TRANS TRIPS. NIL IN REPAIR BOOK NFF. | | | |
| SALISBURY | | | 29/8 | W) TO | 29/8 WBY | FLD SALISBURY WKG 01.43 WBY– | | | |
| WBY | | | 29/8 | / | 29/8 | MERSTHAM. B ENG COOL HOSE BURST. | | | |
| LA | | 15.00 | 10/9 | | | CMF LA STATES EXAM WILL BE 'PRUNED' BUT | | Fx | |
| | | | | 10.45 | 12/9 | WILL EMBRACE MORE THAN Bx SHOWN ON PROG. | | | |
| | | | | | | REQUEST TO SHOW AS Fx ON TEMEX! | | | |
| LA | | 15.00 | 15/9 | 17.00 | 15/9 | 'A' fuel L/P pump U/S | | | |
| | | | | | | A trans trips | | | |
| LA | | 2100 | 10/10 | 0130 | 11/10 | AWS DEF | | | |
| SALISBURY | | | 14/10 | HAULED BY 818 TO WBY | 14/10 | FLD SHERBORNE WKG 07.38 FENITON– | | | |
| | | | | | | W'LOO. 65XX WKD FWD. 63' DELAY. | | | |
| WBY | | – | 14/10 | W) TO LA. 10.00 | 16/10 | HAULED TO SALIS. | | | |
| | | | | | | 'A' VW WATER JACKET FRAC | | | |
| LA | | 12.00 | 16/10 | 0500 | 18/10 | 'A' VW CH WKG T/RUN | | Bx | |
| WBY | | 20.00 | 19/10 | | | HEAT EX DEF. OEO HFR | | | |
| LA | | 20.30 | 20/10 | 0500 | 21/10 | 'A' H/EXCH. DEF | | | |
| LA | | 1100 | 27/10 | 1600 | 27/10 | TRANS FAULT | | | |
| WBY | | 07.00 | 3/11 | – | 3/11 | COOLANT LEAKS. | | | |
| LA | | 01.00 | 5/11 | 11.30 | 7/11 | 'A' TRANS GOV CH | | | |
| | | | | | | WTG TRIAL RUN FOR TRANS CHECK OK. | | | |

The Repair card from 4 May to 5 November 1971 for 810 COCKADE.

# D600 ACTIVE

| | |
|---|---|
| Lot no./Works no. | 425/27660 |
| **Significant dates and allocations** | |
| Delivered | 16/01/58 |
| Into traffic - Swindon | 24/01/58 |
| Laira | 05/58 |
| Withdrawn (Laira) | 31/12/67 |
| (Woodhams Barry) | 28/07/68 |
| Date cut-up | 03/70 |

| | |
|---|---|
| **Modifications** | |
| Vertical air intakes | 16/11/60 |
| 4 character train identification indicators | 08/05/67 |
| **Livery and insignia changes** | |
| Green | 14/01/58 |
| OHLW flashes | ? |
| Yellow warning panels | 10/05/62 |
| Blue - full yellow ends | 08/05/67 |
| **Recorded mileage** | 637,000 |

**Works visits and depot repairs**

| Stopped | At | On Works | Off Works | At | Type | Days | Work carried out |
|---|---|---|---|---|---|---|---|
| 14/01/58 | NBL | 16/01/58 | 24/01/58 | SW | D/A | 10 | Delivery inspection and acceptance; ATC equipment fitted and name plates fitted. |
| 02/04/58 | Ex-T | 08/04/58 | 17/04/58 | SW | L/C | 15 | Engine defects |
| ? | ? | 06/58 | 06/58 | SW | ? | 1 | Received unknown modifications |
| 01/04/59 | Ex-T | 01/04/59 | 03/07/59 | SW | L/C | 93 | A & B Engines repaired; A & B Bogies repaired; Modifications carried out in accordance with N.B.L. Co. instructions. |
| 19/12/59 | Ex-T | 19/12/59 | 22/12/59 | SW | L/C | 3 | B Bogie changed (left hand inner tyre loose) |
| 11/04/60 | LA | 13/04/60 | 12/05/60 | SW | L/C | 31 | |
| 07/08/60 | Ex-T | 07/08/60 | 16/11/60 | SW | L/C | 101 | 5,000 hour exam; B Bogie changed; B Transmission changed; vertical air intakes |
| 23/12/60 | Ex-T | 24/12/60 | 06/01/61 | LA | Unsch | 14 | The loco was out of traffic for a long period awaiting materials from Swindon Works. |
| 11/01/61 | Ex-T | 11/01/61 | 17/02/61 | SW | L/C | 37 | B Transmission changed (returned to NBL under guarantee) |
| 16/03/61 | Ex-T | 23/03/61 | 27/03/61 | SW | Unsch | 11 | A Bogie changed (following derailment at Newbury on down 'CRE') |
| 14/06/61 | Ex-T | 14/06/61 | 20/06/61 | LA | L/C | 6 | A Bogie tyres turned |
| 04/08/61 | LA | 08/08/61 | 31/08/61 | SW | U/C | 27 | A & B Engines repaired |
| 01/10/61 | Ex-T | 01/10/61 | 16/10/61 | LA | L/C | 15 | A & B Engines fuel pumps changed |
| 28/11/61 | Ex-T | 28/11/61 | 14/12/61 | LA | L/C | 17 | B Engine changed |
| 29/01/62 | Ex-T | 29/01/62 | 31/01/62 | LA | L/C | 2 | A & B Bogie tyres turned |
| 02/02/62 | LA | 13/02/62 | 10/05/62 | SW | H/C | 97 | A Engine changed; A & B Transmissions changed; A & B Bogie tyres renewed; Boiler changed; Exhausters and compressors changed. A & B dynostarters removed, modified and refitted, all cardan shafts examined in 'AM' and refitted, Serck radiators removed, cleaned and refitted and fan motors serviced; all heat exchangers examined and tested |
| 26/06/62 | LA | 29/06/62 | 12/07/62 | SW | H/C | 16 | A Engine changed (removed for repair by N.B.L. Co. Engineers) |
| 18/09/62 | LA | 24/09/62 | 01/11/62 | SW | H/C | 44 | A Engine changed (engine bed removed, damage repaired, realigned and re-bolted) |
| 25/01/63 | Ex-T | 25/01/63 | 13/02/63 | LA | U/C | 19 | 5,250 hour exam |
| 07/03/63 | LA | 18/03/63 | 02/04/63 | SW | H/C | 26 | A Bogie changed; Exhausters and compressor changed |
| 08/04/63 | Ex-T | 08/04/63 | 08/04/63 | LA | L/C | 1 | B Bogie tyres turned |
| 06/10/63 | Ex-T | 06/10/63 | 12/10/63 | LA | L/C | 6 | 7,500 hour exam; A & B Bogie tyres turned |
| 10/04/64 | Ex-T | 10/04/64 | 22/04/64 | LA | L/C | 12 | B Engine changed (low oil pressure) |
| 28/07/64 | Ex-T | 28/07/64 | 12/08/64 | LA | L/C | 15 | B Transmission changed (control piston seizure and metal particles in filters) |
| 01/09/64 | Ex-T | 01/09/64 | 17/10/64 | LA | Unsch | 46 | B Transmission changed (metal particles in filters from coupling clutch selector ring) |
| 02/02/65 | Ex-T | 02/02/65 | 13/02/65 | LA | L/C | 11 | A Engine changed (Nos. 1-6 bank cylinder liners leaking) |
| 04/04/65 | Ex-T | 04/04/65 | 17/04/65 | LA | Unsch | 13 | A Bogie changed (intermediate axle box damaged and compensating beam displaced by collision) |
| 18/08/65 | Ex-T | 18/08/65 | 29/08/65 | LA | L/C | 11 | A Bogie tyres turned; B Bogie changed |
| 03/11/65 | Ex-T | 03/11/65 | 05/11/65 | LA | L/C | 2 | Boiler changed (seriously overheated) |
| 03/01/66 | Ex-T | 03/01/66 | 10/01/66 | LA | L/C | 7 | B Transmission changed (governor drive wheel teeth stripped) |
| 24/05/66 | Ex-T | 24/05/66 | 21/06/66 | LA | L/C | 28 | B Engine changed |
| 21/11/66 | Ex-T | 21/11/66 | 08/05/67 | SW | Int | 168 | A & B Engines changed; A Transmission changed; A & B Bogies changed; Headcode discs replaced with four character train identification indicators |
| 22/11/67 | Ex-T | 22/11/67 | 28/11/67 | LA | L/C | 6 | B Transmission changed (all teeth stripped from oil filling pump drive gear and bearing collapsed |
| 31/12/67 | Ex-T | | | LA | | | Withdrawn |

D600 ACTIVE in 1958 at Reading General with a parcels train. It still has its original non-serif 'D' prefix and horizontal ventilator louvres. The crude metal brackets to hold the train headboard were only fitted to D600 and D601 for a short time. The headboards were then suspended from the top lamp bracket to allow the train reporting numbers introduced in late-1958 to be displayed below. (www.rail-online.co.uk)

D600 ACTIVE at Plymouth in June 1967. It was the only one of the class to be given the complete BR corporate blue treatment with full yellow ends. When it was repainted in April 1967 the worksplates were moved to the solebars on the centre line to accommodate the double arrow symbols on the cabside. (www.rail-online.co.uk)

# D601 ARK ROYAL

| Lot no./Works no. | 425/27661 |
|---|---|
| **Significant dates and allocations** | |
| Delivered | 24/03/58 |
| Into traffic - Swindon | |
| Laira | 06/58 |
| Landore | 08/67 |
| Laira | 11/67 |
| Withdrawn (Laira) | 31/12/67 |
| (Woodhams Barry) | 28/07/68 |
| Date cut-up | 06/80 |

| **Modifications** | |
|---|---|
| Vertical air intakes | ? |
| 4 character train identification indicators | 23/01/66 |
| **Livery and insignia changes** | |
| Green | 24/03/58 |
| OHLW flashes | ? |
| Yellow warning panels (assumed) | 03/08/62 |
| Full yellow ends | - |
| Blue | - |
| **Recorded mileage** | 587,000 |

**Works visits and depot repairs**

| Stopped | At | On Works | Off Works | At | Type | Days | Work carried out |
|---|---|---|---|---|---|---|---|
| | | 24/03/58 | 28/03/58 | SW | D/A | 4 | Delivery inspection and acceptance |
| | Ex-T | 15/04/58 | 22/04/58 | SW | L/C | 8 | Unrecorded modifications carried out. |
| 15/05/58 | Ex-T | 05/58 | 02/06/58 | ? | Unsch | 18 | |
| 02/10/59 | Ex-T | 05/10/59 | 07/12/59 | SW | H/I | 66 | |
| 10/03/60 | LA | 22/03/60 | 04/05/60 | SW | L/C | 55 | |
| 23/08/60 | LA | 24/08/60 | 30/09/60 | SW | Unsch | 38 | |
| 12/11/60 | LA | 18/11/60 | 05/01/61 | SW | L/C | 54 | |
| 20/03/61 | LA | 22/03/61 | 15/05/61 | SW | L/C | 56 | |
| 23/05/61 | LA | 07/06/61 | 18/07/61 | SW | L/C | 56 | |
| 14/09/61 | Ex-T | 14/09/61 | 27/09/61 | LA | U/C | 13 | |
| 27/10/61 | LA | 05/12/61 | 21/12/61 | SW | Unsch | 55 | |
| 01/08/62 | Ex-T | 01/08/62 | 03/08/62 | LA | L/C | 2 | |
| 19/09/62 | Ex-T | 19/09/62 | 06/10/62 | StB | Unsch | 17 | |
| 19/09/63 | LA | 26/09/63 | 25/10/63 | SW | H/C | 36 | Loco stopped at Laira due to derailment damage. A & B bogies, B engine and boiler recommended for change. |
| 23/01/64 | Ex-T | 23/01/64 | 01/02/64 | LA | ? | 9 | |
| 09/03/64 | Ex-T | 09/03/64 | 26/03/64 | LA | L/C | 17 | A Engine changed (low oil pressure) |
| | Ex-T | 08/65 | 23/01/66 | SW | Int | 145+ | Estimated dates – assumed Route Indicator panels fitted at this visit |
| | | 09/66 | | SW | | | Transmission removed (Forward / Reverse dog seized) |
| | | | | | | | (1964-1967 No detailed information available) |
| 31/12/67 | Ex-T | | | LA | | | Withdrawn |

D601 ARK ROYAL on 13 June 1958 at Penzance. Three days later it was put on the up 'Cornish Riviera Express' from Plymouth returning west overnight, but failed after a few days and resumed its previous Plymouth-Penzance routine. (JH Aston)

D601 ARK ROYAL at Plymouth in 1966-67. It was fitted with route indicator boxes in January 1966. (www.rail-online.co.uk)

# D602 BULLDOG

| Lot no./Works no. | 425/27662 |
|---|---|
| **Significant dates and allocations** | |
| Delivered | 10/58 |
| Into traffic - Laira | 03/11/58 |
| Landore | 08/67 |
| Laira | 11/67 |
| Withdrawn (Laira) | 31/12/67 |
| (J Cashmore Newport) | 29/07/68 |
| Date cut-up | 11/68 |

| **Modifications** | |
|---|---|
| Vertical air intakes | 04/11/60 |
| 4 character train identification indicators fitted | 18/12/64 |
| **Livery and insignia changes** | |
| Green | 03/11/58 |
| OHLW flashes | ? |
| Yellow warning panels | 04/04/62 |
| Blue – yellow warning panel | 06/02/67 |
| **Recorded mileage** | 500,000 |

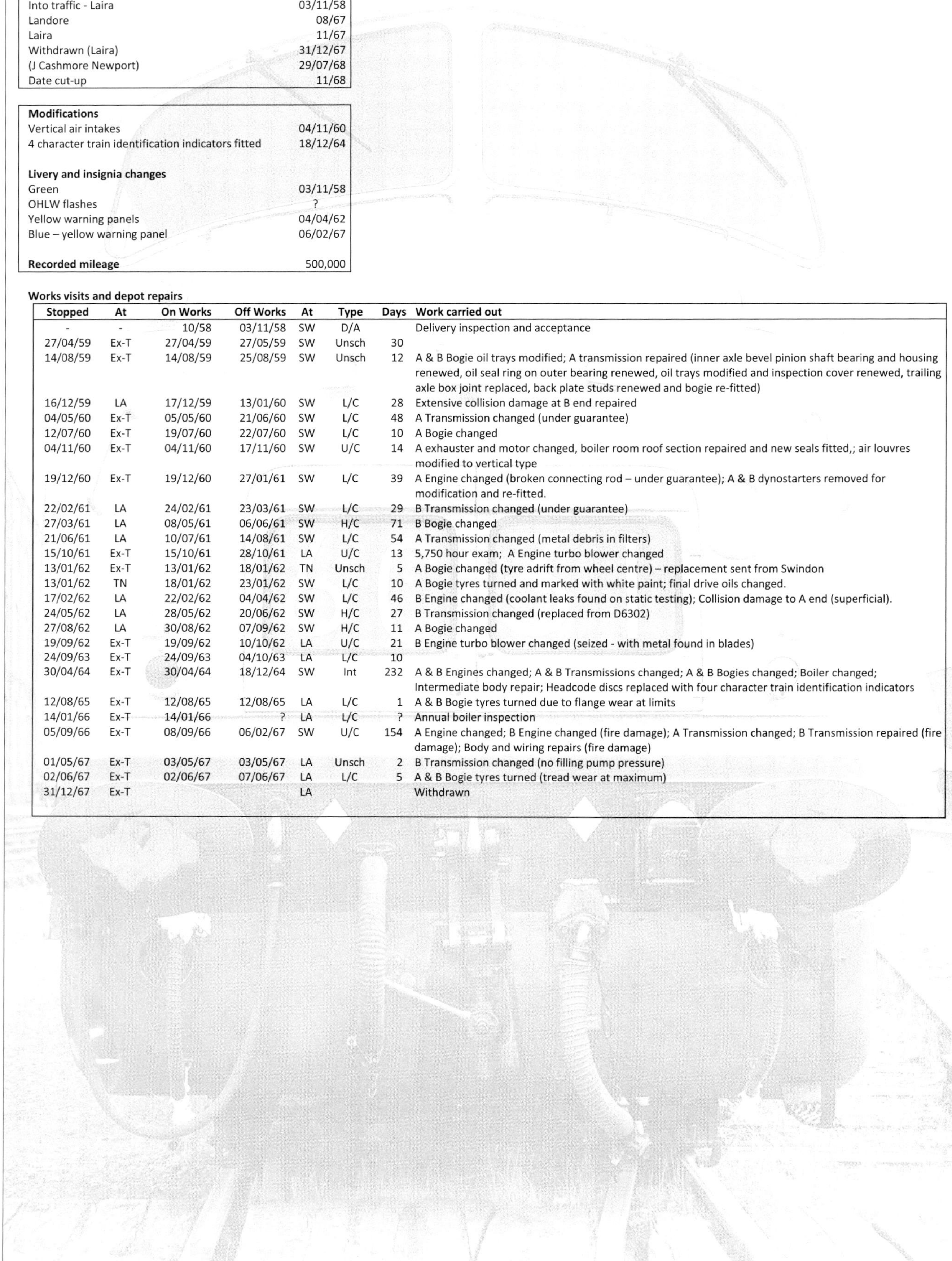

**Works visits and depot repairs**

| Stopped | At | On Works | Off Works | At | Type | Days | Work carried out |
|---|---|---|---|---|---|---|---|
| - | - | 10/58 | 03/11/58 | SW | D/A | | Delivery inspection and acceptance |
| 27/04/59 | Ex-T | 27/04/59 | 27/05/59 | SW | Unsch | 30 | |
| 14/08/59 | Ex-T | 14/08/59 | 25/08/59 | SW | Unsch | 12 | A & B Bogie oil trays modified; A transmission repaired (inner axle bevel pinion shaft bearing and housing renewed, oil seal ring on outer bearing renewed, oil trays modified and inspection cover renewed, trailing axle box joint replaced, back plate studs renewed and bogie re-fitted) |
| 16/12/59 | LA | 17/12/59 | 13/01/60 | SW | L/C | 28 | Extensive collision damage at B end repaired |
| 04/05/60 | Ex-T | 05/05/60 | 21/06/60 | SW | L/C | 48 | A Transmission changed (under guarantee) |
| 12/07/60 | Ex-T | 19/07/60 | 22/07/60 | SW | L/C | 10 | A Bogie changed |
| 04/11/60 | Ex-T | 04/11/60 | 17/11/60 | SW | U/C | 14 | A exhauster and motor changed, boiler room roof section repaired and new seals fitted,; air louvres modified to vertical type |
| 19/12/60 | Ex-T | 19/12/60 | 27/01/61 | SW | L/C | 39 | A Engine changed (broken connecting rod – under guarantee); A & B dynostarters removed for modification and re-fitted. |
| 22/02/61 | LA | 24/02/61 | 23/03/61 | SW | L/C | 29 | B Transmission changed (under guarantee) |
| 27/03/61 | LA | 08/05/61 | 06/06/61 | SW | H/C | 71 | B Bogie changed |
| 21/06/61 | LA | 10/07/61 | 14/08/61 | SW | L/C | 54 | A Transmission changed (metal debris in filters) |
| 15/10/61 | Ex-T | 15/10/61 | 28/10/61 | LA | U/C | 13 | 5,750 hour exam; A Engine turbo blower changed |
| 13/01/62 | Ex-T | 13/01/62 | 18/01/62 | TN | Unsch | 5 | A Bogie changed (tyre adrift from wheel centre) – replacement sent from Swindon |
| 13/01/62 | TN | 18/01/62 | 23/01/62 | SW | L/C | 10 | A Bogie tyres turned and marked with white paint; final drive oils changed. |
| 17/02/62 | LA | 22/02/62 | 04/04/62 | SW | L/C | 46 | B Engine changed (coolant leaks found on static testing); Collision damage to A end (superficial). |
| 24/05/62 | LA | 28/05/62 | 20/06/62 | SW | H/C | 27 | B Transmission changed (replaced from D6302) |
| 27/08/62 | LA | 30/08/62 | 07/09/62 | SW | H/C | 11 | A Bogie changed |
| 19/09/62 | Ex-T | 19/09/62 | 10/10/62 | LA | U/C | 21 | B Engine turbo blower changed (seized - with metal found in blades) |
| 24/09/63 | Ex-T | 24/09/63 | 04/10/63 | LA | L/C | 10 | |
| 30/04/64 | Ex-T | 30/04/64 | 18/12/64 | SW | Int | 232 | A & B Engines changed; A & B Transmissions changed; A & B Bogies changed; Boiler changed; Intermediate body repair; Headcode discs replaced with four character train identification indicators |
| 12/08/65 | Ex-T | 12/08/65 | 12/08/65 | LA | L/C | 1 | A & B Bogie tyres turned due to flange wear at limits |
| 14/01/66 | Ex-T | 14/01/66 | ? | LA | L/C | ? | Annual boiler inspection |
| 05/09/66 | Ex-T | 08/09/66 | 06/02/67 | SW | U/C | 154 | A Engine changed; B Engine changed (fire damage); A Transmission changed; B Transmission repaired (fire damage); Body and wiring repairs (fire damage) |
| 01/05/67 | Ex-T | 03/05/67 | 03/05/67 | LA | Unsch | 2 | B Transmission changed (no filling pump pressure) |
| 02/06/67 | Ex-T | 02/06/67 | 07/06/67 | LA | L/C | 5 | A & B Bogie tyres turned (tread wear at maximum) |
| 31/12/67 | Ex-T | | | LA | | | Withdrawn |

D602 BULLDOG waits to depart from Paddington with the 'Mayflower' on 26 June 1959, after its long stay in Scotland for rectification work. The train headboard is fitted on the top lamp bracket and is off-centre to the right. (www.rail-online.co.uk)

D602 BULLDOG rests at Plymouth on 4 April 1967. It received an early version of the new BR blue livery with a small warning panel in December 1966. (Alec Swain, www.transporttreasury.co.uk)

# D603 CONQUEST

| Lot no./Works no. | 425/27663 |
|---|---|
| **Significant dates and allocations** | |
| Delivered | 11/58 |
| Into traffic - Laira | 21/11/58 |
| Withdrawn (Laira) | 31/12/67 |
| (J Cashmore Newport) | 29/07/68 |
| Date cut-up | 11/68 |

| **Modifications** | |
|---|---|
| Vertical air intakes | 01/12/60 |
| 4 character train identification indicators fitted | 14/10/65 |
| **Livery and insignia changes** | |
| Green | 21/11/58 |
| OHLW flashes | 01/12/60 |
| Yellow warning panels | 11/04/62 |
| Full yellow ends | - |
| Blue | - |
| **Recorded mileage** | 512,000 |

**Works visits and depot repairs**

| Stopped | At | On Works | Off Works | At | Type | Days | Work carried out |
|---|---|---|---|---|---|---|---|
| - | - | ? | 21/11/58 | SW | D/A | | Delivery inspection and acceptance |
| 08/12/58 | Ex-T | 09/12/58 | 03/02/59 | SW | Unsch | 57 | Minor repairs carried out before the loco was returned to N.B.L. Co. |
| 03/02/59 | SW | ? | 04/59 | NBL | | 60 | |
| 28/05/59 | Ex-T | 28/05/59 | 19/06/59 | LA | Unsch | 22 | A & B Engines removed (defective con rods. Twelve con rods and large end bearing renewed) |
| 29/10/59 | Ex-T | 29/10/59 | 18/11/59 | SW | L/C | 20 | A Engine changed |
| 17/12/59 | Ex-T | 17/12/59 | 18/12/59 | LA | | 1 | Turbo blower changed |
| 15/02/60 | Ex-T | 15/02/60 | 04/03/60 | NTH | Unsch | 18 | A & B Bogies examined for damage from hot boxes |
| 21/11/60 | Ex-T | 21/11/60 | 01/12/60 | SW | Unsch | 10 | B Transmission changed; Body side panels removed for access to exhauster and refitted, A exhauster & motor changed; air intake louvres modified to vertical type |
| 08/08/61 | LA | 09/08/61 | 13/09/61 | SW | L/C | 36 | B Engine changed (No. 2 cylinder seized); A Transmission heat exchanger changed; A & B dynostarters changed |
| 15/09/61 | Ex-T | 15/09/61 | 20/09/61 | LA | L/C | 5 | A & B Bogie tyres turned and reprofiled |
| 18/10/61 | Ex-T | 19/10/61 | 15/12/61 | SW | L/C | 58 | A Engine changed (No. 7 cylinder head leaking badly and engine rpm too high on idling); B Engine changed (damage to No. 6 cylinder con rod, piston and crankcase) |
| 05/02/62 | LA | 26/02/62 | 11/04/62 | SW | L/C | 65 | B Engine changed; A Transmission changed; A end nose section front doors levelled and one buffer replaced |
| 05/10/62 | LA | 09/10/62 | 02/11/62 | SW | H/C | 28 | A Engine changed; B Bogie changed (removed after trial run - outer final drive gear suspect); Compressors & exhausters changed; B Transmission to final drive cardan shaft changed |
| 20/02/63 | LA | 25/02/63 | 20/03/63 | SW | H/C | 28 | A & B Engines changed; A & B engine heat exchangers changed, A & B transmission heat exchangers removed, tested and replaced |
| 10/04/63 | Ex-T | 10/04/63 | ? | LA | L/C | | A end A V R changed |
| 26/08/63 | Ex-T | 26/08/63 | 05/09/63 | LA | L/C | 10 | 9,750 hour exam |
| 09/03/64 | Ex-T | 09/03/64 | 26/03/64 | LA | Unsch | 15 | B Transmission changed (no filling pump pressure; 6,000 hour exam |
| 23/04/64 | Ex-T | 28/04/64 | 21/05/64 | LA | L/C | 28 | B Engine changed |
| 23/06/64 | Ex-T | 23/06/64 | 26/06/64 | LA | L/C | 3 | A Engine Turbo blower changed |
| ? | LA | 10/11/64 | 14/10/65 | SW | Int | 338 | A Engine changed; Intermediate body repair; Fitted with 4 character train identification indicators |
| 28/12/65 | Ex-T | 28/12/65 | 05/01/66 | LA | Unsch | 8 | A Engine changed (fractured connecting rod) |
| 25/01/67 | Ex-T | 25/01/67 | 31/01/67 | LA | L/C | 6 | B Engine changed |
| 09/06/67 | Ex-T | 09/06/67 | 09/06/67 | LA | Unsch | 1 | A & B Bogie tyres turned |
| 30/07/67 | Ex-T | 30/07/67 | 22/08/67 | LA | Unsch | 23 | A Engine changed (low oil pressure); A Transmission changed |
| 31/12/67 | Ex-T | | | LA | | | Withdrawn |

D603 CONQUEST at Plymouth on 4 July 1961. The support for the train reporting number frame had every appearance of an afterthought; it did nothing for the front-end appearance and the brackets to support the train headboard are just dangling. It now has vertical louvres but still no yellow warning panels, which were applied when it went into works in February 1962. (www.rail-online.co.uk)

D603 CONQUEST at Plymouth North Road in the mid-1960s on the 1A94 2.0pm Penzance-Paddington. The route indicator boxes were probably fitted during an 11 month stay in Swindon between October 1964 and November 1965.

## D604 COSSACK

| | |
|---|---|
| Lot no./Works no. | 425/27664 |
| **Significant dates and allocations** | |
| Delivered | 1/59 |
| Into traffic - Laira | 20/01/59 |
| Landore | 08/67 |
| Laira | 11/67 |
| Withdrawn (Laira) | 31/12/67 |
| (J Cashmore Newport) | 29/07/68 |
| Date cut-up | 09/68 |

| | |
|---|---|
| **Modifications** | |
| Vertical air intakes | 06/01/61 |
| 4 character train identification indicators fitted | 18/11/66 |
| **Livery and insignia changes** | |
| Green | 20/01/59 |
| OHLW flashes | 18/10/61 |
| Yellow warning panels | 27/02/62 |
| Full yellow ends | - |
| Blue | - |
| **Recorded mileage** | 480,000 |

**Works visits and depot repairs**

| Stopped | At | On Works | Off Works | At | Type | Days | Work carried out |
|---|---|---|---|---|---|---|---|
| - | - | ? | 20/01/59 | SW | D/A | | Delivery inspection and acceptance |
| 08/05/59 | Ex-T | 12/05/59 | 29/05/59 | SW | Unsch | 21 | |
| 06/10/59 | Ex-T | 06/10/59 | 28/10/59 | SW | Unsch | 22 | A Engine repaired (12 burner inserts renewed (new type pattern), 2 fuel pump couplings replaced and retimed); B Engine repaired (Turbo blower changed, Nos. 1, 2, 5, 6 & 7 pistons renewed, 3 cylinder liners renewed, 12 con rods renewed, 12 burner inserts renewed , 4 cylinder head core plugs renewed, 2 fuel pump couplings replaced and retimed) |
| 17/10/60 | LA | 18/10/60 | 06/01/61 | SW | L/C | 80 | A Transmission changed; air intake louvres modified vertical type fitted; all electrical controls checked and tested |
| 19/01/61 | Ex-T | 19/01/61 | 14/04/61 | SW | L/C | 85 | A Engine (Modified fuel pump fitted); B Engine changed (broken connecting rod on test); B Transmission changed (suspected bearing collapse and then changed again after failure on stationary works tests due to over-speeding) |
| 07/06/61 | LA | 27/06/61 | 24/08/61 | SW | L/C | 78 | A Transmission changed (transmission casing fractured near governor during servicing at Laira, repaired at Swindon and then failed on trial) |
| 11/09/61 | LA | 15/09/61 | 18/10/61 | SW | L/C | 37 | A Engine changed; (overheating) – removed from D6304 |
| 21/10/61 | Ex-T | 21/10/61 | 23/10/61 | LA | L/C | 2 | A & B Bogie tyres turned and reprofiled |
| 18/01/62 | LA | 29/01/62 | 27/02/62 | SW | L/C | 40 | B Transmission changed; B Bogie changed (outer final drive defective and cardan shaft damaged) |
| 02/05/62 | LA | 02/05/62 | 06/06/62 | SW | L/C | 35 | A Engine changed; A Bogie changed |
| 13/09/62 | LA | 17/09/62 | 02/10/62 | SW | H/C | 19 | B Transmission changed |
| 07/11/62 | LA | 14/11/62 | 22/11/62 | SW | U/C | 15 | |
| 07/02/63 | Ex-T | 07/02/63 | 16/02/63 | LA | U/C | 9 | |
| 02/04/63 | Ex-T | 02/04/63 | 06/04/63 | LA | L/C | 4 | B Bogie tyres turned and reprofiled |
| 06/04/63 | LA | 08/04/63 | 03/05/63 | SW | H/C | 29 | B Engine Turbo blower changed; A Transmission changed (failed during trials); B Bogie changed; Boiler changed |
| 20/05/63 | LA | 23/05/63 | 18/06/63 | SW | H/C | 29 | A Transmission changed |
| 22/07/63 | LA | 23/07/63 | 20/08/63 | SW | H/C | 29 | B Engine changed |
| 08/05/64 | Ex-T | 08/05/64 | ? | LA | U/C | | Annual boiler inspection carried out. |
| 09/07/64 | Ex-T | 09/07/64 | 16/07/64 | LA | U/C | 7 | B Engine Turbo blower changed |
| 7/07/64 | ? | 17/07/64 | 17/09/64 | LA | Unsch | 72 | A Transmission changed (control piston seized); the change was booked to have been carried out at Swindon but due to delay in acceptance at works it was done at Laira |
| 15/10/64 | Ex-T | 15/10/64 | 01/11/64 | LA | L/C | 17 | A & B Bogies changed |
| 08/12/64 | Ex-T | 08/12/64 | 19/12/64 | LA | Unsch | 11 | A & B Engines changed (cylinder heads and liners leaking) |
| 16/06/65 | Ex-T | 16/06/65 | 26/06/65 | LA | L/C | 10 | Boiler changed |
| 06/10/65 | Ex-T | 06/10/65 | 08/10/65 | LA | L/C | 2 | B Bogie tyres turned |
| 16/01/66 | Ex-T | 16/01/66 | 22/01/66 | LA | Unsch | 6 | B Engine changed (cylinder heads and liners leaking coolant) |
| 04/02/66 | Ex-T | 04/02/66 | 25/02/66 | LA | Unsch | 21 | B Engine changed (No. 12 exhaust cam damaged) |
| 23/05/66 | Ex-T | 23/05/66 | 18/11/66 | SW | Int | 179 | A Engine changed; B Transmission changed; A & B Bogies changed; Intermediate body repair; Headcode discs replaced with four character train identification indicators |
| 28/02/67 | Ex-T | 02/03/67 | 22/03/67 | SW | Unsch | 22 | Collision damage repair to its B end; headcode digit box was torn off, the cast nose casing behind was pushed in; lower skirting from the front corner to the cab door was torn off exposing pipework and cables; buffer shroud missing |
| 31/12/67 | Ex-T | | | LA | | | Withdrawn |

D604 COSSACK passing through Reading in June 1959 with train 054, the 8.15am Perranporth-Paddington. The two white discs indicate a Class 1 express working. (www.rail-online.co.uk)

D604 COSSACK in 1963 at Swindon Works. It was the last of the class to be fitted with route indicator boxes, added at an Intermediate repair in mid-1966.

# D800 SIR BRIAN ROBERTSON

| Lot no./Works no. | 428 / - |
|---|---|
| **Significant dates and allocations** | |
| Built/delivered | 03/06/58 |
| Into traffic - Swindon | 11/08/58 |
| Laira | 09/58 |
| Stored (Laira) until withdrawn | 09/68 |
| Withdrawn | 05/10/68 |
| To Cashmores Newport | 18/07/69 |
| Date cut-up | By 24/07/69 |

| **Modifications** | |
|---|---|
| 4 character train identification indicators fitted | 24/03/64 |
| **Livery and insignia changes** | |
| Green | 03/06/58 |
| OHLW flashes; serif 'D'-prefix | 11/12/61 |
| Yellow warning panels | 01/05/63 |
| Maroon | - |
| Blue | - |
| **Recorded mileage** | 923,870 |

**Works visits and depot repairs**

| Stopped | At | On Works | Off Works | At | Type | Days | Work carried out |
|---|---|---|---|---|---|---|---|
| - | - | - | 03/06/58 | SW | D/A | | Delivery inspection and acceptance |
| 10/10/58 | Ex-T | 10/10/58 | 20/10/58 | SW | U/C | 10 | A & B Bogies removed for modifications and re-fitted; fuel levelling pipe modified |
| 17/07/59 | Ex-T | 17/07/59 | 07/08/59 | SW | U/C | 21 | A & B Transmissions changed, fuel gauges changed to Baynham type, vacuum relief valve and all roof sections changed. |
| 14/09/59 | Ex-T | 14/09/59 | 16/09/59 | SW | Unsch | 2 | |
| 26/10/59 | Ex-T | 26/10/59 | 30/10/59 | SW | Unsch | 4 | A & B Bogies changed |
| 01/12/59 | Ex-T | 01/12/59 | 07/12/59 | SW | U/C | 6 | Turbo blowers changed |
| 08/01/60 | Ex-T | 08/01/60 | 16/02/60 | SW | L/C | 39 | A Engine repaired, B Engine changed, A & B Bogies changed, Boiler changed |
| 19/02/60 | Ex-T | 23/02/60 | 29/02/60 | SW | L/C | 10 | A Engine repaired (continuation of previous 5000 hour exam) |
| 17/03/60 | LA | 21/03/60 | 31/03/60 | SW | L/C | 14 | A Engine repaired; A & B Bogies changed (A removed due to frame fractures at well plate) |
| 28/04/60 | Ex-T | 28/04/60 | 28/04/60 | SW | U/C | 1 | |
| 05/09/60 | Ex-T | 06/09/60 | 16/09/60 | SW | L/C | 11 | B Transmission changed; A and B end engine exhaust elbows fitted with modified drain pipes and rapid closing gate valves and system removed. |
| 02/11/60 | Ex-T | 02/11/60 | 02/11/60 | SW | U/C | 1 | |
| 12/11/60 | LA | 12/11/60 | 23/11/60 | SW | L/C | 11 | A Engine repaired, B Engine changed; A & B Bogies changed |
| 09/12/60 | Ex-T | 09/12/60 | 15/12/60 | SW | U/C | 6 | A Engine repaired |
| 14/02/61 | Ex-T | 14/02/61 | 06/03/61 | SW | L/C | 20 | A and B end engine speed motors modified; Over bogie structure and thrust pads re-set (shopped due to reported vibrations at the B end during acceleration and being noisy at the output end); body repairs |
| 20/03/61 | LA | 27/03/61 | 13/04/61 | SW | U/C | 23 | B engine repaired and modified type exhaust manifold pipes fitted. |
| 21/07/61 | Ex-T | 25/07/61 | 12/08/61 | SW | L/C | 22 | B Bogie changed |
| 13/11/61 | Ex-T | 13/11/61 | 11/12/61 | SW | L/C | 28 | B Engine changed; A Bogie changed |
| 21/05/62 | Ex-T | 21/05/62 | 23/05/62 | LA | L/C | 2 | Boiler changed |
| 07/08/62 | Ex-T | 07/08/62 | 15/08/62 | LA | H/C | 8 | A Engine changed (No. 2 cylinder head fractured) |
| 06/11/62 | LA | 09/11/62 | 14/11/62 | SW | H/C | 8 | A Bogie changed |
| 14/01/63 | LA | 22/01/63 | 13/02/63 | SW | H/C | 30 | B Transmission changed; A Bogie repaired; B Bogie changed; body repairs |
| 06/04/63 | BS | 08/04/63 | 01/05/63 | SW | H/C | 25 | A Engine changed (Nos. 2 and 5 cylinder liners fractured); A Transmission changed |
| 05/09/63 | Ex-T | 05/09/63 | 05/09/63 | LA | U/C | 1 | A exhauster changed (knocking badly) |
| 01/10/63 | Ex-T | 01/10/63 | 02/10/63 | LA | L/C | 2 | |
| 11/10/63 | Ex-T | 10/63 | 17/10/63 | LA | H/C | 6 | B Engine changed |
| 23/10/63 | Ex-T | ? | 15/11/63 | LA | H/C | 23 | B Bogie changed |
| 07/02/64 | Ex-T | 02/64 | 19/02/64 | LA | Unsch | 12 | B Bogie changed |
| 07/02/64 | LA | 19/02/64 | 24/03/64 | SW | Unsch | 46 | A & B Bogies changed; Headcode discs replaced with route indicators; frame fractures welded up |
| 07/10/64 | Ex-T | 10/64 | 18/10/64 | LA | L/C | 11 | B Transmission changed |
| 09/01/65 | Ex-T | 10/01/65 | 20/01/65 | LA | H/C | 11 | A Engine changed; A Transmission changed (due to being noisy and metal debris in filter)' Boiler changed |
| 01/02/65 | Ex-T | 05/02/65 | 06/08/65 | SW | Int | 186 | B Engine changed (Nos. 4 and 5 cylinder heads leaking coolant); A & B Transmissions changed; A & B Bogies changed; Modifications |
| 20/09/65 | Ex-T | 20/09/65 | 23/09/65 | LA | L/C | 3 | A Transmission changed (No. 1 clutch bolt ring defective) |
| 27/10/65 | Ex-T | 27/10/65 | 29/10/65 | LA | L/C | 2 | A Transmission changed (metal in filters) |
| 08/04/66 | Ex-T | 08/04/66 | 17/04/66 | LA | H/C | 9 | A & B Engines changed; A Transmission changed (seized ) |
| 25/08/66 | Ex-T | 25/08/66 | 31/08/66 | LA | L/C | 6 | A Transmission changed (directional clutches worn) |
| 30/12/66 | Ex-T | 30/12/66 | 04/01/67 | SW | Unsch | 5 | A & B Bogies changed |
| 05/01/67 | SW | 05/01/67 | 17/02/67 | SW | Unsch | 43 | A & B Bogies changed; collision damage at B end repaired |
| 14/03/67 | Ex-T | 14/03/67 | 17/03/67 | LA | H/C | 3 | B Engine changed (10 cylinder heads fractured) |
| 22/04/67 | Ex-T | 22/04/67 | 27/04/67 | LA | L/C | 5 | B Transmission changed (metal in filters) |
| 07/03/68 | Ex-T | 07/03/68 | 18/03/68 | LA | H/C | 11 | A Engine changed; B Transmission changed (No. 6 clutch defective) |
| 03/06/68 | Ex-T | 03/06/68 | 05/06/68 | LA | L/C | 2 | A Transmission changed (No. 1 gear wheel bearing had excess lift) |
| 26/06/68 | Ex-T | 26/06/68 | 28/06/68 | LA | L/C | 2 | |
| 05/10/68 | | | | LA | - | | Withdrawn |

**D800 SIR BRIAN ROBERTSON** carried a headboard which proclaimed it the **FIRST 2,200 H.P. DIESEL HYDRAULIC LOCOMOTIVE BUILT IN BRITISH RAILWAYS WORKSHOPS - SWINDON 1958** (the actual rating was 2,100hp – D803 was the first at 2,200hp). The special headboard was carried from 14 July 1958 until it returned to Swindon on the 17th when it was photographed on the first of the three reception roads at the end of 'A' shop. (www.rail-online.co.uk)

**D800 SIR BRIAN ROBERTSON** working the 1A98 15.20 Penzance-Paddington after crossing Tresulgan Viaduct east of Menheniot in the mid-1960s. It was the only one of the D800s to be withdrawn in green, coming to a premature end in October 1968. The changes since its days as 'the first 2,200 h.p. diesel hydraulic locomotive built in British Railways workshops' are many, including the removal of multiple working equipment, the addition of a yellow warning panel and the fitting of a standard headcode box. (www.rail-online.co.uk)

# D801 VANGUARD

| Lot no./Works no. | 428 / - |
|---|---|
| **Significant dates and allocations** | |
| Built/delivered | 18/09/58 |
| Into traffic - Laira | 07/11/58 |
| Stored (Laira) | 31/07/68 |
| Withdrawn (Laira) | 03/08/68 |
| (Newton Abbot) | 4/10/69 |
| (Swindon) | 21/07/70 |
| Date cut-up | By 24/10/70 |

| **Modifications** | |
|---|---|
| 4 character train identification indicators fitted | 16/10/63 |
| Multiple working cables and receptors removed | 16/10/63 |
| **Livery and insignia changes** | |
| Green | 18/09/58 |
| OHLW flashes | 18/09/61 |
| Yellow warning panels | 16/02/62 |
| Maroon - yellow warning panels | 24/06/66 |
| Blue | - |
| **Recorded mileage** | 855,560 |

**Works visits and depot repairs**

| Stopped | At | On Works | Off Works | At | Type | Days | Work carried out |
|---|---|---|---|---|---|---|---|
| - | - | - | 18/09/58 | SW | D/A | | Released from Swindon for special tests; Delivery inspection and acceptance |
| 07/03/59 | Ex-T | 07/03/59 | 23/03/59 | SW | Unsch | 16 | B Engine repaired; A & B Bogies changed (removed for special examination and experiment) |
| 09/09/59 | Ex-T | 09/09/59 | 14/09/59 | SW | Unsch | 5 | Bogie lubrication experiment |
| 09/12/59 | Ex-T | 09/12/59 | 16/12/59 | SW | U/C | 7 | A Transmission modified; B Transmission changed |
| 01/02/60 | Ex-T | 01/02/60 | 05/03/60 | SW | H/I | 33 | A & B Engines repaired; A & B Transmissions repaired; A & B Bogies repaired; Body repaired |
| 29/03/60 | Ex-T | 29/03/60 | 31/03/60 | SW | U/C | 2 | A & B Bogies examined in position for frame fractures, outside laminated springs changed and hand brake cross stay nuts tightened |
| 20/04/60 | Ex-T | 20/04/60 | 22/04/60 | SW | U/C | 2 | B Bogie laminated axle box springs changed |
| 02/06/60 | Ex-T | 07/06/60 | 15/06/60 | SW | L/C | 13 | A Transmission changed; body repairs |
| 16/07/60 | Ex-T | 19/07/60 | 25/07/60 | SW | U/C | 9 | B Engine repaired (No. 1 cylinder head changed and all tappet clearances checked) |
| 03/08/60 | Ex-T | 03/08/60 | 12/08/60 | SW | U/C | 9 | B Engine repaired (all cylinder heads changed) |
| 24/10/60 | Ex-T | 24/10/60 | 01/11/60 | SW | U/C | 8 | B Engine repaired (coolant in engine; No. 4 cylinder head and No. 2 fuel injector changed) |
| 24/11/60 | LA | 25/11/60 | 21/12/60 | SW | L/C | 27 | A Engine repaired (coolant in engine. No. 7 cylinder liner and head changed due to fractures, remainder overhauled); Boiler changed |
| 06/01/61 | LA | 06/01/61 | 24/01/61 | SW | Unsch | 18 | B Engine repaired (No. 4 cylinder head leaking coolant. No. 4 cylinder head changed and remainder checked); Transmissions repaired; B end Serck cooler group radiator unit removed due to a defective flexible pipe, pipe modified and cooler group unit re-fitted and battery fault rectified. |
| 10/03/61 | OOC | 17/03/61 | 11/04/61 | SW | L/C | 32 | A Engine repaired; B Engine changed (fractured cylinder heads); A Bogie repaired; B Bogie changed |
| 14/04/61 | Ex-T | 14/04/61 | 24/04/61 | SW | L/C | 10 | B Engine repaired (No. 3 cylinder head leaking coolant) |
| 18/05/61 | Ex-T | 18/05/61 | 06/06/61 | SW | L/C | 19 | B Bogie changed |
| 14/06/61 | Ex-T | 16/06/61 | 19/09/61 | SO | Unsch | 5 | A Bogie removed (inner axle broken) and replaced with spare from Swindon |
| - | SO | 19/06/61 | 24/06/61 | SW | L/C | 5 | A Bogie changed; B Bogie repaired |
| 26/08/61 | LA | 11/09/61 | 18/09/61 | SW | L/C | 23 | A Engine repaired (No. 11 cylinder head changed due to fractures and water pump changed) |
| 11/10/61 | Ex-T | 17/10/61 | 03/11/61 | SW | L/C | 23 | A Engine changed (No. 6 cylinder head fractured); A Transmission repaired; B Transmission changed (steel particles in filters); Body repaired |
| 29/01/62 | Ex-T | 02/02/62 | 16/02/62 | SW | L/C | 18 | B Engine changed (No. 27 exhaust cam damaged) |
| 11/03/62 | Ex-T | 11/03/62 | 14/03/62 | LA | L/C | 3 | B Bogie tyres turned |
| 27/04/62 | LA | 01/05/62 | 08/05/62 | SW | H/C | 11 | A & B Transmissions repaired; Bogie B (frame modifications, final drives stripped and examined and tyres renewed) |
| 14/06/62 | BS | 21/06/62 | 28/06/62 | SW | H/C | 14 | A Bogie changed (inner final drive input shaft bearing collapsed); B Bogie changed |
| 16/12/62 | Ex-T | 16/12/62 | 22/12/62 | LA | L/C | 6 | Boiler changed |
| 08/01/63 | Ex-T | 08/01/63 | 23/01/63 | LA | H/C | 15 | B Transmission changed (front suspension mounting foot broken up) |
| 17/04/63 | Ex-T | 17/04/63 | 17/04/63 | LA | L/C | 1 | B Bogie tyres turned |
| 22/05/63 | Ex-T | 22/05/63 | 30/05/63 | LA | H/C | 8 | A Engine changed; A Transmission changed; A Bogie tyres turned |
| 01/06/63 | Ex-T | 01/06/63 | 05/06/63 | LA | H/C | 4 | B Engine changed (No. 4 cylinder liner leaking coolant; during this repair D801 sustained severe fire damage to the boiler compartment and components within and was sent to works. |
| 05/06/63 | Ex-T | 11/06/63 | 16/10/63 | SW | H/C | 133 | A & B Bogies changed ; Repairs to fire damaged upper structure frame work and inner and outer skins of boiler compartment, internal pipe work and ducting renewed, electrical control cubicles removed, checked and re-fitted, extensive re-wiring carried out, headcode discs replaced with four character train identification indicators, multiple working jumper cables and receptacles removed. |
| 17/11/63 | Ex-T | 17/11/63 | 22/11/63 | LA | U/C | 5 | B exhauster changed (commutator grooved) |
| 28/06/64 | Ex-T | 28/06/64 | 01/07/64 | LA | Unsch | 3 | A Engine Turbo blower changed |
| 14/08/64 | LA | 20/08/64 | 01/09/64 | SW | Unsch | 18 | A & B Engines repaired; A & B Bogies changed; Body repaired |
| 14/01/65 | Ex-T | 14/01/65 | 25/02/65 | SW | Unsch | 42 | A & B Engines changed; A Bogie changed; B Bogie repaired; A Transmission repaired |
| 27/07/65 | Ex-T | 27/07/65 | 30/07/65 | LA | L/C | 3 | B Engine changed |
| 06/10/65 | Ex-T | 06/10/65 | 08/10/65 | LA | U/C | 2 | B Bogie tyres turned |
| 22/01/66 | Ex-T | 22/01/66 | 03/02/66 | LA | L/C | 11 | Boiler changed |
| 13/04/66 | Ex-T | 13/04/66 | 24/06/66 | SW | Int | 72 | A Engine changed; B Engine repaired; A Bogie repaired ; B Bogie changed; A Transmission repaired: B Transmission changed |
| 05/10/67 | Ex-T | 05/10/67 | 05/10/67 | LA | L/C | 1 | A Bogie changed (outer final drive bearing overheating) |
| 21/11/67 | Ex-T | 21/11/67 | 24/11/67 | LA | H/C | 3 | B Engine changed |
| 05/02/68 | Ex-T | 05/02/68 | 10/02/68 | LA | H/C | 5 | A Engine changed; B Transmission changed (overheating); Boiler changed |
| 18/02/68 | Ex-T | 18/02/68 | 27/02/68 | LA | Unsch | 9 | B Transmission changed (directional fault) |
| 05/04/68 | Ex-T | 05/04/68 | 10/04/68 | LA | Unsch | 5 | B Transmission changed (No. 6 clutch defective); B Bogie changed |
| 08/05/68 | Ex-T | 08/05/68 | 09/05/68 | LA | L/C | 1 | A Transmission changed |
| 03/08/68 | | | | LA | | | Withdrawn |

D801 VANGUARD in original condition waits at Bristol Temple Meads around 1960. The short horizontal grab rails which were fitted to the first three D800s can easily be seen; these were replaced by standard ones when the headcode box was fitted. (www.rail-online.co.uk)

D801 VANGUARD on 27 August 1966 at Basingstoke with 1V72 16.00 Waterloo-Exeter. The maroon livery is still in good condition after it was repainted at an Intermediate overhaul completed on 24 June 1966. The multiple working equipment has been removed although its use was limited as the only other Warships that it was compatible with were D800 and D802. VANGUARD was the first of the class to be withdrawn, on 3 August 1968 and retained maroon livery to the end. (P Kerslake, www.transporttreasury.co.uk)

# D802 FORMIDABLE

| | |
|---|---|
| Lot no./Works no. | 428 / - |
| **Significant dates and allocations** | |
| `Into traffic - Laira | 16/12/58 |
| Withdrawn (Laira) | 05/10/68 |
| (Exeter) for component removal | 04/10/69 |
| (Swindon) | 21/07/70 |
| Date cut-up | By 11/70 |

| | |
|---|---|
| **Modifications** | |
| 4 character train identification indicators fitted | 24/04/64 |
| **Livery and insignia changes** | |
| Green | 16/12/58 |
| OHLW flashes | 28/05/62 |
| Yellow warning panels | 28/05/62 |
| Maroon - yellow warning panels | 06/04/66 |
| Blue full yellow ends – double insignia, serif and D | 10/10/67 |
| **Recorded mileage** | 912,880 |

**Works visits and depot repairs**

| Stopped | At | On Works | Off Works | At | Type | Days | Work carried out |
|---|---|---|---|---|---|---|---|
| - | - | - | 16/12/58 | SW | D/A | ? | Delivery inspection and acceptance |
| 15/07/59 | Ex-T | 15/07/59 | 20/07/59 | SW | L/C | 5 | A Transmission repaired; B Transmission removed for special exam and replaced with spare |
| 30/07/59 | Ex-T | 30/07/59 | 31/07/59 | SW | U/C | 1 | B end engine compartment roof section repaired. |
| 12/08/59 | Ex-T | 12/08/59 | 14/08/59 | LA | L/C | 2 | Tyres turned |
| 27/09/59 | Ex-T | 27/09/59 | 03/10/59 | SW | U/C | 5 | A & B engines fitted with modified type governors; A & B Bogies removed for special exam and all coil springs changed; Boiler fitted with modified relays; Body repaired |
| 26/10/59 | Ex-T | 26/10/59 | 29/10/59 | SW | L/C | 3 | B Bogie removed for access to fractured body side control bracket. |
| 13/01/60 | Ex-T | 13/01/60 | 28/01/60 | SW | L/C | 15 | A & B engines repaired; A & B Bogies changed |
| 31/03/60 | NA | 05/04/60 | 02/06/60 | SW | H/C | 63 | A & B engines repaired; A & B Transmissions repaired; A & B Bogies repaired (examined for fractures) |
| 08/06/60 | Ex-T | 08/06/60 | 08/06/60 | SW | U/C | 1 | |
| 01/10/60 | Ex-T | 01/10/60 | 07/10/60 | SW | L/C | 6 | A Transmission repaired (broken mounted bracket causing movement of casing. Foot renewed) |
| 13/04/61 | Ex-T | 13/04/61 | 24/04/61 | SW | L/C | 11 | A Bogie tyres changed; B Bogie changed (worn tyres) |
| 08/06/61 | LA | 15/06/61 | 26/06/61 | SW | L/C | 18 | A Engine changed (No. 6 cylinder liner split); A Bogie changed |
| 28/06/61 | LA | 01/07/61 | 17/07/61 | SW | L/C | 19 | B Engine changed (No. 12 cylinder bore full of coolant) |
| 01/08/61 | Ex-T | 01/08/61 | 01/08/61 | SW | L/C | 1 | |
| 22/03/62 | LA | 06/04/62 | 28/05/62 | SW | H/G | 67 | B Engine changed; A & B Transmissions changed; A & B Bogies changed |
| 11/07/62 | Ex-T | 17/07/62 | 27/07/62 | SW | H/C | 16 | A Engine changed (fractured cylinder liners) |
| 02/10/62 | Ex-T | 09/10/62 | 26/10/62 | SW | H/C | 24 | A Transmission, heat exchanger and dynostarter cardan shaft changed. |
| 14/05/63 | Ex-T | 15/05/63 | 31/05/63 | SW | H/C | 17 | B Bogie changed; Boiler changed |
| 14/06/63 | Ex-T | 14/06/63 | 15/06/63 | LA | L/C | 1 | |
| 28/10/63 | Ex-T | 28/10/63 | 02/11/63 | LA | H/C | 5 | B Engine changed (no oil pressure to the governor and metal in filters) |
| 14/11/63 | Ex-T | 14/11/63 | 20/11/63 | LA | H/C | 6 | A Transmission (front suspension bracket and casing fractured) |
| 06/02/64 | Ex-T | 06/02/64 | 10/02/64 | LA | U/C | 4 | A Bogie changed |
| 16/02/64 | Ex-T | 16/02/64 | 26/02/64 | LA | Unsch | 10 | A Engine changed |
| 11/03/64 | LA | 16/03/64 | 24/04/64 | SW | Unsch | 44 | A & B Transmissions repaired; A & B Bogies changed; A end engine fuel pump changed, A and B end front aprons repaired; headcode discs replaced with four character train identification indicators. |
| 26/09/64 | Ex-T | 26/09/64 | 03/10/64 | LA | L/C | 7 | A Engine changed (No. 2 cylinder liner leaking coolant) |
| 15/04/65 | Ex-T | 15/04/65 | 23/04/65 | LA | H/C | 8 | B Transmission changed (excessive movement in the input thrust bearing) |
| 09/08/65 | Ex-T | 09/08/65 | 16/08/65 | LA | L/C | 7 | B Engine changed |
| 04/09/65 | Ex-T | 04/09/65 | 10/09/65 | LA | L/C | 6 | A Engine changed (No. 9 cylinder cams damaged) |
| 11/11/65 | Ex-T | 11/11/65 | 11/11/65 | LA | L/C | 1 | A & B Bogie tyres turned |
| 14/01/66 | Ex-T | 14/01/66 | 06/04/66 | SW | Int | 72 | A & B engines repaired; A Transmission changed; B Transmission repaired; A & B Bogies changed; Modifications |
| 29/06/66 | Ex-T | 29/06/66 | 30/06/66 | LA | L/C | 1 | B Engine changed (No. 11 cylinder liner leaking coolant) |
| 20/03/67 | Ex-T | 20/03/67 | 04/04/67 | LA | L/C | 14 | A Transmission changed (dynostarter drive coupling becoming loose) |
| 06/06/67 | Ex-T | 06/06/67 | 09/06/67 | LA | L/C | 3 | B Transmission changed (metal in filters) |
| 20/06/67 | Ex-T | 20/06/67 | 22/06/67 | LA | L/C | 2 | Boiler changed |
| 27/07/67 | Ex-T | 27/07/67 | 17/08/67 | LA | L/C | 21 | A Transmission changed (end float on the gear train and not holding in direction) |
| 01/09/67 | Ex-T | 01/09/67 | 13/09/67 | LA | L/C | 12 | A Bogie changed (outer final drive bearing seized) |
| 25/09/67 | Ex-T | 25/09/67 | 29/09/67 | LA | L/C | 4 | B Bogie changed (outer axle of N.B.L. Co. Manufacture) |
| 03/10/67 | Ex-T | 03/10/67 | 10/10/67 | SW | Unsch | 7 | Called to Works for an external repaint (in blue) only |
| 07/03/68 | Ex-T | 12/03/68 | 12/03/68 | LA | H/C | 5 | A & B engines changed |
| 28/04/68 | Ex-T | 28/04/68 | 29/04/68 | LA | L/C | 1 | B Transmission changed (convertor jacket fractured) |
| 29/05/68 | Ex-T | 29/05/68 | 07/06/68 | LA | L/C | 9 | B Bogie changed (lift on the inner final drive bearing) |
| 15/07/68 | Ex-T | 15/07/68 | 18/07/68 | LA | L/C | 3 | A Bogie changed (final drive seizure) |
| 05/10/68 | | | | LA | | | Withdrawn |

**D802 FORMIDABLE, in original condition, runs light at Bristol Temple Meads. The brass worksplate can be easily seen below the nameplate; the Swindon Warships had an oval plate whereas the North British had the traditional 'black diamond.' (www.rail-online.co.uk)**

**D802 FORMIDABLE stands at Laira on 17 May 1964. It had only recently been stopped for unscheduled repairs and Swindon had taken the opportunity to carry out the front end modifications which saw the central lamp bracket, marker light and headboard clips all removed and replaced by the standard headcode box and longer grab rails. FORMIDABLE was released on 24 April and less than a month later the new coat of green paint still looks fresh. D802 was the only one of the first three locomotives to go through the complete green-maroon-blue livery cycle. (SV Blencowe)**

# D803 ALBION

| Lot no./Works no. | 437 / - |
|---|---|
| **Significant dates and allocations** | |
| Into traffic - Laira | 16/03/59 |
| Newton Abbot | 08/67 |
| Laira | 05/68 |
| Newton Abbot | 10/71 |
| Withdrawn (Laira) | 02/01/72 |
| (Bristol St Philips Marsh Junction) | 11/07/72 |
| (Swindon) | 29/08/72 |
| Date cut-up | By 06/10/72 |

| **Modifications** | |
|---|---|
| 4 character train identification indicators fitted | 01/02/65 |
| Dual fitting of BR / WR A.W.S. | 21/11/67 |
| **Livery and insignia changes** | |
| Green | 16/03/59 |
| OHLW flashes | 07/09/61 |
| Yellow warning panels | 01/02/65 |
| Maroon | - |
| Blue full yellow ends – double insignia, serif, D-prefix | 21/11/67 |
| Blue full yellow ends – double insignia, sans serif , no D | 27/12/68 |
| **Recorded mileage** | 1,220,000 |

**Works visits and depot repairs**

| Stopped | At | On Works | Off Works | At | Type | Days | Work carried out |
|---|---|---|---|---|---|---|---|
| - | - | - | 16/03/59 | SW | D/A | | Delivery inspection and acceptance |
| 13/06/59 | Ex-T | 15/06/59 | 16/06/59 | SW | L/C | 3 | A & B Transmissions changed |
| 17/09/59 | Ex-T | 17/09/59 | 25/09/59 | SW | L/C | 8 | A & B Engine governors modified |
| 16/12/59 | Ex-T | 16/12/59 | 18/12/59 | SW | L/C | 2 | B Bogie right hand inner coil spring changed |
| 20/01/60 | Ex-T | 20/01/60 | 27/01/60 | SW | L/C | 7 | A Engine Nos. 5 and 6 cylinder heads changed |
| 28/04/60 | Ex-T | 28/04/60 | 06/05/60 | SW | L/C | 8 | A & B Bogies changed |
| 07/05/60 | LA | 08/05/60 | 17/05/60 | SW | L/C | 10 | B Engine repaired; B Transmission changed (not changing gears correctly) |
| 06/07/60 | Ex-T | 06/07/60 | 13/07/60 | SW | L/C | 7 | A Transmission changed |
| 25/07/60 | Ex-T | 25/07/60 | 28/07/60 | SW | L/C | 3 | A end co-drivers side widow changed, Serck cooling system checked and all electrical connections and controls checked and tested. |
| 02/08/60 | Ex-T | 02/08/60 | 22/08/60 | SW | L/C | 20 | A Engine changed (No. 5 cylinder cracked); B Engine changed |
| 11/11/60 | Ex-T | 11/11/60 | 11/11/60 | SW | L/C | 1 | B Bogie right hand trailing axle box spring changed due to a broken spring top plate |
| 28/07/61 | Ex-T | 28/07/61 | 28/07/61 | LA | L/C | 1 | Boiler removed due to heavy scaling. No replacement fitted |
| 11/08/61 | Ex-T | 23/08/61 | 07/09/61 | SW | H/C | 27 | A & B Bogies changed; Boiler fitted; A & B end Vapor-Watchman preheaters modified. |
| 05/02/62 | Ex-T | 02/62 | 08/02/62 | LA | L/C | 3 | A & B Bogie tyres turned |
| 13/03/62 | Ex-T | 14/03/62 | 16/03/62 | LA | H/C | 3 | B Engine changed (No. 2 cylinder liner leaking coolant) |
| 14/06/62 | Ex-T | 06/62 | 20/06/62 | LA | H/C | 7 | A Engine changed (No. 4 cylinder liner cracked) |
| 18/10/62 | BS | 23/10/62 | 06/11/62 | SW | H/C | 20 | A Bogie changed (inner final drive oil seals leaking); B Bogie changed; A end dynostarter cardan shaft changed, boiler room roof section repaired |
| 05/63 | Ex-T | 02/05/63 | 05/63 | LA | H/C | ? | B Engine changed (valves blowing) |
| 06/63 | Ex-T | 05/06/63 | 06/63 | LA | H/C | ? | A Engine Turbo blower changed (leaking oil) |
| 06/63 | Ex-T | 19/06/63 | 06/63 | LA | L/C | ? | B end dynostarter removed for availability |
| 01/08/63 | Ex-T | | 03/08/63 | LA | H/C | 2 | |
| 06/10/63 | Ex-T | 06/10/63 | 15/10/63 | LA | H/C | 9 | B Transmission changed; Boiler changed |
| 02/64 | Ex-T | 12/02/64 | 02/64 | LA | L/C | ? | A Engine changed |
| 15/08/64 | Ex-T | 15/08/64 | 08/64 | LA | L/C | | B Engine changed (No. 2 cylinder liner cracked) |
| 06/11/64 | Ex-T | 10/11/64 | 01/02/65 | SW | Class | 87 | A Engine changed (crankshaft oil seals leaking); B Engine changed; A Transmission changed; B Transmission repaired; A & B Bogies changed; Modifications; Headcode discs replaced with four character train identification indicators |
| 06/65 | Ex-T | 05/06/65 | 06/65 | LA | L/C | ? | B Engine changed |
| ? | Ex-T | 01/09/65 | 09/65 | LA | H/C | ? | A Transmission changed (output casing damaged by a detached cardan shaft) |
| 09/65 | Ex-T | 30/09/65 | ? | LA | H/C | ? | A Bogie changed (excessive metal in filters of outer final drive) |
| ? | Ex-T | 01/12/65 | 12/65 | LA | L/C | ? | Boiler changed |
| ? | Ex-T | 02/03/66 | 03/66 | LA | L/C | ? | B Transmission changed (incorrect gear change in 2nd gear) |
| 04/04/66 | LA | 06/04/66 | 07/04/66 | SW | Unsch | 3 | A & B Bogies changed (suspected axle flaws) |
| 03/67 | Ex-T | 19/03/67 | 03/67 | LA | H/C | ? | A & B Engines changed |
| 08/67 | Ex-T | 22/08/67 | 08/67 | LA | L/C | ? | A Transmission changed (No. 7 gear collapsed and brass in filters) |
| 10/67 | Ex-T | 17/10/67 | 10/67 | NA | L/C | ? | Boiler changed |
| 10/67 | Ex-T | 27/10/67 | 21/11/67 | SW | Class | ? | A & B Engines repaired; A & B Bogies changed; Dual fitting of BR / WR A.W.S.; Modifications |
| 06/68 | Ex-T | 24/06/68 | 06/68 | LA | L/C | ? | B Transmission changed (removed for availability to use on D824) |
| ? | Ex-T | 02/07/68 | 07/68 | LA | L/C | ? | B Transmission changed (knocking noises in the output section) |
| 09/68 | Ex-T | 04/09/68 | 09/68 | LA | L/C | ? | A Transmission changed (convertor oil leaks) |
| 11/68 | Ex-T | 15/11/68 | 27/12/68 | SW | Int | ? | A & B Engines changed; A Transmission changed (input oil seals leaking); B Transmission changed ; A & B Bogies changed (torn side control rubbers); Collision damage repairs at B end nose; Modifications |
| 08/69 | Ex-T | 16/08/69 | 25/08/69 | LA | L/C | ? | A Transmission changed (output oil seals leaking) |
| 10/69 | Ex-T | 23/10/69 | 10/69 | LA | L/C | ? | Boiler changed |
| 26/02/70 | Ex-T | 03/7 | 05/03/70 | LA | L/C | 8 | B Transmission changed (reported as noisy) |
| 25/04/70 | Ex-T | 26/04/70 | 29/04/70 | LA | L/C | 5 | B Transmission changed (low oil pressure and convertor 'O' ring oil seals leaking) |
| 26/08/70 | Ex-T | 26/08/70 | 28/08/70 | LA | L/C | 3 | A Transmission changed (no oil pressure and several gear wheels teeth pitted) |
| 03/10/70 | Ex-T | 03/7 | 07/10/70 | LA | L/C | 5 | A Transmission changed (overheating in all gears) |
| 20/10/70 | Ex-T | 20/10/70 | 22/10/70 | LA | L/C | 3 | A Engine changed |
| 09/11/70 | Ex-T | 09/11/70 | 10/11/70 | LA | L/C | 2 | B Bogie changed (frame fractures) |
| 08/12/70 | Ex-T | 09/12/70 | 11/12/70 | LA | L/C | 4 | B Engine changed |
| 03/03/71 | Ex-T | 03/03/71 | 06/03/71 | LA | L/C | 4 | A Bogie changed |
| 21/03/71 | Ex-T | 06/04/71 | 03/06/71 | SW | U/C | 75 | A & B Bogies changed; Boiler changed; damage repairs following derailment at Uffington (resulting in the re-appearance of the headboard clips removed in 1965, probably because the nose end from withdrawn D830 was fitted, and headcode doors ex-D841 which had the Old Oak NBL modification of air hole vents under the indicators) |
| 27/09/71 | Ex-T | 27/09/71 | 29/09/71 | LA | L/C | 2 | B Transmission changed (reported as knocking) |
| 07/11/71 | Ex-T | 11/71 | 13/11/71 | NA | L/C | 6 | B Transmission changed (No. 4 clutch being defective and reported knocking.) |
| 02/01/72 | | | | LA | - | | Withdrawn |

First of the production series, D803 ALBION, and D824 HIGHFLYER passing through Brookwood on 10 October 1964 with the 1V72 13.00 Waterloo-Exeter. D824 had failed at Waterloo the previous day and was being returned to the WR for attention. D803 didn't receive a yellow warning panel until February 1965 and was the only one of the first thirteen not to receive the panel before having a standard headcode box fitted. (Alec Swain, www.transporttreasury.com)

803 ALBION in 1970 at Backwell, south of Bristol with a van train. Note the air ventilation holes under the headcode panel; these were normally found only on NBL-built locomotives. 803 had suffered front end damage during 1969 and the headcode box doors from D841 ROEBUCK had been used to effect a repair. It has the multiple working equipment refitted in 1968; a colour photograph would have shown up the maroon front end valance donated by withdrawn D848 SULTAN.

# D804 AVENGER

| Lot no./Works no. | 437 / - |
|---|---|
| **Significant dates and allocations** | |
| Into traffic - Laira | 23/04/59 |
| Newton Abbot | 08/67 |
| Laira | 05/68 |
| Withdrawn (Laira) | 01/10/71 |
| (Swindon) | By 07/10/71 |
| Date cut-up | By 24/03/72 |

| **Modifications** | |
|---|---|
| 4 character train identification indicators fitted | 27/09/63 |
| Dual fitting of BR / WR A.W.S. | 06/11/67 |
| **Livery and insignia changes** | |
| Green | 23/04/59 |
| OHLW flashes | 11/09/61 |
| Yellow warning panels | 10/12/62 |
| Maroon | - |
| Blue full yellow ends – double insignia, serif, D-prefix | 06/11/67 |
| **Recorded mileage** | 1,206,000 |

**Works visits and depot repairs**

| Stopped | At | On Works | Off Works | At | Type | Days | Work carried out |
|---|---|---|---|---|---|---|---|
| - | - | - | 23/04/59 | SW | D/A | | Delivery inspection and acceptance |
| 19/05/59 | Ex-T | 20/05/59 | 03/07/59 | SW | Unsch | 45 | A & B Bogie springs changed |
| 10/59 | Ex-T | 10/59 | 24/10/59 | SW | U/C | ? | |
| 03/60 | Ex-T | 03/60 | 08/03/60 | SW | L/C | ? | |
| 27/08/60 | LA | 30/08/60 | 05/09/60 | SW | L/C | 9 | |
| 30/12/60 | Ex-T | 30/12/60 | 09/02/61 | SW | L/C | 41 | |
| 03/61 | Ex-T | 03/61 | 21/03/61 | SW | L/C | ? | |
| 26/05/61 | Ex-T | 26/05/61 | 25/07/61 | SW | L/C | 60 | A & B Bogies changed |
| 24/08/61 | Ex-T | 24/08/61 | 11/09/61 | SW | L/C | 18 | A & B Bogies changed |
| 22/11/61 | Ex-T | 22/11/61 | 01/12/61 | SW | L/C | 9 | |
| 01/02/62 | Ex-T | 01/02/62 | 05/02/62 | LA | L/C | 4 | |
| 09/04/62 | Ex-T | 10/04/62 | 19/04/62 | LA | L/C | 10 | |
| 27/06/62 | LA | 27/06/62 | 09/07/62 | SW | L/C | 12 | |
| 12/07/62 | Ex-T | 12/07/62 | 13/07/62 | LA | L/C | 1 | |
| 21/08/62 | Ex-T | 23/08/62 | 06/09/62 | SW | L/C | 16 | |
| 10/11/62 | Ex-T | 27/11/62 | 10/12/62 | SW | H/C | 31 | |
| 06/02/63 | Ex-T | 02/63 | 14/02/63 | LA | H/C | ? | |
| 23/03/63 | Ex-T | 03/63 | 02/04/63 | LA | H/C | 10 | |
| 04/63 | Ex-T | 16/04/63 | 04/63 | LA | L/C | ? | |
| 08/08/63 | Ex-T | 12/08/63 | 27/09/63 | SW | H/C | 50 | A & B nose ends modified; 4 character train identification indicators fitted |
| 13/12/63 | Ex-T | 14/12/63 | 14/12/63 | SW | L/C | 1 | |
| 03/64 | Ex-T | 10/03/64 | 03/64 | LA | H/C | ? | B Transmission changed (top casing fractured) |
| 06/05/64 | Ex-T | 06/05/64 | 09/05/64 | LA | L/C | 3 | |
| 03/65 | Ex-T | 02/03/65 | 04/05/65 | SW | ? | ? | B Bogie changed |
| 05/65 | Ex-T | 05/65 | 05/65 | ? | L/C | ? | A Transmission changed (grinding when off power, Nos. 5 or 7 gearwheel bearings suspect) |
| 07/65 | Ex-T | 07/65 | 07/65 | | | ? | B Bogie changed |
| 09/66 | Ex-T | 09/66 | 66 | LA | L/C | ? | A Engine repaired |
| 11/66 | Ex-T | 16/11/66 | 11/66 | LA | L/C | ? | |
| 03/67 | Ex-T | 01/03/67 | 03/67 | LA | L/C | ? | A Bogie changed (traces on N.B.L. Co. manufactured axles) |
| 03/67 | Ex-T | 03/67 | 03/67 | ? | L/C | ? | B Transmission repaired |
| 04/67 | Ex-T | 04/67 | 04/67 | ? | L/C | ? | Removed due to input oil seals leaking) |
| 09/67 | NA | 19/09/67 | 06/11/67 | SW | Class | ? | Modifications |
| 12/67 | Ex-T | 12/67 | 12/67 | ? | L/C | ? | A Engine repaired |
| 07/68 | Ex-T | 05/07/68 | 07/68 | LA | L/C | ? | A Transmission changed (clutch damage) |
| 09/68 | Ex-T | 09/68 | 09/68 | ? | L/C | ? | B Transmission changed (clutch damage) |
| 02/69 | Ex-T | 02/69 | 02/69 | ? | L/C | ? | B Transmission changed (not changing gear) |
| 08/69 | Ex-T | 08/69 | 08/69 | ? | H/C | ? | A & B Bogies removed |
| 09/69 | Ex-T | 09/69 | 09/69 | ? | L/C | ? | A Engine changed; B Transmission changed (forward / reverse faults) |
| 02/70 | Ex-T | 02/70 | 02/70 | ? | L/C | ? | B Transmission removed (metal debris in the command block and oil) |
| 04/70 | Ex-T | 04/70 | 04/70 | ? | L/C | ? | B Engine repaired |
| 05/70 | Ex-T | 05/70 | 05/70 | ? | L/C | ? | B Bogie repaired |
| 04/08/70 | Ex-T | 04/08/70 | 06/08/70 | LA | L/C | 3 | A Engine changed (fractured crank case) |
| 11/70 | Ex-T | 11/70 | 11/70 | ? | L/C | ? | Boiler repaired |
| 01/71 | Ex-T | 01/71 | 01/71 | ? | L/C | ? | A Engine removed (cylinder head studs seized) |
| 02/71 | Ex-T | 02/71 | 02/71 | ? | L/C | ? | A Bogie changed |
| 02/71 | Ex-T | 02/71 | ? | ? | ? | ? | A Bogie removed outer final drive flange becoming loose) |
| 07/71 | Ex-T | 07/71 | 07/71 | ? | L/C | ? | B Transmission removed (overheating) |
| 01/10/71 | LA | | | | | | Withdrawn (B end dynostarter cardan shaft faults) |

D804 AVENGER arrives at Bristol in early 1961 with the 1B02 8.45am Paddington-Bristol 'Bristolian'; chocolate and cream coaches, three character train identifier – almost a pure Great Western scene. AVENGER was used on the first up run of the accelerated 100 minutes schedule on 15 June 1959 when it recorded the fastest time yet achieved to that date, with speeds in excess of 100mph at three points on the journey. (www.rail-online.co.uk)

D804 AVENGER at Gloucester Central with a class 4 freight on 17 September 1969. D804 remained in green until November 1967 when it was painted straight into blue. A relatively early convert to corporate livery, it had double arrow symbols on each cab and the serif numbers until its withdrawal in October 1971. (www.rail-online.co.uk)

# D805 BENBOW

| Lot no./Works no. | 437 / - |
|---|---|
| **Significant dates and allocations** | |
| Into traffic - Laira | 13/05/59 |
| Newton Abbot | 08/67 |
| Laira | 05/68 |
| Newton Abbot | 06/68 |
| Laira | 11/68 |
| Newton Abbot | 11/68 |
| Laira | 10/69 |
| Newton Abbot | 10/71 |
| Laira | 01/72 |
| Withdrawn (Laira) | 23/10/72 |
| (Swindon) | 31/10/72 |
| Date cut-up | By 16/05/73 |

| **Modifications** | |
|---|---|
| 4 character train identification indicators fitted | 31/03/64 |
| Multiple working jumper cables and sockets removed | 07/01/66 |
| Dual fitting of BR/WR AWS | 02/02/68 |
| **Livery and insignia changes** | |
| Green | 13/05/59 |
| OHLW flashes | 28/07/61 |
| Yellow warning panels | 03/05/63 |
| Maroon - yellow warning panels | 07/01/66 |
| Maroon - full yellow ends | 02/02/68 |
| Data panels | By 06/69 |
| Blue full yellow ends – single insignia, sans serif , no D | 24/10/70 |
| **Recorded mileage** | 1,281,000 |

## Works visits and depot repairs

| Stopped | At | On Works | Off Works | At | Type | Days | Work carried out |
|---|---|---|---|---|---|---|---|
| - | - | - | 13/05/59 | SW | D/A | | Delivery inspection and acceptance (A & B Bogies were ex-D801) |
| 02/09/59 | Ex-T | 02/09/59 | 05/09/59 | SW | L/C | 3 | A & B Bogie tyres turned; B Bogie frames welded |
| 07/09/59 | Ex-T | 07/09/59 | 11/09/59 | SW | L/C | 4 | A & B Bogies all springs changed |
| 05/12/59 | Ex-T | 05/12/59 | 08/12/59 | SW | L/C | 3 | Shopped after reported loose tyres but a trial run found all tyres to be satisfactory |
| 12/01/60 | Ex-T | 12/01/60 | 15/01/60 | SW | L/C | 3 | A Bogie tyres turned; B Bogie changed |
| 05/04/60 | Ex-T | 05/04/60 | 14/04/60 | SW | L/C | 9 | A & B Bogie tyres turned |
| 30/04/60 | Ex-T | 30/04/60 | 02/05/60 | SW | L/C | 2 | A Transmission (command box fault rectified in situ) |
| 26/05/60 | LA | 26/05/60 | 27/05/60 | SW | L/C | 1 | A Bogie removed (component support brackets welded to main frames found fractured) |
| 12/07/60 | Ex-T | 12/07/60 | 22/07/60 | SW | L/C | 11 | A Engine (No. 7 cylinder head changed) |
| 05/09/60 | Ex-T | 05/09/60 | 09/09/60 | SW | L/C | 4 | A & B Bogies (shopped for reported body riding on the bogie coil spring stops. After a trial run it was found that the bumping was being caused by heavy flats, as a result all tyres were turned and all springs changed) |
| 27/09/60 | Ex-T | 27/09/60 | 29/09/60 | SW | L/C | 2 | B Transmission (low oil pressure switch changed); A pre-heater changed |
| 10/10/60 | Ex-T | 10/10/60 | 14/10/60 | SW | L/C | 4 | B Bogie (worn torque arm) |
| 07/11/60 | Ex-T | 07/11/60 | 01/12/60 | SW | L/C | 24 | A & B Engines changed; A Bogie tyres turned; B Bogie special examination |
| 06/12/60 | Ex-T | 06/12/60 | 08/12/60 | SW | L/C | 2 | A Engine changed (sump contaminated with coolant water) |
| 21/03/61 | LA | 27/03/61 | 26/04/61 | SW | L/C | 36 | A Engine modification; B Engine (No. 5 cylinder head changed; A & B Bogies changed |
| 12/07/61 | LA | 17/07/61 | 28/07/61 | SW | U/C | 16 | A Engine repaired; A Bogie repaired; A and B exhausters and A pre-heater changed |
| 23/11/61 | Ex-T | 23/11/61 | 25/11/61 | LA | L/C | 2 | B Engine changed (No. 8 cylinder head fractured) |
| 27/07/62 | Ex-T | 29/07/62 | 04/08/62 | LA | L/C | 8 | Boiler changed (heavy scaling) |
| 21/10/62 | Ex-T | 10/62 | 30/10/62 | LA | H/C | 9 | A Engine changed (No. 6 cylinder liner fractured) |
| 08/04/63 | LA | 10/04/63 | 03/05/63 | SW | H/C | 25 | B Transmission changed (oil seals leaking); A & B Bogies changed; B pre-heater changed |
| 22/05/63 | Ex-T | 22/05/63 | 25/05/63 | LA | H/C | 3 | B Engine changed |
| 09/10/63 | Ex-T | 10/63 | 18/10/63 | LA | H/C | 9 | B Engine changed (fractures adjacent to No. 3 cylinder and coolant leaking); A Transmission changed |
| 03/02/64 | LA | 20/02/64 | 31/03/64 | SW | Unsch | 57 | A Engine changed (cooling water pump faults; B Engine changed (Nos. 1 and 2 cylinder heads blowing); B Transmission changed (grinding on gear changes); A & B Bogies changed; Headcode discs replaced with four character train identification indicators, A pre-heater changed, A and B end main frame fractures welded |
| 02/06/64 | Ex-T | 02/06/64 | 03/06/64 | LA | L/C | 1 | A end dynostarter changed (commutator bearings breaking up) |
| ? | Ex-T | 10/11/64 | 11/64 | LA | L/C | ? | B Bogie (inner final drive torque arm suspension pads collapsed or missing |
| 14/12/64 | Ex-T | 14/12/64 | 15/12/64 | LA | L/C | 1 | A Engine changed (low on power) |
| 12/64 | Ex-T | 29/12/64 | 12/64 | LA | L/C | ? | B Transmission changed (threads stripped in mounting holding feet) |
| 07/65 | Ex-T | 26/07/65 | 07/65 | LA | L/C | ? | A Engine changed (suspected leaking of cylinder heads and liners) |
| 10/08/65 | Ex-T | 08/65 | 25/08/65 | ? | H/C | 15 | A Transmission changed (dynostarter cardan shaft seizing inside the transmission, smashing the top casing) |
| 30/09/65 | Ex-T | 04/10/65 | 07/01/66 | SW | Int | 100 | B Engine changed; A & B Bogies changed; Boiler changed (fire damage); Modifications |
| ? | Ex-T | 27/06/66 | 06/66 | LA | L/C | ? | Boiler changed (split tube) |
| 21/07/66 | Ex-T | 07/66 | 01/08/66 | LA | L/C | 11 | A Transmission changed (direction clutch seized) |
| 24/08/66 | Ex-T | 24/08/66 | 24/08/66 | SW | Unsch | 1 | Sent to Swindon for weighing |
| 20/02/67 | Ex-T | 20/02/67 | 22/02/67 | LA | L/C | 2 | B Transmission changed (input oil seals leaking) |
| 03/67 | Ex-T | 30/03/67 | 04/67 | LA | L/C | ? | B Transmission changed (Nos. 3 & 4 clutches worn & teeth stripped on No. 3 baulk ring) |
| 06/67 | Ex-T | 06/06/67 | 06/67 | LA | H/C | ? | A Bogie changed; B Bogie changed (frame fractures) |
| 06/67 | Ex-T | 30/06/67 | 07/67 | LA | L/C | ? | B Transmission changed (No. 4 clutch faults) |
| 10/67 | Ex-T | 30/10/67 | 11/67 | LA | L/C | ? | B Dynostarter changed |
| 12/67 | Ex-T | 03/12/67 | 12/67 | LA | H/C | ? | A & B Engines changed |
| 08/01/68 | Ex-T | 09/01/68 | 11/01/68 | LA | L/C | 3 | A Transmission changed (severe ratcheting on change of direction and metal in filters) |
| 08/01/68 | LA | 15/01/68 | 02/02/68 | SW | U/C | 20 | A & B Bogies removed (torn side control rubbers and worn bushes on springs); Dual fitting of BR/WR AWS |
| 02/68 | Ex-T | 13/02/68 | 02/68 | NA | L/C | ? | A Exhauster changed (overheated brush gear) |
| 04/68 | Ex-T | 23/04/68 | 04/68 | LA | H/C | ? | B Transmission changed (ratcheting, No. 3 gear collapsed, Nos. 1, 3 and 5 clutches worn and metal in filters) |
| 10/68 | Ex-T | 21/10/68 | 10/68 | LA | H/C | ? | A Bogie changed (thrust pad missing); B Bogie changed |
| 10/68 | Ex-T | 25/10/68 | 10/68 | NA | L/C | ? | A Exhauster changed (motor gone to 'earth') |
| 03/69 | Ex-T | 27/03/69 | 03/69 | NA | L/C | ? | A Engine Turbo blower changed |
| 04/69 | Ex-T | 18/04/69 | 04/69 | NA | L/C | ? | Boiler changed |
| 06/69 | Ex-T | 11/06/69 | 06/69 | LA | L/C | ? | A Engine changed (Nos. 4 and 5 cylinder liners leaking coolant) |
| 05/10/69 | Ex-T | 13/10/69 | 13/10/69 | OOC | H/C | 8 | B Transmission changed (output casing fractured by a detached cardan shaft); B Bogie changed (damaged by detached cardan shaft) |
| 17/11/69 | Ex-T | 11/69 | 24/11/69 | LA | L/C | 7 | B Engine changed (low lub. oil pressure, severe knocking reported and coolant in sump) |
| 13/01/70 | Ex-T | 13/01/70 | 14/01/70 | LA | L/C | 1 | A Transmission changed (metal in filters) |
| 10/03/70 | Ex-T | 03/70 | 16/03/70 | LA | L/C | 6 | B Transmission changed (ratcheting) |
| 16/04/70 | Ex-T | 16/04/70 | 18/04/70 | LA | L/C | 2 | A Transmission changed (input shaft bearing faults) |
| 28/04/70 | Ex-T | 28/04/70 | 30/04/70 | LA | L/C | 2 | A Transmission changed (overheating when changing gear) |
| 04/08/70 | Ex-T | 04/08/70 | 06/08/70 | LA | L/C | 2 | B Engine changed (for availability prior to Intermediate at Swindon) |
| 04/08/70 | LA | 12/08/70 | 24/10/70 | SW | Int | 78 | A & B Engines changed; A & B Transmissions changed; A & B Bogies changed; all hoses and cardan shafts changed, exhausters and compressor changed; Modifications |
| 15/01/71 | Ex-T | 01/71 | 19/01/71 | LA | L/C | 4 | B Transmission changed (metal in filters) |
| 21/01/71 | Ex-T | 01/71 | 25/01/71 | LA | L/C | 4 | B Transmission changed (clutch seized) |
| 19/10/71 | WES | 25/10/71 | 02/11/71 | NA | Unsch | 14 | A Transmission changed (output casing fractured) |
| 10/11/71 | BS | 11/11/71 | 17/11/71 | NA | L/C | 7 | A Transmission changed (direction clutch damaged and reported knocking) |
| 03/01/72 | Ex-T | 03/01/72 | 06/01/72 | NA | L/C | 3 | A Transmission changed (casing fractured) |
| 06/03/72 | Ex-T | 06/03/72 | 10/03/72 | LA | L/C | 4 | A Bogie changed (lift in the inner final drive input bearing) |
| 27/04/72 | Ex-T | 27/04/72 | 02/05/72 | LA | L/C | 5 | B Transmission changed (metal in filters); Boiler changed |
| 18/05/72 | Ex-T | 05/72 | 26/05/72 | LA | L/C | 8 | A Bogie changed (No. 4 clutch defective) |
| 04/07/72 | Ex-T | 05/07/72 | 11/07/72 | LA | L/C | 7 | B Engine changed (fractured crank case) |
| 30/08/72 | Ex-T | 30/08/72 | 31/08/72 | LA | L/C | 1 | B Bogie changed (thin tyres and worn brake gear). |
| 28/09/72 | Ex-T | 28/09/72 | 29/09/72 | LA | L/C | 1 | A Transmission repaired (Forward / reverse mechanism seized); Boiler changed |
| 23/10/72 | | | | LA | | | Stopped 20/10/72 with A Transmission faults and returned to traffic working as a type '2' locomotive (*O E O*) awaiting materials, but withdrawn before the transmission change took place. |

*Left.* D805 BENBOW on 2 July 1960 stabled at the old Laira steam shed, before the new diesel building was completed. The photograph perfectly illustrates the steam age environment that the new diesels had to inhabit. The nose end detail of the early locomotives is well shown: the frame to hold the train reporting numbers, the multiple working equipment, the headcode discs folded down and the warning horns. (www.rail-online.co.uk)

*Below.* 805 BENBOW alongside 811 at Exeter stabling point on 8 May 1971. The 1O10 in the headcode box relates to the 10.15 Exeter-Waterloo which it had worked the previous day. Working only light duties on that day, BENBOW was called on to run light to Chard to rescue failed D6336 and its train, the 6O19 16.55 Chard Junction- Morden South milk. 805 was one of the last to be withdrawn, surviving until late October 1972. (www.rail-online.co.uk)

# D806 CAMBRIAN

| Lot no./Works no. | 437 / - |
|---|---|
| **Significant dates and allocations** | |
| Into traffic - Laira | 03/06/59 |
| Newton Abbot | 08/67 |
| Laira | 05/68 |
| Newton Abbot | 06/68 |
| Laira | 10/69 |
| Newton Abbot | 05/71 |
| Laira | 01/72 |
| Withdrawn (Laira) | 01/11/72 |
| (Swindon) | 07/12/72 |
| Date cut-up | By 01/05/75 |

| **Modifications** | |
|---|---|
| 4 character train identification indicators fitted | 18/10/63 |
| Multiple working jumper cables and sockets removed | 28/06/66 |
| Dual fitting of BR / WR A.W.S. | 16/01/68 |
| **Livery and insignia changes** | |
| Green | 03/06/59 |
| OHLW flashes | 13/09/61 |
| Yellow warning panels | 02/03/62 |
| Maroon - yellow warning panels | 28/06/66 |
| Maroon - full yellow ends | 16/01/68 |
| Blue full yellow ends - single insignia, sans serif , no D | 04/03/71 |
| **Recorded mileage** | 1,281,000 |

**Works visits and depot repairs**

| Stopped | At | On Works | Off Works | At | Type | Days | Work carried out |
|---|---|---|---|---|---|---|---|
| - | - | - | 03/06/59 | SW | D/A | | Delivery inspection and acceptance |
| 19/08/59 | Ex-T | 19/08/59 | 21/08/59 | SW | Unsch | 2 | B Engine repaired (all cylinder heads removed, valves and seatings refaced, No. 5 exhaust valve on No. 8 cylinder head renewed, all exhaust valve guides renewed and cylinder heads re-fitted, turbo blower change) |
| 04/11/59 | Ex-T | 04/11/59 | 13/11/59 | SW | L/C | 9 | B Engine changed (removed for examination by Bristol Siddeley engineers); A & B Bogies repaired |
| 17/02/60 | Ex-T | 18/02/60 | 26/02/60 | SW | L/C | 9 | B Engine preheater changed, drain bosses fitted to manifold pipes and governor modified; A & B Bogies repaired |
| 03/03/60 | LA | 04/03/60 | 05/03/60 | SW | L/C | 3 | A & B Engines repaired |
| 26/04/60 | Ex-T | 26/04/60 | 12/05/60 | SW | L/C | 16 | A & B Engines repaired; Modified arm type A T C gear fitted |
| 19/08/60 | LA | 19/08/60 | 24/08/60 | SW | L/C | 6 | B Bogie repaired; Modified exhaust elbow drains fitted |
| 01/09/60 | Ex-T | 01/09/60 | 02/09/60 | SW | L/C | 1 | A Bogie (coil and laminated springs changed) |
| 06/09/60 | Ex-T | 06/09/60 | 07/09/60 | SW | L/C | 1 | A Transmission repaired (Defective command box) |
| 03/10/60 | Ex-T | 03/10/60 | 04/11/60 | SW | Gen | 32 | A & B Engines changed; A Bogie changed; B Bogie repaired; A & B preheaters changed, A & B dynostarters serviced |
| 15/11/60 | BS | 16/11/60 | 17/11/60 | SW | L/C | 2 | Burnt out A end preheater changed and B end preheater examined. |
| 19/01/61 | Ex-T | 19/01/61 | 01/02/61 | SW | L/C | 13 | B Engine repaired; A Transmission changed |
| 02/02/61 | LA | 07/02/61 | 16/02/61 | SW | L/C | 14 | B Engine changed (Nos. 2 and 11 exhaust valves not seating correctly) |
| 13/03/61 | LA | 18/03/61 | 25/03/61 | SW | L/C | 12 | A Engine changed (No. 2 cylinder head fractured); A end preheater changed; A and B end dynostarter cardan shafts changed |
| 17/05/61 | LA | 17/05/61 | 19/05/61 | SW | L/C | 2 | A Bogie (Bent body spring support hangers changed, tyres examined) |
| 28/08/61 | LA | 06/09/61 | 13/09/61 | SW | L/C | 16 | A & B Bogies changed |
| 11/10/61 | Ex-T | 12/10/61 | 14/10/61 | LA | L/C | 3 | A Engine changed (exhaust valves sticking on Nos. 5, 8 and 11 heads) |
| 14/02/62 | LA | 19/02/62 | 02/03/62 | SW | L/C | 16 | B Engine changed (No. 8 cylinder head fractured) |
| 18/07/62 | Ex-T | 19/07/62 | 25/07/62 | LA | L/C | 7 | A & B Engines Turbo Blowers changed; Boiler changed |
| 09/62 | Ex-T | 12/09/62 | 09/62 | LA | L/C | ? | B Transmission changed |
| 09/62 | Ex-T | 20/09/62 | 09/62 | LA | L/C | ? | A end dynostarter changed (burnt out) |
| 30/04/63 | Ex-T | 30/04/63 | 01/05/63 | LA | L/C | 1 | Boiler changed (crown split) |
| 08/05/63 | Ex-T | 05/63 | 15/05/63 | LA | L/C | 7 | A Engine changed |
| 29/08/63 | LA | 02/09/63 | 18/10/63 | SW | H/C | 50 | A & B Engines changed ; A Transmission changed; A & B Bogies changed; Headcode discs replaced with four character train identification indicators, body repaired |
| 11/63 | Ex-T | 06/11/63 | 11/63 | LA | L/C | ? | A Transmission changed (low oil pressure) |
| 05/64 | Ex-T | 07/05/64 | 05/64 | LA | L/C | ? | A Transmission changed (overheating) |
| 17/07/64 | LA | 22/07/64 | 14/08/64 | SW | Unsch | 28 | A & B Engines modified (fitted with exhaust stack drain); A & B Transmissions changed (Output shaft oil seals renewed); A & B Bogies changed; Boiler changed |
| 06/09/64 | LA | 07/09/64 | 30/10/64 | SW | Unsch | 55 | A Transmission changed (top casing smashed caused by a detached cardan shaft); A & B Bogies changed; A end body repairs (from detached cardan shaft) |
| 07/65 | Ex-T | 26/07/65 | 07/65 | LA | L/C | ? | A Transmission changed (overheating, oil emulsified due to the presence of water, No. 3 clutch slipper pieces badly worn and metal in filters) |
| 08/65 | Ex-T | 19/08/65 | 08/65 | LA | L/C | ? | B Transmission changed (directional clutches seized) |
| 09/65 | Ex-T | 07/09/65 | 09/65 | LA | H/C | ? | A & B Engines changed |
| 21/01/66 | Ex-T | 21/01/66 | 26/01/66 | LA | L/C | 5 | A Engine changed (No. 3 con rod fractured, crank case holed and coolant in sump) |
| 14/04/66 | LA | 21/04/66 | 28/06/66 | SW | Int | 76 | A Engine repaired; B Engine changed; A & B Transmissions changed; A & B Bogies changed; Boiler changed; Multiple working equipment removed |
| 02/67 | Ex-T | 28/02/67 | 02/67 | NA | L/C | ? | A end dynostarter changed |
| 04/67 | Ex-T | 26/04/67 | 04/67 | LA | H/C | ? | A & B Engines changed |
| 08/67 | Ex-T | 24/08/67 | 08/67 | LA | L/C | ? | Boiler changed |
| 18/12/67 | Ex-T | 18/12/67 | 16/01/68 | SW | U/C | 30 | A & B Bogies changed; Boiler repaired; Dual fitting of BR/WR A.W.S; D806 sustained collision damage inside Swindon Works. Fitting staff attending the loco on 20/12/67 and started the A Engine. On starting B Engine it moved towards the closed shop doors and collided with them. Reverse was selected by the staff onboard in an attempt to stop the loco but it was too late to prevent the collision. The cause was found to be the A end transmission 'Back blading' when going into the direction selected. |
| 01/02/68 | Ex-T | 05/02/68 | 02/68 | LA | L/C | ? | A Transmission changed (output bearing seizing and fire damage) |
| 05/68 | Ex-T | 16/05/68 | 05/68 | LA | L/C | ? | A Transmission changed (No. 4 clutch defective) |
| 07/68 | Ex-T | 05/07/68 | 07/68 | LA | H/C | ? | A Transmission changed (No. 6 clutch ratcheting); B Transmission changed |
| 08/68 | Ex-T | 08/68 | 08/68 | LA | L/C | ? | A Transmission changed (heavy ratcheting) |
| 09/68 | Ex-T | 06/09/68 | 09/68 | NA | L/C | ? | A Engine Turbo blower changed |
| 11/68 | Ex-T | 13/11/68 | 11/68 | LA | L/C | ? | B Transmission changed (ratcheting in all gears) |
| 12/68 | Ex-T | 12/12/68 | 12/68 | LA | H/C | ? | A & B Engines changed |
| 31/12/68 | Ex-T | 01/01/69 | 17/01/69 | SW | U/C | 17 | A Transmission changed (oil leaks); B Transmission changed (damaged by a detached cardan shaft); A Bogie changed (worn bushes and laminated springs); B Bogie changed (damaged by a detached cardan shaft); Body repairs |
| 03/69 | Ex-T | 25/03/69 | 03/69 | LA | L/C | ? | A Transmission changed (excessive movement on the forward / reverse lever ) |
| 04/69 | Ex-T | 24/04/69 | 04/69 | NA | L/C | ? | B Engine Turbo blower changed |
| 06/69 | Ex-T | 06/06/69 | 06/69 | NA | L/C | ? | A end dynostarter changed (reported as noisy) |
| 11/09/69 | Ex-T | 11/09/69 | 11/09/69 | NA | L/C | 1 | Boiler changed |
| 20/09/69 | Ex-T | 20/09/69 | 22/09/69 | LA | L/C | 2 | B Transmission changed (output oil seals leaking) |
| 27/11/69 | Ex-T | 02/12/69 | 03/12/69 | LA | H/C | 6 | A & B Bogies changed |
| 17/07/70 | Ex-T | 17/07/70 | 20/07/70 | LA | L/C | 3 | B Bogie changed (inner final drive input bearing overheated) |
| 02/12/70 | NA | 04/12/70 | 04/03/71 | SW | Int | 93 | A & B Engines changed ; A & B Transmissions changed; A & B Bogies changed |
| 24/03/71 | Ex-T | 28/03/71 | 31/03/71 | LA | L/C | 7 | B Transmission changed (coming out of direction). |
| 01/06/71 | Ex-T | 01/06/71 | 03/06/71 | LA | L/C | 2 | B Transmission changed (governor defects) |
| 03/01/72 | LA | 04/01/72 | 10/01/72 | NA | L/C | 7 | B Transmission changed (reported trips and stress bolt broken) |
| 02/02/72 | Ex-T | 07/02/72 | 08/02/72 | LA | L/C | 6 | B Transmission changed (clutches seizing) |
| 19/04/72 | Ex-T | 20/04/72 | 21/04/72 | LA | L/C | 2 | Boiler changed |
| 25/08/72 | Ex-T | 25/08/72 | 27/08/72 | LA | L/C | 2 | B Transmission changed (overheating) |
| 01/11/72 | LA | | | | | | Withdrawn |

*Above*. D806 CAMBRIAN, then less than two weeks old, enters Bristol Temple Meads on 18 June 1959. It displays the first pattern of train reporting codes introduced in 1958 – train 204 was the Monday-Friday 'Bristolian', the 8.45am Paddington-Bristol. The new four digit headcodes came into use during early 1960. (www.rail-online.co.uk)

*Left*. 806 CAMBRIAN on 20 May 1972 at Plymouth North Road. At first sight it would appear to be a train to the Midlands but actually 806 is being removed from the 1M01 16.00 St Austell-Kensington Olympia 'Motorail', Class 47 1673 CYCLOPS taking the train forward. CAMBRIAN had worked down with the 08.10 off Olympia that morning through to St Austell. 806 retains its central lamp bracket but had lost its headboard clips, one of several combinations found within the first 13 locomotives when they had headcode boxes fitted. (www.rail-online.co.uk)

# D807 CARADOC

| Lot no./Works no. | 437 / - |
|---|---|
| **Significant dates and allocations** | |
| Into traffic – Laira | 24/06/59 |
| Newton Abbot | 08/67 |
| Laira | 06/68 |
| Newton Abbot | 05/71 |
| Laira | 01/72 |
| Withdrawn (Laira) | 26/09/72 |
| (Swindon) | 05/10/72 |
| Date cut-up | By 3/11/72 |

| **Modifications** | |
|---|---|
| 4 character train identification indicators fitted | 17/02/65 |
| Dual fitting of BR / WR A.W.S. | 06/11/67 |
| **Livery and insignia changes** | |
| Green | 24/06/59 |
| OHLW flashes | 09/12/61 |
| Yellow warning panels | 18/04/63 |
| Maroon | - |
| Blue full yellow ends – double insignia, serif, D-prefix | 06/11/67 |
| Blue full yellow ends – single insignia, sans serif , no D | 06/10/70 |
| **Recorded mileage** | 1,317,000 |

**Works visits and depot repairs**

| Stopped | At | On Works | Off Works | At | Type | Days | Work carried out |
|---|---|---|---|---|---|---|---|
| - | - | - | 24/06/59 | SW | D/A | | Delivery inspection and acceptance |
| 31/08/59 | Ex-T | 31/08/59 | 08/09/59 | SW | L/C | 8 | |
| 10/10/59 | Ex-T | 10/10/59 | 17/10/59 | SW | L/C | 7 | Shopped for an engine change |
| 17/11/59 | Ex-T | 17/11/59 | 01/12/59 | SW | L/C | 14 | |
| 08/04/60 | LA | 08/04/60 | 26/04/60 | SW | L/C | 18 | B Engine changed (fuel oil found in the sump) |
| 19/05/60 | Ex-T | 19/05/60 | 30/05/60 | SW | L/C | 11 | Shopped for bogie faults. |
| 10/06/60 | Ex-T | 10/06/60 | 10/06/60 | SW | Unsch | | Shopped for weighing |
| 30/06/60 | LA | 18/07/60 | 20/07/60 | SW | L/C | 20 | Shopped for bogie faults. |
| 04/03/61 | LA | 07/03/61 | 06/04/61 | SW | L/C | 33 | |
| 21/04/61 | LA | 21/04/61 | 05/05/61 | SW | Unsch | 14 | |
| 14/11/61 | LA | 14/11/61 | 09/12/61 | SW | H/C | 25 | |
| 15/03/62 | LA | 30/03/62 | 10/04/62 | SW | L/C | 26 | |
| 29/11/62 | Ex-T | 11/62 | 10/12/62 | LA | L/C | 11 | |
| 22/03/63 | Ex-T | 26/03/63 | 18/04/63 | SW | H/C | 26 | Headcode discs were to be replaced with four character train identification indicators but this did not take place |
| 04/06/63 | TN | 06/06/63 | 24/06/63 | SW | H/C | 20 | Shopped due to broken cardan shafts. |
| 06/07/63 | LA | 10/07/63 | 15/07/63 | SW | H/C | 9 | Shopped for bogie rectification work. |
| 23/08/63 | Ex-T | 08/63 | 02/09/63 | LA | L/C | 10 | |
| 11/02/64 | Ex-T | 11/02/64 | 12/02/64 | LA | L/C | 1 | A Bogie changed (suspected axle flaws); B Engine Turbo blower changed (oil seals leaking) |
| 21/04/64 | Ex-T | 21/04/64 | 22/04/64 | LA | L/C | 1 | Dynostarter changed |
| 02/12/64 | Ex-T | 02/12/64 | 17/02/65 | SW | Int | 77 | A Engine changed; A Transmission changed; A & B Bogies changed (worn tyres); Headcode discs replaced with four character train identification indicators |
| 07/65 | Ex-T | 12/07/65 | 07/65 | LA | L/C | ? | |
| 01/66 | Ex-T | 05/01/66 | 01/66 | LA | L/C | ? | A Bogie changed (worn tyres) |
| 01/66 | Ex-T | 31/01/66 | 02/66 | LA | L/C | ? | B Engine changed (cylinder liners leaking) |
| 19/07/66 | Ex-T | 19/07/66 | 21/07/66 | LA | L/C | 2 | A Engine changed; B Engine changed (oil throwing from the exhaust) |
| 08/66 | Ex-T | 31/08/66 | 09/66 | LA | L/C | ? | |
| 09/66 | Ex-T | 13/09/66 | 09/66 | LA | L/C | ? | A Transmission changed (directional clutches overheated) |
| 10/66 | Ex-T | 07/10/66 | 10/66 | LA | L/C | ? | |
| 03/67 | Ex-T | 23/03/67 | 03/67 | LA | L/C | ? | |
| 05/67 | Ex-T | 24/05/67 | 05/67 | LA | L/C | ? | |
| 08/67 | Ex-T | 15/08/67 | 08/67 | LA | L/C | ? | A Transmission changed (input shaft bearings overheated) |
| 10/10/67 | Ex-T | 10/10/67 | 06/11/67 | SW | U/C | 26 | A & B Bogies changed; body repairs; modifications |
| 05/68 | Ex-T | 01/05/68 | 05/68 | LA | H/C | ? | A & B Engines changed |
| 08/68 | Ex-T | 09/08/68 | 08/68 | LA | L/C | ? | B Transmission changed (broken belt inside the casing) |
| 23/09/68 | Ex-T | 23/09/68 | 30/09/68 | SW | Unsch | 7 | Main frame bracket platform broken |
| 09/05/69 | Ex-T | 12/05/69 | 23/05/69 | SW | Unsch | 14 | A Transmission changed (output oil seals leaking); Body repairs (derailment damage) |
| 08/69 | Ex-T | 26/08/69 | 08/69 | NA | L/C | ? | |
| 01/02/70 | Ex-T | 02/09/70 | 09/02/70 | LA | L/C | 8 | |
| 20/02/70 | Ex-T | 02/70 | 26/02/70 | LA | H/C | 6 | A Transmission changed (directional clutches seized) |
| 07/03/70 | Ex-T | 03/70 | 7/03/70 | LA | L/C | 10 | B Bogie changed (tyres moved) |
| 12/04/70 | Ex-T | 12/04/70 | 13/04/70 | LA | L/C | 1 | A Engine changed (overheating at Nos. 3 and 4 cylinder heads) |
| 30/06/70 | Ex-T | 01/07/70 | 06/10/70 | SW | Int | 97 | B Engine changed (coolant leaking from the No. 4 cylinder stud holes) |
| 13/03/71 | Ex-T | 13/03/71 | 16/03/71 | LA | L/C | 3 | |
| 01/04/71 | Ex-T | 01/04/71 | 05/04/71 | LA | L/C | 4 | |
| 23/04/71 | Ex-T | 23/04/71 | 29/04/71 | LA | L/C | 6 | B Transmission changed (not engaging in power) |
| 06/08/71 | Ex-T | 06/08/71 | 08/08/71 | LA | L/C | 2 | A Transmission changed (no control from No. 2 piston) |
| 14/10/71 | Ex-T | 14/10/71 | 19/10/71 | LA | L/C | 5 | B Engine changed (turbo blower fractured); A & B Bogies (tyres turned) |
| 16/11/71 | Ex-T | 11/71 | 29/11/71 | NA | L/C | 13 | B Transmission changed (output oil seals leaking) |
| 26/09/72 | | | | | | - | Withdrawn |

D807 CARADOC works an up express through West Drayton in July 1962. The locomotive is as introduced apart from the application of overhead live wire warning flashes. These started appearing on Warships from August 1961; D807 got them in December of that year. (www.rail-online.co.uk)

D807 CARADOC on 1 July 1967 passing the tower blocks at Vauxhall shortly after leaving Waterloo with the 1B43 11.00 Waterloo-Salisbury. By virtue of its early introduction and late survival, until September 1972, CARADOC held the distinction of recording the highest Warship mileage, over 1.3 million miles. (www.rail-online.co.uk)

# D808 CENTAUR

| Lot no./Works no. | 437 / - |
|---|---|
| **Significant dates and allocations** | |
| Into traffic - Laira | 08/07/59 |
| Newton Abbot | 08/67 |
| Laira | 09/68 |
| Newton Abbot | 05/71 |
| Withdrawn (Newton Abbot) | 03/10/71 |
| (Bristol St Philips Marsh Junction) | 20/10/71 |
| (Swindon) | 06/01/72 |
| Date cut-up | By 25/02/72 |

| **Modifications** | |
|---|---|
| 4 character train identification indicators fitted | 12/64 |
| Dual fitting of B.R. / W.R. A.W.S. | 12/67 |
| **Livery and insignia changes** | |
| Green | 08/07/59 |
| OHLW flashes | 30/09/61 |
| Yellow warning panels | 09/03/62 |
| Full yellow ends | 12/67 |
| Maroon | - |
| Blue full yellow ends – double insignia, sans serif, D-prefix | 07/68 |
| Blue full yellow ends – single insignia, sans serif , no D | 19/06/70 |
| **Recorded mileage** | 1,238,000 |

**Works visits and depot repairs**

| Stopped | At | On Works | Off Works | At | Type | Days | Work carried out |
|---|---|---|---|---|---|---|---|
| - | - | - | 08/07/59 | SW | D/A | | Delivery inspection and acceptance |
| 26/10/59 | Ex-T | 28/10/59 | 10/11/59 | SW | Unsch | 15 | B end Vapor-Watchman preheater changed |
| 03/60 | LA | 03/60 | 22/03/60 | SW | L/C | 15 | A.T.C. 'Shoe type' arm apparatus fitted (Experiment W/SW/L/172) |
| 10/05/60 | LA | 11/05/60 | 26/05/60 | SW | L/C | 16 | |
| 09/01/61 | LA | 10/01/61 | 23/01/61 | SW | L/C | 14 | |
| 29/04/61 | LA | 09/05/61 | 01/06/61 | SW | L/C | 33 | |
| 14/06/61 | LA | 23/06/61 | 29/06/61 | SW | Unsch | 15 | |
| 11/09/61 | LA | 19/09/61 | 30/09/61 | SW | L/C | 19 | |
| 13/01/62 | Ex-T | 15/01/62 | 19/01/62 | LA | L/C | 6 | |
| 23/02/62 | Ex-T | 01/03/62 | 09/03/62 | SW | L/C | 14 | A & B Bogies changed |
| 07/62 | Ex-T | 18/07/63 | 29/07/62 | LA | L/C | ? | Experiments W/SW/L/196,199,203 |
| 05/10/62 | LA | 09/10/62 | 26/10/62 | SW | H/C | 21 | B Bogie changed (final drive defects) |
| 27/12/62 | Ex-T | 01/63 | 15/01/63 | LA | H/C | 19 | |
| 28/02/63 | Ex-T | 03/63 | 05/03/63 | LA | L/C | 5 | |
| 20/05/63 | Ex-T | 20/05/63 | 23/05/63 | LA | L/C | 3 | Compressor changed ( valves blowing back) |
| 06/63 | Ex-T | 02/05/63 | 06/63 | LA | L/C | 3 | Exhauster changed (knocking badly) |
| 29/07/63 | LA | 31/07/63 | 21/08/63 | SW | H/C | 23 | A Engine changed (exhaust valves sticking); B Bogie changed (frame damaged) |
| 29/01/64 | Ex-T | 29/01/64 | 01/02/64 | LA | ? | 3 | |
| 10/64 | Ex-T | 24/10/64 | 10/64 | LA | ? | ? | B Bogie changed |
| 10/64 | LA | 10/64 | 12/64 | SW | L/C | ? | Engine changed; Headcode discs replaced with four character train identification indicators |
| 03/08/65 | Ex-T | 08/65 | 10/65 | SW | Class | ? | B Engine changed |
| 11/65 | Ex-T | 11/65 | 11/65 | ? | ? | ? | A Transmission changed (continually overheating) |
| 02/66 | Ex-T | 07/02/66 | 02/66 | ? | ? | ? | A Engine changed |
| 03/66 | Ex-T | 04/03/66 | 03/66 | LA | ? | ? | A Transmission changed (overheating) |
| 04/67 | Ex-T | 04/67 | 04/67 | ? | ? | ? | Boiler changed (fire damage) |
| 11/67 | Ex-T | 11/67 | 12/67 | SW | L/C | ? | A Engine changed; Dual fitting of B.R. / W.R. A.W.S. |
| 12/67 | Ex-T | 27/12/67 | 01/68 | LA | L/C | ? | B Transmission changed (fractured casing) |
| 04/68 | Ex-T | 04/68 | 04/68 | ? | ? | ? | A Transmission changed (unable to reverse) |
| ? | Ex-T | ? | 07/68 | SW | ? | ? | |
| 09/09/68 | Ex-T | 09/68 | 09/68 | ? | L/C | ? | B Bogie changed (input bearing to a final drive breaking up) |
| 02/69 | Ex-T | 02/69 | 02/69 | ? | ? | ? | B Engine changed |
| 05/69 | Ex-T | 05/69 | 05/69 | ? | ? | ? | Boiler changed |
| 10/69 | Ex-T | 10/69 | 10/69 | ? | ? | ? | A Transmission changed ( No. 4 baulk ring seized) |
| 01/70 | Ex-T | 01/70 | 01/70 | ? | ? | ? | B Transmission changed (No. 4 clutch worn) |
| 04/70 | Ex-T | 04/70 | 04/70 | ? | ? | ? | A Engine changed |
| 28/05/70 | Ex-T | 28/05/70 | 20/06/70 | ? | ? | ? | Bogie changed |
| 01/71 | Ex-T | 01/71 | 01/71 | ? | ? | ? | B Engine changed |
| 03/10/71 | | | | NA | - | | Withdrawn |

D808 CENTAUR arrives at Paddington with the 1A92 4.15pm Bristol-Paddington 'Bristolian' in the summer of 1960. D808 has its buffers painted silver which was an embellishment bestowed on a few of the class, usually in association with an open day or similar event. With its silver buffers, the ornate 'Bristolian' headboard and the old steam-style reporting numbers, CENTAUR really looks the part. (www.rail-online.co.uk)

D808 CENTAUR at Exeter St David's on 12 July 1969. Unusually, it had the TOPS information panel at the 'wrong' end, just behind the BR symbol. It also has white diamonds on the buffer beam which denotes it is fitted for multiple working, these fittings having been reinstated in 1968. (GW)

# D809 CHAMPION

| Lot no./Works no. | 437 / - |
|---|---|
| **Significant dates and allocations** | |
| Into traffic - Laira | 19/08/59 |
| Newton Abbot | 08/67 |
| Withdrawn (Old Oak Common) | 03/10/71 |
| (Laira) | 16/06/72 |
| (Bristol St Philips Marsh Junction) | 11/07/72 |
| (Swindon) | 29/08/72 |
| Date cut-up | By 06/10/72 |

| **Modifications** | |
|---|---|
| 4 character train identification indicators fitted | 24/02/64 |
| Multiple working jumper cables and sockets removed | 04/03/66 |
| Dual fitting of B.R. / W.R. A.W.S. | 08/03/68 |
| **Livery and insignia changes** | |
| Green | 19/08/59 |
| OHLW flashes | 04/10/61 |
| Yellow warning panels | 15/03/63 |
| Maroon yellow warning panels | 04/03/66 |
| Maroon full yellow ends | 08/03/68 |
| Blue | - |
| **Recorded mileage** | 1,135,000 |

**Works visits and depot repairs**

| Stopped | At | On Works | Off Works | At | Type | Days | Work carried out |
|---|---|---|---|---|---|---|---|
| - | - | - | 19/08/59 | SW | D/A | | Delivery inspection and acceptance |
| 22/10/59 | Ex-T | 22/10/59 | 04/11/59 | SW | Casual | 13 | B Engine repaired; A & B Bogies (All coil and laminated springs changed) |
| 04/01/60 | Ex-T | 04/01/60 | 08/01/60 | SW | ? | 4 | A & B Engines and Transmissions modified |
| 22/04/60 | Ex-T | 23/04/60 | 26/04/60 | SW | L/C | 4 | A Bogie (broken right and left hand inside laminated springs changed); A end Vapor-Watchman preheater changed |
| 04/05/60 | Ex-T | 04/05/60 | 06/05/60 | SW | U/C | 2 | Damaged right hand leading battery box door repaired |
| 23/05/60 | ? | 23/05/60 | 26/05/60 | SW | ? | 3 | A Engine repaired; A & B Bogies repaired |
| 31/05/60 | Ex-T | 31/05/60 | 03/06/60 | SW | Unsch | 3 | B Engine repaired (No. 3 cylinder head changed - leaking coolant) |
| 19/08/60 | Ex-T | 19/08/60 | 30/08/60 | SW | ? | 11 | A Engine modified; B engine (All cylinder heads changed due to leaking coolant and modification completed) |
| 08/11/60 | BS | 11/11/60 | 10/12/60 | SW | L/C | 32 | A & B Engines changed; A & B Transmission repaired; A & B Bogies repaired; collision damage to the A end front apron and nose section repaired; A end cab side collision damage repaired; A and B end Vapor-Watchman preheaters changed |
| 10/02/61 | Ex-T | 10/02/61 | 20/02/61 | SW | L/C | 10 | A & B Bogies removed (for reported rough riding; brake blocks changed and adjusted, tyres turned) |
| 28/02/61 | LA | 02/03/61 | 11/03/61 | SW | L/C | 11 | A Engine changed (coolant contamination); A & B Engines modification completed. |
| 31/05/61 | LA | 01/06/61 | 22/06/61 | SW | L/C | 22 | A & B Bogies repaired; Boiler changed (heavy scaling) |
| 20/09/61 | LA | 22/09/61 | 04/10/61 | SW | ? | 14 | B Engine (No. 6 cylinder head and turbo blower changed); A & B Bogies changed |
| 21/01/62 | Ex-T | 21/01/62 | 28/01/62 | LA | L/C | 7 | B Engine changed (No. 4 cylinder head fractured) |
| 25/02/63 | LA | 27/02/63 | 15/03/63 | SW | H/C | 18 | A Engine changed; A & B Bogies changed; Boiler changed; Engine to transmission cardan shafts and transmission to final drive cardan shafts changed; body to bogie side control linkage fitted |
| 15/03/63 | SW | 15/03/63 | 20/03/63 | SW | Unsch | 5 | A Engine repaired (No. 9 cylinder head and Nos. 7-12 cam box changed) |
| 05/63 | Ex-T | 22/05/63 | 05/63 | LA | Unsch | ? | Compressor changed (valves blowing) |
| 06/63 | Ex-T | 27/06/63 | 06/63 | LA | Unsch | ? | B exhauster changed (knocking badly) |
| 06/63 | Ex-T | 29/06/63 | 06/63 | LA | Unsch | ? | B exhauster changed (continually blowing fuses) |
| 25/07/63 | Ex-T | 25/07/63 | 03/08/63 | LA | H/C | 9 | A & B Engines changed; A Transmission changed |
| 10/63 | Ex-T | 03/10/63 | 10/63 | LA | Unsch | ? | B Engine (Turbo blower changed) |
| 19/10/63 | Ex-T | 19/10/63 | 28/10/63 | LA | H/C | 9 | B Transmission changed (casing damaged) |
| 09/01/64 | LA | 15/01/64 | 24/02/64 | SW | Casual | 46 | A & B Bogies changed; Headcode discs replaced with four character train identification indicators |
| 10/64 | Ex-T | 10/10/64 | 10/64 | LA | L/C | ? | B Engine changed (cylinder heads blowing) |
| 01/65 | Ex-T | 26/01/65 | 01/65 | LA | Unsch | ? | B Engine Turbo blower changed (noisy on run down) |
| 03/65 | Ex-T | 13/03/65 | 03/65 | LA | L/C | ? | A Engine changed |
| 25/03/65 | Ex-T | 26/03/65 | 03/65 | LA | L/C | ? | A Transmission changed (input shaft bearing from the dynostarter collapsed ); B Transmission changed |
| 04/65 | Ex-T | 30/04/65 | 04/65 | LA | L/C | ? | Boiler changed |
| 08/65 | Ex-T | 16/08/65 | 08/65 | LA | L/C | ? | B Engine changed (No. 12 cylinder liner fractured) |
| 22/12/65 | Ex-T | 31/12/65 | 04/03/66 | SW | Int | 72 | A & B Engines changed; A & B Bogies changed; Boiler changed; Modifications; Multiple working jumper cables and sockets removed from buffer beam |
| 03/66 | Ex-T | 31/03/66 | 03/66 | LA | L/C | ? | B Transmission changed (output oil seals leaking, oil emulsified by the presence of water and Nos. 1 and 2 dog clutches overheated and worn) |
| 06/66 | Ex-T | 01/06/66 | 06/66 | LA | L/C | ? | A Transmission changed (output oil seals leaking) |
| 19/07/66 | Ex-T | 19/07/66 | 22/07/66 | SW | Unsch | 3 | B Bogie changed (inner axle flaws) |
| 11/66 | Ex-T | 25/11/66 | 11/66 | LA | L/C | ? | A Engine changed |
| 01/67 | Ex-T | 16/01/67 | 01/67 | LA | L/C | ? | B Bogie changed (flaw trace at No. 2 groove) |
| 02/67 | Ex-T | 28/02/67 | 02/67 | NA | Unsch | ? | A end dynostarter changed |
| 05/67 | Ex-T | 14/05/67 | 05/67 | LA | L/C | ? | A Bogie changed (outer final drive gear wheel having a tooth missing) |
| 05/67 | Ex-T | 23/05/67 | 30/05/67 | LA | H/C | ? | A Transmission changed (output coupling flange holes elongated); B Transmission changed (failed on fitting - metal in filters); B Bogie changed (inner final drive input shaft sheared) |
| 06/67 | Ex-T | 11/06/67 | 06/67 | LA | L/C | ? | B Transmission changed (No. 2 clutch damaged) |
| 09/67 | Ex-T | 04/09/67 | 09/67 | NA | Unsch | ? | B Engine (Turbo blower changed) |
| 11/67 | Ex-T | 30/11/67 | 11/67 | LA | L/C | ? | B Engine changed |
| 12/67 | Ex-T | 12/12/67 | 12/67 | LA | L/C | ? | B Bogie changed (due to being fitted with N.B.L. Co. Axles) |
| 05/02/68 | Ex-T | 05/02/68 | 08/03/68 | SW | U/C | 32 | A Transmission changed (input oil seals leaking); Modifications; Body repairs |
| 09/68 | Ex-T | 09/09/68 | 09/68 | LA | L/C | ? | A Engine changed (fractured block) |
| 10/68 | Ex-T | 14/10/68 | 10/68 | NA | L/C | ? | B Transmission changed (fire damage with the gear train black and overheated) |
| 02/69 | Ex-T | 19/02/69 | 02/69 | LA | L/C | ? | B Transmission changed (input bearing running hot) |
| 05/69 | Ex-T | 02/05/69 | 05/69 | LA | L/C | ? | B Transmission changed (lift in the input bearing) |
| 05/69 | Ex-T | 16/05/69 | 05/69 | NA | Unsch | ? | A end dynostarter changed |
| 06/69 | Ex-T | 03/06/69 | 06/69 | NA | Unsch | ? | A Engine (Turbo blower changed) |
| 08/69 | Ex-T | 17/08/69 | 08/69 | NA | Unsch | ? | A Engine (Turbo blower changed) |
| 01/11/69 | Ex-T | 01/11/69 | 03/11/69 | LA | L/C | 2 | B Engine changed (venting coolant) |
| 03/02/70 | Ex-T | 03/02/70 | 05/02/70 | NA | L/C | 2 | B Transmission changed (overheating) |
| 20/02/70 | Ex-T | 20/02/70 | 22/02/70 | LA | L/C | 2 | B Bogie changed (thrust pad missing) |
| 04/70 | Ex-T | 02/04/70 | 04/70 | NA | Unsch | ? | A Engine (Turbo blower changed) |
| 05/70 | Ex-T | 01/05/70 | 05/70 | NA | Unsch | ? | Batteries changed (not holding a sufficient charge) |
| 05/70 | Ex-T | 14/05/70 | 05/70 | NA | Unsch | ? | A & B Engines (Turbo blower changed) |
| 06/70 | Ex-T | 05/06/70 | 06/70 | NA | Unsch | ? | B Engine (Turbo blower changed due to fractures,) |
| 07/70 | Ex-T | 07/07/70 | 07/70 | NA | Unsch | ? | B Engine (Turbo blower changed) |
| 18/08/70 | Ex-T | 08/70 | 26/08/70 | NA | L/C | 8 | Boiler changed |
| 03/09/70 | Ex-T | 03/09/70 | 09/09/70 | NA | L/C | 6 | A Transmission changed (ratcheting) |
| 04/11/70 | Ex-T | 04/11/70 | 05/11/70 | LA | L/C | 1 | A Engine changed |
| 12/02/71 | Ex-T | 12/02/71 | 13/02/71 | LA | L/C | 1 | A Bogie changed |
| 27/07/71 | Ex-T | 27/07/71 | 29/07/71 | LA | L/C | 2 | A Engine changed (loss of power) |
| 03/10/71 | OOC | | | | - | | Withdrawn (due to a broken bogie spring, failed at Waterloo for 1V09 to Exeter) |

D809 CHAMPION on 22 August 1959, when it was just three days into traffic. D809 is joined at Ranelagh Bridge stabling point by D807, a seasoned hand of exactly two months service. (RC Riley, www.transporttreasury.co.uk)

D809 CHAMPION, still in maroon livery, albeit with full yellow ends, takes the 1V17 17.00 Waterloo-Exeter out of the London terminus on 31 July 1971. This train was actually topped by D7040 from Salisbury through to Exeter; Warships and Hymeks in tandem were a fairly regular occurrence west of Salisbury. (PH Groom)

# D810 COCKADE

| Lot no./Works no. | 437 / - |
|---|---|
| **Significant dates and allocations** | |
| Into traffic - Laira | 16/09/59 |
| Newton Abbot | 08/67 |
| Laira | 01/72 |
| Withdrawn (Laira) | 04/12/72 |
| (Swindon) | 08/12/72 |
| Date cut-up | By 26/09/73 |

| **Modifications** | |
|---|---|
| 4 character train identification indicators fitted | 09/65 |
| B.R. A W S fitted | O1/68 |
| **Livery and insignia changes** | |
| Green | 16/09/59 |
| OHLW flashes | 08/11/61 |
| Yellow warning panels | 21/09/62 |
| Full yellow ends | By 06/01/68 |
| Maroon | - |
| Blue full yellow ends – single insignia, sans serif , no D | 06/04/70 |
| **Recorded mileage** | 1,308,000 |

**Works visits and depot repairs**

| Stopped | At | On Works | Off Works | At | Type | Days | Work carried out |
|---|---|---|---|---|---|---|---|
| - | - | - | 16/09/59 | SW | D/A | | Delivery inspection and acceptance |
| 20/04/60 | LA | 21/04/60 | 07/05/60 | SW | L/C | 17 | |
| 01/11/60 | Ex-T | 01/11/60 | 08/11/60 | SW | L/C | 7 | |
| 07/03/61 | LA | 10/03/61 | 05/04/61 | SW | ? | 29 | |
| 30/10/61 | Ex-T | 30/10/61 | 08/11/61 | SW | L/C | 9 | |
| 28/12/61 | LA | 02/01/62 | 12/01/62 | SW | L/C | 15 | Pipework repaired (severe frost damage) |
| 16/01/62 | Ex-T | 16/01/62 | 16/01/62 | LA | L/C | 1 | |
| 16/05/62 | Ex-T | 16/05/62 | 23/05/62 | LA | Unsch | 7 | B Engine Turbo blower changed (several turbine blades broken) |
| 03/09/62 | LA | 05/09/62 | 21/09/62 | SW | H/C | 18 | B Engine changed; B Transmission changed |
| 28/09/62 | LA | 05/10/62 | 16/10/62 | SW | H/C | 18 | |
| 10/01/63 | LA | 22/01/63 | 15/02/63 | SW | H/C | 36 | |
| 23/07/63 | Ex-T | 23/07/63 | 26/07/63 | LA | H/C | 3 | |
| 04/09/63 | LA | 09/09/63 | 26/09/63 | SW | H/C | 22 | |
| 10/64 | Ex-T | 26/10/64 | 01/65 | ? | ? | ? | B Transmission changed (brass particles in the filters) |
| 11/06/65 | Ex-T | 06/65 | 09/65 | SW | ? | ? | B Engine changed (turbo blower faults); Headcode discs replaced with four character train identification indicators |
| 09/66 | Ex-T | 09/66 | 09/66 | ? | ? | ? | B Bogie changed (frame damaged by a detached cardan shaft) |
| 04/67 | Ex-T | 04/67 | 04/67 | ? | ? | ? | Boiler changed |
| ? | Ex-T | | 01/68 | SW | Class | ? | Modifications |
| 04/68 | Ex-T | 04/68 | 04/68 | ? | ? | ? | Engine changed |
| 09/68 | Ex-T | 09/68 | 09/68 | ? | ? | ? | B Transmission changed (coming out of direction) |
| 11/68 | Ex-T | 18/11/68 | 11/68 | ? | ? | ? | B Engine changed air in the cooling system and overheating) |
| 01/69 | Ex-T | 01/69 | 01/69 | ? | ? | ? | Transmission changed (Nos. 7 and 8 gear wheels having broken teeth and Nos. 5 and 6 clutches having broken teeth) |
| 09/69 | Ex-T | 03/09/69 | 09/69 | NA | L/C | ? | A Transmission changed; B Transmission changed (coming out of direction) |
| 01/70 | Ex-T | 01/70 | 01/70 | LA | L/C | ? | A Transmission changed (reported as noisy) |
| 03/02/70 | Ex-T | 04/02/70 | 02/70 | NA | L/C | ? | A Transmission changed |
| 02/70 | NA | 02/70 | 06/04/70 | SW | ? | ? | Engine changed; A Transmission changed (overheating); B Transmission changed |
| 08/70 | Ex-T | 08/70 | 08/70 | ? | ? | ? | A Transmission changed (metal in filters) |
| 08/70 | Ex-T | 08/70 | 08/70 | ? | ? | ? | B Transmission changed (reversing arm seized) |
| 10/70 | Ex-T | 10/70 | 10/70 | ? | ? | ? | Engine changed (No. 3 cylinder liner damaged and the crank case fractured) |
| 04/71 | Ex-T | 04/71 | 04/71 | LA | ? | ? | A Transmission changed (outer ball race fractured) |
| 07/71 | Ex-T | 07/71 | 07/71 | ? | ? | ? | B Transmission changed (overheating and unable to reverse) |
| 12/10/71 | Ex-T | 12/10/71 | 17/10/71 | LA | ? | 5 | B Engine changed (crank case fractured) |
| 23/12/71 | Ex-T | 23/12/71 | 30/12/71 | NA | L/C | 7 | B Transmission changed (defective) |
| 05/01/72 | Ex-T | 05/01/72 | 05/01/72 | LA | L/C | 1 | B Bogie changed (frame fractures) |
| 04/05/72 | Ex-T | 04/05/72 | 07/05/72 | NA | L/C | 3 | Boiler removed |
| 04/12/72 | LA | | | | | - | Withdrawn |

D810 COCKADE keeps D817 FOXHOUND company at Old Oak Common on 5 June 1960. COCKADE was second only to D807 in the mileage stakes, also with a total of over 1.3 million miles. (PH Groom)

D810 COCKADE stands on one of the turntable roads at Old Oak Common on 22 June 1969. It was one of only two Warships to receive full yellow ends while still in green. However COCKADE was *the* green full yellow locomotive because the other one, D808 CENTAUR, only dabbled with the livery for around six months leaving D810 to soldier on as a novelty for nearly two years. (Alec Swain, www.transporttreasury.co.uk)

# D811 DARING

| Lot no./Works no. | 437 / - |
|---|---|
| **Significant dates and allocations** | |
| Into traffic - Laira | 14/10/59 |
| Newton Abbot | 08/67 |
| Withdrawn (Newton Abbot) | 02/01/72 |
| (Laira) | By 25/01/72 |
| (Swindon) | 12/09/72 |
| Date cut-up | By 13/10/72 |

| **Modifications** | |
|---|---|
| 4 character train identification indicators fitted | 11/03/64 |
| Dual fitting of B.R. / W.R. A.W.S | 30/08/67 |
| **Livery and insignia changes** | |
| Green | 14/10/59 |
| OHLW flashes | 20/10/61 |
| Yellow warning panels | 29/09/62 |
| Maroon yellow warning panels | 05/11/65 |
| Maroon full yellow ends | 30/08/67 |
| Blue full yellow ends – single insignia, sans serif , no D | 09/01/70 |
| **Recorded mileage** | 1,092,000 |

**Works visits and depot repairs**

| Stopped | At | On Works | Off Works | At | Type | Days | Work carried out |
|---|---|---|---|---|---|---|---|
| - | - | - | 14/10/59 | SW | D/A | | Delivery inspection and acceptance |
| 09/11/59 | Ex-T | 09/11/59 | 13/11/59 | SW | Unsch | 4 | A & B Bogies (examined and thrust pads reset); A end collision damage to cab exterior rectified |
| 09/12/59 | Ex-T | 09/12/59 | 16/12/59 | SW | Unsch | 7 | A Engine (all cylinder heads changed for modified heads) |
| 10/02/60 | LA | 10/02/60 | 16/02/60 | SW | Casual | 6 | A Engine (Turbo blower changed - defective top bearings); A & B Bogies (Tyres turned, brake gear checked and adjusted) |
| 28/03/60 | Ex-T | 28/03/60 | 01/04/60 | SW | Casual | 3 | B Bogie (One coil spring changed) |
| 13/05/60 | LA | 14/05/60 | 18/05/60 | SW | L/C | 5 | A Bogie (small frame fracture cut out and repaired, worn bushes replaced, brake hangers, cross stays and adjusters changed) |
| 29/06/60 | LA | 01/07/60 | 16/07/60 | SW | Unsch | 17 | A Engine (No. 12 cylinder exhaust valve stuck open and main lub. oil handle broken. All cylinder heads changed for 'stage 4' type) |
| 23/10/60 | LA | 24/10/60 | 08/11/60 | SW | L/C | 16 | A Engine (No. 8 cylinder head fractured); A & B Engines modified |
| 14/02/61 | Ex-T | 14/02/61 | 28/02/61 | SW | L/C | 14 | A Engine (Turbo blower changed - reported as noisy); A Bogie repaired; B Bogie repaired (flats on tyres and inner final drive gear box oil consumption reported as high. Broken inner axle spring changed, inner final drive checked and found satisfactory; brake blocks changed.) |
| 06/03/61 | LA | 15/03/61 | 25/03/61 | SW | L/C | 19 | B Bogie repaired (inner left hand axle box spring fractured. All coils springs changed) |
| 24/05/61 | Ex-T | 24/05/61 | 24/05/61 | SW | Unsch | 1 | |
| 19/07/61 | Ex-T | 19/07/61 | 31/07/61 | SW | Unsch | 12 | A Engine repaired (oil leaks from heat exchanger rectified); A Bogie changed (worn brake gear); B Bogie changed (worn brake gear and final drives using excessive amounts of oil – 90 pints on the inner drive and 104 pints on the outer in 40 days) |
| 09/10/61 | LA | 10/10/61 | 20/10/61 | SW | L/C | 11 | A Engine changed (No. 4 cylinder containing coolant); Boiler changed) |
| 01/01/62 | LA | 09/01/62 | 10/01/62 | SW | L/C | 9 | |
| 03/09/62 | NA | 13/09/62 | 26/09/62 | SW | H/C | 23 | A & B Bogies changed (worn tyre profiles); B end dynostarter cardan shaft changed, B end Vapor-Watchman preheater changed, transmission to final drive cardan shafts changed) |
| 07/10/62 | Ex-T | 10/62 | 20/10/62 | LA | L/C | 13 | B Transmission changed (excessive metal in filters) |
| 08/01/63 | OOC | 11/01/63 | 30/01/63 | LA | L/C | 22 | B Engine changed (No. 4 cylinder head fractured) |
| 30/08/63 | LA | 02/09/63 | 23/09/63 | SW | H/C | 24 | A Engine changed; A & B Bogies changed; Boiler changed |
| 16/10/63 | Ex-T | 10/63 | 25/10/63 | LA | L/C | 9 | B Transmission changed (not changing gear and output shaft to dynostarter seal leaking) |
| 16/01/64 | LA | 20/01/64 | 11/03/64 | SW | Unsch | 55 | A & B Transmissions changed; A & B Bogies changed; A and B end transmission heat exchangers changed; Headcode discs replaced with four character train identification indicators |
| 04/64 | Ex-T | 06/04/64 | 04/64 | LA | H/C | ? | A Engine changed (cracked cylinder liners) |
| 06/64 | Ex-T | 19/06/64 | 06/64 | LA | H/C | ? | A Transmission changed; B Transmission changed (output shaft oil seal leaking) |
| 16/07/64 | Ex-T | 16/07/64 | 24/07/64 | LA | L/C | 8 | B Transmission changed (output shaft oil seal leaking) |
| 17/08/64 | BS | 17/08/64 | 07/09/64 | SW | Unsch | 21 | A Bogie changed (inner final drive input bearing defective); B Bogie changed (hand brake defect); A & B end nose end foot-steps levelled, fracture in the A end over bogie structure welded, A & B end thrust pads reset |
| 17/12/64 | Ex-T | 17/12/64 | 18/12/64 | LA | L/C | 1 | B Engine changed |
| 26/08/65 | Ex-T | 31/08/65 | 05/11/65 | SW | Int | 70 | A Engine changed; A Bogie changed; B Bogie changed (inner final drive bearing defective); Modifications |
| 05/66 | Ex-T | 25/05/66 | 05/66 | LA | L/C | ? | B Engine changed (No. 3 cylinder head tappet broken off and the camshaft damaged) |
| 14/06/66 | Ex-T | 14/06/66 | 24/06/66 | LA | L/C | 10 | A Transmission changed |
| 08/66 | Ex-T | 25/08/66 | 08/66 | LA | L/C | ? | A Engine changed (No. 9 cylinder liner fractured) |
| 11/09/66 | Ex-T | 11/09/66 | 16/09/66 | LA | L/C | 5 | B Engine changed (fractured cylinder liner) |
| 11/04/67 | Ex-T | 04/67 | 20/04/67 | LA | L/C | 9 | B Bogie changed (tyres at scrapping size) |
| 03/08/67 | Ex-T | 07/08/67 | 30/08/67 | SW | Unsch | 26 | A Bogie changed; B Bogie changed (outer final drive input bearing overheated); Modifications; Body repairs; Dual fitting of B.R. / W.R. A.W.S |
| 09/67 | Ex-T | 05/09/67 | 09/67 | LA | L/C | ? | Boiler changed |
| 10/67 | Ex-T | 09/10/67 | 10/67 | NA | L/C | ? | Turbo blower changed |
| 09/68 | Ex-T | 23/09/68 | 09/68 | LA | H/C | ? | A & B Engines changed; A Transmission changed (internal oil pump defective) |
| 10/68 | Ex-T | 15/10/68 | 10/68 | LA | H/C | ? | A Transmission changed; B Transmission changed (overheating) |
| 02/69 | Ex-T | 19/02/69 | 02/69 | LA | L/C | ? | A Engine changed (losing coolant and oil leaking from behind the flywheel) |
| 05/69 | Ex-T | 09/05/69 | 05/69 | LA | L/C | ? | B Transmission changed (reversing solenoids being broken and metal in filters) |
| 08/69 | Ex-T | 01/08/69 | 08/69 | OOC | L/C | ? | A Bogie changed (final drive pinion broken) |
| 10/69 | Ex-T | 30/10/69 | 09/01/70 | SW | Int | 71 | A & B Engines changed; A & B Transmissions changed; A & B Bogies changed; Boiler changed; Modifications; All hoses and cardan shafts changed; exhausters and compressor changed and a new nameplate manufactured |
| 15/01/70 | Ex-T | 15/01/70 | 16/01/70 | LA | L/C | 1 | B Bogie changed (inner final drive cardan shaft broken and bogie frame damage) |
| 02/70 | Ex-T | 23/02/70 | 02/70 | NA | L/C | ? | A end dynostarter changed |
| 05/70 | Ex-T | 24/05/70 | 05/70 | NA | L/C | ? | B end dynostarter changed (holding down bolt holes in mounting feet worn) |
| 10/12/70 | Ex-T | 12/70 | 22/12/70 | NA | L/C | 12 | Boiler changed |
| 06/07/71 | Ex-T | 06/07/71 | 08/07/71 | LA | L/C | 2 | A Engine changed (low lub. oil pressure) |
| 17/09/71 | Ex-T | 17/09/71 | 18/09/71 | LA | L/C | 1 | Turbo blower changed |
| 02/01/72 | Ex-T | | | NA | - | | Withdrawn |

In 1960 D811 DARING runs into Bristol Temple Meads from the west past the old Bath Road steam shed which was replaced by the new diesel depot two years later. D811 was a Laira engine at this time and would remain so until its one and only re-allocation, to Newton Abbot, in August 1967. (www.rail-online.co.uk)

811 DARING enters Exeter St David's on 4 September 1971 with the 2B99 12.22 Barnstaple-Exeter. 811 had worked down from Salisbury in the morning and was co-opted to work the 09.23 to Barnstaple. However DARING was back on front-line work later in the day, on the 1O16 16.00 to Waterloo. (www.rail-online.co.uk)

# D812 ROYAL NAVAL RESERVE 1859 - 1959

| Lot no./Works no. | 437 / - |
|---|---|
| **Significant dates and allocations** | |
| Into traffic - Laira | 12/11/59 |
| Newton Abbot | 08/67 |
| Laira | 01/72 |
| Withdrawn (Laira) | 01/12/72 |
| (Swindon) | 08/12/72 |
| Date cut-up | By 04/07/73 |

| **Modifications** | |
|---|---|
| 4 character train identification indicators fitted | 27/01/64 |
| Dual fitting of B.R. / W.R. A.W.S | 09/04/68 |
| **Livery and insignia changes** | |
| Green | 12/11/59 |
| OHLW flashes | 22/02/63 |
| Yellow warning panels | 18/04/62 |
| Maroon yellow warning panels | 31/12/65 |
| Maroon full yellow ends | 09/04/68 |
| Blue full yellow ends – single insignia, sans serif , no D | 13/03/70 |
| **Recorded mileage** | 1,243,000 |

**Works visits and depot repairs**

| Stopped | At | On Works | Off Works | At | Type | Days | Work carried out |
|---|---|---|---|---|---|---|---|
| - | - | - | 12/11/59 | SW | D/A | | Delivery inspection and acceptance |
| 17/01/60 | Ex-T | 18/01/60 | 22/01/60 | SW | L/C | 5 | A & B bogies fitted with contact brackets; Boiler room roof section repaired |
| 22/03/60 | Ex-T | 22/03/60 | 01/04/60 | SW | Casual | 10 | A & B bogies tyres turned; A & B end dynostarter cardan shafts changed |
| 08/08/60 | LA | 10/08/60 | 22/08/60 | SW | Casual | 14 | B Engine changed (No. 6 piston, liner and con rod fractured and a fractured crank case) |
| 27/08/60 | LA | 31/08/60 | 08/09/60 | SW | L/C | 12 | A bogie changed (outer final drive bearing collapsed); B bogie changed |
| 07/10/60 | Ex-T | 07/10/60 | 13/10/60 | SW | Casual | 6 | A Engine changed (Fractured No. 6 cylinder head) |
| 10/12/60 | Ex-T | 10/12/60 | 16/12/60 | SW | Unsch | 6 | A Engine No. 12 cylinder head changed |
| 02/01/61 | OOC | 04/01/61 | 13/01/61 | SW | L/C | 11 | A Engine changed (coolant leaks) |
| 02/05/61 | Ex-T | 02/05/61 | 12/05/61 | SW | L/C | 10 | Boiler changed; A & B Engines fitted with Engine to idle modification; A & B end Vapor-Watchman preheaters changed; loco height checked due to reported as 'riding low' |
| 27/06/61 | Ex-T | 29/06/61 | 06/07/61 | SW | L/C | 9 | A Engine changed (No. 3 cylinder liner fractured) |
| 25/08/61 | LA | | 27/08/61 | ? | L/C | 2 | |
| 23/03/62 | BS | 06/04/62 | 18/04/62 | SW | L/C | 26 | A bogie changed (outer final drive input shaft bearing collapsed); B bogie changed; A & B end Vapor-Watchman preheaters changed |
| 13/10/62 | LA | 13/10/62 | 19/10/62 | LA | H/C | 6 | B Engine changed (fractured liner) |
| 18/12/62 | Ex-T | 27/12/62 | 09/01/63 | SW | H/C | 22 | A & B bogies changed (final drive oil seals leaking) |
| 07/02/63 | Ex-T | 11/02/63 | 22/02/63 | SW | H/C | 15 | A Engine changed (No. 4 cylinder liner fractured); Boiler changed |
| 10/06/63 | Ex-T | 10/06/63 | 13/06/63 | LA | L/C | 3 | B Transmission changed (suffering temperature trips and metal in filters) |
| 06/63 | Ex-T | 19/06/63 | 06/63 | LA | Unsch | ? | B end dynostarter changed |
| 02/12/63 | Ex-T | 06/12/63 | 27/01/64 | SW | Casual | 56 | A & B bogies changed; Headcode discs replaced with four character train identification indicators, B end engine to transmission and all transmission to final drive cardan shafts changed, fractured B end main frame welded and external body repaint |
| 02/64 | Ex-T | 25/02/64 | 02/64 | LA | Unsch | ? | B end dynostarter changed - armature shaft worn |
| 10/04/64 | Ex-T | 10/04/64 | 15/04/64 | LA | L/C | 5 | A Transmission changed; A engine removed (see below) |
| 10/04/64 | LA | 17/04/64 | 08/05/64 | SW | Unsch | 23 | A Engine changed (cylinder heads blowing badly on Nos. 7-12 bank); A & B bogies changed; Fractured A end engine room floor decking welded, transmission to final drive cardan shafts changed, A and B end engine room roof sections repaired |
| 08/64 | Ex-T | 21/08/64 | 08/64 | LA | L/C | ? | B Engine changed |
| 02/65 | Ex-T | 09/02/65 | 02/65 | LA | L/C | ? | A Engine changed (oil leaking from the crank shaft fly wheel, mounting found broken) |
| 07/65 | Ex-T | 12/07/65 | 07/65 | LA | L/C | ? | Boiler changed |
| 08/65 | Ex-T | 28/08/65 | 08/65 | LA | L/C | ? | A Engine changed (coolant in the No. 1 cylinder, liner fractures suspected) |
| 23/09/65 | Ex-T | 28/09/65 | 31/12/65 | SW | Int | 99 | A Engine changed (low lub. oil pressure); A & B bogies changed; Modifications; all hoses and cardan shafts changed, exhausters and compressor changed |
| 10/66 | Ex-T | 22/10/66 | 10/66 | LA | L/C | ? | B Engine changed (water pump idler gear bearing loose) |
| 11/66 | Ex-T | 23/11/66 | 11/66 | LA | L/C | ? | A Transmission changed (forward / reverse gear defective) |
| 01/67 | Ex-T | 26/01/67 | 01/67 | LA | L/C | ? | B Transmission changed |
| 20/02/67 | Ex-T | 21/02/67 | 23/02/67 | SW | Class | 3 | A & B bogies changed (traces on axles) |
| 07/67 | Ex-T | 04/07/67 | 07/67 | LA | L/C | ? | B Transmission changed (forward / reverse mechanism seized) |
| 11/67 | Ex-T | 11/11/67 | 11/67 | LA | H/C | ? | A Engine changed (low lub. oil pressure); B Transmission changed (ratcheting); Boiler changed |
| 05/03/68 | Ex-T | 08/03/68 | 09/04/68 | SW | U/C | 35 | A & B bogies repaired; Modifications; Dual fitting of B.R. / W.R. A.W.S |
| 16/09/68 | Ex-T | 17/09/68 | 11/10/68 | SW | Class | 25 | B Engine changed; A & B bogies changed (worn tyres) |
| 11/68 | Ex-T | 22/11/68 | 11/68 | NA | Unsch | ? | B Engine Turbo blower changed |
| 11/68 | Ex-T | 29/11/68 | 11/68 | NA | Unsch | ? | B Engine Turbo blower changed (leaking oil) |
| 02/69 | Ex-T | 14/02/69 | 02/69 | NA | Unsch | ? | B Engine Turbo blower changed |
| 02/69 | Ex-T | 21/02/69 | 02/69 | LA | L/C | ? | B Engine changed (No. 4 piston being damaged) |
| 26/08/69 | Ex-T | 08/69 | 14/09/69 | LA | H/C | 19 | A Engine changed (Nos. 1 and 7 bottom registers eroded); B Engine changed; Boiler changed |
| 10/69 | Ex-T | 24/10/69 | 10/69 | NA | Unsch | ? | A Engine Turbo blower changed |
| 12/69 | Ex-T | 17/12/69 | 12/69 | NA | Unsch | ? | A Engine Turbo blower changed |
| 08/01/70 | Ex-T | 12/01/70 | 13/03/70 | SW | Int | 64 | A & B Engine changed ; A Transmission changed ; B Transmission changed (damage caused by a detached cardan shaft); A bogie changed; B bogie changed (final drive universal joint fractured); all hoses and cardan shafts changed, exhausters and compressor changed and fire damage to left hand side paint work rectified |
| 04/70 | Ex-T | 02/04/70 | 04/70 | NA | Unsch | ? | B Engine Turbo blower changed |
| 06/05/70 | Ex-T | 06/05/70 | 08/05/70 | LA | L/C | 2 | B Transmission changed (defective gear train) |
| 11/05/70 | Ex-T | 11/05/70 | 14/05/70 | LA | L/C | 3 | A bogie changed (outer final drive coupling loose) |
| 16/10/70 | Ex-T | 16/10/70 | 17/10/70 | LA | L/C | 1 | B Engine changed (No. 5 piston crown smashed and No. 12 piston partially seized) |
| 01/04/71 | Ex-T | 01/04/71 | 02/04/71 | LA | L/C | 1 | B Transmission changed (not changing gear) |
| 14/05/71 | Ex-T | 14/05/71 | 18/05/71 | LA | L/C | 4 | B Transmission changed (ratcheting) |
| 08/09/71 | Ex-T | 08/09/71 | 10/09/71 | LA | L/C | 2 | B Transmission changed (metal in filters) |
| 07/10/71 | NA | 08/10/71 | 12/10/71 | LA | L/C | 5 | B Transmission changed (not changing gear) |
| 11/05/72 | Ex-T | 11/05/72 | 16/05/72 | LA | L/C | 5 | Boiler changed |
| 08/08/72 | Ex-T | 09/08/72 | 11/08/72 | LA | L/C | 3 | A Transmission changed (defective clutches) |
| 23/08/72 | Ex-T | 23/08/72 | 26/08/72 | LA | L/C | 3 | B Transmission repaired (not changing gear) |
| 02/09/72 | Ex-T | 02/09/72 | 05/09/72 | LA | L/C | 3 | B Transmission changed (metal in filters); A end dynostarter changed |
| 25/09/72 | Ex-T | 25/09/72 | 26/09/72 | LA | L/C | 1 | A Transmission changed (defective clutches) |
| 29/11/72 | Ex-T | | 01/12/72 | LA | | | B Transmission governor collapsed; Withdrawn |

D812 ROYAL NAVAL RESERVE 1859-1959 stands at Plymouth on 11 March 1961. D800 and D812 were the only two of the class not to carry a straightforward warship name, and the length of the plates meant the sub title WARSHIP CLASS could not be carried. Before the fitting of the headcode box it was common to see chalked reporting numbers on the front of the first thirteen D800s; unfortunately they often referred to the previous working or worse. (www.rail-online.co.uk)

812 ROYAL NAVAL RESERVE 1859-1959 on 4 September 1971 at Exeter St David's. 812 had worked the 1A24 10.25 Newquay-Paddington from Plymouth where it had relieved sister engine D815 DRUID. Locomotive changes at Plymouth were more of a hangover from steam age practice than a real necessity. The Crompton had worked in on the Brighton-Exeter, a turn which was booked for a pair of these locomotives for many years. (www.rail-online.co.uk)

# D813 DIADEM

| Lot no./Works no. | 437 / - |
|---|---|
| **Significant dates and allocations** | |
| Into traffic - Laira | 09/12/59 |
| Withdrawn (Newton Abbot) | 01/01/72 |
| (Laira) | By 23/06/72 |
| (Bristol St Philips Marsh Junction) | 11/07/72 |
| (Swindon) | 29/08/72 |
| Date cut-up | By 30/09/72 |

| **Modifications** | |
|---|---|
| **Livery and insignia changes** | |
| Green | 09/12/59 |
| OHLW flashes | 21/08/62 |
| Yellow warning panels | 10/04/63 |
| Maroon - yellow warning panels | 11/65 |
| Blue full yellow ends – double insignia, serif, D-prefix | 05/07/67 |
| Blue full yellow ends – single insignia, sans serif, no D | 28/11/69 |
| **Recorded mileage** | 1,099,000 |

**Works visits and depot repairs**

| Stopped | At | On Works | Off Works | At | Type | Days | Work carried out |
|---|---|---|---|---|---|---|---|
| - | - | - | 09/12/59 | SW | D/A | | Delivery inspection and acceptance |
| 01/60 | Ex-T | 01/61 | 01/60 | SW | L/C | ? | |
| 02/01/61 | Ex-T | 02/01/61 | 14/01/61 | SW | L/C | 12 | Bogie changed |
| 23/01/61 | OOC | 25/01/61 | 14/02/61 | SW | L/C | 22 | Bogie changed |
| 08/04/61 | LA | 11/04/61 | 26/04/61 | SW | L/C | 18 | |
| 06/12/61 | LA | 15/12/61 | 01/01/62 | SW | L/C | 26 | |
| 13/03/62 | Ex-T | 13/03/62 | 23/03/62 | LA | L/C | 10 | |
| 20/07/62 | Ex-T | 24/07/62 | 21/08/62 | SW | L/C | 28 | Boiler removed |
| 22/10/62 | Ex-T | 23/10/62 | 23/10/62 | LA | L/C | 1 | Tyres turned |
| 02/01/63 | LA | 13/01/63 | 10/04/63 | SW | H/C | 98 | Collision damage repaired |
| 22/07/63 | Ex-T | 22/07/63 | 31/07/63 | LA | H/C | 9 | |
| 03/12/63 | Ex-T | 03/12/63 | 08/12/63 | LA | H/C | 5 | |
| 10/12/63 | Ex-T | 10/12/63 | 12/12/63 | LA | H/C | 2 | A Engine changed (No. 5 cylinder liner fractured) |
| 03/02/64 | Ex-T | 03/02/64 | 03/02/64 | LA | Unsch | 1 | |
| 10/64 | Ex-T | 23/10/64 | 10/64 | ? | ? | ? | Boiler changed |
| 02/09/65 | Ex-T | 02/09/65 | 11/65 | SW | ? | ? | A & B Engines removed (unscheduled repair); A Bogie removed (an inner final drive bearing defect); B Bogie removed (3" fractures adjacent to the inner torque arm bracket); Boiler removed; Modifications |
| ? | Ex-T | ? | 05/66 | SW | ? | ? | |
| 03/67 | Ex-T | 03/67 | 03/67 | ? | ? | ? | A Transmission removed |
| 04/67 | Ex-T | 04/67 | 04/67 | ? | ? | ? | Boiler removed |
| 06/67 | Ex-T | 06/67 | 06/67 | ? | ? | ? | A Bogie removed ( 4cm trace at No. 1 groove outer axle); B Bogie removed |
| 06/67 | Ex-T | 07/06/67 | 05/07/67 | SW | Class | 28 | B Engine removed; A & B Bogies removed; Modifications; slight collision damage to A end right hand nose corner made good |
| 04/68 | Ex-T | 04/68 | 04/68 | ? | ? | ? | B Transmission removed (teeth broken off from the No. 4 baulk ring) |
| 05/68 | Ex-T | 05/68 | 05/68 | ? | ? | ? | A Engine removed |
| 11/68 | Ex-T | 20/11/68 | 11/68 | ? | ? | ? | A Transmission changed (reported as noisy and metal in filters); replacement failed on fitting (direction selector piston seized) |
| 12/68 | Ex-T | 16/12/68 | 12/68 | NA | ? | ? | A end dynostarter changed (going 'open circuit') |
| 12/68 | Ex-T | 12/68 | 12/68 | ? | ? | ? | A Transmission removed (ratcheting) |
| 04/69 | Ex-T | 04/69 | 04/69 | ? | ? | ? | Engine removed (No. 9 cylinder liner fractured) |
| 05/69 | Ex-T | 13/05/69 | 05/69 | NA | ? | ? | A Engine Turbo blower changed (leaking coolant) |
| ? | Ex-T | ? | 28/11/69 | ? | ? | ? | |
| 04/70 | Ex-T | 04/70 | 04/70 | NA | ? | ? | A Engine Turbo blower changed (oil leaking from a fractured casing) |
| 05/70 | Ex-T | 15/05/70 | 05/70 | ? | ? | ? | A Engine Turbo blower changed (oil leaks) |
| 08/70 | Ex-T | 08/70 | 08/70 | ? | ? | ? | A Transmission removed (convertor seizing and metal in filters) |
| 11/70 | Ex-T | 11/70 | 11/70 | ? | ? | ? | A Transmission removed (overheating) |
| 22/08/71 | Ex-T | 22/08/71 | 23/08/71 | LA | L/C | 1 | B Transmission changed (metal in filters); B end dynostarter changed |
| 03/09/71 | Ex-T | 03/09/71 | 06/09/71 | LA | L/C | 3 | B Transmission removed (baulk ring seized) |
| 01/01/72 | NA | | | | - | | Withdrawn |

D813 DIADEM in April 1962 at Bristol Temple Meads having just arrived with the 1A30 7.50am Taunton-Paddington. The train was booked to change locomotive here and D852 TENACIOUS waits on one of the through roads to take it forward. DIADEM was the first Warship to be introduced with headcode boxes already fitted. (www.rail-online.co.uk)

813 DIADEM on 11 March 1971 at Bristol Temple Meads carrying the final version of blue with sans serif numbers and a single double arrow symbol. 813 had also carried the earlier version with serif numbers and BR symbols on the cabs between July 1967 and November 1969. (www.rail-online.co.uk)

# D814 DRAGON

| Lot no./Works no. | 437 / - |
|---|---|
| **Significant dates and allocations** | |
| Into traffic - Laira | 01/01/60 |
| Newton Abbot | 08/67 |
| Laira | 06/68 |
| Newton Abbot | 03/70 |
| Withdrawn (Newton Abbot) | 01/01/72 |
| Reinstated – Laira (*officially 01/05/72*) | 20/03/72 |
| Stored (Bristol Bath Road) | 04/11/72 |
| Withdrawn (Laira) | 07/11/72 |
| (Swindon) | 12/12/72 |
| Date cut-up | By 20/02/74 |

| **Modifications** | |
|---|---|
| Dual fitting of B.R. / W.R. A.W.S | 25/08/67 |
| **Livery and insignia changes** | |
| Green | 01/01/60 |
| OHLW flashes | 06/10/61 |
| Yellow warning panels | 25/02/63 |
| Maroon | - |
| Blue full yellow ends – double insignia, serif, D-prefix | 25/08/67 |
| Blue full yellow ends – single insignia, sans serif, no D | 23/05/69 |
| **Recorded mileage** | 1,238,000 |

**Works visits and depot repairs**

| Stopped | At | On Works | Off Works | At | Type | Days | Work carried out |
|---|---|---|---|---|---|---|---|
| - | - | - | 01/01/60 | SW | D/A | | For record purposes this locomotive was considered as a 1959 built locomotive |
| 01/60 | Ex-T | 01/60 | 06/01/60 | SW | Unsch | | |
| 04/03/60 | Ex-T | 07/03/60 | 09/03/60 | SW | Unsch | 5 | A Engine repaired (Leaking No. 1 cylinder head core plug and governor servo piston spring changed); Boiler Spray head assembly changed |
| 25/06/60 | Ex-T | 28/06/60 | 30/06/60 | SW | L/C | 5 | A & B Bogies removed and examined for fractures following derailment damage; brake hangers changed |
| 27/07/60 | Ex-T | 27/07/60 | 27/07/60 | SW | Unsch | 1 | B Engine speed regulator motor changed |
| 08/08/60 | Ex-T | 10/08/60 | 17/08/60 | SW | Unsch | 9 | B Engine changed (worn valve guides) |
| 30/08/60 | LA | 01/09/60 | 13/09/60 | SW | Unsch | 14 | A Engine changed (cylinders and sump full of coolant, liners suspect) |
| 17/10/60 | LA | 18/10/60 | 20/10/60 | SW | L/C | 3 | A Bogie changed (inner final drive bevel wheel teeth and pinion teeth pitted) |
| 04/04/61 | LA | 06/04/61 | 19/04/61 | SW | L/C | 15 | A & B Engines modified; A & B Transmissions repaired; A & B Bogies repaired |
| 16/05/61 | Ex-T | 30/05/61 | 13/06/61 | SW | Casual | 28 | A Engine changed (rocker gear rusty); B Engine repaired |
| 17/06/61 | LA | 20/06/61 | 28/06/61 | SW | L/C | 11 | A Engine changed (No. 2 cylinder head leaking coolant) |
| 26/09/61 | Ex-T | 29/09/61 | 06/10/61 | SW | L/C | 10 | A Bogie removed, four coil springs and all brake blocks changed |
| 25/11/61 | NA | 11/12/61 | 15/12/61 | SW | L/C | 20 | A & B Engines modified; A Bogie changed (inner final drive pinion bearing collapsed); B Bogie changed (outer final drive input shaft and axle seals leaking) |
| 01/62 | Ex-T | 04/01/62 | 01/62 | LA | Unsch | ? | A Engine Turbo blower removed, repaired and re-fitted |
| 27/03/62 | BS | 29/03/62 | 02/04/62 | LA | L/C | 6 | B Engine changed (No. 5 cylinder head fractured) |
| 26/08/62 | BS | 27/08/62 | 05/09/62 | LA | H/C | 10 | A Transmission changed (metal in filters); B Transmission changed (dog clutch not engaging in 4th gear) |
| 05/12/62 | Ex-T | 05/12/62 | 5/12/62 | LA | L/C | 1 | |
| 05/02/63 | LA | 08/02/63 | 25/02/63 | SW | H/C | 20 | A Engine changed; B Engine changed (low lub. oil pressure); Boiler changed; Exhausters changed; compressor changed |
| 21/03/63 | Ex-T | 21/03/63 | 24/03/63 | LA | H/C | 3 | A Engine changed (piston and con rod damage) |
| 05/63 | Ex-T | 06/05/63 | 05/63 | LA | Unsch | ? | B Engine Turbo blower changed |
| 06/09/63 | BS | 09/09/63 | 18/09/63 | SW | H/C | 12 | B Transmission changed (Nos. 3 and 5 gears seized and multiple damage to teeth and bearings); A & B Bogies changed |
| 20/11/63 | LA | 22/11/63 | 13/12/63 | SW | H/C | 23 | A Engine changed (deep porosity of the crank case); A & B Bogies changed; Engine to transmission and inner final drive cardan shafts changed; A and B end Vapor-Watchman preheaters changed; B exhauster changed |
| 18/12/63 | Ex- | 18/12/63 | 19/12/63 | LA | H/C | 1 | |
| 03/64 | Ex-T | 28/03/64 | 03/64 | LA | Unsch | ? | A Engine Turbo blower changed |
| 04/64 | Ex-T | 22/04/64 | 04/64 | LA | Unsch | ? | B Engine Turbo blower changed (coolant leaking from the casing) |
| 04/11/64 | Ex-T | 12/11/64 | 11/02/65 | SW | Int | 98 | A & B Engines changed; A & B Transmissions changed; A & B Bogies changed; all hoses and cardan shafts changed; exhausters changed |
| 06/65 | Ex-T | 09/06/65 | 06/65 | NA | Unsch | ? | A end dynostarter changed (damaged coupling) |
| 30/07/65 | Ex-T | 06/08/65 | 08/65 | LA | L/C | ? | A Engine changed (No. 6 cylinder liner fractured) |
| 12/65 | Ex-T | 13/12/65 | 12/65 | LA | L/C | ? | B Bogie changed (outer final drive defective) |
| 01/66 | Ex-T | 18/01/66 | 01/66 | LA | L/C | ? | B Engine changed (exhaust cams worn) |
| 11/66 | Ex-T | 21/11/66 | 24/11/66 | SW | Class | ? | A & B Engines repaired; A & B Transmissions repaired (leaking input oil seals); A & B Bogies repaired |
| 03/67 | Ex-T | 01/03/67 | 03/67 | LA | H/C | ? | A Engine changed; A & B Transmissions changed |
| 03/67 | Ex-T | 16/03/67 | 03/67 | LA | L/C | ? | Boiler changed |
| 13/07/67 | Ex-T | 20/07/67 | 25/08/67 | SW | U/C | 51 | A Engine changed (reported knocking between Nos. 3 and 4 cylinders, low lub. oil pressure and the No. 5 crank pin journal damaged by a rod bearing failure); B Engine repaired (all cylinder heads changed and exhaust joints tightened); A & B Bogies changed; Modifications; Dual fitting of B.R. / W.R. A.W.S; A and B end dynostarters replaced |
| 12/67 | Ex-T | 22/12/67 | 12/67 | LA | L/C | ? | B Engine changed |
| 01/68 | Ex-T | 03/01/68 | 01/68 | LA | Unsch | ? | B Engine Turbo blower changed |
| 06/68 | Ex-T | 25/06/68 | 06/68 | NA | L/C | ? | Boiler changed (coil splitting and in generally poor condition) |
| 12/68 | Ex-T | 19/12/68 | 12/68 | NA | Unsch | ? | A end dynostarter changed |
| 02/69 | Ex-T | 20/02/69 | 02/69 | NA | Unsch | ? | B Engine Turbo blower changed |
| 04/69 | Ex-T | 09/04/69 | 23/05/69 | SW | Int | 44 | A Engine changed (several liners loose in the crank case); A Bogie changed; Fitting of TOPS data panels; all hoses and cardan shafts changed; exhausters and compressor changed |
| 13/11/69 | Ex-T | 13/11/69 | 15/11/69 | LA | L/C | 2 | B Transmission changed (ratcheting and not selecting gear) |
| 01/70 | Ex-T | 30/01/70 | 01/70 | LA | L/C | ? | Boiler changed (coil blocked) |
| 16/04/70 | Ex-T | 16/04/70 | 24/04/70 | LA | L/C | 8 | B Engine changed (coolant in the sump and No. 4 crank pin damaged) |
| 14/10/70 | Ex-T | 14/10/70 | 15/10/70 | LA | L/C | 1 | B Transmission changed (metal in filters) |
| 15/01/71 | Ex-T | 15/01/71 | 20/01/71 | LA | L/C | 5 | B Transmission changed (No. 4 clutch slipper piece worn) |
| 05/02/71 | Ex-T | 05/02/71 | 08/02/71 | LA | H/C | 3 | A Engine changed; B Transmission changed (input oil seals leaking) |
| 21/04/71 | Ex-T | 21/04/71 | 22/04/71 | LA | H/C | 1 | A & B Bogies changed |
| 08/06/71 | NA | 11/06/71 | 12/06/71 | LA | L/C | 4 | A Transmission changed (input shaft bearing collapsed and casing fractured) |
| 30/06/71 | Ex-T | 30/06/71 | 02/07/71 | LA | L/C | 2 | A Engine changed (No. 8 cylinder liner leaking) |
| 14/07/71 | Ex-T | 14/07/71 | 15/07/71 | LA | L/C | 1 | B Transmission changed (forward / reverse defects) |
| 17/07/71 | SB | 20/07/71 | 03/08/71 | LA | L/C | 17 | A Transmission changed (output sump detached) |
| 01/01/72 | NA | 16/03/72 | 25/03/72 | LA | | 84 | Withdrawn and then on 16/03/72 hauled from Newton Abbot to Laira with D825 and D829 for re-instatement to traffic |
| 02/05/72 | Ex-T | 02/05/72 | 04/05/72 | LA | L/C | 2 | A Transmission changed (overheating) |
| 21/06/72 | Ex-T | 21/06/72 | 23/06/72 | LA | L/C | 2 | A & B Bogies Tyres turned; B end dynostarter changed (reported vibrations) |
| 09/10/72 | Ex-T | 09/10/72 | 10/10/72 | LA | Unsch | 1 | A Engine Turbo blower changed |
| 07/11/72 | LA | 07/11/72 | | | - | | Withdrawn (A Engine Water pump defective and turbo blower defective) |

D814 DRAGON on 17 September 1960 at Exeter St David's with the 1.30pm Paddington-Penzance. The train was the 'Royal Duchy' but no headboard was being carried on this occasion. Although only introduced In January 1960 DRAGON had already received two replacement engines, the last one three days before this photograph. (www.rail-online.co.uk)

814 DRAGON on 22 May 1971 at Exeter St David's waiting to back down on to the 16.00 for Barnstaple. DRAGON worked two trips to Barnstaple that day, also working the 06.30. D814 is in its final livery, still with the multiple working equipment which was refitted for the double headed workings in 1968. It was withdrawn at the end of 1971 but was one of three Class 42s, along with 825 and 829, to be reinstated in March 1972, although officialdom regarded the date as 1 May, no doubt for 'statistical reasons'. (www.rail-online.co.uk)

# D815 DRUID

| Lot no./Works no. | 437 / - |
|---|---|
| **Significant dates and allocations** | |
| Into traffic - Laira | 20/01/60 |
| Newton Abbot | 08/67 |
| Stored (Newton Abbot) | 29/09/71 |
| Withdrawn (Newton Abbot) | 03/10/71 |
| (Bristol St Philips Marsh Junction) | 21/10/71 |
| (Laira) | 04/07/72 |
| (Bristol St Philips Marsh Junction) | 18/08/72 |
| (Swindon) | 22/08/72 |
| Date cut-up | By 13/10/72 |

| **Modifications** | |
|---|---|
| Multiple working jumper equipment removed | 23/08/66 |
| Dual fitting of B.R. / W.R. A.W.S. | 29/01/68 |
| **Livery and insignia changes** | |
| Green | 20/01/60 |
| OHLW flashes | By 04/62 |
| Yellow warning panels | 29/11/62 |
| Maroon yellow warning panels | 23/08/66 |
| Maroon full yellow ends | 29/01/68 |
| Blue | - |
| **Recorded mileage** | 1,087,000 |

**Works visits and depot repairs**

| Stopped | At | On Works | Off Works | At | Type | Days | Work carried out |
|---|---|---|---|---|---|---|---|
| - | - | - | 20/01/60 | SW | D/A | | Delivery inspection and acceptance |
| 03/60 | Ex-T | 26/03/60 | 05/04/60 | SW | L/C | ? | |
| 05/60 | Ex-T | 27/05/60 | 02/06/60 | SW | L/C | ? | |
| 04/08/60 | Ex-T | 04/08/60 | 04/08/60 | SW | Unsch | 1 | |
| 08/60 | Ex-T | 31/08/60 | 07/09/60 | SW | L/C | ? | Attention to engines |
| 01/61 | Ex-T | 11/01/61 | 19/01/61 | SW | L/C | ? | Attention to engines |
| 02/02/61 | LA | 06/02/61 | 17/02/61 | SW | L/C | 15 | |
| 02/05/61 | LA | 08/05/61 | 14/06/61 | SW | Int | 43 | |
| 16/06/61 | LA | 20/06/61 | 26/06/61 | SW | L/C | 10 | |
| 16/07/61 | Ex-T | 19/07/61 | 24/07/61 | SW | Unsch | 8 | Attention to exhausters |
| 08/61 | Ex-T | 18/08/61 | 22/08/61 | SW | L/C | ? | Attention to engines |
| 02/62 | Ex-T | 18/02/62 | 02/62 | LA | L/C | ? | B Engine Turbo blower changed |
| 19/05/62 | LA | 22/05/62 | 31/05/62 | SW | U/C | 12 | Attention to bogies |
| 15/06/62 | Ex-T | 15/06/62 | 16/06/62 | LA | L/C | 1 | |
| 07/62 | Ex-T | 19/07/62 | 07/62 | LA | Casual | ? | A Engine Turbo blower changed |
| 16/11/62 | LA | 19/11/62 | 29/11/62 | SW | H/C | 13 | Attention to transmissions; Attention to boiler |
| 10/12/62 | LA | 11/12/62 | 21/12/62 | SW | H/C | 11 | B Transmission changed (unable to reverse and metal in filter); B Bogie changed (main frame distorted after derailment damage) |
| 01/04/63 | Ex-T | 01/04/63 | 05/04/63 | LA | H/C | 4 | |
| 11/06/63 | LA | 13/06/63 | 02/07/63 | SW | H/C | 21 | B Transmission removed; Compressor changed |
| 11/01/64 | Ex-T | 01/64 | 05/02/64 | LA | ? | 25 | |
| 04/02/64 | Ex-T | 12/02/64 | 03/03/64 | SW | Unsch | 28 | A & B Bogies removed |
| 12/06/64 | Ex-T | 12/06/64 | 12/06/64 | ? | ? | 1 | |
| 09/64 | Ex-T | 01/10/64 | 29/10/64 | SW | Unsch | ? | A & B Bogies - attention to final drives |
| 08/65 | Ex-T | 08/65 | 08/65 | LA | L/C | ? | A Engine changed |
| 06/66 | Ex-T | 17/06/66 | 23/08/66 | SW | Class | 67 | Transmission removed; A Bogie removed; B Bogie removed (inner final drive bearing collapsed); Boiler removed; Modifications; Multiple working jumper cables and sockets removed from buffer beam |
| 02/67 | Ex-T | 23/02/67 | 02/67 | LA | ? | ? | A Transmission changed (excessive clearances on Nos. 3 & 4 clutches) |
| 10/67 | Ex-T | 10/67 | 10/67 | LA | L/C | ? | A Engine removed (outlet manifold exhaust joints overheating) |
| 01/68 | Ex-T | 04/01/68 | 29/01/68 | SW | Class | ? | B Engine changed; Boiler changed; Dual fitting of B.R. / W.R. A.W.S. |
| 03/68 | Ex-T | 28/03/68 | 03/68 | LA | ? | ? | A Transmission removed (not changing gear) |
| 02/08/68 | Ex-T | 02/08/68 | 03/08/68 | LA | ? | 1 | B Engine changed (No. 11 cylinder liner fractured) |
| 03/69 | Ex-T | 03/69 | 03/69 | LA | ? | ? | Transmission removed (lift on input shaft to dynostarter) |
| 21/11/69 | Ex-T | 21/11/69 | 22/11/69 | LA | Unsch | ? | Bogie removed |
| 16/03/70 | Ex-T | 16/03/70 | 18/03/70 | LA | L/C | 2 | Boiler removed (split coils, overheating and in generally poor condition) |
| 07/05/70 | Ex-T | 05/70 | 11/05/70 | LA | H/C | 4 | Engine removed; B Engine Turbo blower changed |
| 06/06/70 | Ex-T | 06/06/70 | 09/06/70 | LA | H/C | 3 | A & B Bogies changed (loose tyres) |
| 21/07/70 | Ex-T | 21/07/70 | 22/07/70 | LA | Unsch | 1 | A & B Bogies removed |
| 12/70 | Ex-T | 12/70 | 12/70 | LA | Unsch | 1 | A Bogie removed (outer input flange loose) |
| 30/01/71 | Ex-T | 30/01/71 | 01/02/71 | LA | H/C | 1 | B Transmission removed (output casing fractured); A Bogie removed (outer input flange damaged) |
| 22/05/71 | Ex-T | 22/05/71 | 24/05/71 | LA | L/C | 2 | B Engine changed (low lub. oil pressure) |
| 06/71 | Ex-T | 06/71 | 06/71 | LA | L/C | ? | B Engine changed (No. 11 cylinder liner fractured) |
| 03/10/71 | NA | | | | - | | Withdrawn |

D815 DRUID on 9 March 1961 watched by three well dressed platform enders runs into Paddington under the Bishops Bridge. The train is the 8.30am Plymouth-Paddington 'Mayflower'. It was to spend over 90 days stopped during this, its second year in traffic. (www.rail-online.co.uk)

D815 DRUID on 29 May 1971 takes the 1A45 12.18 Penzance-Paddington out of Exeter St David's. When taken out of service in October 1971 DRUID was one of four Warships to be withdrawn in maroon with full yellow ends, the others being D809, D817 and D838. (www.rail-online.co.uk)

# D816 ECLIPSE

| Lot no./Works no. | 437 / - |
|---|---|
| **Significant dates and allocations** | |
| Into traffic - Laira | 17/02/60 |
| Newton Abbot | 08/67 |
| Withdrawn (Newton Abbot) | 01/01/72 |
| (Laira) | By 23/06/72 |
| (Bristol St Philips Marsh Junction) | 18/08/72 |
| (Swindon) | 22/08/72 |
| Date cut-up | By 22/09/72 |

| **Modifications** | |
|---|---|
| Dual fitting of B.R. / W.R. A.W.S | 27/09/67 |
| Multiple Working jumper equipment re-fitted | 26/02/69 |
| **Livery and insignia changes** | |
| Green | 17/02/60 |
| OHLW flashes | 27/09/61 |
| Yellow warning panels | 23/02/62 |
| Maroon | - |
| Blue full yellow ends – double insignia, serif, D-prefix | 27/09/67 |
| Blue full yellow ends – single insignia, sans serif, no D | 26/02/69 |
| **Recorded mileage** | 1,144,000 |

## Works visits and depot repairs

| Stopped | At | On Works | Off Works | At | Type | Days | Work carried out |
|---|---|---|---|---|---|---|---|
| - | - | - | 17/02/60 | SW | D/A | | Delivery inspection and acceptance |
| 10/05/60 | LA | 10/05/60 | 25/05/60 | SW | L/C | 15 | A Engine changed; B Engine changed (No. 9 exhaust valve stuck open) |
| 29/11/60 | Ex-T | 29/11/60 | 05/12/60 | SW | U/C | 6 | A Engine Fractured No. 5 cylinder head changed; A & B Bogies Hangers, cross stays, brake adjusters and brake blocks changed. |
| 14/12/60 | OOC | 15/12/60 | 15/12/60 | SW | L/C | 8 | A Bogie removed, brake gear repaired; B Bogie (final drive oil seals leaking) |
| 25/03/61 | LA | 27/03/61 | 17/04/61 | SW | L/C | 23 | A Engine New coolant water pump fitted; B Engine Turbo blower changed; A Bogie right hand spring plates loose (all spring gear checked and adjusted); B end Vapor-Watchman preheater changed |
| 31/08/61 | LA | 01/09/61 | 27/09/61 | SW | L/C | 27 | B Engine changed (No. 8 cylinder head valves stuck open); B Transmission Input flange changed after trial run ( excessive end float, output flange examined); B Bogie changed (frame fractures) |
| 01/02/62 | BS | 02/02/62 | 23/02/62 | SW | L/C | 22 | A Engine changed (No. 3 cylinder head fractured); A Transmission changed (metal in filters) |
| 06/05/62 | Ex-T | 07/05/62 | 13/05/62 | LA | L/C | 7 | |
| 13/06/62 | SW | 18/06/62 | 21/06/62 | SW | H/C | 8 | A Bogie changed (thin tyres); B Bogie changed (left hand inner spring broken) |
| 28/03/63 | Ex-T | 28/03/63 | 29/03/63 | LA | L/C | 1 | |
| 09/04/63 | Ex-T | 09/04/63 | 16/04/63 | LA | H/C | 7 | A Transmission changed (not selecting direction) |
| 27/05/63 | Ex-T | 27/05/63 | 27/05/63 | LA | L/C | 1 | |
| 16/07/63 | Ex-T | 23/07/63 | 23/07/63 | LA | H/C | 7 | B Engine changed |
| 07/11/63 | Ex-T | 07/11/63 | 16/11/63 | LA | H/C | 9 | A Engine changed ; B Engine removed, failed on fitting, changed (Nos. 3 & 9 big ends knocking) |
| 04/12/63 | Ex-T | 04/12/63 | 09/12/63 | LA | H/C | 5 | A Engine changed (No. 1 cylinder liner fractured) |
| 02/02/64 | Ex-T | 02/04/64 | 06/02/64 | LA | H/C | 4 | A Engine Turbo blower changed (oil leaks) |
| 27/02/64 | Ex-T | 03/64 | 25/03/64 | LA | Unsch | 27 | Boiler changed (excessive temperatures recorded on dome and sealed tube of exhaust not correct); B end dynostarter removed |
| - | LA | 01/04/64 | 24/04/64 | SW | Unsch | 30 | A Bogie changed ; B Bogie changed (inner final drive suspected fault); Modifications; Bogie side control linkage replaced with hydraulic shock absorbers; fractures in over bogie structure repaired and thrust pads reset; B end dynostarter fitted |
| 09/05/64 | Ex-T | 09/05/6 | 09/05/64 | LA | Unsch | 1 | A exhauster changed (fractured sump) |
| 03/06/64 | Ex-T | 03/06/64 | 08/06/64 | LA | L/C | 5 | A Engine Turbo blower changed ) top casing fractured) |
| 10/06/64 | Ex-T | 10/06/64 | 13/06/64 | LA | ? | 3 | |
| 12/64 | Ex-T | 09/12/64 | 12/64 | LA | L/C | ? | B Engine Turbo blower changed ('blow through') |
| 10/03/65 | Ex-T | 10/03/65 | 19/03/65 | LA | Unsch | 9 | B Bogie changed |
| 10/03/65 | LA | 19/03/65 | 12/06/65 | SW | Int | 94 | A Engine changed (oil leaks from the crankshaft oil seals); B Engine changed; A Transmission changed (output oil seals leaking); B Transmission changed; A & B Bogies changed (axle flaws); Boiler changed; Modifications; Exhauster changed, compressor and heat exchangers fitted (missing on arrival); A & B end Vapor-Watchman preheaters changed; all hoses and cardan shafts changed; battery box door collision damage repaired |
| 03/66 | Ex-T | 14/03/66 | 03/66 | LA | H/C | ? | B Transmission changed (No. 3 gear wheal collapsed, No. 5 gear outer track broken and metal in filter) |
| 03/66 | Ex-T | 30/03/66 | 04/66 | LA | L/C | ? | A Engine changed |
| 06/66 | Ex-T | 07/06/66 | 06/66 | LA | L/C | ? | A Engine changed (No. 6 cylinder liner fractured) |
| 11/66 | Ex-T | 17/11/66 | 11/66 | LA | L/C | ? | B Transmission changed (metal in filters) |
| 12/12/66 | Ex-T | 13/12/66 | 12/66 | LA | H/C | ? | B Transmission changed (No. 4 clutch defective and metal in filters) |
| 06/02/67 | Ex-T | 07/02/67 | 02/67 | LA | L/C | ? | B Engine changed (a cam shaft gear damaged) |
| 04/67 | Ex-T | 10/04/67 | 04/67 | LA | H/C | ? | A Bogie changed; B Bogie changed (inner final drive defects) |
| 05/67 | Ex-T | 22/05/67 | 05/67 | LA | L/C | ? | Boiler changed |
| 17/08/67 | LA | 24/08/67 | 27/09/67 | SW | U/C | 41 | A Engine repaired (leaking fuel lines at Nos. 1-2, 9-10 & 11-12 cam box covers, all coolant hoses tightened and exhaust system relagged); B Bogie changed; Modifications; Dual fitting of B.R. / W.R. A.W.S. |
| 10/67 | Ex-T | 18/10/67 | 10/67 | NA | L/C | ? | B end dynostarter changed |
| 08/03/68 | Ex-T | 10/03/68 | 03/68 | LA | H/C | ? | B Bogie changed (reported heavy vibrations) |
| 05/68 | Ex-T | 10/05/68 | 05/68 | SW | L/C | ? | A Engine Turbo blower changed |
| 04/06/68 | Ex-T | 06/68 | 12/06/68 | LA | H/C | 8 | A Engine changed; B Transmission changed (forward / reverse mechanism defects and overheating) |
| 09/68 | Ex-T | 28/09/68 | 09/68 | NA | L/C | ? | Compressor changed |
| 12/68 | Ex-T | 31/12/68 | 01/69 | NA | L/C | ? | B Engine Turbo blower changed |
| 09/01/69 | Ex-T | 13/01/69 | 26/02/69 | SW | Int | 48 | B Engine changed; A Transmission changed; B Transmission changed (output shaft oil seals leaking); A Bogie changed; B Bogie changed (trace on the outer axle, fractured thrust pads, fractured inner laminated spring and side control rubbers torn); Modifications; all hoses and cardan shafts changed, exhausters and compressor changed; multiple working jumper cables and receptacles re-fitted |
| 03/69 | Ex-T | 26/03/69 | 03/69 | NA | L/C | ? | B Transmission changed (collapsed bearings on the oil pump drive) |
| 04/69 | Ex-T | 22/04/69 | 04/69 | NA | L/C | ? | B Engine Turbo blower changed |
| 04/69 | Ex-T | 28/04/69 | 04/69 | LA | L/C | ? | A Transmission changed (governor drive defective) |
| 05/69 | Ex-T | 15/05/69 | 05/69 | NA | L/C | ? | Boiler changed |
| 07/69 | Ex-T | 17/07/69 | 17/07/69 | LA | L/C | ? | A Engine changed (fractured cylinder heads) |
| 09/69 | Ex-T | 29/09/69 | 09/69 | NA | L/C | ? | A exhauster changed (noisy) |
| 10/69 | Ex-T | 20/10/69 | 10/69 | NA | L/C | ? | B Engine Turbo blower changed; Compressor changed |
| 02/12/69 | Ex-T | 02/12/69 | 03/12/69 | LA | H/C | ? | A Engine changed (No. 8 fork rod fractured causing the fracture of No. 2 blade rod) |
| 01/70 | Ex-T | 07/01/70 | 01/70 | NA | L/C | ? | A Engine Turbo blower changed |
| 01/04/70 | Ex-T | 01/04/70 | 03/04/70 | LA | H/C | 2 | A Transmission changed ; B Transmission changed (control piston seized ) |
| 23/11/70 | Ex-T | 23/11/70 | 24/11/70 | LA | H/C | 1 | A & B Bogies changed |
| 28/05/71 | Ex-T | 28/05/71 | 31/05/71 | LA | L/C | 3 | B Engine changed (hydraulicing) |
| 17/06/71 | Ex-T | 17/06/71 | 18/06/71 | LA | H/C | 2 | A Transmission changed (dynostarter shaft input casing fractured) |
| 01/12/71 | Ex-T | 16/12/71 | 31/12/71 | NA | L/C | 30 | D816 was stopped at 03.00 due to the A end dynostarter cardan shaft being defective, a bogie side pad defect and B.R. AWS receiver faults. B Transmission changed; released on 31/12/71 D816 went straight into store pending withdrawal |
| 01/01/72 | NA | | | | | | Withdrawn |

D816 ECLIPSE has just arrived at Bristol Temple Meads on 15 September 1960 with a class A working. This annotation was used for a short time in lieu of the full headcode. Unfortunately it didn't do much for identifying the specific working. (www.rail-online.co.uk)

816 ECLIPSE during its final summer in 1971 at Exeter St David's having just arrived with the 13.00 Waterloo-Exeter. This locomotive had its multiple working equipment refitted, complete with white diamonds on the buffer beam, during early 1969 but there is little evidence that it was put to practical use. (www.rail-online.co.uk)

# D817 FOXHOUND

| Lot no./Works no. | 437 / - |
|---|---|
| **Significant dates and allocations** | |
| Into traffic - Laira | 09/03/60 |
| Newton Abbot | 03/67 |
| Withdrawn (Old Oak Common) | 05/10/71 |
| (Swindon) | 15/12/71 |
| Date cut-up | By 10/03/72 |

| **Modifications** | |
|---|---|
| Multiple working jumper equipment removed | 09/66 |
| **Livery and insignia changes** | |
| Green | 09/03/60 |
| OHLW flashes | 14/12/61 |
| Yellow warning panels | 08/03/63 |
| Maroon yellow warning panels | 09/66 |
| Maroon full yellow ends | 12/67 |
| Blue | - |
| **Recorded mileage** | 1,078,000 |

**Works visits and depot repairs**

| Stopped | At | On Works | Off Works | At | Type | Days | Work carried out |
|---|---|---|---|---|---|---|---|
| - | - | - | 09/03/60 | SW | D/A | | Delivery inspection and acceptance |
| 17/03/60 | LA | 17/03/60 | 22/03/60 | SW | L/C | 5 | A.T.C. 'Shoe type' arm apparatus fitted |
| 20/10/60 | LA | 20/10/60 | 04/11/60 | SW | L/C | 15 | |
| 18/02/61 | LA | 22/02/61 | 03/03/61 | SW | L/C | 13 | |
| 07/03/61 | Ex-T | 07/03/61 | 17/03/61 | SW | ? | 10 | |
| 26/04/61 | LA | 28/04/61 | 11/05/61 | SW | L/C | 15 | |
| 21/05/61 | LA | 05/06/61 | 16/06/61 | SW | L/C | 26 | |
| 03/09/61 | LA | 11/09/61 | 22/09/61 | SW | Unsch | 19 | |
| 17/11/61 | LA | 21/11/61 | 14/12/61 | SW | L/C | 27 | |
| 16/01/62 | Ex-T | 16/01/62 | 18/01/62 | LA | Unsch | 2 | |
| 08/06/62 | Ex-T | 06/62 | 15/06/62 | LA | L/C | 7 | |
| 5/02/63 | Ex-T | 20/02/63 | 08/03/63 | SW | H/C | 21 | A & B Bogies changed |
| 04/63 | Ex-T | 07/04/63 | 04/63 | LA | Unsch | ? | Compressor changed (overheating) |
| 11/63 | Ex-T | 09/11/63 | 11/63 | LA | Unsch | ? | A Engine Turbo blower changed. |
| 07/01/64 | Ex-T | 07/01/64 | 28/01/64 | SW | Casual | 21 | A & B Bogies removed |
| 22/05/64 | Ex-T | 23/05/64 | 28/05/64 | LA | ? | 6 | Component change |
| 14/06/64 | Ex-T | 14/06/64 | 26/06/64 | ? | ? | 12 | Component change |
| 09/64 | Ex-T | 14/09/64 | 09/64 | LA | L/C | ? | B Transmission changed (No. 1 clutch defective) |
| 09/64 | Ex-T | 09/64 | 23/10/64 | SW | ? | ? | A & B Bogies changed; Boiler changed |
| 09/65 | Ex-T | 09/6 | 09/65 | ? | ? | ? | Engine removed for routine overhaul |
| 01/66 | Ex-T | 20/01/66 | 01/66 | ? | ? | ? | A Transmission removed (No. 3 clutch chipped and excess metal in filters) |
| 07/66 | Ex-T | 21/07/66 | 09/66 | SW | Int | ? | A Engine removed (heavy fuel leak under Nos. 2 and 3 cam boxes and bottom joint of turbo blower leaking lub. oil into the 'vee' of the engine); B Engine removed; A & B Bogies removed; Boiler removed; Modifications; Multiple working jumper cables and sockets removed from buffer beam |
| 09/67 | Ex-T | 13/09/67 | ? | SW | U/C | ? | A Transmission removed (seized); B Transmission changed (heavy metal in filters) |
| 11/67 | Ex-T | 11/67 | 11/67 | ? | ? | ? | B Transmission removed (metal in filters) |
| 03/68 | Ex-T | 03/68 | 03/68 | ? | ? | ? | B Transmission removed (overheating) |
| 06/68 | Ex-T | 22/06/68 | 06/68 | LA | L/C | ? | B Bogie changed (inner final drive bearing collapsed) |
| 05/69 | Ex-T | 06/05/69 | 05/69 | ? | ? | ? | A Engine Turbo blower changed |
| 10/69 | Ex-T | 10/69 | 10/69 | LA | ? | | B Bogie changed (fractures in the frame around the inner torque arm) |
| 03/70 | Ex-T | 12/03/70 | 03/70 | NA | Unsch | ? | B end dynostarter changed ( broken mounting foot) |
| 06/70 | Ex-T | 06/70 | 06/70 | LA | ? | ? | B Bogie removed ( inner final drive being seized) |
| 09/70 | Ex-T | 09/70 | 09/70 | ? | ? | ? | A Engine removed |
| 11/70 | Ex-T | 11/70 | 11/70 | ? | ? | ? | Boiler removed |
| 05/10/71 | Ex-T | | | | | | Withdrawn |

At Swindon Works D817 FOXHOUND is shown off at what appears to be an open day or large group visit. The date is 18 March 1960 and D817 had been released to traffic just over a week before, on the 9th. (www.rail-online.co.uk)

D817 FOXHOUND on the 31 July 1971 departs from Exeter St David's with the 16.00 for Waterloo; it will be back again the following day on the 11.08 off Waterloo after spending the night at Stewarts Lane. D817 was another of the class withdrawn in maroon with full yellow ends. (www.rail-online.co.uk)

# D818 GLORY

| Lot no./Works no. | 437 / - |
|---|---|
| **Significant dates and allocations** | |
| Into traffic - Laira | 30/03/60 |
| Newton Abbot | 03/67 |
| Laira | 01/72 |
| Withdrawn (Laira) | 31/10/72 |
| (Swindon) | 26/04/73 |
| Date cut-up | By 25/10/85 |

| **Modifications** | |
|---|---|
| Multiple working jumper equipment removed | 13/04/66 |
| Dual fitting of B.R. / W.R. A.W.S. | 08/06/67 |
| **Livery and insignia changes** | |
| Green | 30/03/60 |
| OHLW flashes | 03/10/61 |
| Yellow warning panels | 18/03/63 |
| Maroon | - |
| Blue full yellow ends – double insignia, serif, D-prefix | 08/06/67 |
| Blue full yellow ends – single insignia, sans serif , no D | 10/08/71 |
| **Recorded mileage** | 1,137,000 |

**Works visits and depot repairs**

| Stopped | At | On Works | Off Works | At | Type | Days | Work carried out |
|---|---|---|---|---|---|---|---|
| - | - | - | 30/03/60 | SW | D/A | | Delivery inspection and acceptance |
| 27/04/60 | Ex-T | 27/04/60 | 30/04/60 | SW | Unsch | 3 | |
| 26/06/60 | Ex-T | 26/09/60 | 30/09/60 | SW | L/C | 4 | A Engine changed (turbo blower blade broken and leaking coolant); A & B Bogies - brake hangers, cross stays and adjuster tightened |
| 03/11/60 | LA | 07/11/60 | 11/11/60 | SW | L/C | 8 | A & B Bogies removed and examined for fractures; Boiler changed (due to the number of items missing on arrival at shops, removed items 'robbed' for other locomotives) |
| 24/01/61 | Ex-T | 26/01/61 | 03/02/61 | SW | L/C | 10 | A & B Bogies changed (inner final drive oil seals leaking) |
| 12/02/61 | OOC | 15/02/61 | 27/02/61 | SW | L/C | 15 | B Engine changed (No. 5 cylinder liner leaking and turbo blower water jacket fractured) |
| 26/04/61 | Ex-T | 26/04/61 | 14/06/61 | SW | L/C | 49 | B Engine cooling water pump changed, experimental valve seals examined and No. 5 sleeve on No. 1 cylinder renewed; A Bogie removed ( hole in right hand outer tyre); B Bogie changed (left hand outer bearing axle seal leaking); Boiler changed |
| 11/08/61 | LA | 15/08/61 | 24/08/61 | SW | L/C | 13 | A Engine changed (coolant leaking from tell-tale holes of Nos. 7 to 12 cylinder heads); A & B end dynostarter cardan shafts replaced |
| 19/09/61 | LA | 19/09/61 | 03/10/61 | SW | L/C | 14 | B Engine changed (No. 11 cylinder exhaust valve stuck open); A & B Transmissions repaired; A Bogie changed; B Bogie repaired |
| 09/11/61 | LA | 14/11/61 | 20/11/61 | SW | L/C | 11 | A Bogie changed (loose tyres, right hand inner tyre inside surface of wheel bright and shiny markings (made by wheel turning against circlip or Gibson ring) |
| 01/01/62 | Ex-T | 01/62 | 08/01/62 | TN | Unsch | 7 | B Bogie changed (left hand inner axle box overheated); the replacement bogie was sent to Taunton from Swindon by 'Green Arrow' on wagon B.909052 on 03/01/62 and once the change was completed D818 was sent to Swindon |
| | TN | 09/01/62 | 10/01/62 | SW | L/C | 1 | |
| 28/03/62 | BS | 30/03/62 | 12/04/62 | SW | L/C | 15 | A Transmission changed (excessive metals particles in filters); A & B Bogies - brake blocks and adjusters changed |
| 02/05/62 | LA | 08/05/62 | 18/05/62 | SW | ? | 16 | A Transmission changed (overheating) |
| 24/02/63 | OOC | 28/02/63 | 18/03/63 | SW | H/C | 22 | A Engine changed (No. 3 cylinder liner fractured and coolant in the cylinder); B Engine Turbo blower changed; A & B Bogies changed; Boiler changed; body to bogie side control linkage fitted, one engine to transmission cardan shaft changed, all transmission to final drive cardan shafts changed |
| 16/09/63 | Ex-T | 16/09/63 | 18/09/63 | LA | H/C | 2 | A Engine changed; B exhauster changed |
| 11/63 | Ex-T | 18/11/63 | 11/63 | LA | Unsch | ? | A end dynostarter changed (going 'open circuit' on starter windings) |
| 10/12/63 | Ex-T | 10/12/63 | 13/12/63 | LA | H/C | 3 | A Engine changed (cracks in Nos. 7, 8 and 9 cylinder heads); A exhauster changed (earth on the exhauster motor) |
| 06/02/64 | LA | 07/02/64 | 06/03/64 | SW | Unsch | 29 | A Bogie removed (both axles fractured); B Bogie changed (outer axle fractured) |
| 04/64 | Ex-T | 10/04/64 | 04/64 | LA | Unsch | ? | Boiler changed (overheating) |
| 01/65 | Ex-T | 14/01/65 | 01/65 | LA | H/C | ? | A Engine changed; A Transmission changed; B Transmission changed (metal in filters) |
| 03/65 | Ex-T | 14/03/65 | 03/65 | LA | L/C | ? | B Engine changed |
| 24/05/65 | LA | 04/05/65 | 30/07/65 | SW | Int | 67 | A & B Engines changed; A Transmission changed; A Bogie changed (derailment damage); B Bogie changed; Modifications; twisted and damaged right hand side main frame and body support seating above A end bogie repaired; all hoses and cardan shafts changed; exhausters changed |
| 14/03/66 | Ex-T | 15/03/66 | 13/04/66 | SW | Unsch | 30 | A Engine changed (oil leaks); B Engine changed (change cooling water transmitter);Modifications; Multiple working jumper cables and sockets removed from buffer beam; A end right hand body main frame section repaired, |
| 06/66 | Ex-T | 28/07/66 | 06/66 | LA | L/C | ? | Boiler changed |
| 02/09/66 | Ex-T | 08/09/66 | 09/66 | LA | Unsch | ? | B Transmission changed (No. 5 gear wheel bearing collapsed, brass bushes fitted to No. 7 gear wheel broken up and teeth chipped and metal in filters) |
| 28/10/66 | Ex-T | 02/11/66 | 11/66 | LA | H/C | ? | B Engine changed; A Transmission changed (No. 5 shaft broken, bearings on No. 5 gear wheel collapsed, brass bushes fitted to No. 7 gear wheel broken up and teeth chipped) |
| 28/04/67 | Ex-T | 01/05/67 | 08/06/67 | SW | Class | 41 | A Engine changed; A Transmission changed (Nos. 5 and 6 dog clutches and flange ring teeth badly damaged with excessive metal particles in primary filters); A & Bogies changed; Modifications; Dual fitting of B.R. / W.R. A.W.S. |
| 07/67 | Ex-T | 20/07/67 | 07/67 | NA | L/C | ? | A end dynostarter changed (mountings out of true) |
| 08/67 | Ex-T | 01/08/67 | 08/67 | NA | L/C | ? | A end dynostarter changed |
| 09/67 | Ex-T | 04/09/67 | 09/67 | NA | Unsch | ? | B Transmission changed (overheating and oil leaks) |
| 10/67 | Ex-T | 01/10/67 | 10/67 | NA | L/C | ? | A Engine Turbo blower changed |
| 09/10/67 | Ex-T | 10/10/67 | 10/67 | LA | L/C | ? | B Transmission changed (overheating and an 8" steel pipe lost inside the casing) |
| 10/67 | Ex-T | 18/10/67 | 10/67 | NA | Unsch | ? | Batteries changed (life expired) |
| 02/68 | Ex-T | 13/02/68 | 02/68 | LA | L/C | ? | B Engine changed (No. 3 piston damaged) |
| 03/68 | Ex-T | 20/03/68 | 03/68 | NA | L/C | ? | B Engine Turbo blower changed |
| 07/68 | Ex-T | 16/07/68 | 07/68 | NA | L/C | ? | A Transmission changed (overheating and metal in filters) |
| 22/11/68 | Ex-T | 22/11/68 | 28/11/68 | NA | H/C | 6 | B Engine Turbo blower changed (oil joints leaking); A Transmission changed (heavy ratcheting on changing direction) |
| 03/69 | Ex-T | 14/03/69 | 03/69 | LA | H/C | ? | A Engine changed; A Transmission changed (ratcheting and gear selector stiff) |
| 05/69 | Ex-T | 08/05/69 | 05/69 | NA | L/C | ? | A Engine Turbo blower changed |
| 25/06/69 | Ex-T | 26/06/69 | 16/07/69 | SW | Class | 21 | A & B Engines - coolant flexible hoses tightened; A & B Bogies changed; damaged A end over bogie structure repaired |
| 20/01/70 | Ex-T | 20/01/70 | 25/01/70 | LA | H/C | 5 | B Engine changed; B Transmission changed (input oil seals leaking) |
| 14/05/70 | Ex-T | 14/05/70 | 14/05/70 | NA | Unsch | 1 | A Engine Turbo blower changed |
| 31/08/70 | Ex-T | 09/70 | 11/09/70 | LA | L/C | 11 | A Engine changed |
| 08/01/71 | Ex-T | 08/01/71 | 12/01/71 | LA | H/C | 4 | A Transmission changed (output oil seals leaking); A Bogie changed (frame damage caused by a detached cardan shaft); B Bogie changed |
| 15/01/71 | Ex-T | 15/01/71 | 16/01/71 | LA | L/C | 1 | B Engine changed (crank case fracture adjacent to No. 2 cylinder) |
| 21/01/71 | Ex-T | 21/01/71 | 24/01/71 | LA | L/C | 3 | B Transmission changed (overheating with gears and bearings 'blue') |
| 22/03/71 | Ex-T | 22/03/71 | 23/03/71 | LA | L/C | 1 | A Engine changed (No. 7 piston crown loose and bolt fractured) |
| 19/04/71 | Ex-T | 04/71 | 12/05/71 | LA | Unsch | 24 | A & B Engine Turbo blowers changed; A & B Transmissions changed |
| | LA | 18/05/71 | 10/08/71 | SW | Int | 83 | A & B Engines changed; A & B Transmissions changed; A & B Bogies changed (derailment damage); Modifications; fractured A end right side frame above pedestal bracket repaired, A & B end dynostarters replaced (originals missing on arrival); all pipe work and connections stripped and examined; exhausters and compressor changed; B engine fuel pump replaced (original missing on arrival); boiler room lining plates replaced due to distortion from heat, all hoses and cardan shafts changed; external repaint due to poor condition of paint work, flaking and peeled |
| 27/08/71 | Ex-T | 27/08/71 | 30/08/71 | LA | H/C | 3 | A Transmission changed (overheating and metal in filters) |
| 21/06/72 | Ex-T | 21/06/72 | 22/06/72 | LA | L/C | 1 | B Transmission changed (ratcheting) |
| 16/08/72 | Ex-T | 16/08/72 | 18/08/72 | LA | L/C | 2 | B Engine changed (no lub. oil pressure) |
| 31/10/72 | LA | | | | - | | Withdrawn due to the outer final drive pinion collapsed on A end bogie |

D818 GLORY on 30 July 1961 at Old Oak Common. The headcode indicates that it has worked up overnight from the West Country with the 7pm Penzance 'postal'. (Alec Swain, www.transporttreasury.co.uk)

818 GLORY at Bristol Bath Road on 21 October 1972 with just ten days left in traffic. It carried both variants of blue livery but missed out on maroon. GLORY's chief claim to fame was that it escaped the cutters torch until 1985 when it was finally disposed of at Swindon Works. (www.rail-online.co.uk)

# D819 GOLIATH

| | |
|---|---|
| Lot no./Works no. | 437 / - |
| **Significant dates and allocations** | |
| Into traffic - Laira | 25/04/60 |
| Newton Abbot | 03/67 |
| Laira | 06/68 |
| Newton Abbot | 03/70 |
| Withdrawn (Newton Abbot) | 01/10/71 |
| (Bristol St Philips Marsh Junction) | 20/10/71 |
| (Swindon) | 06/01/72 |
| Date cut-up | By 03/03/72 |

| | |
|---|---|
| **Modifications** | |
| Dual fitting of B.R. / W.R. A.W.S | 05/67 |
| **Livery and insignia changes** | |
| Green | 25/04/60 |
| OHLW flashes | 02/02/62 |
| Yellow warning panels | 23/05/63 |
| Maroon | - |
| Blue full yellow ends – double insignia, serif, D-prefix | 05/67 |
| Blue full yellow ends – double insignia, sans serif, D-prefix | 24/03/68 |
| **Recorded mileage** | 1,125,000 |

**Works visits and depot repairs**

| Stopped | At | On Works | Off Works | At | Type | Days | Work carried out |
|---|---|---|---|---|---|---|---|
| - | - | - | 25/04/60 | SW | D/A | | Delivery inspection and acceptance |
| 27/01/61 | LA | 01/02/61 | 15/02/61 | SW | L/C | 19 | |
| 06/61 | Ex-T | 05/06/61 | 12/07/61 | SW | H/C | 37 | |
| 09/01/62 | LA | 15/01/62 | 02/02/62 | SW | L/C | 24 | |
| 04/07/62 | Ex-T | 04/07/62 | 09/07/62 | LA | H/C | 5 | |
| 13/08/62 | Ex-T | 13/08/62 | 14/08/62 | TYS | L/C | 1 | |
| 29/04/63 | LA | 03/05/63 | 23/05/63 | SW | H/C | 24 | A & B Bogies changed; Modifications ;fractured dynostarter cardan shaft changed and damaged wiring replaced |
| 08/09/63 | Ex-T | 08/09/63 | 11/09/63 | LA | H/C | 3 | A Engine changed (No. 12 cylinder liner fractured) |
| 10/63 | Ex-T | 16/10/63 | 10/63 | LA | Unsch | ? | Compressor changed (noisy and overheating) |
| 26/11/63 | LA | 05/12/63 | 17/01/64 | SW | Casual | 52 | |
| 02/09/64 | Ex-T | 09/64 | ? | SW | ? | ? | Boiler removed; A end nose section compartment damage repaired |
| 06/65 | Ex-T | 06/65 | 06/65 | LA | ? | ? | A Engine changed |
| 09/65 | Ex-T | 09/65 | 09/65 | ? | ? | ? | B Engine changed |
| 02/66 | Ex-T | 02/66 | 02/66 | ? | ? | ? | Transmission removed (No. 4 dog clutch teeth broken) |
| 03/67 | Ex-T | 03/67 | 05/67 | SW | ? | ? | A & B Engines changed; Dual fitting of B.R. / W.R. A.W.S. |
| 01/68 | Ex-T | 02/01/68 | 01/68 | LA | Unsch | ? | A Transmission changed (not reversing and metal in filters) |
| 07/68 | Ex-T | 31/07/68 | 07/68 | ? | ? | ? | A Transmission removed (baulk ring seized) |
| 08/68 | Ex-T | 08/68 | 08/68 | ? | ? | ? | Transmission removed (heavy ratcheting and overheating) |
| 02/69 | Ex-T | 02/69 | 02/69 | ? | ? | ? | Boiler removed |
| 01/70 | Ex-T | 01/70 | 01/70 | ? | ? | ? | A & B Engines changed |
| 02/70 | Ex-T | 24/02/70 | 02/70 | ? | ? | ? | B Transmission removed ( forward / reverse faults) |
| 11/70 | Ex-T | 11/70 | 11/70 | ? | ? | ? | A Bogie removed; B Bogie removed (excessive wear on the outer torque arm pivot pin) |
| 04/71 | Ex-T | 04/71 | 04/71 | ? | ? | | A Transmission changed (metal in filters); B Transmission removed (oil leaking from the convertor tell-tale holes) |
| 01/10/71 | Ex-T | | | NA | - | | Withdrawn |

**D819 GOLIATH stands at Salisbury shed (photographs of them here are few and far between) on 16 May 1965. (www.rail-online.co.uk)**

**D819 GOLIATH on 9 October 1969 at Gloucester Central with a van train. GOLIATH was one of the first Warships in blue when released from Swindon in April 1967. Along with D857 it originally carried a much smaller BR symbol under the number. The livery pictured here with the standard symbol was carried by D819 from March 1968. (www.rail-online.co.uk)**

# D820 GRENVILLE

| Lot no./Works no. | 437 / - |
|---|---|
| **Significant dates and allocations** | |
| Into traffic - Laira | 04/05/60 |
| Newton Abbot | 03/63 |
| Laira | 06/65 |
| Newton Abbot | 03/67 |
| Laira | 01/72 |
| Withdrawn (Laira) | 01/11/72 |
| (Bristol St Philips Marsh Junction) | 08/12/72 |
| (Swindon) | 11/12/72 |
| Date cut-up | By 15/08/73 |

| **Modifications** | |
|---|---|
| Dual fitting of B.R. W.R. A.W.S. | 04/07/67 |
| **Livery and insignia changes** | |
| Green | 04/05/60 |
| OHLW flashes | 26/09/61 |
| Yellow warning panels | 29/01/62 |
| Maroon | - |
| Blue full yellow ends – double insignia, serif, D-prefix | 04/07/67 |
| Blue full yellow ends – double insignia, sans serif, D-prefix | 21/05/68 |
| Blue full yellow ends – single insignia, sans serif, no-D | 06/09/71 |
| **Recorded mileage** | 1,126,000 |

**Works visits and depot repairs**

| Stopped | At | On Works | Off Works | At | Type | Days | Work carried out |
|---|---|---|---|---|---|---|---|
| - | - | - | 04/05/60 | SW | D/A | | Delivery inspection and acceptance |
| 06/60 | Ex-T | 15/06/60 | 20/06/60 | SW | L/C | 5 | |
| 07/01/61 | LA | 09/01/61 | 01/02/61 | SW | L/C | 25 | |
| 02/61 | Ex-T | 17/02/61 | 08/03/61 | SW | L/C | 19 | |
| 01/05/61 | LA | 04/05/61 | 17/05/61 | SW | L/C | 16 | |
| 31/08/61 | LA | 15/09/61 | 26/09/61 | SW | U/C | 26 | |
| 23/10/61 | LA | 24/10/61 | 02/11/61 | SW | L/C | 10 | |
| 15/01/62 | LA | 15/01/62 | 29/01/62 | SW | L/C | 14 | |
| 14/08/62 | LA | 15/08/62 | 22/08/62 | SW | L/C | 8 | |
| 24/11/62 | Ex-T | 24/11/62 | 06/12/62 | LA | H/C | 12 | |
| 01/07/63 | Ex-T | 01/07/63 | 15/07/63 | LA | H/C | 14 | Boiler changed (super heating and burnt coils) |
| 28/09/63 | Ex-T | 28/09/63 | 29/09/63 | LA | L/C | 1 | |
| 22/11/63 | Ex-T | 22/11/63 | 24/11/63 | LA | H/C | 2 | A Bogie changed |
| 18/02/64 | NA | 25/02/64 | 17/03/64 | SW | Unsch | 28 | |
| 07/07/64 | Ex-T | 07/07/64 | 17/07/64 | BS | Unsch | 10 | |
| 12/64 | Ex-T | 12/64 | 12/64 | ? | ? | ? | A transmission removed |
| 05/65 | Ex-T | 20/05/65 | 05/65 | LA | ? | ? | A transmission changed (having casing bolts sheared) |
| 11/65 | Ex-T | 11/65 | 11/65 | ? | ? | ? | Engine removed ( crank case fractures) |
| 11/05/67 | Ex-T | 14/05/67 | 15/05/67 | LA | ? | ? | B Engine changed |
| 11/05/67 | Ex-T | 15/05/67 | 04/07/67 | SW | Class | 54 | A Engine changed (crank case fractures); B Engine (fractured No. 5 cylinder liner); A & B Bogies removed; Modifications; Dual fitting of B.R. W.R. A.W.S.; Compressor changed; B dynostarter changed |
| 08/67 | Ex-T | 08/67 | 08/67 | ? | ? | ? | A Engine removed (No. 1 cylinder liner fractured) |
| ? | Ex-T | ? | 21/05/68 | SW | ? | ? | |
| 07/68 | Ex-T | 16/07/68 | 07/68 | LA | L/C | ? | B Bogie changed (outer final drive input bearing broken up) |
| 02/69 | Ex-T | 02/69 | 02/69 | ? | ? | ? | B Transmission removed (output oil seals leaking) |
| 03/69 | Ex-T | 03/69 | 03/69 | ? | ? | ? | A Bogie removed (final drive oil seals leaking) |
| 10/69 | Ex-T | 10/69 | 10/69 | ? | ? | ? | A Transmission removed (overheating in 3rd convertor) |
| 11/69 | Ex-T | 11/69 | 11/69 | ? | ? | ? | Transmission removed |
| 10/70 | Ex-T | 20/10/70 | 10/70 | ? | ? | ? | A Transmission removed (not selecting reverse) |
| 02/71 | Ex-T | 02/71 | 02/71 | ? | ? | ? | B Bogie removed |
| 03/71 | Ex-T | 05/03/71 | 03/71 | ? | ? | ? | A Engine removed (defective cam boxes and the No. 1 bottom register eroded) |
| 26/03/71 | Ex-T | 01/04/71 | 06/09/71 | SW | Int | 162 | Engine removed (fire damage); A Transmission removed; A Bogie removed (worn brake hangers and laminated springs) |
| 30/09/71 | Ex-T | | 07/10/71 | NA | ? | 7 | B Transmission changed |
| 08/05/72 | Ex-T | 08/05/72 | 09/05/72 | LA | ? | 1 | A Engine Turbo blower changed |
| 20/07/72 | Ex-T | 20/07/72 | 23/07/72 | LA | ? | 3 | B Engine Turbo blower changed |
| 09/07/72 | Ex-T | 09/07/72 | 14/07/72 | LA | L/C | 5 | Boiler inoperable (split coils) |
| 04/10/72 | Ex-T | 04/10/72 | 07/10/72 | LA | L/C | 3 | |
| 01/11/72 | Ex-T | | | | - | | Withdrawn |

A wet day at Bristol in 1961 as D820 GRENVILLE draws forward from its stock after bringing in the 1B02 8.45am Paddington-Bristol 'Bristolian'. Steam was very much the norm at this time and these gleaming green diesels must have looked very odd to those brought up with the (G)WR. (www.rail-online.co.uk)

820 GRENVILLE stands at Exeter Central with the 17.37 Exeter-Waterloo Bank Holiday Relief on 29 May 1972. Warships had been replaced on the line the previous October by the less powerful BRCW Type 3s so this working would have been of special interest. GRENVILLE worked back the following day on the 1V17 17.05 Waterloo-Exeter. It was one of the few to carry all three variants of the rail blue livery; this was the final one, applied in September 1971. (Andy Bevington)

# D821 GREYHOUND

| Lot no./Works no. | 437 / - |
|---|---|
| **Significant dates and allocations** | |
| Into traffic - Laira | 25/05/60 |
| Newton Abbot | 03/67 |
| Laira | 03/70 |
| Newton Abbot | 10/71 |
| Laira | 01/72 |
| Withdrawn (Laira) | 04/12/72 |
| Preserved (Didcot Railway Centre) | 25/05/73 |

| **Modifications** | |
|---|---|
| Multiple working equipment removed | 06/05/66 |
| Dual fitting of B.R. / W.R. A.W.S. | 11/01/68 |
| **Livery and insignia changes** | |
| Green | 25/05/60 |
| OHLW flashes | 04/10/61 |
| Yellow warning panels | 07/02/64 |
| Maroon yellow warning panels | 06/05/66 |
| Blue full yellow ends – double insignia, serif, D-prefix | 11/01/68 |
| Blue full yellow ends – single insignia, sans serif, no D | 18/08/71 |
| **Recorded mileage** | 1,088,000 |

**Works visits and depot repairs**

| Stopped | At | On Works | Off Works | At | Type | Days | Work carried out |
|---|---|---|---|---|---|---|---|
| - | - | - | 25/05/60 | SW | D/A | | Delivery inspection and acceptance |
| 15/07/60 | Ex-T | 19/07/60 | 21/07/60 | SW | Casual | 6 | Collision damage repairs to A end (front headstock apron bent back approx. 12", steam heating pipe and cock broken off, left hand buffer step bent, right hand jumper cable elbow fractured, right hand through air pipe fractured, straight air pipe outlet broken, jumper receptacle broken off and both air warning horns damaged) |
| 07/08/60 | LA | 09/08/60 | 12/08/60 | SW | Casual | 5 | A Engine (all cylinder heads changed, No. 5 exhaust valve reported stuck open) ; A & B Engines modification completed |
| 21/09/60 | Ex-T | 22/09/60 | 29/09/60 | SW | L/C | 8 | B Engine changed (No. 5 exhaust valve stuck open); A Bogie removed for examination and one inner laminated spring changed ; B Bogie removed for examination and side control linkage changed |
| 01/12/60 | Ex-T | 01/12/60 | 07/12/60 | SW | L/C | 6 | A Engine (cam blocks removed, checked and replaced, No. 12 cylinder head changed, all tappet clearances checked, lub. oil changed and filters serviced) |
| 17/04/61 | Ex-T | 17/04/61 | 03/05/61 | SW | L/C | 16 | A & B Engines modification completed; A Transmission repaired (Output shaft oil seals renewed and oil changed); B end engine fuel pump changed |
| 14/08/61 | Ex-T | 14/08/61 | 04/10/61 | SW | L/C | 51 | A & B Engines changed; A & B Transmissions (Primary and secondary filters cleaned and examined for brass swarf);Boiler changed |
| 04/07/62 | BS | 10/07/62 | 14/07/62 | SW | H/C | 10 | A Bogie changed; B Bogie removed inner and outer final drive oil seals leaking) |
| 23/08/62 | Ex-T | 08/62 | 31/08/62 | LA | H/C | 8 | A Engine changed; B Engine (No. 6 cylinder liner fractured and coolant in sump) |
| 26/03/63 | Ex-T | 26/03/63 | 26/03/63 | SW | Unsch | 1 | |
| 03/04/63 | Ex-T | 03/04/63 | 06/04/63 | LA | H/C | 3 | |
| 10/04/63 | Ex-T | 10/04/63 | 12/04/63 | LA | H/C | 2 | A Engine changed (No. 5 cylinder liner fractured) |
| 17/05/63 | Ex-T | 17/05/63 | 21/05/63 | LA | H/C | 4 | A Transmission changed (metal in filters) |
| 17/09/63 | Ex-T | 17/09/63 | 17/09/63 | LA | L/C | 1 | B Engine Turbo blower changed (oil leaks from top casing) |
| 20/10/63 | Ex-T | 10/63 | 29/10/63 | LA | H/C | 9 | A Engine changed |
| 15/01/64 | LA | 16/01/64 | 12/02/64 | SW | Unsch | 28 | A & B Bogies changed; Boiler changed; Modifications |
| 13/02/64 | Ex-T | 02/64 | 24/02/64 | LA | H/C | 11 | A Engine changed (No. 10 cylinder liner fractured) |
| 26/02/64 | Ex-T | 26/02/64 | 02/64 | LA | H/C | ? | A Engine changed (No. 5 cylinder liner fractured ) |
| 07/09/64 | Ex-T | 08/09/64 | 09/64 | LA | L/C | ? | A Transmission changed (forward / reverse clutch defective) |
| 04/11/64 | Ex-T | 05/11/64 | 11/64 | LA | H/C | ? | B Engine changed; B Transmission changed (unable to select direction) |
| 08/65 | Ex-T | 08/65 | 08/65 | LA | L/C | ? | B Engine changed |
| 09/09/65 | Ex-T | 09/09/65 | 23/09/65 | LA | H/C | 14 | A Engine changed; A Bogie changed (outer final drive input bearing collapsed); replacement failed on fitting (outer final drive defective with excessive metal particles found in the sump) |
| 04/03/66 | Ex-T | 09/03/66 | 06/05/66 | SW | Int | 63 | B Engine changed (oil spraying from engine flywheel); A Transmission changed (double row bearing fitted to No. 3 gear wheel collapsed, roller bearings fitted to Nos. 4 and 5 gear wheels having fractured outer tracks and steel and brass debris in filters); B Transmission changed (No. 8 gearwheel, intermediate and output gear wheels having broken teeth and aluminium particles in filters); Boiler changed; Modifications; Multiple working jumper cables and sockets removed from buffer beam; all hoses and cardan shafts changed, exhausters and compressor changed |
| 06/66 | Ex-T | 03/06/66 | 06/66 | NA | Unsch | ? | A end dynostarter removed (shorting out) |
| 06/66 | Ex-T | 10/06/66 | 06/66 | NA | Unsch | ? | A end dynostarter changed |
| 04/67 | Ex-T | 20/04/67 | 04/67 | LA | L/C | ? | B Transmission changed (excessive clearance on No. 2 gear change lever) |
| 05/67 | Ex-T | 15/05/67 | 05/67 | LA | L/C | ? | B Transmission changed (forward / reverse lever seized) |
| 03/10/67 | Ex-T | 04/10/67 | 10/67 | LA | H/C | ? | A Engine changed |
| 21/10/67 | Ex-T | 22/10/67 | 27/10/67 | NA | L/C | 6 | B end dynostarter changed; compressor changed |
| 01/11/67 | Ex-T | 01/11/67 | 11/67 | NA | H/C | ? | A Transmission changed (erratic gear changes); B Transmission changed (noisy in one direction and metal in filters); compressor changed ( defective bearings) |
| 07/12/67 | Ex-T | 08/12/67 | 11/01/68 | SW | U/C | 35 | A Engine speed regulator guard refitted and exhaust elbow relagged; B Engine changed; B Transmission changed (ratcheting and gear trains stripped); A & B Bogies changed; Modifications; Dual fitting of B.R. / W.R. A.W.S. |
| 02/68 | Ex-T | 01/02/68 | 02/68 | LA | L/C | ? | A Engine changed (No. 4 liner fractured) |
| 02/68 | Ex-T | 03/02/68 | 02/68 | NA | L/C | ? | B end dynostarter changed (worn holes in the cardan shaft flange causing vibrations) |
| 05/68 | Ex-T | 19/05/68 | 05/68 | NA | L/C | ? | Boiler changed |
| 14/06/68 | Ex-T | 06/68 | 06/07/68 | LA | H/C | 22 | A Transmission changed; B Transmission changed (ratcheting on engagement of gears and heavy bronze debris in filter) |
| 24/07/68 | Ex-T | 25/07/68 | 07/68 | LA | L/C | ? | B Transmission changed (No. 3 piston cover fractured) |
| 10/68 | Ex-T | 03/10/68 | 10/68 | NA | L/C | ? | B Engine Turbo blower changed (coolant leaks) |
| 12/68 | Ex-T | 11/12/68 | 12/68 | LA | L/C | ? | B Transmission changed (no filling pump pressure) |
| 01/69 | Ex-T | 02/01/69 | 01/69 | LA | L/C | ? | B Transmission changed (ratcheting) |
| 03/69 | Ex-T | 20/03/69 | 03/69 | NA | U/C | ? | A Engine Turbo blower changed (coolant leaks) |
| 03/09/69 | Ex-T | 04/09/69 | 05/09/69 | NA | L/C | 2 | A Transmission changed (overheating in 3rd gear, teeth broken from No. 3 baulk ring, No. 3 dog clutch and flange ring teeth chipped and damaged and metal debris in sump) |
| 10/69 | Ex-T | 13/10/69 | 10/69 | LA | H/C | ? | A Bogie changed |
| 13/11/69 | Ex-T | 13/11/69 | 13/11/69 | LA | L/C | 1 | A Engine changed (crankcase compression) |
| 17/12/69 | Ex-T | 17/12/69 | 17/12/69 | NA | Unsch | 1 | B Engine Turbo blower changed |
| 19/01/70 | Ex-T | 19/01/70 | 20/01/70 | LA | L/C | 1 | B Bogie changed (thrust pad missing) |
| 28/02/70 | Ex-T | 28/02/70 | 28/02/70 | NA | Unsch | 1 | Batteries changed |
| 06/03/70 | Ex-T | 06/03/70 | 09/03/70 | LA | L/C | 3 | B Engine changed (blowing oil) |
| 22/05/70 | Ex-T | 23/05/70 | 29/05/70 | LA | L/C | 7 | B Transmission changed |
| 27/06/70 | Ex-T | 27/06/70 | 27/06/70 | LA | L/C | 1 | B Bogie changed (outer final drive flange missing) |
| 18/09/70 | Ex-T | 18/09/70 | 20/09/70 | NA | L/C | 2 | Boiler changed (split coils) |
| 21/09/70 | Ex-T | 21/09/70 | 24/09/70 | LA | L/C | 3 | A Transmission changed (metal in filters) |
| 18/02/71 | Ex-T | 18/02/71 | 19/02/71 | LA | L/C | 1 | B Bogie changed (lift on the outer final drive input bearing) |
| 14/04/71 | Ex-T | 15/04/71 | 19/04/71 | LA | Unsch | ? | B Transmission removed |
| 14/04/71 | LA | 20/04/71 | 18/08/71 | SW | Class | 126 | A & B Engines changed; A Transmission changed (ratcheting); B Transmission changed; A & B Bogies changed; Modifications; Fire damage repaired (in B end engine room adjacent to compressor, inner and outer skins scorched, external paintwork flaking and in poor condition); All cardan shafts and hoses changed; exhausters and compressor changed; serck pumps changed; all pipe work stripped and examined |
| 03/01/72 | LA | 03/01/72 | 07/01/72 | NA | L/C | 4 | Boiler changed (split coils) |
| 27/04/72 | Ex-T | 27/04/72 | 30/04/72 | LA | L/C | 3 | A Transmission changed (convertor seals leaking) |
| 30/08/72 | Ex-T | 30/08/72 | 01/09/72 | LA | Unsch | 2 | A Transmission changed (ratcheting) |
| 25/10/72 | Ex-T | 25/10/72 | 27/10/72 | LA | L/C | 2 | B Transmission changed (forward / reverse defects) |
| 04/12/72 | Ex-T | | | LA | - | | Withdrawn |

D821 GREYHOUND brings the 1A24 6.30am Plymouth-Paddington through West Drayton in July 1961; the first two coaches are ex-GWR stock. This locomotive is one of only two survivors and has been in the care of the Diesel Traction Group for much longer than its relatively short life in BR service. (www.rail-online.co.uk)

821 GREYHOUND on 17 June 1972 at Bristol Bath Road where it received an 'A' exam before working off the following Monday morning on the 1B78 06.30 Bristol-Plymouth. The final blue livery shown here did little for the Warships and tended to make them look shorter than their 60 feet. The loco was withdrawn on 4 December 1972 and moved to Didcot for preservation in May 1973. (www.rail-online.co.uk)

# D822 HERCULES

| Lot no./Works no. | 437 / - |
|---|---|
| **Significant dates and allocations** | |
| Into traffic - Laira | 15/06/60 |
| Newton Abbot | 09/62 |
| Laira | 06/65 |
| Newton Abbot | 03/67 |
| Laira | 08/67 |
| Withdrawn (Newton Abbot) | 04/10/71 |
| (Bristol St Philips Marsh Junction) | 20/10/71 |
| (Swindon) | 06/01/72 |
| Date cut-up | By 18/02/72 |

| **Livery and insignia changes** | |
|---|---|
| Green | 15/06/60 |
| OHLW flashes | 20/03/62 |
| Yellow warning panels | 26/01/62 |
| Maroon | - |
| Blue full yellow ends – double insignia, sans serif, D-prefix | 27/03/68 |
| **Recorded mileage** | 1,098,000 |

## Works visits and depot repairs

| Stopped | At | On Works | Off Works | At | Type | Days | Work carried out |
|---|---|---|---|---|---|---|---|
| - | - | - | 15/06/60 | SW | D/A | | Delivery inspection and acceptance |
| 06/07/60 | Ex-T | 06/07/60 | 08/07/60 | SW | Unsch | 2 | A Engine (all cylinder heads changed for 'stage 4' type); B Engine (No. 5 exhaust valve stuck open, rectified in situ) |
| 22/07/60 | Ex-T | 22/07/60 | 28/07/60 | SW | L/C | 6 | |
| 14/12/60 | Ex-T | 14/12/60 | 10/01/61 | SW | Unsch | 27 | |
| 10/03/61 | Ex-T | 10/03/61 | 17/04/61 | SW | L/C | 38 | A Engine changed (No. 12 exhaust valve sticking); A Bogie right hand body support springs changed (bottom plate slipping through the buckle); B Bogie removed (all coil springs, brake gear, hangers, cross stays and brake blocks changed) |
| 01/06/61 | Ex-T | 01/06/61 | 02/06/61 | SW | Unsch | 1 | |
| 18/07/61 | Ex-T | 18/07/71 | 20/07/61 | LA | L/C | 2 | A & B Bogies (tyres turned) |
| 21/09/61 | Ex-T | 21/09/61 | 22/09/61 | LA | L/C | 1 | A & B Bogies (tyres turned) |
| 15/12/61 | LA | 19/12/61 | 26/01/62 | SW | L/C | 42 | A & B Engine modifications completed; A Transmission changed (metal particles in filters); replacement failed after trial run; B Transmission changed (metal particles in filters); A & B Bogies changed (worn brake gear and tyres at minimum thickness); A & B end cooler group frost damage repaired, A & B end transmission heat exchangers removed, tested and re-fitted; A & B end Vapor-Watchman preheaters changed due to frost damage (It was left outside the 'Foundry' over the week-end of 16th / 17th December without being drained. As a result of the severe cold weather several locos, sustained damage to pipe work caused by the freezing temperatures) |
| 05/03/62 | Ex-T | 06/03/62 | 20/03/62 | SW | L/C | 15 | A Engine changed (6 cylinder heads leaking coolant ); B Engine leaking core plug under the turbo blower renewed |
| 17/04/62 | Ex-T | 26/04/62 | 07/05/62 | SW | H/C | 20 | B Engine removed (No. 12 centre inlet valve clearance at minimum); B Transmission changed (excessive metal debris found in the primary filter) |
| 24/09/62 | Ex-T | 24/09/62 | 16/10/62 | SW | H/C | 22 | A Engine Turbo blower changed; A & B Transmissions changed (steel debris in the primary filters); Boiler changed; Compressor changed; 3 final drive cardan shafts changed |
| 10/12/62 | LA | 13/12/62 | 28/12/62 | SW | H/C | 18 | B Transmission changed (not returning to neutral); B exhauster changed |
| 10/03/63 | Ex-T | 10/03/63 | 15/03/63 | LA | H/C | 5 | B Transmission changed (not changing gear) |
| 10/06/63 | Ex-T | 10/06/63 | 14/06/63 | LA | H/C | 4 | B Engine removed (No. 5 cylinder top left hand corroded into the coolant space) |
| 18/06/63 | Ex-T | 18/06/63 | 04/07/63 | NA | Unsch | 16 | |
| 18/09/63 | Ex-T | 18/09/63 | 27/09/63 | LA | H/C | 9 | A Transmission changed (ingress of coolant and bronze debris in filters) |
| 10/63 | Ex-T | 08/10/63 | 10/63 | LA | Unsch | ? | A & B Engine Turbo blowers changed (oil leaks) |
| 03/12/63 | Ex | 03/12/63 | 19/12/63 | NA | Unsch | 16 | |
| 19/02/64 | Ex | 19/02/64 | 04/03/64 | NA | Unsch | 14 | |
| 01/06/64 | Ex-T | 05/06/64 | 29/06/64 | SW | Unsch | 28 | A Engine changed; A Bogie changed; B Bogie changed (outer final drive overheated and the oil pump full of steel particles); Boiler changed; Modifications; Bogie side control linkage replaced with hydraulic shock absorbers |
| 10/64 | Ex-T | 22/10/64 | 10/64 | LA | L/C | ? | B Transmission changed (debris in filters) |
| 01/65 | Ex-T | 19/01/65 | 01/65 | NA | Unsch | ? | A exhauster changed (seized) |
| 02/65 | Ex-T | 23/02/65 | 02/65 | LA | L/C | ? | B Engine changed |
| 21/07/65 | Ex-T | 23/07/65 | 08/09/65 | SW | Unsch | 49 | B Engine repaired (Flexible hose to the heat exchanger changed in situ and exhaust drain pipe renewed); A Transmission changed (output casing fracturing after an internal seizure); A Bogie changed (damage sustained by a fractured cardan shaft after a seizure); B Bogie changed; Modifications; Fractures in the A end main frame around the area of the bogie control brackets repaired; over bogie structure repaired; B exhauster changed |
| 09/65 | Ex-T | 22/09/65 | 09/65 | LA | L/C | ? | A Bogie changed (outer final drive overheated) |
| 12/65 | Ex-T | 20/12/65 | 12/65 | LA | L/C | ? | B Transmission changed (No. 1 clutch defective) |
| 03/66 | Ex-T | 07/03/66 | 03/66 | LA | H/C | ? | A Engine changed; Boiler changed |
| 06/66 | Ex-T | 30/06/66 | 06/66 | LA | L/C | ? | A Transmission changed (directional clutch worn) |
| 10/66 | Ex-T | 24/10/66 | 10/66 | LA | L/C | ? | B Engine changed |
| 11/66 | Ex-T | 14/11/66 | 11/66 | LA | H/C | ? | A & B Bogies changed |
| 06/67 | Ex-T | 19/06/67 | 06/67 | LA | H/C | ? | A Transmission changed (No. 4 clutch defective); A Bogie changed (3cm trace on the inner axle at 15B groove) |
| 09/67 | Ex-T | 09/67 | 09/67 | LA | L/C | ? | B Transmission changed (output oil seals leaking) |
| 10/67 | Ex-T | 06/10/67 | 10/67 | LA | L/C | ? | B Transmission changed (forward / reverse bearing mechanism seized and brass in filters) |
| 10/67 | Ex-T | 27/10/67 | 10/67 | NA | L/C | ? | A Transmission changed (forward / reverse bearing being defective) |
| 11/67 | Ex-T | 29/11/67 | ? | LA | L/C | ? | A Engine changed |
| 01/68 | Ex-T | 24/01/68 | 27/03/68 | SW | Int | 63 | A & B Engines repaired; B Transmission changed; A Bogie changed (4cm trace on Nos. 2 and 11 grooves, outer axle); B Bogie changed (1.2cm trace on No. 11 groove, inner axle, and 1.4cm trace on No. 11 groove, outer axle); Boiler changed; Modifications; slight damage to B end left hand side nose section repaired; all hoses and cardan shafts changed; exhausters and compressor changed; B end dynostarter changed |
| 10/68 | Ex-T | 30/10/68 | 10/68 | LA | L/C | ? | B Engine changed |
| 11/68 | Ex-T | 14/11/68 | 11/68 | ? | Unsch | ? | Compressor changed (knocking badly) |
| 02/69 | Ex-T | 19/02/69 | 02/69 | NA | ? | ? | A Engine Turbo blower changed (oil leaking from the bottom joint) |
| 15/08/69 | Ex-T | 15/08/69 | 18/08/69 | LA | H/C | 3 | A Transmission changed (overheating in 3rd gear); B Transmission changed (directional fault) |
| 06/12/69 | Ex-T | 08/12/69 | 11/12/69 | LA | H/C | 5 | B Bogie changed; Boiler changed (split coil) |
| 11/69 | Ex-T | 24/11/69 | 11/69 | LA | L/C | ? | B Transmission changed (5 teeth broken from the No. 1 gear wheel) |
| 29/01/70 | Ex-T | 29/01/70 | 06/02/70 | LA | L/C | 8 | B Transmission changed (No. 6 clutch seized) |
| 12/02/70 | Ex-T | 12/02/70 | 19/02/70 | LA | L/C | 7 | B Engine changed (leaking coolant from cylinder head studs) |
| 02/03/70 | Ex-T | 02/03/70 | 03/03/70 | LA | L/C | 1 | A Bogie changed (final drive pinion bearing collapsed) |
| 02/04/70 | Ex-T | 02/04/70 | 06/04/70 | LA | L/C | 4 | B Transmission changed (defective clutch) |
| 15/06/70 | Ex-T | 15/06/70 | 18/06/70 | LA | L/C | 3 | A Engine changed |
| 17/07/70 | Ex-T | 17/07/70 | 20/07/70 | LA | L/C | 3 | B Transmission changed (metal in filters) |
| 16/11/70 | Ex-T | 16/11/70 | 18/11/70 | LA | L/C | 2 | A Engine changed (No. 2 cylinder liner broken up damaging the crank case) |
| 18/12/70 | Ex-T | 18/12/70 | 21/12/70 | LA | L/C | 3 | B Engine changed |
| 31/03/71 | Ex-T | 31/03/71 | 01/04/71 | LA | H/C | 1 | A & B Bogies changed |
| 25/04/71 | Ex-T | 25/04/71 | 28/04/71 | LA | L/C | 3 | Boiler changed (split coil) |
| 12/08/71 | Ex-T | 12/08/71 | 13/08/71 | LA | L/C | 1 | B Bogie changed (right hand Gibson ring fractured) |
| 04/10/71 | Ex-T | | | NA | - | | Withdrawn |

D822 HERCULES has just made the 1 in 37 climb from St David's to Exeter Central with the 1O88 14.20 Exeter-Waterloo. It was the summer of 1966 and the Warships were now fully in control of the ex-L&SWR route to Waterloo, two years into their tenure and five still before they were replaced by Class 33s. D822 was one of the class never to have maroon livery, going straight from green to blue in the spring of 1968. (www.rail-online.co.uk)

In November 1969 D822 HERCULES keeps company at Bristol Bath Road with D1011 WESTERN THUNDERER, Peak D193 and Brush Type 4 D1957. This photograph illustrates the point made previously; the simple placing of the BR symbols under the cab numbers creates an illusion of greater length when compared with the single symbol amidships. By the date of this photograph HERCULES had been reunited with its multiple working equipment, for the accelerated West of England services the previous year. (www.rail-online.co.uk)

# D823 HERMES

| Lot no./Works no. | 437 / - |
|---|---|
| **Significant dates and allocations** | |
| Into traffic - Laira | 06/07/60 |
| Newton Abbot | 09/62 |
| Laira | 06/65 |
| Newton Abbot | 03/67 |
| Withdrawn (Old Oak Common) | 04/10/71 |
| (Swindon) | 15/12/71 |
| Date cut-up | By 19/05/72 |

| **Livery and insignia changes** | |
|---|---|
| Green | 06/07/60 |
| OHLW flashes | 21/09/61 |
| Yellow warning panels | 23/04/63 |
| Maroon yellow warning panels | 05/66 |
| Maroon full yellow ends | By 05/68 |
| Blue full yellow ends – single insignia, sans serif , no D | 19/09/69 |
| **Recorded mileage** | 1,058,000 |

**Works visits and depot repairs**

| Stopped | At | On Works | Off Works | At | Type | Days | Work carried out |
|---|---|---|---|---|---|---|---|
| - | - | - | 06/07/60 | SW | D/A | | Delivery inspection and acceptance |
| 10/03/61 | Ex-T | 10/03/61 | 17/03/61 | SW | L/C | 7 | |
| 18/07/61 | LA | 21/07/61 | 04/08/61 | SW | L/C | 17 | |
| 25/08/61 | LA | 11/09/61 | 21/09/61 | SW | U/C | 27 | |
| 25/09/61 | LA | 25/09/61 | 05/10/61 | SW | L/C | 13 | |
| 04/08/62 | Ex-T | 04/08/62 | 09/08/62 | LA | H/C | 5 | |
| 10/62 | Ex-T | 13/10/62 | 10/62 | LA | Unsch | 5 | Compressor changed |
| 25/03/63 | NA | 28/03/63 | 23/04/63 | SW | H/C | 29 | |
| 17/07/63 | Ex-T | 17/07/63 | 26/07/63 | LA | H/C | 9 | |
| 19/05/64 | NA | 21/05/64 | 16/06/64 | SW | Unsch | 26 | Boiler removed; Modifications; Bogie side control linkage replaced with hydraulic shock absorbers |
| 08/64 | Ex-T | 05/08/64 | ? | ? | ? | ? | B Engine changed (engine bedplate fractured) |
| 01/65 | Ex-T | 01/65 | 01/65 | LA | L/C | ? | A Engine changed ; B Engine changed (irregular running, wrong camshaft fitted to Nos. 1-7 bank) |
| 02/66 | Ex-T | 07/02/66 | ? | SW | ? | ? | Boiler removed for modifications |
| 06/66 | Ex-T | 30/06/66 | ? | ? | ? | ? | B Transmission removed (metal in filters) |
| ? | Ex-T | ? | 30/08/66 | SW | ? | ? | |
| 09/66 | Ex-T | 01/09/66 | 09/66 | ? | ? | ? | A Engine changed (No. 8 cylinder liner fractured) |
| 11/66 | Ex-T | 11/66 | 11/66 | ? | ? | ? | B Engine removed (fractured liner) |
| 01/67 | Ex-T | 01/67 | 01/67 | ? | ? | ? | A Engine changed |
| 06/67 | Ex-T | 06/67 | 06/67 | ? | ? | ? | Engine removed (metallic debris throughout the engine caused by a failed turbo blower);Turbo blower removed (output bearing damaged) |
| 16/04/68 | WB | 17/04/68 | 06/68 | SW | Unsch | ? | Collision at Westbury on 16/04/68 with Class 08 D3964 and hauled to Swindon the following day, both locomotives received considerable damage |
| 08/68 | Ex-T | 08/68 | 08/68 | ? | ? | ? | A Transmission removed (throwing out the clutch in one direction ) |
| 09/68 | Ex-T | 09/68 | 09/68 | ? | ? | ? | Boiler changed |
| 03/69 | Ex-T | 03/69 | 03/69 | ? | ? | ? | A Engine changed; A Bogie removed (final drive input shaft sheared) |
| 11/69 | Ex-T | 11/69 | 11/69 | ? | ? | ? | A Transmission removed (dynostarter drive shaft bearing collapsed) |
| 02/70 | Ex-T | 02/70 | 02/70 | ? | ? | ? | B Bogie removed |
| 06/70 | Ex-T | 17/06/70 | 06/70 | ? | ? | ? | A Transmission removed (not changing gear) |
| 10/70 | Ex-T | 10/70 | 10/70 | ? | ? | ? | Transmission removed (output casing broken away from transmission) |
| 10/70 | Ex-T | 10/70 | 10/70 | ? | ? | ? | Transmission removed (No. 2 clutch defective) |
| 03/71 | Ex-T | 03/71 | 03/71 | ? | ? | ? | Boiler removed (split coil) |
| 04/71 | Ex-T | 04/71 | 04/71 | ? | ? | ? | B Engine removed (crank case compression) |
| 04/10/71 | Ex-T | | | OOC | - | | Withdrawn |

D823 HERMES taking an up service out of Bristol Temple Meads in 1961. D823 went into traffic on 6 July 1960 and retained the all over green livery until gaining a yellow panel in April 1963. HERMES went through the whole spectrum of liveries, carrying maroon with both small panel and full yellow ends and finally blue with full yellow ends in September 1969. (www.rail-online.co.uk)

823 HERMES was the only Warship to carry a ship's crest, which it gained during a ceremony at Plymouth on 29 October 1965. Some five years later, with crests still firmly in place, 823 waits for the off at Paignton with the 1M61 16.20 Paignton-Kensington Motorail. HERMES carried the crests while in four different liveries, from green through both maroon variants to the final blue variant. (Paul Chancellor Collection)

# D824 HIGHFLYER

| Lot no./Works no. | 437 / - |
|---|---|
| **Significant dates and allocations** | |
| Into traffic – Laira | 27/07/60 |
| Newton Abbot | 02/61 |
| Laira | 06/65 |
| Newton Abbot | 03/67 |
| Laira | 08/67 |
| Newton Abbot | 10/71 |
| Laira | 01/72 |
| Withdrawn (Laira) | 01/12/72 |
| (Bristol Bath Road – for possible use by Derby RTC) | 08/12/72 |
| (Bristol St Philips Marsh Junction) | By 05/02/73 |
| (Swindon) | 18/12/73 |
| Date cut-up | By 18/06/75 |

| Livery and insignia changes | |
|---|---|
| Green | 27/07/60 |
| OHLW flashes | 16/10/61 |
| Yellow warning panels | 31/05/62 |
| Maroon | - |
| Blue full yellow ends – double insignia, sans serif , no D | 23/04/69 |
| **Recorded mileage** | 1,077,000 |

## Works visits and depot repairs

| Stopped | At | On Works | Off Works | At | Type | Days | Work carried out |
|---|---|---|---|---|---|---|---|
| - | - | - | 27/07/60 | SW | D/A | | Delivery inspection and acceptance |
| 21/01/61 | OOC | 24/01/61 | 11/02/61 | SW | L/C | 21 | A & B Engines modified; A & B Bogies modified |
| 29/03/61 | Ex-T | 29/03/61 | 14/04/61 | SW | Unsch | 21 | A & B Engines changed (rocker eccentrics at maximum wear; Nos. 6 and 12 cylinder heads changed, all remaining heads checked and cam boxes rectified) |
| 02/10/61 | NA | 04/10/61 | 16/10/61 | SW | L/C | 14 | A & B Transmissions (secondary filters cleaned and examined); B Bogie removed (severe derailment damage); derailment damage to B end repaired, |
| 08/02/62 | Ex-T | 08/02/62 | 08/02/62 | NA | L/C | 1 | Boiler changed |
| 11/05/62 | Ex-T | 11/05/62 | 31/05/62 | SW | H/C | 20 | B Transmission changed (high metal content in filters); A & B Bogies changed (loss of profiles) |
| 08/11/62 | Ex-T | 08/11/62 | 16/11/62 | LA | H/C | 8 | A Engine changed (No. 1 cylinder head internal coolant leak) |
| 17/03/63 | Ex-T | 17/03/63 | 31/03/63 | LA | H/C | 14 | B Engine changed; B Transmission changed (operating arm broken, not selecting gear) |
| 23/08/63 | LA | 27/08/63 | 17/09/63 | SW | L/C | 25 | B Engine changed; A Transmission changed; A & B Bogies changed; Boiler changed; Modifications; all cardan shafts changed; exhausters changed |
| 06/11/63 | NA | 11/11/63 | 17/01/64 | SW | Unsch | 72 | A & B Engine Turbo blower joints renewed; B Transmission changed; A & B Bogies changed (derailment damage, pipe work bent and buckled); damaged underframe repaired; A end over bogie structure repaired and fractures welded; A end front apron removed, repaired and re-fitted; fuel tanks removed, welded and re-fitted) |
| 02/64 | Ex-T | 26/02/64 | 02/64 | LA | Unsch | ? | B Transmission changed (heavy bronze and steel debris in the primary filter) |
| 03/65 | Ex-T | 07/03/65 | 03/65 | LA | L/C | ? | A Engine changed |
| 20/04/65 | Ex-T | 20/04/65 | 27/04/65 | NA | Unsch | 7 | B Bogie changed (outer axle flawed) |
| 12/05/65 | Ex-T | 17/05/65 | 16/08/65 | SW | Int | 96 | B Engine changed (No. 6 cylinder head fractured); A Transmission changed (output oil seals leaking); B Transmission changed (lumps of brass found in the sump, bearing cage suspect); A Bogie changed (brake gear in bad condition causing tyre damage); B Bogie changed; Boiler changed; Modifications; all hoses and cardan shafts changed; exhausters and compressor changed |
| 04/66 | Ex-T | 16/04/66 | 04/66 | LA | L/C | ? | Boiler changed (coil blocked) |
| 08/66 | Ex-T | 12/08/66 | 08/66 | LA | L/C | ? | B Transmission changed (metal in filters) |
| 04/67 | Ex-T | 09/04/67 | 04/67 | LA | L/C | ? | A Transmission changed (output oil seals leaking) |
| 06/67 | Ex-T | 26/06/67 | 06/67 | NA | H/C | ? | A & B Engines changed; B Transmission changed (No. 4 baulk ring defective) |
| 07/67 | Ex-T | 15/07/67 | 07/67 | NA | L/C | ? | A Transmission changed (overheating in 4th gear) |
| 08/67 | Ex-T | 02/08/67 | 08/67 | LA | L/C | ? | A Bogie changed; B Bogie changed (outer final drive bearing collapsed) |
| 24/03/68 | Ex-T | 24/03/68 | 25/03/68 | LA | L/C | 1 | B Transmission removed (oil leaks in the convertor, Nos. 5 and 6 gear teeth fractured and slipper blocks worn) |
| 04/68 | Ex-T | 08/04/68 | 04/68 | LA | L/C | ? | B Transmission changed (oil leaking from between the convertor and casing) |
| 06/68 | Ex-T | 19/06/68 | 06/68 | LA | L/C | ? | Boiler changed |
| 06/68 | Ex-T | 24/06/68 | 06/68 | LA | L/C | ? | B Transmission removed (direction clutch defects, collapsed bearings and all teeth stripped off No. 7 gear) |
| 07/68 | Ex-T | 24/07/68 | 07/68 | LA | L/C | ? | B Transmission changed (coming out of direction and metal in filters) |
| 10/68 | Ex-T | 08/10/68 | 10/68 | LA | L/C | ? | A Engine changed (coolant leaking from No. 13 stud hole adjacent to No. 9 cylinder) |
| 11/68 | Ex-T | 19/11/68 | 11/68 | LA | L/C | ? | Boiler changed (blocked coils) |
| 12/68 | Ex-T | 02/12/68 | 02/68 | LA | L/C | ? | B Transmission changed (ratcheting in 4th gear, No. 5 shaft broken, bushes seized on Nos. 5 and 7 shafts, teeth broken from the intermediate gear and metal in filters) |
| 01/69 | Ex-T | 24/01/69 | 01/69 | LA | L/C | ? | A Transmission changed (forward / reverse defects) |
| 03/69 | Ex-T | 14/03/69 | 18/03/69 | LA | Unsch | ? | B Transmission changed |
| 03/69 | Ex-T | 27/03/69 | 23/04/69 | SW | Class | 27 | B Engine changed; A Transmission changed (metal in filters); B Transmission changed (lift in the input shaft from the dynostarter): A & B Bogies changed; fitting of TOPS data panels; bodywork repairs |
| 13/10/69 | Ex-T | 13/10/69 | 15/10/69 | LA | L/C | 2 | A Transmission changed (directional fault, No. 6 shaft broken, double row bearing fitted to No. 6 shaft collapsed and teeth broken stripped from the intermediate gear) |
| 15/07/70 | Ex-T | 15/07/70 | 17/07/70 | LA | L/C | 2 | A Engine changed (fractures adjacent to the No. 5 crank case door) |
| 09/70 | Ex-T | 17/09/70 | 10/11/70 | SW | Int | 54 | A & B Engines changed; A Transmission changed (oil leaking from the convertor); B Transmission changed; A & B Bogies changed; Modifications; all hoses and cardan shafts changed; exhausters and compressor changed |
| 18/03/71 | Ex-T | 18/03/71 | 30/03/71 | LA | L/C | 12 | A Transmission changed (excessive metal in filters) |
| 02/07/71 | Ex-T | 02/07/71 | 05/07/71 | LA | L/C | 3 | A Transmission changed (metal in filters, No. 6 flange clutch teeth fractured and water contamination) |
| 16/08/71 | Ex-T | 16/08/71 | 17/08/71 | LA | L/C | 1 | A Transmission changed (metal in filters) |
| 04/10/71 | Ex-T | 04/10/71 | 05/10/71 | LA | L/C | 1 | Boiler changed |
| 07/04/72 | Ex-T | 07/04/72 | 12/04/72 | LA | L/C | 5 | A Transmission changed (defective clutches); A end engine to transmission cardan shaft changed |
| 01/06/72 | TN | 09/06/72 | 13/06/72 | LA | L/C | 12 | A Transmission changed (seizure) |
| 11/08/72 | Ex-T | 11/08/72 | 16/08/72 | LA | L/C | 5 | A Engine changed (fractured liner) |
| 14/09/72 | Ex-T | 14/09/72 | 18/09/72 | LA | L/C | 4 | A Engine changed (fractured liner and sump contaminated with coolant ); Batteries changed |
| 17/10/72 | Ex-T | 17/10/72 | 19/10/72 | LA | L/C | 2 | Boiler changed (split tube); A exhauster changed |
| 22/11/72 | Ex-T | 22/11/72 | 25/11/72 | LA | H/C | 3 | A Engine changed (No. 8 cylinder liner seal leaking) |
| 01/12/72 | Ex-T | | | LA | - | | Withdrawn |

D824 HIGHFLYER passes Laira Junction on 30 August 1961 with the 1F38 7.55am Penzance-Swansea, and would most likely have worked through to Bristol. The old Laira steam shed is in the background, now populated by a good selection of hydraulics. (RC Riley, www.transporttreasury.co.uk)

824 HIGHFLYER trundles through Newton Abbot on 22 June 1972 with the 6B59 08.40 Plymouth Friary-Exeter Riverside, a regular turn for the remaining D800s at the time. After pausing at Riverside HIGHFLYER went forward with the 7C52 13.26 Exeter Riverside Yard-Severn Tunnel Junction. 824 was one of the very last Warships in service, being withdrawn in December 1972, although this was not quite the end as the loco escaped the cutter's torch for a further two and a half years at Swindon until finally succumbing in June 1975. It had been sent to Bath Road after withdrawal for possible use by Derby RTC but D832 went there instead. (www.rail-online.co.uk)

# D825 INTREPID

| Lot no./Works no. | 437 / - |
|---|---|
| **Significant dates and allocations** | |
| Into traffic - Laira | 24/08/60 |
| Newton Abbot | 01/61 |
| Laira | 06/65 |
| Newton Abbot | 03/67 |
| Laira | 08/67 |
| Newton Abbot | 10/71 |
| Withdrawn (Newton Abbot) | 01/01/72 |
| Reinstated - Laira *(officially 01/05/72)* | 20/03/72 |
| Withdrawn (Laira) | 23/08/72 |
| (Swindon) | 05/10/72 |
| Date cut-up | By 27/10/72 |

| **Livery and insignia changes** | |
|---|---|
| Green | 24/08/60 |
| OHLW flashes | 11/12/61 |
| Yellow warning panels | 28/03/63 |
| Maroon | - |
| Blue full yellow ends – double insignia, sans serif , no D | 27/11/68 |
| **Recorded mileage** | 1,014,000 |

**Works visits and depot repairs**

| Stopped | At | On Works | Off Works | At | Type | Days | Work carried out |
|---|---|---|---|---|---|---|---|
| - | - | - | 24/08/60 | SW | D/A | | Delivery inspection and acceptance |
| 02/03/61 | Ex-T | 02/03/61 | 11/03/61 | SW | L/C | 9 | A & B Engines modified |
| 18/03/61 | OOC | 04/04/61 | 19/04/61 | SW | L/C | 32 | A Engine changed (No. 6 cylinder head cracked and liner damaged) |
| 13/08/61 | NA | 05/09/61 | 11/12/61 | SW | L/C | 120 | A & B Engines removed for exam, lub. oil changed and filter examined for debris; A & B Bogies removed for collision damage examination; A end collision damage repaired (A nose end dropped approx. 2", main tubes buckled, dynostarter decking plate pushed down, headcode doors pushed back and cab sides and nose skins creased and distorted); all cardan shafts removed, examined and re-fitted; B end engine to transmission cardan shaft changed; compressor and exhausters serviced; A & B drivers brake valves changed (experimental type fitted) |
| 08/08/62 | NA | 16/08/62 | 31/08/62 | SW | H/C | 23 | A Bogie changed (right hand outer tyre shelling); B Bogie changed; Boiler changed |
| 19/12/62 | OOC | 19/12/62 | 03/01/63 | SW | H/C | 15 | A Engine changed (No. 10 cylinder liner cracked; B Engine changed |
| 13/02/63 | NA | 21/02/63 | 28/03/63 | SW | H/C | 43 | A & B Transmissions changed; B Bogie changed; A & B end dynostarters removed, serviced and replaced; dynostarter platforms repaired; transmission to dynostarter cardan shafts replaced; A & B end thrust pads reset |
| 24/04/63 | NA | 03/05/63 | 24/05/63 | SW | H/C | 30 | B Engine changed; A & B Bogies changed; Modifications; A & B engine to transmission and transmission to final drives cardan shafts changed; A & B dynostarters removed, serviced and replaced |
| 13/09/63 | Ex-T | 13/09/63 | 15/09/63 | LA | H/C | 2 | B Transmission changed (not reversing, gears grinding and metal debris in filters) |
| 21/11/63 | Ex-T | 21/11/63 | 11/12/63 | NA | Unsch | 20 | |
| 03/64 | Ex-T | 02/03/64 | 03/64 | LA | L/C | ? | B Engine changed (turbo blower blades breaking up) |
| 05/64 | Ex-T | 26/05/64 | 05/64 | NA | L/C | ? | A Engine changed (No. 1 cylinder liner fractured) |
| 25/06/64 | Ex-T | 25/06/64 | 27/06/64 | NA | L/C | 2 | B Transmission changed |
| 07/64 | Ex-T | 21/07/64 | 07/64 | NA | L/C | ? | Boiler changed |
| 09/64 | Ex-T | 16/09/64 | 09/64 | LA | H/C | ? | A Engine changed (water contamination and engine seizure); B Transmission repaired (failing to engage gears and direction selection difficult) |
| 26/01/65 | Ex-T | 28/01/65 | 15/04/65 | SW | Class | 79 | A Transmission changed (casing fractured by detached cardan shaft); B Transmission changed; A Bogie changed (frame damage caused by a detached cardan shaft); B Bogie changed; Modifications; Bogie side control linkage replaced with hydraulic shock absorbers |
| 02/66 | Ex-T | 18/02/66 | 02/66 | LA | L/C | ? | Boiler changed |
| 03/66 | Ex-T | 23/03/66 | 03/66 | LA | L/C | ? | A Engine changed (No. 12 con rod pushed through the crankcase) |
| 04/66 | Ex-T | 20/04/66 | 04/66 | LA | L/C | ? | B Engine changed |
| 07/66 | Ex-T | 18/07/66 | 07/66 | LA | L/C | ? | B Engine changed (cylinder heads leaking) |
| 01/11/66 | Ex-T | 08/11/66 | 11/11/66 | SW | Class | 10 | A & B Bogies changed |
| 09/12/66 | Ex-T | 12/66 | 14/12/66 | LA | L/C | 5 | B Transmission changed (output shaft oil seals leaking) |
| 16/12/66 | Ex-T | 16/12/66 | 12/66 | LA | L/C | ? | B Transmission changed (No. 3 baulk ring defective) |
| 07/67 | Ex-T | 18/07/67 | 07/67 | NA | Unsch | ? | A Engine Turbo blower changed |
| 01/68 | Ex-T | 02/01/68 | 01/68 | LA | H/C | ? | A & B Engines changed; Boiler changed (cutting out on the steam temperature switch) |
| 05/68 | Ex-T | 02/05/68 | 05/68 | LA | H/C | ? | A & B Bogies changed |
| 04/09/68 | Ex-T | 12/09/68 | 27/11/68 | SW | Int | 83 | A & B Engines changed; A & B Transmissions changed; A Bogie changed (torn side control rubbers and fractured thrust pad welds); B Bogie changed (fractured thrust pad welds and worn laminated springs); Modifications; all hoses and cardan shafts changed; exhausters and compressor changed |
| 12/6 | Ex-T | 16/12/68 | 12/68 | NA | Unsch | ? | B end dynostarter changed (going open circuit) |
| 01/69 | Ex-T | 05/01/69 | 01/69 | NA | Unsch | ? | B end dynostarter changed |
| 01/69 | Ex-T | 27/01/69 | 01/69 | LA | L/C | ? | B Bogie changed (inner final drive bearing collapsed) |
| 05/69 | Ex-T | 16/05/69 | 05/69 | LA | L/C | ? | B Transmission changed (gear change defects) |
| 24/09/69 | Ex-T | 24/09/69 | 25/09/69 | LA | L/C | 1 | B Transmission changed (input shaft oil seals leaking) |
| 28/09/69 | Ex-T | 28/09/69 | 30/09/69 | LA | L/C | 2 | B Transmission changed (seized: command block actuating piston for No. 3 fork arm controlling the forward / reverse clutches locked solid) |
| 26/10/69 | Ex-T | 26/10/69 | 28/10/69 | LA | L/C | 2 | A Transmission changed (output oil seals leaking, transmission full of emulsified oil, slipper blocks worn, No. 5 dog clutch overheated and worn in groove) |
| 17/11/69 | Ex-T | 17/11/69 | 20/11/69 | LA | L/C | 3 | Boiler changed (split coil) |
| 20/04/70 | Ex-T | 20/04/70 | 22/04/70 | LA | H/C | 2 | A & B Bogies changed |
| 18/06/70 | Ex-T | 18/06/70 | 22/06/70 | LA | L/C | 4 | A Engine changed (several cylinder heads blowing) |
| 19/09/70 | Ex-T | 19/09/70 | 25/09/70 | LA | H/C | 6 | B Engine changed; A & B Transmissions changed |
| 11/12/70 | Ex-T | 11/12/70 | 14/12/70 | LA | L/C | 3 | B Transmission changed (not selecting 3rd gear) |
| 08/03/71 | Ex-T | 08/03/71 | 13/03/71 | LA | L/C | 5 | A Bogie changed |
| 02/04/71 | Ex-T | 02/04/71 | 14/04/71 | LA | L/C | 11 | A Transmission changed (oil leaks below the input shaft and not changing gear) |
| 01/01/72 | Ex-T | ? | 16/03/72 | NA | ? | 75 | Withdrawn then subsequently reinstated on 20/03/72 |
| 16/03/72 | | 24/03/72 | 29/03/72 | LA | L/C | 13 | A Transmission changed (metal in filters) |
| 12/04/72 | Ex-T | 12/04/72 | 15/04/72 | LA | L/C | 3 | A Transmission changed (metal in filters) |
| 15/08/72 | Ex-T | 15/08/72 | 22/08/72 | LA | H/C | 7 | A Engine changed; A Transmission changed (clutches ratcheting) |
| 22/08/72 | Ex-T | | 23/08/72 | LA | - | | Withdrawn |

**D825 INTREPID at Marazion on 1 April 1963 with the 1M06 11.40am Penzance-Crewe perishables. D825 was not long out of the paint shop and this is probably the reason it was chosen to feature in several official BR shots of this particular train taken at various points along its route. This is a good illustration of the fittings at the front end, most obviously the multiple working equipment, which was removed in 1965 only to be replaced in spring 1968 for the double-headed West of England services.**

**825 INTREPID at the Exeter stabling point on 5 May 1971 with D815 DRUID and D6331 for company, in a typical line up of the period. Both Warships were engaged on 'LSW' main line duties; 825 would work the 1O20 20.07 Exeter-Basingstoke and D815 had arrived on the 1V11 11.08 Waterloo-Exeter.** (www.rail-online.co.uk)

# D826 JUPITER

| Lot no./Works no. | 437 / - |
|---|---|
| **Significant dates and allocations** | |
| Into traffic - Laira | 07/09/60 |
| Newton Abbot | 01/61 |
| Laira | 06/65 |
| Newton Abbot | 03/67 |
| Laira | 08/67 |
| Withdrawn (Newton Abbot) | 18/10/71 |
| (Bristol St Philips Marsh Junction) | 26/10/71 |
| (Swindon) | 30/12/71 |
| Date cut-up | By 21/01/72 |

| **Modifications** | |
|---|---|
| Multiple working jumper cables and sockets removed | 04/08/66 |
| **Livery and insignia changes** | |
| Green | 07/09/60 |
| OHLW flashes | By 03/62 |
| Yellow warning panels | 30/10/62 |
| Maroon | - |
| Blue full yellow ends – double insignia, sans serif, D-prefix | 19/01/68 |
| Blue full yellow ends – single insignia, serif, no D | 07/07/71 |
| **Recorded mileage** | 1,097,000 |

## Works visits and depot repairs

| Stopped | At | On Works | Off Works | At | Type | Days | Work carried out |
|---|---|---|---|---|---|---|---|
| - | - | - | 07/09/60 | SW | D/A | | Delivery inspection and acceptance |
| 26/08/61 | NA | 05/09/61 | 15/09/61 | SW | Casual | 20 | A & B Engines (Modification and Nos. 6 and 12 cylinder heads changed) |
| 29/09/61 | Ex-T | 29/09/61 | 02/10/61 | LA | L/C | 3 | A & B Bogies (Tyres turned and measured) |
| 18/12/61 | NA | 12/61 | 06/01/62 | LA | L/C | 19 | |
| 20/03/62 | NA | 26/03/62 | 26/03/62 | SW | Unsch | 6 | B Transmission (Fractured top casing changed in situ) |
| 04/06/62 | Ex-T | 04/06/62 | 06/06/62 | NA | H/C | 2 | B Engine changed (No. 9 cylinder head cracked and liner damaged) |
| 19/10/62 | NA | 23/10/62 | 30/10/62 | SW | H/C | 11 | A Bogie changed (outer final drive pinion collapsed) |
| 03/11/62 | Ex-T | 03/11/62 | 13/11/62 | LA | L/C | 10 | A Transmission changed (not changing gear, reported as noisy and metal in filters) |
| 27/11/62 | Ex-T | 27/11/62 | 27/11/62 | LA | L/C | 1 | |
| 11/12/62 | Ex-T | 11/12/62 | 13/12/62 | LA | H/C | 2 | A Engine changed; B Engine changed (No. 8 cylinder liner fractured) |
| 20/05/63 | NA | 23/05/63 | 14/06/63 | SW | L/C | 25 | A & B Bogies changed; Boiler changed; Modifications; A end control cubicle and trunking repaired after damage sustained from a broken A end dynostarter cardan shaft; A end dynostarter platform mounting fracture welded; transmission to final drive cardan shafts replaced |
| 13/07/63 | Ex-T | 13/07/63 | 15/07/63 | LA | H/C | 2 | B Engine changed (No. 2 cylinder liner fractured and scored) |
| 09/04/64 | Ex-T | 09/04/64 | 04/64 | LA | L/C | ? | B Transmission changed (not changing gear and loss of oil) |
| 02/05/64 | Ex-T | 02/05/64 | 04/05/64 | LA | Unsch | 2 | B end dynostarter changed (flange coupling defects) |
| 20/05/64 | Ex-T | 20/05/64 | 05/06/64 | SW | Unsch | 16 | A & B Bogies changed; Boiler changed; Modifications; Bogie side control linkage replaced with hydraulic shock absorbers |
| 23/07/64 | Ex-T | 20/08/64 | 11/09/64 | SW | Unsch | 49 | A & B Engines repaired; A & B Transmissions repaired; A & B Bogies changed; collision damage repaired (right hand battery box doors and adjacent panels repaired and repainted; four final drive cardan shafts replaced; A end Vapor-Watchman preheater repaired in situ) |
| 30/10/64 | Ex-T | 03/11/64 | 04/11/64 | LA | H/C | 5 | A Engine changed (low lub. oil pressure) |
| 11/64 | Ex-T | 18/11/64 | 11/64 | LA | H/C | ? | A Engine changed (No. 9 cylinder liner fractured) |
| 11/64 | Ex-T | 29/11/64 | ? | LA | L/C | ? | B Engine changed (No. 2 cylinder liner leaking) |
| 03/65 | Ex-T | 23/03/65 | 03/65 | LA | L/C | ? | Compressor changed (seized) |
| 24/06/65 | Ex-T | 28/06/65 | 29/06/65 | LA | H/C | 5 | B Engine changed (low lub. oil pressure and knocking at No. 3 cylinder caused by a worn crank pin) |
| 03/09/65 | Ex-T | 03/09/65 | 04/09/65 | LA | L/C | 1 | B Transmission changed (not changing gear and metal in filters) |
| 01/02/66 | Ex-T | 01/02/66 | 02/66 | LA | H/C | ? | B Bogie changed (outer axle suspected flaw) |
| 03/66 | Ex-T | 14/03/66 | 03/66 | LA | H/C | ? | B Engine changed (No. 1 cylinder head and liner fractured with rusty bores) |
| 04/66 | Ex-T | 04/04/66 | 04/66 | LA | L/C | ? | B Transmission changed (ratcheting in all gears) |
| 05/66 | Ex-T | 26/05/66 | 05/66 | NA | L/C | ? | B exhauster changed (low insulation on the motor) |
| 01/06/66 | Ex-T | 02/06/66 | 04/08/66 | SW | Int | 64 | A & B Engines changed; A Transmission changed; B Transmission changed (output shaft oil seals leaking); A & B Bogies changed; Boiler changed; Modifications; Multiple working jumper cables and sockets removed from buffer beam; repair of fire damage behind B exhauster, main 2" tubes scorched; B end exhauster changed due to fire damage, complete external repaint (green), one coat only |
| 06/67 | Ex-T | 02/06/67 | 06/67 | LA | H/C | ? | B Transmission changed (water contamination, Nos. 7 & 8 gear wheel teeth damaged and badly worn, broken teeth on the intermediate gears and dog clutches overheated) |
| 06/67 | Ex-T | 27/06/67 | 06/67 | LA | L/C | ? | A Bogie changed (outer final drive seized) |
| 23/11/67 | Ex-T | 23/11/67 | 27/11/67 | LA | H/C | 4 | A & B Transmissions changed |
| 23/11/67 | LA | 27/11/67 | 19/01/68 | SW | Int | 57 | A & B Transmissions changed (defective clutches); A Bogie changed (traces on the inner axle); B Bogie changed; Boiler removed (leaking fuel pipes and burner defects); Modifications; collision damage repaired ( A end left hand nose corner damage and left hand side of body outer skin scored badly); all hoses and cardan shafts changed; exhauster and compressor changed |
| 01/68 | Ex-T | 31/01/68 | 01/68 | LA | L/C | ? | B Transmission changed (not changing gear) |
| 04/68 | Ex-T | 03/04/68 | 04/68 | LA | L/C | ? | A Engine changed (losing oil and coolant); B Transmission changed (not selecting drive) |
| 23/04/68 | Ex-T | 23/04/68 | 24/04/68 | LA | L/C | 1 | B Transmission changed (rejecting Nos. 3 & 4 clutches) |
| 05/68 | Ex-T | 13/05/68 | 05/68 | LA | L/C | ? | B Bogie changed (frame damage, inner final drive overheated and worn pivot pin bushes) |
| 07/68 | Ex-T | 01/07/68 | 07/68 | LA | L/C | ? | B Engine changed |
| 08/68 | Ex-T | 13/08/68 | 08/68 | LA | H/C | ? | A Transmission changed (No. 2 clutch seized, double row bearing fitted to No. 4 gear completely collapsed, bushes fitted to Nos. 7 & 8 gears broken and seized and governor casing fractured); Boiler changed |
| 04/69 | Ex-T | 01/04/69 | 04/69 | LA | L/C | ? | A Bogie changed (tyres pitted too thin to turn) |
| 06/69 | Ex-T | 16/06/69 | 06/69 | LA | H/C | ? | B Transmission changed (output oil seals leaking and metal in filters) |
| 08/09/69 | Ex-T | 08/09/69 | 10/09/69 | LA | L/C | 2 | A Transmission changed (metal in filters) |
| 25/02/70 | Ex-T | 28/02/70 | 02/03/70 | LA | L/C | 6 | A Transmission changed (metal in filters) |
| 29/03/70 | Ex-T | 29/03/70 | 29/03/70 | LA | L/C | 1 | A Engine changed |
| 04/05/70 | Ex-T | 20/05/70 | 23/05/70 | LA | H/C | 19 | B Bogie changed (tyres worn too thin to turn) |
| 12/07/70 | Ex-T | 12/07/70 | 13/07/70 | LA | L/C | 1 | A Transmission changed (metal in filters) |
| 13/08/70 | Ex-T | 13/08/70 | 13/08/70 | NA | Casual | 1 | B end dynostarter changed |
| 23/08/70 | Ex-T | 23/08/70 | 25/08/70 | LA | H/C | 2 | B Engine changed (fractured crankcase and tip registers in gear case out of limits) |
| 09/70 | Ex-T | 21/09/70 | 09/70 | NA | L/C | ? | Boiler changed (fractured pipe in separator) |
| 04/01/71 | Ex-T | 04/01/71 | 07/01/71 | LA | H/C | 3 | A Bogie changed |
| 16/02/71 | Ex-T | 16/02/71 | 18/02/71 | LA | L/C | 2 | B Engine changed (No. 6 cylinder liner fractured) |
| 21/04/71 | Ex-T | 21/04/71 | 21/04/71 | LA | L/C | 1 | B Engine changed (crank case fractured) |
| 17/05/71 | Ex-T | 24/05/71 | 26/05/71 | LA | L/C | 9 | B Transmission changed (fractures around the output section) |
| 15/06/71 | Ex-T | 19/06/71 | 07/07/71 | LA | H/C | 22 | A Engine changed (coolant leaks from cylinder stud holes); A Transmission changed (metal in filters); B Transmission changed; external repaint in blue livery |
| 13/07/71 | Ex-T | 13/07/71 | 14/07/71 | LA | L/C | 1 | A Bogie changed (3cm trace on No. 1 axle) |
| 04/08/71 | Ex-T | 04/08/71 | 05/08/71 | LA | L/C | 1 | B Transmission changed (overheating and metal in filters) |
| 18/10/71 | NA | | | | - | | Withdrawn |

D826 JUPITER at Clapham with the 11.00 Waterloo-Salisbury in 1965/66. The green Bulleid stock seemed to blend well with the Warships, but was less harmonious when they began to appear in maroon. The photograph shows clearly the Swindon style of roof ventilators and grills. (JG Walmsley, www.transporttreasury.co.uk)

D826 JUPITER, now in corporate blue, passes Bedminster Park just outside Bristol Temple Meads on 7 June 1969 with the 1V68 08.23 Nottingham-Paignton. D826 was one of 22 Warships which had their multiple working reinstated to work the accelerated West of England services in 1968, but unfortunately the twin Class 42 diagrams only lasted for two years. JUPITER itself lasted until October 1971, gaining a Laira repaint in July because of the dreadful condition of its paintwork by that date. (www.rail-online.co.uk)

# D827 KELLY

| Lot no./Works no. | 437 / - |
|---|---|
| **Significant dates and allocations** | |
| Into traffic - Laira | 04/10/60 |
| Newton Abbot | 01/61 |
| Laira | 03/63 |
| Newton Abbot | 05/66 |
| Laira | 08/67 |
| Newton Abbot | 10/71 |
| Withdrawn (Newton Abbot) | 01/01/72 |
| (Laira) | By 25/01/72 |
| (Swindon) | 12/09/72 |
| Date cut-up | By 13/10/72 |

| **Modifications** | |
|---|---|
| **Livery and insignia changes** | |
| Green | 04/10/60 |
| OHLW flashes | 20/10/61 |
| Yellow warning panels | 02/05/62 |
| Maroon | - |
| Blue full yellow ends – double insignia, serif, D-prefix | 11/08/67 |
| Blue full yellow ends – double insignia, sans serif, no D | 23/04/71 |
| **Recorded mileage** | 1,071,000 |

**Works visits and depot repairs**

| Stopped | At | On Works | Off Works | At | Type | Days | Work carried out |
|---|---|---|---|---|---|---|---|
| - | - | - | 04/10/60 | SW | D/A | | Delivery inspection and acceptance (B Bogie was ex-D803 and had done 148,260 miles) |
| 20/06/61 | BS | 22/06/61 | 01/07/61 | SW | L/C | 11 | B Engine changed (coolant in No. 4 cylinder) |
| 05/09/61 | LA | 06/09/61 | 07/09/61 | LA | L/C | 2 | A & B Bogies tyres turned |
| 28/09/61 | NA | 05/10/61 | 20/10/61 | SW | L/C | 22 | A Engine repaired; B Bogie changed |
| 09/12/61 | NA | 12/12/61 | 21/12/61 | SW | L/C | 12 | B Transmission changed (brass particles in filters) |
| 14/04/62 | NA | 26/04/62 | 02/05/62 | SW | H/C | 18 | A Bogie changed (inner final drive input shaft bearing collapsed) |
| 16/11/62 | NA | 16/11/62 | 18/11/62 | LA | H/C | 2 | A Engine changed (coolant in left and right hand cylinder heads) |
| 29/11/62 | OOC | 03/12/62 | 20/12/62 | SW | H/C | 21 | A Transmission changed (defective oil pump); A & B Bogies removed (to access thrust pads and reset to correct clearances); Boiler changed |
| 01/04/63 | Ex-T | 01/04/63 | 10/04/63 | LA | H/C | 9 | A Engine changed (No. 10 cylinder liner fractured) |
| 05/05/63 | Ex-T | 05/05/63 | 09/05/63 | LA | H/C | 4 | B Engine changed (No. 5 cylinder head fractured) |
| 01/10/63 | Ex-T | 01/10/63 | 04/10/63 | LA | H/C | 3 | A Engine changed (particles of metal found in the inlet manifolds) |
| 15/01/64 | Ex-T | 15/01/64 | 31/01/64 | SW | Casual | 16 | A & B Bogies changed; Modifications; Bogie side control linkage replaced with hydraulic shock absorbers |
| 29/05/64 | LA | 03/03/64 | 02/07/64 | SW | Unsch | 34 | A & B Engines repaired; B Transmission changed; B Bogie changed (inner final drive defects); Boiler changed; Modifications |
| 09/64 | Ex-T | 23/09/64 | 09/64 | NA | L/C | ? | Boiler changed (hole in the coil) |
| 01/11/64 | Ex-T | 01/11/64 | 02/11/64 | LA | Unsch | 1 | A & B Bogies U A T |
| 17/11/64 | Ex-T | 19/11/64 | 12/02/65 | SW | Unsch | 87 | A Engine changed (turbo blower leaking oil); B Engine changed; A Transmission changed (output shaft oil seals leaking and excessive travel on No. 2 gear shift lever);B Transmission changed (output shaft oil seals leaking); A Bogie changed (flats); B Bogie changed (bogie thrust pad cross member twisted); Modifications |
| 03/65 | Ex-T | 04/03/65 | 03/65 | LA | L/C | ? | B Bogie changed (suspected axle flaw) |
| 04/65 | Ex-T | 28/04/65 | 04/65 | LA | L/C | ? | B Transmission changed (No. 4 clutch or convertor thrust bearing collapsed and metal in filters) |
| 09/65 | Ex-T | 29/07/65 | 07/65 | LA | L/C | ? | B Bogie changed (trace on No. 5 groove on the inner axle) |
| 01/66 | Ex-T | 26/01/66 | 01/66 | LA | L/C | ? | A Engine changed |
| 06/66 | Ex-T | 09/06/66 | 06/66 | LA | L/C | ? | B Engine changed (cylinder liners fractured and coolant in the sump) |
| 09/66 | Ex-T | 26/09/66 | 09/66 | NA | Unsch | ? | A Engine Turbo blower changed |
| 10/66 | Ex-T | 05/10/66 | 10/66 | LA | H/C | ? | A Transmission changed (dynostarter input flange bearing collapsed and top casing fractured) |
| 01/67 | Ex-T | 31/01/67 | 01/67 | NA | L/C | ? | Boiler changed |
| 04/67 | Ex-T | 08/04/67 | 04/67 | NA | Unsch | ? | A & B Engines Turbo blowers changed |
| 21/07/67 | Ex-T | 27/07/67 | 11/08/67 | SW | U/C | 21 | A Bogie changed (fractured coil spring) |
| 08/67 | Ex-T | 25/08/67 | 08/67 | LA | H/C | ? | A & B Bogies changed (worn tyres) |
| 11/67 | Ex-T | 08/11/67 | 11/67 | NA | H/C | ? | A Engine changed; B Engine Turbo blower changed (oil leaks) |
| 03/68 | Ex-T | 28/03/68 | 03/68 | LA | L/C | ? | B Engine changed (fracture in No. 6 bore near the previous 'Metalock' repair) |
| 05/68 | Ex-T | 17/05/68 | 05/68 | LA | L/C | ? | B Bogie changed (excessive lift on the inner final drive shaft) |
| 06/68 | Ex-T | 06/06/68 | 06/68 | LA | L/C | ? | A Transmission changed (oil seals leaking) |
| 11/68 | Ex-T | 07/11/68 | 11/68 | NA | Unsch | ? | A end dynostarter changed (fractured mounting foot) |
| 01/69 | Ex-T | 17/01/69 | 01/69 | LA | L/C | ? | A Transmission changed (defective bearings on the output drive shaft to the dynostarter) |
| 03/02/69 | Ex-T | 03/02/69 | 07/02/69 | LA | H/C | 4 | A & B Bogies changed; Boiler changed |
| 04/69 | Ex-T | 09/04/69 | 04/69 | LA | L/C | ? | B Transmission changed |
| 25/09/69 | Ex-T | 09/69 | 30/09/69 | LA | L/C | 5 | A Engine changed |
| 19/11/69 | Ex-T | 19/11/69 | 20/11/69 | LA | L/C | 1 | B Transmission changed (overheating in 2nd convertor) |
| 02/70 | Ex-T | 26/02/70 | 02/70 | LA | L/C | ? | A Bogie changed (brake gear wearing badly and a moved tyre) |
| 05/03/70 | Ex-T | 05/03/70 | 10/03/70 | LA | L/C | 5 | A Transmission changed (reported as noisy) |
| 13/04/70 | Ex-T | 13/04/70 | 16/04/70 | LA | L/C | 3 | B Transmission changed (forward / reverse defects) |
| 22/05/70 | Ex-T | 05/70 | 28/05/70 | LA | L/C | 6 | B Bogie changed (wheel tread wear at the maximum and thin tyres) |
| 16/06/70 | Ex-T | 16/06/70 | 19/06/70 | LA | L/C | 3 | A Engine changed (cylinder block broken away from No. 5 bore in the crankcase) |
| 22/06/70 | Ex-T | 22/06/70 | 23/06/70 | LA | L/C | 1 | A Engine changed (No. 1 cylinder liner fractured) |
| 16/07/70 | Ex-T | 07/70 | 21/07/70 | LA | L/C | 5 | Boiler changed (badly corroded coil and generator in generally poor condition) |
| 09/70 | Ex-T | 29/09/70 | 09/70 | LA | H/C | ? | A Transmission changed (top casing smashed caused by a loose dynostarter cardan shaft) |
| 28/10/70 | Ex-T | 28/10/70 | 30/10/70 | LA | L/C | 2 | B Engine changed (coolant contamination in the lub.oil) |
| 12/11/70 | Ex-T | 11/70 | 13/11/70 | LA | L/C | 1 | B Bogie changed (flats and tyres too thin to turn) |
| 30/12/70 | Ex-T | 30/12/70 | 02/01/71 | LA | L/C | 3 | B Transmission changed (metal in filters) |
| 05/02/71 | LA | 08/02/71 | 23/04/71 | SW | Int | 77 | A & B Engines changed; A Transmission changed; B Transmission changed (not changing gear); A Bogie changed; B Bogie changed (torn side control rubbers); Modifications; over bogie structures repaired; loco rewired; all hoses and cardan shafts changed, exhausters and compressor changed; A and B end dynostarters fitted (missing on arrival) |
| 26/04/71 | Ex-T | 26/04/71 | 11/05/71 | SW | Rectfn | 15 | D827 returned to Swindon due to temperature trips of engine(s) and/or transmission(s) |
| 06/08/71 | Ex-T | 06/08/71 | 10/08/71 | LA | L/C | 4 | A Transmission changed (overheating and metal in filters) |
| 24/12/71 | BS | 24/12/71 | 29/12/71 | NA | H/C | 5 | B Transmission changed |
| 01/01/72 | NA | | | | - | | Withdrawn after collision with D7047 at Bristol Bath Road on 24/12/71 |

D827 KELLY stands at Bristol Temple Meads in the rain in 1965 with a local service to Taunton. KELLY received a new coat of green paint as late as February 1965 which ensured that it would not require a repaint during the time that maroon was in vogue. D827 retains its multiple working equipment in this shot but would lose it the following year. (www.rail-online.co.uk)

D827 KELLY at Plymouth North Road in June 1968 with the 1M39 08.40 Penzance-Wolverhampton. Note that the electrification flashes are missing from the side; when these were replaced they appeared in front of the doors rather than behind which made KELLY unique among Swindon Warships. The multiple working equipment has reappeared courtesy of the 1968 paired diagrams. (www.rail-online.co.uk)

## D828 MAGNIFICENT

| Lot no./Works no. | 437 / - |
|---|---|
| **Significant dates and allocations** | |
| Into traffic - Laira | 19/10/60 |
| Newton Abbot | 01/61 |
| Laira | 06/65 |
| Newton Abbot | 09/65 |
| Laira | 08/67 |
| Stored (Laira) | 13/07/71 |
| Withdrawn (Newton Abbot) | 28/08/71 |
| (Swindon) | 15/10/71 |
| Date cut-up | By 07/04/72 |

| **Livery and insignia changes** | |
|---|---|
| Green | 19/10/60 |
| OHLW flashes | 01/02/62 |
| Yellow warning panels | 09/05/62 |
| Maroon yellow warning panels | By 06/03/66 |
| Blue full yellow ends – double insignia, sans serif , no D | 12/07/69 |
| **Recorded mileage** | 922,000 |

**Works visits and depot repairs**

| Stopped | At | On Works | Off Works | At | Type | Days | Work carried out |
|---|---|---|---|---|---|---|---|
| - | - | - | 19/10/60 | SW | D/A | | Delivery inspection and acceptance |
| 07/61 | Ex-T | 18/07/61 | 26/07/61 | SW | L/C | 8 | |
| 20/08/61 | Ex-T | 20/08/61 | 21/08/61 | LA | L/C | 1 | |
| 19/10/61 | Ex-T | 19/10/61 | 20/10/61 | LA | ? | 1 | |
| 29/12/61 | NA | 03/01/62 | 01/02/62 | SW | L/C | 34 | As a result of the severe cold weather several locos, including D828, sustained damage to pipe work caused by the freezing temperatures |
| 08/03/62 | NA | 15/03/62 | 09/05/62 | SW | L/C | 62 | |
| 02/08/62 | NA | 10/08/62 | 13/08/62 | SW | H/C | 11 | B Bogie removed ( tyres worn to minimum size) |
| 09/11/62 | Ex-T | 09/11/62 | 13/11/62 | NA | L/C | 4 | |
| 21/01/63 | Ex-T | 01/63 | 05/02/63 | NA | U/C | 15 | |
| 14/03/63 | NA | 21/03/63 | 05/04/63 | SW | H/C | 22 | |
| 29/10/63 | Ex-T | 29/10/63 | 30/10/63 | LA | ? | 1 | |
| 11/02/64 | Ex-T | | 03/64 | LA | Unsch | | Bogie changed |
| 11/02/64 | LA | 03/03/64 | 07/04/64 | SW | Unsch | 55 | A & B Engines removed; Bogie removed (suspected axle flaws and the outer final drive thrust bearing fractured; Modifications; Bogie side control linkage replaced with hydraulic shock absorbers |
| 30/06/64 | Ex-T | 30/06/64 | 03/07/64 | NA | ? | 3 | Component change |
| 24/07/64 | Ex-T | 07/64 | ? | SW | U/C | ? | A end collision damage repaired; drivers side buffer 1/2" high, B end co-drivers side buffer 2" high, drivers side 3/4" high, co-drivers cab door distorted and panel work distorted |
| 18/08/64 | Ex-T | 18/08/64 | 23/08/64 | NA | ? | 5 | Component change |
| 12/65 | Ex-T | 07/12/65 | 12/65 | LA | L/C | ? | B Transmission changed (metal in filters) |
| ? | Ex-T | ? | 03/66 | SW | ? | ? | |
| 05/66 | Ex-T | 15/05/66 | 05/66 | NA | Unsch | ? | A end dynostarter changed due to fluctuating voltages |
| 06/67 | Ex-T | 06/67 | 06/67 | ? | L/C | ? | Boiler removed for routine overhaul |
| 06/67 | Ex-T | 29/06/67 | 06/67 | NA | L/C | ? | A Transmission changed (output oil seals leaking) |
| 11/67 | Ex-T | 22/11/67 | 11/67 | ? | ? | ? | A & B Engines removed for routine overhaul |
| 12/67 | Ex-T | 29/12/67 | 12/67 | LA | H/C | ? | A & B Bogies changed |
| 04/68 | Ex-T | 04/68 | 04/68 | ? | L/C | ? | A Engine removed (No. 2 cylinder head leaking) |
| 06/68 | Ex-T | 06/68 | 06/68 | ? | L/C | ? | A Transmission removed (overheating in 3rd gear and the output oil seals leaking) |
| 03/69 | Ex-T | 03/69 | 03/69 | ? | ? | ? | A Transmission removed (ratcheting and metal in filters) |
| 04/69 | Ex-T | 04/69 | 04/69 | ? | ? | ? | Engine removed (fractured liners and rusty bores) |
| ? | Ex-T | ? | 12/07/69 | SW | ? | ? | |
| 08/70 | Ex-T | 08/70 | 08/70 | ? | ? | ? | A Engine removed (No. 8 cylinder liner seals leaking) |
| 11/70 | Ex-T | 11/70 | 11/70 | ? | ? | ? | A & B Transmissions removed |
| 03/07/71 | BS | 04/07/71 | 28/08/71 | NA | - | | Withdrawn (caught fire 02/07/71 when fuel from an open bleed screw on a fuel line sprayed over the compressor motor and then ignited from the sparks off the commutation ring) |

D828 MAGNIFICENT in the summer of 1961 at Chippenham in a scene full of GWR atmosphere. The water column was not just used for steam locomotives, but was occasionally served to top up the boiler of a diesel. (www.rail-online.co.uk)

828 MAGNIFICENT sits on Exeter stabling point on 16 May 1971. The headcode is the 12.50 Penzance-Bristol perishables which it had worked as far as Exeter the previous day. The livewire flash has now been moved to the 'correct' position, and the multiple working equipment is intact, as denoted by the white diamonds; MAGNIFICENT has the final version blue livery and was stored in July after fire damage before withdrawal on 28 August. (www.rail-online.co.uk)

# D829 MAGPIE

| Lot no./Works no. | 437 / - |
|---|---|
| **Significant dates and allocations** | |
| Into traffic - Laira | 23/11/60 |
| Newton Abbot | 01/61 |
| Laira | 06/65 |
| Newton Abbot | 09/65 |
| Laira | 08/67 |
| Newton Abbot | 10/71 |
| Withdrawn (Newton Abbot) | 01/01/72 |
| Laira (Reinstated – *officially 01/05/72* | 17/03/72 |
| Withdrawn (Westbury) | 25/08/72 |
| (Laira) | 26/08/72 |
| (Bristol Bath Road) – for possible preservation by the TV programme 'Magpie' | 05/10/72 |
| (Swindon) | 12/12/72 |
| Date cut-up | By 30/01/74 |

| **Livery and insignia changes** | |
|---|---|
| Green | 23/11/60 |
| OHLW flashes | 05/10/61 |
| Yellow warning panels | 13/09/62 |
| Maroon yellow warning panels | 12/65 |
| Maroon full yellow ends | 06/68 |
| Blue full yellow ends – double insignia, sans serif, no D | 10/69 |
| **Recorded mileage** | 975,000 |

### Works visits and depot repairs

| Stopped | At | On Works | Off Works | At | Type | Days | Work carried out |
|---|---|---|---|---|---|---|---|
| - | - | - | 23/11/60 | SW | D/A | | Delivery inspection and acceptance |
| 01/61 | Ex-T | 16/01/61 | 17/02/61 | SW | H/C | 32 | |
| 04/61 | Ex-T | 24/04/61 | 08/05/61 | SW | U/C | 14 | |
| 06/61 | Ex-T | 21/06/61 | 30/06/61 | SW | L/C | 9 | |
| 22/09/61 | Ex-T | 22/09/61 | 05/10/61 | SW | U/C | 13 | |
| 08/62 | Ex-T | 30/08/62 | 13/09/62 | SW | H/C | 15 | A Transmission removed (excessive metal in filters); A & B Bogies changed |
| 13/03/63 | NA | 15/03/63 | 03/04/63 | SW | H/C | 21 | |
| 24/04/63 | NA | 29/04/63 | 09/05/63 | SW | L/C | 15 | |
| 09/63 | Ex-T | 09/63 | 09/63 | LA | L/C | ? | A & B Bogies tyres turned |
| 23/09/63 | Ex-T | 24/09/63 | 26/09/63 | SW | L/C | 3 | A & B Bogies removed |
| 05/11/63 | NA | 11/11/63 | 26/11/63 | SW | H/C | 21 | |
| 24/03/64 | LA | 31/03/64 | 17/04/64 | SW | Unsch | 24 | Transmission removed (ratcheting on the Down gear change) |
| 05/64 | Ex-T | 05/64 | 05/64 | ? | ? | ? | B Transmission removed (casing fractured) |
| 09/65 | Ex-T | 14/09/65 | 12/65 | SW | Int | ? | A Engine removed; B Engine changed; A & B Transmissions removed; A Bogie removed; B Bogie removed (outer final drive oil pump bearing defective) |
| 01/66 | Ex-T | 21/01/66 | 01/66 | NA | ? | ? | Compressor changed |
| 05/66 | Ex-T | 10/05/66 | 05/66 | NA | ? | ? | A exhauster changed |
| 10/66 | Ex-T | 10/66 | 10/66 | ? | ? | ? | A Transmission removed (dynostarter input flange bearing breaking up) |
| 10/67 | Ex-T | 10/67 | 10/67 | ? | ? | ? | B Engine removed for general repair |
| 04/68 | Ex-T | 04/68 | 04/68 | ? | ? | ? | B Transmission removed for general repair |
| ? | Ex-T | ? | 06/68 | SW | ? | ? | |
| 07/69 | Ex-T | 07/69 | 07/69 | ? | ? | ? | Bogie removed (worn bushes on the outer laminated spring) |
| 08/69 | Ex-T | 06/08/69 | 10/69 | SW | ? | ? | A B Engines removed for routine overhaul; B Transmission removed routine overhaul |
| 10/69 | Ex-T | 10/69 | 10/69 | ? | ? | ? | B Transmission removed (metal in filters) |
| 12/69 | Ex-T | 12/69 | 12/69 | ? | ? | ? | B Transmission removed (excessive ratcheting and metal in filters) |
| 08/70 | Ex-T | 08/70 | 08/70 | ? | ? | ? | B Transmission removed (defective clutches) |
| 09/70 | Ex-T | 09/70 | 09/70 | ? | ? | ? | B Transmission removed (ratcheting) |
| 01/71 | Ex-T | 01/71 | 01/71 | ? | ? | ? | A Transmission removed (output oil seals leaking) |
| 07/71 | Ex-T | 07/71 | 07/71 | ? | ? | ? | A Engine removed for general repair |
| 22/08/71 | Ex-T | 22/08/71 | 23/08/71 | LA | H/C | 1 | A & B Engines removed |
| 01/01/72 | NA | 16/03/72 | 17/03/72 | LA | ? | 76 | Withdrawn on 01/01/72, D829 was hauled from Newton Abbot to Laira with D814 and D825 for re-instatement to traffic on 16/03/72. After repair D829 was released on 17/03/72 |
| 15/07/72 | Ex-T | 15/07/72 | 17/07/72 | LA | L/C | 2 | B Transmission removed |
| 25/08/72 | WES | 26/08/72 | 26/08/72 | LA | - | | D829 was withdrawn at Westbury on 25/08/72 and travelled under its own power to Laira on 26/08/72 |

D829 MAGPIE at Swindon Works on 24 September 1961, during a Light Classified overhaul lasting from 22 September until 5 October. The class visited Swindon much more frequently in the early years for minor repairs, until facilities became available at Laira and the other depots to carry out more of the lighter work. (EW Fry)

829 MAGPIE at Didcot GWS, smartened up for the Open Day on 18 September 1971. The 1B25 headcode was from the previous Wednesday when it had taken the 13.30 down to Paignton, worked back up to London with the Chard milk and then spent a couple of days at Old Oak being specially cleaned in preparation for the event. Regal treatment for a loco which would be withdrawn in three months, although MAGPIE was one of three Class 42s to get a reprieve over the summer of 1972. An abortive preservation attempt was made by the namesake ITV childrens programme in October 1972. (www.rail-online.co.uk)

# D830 MAJESTIC

| Lot no./Works no. | 437 / - |
|---|---|
| **Significant dates and allocations** | |
| Into traffic - Newton Abbot | 19/01/61 |
| Stored (Newton Abbot) | 02/69 |
| Withdrawn (Newton Abbot) | 26/03/69 |
| (Laira) | By 25/06/69 |
| (Exeter) | 4/10/69 |
| (Swindon) | 27/07/70 |
| Date cut-up | By 22/10/71 |

| **Livery and insignia changes** | |
|---|---|
| Green | 19/01/61 |
| OHLW flashes | 09/04/62 |
| Yellow warning panels | 09/04/62 |
| Maroon | - |
| Blue yellow panels – single insignia, serif, D-prefix | 08/01/67 |
| Blue full yellow ends – single insignia, serif, D-prefix | 08/67 |
| **Recorded mileage** | 447,000 |

**Works visits and depot repairs**

| Stopped | At | On Works | Off Works | At | Type | Days | Work carried out |
|---|---|---|---|---|---|---|---|
| - | - | - | 19/01/61 | SW | D/A | | Delivery inspection and acceptance |
| 04/61 | Ex-T | 17/04/61 | 05/05/61 | SW | L/C | 18 | |
| 04/09/61 | Ex-T | 04/09/61 | 06/09/61 | LA | L/C | 2 | |
| 23/10/61 | NA | 24/10/61 | 02/11/61 | SW | L/C | 10 | |
| 26/03/62 | Ex-T | 26/03/62 | 09/04/62 | SW | L/C | 14 | A Engine removed; B Engine repaired in situ with Paxman Engineers |
| 08/62 | Ex-T | 16/08/62 | 08/62 | NA | Unsch | ? | |
| 10/62 | Ex-T | 02/10/62 | 17/10/62 | SW | H/C | 15 | |
| 08/11/62 | NA | 09/11/62 | 16/11/62 | SW | H/C | 8 | B Transmission removed |
| 14/05/63 | NA | 16/05/63 | 18/07/63 | SW | H/C | 65 | |
| 18/12/63 | NA | 19/12/63 | 24/12/63 | LA | H/C | 5 | A Transmission removed (input bearings defective) |
| 03/02/64 | NA | 13/02/64 | 11/03/64 | SW | Unsch | 37 | A Engine removed (fractures found at the No. 3 crank web) |
| 13/03/64 | 999 | 26/03/64 | 19/06/64 | SW | Unsch | 98 | A Engine removed (low lub. oil pressure); B Engine removed for sump modification |
| 07/10/64 | Ex-T | 10/64 | ? | SW | ? | ? | A Engine oil leaking from lub. oil pipes to cylinder heads and liners began to lift on removing the heads; B Engine attention to liners and heads |
| 02/02/65 | Ex-T | 02/65 | ? | SW | Unsch | ? | A & B Engines unscheduled repairs carried out in situ |
| 07/65 | Ex-T | 17/07/65 | 07/65 | NA | Unsch | ? | A exhauster changed |
| 09/65 | Ex-T | 20/09/65 | 09/65 | NA | Unsch | ? | A end dynostarter changed (broken mounting foot) |
| 05/66 | Ex-T | 23/05/66 | 05/66 | LA | ? | ? | B Transmission changed (not changing gear) |
| 11/66 | Ex-T | 11/66 | 11/66 | ? | ? | ? | A & B Bogies removed |
| ? | Ex-T | ? | 08/01/67 | SW | Int | ? | |
| 04/67 | Ex-T | 04/67 | 04/67 | ? | ? | ? | B Transmission removed (Nos. 2 and 6 dog clutches worn) |
| ? | Ex-T | ? | 08/67 | SW | ? | ? | |
| 11/67 | Ex-T | 11/67 | 11/67 | ? | ? | ? | A Transmission changed (lift in the dynostarter input bearing) |
| 01/68 | Ex-T | 01/68 | 01/68 | ? | ? | ? | A Transmission removed (No. 2 gear control piston seized) |
| 04/68 | Ex-T | 04/68 | 04/68 | ? | ? | ? | A Bogie removed due to frame fractures |
| 21/03/69 | Ex-T | | 26/03/69 | NA | | | Withdrawn |

1. AIR INLET TRUNKING
2. WATER OUTLET MANIFOLD
3. CYLINDER HEAD
4. ROCKER LEVER
5. THERMOSTATIC CONTROL VALVE
6. CYLINDER HEAD COVER
7. FUEL INJECTOR
8. BRIDGE PIECE FOR CYLINDER HEAD STUD
9. INLET VALVE
10. AIR VESSEL
11. AIR INLET MANIFOLD
12. EXHAUST VALVE
13. FUEL OIL FILTER
14. FUEL FEED PUMP
15. LUBRICATING OIL FILLER
16. CRANKCASE INSPECTION DOOR
17. CRANKCASE
18. FUEL-INJECTION PUMP
19. LUBRICATING OIL SUMP
20. OVERSPEED TRIP UNIT
21. FUEL PUMP CONTROL ROD
22. WATER INLET MANIFOLD
23. FUEL INJECTOR DRAIN RAIL
24. CYLINDER LINER
25. FUEL PUMP DRIVE CARDAN SHAFT
26. PISTON
27. CRANKCASE TRANSVERSE WEB
28. GUDGEON PIN
29. LARGE-END BEARING BLOCK
30. CENTRE CONNECTING ROD
31. FORKED CONNECTING ROD
32. CRANKSHAFT
33. SAFETY VALVE
34. CRANKSHAFT BALANCE WEIGHT
35. PRESSURE OIL PUMP
36. PRESSURE OIL PUMP GEARWHEEL
37. MAIN BEARING CAP SOCKET-HEAD SCREW
38. SUCTION STRAINER
39. COOLING OIL PUMP GEARWHEEL
40. DRIVE-END SPLASH PLATE
41. IDLER GEARWHEEL
42. MAIN BEARING CAP
43. CRANKSHAFT GEARWHEEL
44. OUTER MAIN BEARING
45. FUEL PUMP DRIVE GEARWHEEL
46. DOUBLE IDLER GEARWHEEL
47. SPRAYER FOR GEARS
48. DOUBLE IDLER GEARWHEEL
49. LUBRICATING OIL GALLERY
50. CAMSHAFT DRIVE GEARWHEEL
51. IDLER GEARWHEEL
52. CAMSHAFT
53. GOVERNOR DRIVE BEVEL GEARS
54. VALVE TAPPET HOUSING
55. WATER PUMP DRIVE GEARWHEEL
56. WATER PUMP DRIVE SHAFT
57. PUSH ROD
58. GOVERNOR LUBRICATING OIL FILTER
59. TURBO-BLOWER BRACKETS
60. EXHAUST MANIFOLD
61. GOVERNOR
62. TURBO-BLOWER

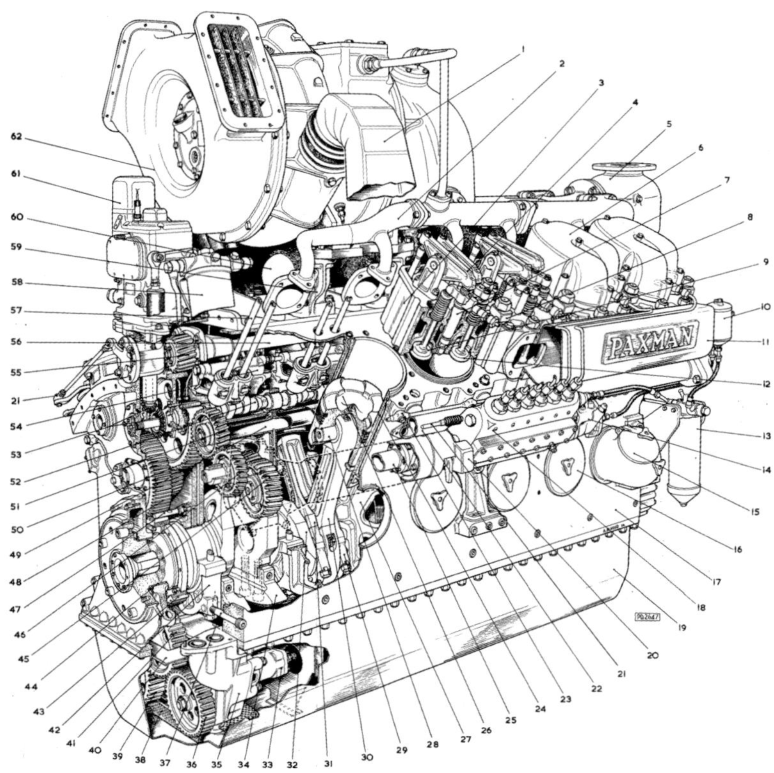


**For the story of MAJESTIC's Paxman engines, see page 108.**

**D830 MAJESTIC stands in the reception/despatch area at Swindon Works in 1965; the doors to the rear of the locomotive lead into 'A' Shop. MAJESTIC was unique amongst the Warships in having Paxman engines instead of the standard Maybachs. D830 covered around half the average distance for a D800 during its relatively short life. This was not as a result of any inherent unreliability but the inevitable consequence of maintaining a unique locomotive. (www.rail-online.co.uk)**

**D830 MAJESTIC in Dorset, north of Monkton and Came Halt with a Footex from Bristol to Weymouth on 4 June 1967. Its power units were not the only unique aspect of D830, the combination of blue livery with BR emblems above the nameplate and small yellow panels was carried by no other Warship. MAJESTIC received this livery at Swindon during December 1966 but by August of the following year a full yellow end had been applied; the small BR symbol above the nameplate remained until its withdrawal in March 1969. (Michael Mensing)**

# D831 MONARCH

| | |
|---|---|
| Lot no./Works no. | 437 / - |
| **Significant dates and allocations** | |
| Into traffic - Laira | 11/01/61 |
| Newton Abbot | 07/61 |
| Laira | 06/65 |
| Newton Abbot | 09/65 |
| Laira | 08/67 |
| Withdrawn (Laira) | 08/10/71 |
| (Bristol St Philips Marsh Junction) | 18/10/71 |
| (Swindon) | 16/03/72 |
| Date cut-up | By 23/06/72 |

| | |
|---|---|
| **Modifications** | |
| Multiple working jumper cables and sockets removed | 30/11/66 |
| **Livery and insignia changes** | |
| Green | 11/01/61 |
| OHLW flashes | 13/10/61 |
| Yellow warning panels | 17/01/63 |
| Maroon | - |
| Blue yellow panels – double insignia, serif numbers positioned underneath bodyside windows, D-prefix | 30/11/66 |
| Blue full yellow ends – single insignia, sans serif, no D | 04/03/69 |
| **Recorded mileage** | 1,011,000 |

**Works visits and depot repairs**

| Stopped | At | On Works | Off Works | At | Type | Days | Work carried out |
|---|---|---|---|---|---|---|---|
| - | - | - | 11/01/61 | SW | D/A | | Delivery inspection and acceptance |
| 10/03/61 | LA | 10/03/61 | 22/03/61 | SW | Casual | 12 | A & B Engines (excessive valve cam clearance, new rocker boxes fitted; A end dynostarter cardan shaft changed) |
| 28/03/61 | Ex-T | 28/03/61 | 14/04/61 | SW | L/C | 17 | B Bogie changed (left hand outer axle bearing overheated) |
| 25/07/61 | Ex-T | 25/07/61 | 04/08/61 | SW | Casual | 10 | A Engine (leaking No. 1 cylinder head gasket repaired and Nos. 1 - 6 cylinder heads inclusive changed); B Engine (water pump changed and Nos. 1 - 6 cylinder heads inclusive changed) |
| 06/10/61 | BS | 06/10/61 | 13/10/61 | SW | L/C | 7 | A & B Engine air manifolds fitted with Griflex drains; B Bogie changed (steel and bronze particles found in the inner final drive) |
| 23/10/61 | NA | 23/10/61 | 24/10/61 | LA | L/C | 1 | A Bogie tyres turned |
| 03/11/61 | NA | 03/11/61 | 14/11/61 | SW | L/C | 11 | A Transmission changed (failing to reverse and metal in filters) |
| 14/12/61 | Ex-T | 18/12/61 | 23/12/61 | NA | L/C | 9 | A Bogie changed (final drive defects) |
| 04/01/62 | Ex-T | 04/01/62 | 18/01/62 | SW | L/C | 14 | Boiler changed; B end Vapor-Watchman preheater repaired, A end Vapor-Watchman preheater changed (both due to frost damage- D831 was left outside the depot at Newton Abbot over the week-end of 16 /17 December without being drained at the A end because the drain cock had frozen solid, although the B end had been drained. As a result of the severe cold weather several locos, including D831, sustained damage to pipe work caused by the freezing temperatures) |
| 12/01/62 | Ex-T | 12/10/62 | 13/10/62 | LA | L/C | 1 | |
| 18/12/62 | LA | 21/12/62 | 17/01/63 | SW | H/C | 30 | A & B Engines changed; B Bogie changed (outer final drive gears extensively damaged) |
| 20/08/63 | NA | 20/08/63 | 21/08/63 | LA | H/C | 1 | A Engine changed (Nos. 8, 9 and 10 cylinders full of coolant) |
| 04/11/63 | Ex-T | 04/11/63 | 18/11/63 | NA | Unsch | 14 | |
| 04/01/64 | Ex-T | 08/01/64 | 31/01/64 | NA | Unsch | 27 | Boiler changed (both inner and outer coils burst) |
| 13/04/64 | Ex-T | 04/64 | 20/04/64 | NA | Unsch | 7 | Boiler changed (defective coils) |
| 20/04/64 | NA | 21/04/64 | 14/05/64 | SW | Unsch | 24 | A Engine changed; B Engine Turbo blower changed; A Transmission changed; B Transmission changed (suffering from occasional 'trips'); A & B Bogies changed; Boiler changed; Modifications; Bogie side control linkage replaced with hydraulic shock absorbers |
| 07/64 | Ex-T | 28/07/64 | 07/64 | LA | L/C | ? | A Engine changed (broken valve rocker gear lugs) |
| 05/65 | Ex-T | 14/05/65 | 05/65 | LA | H/C | ? | A Transmission changed (suffering from excessive lift on the output shaft to the dynostarter, pressure in the suction pump, twin gear drive shaft bearing collapsed and metal in filters) |
| 16/06/65 | Ex-T | 18/06/65 | 06/65 | LA | L/C | ? | B Bogie changed (the outer final drive seized and all gears stripped) |
| 09/65 | Ex-T | 20/09/65 | 09/65 | LA | L/C | ? | B Bogie changed (inner final drive seriously overheated) |
| 10/65 | Ex-T | 15/10/65 | 10/65 | LA | L/C | ? | A Engine changed (exhaust and coolant leaks from Nos. 5, 6 and 8 cylinder heads) |
| 05/66 | Ex-T | 13/05/66 | 05/66 | LA | H/C | ? | B Engine changed; Boiler changed |
| 27/09/66 | Ex-T | 28/09/66 | 09/66 | LA | L/C | ? | B Engine changed (low lub. oil pressure) |
| 10/66 | Ex-T | 10/10/66 | 30/11/66 | SW | Int | 51 | A & B Engines repaired; A & B Transmissions repaired; A & B Bogies changed; Modifications; Multiple working jumper cables and sockets removed from buffer beam; all hoses and cardan shafts changed; exhausters and compressor changed |
| 01/67 | Ex-T | 14/01/67 | 01/67 | ? | L/C | ? | A Bogie changed (flaw trace on No. 2 groove on the inner axle) |
| 04/67 | Ex-T | 19/04/67 | 04/67 | LA | Unsch | ? | A end dynostarter changed |
| 24/04/67 | Ex-T | 24/04/67 | 04/67 | NA | L/C | ? | A Engine Turbo blower changed |
| 27/04/67 | Ex-T | 28/04/67 | 04/67 | LA | L/C | ? | B Engine changed (Nos. 3 and 4 cylinder heads blowing) |
| 05/67 | Ex-T | 13/05/67 | 05/67 | LA | L/C | ? | A Engine changed (crank shaft fracturing at No. 3 crank pin) |
| 02/11/67 | Ex-T | 06/11/67 | 11/67 | LA | L/C | ? | A Transmission changed (coming out of direction) |
| 08/12/67 | Ex-T | 08/12/67 | 12/67 | LA | L/C | ? | B Transmission changed |
| 02/68 | Ex-T | 13/02/68 | 02/68 | LA | L/C | ? | B Bogie changed (a fracture in the bogie frame) |
| 05/68 | Ex-T | 22/05/68 | 05/68 | LA | L/C | ? | Boiler changed |
| 10/09/68 | Ex-T | 10/09/68 | 09/68 | LA | L/C | ? | A Bogie changed |
| 10/68 | Ex-T | 03/10/68 | 10/68 | LA | L/C | ? | B Transmission changed (metal in filters) |
| 11/68 | Ex-T | 13/11/68 | 11/68 | NA | Unsch | ? | B end dynostarter changed (damaged coupling) |
| 03/02/69 | BS | 04/02/69 | 04/03/69 | SW | U/C | 29 | A & B Engines changed; B Transmission changed (bottom casing disintegrated, main casing fractured, sump plate broken and Nos. 1 and 4 clutches overheated and worn); A Bogie repaired (torn side control rubbers, thrust pads worn and hydraulic dampers missing); B Bogie repaired (frame damage caused by a broken cardan shaft); Modifications |
| 04/69 | Ex-T | 14/04/69 | 04/69 | LA | L/C | ? | B Engine changed (low lub. oil pressure) |
| 04/69 | Ex-T | 18/04/69 | 04/69 | NA | L/C | ? | Boiler changed (coil splitting) |
| 10/12/69 | Ex-T | 10/12/69 | 11/12/69 | LA | L/C | 1 | A Engine changed (No. 7 cylinder liner leaking) |
| 05/70 | Ex-T | 07/05/70 | 05/70 | LA | Unsch | ? | B Engine Turbo blower changed |
| 11/05/70 | Ex-T | 11/05/70 | 13/05/70 | LA | L/C | 2 | B Transmission changed (output oil seals and convertor 'O' rings leaking) |
| 28/06/70 | Ex-T | 28/06/70 | 30/06/70 | LA | L/C | 2 | B Transmission changed (loss of oil pressure) |
| 19/08/70 | Ex-T | 08/70 | 25/08/70 | LA | L/C | 6 | B Engine changed (Nos. 5 and 6 cylinder heads studs seized) |
| 15/09/70 | Ex-T | 15/09/70 | 20/09/70 | LA | L/C | 5 | A Transmission changed |
| 05/11/70 | Ex-T | 05/11/70 | 08/11/70 | LA | L/C | 3 | B Transmission changed (clutches becoming disconnected) |
| 27/11/70 | Ex-T | 27/11/70 | 28/11/70 | LA | H/C | 1 | A & B Bogies changed |
| 04/03/71 | Ex-T | 04/03/71 | 06/03/71 | NA | L/C | 2 | Boiler changed (coil splitting) |
| 23/04/71 | Ex-T | 23/04/71 | 26/04/71 | LA | L/C | 3 | B Transmission changed (metal in filters) |
| 26/07/71 | Ex-T | 26/07/71 | 29/07/71 | LA | L/C | 3 | B Engine changed ( fractured crankcase) |
| 08/10/71 | LA | | | | - | | Withdrawn (B Transmission defective) |

**D831 MONARCH crosses into Devon over the Royal Albert Bridge at Saltash with a mixed freight from St Blazey on 29 May 1968. This was another unique livery as Swindon struggled to come to terms with the conflicting instructions from on high as to the new blue livery. D831 was the second Warship to receive blue when it left Swindon on 30 November 1966, and remained in this livery until March 1969. It was understandably a favourite with photographers, especially as it was also multiple working fitted and was often to be seen paired up on the West of England expresses during 1968/9. (Alec Swain, www.transporttreasury.co.uk).**

**831 MONARCH on 30 November 1969 at Bristol Temple Meads; its unique livery has gone but the multiple working equipment remains. It lasted until October 1971 when it was withdrawn with a defective transmission. (www.rail-online.co.uk)**

# D832 ONSLAUGHT

| Lot no./Works no. | 437 / - |
|---|---|
| **Significant dates and allocations** | |
| Into traffic - Laira | 08/02/61 |
| Newton Abbot | 07/61 |
| Laira | 06/65 |
| Newton Abbot | 09/65 |
| Laira | 08/67 |
| Newton Abbot | 10/71 |
| Laira | 01/72 |
| Stored (Laira) | 07/11/72 |
| Withdrawn (Laira) | 16/12/72 |
| Derby RTC | 10/01/73 |
| Preserved | 04/79 |

| **Modifications** | |
|---|---|
| **Livery and insignia changes** | |
| Green | 08/02/61 |
| OHLW flashes | 14/11/61 |
| Yellow warning panels | 01/12/62 |
| Maroon yellow warning panels | 01/04/66 |
| Maroon full yellow ends | 03/69 |
| Blue full yellow ends – double insignia, sans serif, no D | 11/70 |
| **Recorded mileage** | 1,131,000 |

**Works visits and depot repairs**

| Stopped | At | On Works | Off Works | At | Type | Days | Work carried out |
|---|---|---|---|---|---|---|---|
| - | - | - | 08/02/61 | SW | D/A | | Delivery inspection and acceptance |
| 05/05/61 | OOC | 11/05/61 | 17/05/61 | SW | L/C | 12 | |
| 01/11/61 | Ex-T | 01/11/61 | 14/11/61 | SW | L/C | 13 | |
| 06/04/62 | LA | 06/04/62 | 11/04/62 | ? | L/C | 5 | |
| 15/07/62 | Ex-T | 15/07/62 | 17/07/62 | LA | H/C | 2 | A Engine changed (cracked liner) |
| 19/11/62 | NA | 22/11/62 | 01/12/62 | SW | L/C | 12 | |
| 07/01/63 | Ex-T | 07/01/63 | 25/01/63 | LA | H/C | 18 | |
| 12/06/63 | Ex-T | 12/06/63 | 12/06/63 | LA | L/C | 1 | |
| 18/06/63 | NA | 19/06/63 | 05/07/63 | SW | H/C | 17 | A Transmission removed |
| 29/07/63 | Ex-T | ? | 16/08/63 | NA | U/C | 18 | |
| 05/09/63 | Ex-T | 05/09/63 | 05/09/63 | LA | L/C | 1 | |
| 22/04/64 | Ex-T | 04/64 | 08/05/64 | NA | U/C | 16 | |
| 20/05/64 | NA | 05/64 | ? | SW | ? | ? | Modifications |
| 09/64 | Ex-T | 09/64 | ? | SW | ? | ? | Boiler removed |
| 08/65 | Ex-T | 08/65 | 08/65 | ? | ? | ? | Transmission removed (bearing cage broken and slipper pieces worn) |
| 12/65 | Ex-T | 12/65 | 12/65 | ? | ? | ? | A Bogie removed (flats);B Bogie removed |
| 01/66 | Ex-T | 04/01/66 | 01/66 | SW | ? | ? | A & B Engines changed |
| 07/66 | Ex-T | 07/66 | 07/66 | ? | ? | ? | A Bogie removed (inner final drive bearing overheated) |
| ? | Ex-T | ? | 10/66 | SW | Int | ? | B Engine removed (No. 3 cylinder head and liner damaged); A Transmission removed (not engaging gears) |
| 11/66 | Ex-T | 21/11/66 | 11/66 | LA | ? | ? | A Engine changed (fractured liners) |
| 11/67 | Ex-T | 23/11/67 | 11/67 | LA | L/C | | A Transmission changed (No. 4 clutch defective) |
| 01/68 | Ex-T | 11/01/68 | 01/68 | LA | ? | ? | A Engine changed; B Transmission changed |
| 03/68 | Ex-T | 03/68 | 03/68 | ? | ? | ? | B Bogie removed |
| 04/68 | Ex-T | 25/04/68 | 04/68 | ? | ? | ? | A Transmission removed (oil seals leaking) |
| 05/68 | Ex-T | 27/05/68 | 05/68 | ? | ? | ? | A Bogie removed |
| 07/68 | Ex-T | 07/68 | 07/68 | ? | ? | ? | A Bogie removed (inner final drive bearing seized) |
| 01/69 | Ex-T | 09/01/69 | 03/69 | SW | U/C | ? | A Transmission removed (output assembly broken off); B Transmission changed; A Bogie removed (frame damage caused by a detached cardan shaft); Modifications |
| 02/70 | Ex-T | 02/70 | 02/70 | ? | ? | ? | B Bogie removed |
| 03/70 | Ex-T | 03/70 | 03/70 | ? | ? | ? | A Bogie removed (traces on the No. 1 axle); B Bogie removed |
| 05/70 | Ex-T | 05/70 | 05/70 | ? | ? | ? | B Engine removed; B Transmission removed; Boiler removed (intermediate coil splitting) |
| 09/70 | Ex-T | 09/70 | 09/70 | ? | ? | ? | B Transmission removed (convertor 'O' rings leaking) |
| ? | Ex-T | ? | 11/70 | SW | ? | ? | B Transmission removed (clutch damaged and metal in filters) |
| 10/11/71 | Ex-T | 10/11/71 | 17/11/71 | NA | L/C | 7 | B Transmission changed (not changing direction) |
| 28/02/72 | Ex-T | 28/07/72 | 01/03/72 | LA | L/C | 2 | |
| 19/05/72 | Ex-T | 19/05/72 | 23/05/72 | LA | L/C | 4 | B Transmission removed (casing smashed) |
| 03/08/72 | Ex-T | 03/08/72 | 10/08/72 | LA | L/C | 7 | A Engine removed (pistons passing oil) |
| 06/11/72 | LA | 07/11/72 | 16/12/72 | | - | | Withdrawn |

D832 ONSLAUGHT stands on Horton Road shed on 29 April 1970. The loco had worked up to Gloucester on the 1E54 13.55 Plymouth-Leeds. Quite what the passengers thought of the abominable state of their train engine can only be imagined. Although none of the paint used on the Warships wore well, the maroon appeared to be particularly prone to deterioration. D6331 stands behind, one of only two NBL type 2s to carry green with a full yellow end. (NE Preedy)

832 ONSLAUGHT at Exeter St David's on 29 May 1971, looking considerably more presentable, corporate blue having been applied in the previous November. ONSLAUGHT has just been released from the stock of the 1V11 11.00 Waterloo-Exeter and will later return on the 1O20 20.07 Exeter-Basingstoke. Officially it was the last Warship in service when withdrawn on 16th December 1972, although it had been in store since 8 November; 810, 812, 821 and 824 all survived in traffic after this date. However it outlived all except fellow survivor 821 by virtue of its use by Derby RTC, which allowed it to be preserved in 1979. (www.rail-online.co.uk)

# D833 PANTHER

| Lot no./Works no. | 443/27962 |
|---|---|
| **Significant dates and allocations** | |
| Delivered | 17/06/60 |
| Into traffic - Laira | 06/07/60 |
| Newton Abbot | 07/61 |
| Old Oak Common | 07/67 |
| Bescot (Temporary) | 08/67 |
| Old Oak Common | 09/67 |
| Newton Abbot | 10/70 |
| Withdrawn (Newton Abbot) | 03/10/71 |
| (Bristol St Philips Marsh Junction) | By 22/10/71 |
| (Swindon) | 30/12/71 |
| Date cut-up | By 05/02/72 |

| **Stored** | From | To |
|---|---|---|
| Old Oak Common | 03/69 | 09/69 |
| Reading | 21/09/71 | 25/09/71 |

| **Livery and insignia changes** | |
|---|---|
| Green | 06/07/60 |
| OHLW flashes | 20/10/61 |
| Yellow warning panels | 26/09/62 |
| Maroon | - |
| Blue full yellow ends – double insignia, serif, D-prefix | - |
| Single insignia, sans serif, no D | 09/69 |
| **Recorded mileage** | 671,000 |

**Works visits and depot repairs**

| Stopped | At | On Works | Off Works | At | Type | Days | Work carried out |
|---|---|---|---|---|---|---|---|
| - | - | 17/06/60 | 06/07/60 | SW | D/A | 18 | Delivery inspection and acceptance |
| 01/11/60 | LA | 03/11/60 | 28/11/60 | SW | L/C | 27 | |
| 16/05/61 | Ex-T | 16/05/61 | 24/05/61 | SW | L/C | 8 | |
| 07/06/61 | LA | 09/06/61 | 08/07/61 | SW | L/C | 31 | |
| 16/08/61 | NA | 21/08/61 | 07/09/61 | SW | Un | 22 | |
| 06/10/61 | NA | 06/10/61 | 20/10/61 | SW | Un | 14 | |
| 29/11/61 | Ex-T | 11/61 | 12/12/61 | NA | Un | 13 | |
| 16/12/61 | Ex-T | 12/61 | 28/12/61 | NA | L/C | 12 | |
| 25/06/62 | Ex-T | 06/62 | 09/07/62 | NA | Unsch | 14 | |
| 15/08/62 | Ex-T | 08/62 | 25/08/62 | LA | H/C | 10 | A Transmission removed (control piston seized) |
| 04/09/62 | BS | 07/09/62 | 26/09/62 | SW | H/C | 22 | B Engine removed (high lub. oil consumption); A Transmission removed; Boiler removed |
| 27/11/62 | Ex-T | 27/11/62 | 28/11/62 | LA | L/C | 1 | |
| 07/03/63 | Ex-T | 03/63 | 15/03/63 | ? | H/C | 8 | |
| 25/03/63 | NA | 29/03/63 | 19/04/63 | SW | H/C | 25 | |
| 05/07/63 | Ex-T | 07/63 | 24/07/63 | LA | H/C | 19 | |
| 26/09/63 | Ex-T | 26/09/63 | 28/09/63 | LA | H/C | 2 | |
| 15/10/63 | LA | 17/10/63 | 11/11/63 | SW | H/C | 17 | B Bogie changed; Modifications |
| 05/64 | Ex-T | 05/05/64 | 05/05/64 | LA | L/C | ? | A Engine changed |
| 20/05/64 | NA | 26/05/64 | 22/06/64 | SW | Unsch | 33 | A & B Bogie removed (inner axle flaw suspected) |
| 10/64 | Ex-T | 24/10/64 | 10/64 | LA | H/C | ? | A Bogie changed |
| 03/65 | Ex-T | 16/03/65 | 03/65 | LA | H/C | ? | A Bogie changed |
| 06/65 | Ex-T | 06/65 | 09/65 | SW | L/C | ? | A Engine changed, A (bottom casing fractured ) & B Transmissions removed |
| 09/65 | Ex-T | ? | 22/09/65 | LA | L/C | 14 | A Engine changed (low lubricating oil pressure) |
| 11/65 | Ex-T | ? | 18/11/65 | ? | ? | ? | A & B Transmissions changed |
| 19/04/66 | Ex-T | 04/66 | 06/66 | SW | H/C | ? | A Engine removed, A Bogie changed ; B Bogie removed (collision damage); Boiler repaired; Body repairs (collision damage) |
| 01/67 | Ex-T | 12/01/67 | 01/67 | LA | L/C | ? | A Transmission changed (no filling pump pressure) |
| 03/68 | Ex-T | 07/03/68 | 03/68 | LA | L/C | ? | A Bogie changed (thin tyres) |
| 05/68 | Ex-T | 05/68 | 05/68 | ? | L/C | ? | A Transmission removed (overheating and metal in filters) |
| 06/68 | Ex-T | 06/68 | 06/68 | ? | ? | ? | Engine removed |
| 07/68 | Ex-T | 07/68 | 07/68 | ? | L/C | ? | A Transmission removed (forward / reverse gear defects) |
| 03/69 | Ex-T | - | 06/69 | OOC | - | ? | To store / Re-instated to traffic |
| 06/69 | Ex-S | 06/69 | 09/69 | SW | Int | ? | A & B Engines removed (passing oil) |
| 09/70 | Ex-T | ? | | ? | L/C | ? | B Transmission removed |
| 10/70 | Ex-T | 10/70 | 10/70 | ? | L/C | ? | A Transmission removed (metal in filters) |
| 11/70 | Ex-T | 11/70 | 11/70 | ? | L/C | ? | Boiler removed |
| 01/71 | Ex-T | 01/71 | 01/71 | ? | L/C | ? | Engine removed (passing oil) |
| 04/71 | Ex-T | 04/71 | 04/71 | ? | L/C | ? | A Bogie removed (lift in the input bearings) |
| 22/09/71 | RG | | 03/10/71 | NA | - | | Stopped after A engine failed, hauled from Reading to NA on 25/09/71; then withdrawn |

**Just over two months old, and with only two of its Glasgow stablemates in traffic, D833 PANTHER departs Paddington on 10 September 1960 with the 11.40am to Penzance. At first glance the NBL-built Warships were identical to those built at Swindon but on closer examination a number of small detail variations come to light. The shedplate which can be seen on the bufferbeam is the easiest to spot; the BR Warships carried them on the side of the valance. (RC Riley, www.transporttreasury.co.uk)**

**On 18 July 1971, two months before its demise, 833 PANTHER is accompanied on to Newton Abbot depot by D7001. PANTHER had failed earlier in the day at Whiteball while working the 1Z30 08.30 Paignton-Weymouth, and D7001 was called on to assist. The pair had continued in tandem to Westbury where they were relieved by 824. The locomotives then returned to Newton Abbot on a Portsmouth-Plymouth military special. There was a minor fault to the water pump which was rectified by the following day. (NE Preedy)**

# D834 PATHFINDER

| Lot no./Works no. | 443/27963 |
|---|---|
| **Significant dates and allocations** | |
| Delivered | 07/07/60 |
| Into traffic - Laira | 26/07/60 |
| Newton Abbot | 07/61 |
| Wolverhampton (Temporary) | 31/07/67 |
| Old Oak Common | 08/67 |
| Newton Abbot | 03/69 |
| Withdrawn (Newton Abbot) | 04/10/71 |
| (Bristol St Philips Marsh Junction) | By 24/10/71 |
| (Swindon) | 30/11/71 |
| Date cut-up | By 18/02/72 |

| **Livery and insignia changes** | |
|---|---|
| Green | 26/07/60 |
| OHLW flashes | 30/09/61 |
| Yellow warning panels | 16/01/62 |
| Maroon yellow warning panels | 10/06/66 |
| Maroon full yellow ends | 08/02/68 |
| Blue full yellow ends – single insignia, sans serif , no D | 31/12/70 |
| **Recorded mileage** | 754,000 |

**Works visits and depot repairs**

| Stopped | At | On Works | Off Works | At | Type | Days | Work carried out |
|---|---|---|---|---|---|---|---|
| - | - | 07/07/60 | 26/07/60 | SW | D/A | 19 | Delivery inspection and acceptance |
| 31/08/60 | Ex-T | 31/08/60 | 01/09/60 | SW | Unsch | 1 | Derailment damage inspected |
| 02/01/61 | LA | 04/01/61 | 23/01/61 | SW | Unsch | 21 | A Engine repaired |
| 26/05/61 | LA | | 10/06/61 | LA | Unsch | 15 | |
| 19/09/61 | Ex-T | 19/09/61 | 30/09/61 | SW | Casual | 11 | A & B Engines repaired (oil leaks); defective paint work and side panels rectified |
| 21/12/61 | LA | 02/01/62 | 16/01/62 | SW | L/C | 26 | B Transmission changed (lack of actuating pressure on the filling pump); A & B Bogies tyres reprofiled; A and B end dynostarters changed |
| 08/02/62 | BS | 14/02/62 | 27/02/62 | SW | L/C | 19 | B Transmission changed (forward / reverse gears defective and sump leaking oil) |
| 03/07/62 | LA | 10/07/62 | 08/08/62 | SW | H/C | 36 | A Transmission changed (output drive bearing collapsed); A & B Bogies repaired; Boiler changed |
| 13/10/62 | LA | 17/10/62 | 13/11/62 | SW | H/C | 31 | A & B Engines changed (bad oil leaks and high lub. oil consumption); A Bogie changed (extensive frame fractures, left hand side); B Bogie changed (worn brake gear); A & B end engine room roof sections repaired and all cardan shafts repaired |
| 11/12/62 | Ex-T | 11/12/62 | 22/12/62 | LA | H/C | 11 | A Transmission changed (no pressure on the filling pump) |
| 23/06/63 | NA | | 09/07/63 | NA | Unsch | 16 | |
| 23/09/63 | NA | 08/10/63 | 17/01/64 | SW | Casual | 119 | A Engine changed (high lub. oil consumption); B Engine changed; A Transmission changed; B Transmission changed (overheating and noisy); A & B Bogies changed (worn tyres); Boiler changed |
| 18/02/64 | NA | 10/03/64 | 26/03/64 | SW | Unsch | 37 | A Bogie changed; B Bogie changed (flawed outer axle); Bogie side control linkage replaced with hydraulic shock absorbers |
| 31/07/64 | Ex-T | 08/64 | 22/08/64 | NA | H/C | 22 | A Engine changed (not venting properly and excessive aeration of the cooling system) |
| 03/65 | Ex-T | 02/03/65 | 03/65 | NA | Unsch | ? | A Engine Turbo blower changed (seizure) |
| 03/65 | Ex-T | 12/03/65 | 03/65 | NA | L/C | ? | Compressor changed (seizure) |
| 23/08/65 | Ex-T | 05/09/65 | 09/65 | LA | H/C | ? | A Bogie changed (inner final drive input bearing collapsed) |
| 12/65 | Ex-T | 07/12/65 | 12/65 | NA | Unsch | | A Engine Turbo blower changed |
| 01/66 | Ex-T | 26/01/66 | 01/66 | NA | L/C | ? | Boiler changed |
| 23/03/66 | Ex-T | 23/03/66 | 10/06/66 | SW | Int | 79 | A & B Engines changed; B Transmission changed (leaking oil seals); A & B Bogies changed; Modifications; all hoses and cardan shafts changed; exhausters and compressor changed |
| 10/66 | Ex-T | 18/10/66 | 19/10/66 | NA | L/C | ? | A & B Engines Turbo blower changed |
| 05/12/66 | Ex-T | 12/66 | 08/12/66 | NA | Unsch | 3 | A Engine Fuel pumps changed |
| 03/67 | Ex-T | 19/03/67 | 03/67 | LA | L/C | | A Transmission changed (low filling pump pressure) |
| 03/67 | Ex-T | 28/03/67 | 03/67 | NA | Unsch | ? | A end dynostarter changed |
| 09/67 | Ex-T | 13/09/67 | 09/67 | OOC | L/C | ? | A Transmission changed (fine metallic debris in the sump, a seized rotor and parts of a broken bearing cage found in the sump, the control piston seized and metal in filters) |
| 10/67 | Ex-T | 09/10/67 | 10/67 | OOC | L/C | ? | A Transmission changed (control piston seized, overheating and metal in filters) |
| 08/12/67 | OOC | 17/01/68 | 08/02/68 | SW | U/C | 61 | A & B Engines changed; B Transmission changed; A & B Bogies changed (traces on the outer axle); Boiler changed; collision damage to the A end repaired, large dent in right hand nose section repaired, buckled side cab sheeting repaired, damaged underframe and tubes straightened |
| 12/02/68 | Ex-T | 12/02/68 | 20/02/68 | SW | U/C | 8 | Draught proofing modifications |
| 07/68 | Ex-T | 23/07/68 | 07/68 | OOC | Unsch | ? | B Transmission changed (suspected output bearing collapsed) |
| 08/68 | Ex-T | 06/08/68 | 08/68 | OOC | L/C | ? | B Engine changed (No. 1 piston fractured) |
| 11/68 | Ex-T | 25/11/68 | 11/68 | OOC | L/C | ? | A Bogie changed (torque arm pivot fractured) |
| 01/69 | Ex-T | 02/01/69 | 01/69 | OOC | L/C | ? | B Transmission changed (clutch arm disconnected) |
| 03/69 | Ex-T | 26/03/69 | 03/69 | LA | L/C | ? | B Engine changed (fumes from the crank case breather) |
| 04/69 | Ex-T | 25/04/69 | 04/69 | NA | Unsch | ? | Turbo blower changed |
| 04/69 | Ex-T | 28/04/69 | 04/69 | LA | L/C | ? | B Engine repaired (passing lub. oil) |
| 05/69 | Ex-T | 07/05/69 | 05/69 | NA | Unsch | ? | B end dynostarter changed |
| 05/69 | Ex-T | 13/05/69 | 05/69 | NA | L/C | ? | A Engine Turbo blower changed (partial seizure) |
| 08/69 | Ex-T | 20/08/69 | 08/69 | NA | Unsch | ? | A exhauster changed |
| 12/11/69 | Ex-T | 11/69 | 18/11/69 | NA | L/C | 6 | B Transmission changed (forward / reverse clutch seized) |
| 02/03/70 | Ex-T | 02/03/70 | 04/03/70 | LA | L/C | 2 | A Transmission changed (No. 2 turbine parted at the rivets) |
| 21/05/70 | Ex-T | 21/05/70 | 23/05/70 | OOC | L/C | 2 | A Bogie changed (torque arm being damaged by loose cardan shafts bolts) |
| 03/06/70 | Ex-T | 06/70 | 25/06/70 | NA | H/C | 22 | Boiler changed; B exhauster changed (resistance on the motor) |
| 07/70 | Ex-T | 21/07/70 | 07/70 | LA | L/C | ? | A Engine changed (emitting fumes) |
| 10/70 | Ex-T | 12/10/70 | 10/70 | LA | L/C | ? | A Transmission changed (seized sliding dog) |
| 11/70 | Ex-T | 09/11/70 | 31/12/70 | SW | Int | 64 | A & B Engines changed; A & B Transmissions changed; A & B Bogies changed; Modifications; A end front apron damage repaired, all hoses and cardan shafts changed, exhausters and compressor changed |
| 01/01/71 | Ex-T | 01/01/71 | 20/01/71 | SW | Int | 19 | |
| 01/05/71 | Ex-T | 01/05/71 | 05/05/71 | LA | L/C | 4 | A Transmission changed (high temperatures in the No. 2 convertor) |
| 30/06/71 | Ex-T | 30/06/71 | 02/07/71 | LA | L/C | 2 | A Transmission changed (standstill detector defective) |
| 04/10/71 | Ex-T | | | NA | | | Fire damage and defective rocker gear; Withdrawn |

D834 PATHFINDER runs light through Bristol Temple Meads during the early summer of 1961. As noted previously, the Warships had a myriad of small detail differences and this even extended to the almost entirely unused driver's card holder beneath the cab window. The card holders were flush with the bottom of the window on the Swindon Warships but dropped down slightly on the NBLs, but it's never that straightforward, because D833-D835 had theirs in the Swindon position! (www.rail-online.co.uk)

D834 PATHFINDER being fuelled at Gloucester Horton Road depot on 9 March 1970. It has worked up on the 1E30 07.40 Plymouth-Newcastle and will return on the 1V87 12.15 Newcastle-Plymouth. This was a regular Warship turn in 1970 and the locomotive change was at the now sadly departed Gloucester Eastgate. PATHFINDER was one of four Class 43s to carry maroon livery with a full yellow end, the others being D838, D842 and D844. (www.rail-online.co.uk)

# D835 PEGASUS

| Lot no./Works no. | 443/27964 |
|---|---|
| **Significant dates and allocations** | |
| Delivered | 22/07/60 |
| Into traffic - Laira | 05/08/60 |
| Newton Abbot | 08/61 |
| Old Oak Common | 08/67 |
| Bescot (Temporary) | 07/08/67 |
| Withdrawn (Bristol Bath Road) | 04/10/71 |
| (Bristol St Philips Marsh Junction) | 10/71 |
| (Swindon) | 13/10/71 |
| Date cut-up | By 11/12/71 |

| **Livery and insignia changes** | |
|---|---|
| Green | 05/08/60 |
| OHLW flashes | 21/06/61 |
| Yellow warning panels | 01/06/62 |
| Maroon | - |
| Blue full yellow ends – double insignia, sans serif, D-prefix | 28/03/68 |
| Blue full yellow ends – single insignia, sans serif , no D | 08/04/71 |
| **Recorded mileage** | 785,000 |

**Works visits and depot repairs**

| Stopped | At | On Works | Off Works | At | Type | Days | Work carried out |
|---|---|---|---|---|---|---|---|
| - | - | 22/07/60 | 05/08/60 | SW | D/A | 14 | Unrecorded modifications carried out to Drawings Office instructions; ATC shoe gear equipment fitted |
| 19/04/61 | BS | 24/04/61 | 05/05/61 | SW | L/C | 16 | A & B Engines repaired; A & B Bogies repaired |
| 02/06/61 | LA | 14/06/61 | 21/06/61 | SW | Unsch | 19 | A & B Bogies reprofiled; B exhauster changed (overheating); B end dynostarter changed |
| 12/61 | Ex-T | 06/12/61 | 12/61 | LA | Unsch | ? | A Engine repaired (unable to create more than 20 p.s.i. lub. oil pressure) |
| 08/05/62 | TN | 14/05/62 | 01/06/62 | SW | H/C | 24 | B Transmission changed (forward/reverse gear 'tight'); B dynostarter cardan shaft changed. |
| 06/62 | Ex-T | 20/06/62 | 06/62 | LA | L/C | ? | B Engine Turbo blower changed |
| 10/07/62 | Ex-T | 13/07/62 | 14/07/62 | LA | L/C | 4 | Transmissions repaired; A & B Bogies Tyres turned |
| 02/08/62 | Ex-T | 03/08/62 | 29/08/62 | SW | L/C | 27 | A Transmission repaired; A & B Bogies repaired; Boiler changed |
| 06/11/62 | Ex-T | 06/11/62 | 07/11/62 | LA | L/C | 1 | A & B Bogies Tyres turned |
| 09/11/62 | NA | 15/11/62 | 22/11/62 | LA | H/C | 13 | A & B Engines changed (high lub. oil consumption, unable to maintain lub. oil pressure and fumes from the crank case breather) |
| 13/12/62 | NA | 21/12/62 | 08/01/63 | SW | H/C | 26 | A & B Bogies repaired (fumes from the crank case breather); B Transmission changed (overheating) |
| 16/07/63 | Ex-T | 16/07/63 | 18/07/63 | LA | H/C | 2 | A Engine changed (high lub. oil consumption and excessive fumes) |
| 05/09/63 | Ex-T | 09/63 | 25/09/63 | NA | Unsch | 20 | Boiler changed |
| 09/12/63 | Ex-T | 10/12/63 | 21/01/64 | SW | Casual | 42 | A & B Bogies changed (derailment damage); Modifications; Bogie side control linkage replaced with hydraulic shock absorbers; collision and derailment damage repaired, torn B end cab skin and valance repaired and damaged main frames repaired |
| 04/64 | Ex-T | 22/04/64 | 04/64 | LA | L/C | ? | A Transmission changed (overheating) |
| 19/05/64 | Ex-T | 28/05/64 | 04/06/64 | LA | L/C | 16 | A Transmission changed (convertor burst) |
| 13/08/64 | Ex-T | 13/08/64 | 13/08/64 | LA | Unsch | 1 | B Engine Turbo blower changed |
| 10/64 | Ex-T | 31/10/64 | 11/64 | LA | L/C | ? | B Engine changed (high lub. oil consumption) |
| 02/65 | Ex-T | 04/02/65 | 02/65 | LA | L/C | ? | A Transmission changed (extension shaft on the stand still detector being loose) |
| 23/03/65 | Ex-T | 26/03/65 | 22/06/65 | SW | Class | 91 | A Engine changed (Nos. 3, 4 and 5 cylinder liners leaking); B Engine changed (cylinder heads leaking); A Transmission changed; B Transmission changed (output flange bolts sheared and output seal housing damaged); A Bogie changed; B Bogie changed (outer final drive detached, main frame damaged by a detached cardan shaft and main side control brackets damaged); Modifications |
| 07/65 | Ex-T | 14/07/65 | 07/65 | NA | L/C | ? | A Engine changed (loose fuel pump drive) |
| 09/65 | Ex-T | 22/09/65 | 09/65 | NA | Unsch | ? | A Engine Fuel pumps changed |
| 11/65 | Ex-T | 01/11/65 | 11/65 | NA | Unsch | ? | Compressor changed (noisy, suspected bearing damage) |
| 10/11/65 | NA | 15/11/65 | 03/01/66 | SW | U/C | 54 | A & B Engines repaired; A Transmission changed (fractured sump); A Bogie changed (snapped outer final drive cardan shaft); B Bogie changed (suspected axle flaws); Boiler changed; Modifications; damaged frame A end caused by a snapped cardan shaft repaired; A end dynostarter changed |
| 02/66 | Ex-T | 24/02/66 | 02/66 | NA | Unsch | ? | B exhauster changed |
| 06/66 | Ex-T | 01/06/66 | 06/66 | NA | Unsch | ? | Compressor changed |
| 07/66 | Ex-T | 30/07/66 | 07/66 | NA | Unsch | ? | B end dynostarter changed |
| 08/66 | Ex-T | 22/08/66 | 08/66 | NA | Unsch | ? | A Engine Fuel pumps changed |
| 01/67 | Ex-T | 16/01/67 | 01/67 | NA | Unsch | ? | Batteries changed (life expired) |
| 02/67 | Ex-T | 17/02/67 | 02/67 | NA | Unsch | ? | A exhauster changed |
| 04/67 | Ex-T | 17/04/67 | 04/67 | LA | L/C | ? | A Transmission changed (control piston seized) |
| 08/05/67 | Ex-T | 11/05/67 | 05/67 | LA | H/C | ? | A & B Engines changed; A Transmission changed (control piston seized and cast iron debris in the sump) |
| 08/67 | Ex-T | 03/08/67 | 08/67 | OOC | H/C | ? | A & B Bogies changed (worn tyres too thin to turn) |
| 01/68 | Ex-T | 10/01/68 | 01/68 | OOC | L/C | ? | Boiler changed |
| 13/02/68 | OOC | 15/02/68 | 28/03/68 | SW | Class | 44 | B Transmission changed; A & B Bogies repaired; Modifications; Collision damage repaired (A left hand bottom of nose ripped open, side decking ripped open and buckled for approx. 18", cab entry step A left hand side partially ripped off and distorted, kick strips ripped away from body, side apron fractured, inner and outer sand box doors distorted and dents in cab nose) |
| 02/69 | Ex-T | 14/02/69 | 02/69 | OOC | L/C | ? | B Engine changed (passing oil) |
| 30/07/69 | Ex-T | 07/69 | 16/08/69 | OOC | H/C | 17 | A & B Engines changed (fuming); A Bogie changed (axle flaw) |
| 11/10/69 | Ex-T | 11/10/69 | 16/10/69 | OOC | L/C | 5 | B Engine changed (big end bearing collapsed) |
| 13/11/69 | Ex-T | 13/11/69 | 15/11/69 | OOC | L/C | 2 | B Bogie changed (suspected axle flaw) |
| 04/12/69 | Ex-T | 04/12/6 | 11/12/69 | OOC | L/C | 7 | A Engine changed (bad internal knocking) |
| 09/06/70 | Ex-T | 09/06/70 | 11/06/70 | NA | L/C | 2 | Boiler changed |
| 21/08/70 | Ex-T | 21/08/70 | 27/08/70 | LA | H/C | 6 | A Transmission changed; B Bogie changed |
| 02/09/70 | Ex-T | 02/09/70 | 04/09/70 | LA | L/C | 2 | B Engine changed (low lub. oil pressure) |
| 16/11/70 | Ex-T | 16/11/70 | 17/11/70 | LA | L/C | 1 | B Transmission changed (forward / reverse mechanism seized) |
| 14/01/71 | LA | 27/01/71 | 08/04/71 | SW | Int | 84 | A & B Engines changed; A Transmission changed (forward / reverse mechanism defective); B Transmission changed (no filling pump pressure); A & B Bogies changed; Modifications; all hoses and cardan shafts, exhausters and compressor changed |
| 28/05/71 | Ex-T | 28/05/71 | 30/05/71 | LA | L/C | 2 | A Engine changed (passing oil) |
| 21/08/71 | Ex-T | 21/08/71 | 24/08/71 | LA | L/C | 3 | B Transmission changed (forward / reverse mechanism seized) |
| 24/09/71 | NA | | 04/10/71 | BS | | | Withdrawn |

D835 PEGASUS outside Swindon works on 12 August 1962 accompanied by D1005 WESTERN VENTURER. This was a 28 day stay at Swindon for a Light Casual overhaul which included attention to the bogies, boiler and one of the transmissions; the works records show that at this point D835 had run 134,000 miles over 5,050 working hours. All major components apart from the other transmission had been in D835 from new, and only the boiler was swapped during this visit to Swindon. (WG Boyden, courtesy F Hornby)

D835 PEGASUS stands on the turntable at Old Oak Common in 1968. It was one of several NBL Warships to be transferred to the London depot in 1967, initially to work on the Birmingham road, but by spring 1968 their principal work was to Worcester and Hereford. A specific Old Oak modification to the NBL variant was the ventilation holes cut in the headcode box and these can clearly be seen in this shot of PEGASUS. It was the last Class 43 to be given a full intermediate at Swindon, taking a full 85 days and being released on 8 April 1971; despite this it was withdrawn less than six months later! (www.rail-online.co.uk)

# D836 POWERFUL

| Lot no./Works no. | 443/27965 |
|---|---|
| **Significant dates and allocations** | |
| Delivered | 31/08/60 |
| Into traffic - Laira | 13/09/60 |
| Newton Abbot | 08/61 |
| Old Oak Common | 08/67 |
| Banbury (Temporary) | 14/08/67 |
| Old Oak Common | 09/67 |
| Newton Abbot | 02/68 |
| Withdrawn (Newton Abbot) | 22/05/71 |
| (Swindon) | 18/10/71 |
| Date cut-up | By 10/03/72 |

| **Stored** | **From** | **To** |
|---|---|---|
| Newton Abbot | 02/05/71 | 22/05/71 |
| **Livery and insignia changes** | | |
| Green | | 13/09/60 |
| OHLW flashes | | 02/12/61 |
| Yellow warning panels | | 23/11/62 |
| Maroon | | - |
| Blue full yellow ends – double insignia, sans serif, D-prefix | | 09/04/68 |
| **Recorded mileage** | | 781,000 |

**Works visits and depot repairs**

| Stopped | At | On Works | Off Works | At | Type | Days | Work carried out |
|---|---|---|---|---|---|---|---|
| - | - | 31/08/60 | 13/09/60 | SW | D/A | 14 | Delivery inspection and acceptance |
| 02/01/61 | OOC | 04/01/61 | 14/01/61 | SW | L/C | 12 | Modified engine speed regulator motors fitted; B bogie changed (cardan shaft and outer final drive defects) |
| 12/04/61 | LA | 24/04/61 | 26/06/61 | SW | L/C | 75 | A Engine changed (blocked coolant system) |
| 20/07/61 | LA | 22/07/61 | 12/08/61 | SW | L/C | 23 | B Engine repaired; B Transmission changed (metal in filters); A & B Bogies repaired |
| 17/11/61 | NA | 20/11/61 | 02/12/61 | SW | L/C | 15 | B Transmission changed (forward / reverse faults) |
| 01/01/62 | Ex-T | | 03/01/62 | LA | L/C | 2 | |
| 13/02/62 | Ex-T | 15/02/62 | 23/02/62 | LA | L/C | 10 | B Engine changed (fuel in the air box) |
| 18/09/62 | NA | 22/09/62 | 08/10/62 | LA | H/C | 20 | B Engine changed (No. 11 cylinder head and piston damaged) |
| 02/11/62 | BS | 05/11/62 | 23/11/62 | SW | H/C | 21 | A Engine repaired (heavy lub. oil leaks); A Transmission repaired (joints leaking); A & B Bogies changed; Boiler changed |
| 30/04/63 | Ex-T | 30/04/63 | 16/05/63 | LA | H/C | 16 | B Engine changed (fractured exhaust valves) |
| 15/09/63 | Ex-T | 16/09/63 | 17/09/63 | LA | L/C | 2 | |
| 11/63 | Ex-T | 27/11/63 | 11/63 | LA | L/C | ? | A Engine changed; B Engine changed (excessive lub. oil consumption) |
| 03/02/64 | Ex-T | 12/02/64 | 13/03/64 | SW | Unsch | 39 | A Engine changed (lub. oil leaks); B Engine changed; A Bogie changed (suspected axle flaws and the inner drive sump contaminated with metal particles); B bogie changed (outer final drive sump contaminated with metal particles); Modifications; all cardan shafts changed |
| 08/06/64 | Ex-T | 06/64 | 25/06/64 | LA | L/C | 17 | B Transmission changed |
| 10/64 | Ex-T | 10/64 | 10/64 | LA | L/C | ? | B Engine changed (high lub. oil consumption) |
| 12/64 | Ex-T | 18/12/64 | 12/64 | NA | L/C | ? | Boiler changed |
| 15/02/65 | Ex-T | 17/02/65 | 07/05/65 | SW | Int | 92 | A Engine changed (Nos. 4, 5 and 9 cylinder heads leaking); B Engine changed (coolant leaks); A Transmission changed; B Transmission changed (teeth on No. 1 convertor drive gear stripped); A & B Bogies changed; Modifications; Bogie side control linkage replaced with hydraulic shock absorbers; All hoses and cardan shafts, exhausters and compressor changed |
| 11/65 | Ex-T | 10/11/65 | 11/65 | NA | Unsch | ? | A end dynostarter changed |
| 11/65 | Ex-T | 13/11/65 | 11/65 | NA | L/C | ? | A Transmission changed (forward / reverse gears seized and metal in filters) |
| 01/66 | Ex-T | 09/01/66 | 01/66 | NA | Unsch | ? | A end dynostarter changed |
| 02/66 | Ex-T | 02/02/66 | 02/66 | NA | Unsch | ? | A exhauster changed (several valve seats breaking up) |
| 04/66 | Ex-T | 12/04/66 | 04/66 | NA | Unsch | ? | A end dynostarter changed (commutator burnt out) |
| 06/66 | Ex-T | 14/06/66 | 06/66 | NA | L/C | ? | A Engine Turbo blower changed |
| 09/66 | Ex-T | 21/09/66 | 09/66 | NA | Unsch | ? | B end dynostarter changed (burnt out) |
| 10/66 | Ex-T | 08/10/66 | 13/10/66 | LA | H/C | ? | A Engine changed; B Transmission changed (primary shaft seizing, thick oil sludge and metal in the sump) |
| 01/67 | Ex-T | 16/01/67 | 01/67 | LA | L/C | ? | B Transmission changed (No. 2 convertor defects and metal in filters) |
| 02/67 | Ex-T | 05/02/67 | 02/67 | NA | Unsch | ? | A exhauster changed |
| 03/67 | Ex-T | 02/03/67 | 03/67 | NA | Unsch | ? | A end dynostarter changed |
| 04/67 | Ex-T | 09/04/67 | 04/67 | LA | H/C | ? | A & B Bogies changed |
| 04/67 | Ex-T | 26/04/67 | 04/67 | NA | L/C | ? | Boiler changed |
| 07/67 | Ex-T | 06/07/67 | 07/67 | NA | Unsch | ? | B end dynostarter changed |
| 11/67 | Ex-T | 22/11/67 | 11/67 | OOC | L/C | ? | B Engine changed |
| 01/68 | Ex-T | 22/01/68 | 01/68 | OOC | L/C | ? | A Engine changed (no compression on No. 5 cylinder) |
| 22/02/68 | Ex-T | 26/02/68 | 09/04/68 | SW | Int | 44 | A Bogie changed (5cm trace recorded on No. 11 groove); B Bogie changed (outer final drive bolt holes elongated); Modifications; all hoses and cardan shafts changed, exhausters and compressor changed |
| 06/68 | Ex-T | 07/06/68 | 06/68 | LA | L/C | ? | A Transmission changed (high temperatures in No. 2 convertor, No. 2 convertor casing fractured, rotor seized, metal debris and oil sludge in the slump) |
| 30/07/68 | Ex-T | 08/68 | 09/08/68 | LA | L/C | 10 | A Transmission changed (main convertor seizing and No. 1 turbine blade rivets broken) |
| 08/68 | Ex-T | 22/08/68 | 08/68 | NA | L/C | ? | B Transmission changed (forward / reverse defects, rotor knocking and metal in sump) |
| 11/68 | Ex-T | 22/11/68 | 11/68 | NA | Unsch | ? | B Engine Turbo blower changed |
| 12/68 | Ex-T | 18/12/68 | 12/68 | BS | Unsch | ? | B Engine Nos. 6, 7 and 8 cylinder heads changed |
| 02/69 | Ex-T | 05/02/69 | 02/69 | NA | L/C | ? | Boiler changed |
| 02/69 | Ex-T | 21/02/69 | 02/69 | LA | L/C | ? | A Engine changed (crank case compression) |
| 19/11/69 | Ex-T | 19/11/69 | 24/11/69 | LA | H/C | 5 | A Engine changed (passing oil); A Transmission changed (forward / reverse faults) |
| 07/12/69 | Ex-T | 07/12/69 | 10/12/69 | LA | L/C | 3 | B Engine changed (passing oil) |
| 19/02/70 | Ex-T | 19/02/70 | 23/02/70 | LA | L/C | 4 | B Engine changed (passing oil) |
| 15/06/70 | Ex-T | 15/06/70 | 16/06/70 | LA | L/C | 1 | B Bogie changed (right hand inner tyres loose) |
| 01/71 | Ex-T | 08/01/71 | 01/71 | LA | L/C | ? | A Transmission changed (dynostarter cardan shaft flange off its taper) |
| 08/02/71 | Ex-T | 08/02/71 | 13/02/71 | LA | H/C | 5 | A Engine changed (passing oil); A & B Bogies changed (thin tyres) |
| 02/05/71 | Ex-T | | 22/05/71 | NA | | | To store/withdrawn |

D836 POWERFUL, during the winter of 1961/62, working a mixed freight at Bradford on Tone just south of Taunton. This photograph shows another difference between the Swindon and Glasgow locomotives: the radiator fan covers on the roof stood proud on the NBLs but were flush on the BR Warships. As with all things Warship it wasn't that clear cut and there were a few exceptions which proved the rule. (www.rail-online.co.uk)

D836 POWERFUL enters Plymouth in 1969 with an unidentified working, though the headcode, 1V67, denoted a Sheffield-Paignton train. The locomotive now carries the first standard blue livery with BR double arrow symbols below the cab numbers. The TOPS panel, introduced widely at the start of 1969, can also been seen below the symbol, in the standard NBL position. The raised fan covers show up better from this angle. (www.rail-online.co.uk)

# D837 RAMILLIES

| Lot no./Works no. | 443/27966 |
|---|---|
| **Significant dates and allocations** | |
| Delivered | 28/10/60 |
| Into traffic - Laira | 08/11/60 |
| Newton Abbot | 11/61 |
| Tyseley (Temporary) | 21/08/67 |
| Old Oak Common | 09/67 |
| Newton Abbot | 02/68 |
| Old Oak Common | 01/69 |
| Newton Abbot | 06/70 |
| Withdrawn (Newton Abbot) | 22/05/71 |
| Component recovery (Laira) | To 16/08/71 |
| (Swindon) | 13/10/71 |
| Date cut-up | By 23/06/72 |

| **Stored** | **From** | **To** |
|---|---|---|
| Newton Abbot | 02/05/71 | 22/05/71 |

| **Livery and insignia changes** | |
|---|---|
| Green | 08/11/60 |
| OHLW flashes | 05/62 |
| Yellow warning panels | 16/07/63 |
| Maroon | - |
| Blue full yellow ends – double insignia, sans serif, D-prefix | 09/07/68 |
| **Recorded mileage** | 701,000 |

**Works visits and depot repairs**

| Stopped | At | On Works | Off Works | At | Type | Days | Work carried out |
|---|---|---|---|---|---|---|---|
| - | - | 28/10/60 | 08/11/60 | SW | D/A | 10 | Delivery inspection and acceptance |
| 05/06/61 | OOC | 07/06/61 | 06/07/61 | SW | L/C | 31 | B Transmission changed (metal particles in filters) – returned to NBL |
| 05/01/62 | Ex-T | | 08/01/62 | LA | L/C | 3 | A & B Bogies Tyres turned |
| 13/01/62 | NA | 15/01/62 | 31/01/62 | SW | L/C | 18 | A Engine repaired (No. 9 piston and cylinder liner damaged by faulty injector; Nos. 1 & 9 cylinder heads changed, twelve injectors changed, turbo blower changed due to damage from debris from No. 9 cylinder) |
| 23/08/62 | Ex-T | 27/08/62 | 07/09/62 | SW | H/C | 15 | B Bogie changed (AWS shoe broken loose and hand brake screw bent ) |
| 29/01/63 | Ex-T | 29/01/63 | 18/02/63 | NA | Unsch | 20 | |
| 23/02/63 | Ex-T | 23/02/63 | 03/03/63 | LA | H/C | 8 | A & B Engines changed |
| 04/05/63 | Ex-T | 04/05/63 | 11/05/63 | NA | H/C | 7 | A Engine changed (No. 3 cylinder exhaust valve head broken off damaging the piston crown; Boiler changed (superheating) |
| 03/07/63 | Ex-T | 03/07/63 | 16/07/63 | SW | H/C | 13 | A Transmission changed (reported as noisy and suffering from trips) |
| 22/08/63 | Ex-T | 08/63 | 30/08/63 | LA | L/C | 8 | A Transmission changed (control piston seizing) |
| 02/64 | Ex-T | 24/02/64 | 02/64 | LA | L/C | ? | B Engine changed (low compression and smoking) |
| 10/03/64 | Ex-T | 10/03/64 | 30/03/64 | NA | Unsch | 20 | |
| 09/04/64 | Ex-T | 04/64 | 05/05/64 | LA | Unsch | 26 | A Transmission changed (control piston and fill valve seizing) |
| 21/06/64 | Ex-T | 21/06/64 | 24/06/64 | LA | L/C | 3 | A Transmission removed – operated as OEO until called to Swindon |
| 21/06/64 | LA | 24/06/64 | 13/10/64 | SW | Int | 114 | A & B Engines changed (several cylinder heads leaking coolant); A Transmission fitted; B Transmission changed (auxiliary drive shaft defects); A & B Bogies changed; Boiler changed; Modifications; Bogie side control linkage replaced with hydraulic shock absorbers; Multiple working jumper cables and sockets removed from buffer beam; all hoses and cardan shafts changed; exhausters and compressor changed |
| 12/64 | Ex-T | 19/12/64 | 12/64 | NA | L/C | ? | A Transmission changed (constantly overheating and difficult to reverse) |
| 09/08/65 | Ex-T | 10/08/65 | 08/65 | LA | L/C | ? | A Engine changed (internal oil leak adjacent to the pressure regulating valve) |
| 10/65 | Ex-T | 19/10/65 | 10/65 | LA | L/C | ? | B Bogie changed (outer axle defect) |
| 11/65 | Ex-T | 18/11/65 | 11/65 | NA | L/C | ? | B Engine No. 158 fuel pumps changed due to overspeed trips |
| 16/12/65 | Ex-T | 20/12/65 | 12/65 | LA | L/C | ? | B Engine changed (No. 10 cylinder burner detaching causing damage to cylinder head and valves) |
| 06/01/66 | Ex-T | 09/01/66 | 11/01/66 | LA | L/C | 5 | A Engine changed (No. 2 cylinder lower oil seal suspect) |
| 06/66 | Ex-T | 27/06/66 | 06/66 | NA | L/C | ? | Boiler changed (heavy internal water leaks) |
| 07/66 | Ex-T | 04/07/66 | 07/66 | NA | Unsch | ? | A end dynostarter changed (armature burning out) |
| 07/66 | Ex-T | 21/07/66 | 07/66 | NA | Unsch | ? | A end dynostarter changed (earth faults) |
| 07/66 | Ex-T | 30/07/66 | 07/66 | NA | Unsch | ? | A end dynostarter changed |
| 23/08/66 | Ex-T | 23/08/66 | 06/09/66 | SW | Class | 14 | A & B Bogies changed |
| 12/66 | Ex-T | 20/12/66 | 12/66 | LA | L/C | ? | A Transmission changed (seized) |
| 01/67 | Ex-T | 11/01/67 | 01/67 | NA | Unsch | ? | A end dynostarter changed |
| 01/67 | Ex-T | 16/01/67 | 01/67 | LA | L/C | ? | B Transmission changed |
| 01/67 | Ex-T | 31/01/67 | 67 | NA | Unsch | ? | B end dynostarter changed |
| 02/67 | Ex-T | 06/02/67 | 02/67 | LA | H/C | ? | B Bogie changed (inner final drive output oil seals leaking) |
| 11/04/67 | Ex-T | 11/04/67 | 14/04/67 | LA | Unsch | 3 | A & B Transmissions changed; locomotive stopped for collision damage |
| 11/04/67 | Ex-T | 14/04/67 | 17/05/67 | SW | Unsch | 36 | A Engine repaired; B Engine changed (heavy contamination of the lub. oil and severe internal knocking); A & B Transmissions changed (not reversing properly, control piston seizing and metal in filters); A Bogie changed (bogie frame being twisted by collision); B Bogie changed; Modifications; A end collision damage repairs; bent main tubes straightened, gussets repaired, distorted buffer beam above the steam pipe flexible straightened, A and B end nose end doors realigned and steam pipe flexible replaced |
| 08/67 | Ex-T | 14/08/67 | 08/67 | LA | L/C | ? | A Engine changed (fumes coming from the crank case breather) |
| 10/67 | Ex-T | 19/10/67 | 10/67 | OOC | L/C | ? | A Engine changed (debris from No. 8 piston found in the sump and in several con rod bearings) |
| 05/68 | Ex-T | 22/05/68 | 09/07/68 | SW | Int | 48 | A Engine repaired; A & B Transmissions changed; A Bogie changed (outer laminated spring buckled and worn side control rubbers); B Bogie changed (debris in the final drive oil sumps and worn side control rubbers); Boiler changed; Modifications; all hoses and cardan shafts changed, exhausters and compressor changed |
| 08/68 | Ex-T | 23/08/68 | 08/68 | LA | L/C | ? | A Bogie changed (outer final drive seized) |
| 11/68 | Ex-T | 29/11/68 | 11/68 | NA | Unsch | ? | A end dynostarter changed (reported vibrations) |
| 12/68 | Ex-T | 17/12/68 | 12/68 | NA | Unsch | ? | A end dynostarter changed (armature overheating) |
| 12/68 | Ex-T | 31/12/68 | 12/68 | LA | H/C | ? | A & B Engines changed (passing oil) |
| 09/06/69 | Ex-T | 09/06/69 | 10/06/69 | SW | Unsch | 1 | B Transmission changed (output assembly and sump cover broken away from the casing); A Bogie changed (scaled tyres and traces on the inner axle); B Bogie changed (extensive frame damage around the pivot pin assembly) |
| 08/69 | Ex-T | 04/08/69 | 08/69 | LA | L/C | ? | B Engine changed breathing badly) |
| 31/12/69 | Ex-T | 01/70 | 13/01/70 | OOC | L/C | 13 | A Engine changed (passing oil) |
| 19/04/70 | Ex-T | 04/70 | 05/05/70 | OOC | H/C | 16 | A Engine changed (partially seized and overheated); B Engine changed; A Transmission changed (reported vibrations); B Transmission changed (overheating); Boiler changed |
| 08/07/70 | Ex-T | 07/70 | 26/07/70 | OOC | H/C | 18 | A Transmission changed (output flange damaged); Boiler changed |
| 17/01/71 | Ex-T | 17/01/71 | 18/01/71 | LA | H/C | 1 | A & B Bogies changed (thin tyres) |
| 17/03/71 | Ex-T | 03/71 | 20/03/71 | LA | L/C | 3 | A Transmission changed (standstill detector shaft flange damaged) |
| 02/05/71 | Ex-T | | 22/05/71 | NA | | | To store / withdrawn |

D837 RAMILLIES stands in the newly converted diesel shed at Bristol Bath Road in 1962; although officially opened on 10 July 1961, it was some time before work was actually completed. Bath Road was a secondary depot in the No.2 Conversion Scheme and in addition to sharing responsibility for the London-South West workings with Laira, it also provided power for the London-South Wales services, and those to Crewe via Hereford and Shrewsbury. The depot also looked after the diesel-electrics handling the southern end of inter-regional workings from the North of England via the Midland line from Birmingham. (www.rail-online.co.uk)

D837 RAMILLIES on 13 July 1968 at Stapleton Road with the 06.30 Plymouth-Newcastle, which had been diverted due to flooding. The locomotive is about to be removed from the train. RAMILLIES is only four days out of Swindon after a full classified repair and repainting into blue. The air intake to the right of the headcode box has been blanked off and D837 is missing one of its redundant headboard clips. A combination of missing headboard clips and location of the overhead livewire flashes can make some locomotives very easy to identify just from a front head-on view. (PJ Fowler)

# D838 RAPID

| Lot no./Works no. | 443/27967 |
|---|---|
| **Significant dates and allocations** | |
| Delivered | 09/60 |
| Into traffic - Laira | 03/10/60 |
| Newton Abbot | 11/61 |
| Old Oak Common | 10/67 |
| Newton Abbot | 02/68 |
| Old Oak Common | 01/69 |
| Newton Abbot | 03/69 |
| Withdrawn (Newton Abbot) | 27/03/71 |
| (Swindon) | 13/10/71 |
| Date cut-up | By 29/07/72 |

| **Livery and insignia changes** | |
|---|---|
| Green | 03/10/60 |
| OHLW flashes | 22/09/61 |
| Yellow warning panels | 21/05/62 |
| Maroon yellow warning panels | 10/66 |
| Maroon full yellow ends | 09/68 |
| Blue | - |
| **Recorded mileage** | 715,000 |

**Works visits and depot repairs**

| Stopped | At | On Works | Off Works | At | Type | Days | Work carried out |
|---|---|---|---|---|---|---|---|
| - | - | 09/60 | 03/10/60 | SW | D/A | | Delivery inspection and acceptance |
| 15/05/61 | Ex-T | 15/05/61 | 30/05/61 | SW | L/C | 15 | |
| 21/06/61 | LA | 27/06/61 | 06/07/61 | SW | L/C | 15 | |
| 20/09/61 | Ex-T | 20/09/61 | 22/09/61 | SW | U/C | 2 | |
| 21/12/61 | Ex-T | 12/61 | 28/12/61 | LA | L/C | 7 | |
| 14/03/62 | Ex-T | 14/03/62 | 26/03/62 | SW | L/C | 12 | |
| 02/05/62 | NA | 04/05/62 | 21/05/62 | SW | H/C | 19 | |
| 16/07/62 | NA | 30/07/62 | 14/08/62 | SW | H/C | 29 | |
| 01/09/62 | NA | 04/09/62 | 10/10/62 | SW | H/C | 39 | A Engine changed (fire damage); A engine room roof section repaired, damaged by fire |
| 08/11/62 | NA | 09/11/62 | 14/12/62 | SW | L/C | 36 | |
| 22/05/63 | NA | 27/05/63 | 05/07/63 | SW | H/C | 44 | A & B Engines changed |
| 14/07/63 | Ex-T | 07/63 | 23/07/63 | LA | L/C | 9 | |
| 06/10/63 | Ex-T | 10/10/63 | 10/10/63 | LA | L/C | 4 | |
| 11/63 | Ex-T | 28/11/63 | 11/63 | ? | L/C | ? | |
| 03/64 | Ex-T | 12/03/64 | 03/64 | LA | L/C | ? | B Transmission changed (output gear casing moved) |
| 04/05/64 | LA | 04/05/64 | 02/06/64 | SW | U/C | 29 | |
| 09/65 | Ex-T | 22/09/65 | 09/65 | NA | Unsch | ? | Fuel pumps changed |
| 11/65 | Ex-T | 11/65 | 11/65 | ? | L/C | ? | A Engine changed (flywheel vibrations) |
| 03/66 | Ex-T | 03/66 | 10/66 | ? | ? | | A & B Engines changed; A & B Transmissions changed; A Bogie changed |
| 11/66 | Ex-T | 10/11/66 | 11/66 | ? | L/C | ? | B Bogie changed (inner final drive axle scored inside the casing) |
| 04/67 | Ex-T | 07/04/67 | 04/67 | LA | L/C | ? | A Transmission changed (control piston seized) |
| 06/67 | Ex-T | 22/06/67 | 06/67 | NA | L/C | ? | Transmission changed (broken mounting foot) |
| 07/67 | Ex-T | 07/67 | 07/67 | ? | L/C | ? | Transmission changed (control piston seized |
| 09/67 | Ex-T | 09/67 | 09/67 | ? | L/C | ? | B Transmission changed (no filling pump pressure) |
| 01/68 | Ex-T | 01/68 | 01/68 | ? | L/C | ? | B Transmission changed (forward / reverse defects) |
| 07/68 | Ex-T | 07/68 | 09/68 | SW | ? | | A Transmission changed (output casing damaged, inner gears scored, No. 12 convertor blackened and overheated, transmission seized); A Bogie changed (frame damaged by a broken cardan shaft caused by a transmission seizure); B Bogie changed (debris in the inner final drive sump and torn side control rubbers); Boiler changed |
| 02/69 | Ex-T | 02/69 | 02/69 | ? | L/C | ? | Engine changed |
| 03/70 | Ex-T | 12/03/70 | 03/70 | NA | Unsch | ? | B end dynostarter changed (bearing defects) |
| 05/70 | Ex-T | | | ? | H/C | | Engine changed; Transmission changed (rotor knocking when turned and metal in filter); B Bogie changed (loose tyres) |
| 27/03/71 | Ex-T | | | | | | Withdrawn |

A fairly common sight in their first few years, though it became rarer; a pair of NBL Warships. D838 RAPID and D849 SUPERB enter Bristol on 4 July 1961 with the 1B11 1.15pm Paddington  to Weston-super-Mare. The multiple working equipment on the NBL Warships was rarely used after the early 1960s and the vast majority lost the fittings in 1965 and 1966. (www.rail-online.co.uk)

D7048 with D838 RAPID at Bristol Bath Road on 10 July 1966. The locomotive is now in maroon with small yellow warning panel, which it would retain until a complete repaint in maroon with full yellow ends in August 1968. It is still one of the enduring Warship mysteries that why, after two years of repainting locomotives in blue, Swindon decided to return D838 back to traffic in a new coat of maroon paint. (www.rail-online.co.uk)

## D839 RELENTLESS

| Lot no./Works no. | 443/27968 |
|---|---|
| **Significant dates and allocations** | |
| Delivered | 06/11/60 |
| Into traffic - Laira | 12/11/60 |
| Newton Abbot | 06/62 |
| Old Oak Common | 09/67 |
| Newton Abbot | 02/68 |
| Old Oak Common | 04/68 |
| Newton Abbot | 06/69 |
| Withdrawn (Newton Abbot) | 04/10/71 |
| (Bristol St Philips Marsh Junction) | By 02/11/71 |
| (Swindon) | 04/01/72 |
| Date cut-up | By 04/08/72 |

| **Stored** | From | To |
|---|---|---|
| Bristol Bath Road (but used on p.way trains and track lifting trains on the old MR route to Bath) | 03/69 | 06/69 |
| **Livery and insignia changes** | | |
| Green | | 12/11/60 |
| OHLW flashes | | 31/08/61 |
| Yellow warning panels | | 17/08/62 |
| Maroon yellow warning panels | | 24/02/66 |
| Blue full yellow ends – single insignia, sans serif , no D | | 11/07/70 |
| **Recorded mileage** | | 790,000 |

### Works visits and depot repairs

| Stopped | At | On Works | Off Works | At | Type | Days | Work carried out |
|---|---|---|---|---|---|---|---|
| - | - | 06/11/60 | 12/11/60 | SW | D/A | 6 | Delivery inspection and acceptance |
| 21/02/61 | LA | 24/02/61 | 15/03/61 | SW | L/C | 22 | A Bogie changed |
| 15/08/61 | Ex-T | 15/08/61 | 15/08/61 | LA | L/C | 1 | |
| 08/61 | Ex-T | 23/08/61 | 31/08/61 | SW | H/C | 8 | |
| 25/07/62 | NA | 30/07/62 | 17/08/62 | SW | H/C | 23 | |
| 29/09/62 | NA | 02/10/62 | 23/10/62 | SW | H/C | 24 | |
| 30/10/62 | NA | 05/11/62 | 16/11/62 | SW | H/C | 17 | |
| 25/10/63 | Ex-T | 10/63 | 29/10/63 | LA | H/C | 4 | B Engine changed |
| 06/02/64 | NA | 14/02/64 | 13/03/64 | SW | Unsch | 36 | A Bogie changed (inner final drive defects); B Bogie changed (axle flaws); Modifications; Bogie side control linkage replaced with hydraulic shock absorbers |
| 12/05/64 | Ex-T | 05/64 | 21/05/64 | NA | ? | 9 | |
| 02/06/64 | Ex-T | 06/64 | 10/06/64 | LA | ? | 8 | |
| 11/64 | Ex-T | 04/11/64 | 11/64 | LA | ? | ? | A Transmission changed (not changing gear) |
| 12/64 | Ex-T | 12/64 | 01/65 | SW | ? | ? | A Transmission changed |
| 07/65 | Ex-T | 16/07/65 | 07/65 | NA | Unsch | ? | A Engine Turbo blower changed |
| 11/65 | Ex-T | 11/65 | 11/65 | ? | L/C | ? | |
| 12/65 | Ex-T | 04/12/65 | 12/65 | LA | H/C | ? | A & B Transmissions changed |
| 12/65 | LA | 12/65 | 24/02/66 | SW | ? | ? | A Transmission changed (output shaft being seized); B Transmission changed (low filling pump pressure) |
| 02/67 | Ex-T | 02/67 | 02/67 | NA | ? | ? | Boiler changed |
| 05/67 | Ex-T | 12/05/67 | 05/67 | LA | L/C | ? | B Engine changed (low lub. oil pressure) |
| 06/67 | Ex-T | 21/06/67 | 06/67 | NA | Unsch | ? | B end dynostarter changed (throwing solder) |
| 06/68 | Ex-T | 06/68 | 06/68 | LA | L/C | ? | A Transmission changed (forward / reverse dog clutch defective) |
| 07/68 | Ex-T | 07/68 | 07/68 | ? | H/C | ? | A & B Bogies changed |
| 11/68 | Ex-T | 01/11/68 | 11/68 | ? | L/C | ? | Boiler changed (split coil) |
| 03/69 | Ex-T | | | ? | L/C | ? | B Engine changed |
| 09/69 | Ex-T | 09/69 | 09/69 | ? | L/C | ? | A Transmission changed (high temperature trips in No. 1 convertor); Bogie changed |
| 01/70 | Ex-T | 01/70 | 01/70 | LA | L/C | ? | B Transmission changed (not reversing) |
| 04/70 | Ex-T | 04/70 | 04/70 | ? | L/C | ? | Engine changed (fuming) |
| 05/70 | Ex-T | 05/70 | 11/07/70 | ? | L/C | ? | Engine changed (defective big end bearings) |
| 27/07/71 | Ex-T | 27/07/71 | 07/71 | NA | L/C | ? | A Transmission changed (broken gear train) |
| 27/08/71 | Ex-T | 27/08/71 | 31/08/71 | LA | L/C | 4 | Transmission changed (forward / reverse dog tight) |
| 04/10/71 | Ex-T | | | | | | Withdrawn |

D839 RELENTLESS at Shrewsbury with the 1V98 3.30pm Manchester-Plymouth; the year is either 1963 or 1964. Shrewsbury was something of a centre for WR hydraulics for a few years in the early 1960s with the Warships on the Crewe-Bristol run and Westerns working through on the Paddington-Birkenhead trains, but by 1965 the diesel-electrics held sway. Another difference between Swindon and Glasgow Warships was the position of the lamp brackets and marker lights, offset on the NBL variant but directly over the marker lights on the BR Warships. (www.rail-online.co.uk)

839 RELENTLESS runs over the level crossing near Gloucester Horton Road depot on 26 September 1970. The train is the 5B73 10.30 Bristol Malago Vale-Worcester vans which called at Gloucester. The locomotive was diagrammed to work forward from Worcester on the 14.15 to Paddington via Evesham and the Cotswold line. 839 was another with ventilation holes cut in the headcode boxes, although with the Warships uniformity was hardly rigid; in this case the holes were square rather than round. (www.rail-online.co.uk)

# D840 RESISTANCE

| Lot no./Works no. | 443/27969 |
|---|---|
| **Significant dates and allocations** | |
| Delivered | 19/01/61 |
| Into traffic - Laira | 03/02/61 |
| Newton Abbot | 06/62 |
| Old Oak Common | 08/67 |
| Withdrawn (Old Oak Common) | 26/04/69 |
| (Swindon) | 21/04/70 |
| Date cut-up | By 07/70 |

| **Stored** | | |
|---|---|---|
| | **From** | **To** |
| Old Oak Common | 01/04/69 | 26/04/69 |
| **Livery and insignia changes** | | |
| Green | | 03/02/61 |
| OHLW flashes | | 31/10/61 |
| Yellow warning panels | | 19/10/62 |
| Maroon - yellow warning panels | | 20/10/66 |
| Blue | | - |
| **Recorded mileage** | | 599,000 |

**Works visits and depot repairs**

| Stopped | At | On Works | Off Works | At | Type | Days | Work carried out |
|---|---|---|---|---|---|---|---|
| | | 19/01/61 | 03/02/61 | SW | D/A | 15 | Delivery inspection and acceptance |
| 11/05/61 | LA | 19/05/61 | 13/06/61 | SW | L/C | 33 | A Engine repaired; B Transmission changed (returned to N.B.L. Co. under guarantee) |
| 07/10/61 | LA | 19/10/61 | 31/10/61 | SW | L/C | 24 | B Transmission changed (output sump oil seals leaking; B Bogie changed (input pinion bearing collapsed on inner final drive and outer final drive torque arm out of position) |
| 03/05/62 | Ex-T | 06/05/62 | 19/05/62 | LA | H/C | 16 | B Engine changed (No. 1 cylinder liner cracked; replacement B Engine failed (sump cracked) on the day it was fitted and changed |
| 25/05/62 | Ex-T | 05/62 | 02/06/62 | LA | H/C | 8 | B Engine changed (push rods bent) |
| 06/62 | Ex-T | 05/06/62 | 05/62 | LA | L/C | ? | B exhauster changed |
| 31/08/62 | LA | 04/09/62 | 19/10/62 | SW | L/C | 49 | B Engine changed; B Transmission changed (defective input bearings) |
| 25/10/62 | OOC | 30/10/62 | 02/11/62 | LA | L/C | 8 | A Engine changed (No. 3 cylinder liner fractured) |
| 21/02/63 | Ex-T | ? | 24/02/63 | LA | L/C | 3 | Compressor changed (motor cable insulation burnt) |
| 16/07/63 | NA | 24/07/63 | 30/08/63 | SW | H/C | 45 | A Engine changed (high lub. oil consumption, low lub. oil pressure, exhaust blows, coolant leaks from cylinder heads and hunting on idle; B Engine changed (high lub. oil consumption, coolant leaks and suspected over-speed); A & B Transmissions repaired ; A Bogie changed; B Bogie changed (reported rough riding and inner final drive torque arm pads defective); Boiler changed; Modifications; Body repairs (chunk of filler (approx 3' x 2') had fallen off the driver's side cab side end) |
| 13/03/64 | NA | 18/03/64 | 10/04/64 | SW | Unsch | 28 | A & B Bogies changed (defective side control dampers); A end front apron repaired |
| 28/05/64 | NA | 02/06/64 | 21/07/64 | SW | Unsch | 54 | A & B Engines repaired; B Transmission changed (metal in filters); A & B Bogies changed; Boiler changed |
| 07/64 | Ex-T | 31/07/64 | 08/64 | LA | Unsch | ? | B Transmission changed (control piston being seized and metal debris in filters) |
| 12/64 | Ex-T | 12/12/64 | 12/64 | LA | L/C | ? | B Bogie changed (frame damage caused by detached cardan shaft) |
| 06/65 | Ex-T | 14/06/65 | 06/65 | NA | L/C | ? | Boiler changed |
| 07/65 | Ex-T | 11/07/65 | 07/65 | LA | H/C | ? | A Transmission changed (not engaging gear correctly in one direction) |
| 12/09/65 | Ex-T | 13/09/65 | 09/65 | LA | H/C | ? | A & B Engines changed |
| 11/10/65 | Ex-T | 11/10/65 | 10/65 | NA | Unsch | ? | B end dynostarter changed (low insulation) |
| 12/65 | Ex-T | 16/12/65 | 12/65 | LA | L/C | ? | B Engine changed (internal oil pipe fractured) |
| 03/66 | Ex-T | 03/06/66 | 06/66 | LA | L/C | ? | A Engine changed (No. 6 con rod pushed through crank case) |
| 15/04/66 | Ex-T | 15/04/66 | 19/04/66 | NA | Unsch | ? | Damaged engine room roof section removed; A exhauster and controller changed |
| 22/08/66 | Ex-T | 26/08/66 | 20/10/66 | SW | Class | 59 | A Engine repaired (No. 4 cylinder head leaking coolant, Nos. 1, 3, 5 and 11 cylinder core plugs leaking and Nos. 7-12 bank coolant outlet pipe fractured); B Engine changed (venting coolant and several liners leaking); A Transmission changed (temperature trips and governor change over block leaking): B Transmission repaired (forward / reverse faults); A & B Bogies changed; Modifications; all hoses and cardan shafts changed, exhausters and compressor changed |
| 11/66 | Ex-T | 10/11/66 | 11/66 | NA | L/C | ? | B end dynostarter changed |
| 01/67 | Ex-T | 25/01/67 | 01/67 | NA | L/C | ? | A end dynostarter changed (low insulation) |
| 08/67 | Ex-T | 02/08/67 | 08/67 | NA | L/C | ? | Boiler changed |
| 10/67 | Ex-T | 13/10/67 | 10/67 | OOC | L/C | ? | A Transmission changed (seized rotor, No. 2 convertor overheated and debris in sump) |
| 02/68 | Ex-T | 01/02/68 | 02/68 | LA | L/C | ? | B Bogie changed inner axle co-drivers side grease seal moving) |
| 02/68 | Ex-T | 12/02/68 | 02/68 | OOC | L/C | ? | A Transmission changed (overheating in No. 2 convertor) |
| 03/68 | Ex-T | 11/03/68 | 03/68 | OOC | L/C | ? | B Transmission changed |
| 04/68 | Ex-T | 05/04/68 | 04/68 | OOC | H/C | ? | A Engine changed; B Engine changed (No. 5 big end bearing collapsed) |
| 05/68 | Ex-T | 13/05/68 | 05/68 | OOC | L/C | ? | B Bogie changed (leading tyres loose on axle) |
| 06/68 | Ex-T | 11/06/68 | 06/68 | OOC | L/C | ? | B Transmission changed (convertor suspected to be breaking up) |
| 06/68 | Ex-T | 20/06/68 | 06/68 | OOC | L/C | ? | A Bogie changed (inner final drive output flange damaged) |
| 08/68 | Ex-T | 05/08/68 | 08/68 | LA | L/C | ? | B Bogie changed (lift in input bearings of both final drives) |
| 02/69 | Ex-T | 03/02/69 | 02/69 | OOC | Unsch | ? | A Engine changed |
| 01/04/69 | Ex-T | | 26/04/69 | OOC | | | Stored and then subsequently withdrawn |

D840 RESISTANCE arrives at Bristol Temple Meads with the down 'Bristolian' in 1961 and D840 hasn't long been in traffic. In fact RESISTANCE was held back at North British and not released until after D843, the existence of a few photographs of D840 carrying out test runs on the G&SW may hold a clue to the reason for this. (www.rail-online.co.uk)

D840 RESISTANCE was one of the first three D833s to be condemned; here it is at Old Oak Common two weeks after, on 9 May 1969. It was one of only seven to be withdrawn in maroon and only three of these still had the small yellow panel, D801, D840 and D848. 1969 was a confusing time for WR traction policy and several of the Warships were stored or even actually withdrawn, only to be resurrected and sent to Swindon. (Alec Swain, www.transporttreasury.co.uk)

# D841 ROEBUCK

| Lot no./Works no. | 443/27970 |
|---|---|
| **Significant dates and allocations** | |
| Delivered | 29/11/60 |
| Into traffic - Laira | 14/12/60 |
| Newton Abbot | 06/62 |
| Old Oak Common | 10/67 |
| Newton Abbot | 10/70 |
| Withdrawn (Laira) | 04/10/71 |
| (Swindon) | 06/10/71 |
| Date cut-up | By 25/02/72 |

| **Stored** | | |
|---|---|---|
| | **From** | **To** |
| Old Oak Common | 03/69 | 03/69 |
| Old Oak Common | 12/11/69 | 18/03/70 |

| **Livery and insignia changes** | |
|---|---|
| Green | 14/12/60 |
| OHLW flashes | By 04/62 |
| Yellow warning panels | 14/09/62 |
| Maroon | - |
| Blue full yellow ends – double insignia, serif, D-prefix | 26/09/67 |
| Blue full yellow ends – single insignia, sans serif , no D | 17/06/70 |
| **Recorded mileage** | 709,000 |

**Works visits and depot repairs**

| Stopped | At | On Works | Off Works | At | Type | Days | Work carried out |
|---|---|---|---|---|---|---|---|
| - | - | 29/11/60 | 14/12/60 | SW | D/A | 15 | Delivery inspection and acceptance |
| 30/03/61 | Ex-T | 04/04/61 | 26/04/61 | SW | L/C | 26 | A & B Engines repaired; B Bogie changed (left hand outer axle box leaking grease) |
| 19/07/61 | Ex-T | 19/07/61 | 29/07/61 | SW | Unsch | 10 | A & B Engines repaired |
| 13/12/61 | Ex-T | - | 28/12/61 | LA | L/C | 15 | |
| 25/03/62 | Ex-T | 25/03/62 | 28/03/62 | LA | L/C | 3 | Boiler changed |
| 18/04/62 | Ex-T | 04/62 | 30/04/62 | OOC | H/C | 11 | A Engine changed (No. 1 gudgeon pin drawn out of the piston) |
| 09/08/62 | NA | 03/09/62 | 14/09/62 | SW | H/C | 36 | A Bogie changed (outer final drive and final drive cardan shafts damaged); Boiler changed |
| 06/10/62 | Ex-T | 07/10/62 | 19/10/62 | LA | H/C | 13 | B Engine changed (No. 8 piston damaged, excessive lub. oil consumption and breather fumes); replacement engine failed (throwing oil from the exhaust) |
| 01/04/63 | Ex-T | 01/04/63 | 03/04/63 | LA | L/C | 2 | B Engine changed (defective oil seals.); A & B Bogies Tyres turned (loss of profile) |
| 30/04/63 | NA | 06/05/63 | 27/05/63 | SW | H/C | 27 | A Transmission changed (metal debris found in the filters); B Transmission changed |
| 10/11/63 | Ex-T | 10/11/63 | 18/11/63 | LA | H/C | 8 | A Engine changed (high lub. oil consumption and overheating.); B Transmission changed (either the secondary shaft or input shaft seized) |
| 02/64 | Ex-T | 06/02/64 | 02/64 | LA | L/C | ? | B Transmission changed (control piston bent and metal in filters) |
| 09/03/64 | LA | 16/03/64 | 10/04/64 | SW | Unsch | 32 | A & B Bogies changed (thin tyres); Modifications; Bogie side control linkage replaced with hydraulic shock absorbers |
| 10/64 | Ex-T | 07/10/64 | 10/64 | LA | L/C | ? | A Transmission changed (drive wheel to the governor having teeth stripped off) |
| 10/64 | Ex-T | 15/10/64 | 10/64 | NA | L/C | ? | Boiler changed |
| 01/65 | Ex-T | 12/01/65 | 01/65 | LA | L/C | ? | A Transmission changed (overheating, No. 2 turbine and impellor damaged and metal debris in filters) |
| 02/65 | Ex-T | 26/02/65 | 02/65 | LA | L/C | ? | B Transmission changed (input shaft and output shaft oil seals leaking) |
| 03/03/65 | Ex-T | 03/03/65 | 06/03/65 | LA | Unsch | ? | A Bogie changed |
| 03/03/65 | Ex-T | 08/03/65 | 08/06/65 | SW | Int | 96 | A Engine changed (Nos. 5 and 9 cylinder heads leaking; B Engine changed (emitting heavy exhaust fumes); A Bogie changed (thin tyres); B Bogie changed (suspected flawed axle); Modifications; all hoses and cardan shafts changed, A & B exhausters changed, compressor changed |
| 22/06/65 | Ex-T | 22/06/65 | 01/07/65 | SW | Unsch | 8 | A Engine repaired; B Engine changed |
| 01/66 | Ex-T | 02/01/66 | 01/66 | NA | Unsch | ? | A Engine fuel pumps changed |
| 27/01/66 | Ex-T | 03/02/66 | 02/66 | LA | L/C | ? | B Bogie changed (outer final drive oil seals leaking) |
| 03/66 | Ex-T | 19/03/66 | 03/66 | NA | Unsch | ? | A Engine fuel pumps changed |
| 04/66 | Ex-T | 25/04/66 | 04/66 | NA | Unsch | ? | B Engine Turbo blower changed |
| 06/66 | Ex-T | 21/06/66 | 06/66 | LA | L/C | ? | B Engine changed (low lub. oil pressure) |
| 07/66 | Ex-T | 21/07/66 | 07/66 | NA | Unsch | ? | B Engine Turbo blower changed |
| 10/66 | Ex-T | 18/10/66 | 10/66 | NA | Unsch | ? | A Engine Turbo blower changed |
| 02/67 | Ex-T | 23/02/67 | 02/67 | NA | L/C | ? | Boiler changed |
| 03/67 | Ex-T | 10/03/67 | 03/67 | NA | Unsch | ? | A Engine fuel pumps changed |
| 04/67 | Ex-T | 16/04/67 | 04/67 | LA | H/C | ? | A Engine changed; B Engine changed (excessive piston blow-by) |
| 04/67 | Ex-T | 28/04/67 | 04/67 | NA | Unsch | ? | A Engine Turbo blower changed |
| 03/09/67 | LA | 04/09/67 | 26/09/67 | SW | Class | 23 | A Bogie changed (4cm trace on outer axle, side axle bearing grease seal revolving on the axle); B Bogie changed |
| 10/67 | Ex-T | 02/10/67 | 10/67 | OOC | L/C | ? | A Engine changed (no compression at No. 7 cylinder and drawing oil from the sump) |
| 03/68 | Ex-T | 25/03/68 | 03/68 | OOC | L/C | ? | B Engine changed |
| 05/68 | Ex-T | 08/05/68 | 05/68 | ? | L/C | ? | B Transmission changed (directional clutch being seized) |
| 07/68 | Ex-T | 07/07/68 | 07/68 | NA | Unsch | ? | A Engine Turbo blower changed (very noisy) |
| 07/68 | Ex-T | 17/07/68 | 07/68 | OOC | L/C | ? | A Engine changed (passing oil through the exhaust) |
| 09/68 | Ex-T | 20/09/68 | 09/68 | OOC | L/C | ? | B Engine changed (low compression) |
| 06/69 | Ex-T | 02/06/69 | 06/69 | LA | L/C | ? | A Engine changed (low on power) |
| 01/10/69 | Ex-T | 01/10/69 | 03/10/69 | OOC | L/C | 2 | Boiler changed |
| 11/69 | Ex-T | 12/11/69 | 18/03/70 | OOC | ? | | To store; A Engine removed; to Swindon for reinstatement |
| 18/03/70 | Ex-T | 19/03/70 | 17/06/70 | SW | Int | 91 | A Engine fitted; B Engine changed (reported smoking); A & B Transmissions changed; A & B Bogies changed; Boiler changed; Modifications; Damaged right hand buffer step repaired; holed A end front apron repaired; A end steam pipe leak repaired; smashed brake cylinder gauges replaced; all hoses and cardan shafts changed; exhausters and compressor changed |
| 30/01/71 | Ex-T | 30/01/71 | 02/02/71 | LA | L/C | 3 | A Transmission changed (no pump pressure) |
| 03/06/71 | Ex-T | 03/06/71 | 08/06/71 | LA | L/C | 5 | B Transmission changed (overheating on 2nd convertor) |
| 01/08/71 | Ex-T | 01/08/71 | 06/08/71 | LA | L/C | 5 | B Transmission changed (standstill detector shaft being damaged) |
| 14/08/71 | NA | 15/08/71 | 18/08/71 | LA | L/C | 4 | B Transmission changed (output oil seals leaking) |
| 02/09/71 | Ex-T | 02/09/71 | 04/09/71 | LA | L/C | 2 | A Transmission changed (control piston seizing and metal in filters) |
| 04/10/71 | LA | | | | | | Withdrawn; ran to Swindon on 06/10/71 under its own power |

D841 ROEBUCK departs Paddington in the summer of 1962 with the 6.45pm Paddington-Bristol. The Warship was the diesel of choice on the Bristol road at this time, the 1963 survey showing no less that thirteen of the class working passenger trains between Bristol and Paddington on Monday 8 July. D841 demonstrates the poetic license given to placement of the electrification flashes; ROEBUCK's are much higher than the normal position, somewhere half way between the horizontal and lower side grab rails. (www.rail-online.co.uk)

841 ROEBUCK coupled to 854 TIGER at the Exeter stabling point, amid the remains of the old steam shed, on Wednesday 28 July 1971. Both had problems and were stopped at Reading the previous weekend, 841 on the Saturday while working the 1B45 09.30 Paddington-Paignton and TIGER with a compressor fault on the Sunday. At least ROEBUCK could muster one engine and it was called on to tow 854 back to Newton Abbot. They paused at Exeter, most likely to change crews before departing at 19.45 for the last leg of their journey. (www.rail-online.co.uk)

# D842 ROYAL OAK

| Lot no./Works no. | 443/27971 |
|---|---|
| **Significant dates and allocations** | |
| Delivered | 08/12/60 |
| Into traffic - Laira | 20/12/60 |
| Newton Abbot | 03/62 |
| Old Oak Common | 08/67 |
| Withdrawn (Old Oak Common) | 26/03/69 |
| Re-instated (Newton Abbot) | w/e 23/07/69 |
| Newton Abbot | 08/69 |
| Withdrawn (Old Oak Common) | 03/10/71 |
| (Swindon) | 29/11/71 |
| Date cut-up | By 17/03/72 |

| **Stored** | | |
|---|---|---|
| | **From** | **To** |
| Old Oak Common | 17/02/69 | 26/03/69 |
| Old Oak Common | 07/07/69 | 23/07/69 |
| **Livery and insignia changes** | | |
| Green | | 20/12/60 |
| OHLW flashes | | 18/10/61 |
| Yellow warning panels | | 14/02/62 |
| Maroon yellow warning panels | | 03/10/66 |
| Maroon full yellow ends | | 02/05/68 |
| Blue full yellow ends – single insignia, sans serif , no D | | 17/10/70 |
| **Recorded mileage** | | 761,000 |

**Works visits and depot repairs**

| Stopped | At | On Works | Off Works | At | Type | Days | Work carried out |
|---|---|---|---|---|---|---|---|
| - | - | 08/12/60 | 20/12/60 | SW | D/A | 12 | Delivery inspection and acceptance |
| 26/09/61 | LA | 27/09/61 | 18/10/61 | SW | L/C | 22 | A Engine repaired (Exhaust leaks rectified in situ, speeds adjusted and bent Nos. 1 - 6 manifold replaced); B Engine repaired (speeds adjusted, water pump changed and oil leaks rectified in situ); B Transmission changed (reversing dog tight on the spline) |
| 01/01/62 | Ex-T | 01/01/62 | 04/01/62 | LA | L/C | 3 | A & B Bogies Tyres turned |
| 05/02/62 | Ex-T | 05/02/62 | 14/02/62 | SW | L/C | 9 | Attention to external paint work on the left hand side panels at B end (On 30/01/62 a letter requesting D842 and D850 to go to Works was issued, attention to be given to the appalling condition of the external paint work) |
| 16/02/62 | Ex-T | 19/02/62 | 28/02/62 | SW | L/C | 12 | A & B Bogies repaired (damaged in a collision after running through level crossing gates) |
| 07/04/62 | Ex-T | 07/04/62 | 16/04/62 | LA | L/C | 9 | A Engine changed (No. 5 cylinder partially seized) |
| 25/06/62 | Ex-T | 27/06/62 | 28/06/62 | LA | L/C | 3 | B Engine changed (No. 5 piston collapsed) |
| 28/03/63 | Ex-T | | 30/03/63 | LA | L/C | 2 | |
| 01/04/63 | BS | 02/04/63 | 01/05/63 | SW | H/C | 30 | A Bogie changed (inner final drive running hot); B Bogie changed (worn tyres); all four transmission to final drive cardan shafts changed; engine room roof sections repaired |
| 15/06/63 | Ex-T | 15/06/63 | 21/06/63 | LA | L/C | 6 | A Transmission changed (overheating and particles of tab washers and wire found on magnetic plug) |
| 11/63 | Ex-T | 05/11/63 | 11/63 | LA | ? | ? | A & B Engines changed (high lub. oil consumption, coolant leaks and excessive fumes) |
| 11/02/64 | Ex-T | 06/03/64 | 03/04/64 | SW | Unsch | 52 | A Engine changed; A & B Transmissions repaired (output shaft oil seals leaking); A & B Bogies changed (suspected axle fractures); Modifications |
| 05/64 | Ex-T | 12/05/64 | 05/64 | LA | L/C | ? | A Engine changed (low lub. oil pressure) |
| 24/06/64 | Ex-T | 24/06/64 | 29/06/64 | LA | Unsch | 5 | B Transmission changed (reported as noisy) |
| 08/64 | Ex-T | 25/08/64 | 08/64 | LA | H/C | ? | A Transmission changed (reported as excessively noisy); B Bogie changed (inner axle suspected fractures) |
| 22/02/65 | Ex-T | 26/02/65 | 02/65 | LA | L/C | ? | A Bogie changed (suspect outer axle flaw at No. 5 groove) |
| 12/04/65 | Ex-T | 13/04/65 | 04/65 | NA | L/C | ? | A Engine changed (leaking badly from the end cover joint): Boiler changed |
| 07/65 | Ex-T | 03/07/65 | 09/07/65 | NA | Unsch | ? | A Engine Turbo blower changed (partly seized rotor shaft); A end dynostarter changed (earth on the motor) |
| 11/65 | Ex-T | 10/11/65 | 11/65 | NA | Unsch | ? | Compressor changed |
| 14/11/65 | Ex-T | 14/11/65 | 19/11/65 | LA | H/C | 5 | A Engine changed (No. 6 cylinder liner cracked); B Engine changed |
| 04/66 | Ex-T | 03/04/66 | 04/66 | NA | Unsch | ? | Compressor changed |
| 05/66 | Ex-T | 20/05/66 | 05/66 | NA | Unsch | ? | B end dynostarter changed |
| 07/66 | Ex-T | 27/07/66 | 03/10/66 | SW | Int | 68 | A & B Engines repaired; A & B Transmissions changed (output shaft oil seals leaking); A & B Bogies changed; Modifications; Multiple working jumper cables and sockets removed from buffer beam |
| 20/10/66 | Ex-T | 24/10/66 | 17/11/66 | SW | U/C | 28 | Collision damage repaired (A end left hand side tube repaired, left hand buffer replaced, left hand corner of cab nose skin replaced left hand leading side access panel door changed and left hand buffer step replaced) |
| 02/12/66 | Ex-T | 02/12/66 | 03/12/66 | LA | L/C | 1 | B Engine changed (no lub. oil pressure to the pressure switch) |
| 01/67 | Ex-T | 03/01/67 | 01/67 | LA | L/C | ? | B Transmission changed (low filling pump pressure and teeth broken from the filling pump drive gear and intermediate drive gear) |
| 02/67 | Ex-T | 05/02/67 | 02/67 | LA | L/C | ? | B Engine changed (excessive lift in the No. 12 big end bearing) |
| 07/67 | Ex-T | 18/07/67 | 07/67 | LA | L/C | ? | A Transmission changed (high temperatures in No. 2 convertor, metal debris in the sump from suspected bearing or labyrinth failure in the convertor) |
| 07/67 | Ex-T | 27/07/67 | 07/67 | NA | L/C | ? | Boiler changed |
| 08/67 | Ex-T | 01/08/67 | 08/67 | LA | L/C | ? | B Bogie changed (inner final drive bearing grease seal retaining ring fractured) |
| 08/67 | Ex-T | 09/08/67 | 08/67 | LA | L/C | ? | B Bogie changed |
| 19/11/67 | Ex-T | 19/11/67 | 21/11/67 | LA | L/C | 2 | A Engine changed (internal water leak from the No. 9 cylinder liner) |
| 11/01/68 | Ex-T | 01/68 | 16/01/68 | OOC | H/C | 5 | A Engine changed (No. 11 big end bearing defective); B Engine changed (no compression at No. 3 cylinder) |
| 02/68 | Ex-T | 02/02/68 | 02/68 | NA | Unsch | ? | B end dynostarter changed |
| 13/02/68 | OX | 15/02/68 | 02/05/68 | SW | U/C | 79 | A & B Bogies changed; Collision damage repaired (A end left and right hand main tubes and gussets distorted, right hand badly damaged and fractured, side decking and nose skin distorted, nose end forced downwards and decking buckled, intermediate decking buckled, nose access flaps and frames distorted, left hand cab door jammed shut, nose door frame distorted, intermediate decking right hand side below cab door fractured, air pipes to operating cylinder broken, cab side sliding window frames distorted and new buffers wanted. A new front end to be fitted) |
| 05/68 | Ex-T | 15/05/68 | 05/68 | OOC | L/C | ? | B Transmission changed (gear not fully engaging) |
| 06/68 | Ex-T | 05/06/68 | 06/68 | OOC | L/C | ? | A Engine changed (throwing oil fumes from the crankcase) |
| 08/68 | Ex-T | 05/08/68 | 08/68 | OOC | L/C | ? | B Transmission changed (no oil pressure) |
| 17/02/69 | Ex-T | 26/06/69 | 17/07/69 | OOC | | 150 | Stored on 17/02/69 and withdrawn on 27/03/69; D842 was re-instated to replace D853 which had caught fire and been put into store on 07/07/69; A & B Bogies changed |
| 08/69 | Ex-T | 22/08/69 | 08/69 | NA | Unsch | ? | Compressor changed (noisy) |
| 12/69 | Ex-T | 17/12/69 | 12/69 | NA | Unsch | ? | B exhauster changed |
| 28/12/69 | Ex-T | 28/12/69 | 03/01/70 | LA | H/C | 6 | A Engine changed (passing oil); Boiler changed |
| 03/70 | Ex-T | 04/03/70 | 03/70 | LA | L/C | ? | B Engine changed (throwing oil) |
| 06/70 | Ex-T | 17/06/70 | 06/70 | NA | Unsch | ? | A end dynostarter changed |
| 16/07/70 | Ex-T | 16/07/70 | 22/07/70 | LA | H/C | 6 | A & B Engines changed |
| 16/07/70 | LA | 27/07/70 | 17/10/70 | SW | Class | 93 | A Engine changed (fractures between Nos. 2 and 3 and 8 and 9 crank case doors); B Engine changed (defective fuel pump drive); A Transmission changed (casing fractured); B Transmission changed; A & B Bogies changed; Modifications |
| 06/03/71 | Ex-T | 06/03/71 | 09/03/71 | LA | L/C | 3 | A Transmission changed (control piston seized, rotor knocking and fine metal debris in sump) |
| 06/04/71 | Ex-T | 06/04/71 | 06/04/71 | LA | L/C | 1 | A Engine changed (camshaft fractured) |
| 25/08/71 | Ex-T | 25/08/71 | 26/08/71 | LA | L/C | 1 | A Engine changed (No. 12 cylinder head and piston smashed) |
| 29/09/71 | Ex-T | 29/09/71 | 03/10/71 | OOC | | | Withdrawn |

As pristine as when it was delivered in December 1960 D842 ROYAL OAK backs into the platform at Bristol Temple Meads in 1961. Unfortunately, like the other NBL-built locomotives, the glossy finish was not what it seemed and D842 was recalled to works in January 1962 specifically because of 'the appalling condition of the external paint work'. ROYAL OAK has worked in from London on the premier train of the day, the 8.45am Paddington-Bristol 'Bristolian'. The 83D Laira shedplate can be clearly seen on the bufferbeam; the Plymouth depot was its home until March 1962 when D842 moved to Newton Abbot. (www.rail-online.co.uk)

D842 ROYAL OAK at Gloucester Central on 8 October 1969. The maroon full yellow locomotives always had a tendency to look a little tatty but this was probably because a nice new shiny yellow end was applied to an already weather-worn maroon locomotive. The front looked fine whereas after a while the paint was literally falling off the sides. Both headboard clips are missing and it has the Old Oak modification of headcode box ventilation holes. (www.rail-online.co.uk)

# D843 SHARPSHOOTER

| Lot no./Works no. | 443/27972 |
|---|---|
| **Significant dates and allocations** | |
| Delivered | 12/60 |
| Into traffic – Laira | 02/01/61 |
| Newton Abbot | 03/62 |
| Old Oak Common | 08/67 |
| Newton Abbot | 10/70 |
| Withdrawn (Newton Abbot) | 22/05/71 |
| (Bristol St Philips Marsh Junction) | By 22/10/71 |
| (Swindon) | 30/12/71 |
| Date cut-up | By 21/04/72 |

| **Stored** | From | To |
|---|---|---|
| Newton Abbot | 02/05/71 | 22/05/71 |

| **Livery and insignia changes** | |
|---|---|
| Green | 02/01/61 |
| OHLW flashes | 21/09/61 |
| Yellow warning panels | 12/05/62 |
| Maroon | - |
| Blue full yellow ends – double insignia, sans serif, D-prefix | 02/68 |
| Blue full yellow ends – single insignia, sans serif , no D | 2/11/70 |
| **Recorded mileage** | 634,000 |

**Works visits and depot repairs**

| Stopped | At | On Works | Off Works | At | Type | Days | Work carried out |
|---|---|---|---|---|---|---|---|
| - | - | 12/60 | 02/01/61 | SW | D/A | ? | Delivery inspection and acceptance |
| 19/04/61 | Ex-T | 19/04/61 | 05/05/61 | SW | L/C | 16 | |
| 25/05/61 | Ex-T | 25/05/61 | 07/06/61 | SW | L/C | 13 | |
| 25/08/61 | LA | 31/08/61 | 21/09/61 | SW | L/C | 27 | |
| 04/04/62 | Ex-T | 04/04/62 | 05/04/62 | LA | L/C | 1 | |
| 14/04/62 | NA | 18/04/62 | 12/05/62 | SW | L/C | 28 | |
| 25/06/62 | NA | 26/06/62 | 02/07/62 | SW | L/C | 7 | |
| 01/04/63 | Ex-T | 01/04/63 | 05/04/63 | LA | Unsch | 4 | A Engine Turbo blower changed (broken blades) |
| 24/05/63 | Ex-T | 24/05/63 | 30/05/63 | LA | H/C | 6 | |
| 06/12/63 | Ex-T | 12/63 | 31/12/63 | LA | H/C | 25 | |
| 09/01/64 | NA | 17/01/64 | 07/02/64 | SW | U/C | 29 | A Bogie changed; B Bogie changed (outer final drive defective) |
| 02/05/64 | Ex-T | 05/64 | 15/05/64 | NA | L/C | 13 | A Transmission changed |
| 08/06/64 | Ex-T | 06/64 | 16/06/64 | LA | Unsch | 8 | |
| 08/64 | Ex-T | 08/64 | 16/11/64 | SW | ? | 90 | A & B Engines changed (cylinder heads leaking); A Transmission changed; B Transmission changed (output flange damaged); A Bogie changed (worn side pads); B Bogie changed (outer final drive cardan shaft fractured); Main frame damage at B end repaired |
| 06/65 | Ex-T | 18/06/65 | | NA | ? | ? | B end dynostarter changed (low insulation) |
| 07/65 | Ex-T | 13/07/65 | | NA | ? | ? | B exhauster changed |
| 07/65 | Ex-T | 07/65 | 07/65 | LA | ? | ? | A Transmission changed (high oil temperature in No. 2 convertor and grating noise) |
| 08/65 | Ex-T | 17/08/65 | 08/65 | LA | ? | ? | A Transmission changed (unable to select direction and overheating) |
| 09/65 | Ex-T | 09/65 | 09/65 | ? | ? | ? | Boiler changed |
| 01/66 | Ex-T | 01/66 | 03/66 | SW | ? | ? | A Engine changed |
| ? | Ex-T | ? | 07/10/66 | ? | ? | ? | B Engine changed |
| ? | Ex-T | 20/10/66 | 10/66 | NA | ? | ? | B end dynostarter changed |
| 11/67 | Ex-T | 12/67 | 02/68 | SW | ? | ? | A Engine changed; B Engine changed (damaged flywheel); A & B Transmissions changed; B Bogie changed; Modifications; Multiple working jumper cables and sockets removed from buffer beam |
| 07/68 | Ex-T | 07/68 | 07/68 | ? | ? | ? | A Engine changed (loss of power) |
| 08/68 | Ex-T | 08/68 | 08/68 | ? | ? | ? | B Transmission changed (output bearing collapsed) |
| 11/68 | Ex-T | 11/68 | 11/68 | ? | ? | ? | B Transmission changed (output flange damaged) |
| 04/69 | Ex-T | 11/04/69 | 04/69 | ? | ? | ? | B Engine changed (passing oil) |
| 06/69 | Ex-T | 19/06/69 | 06/69 | ? | ? | ? | B Transmission changed (no filling pump pressure) |
| 08/69 | Ex-T | 08/69 | 08/69 | ? | ? | ? | A Engine changed (fractured cylinder head) |
| 09/69 | Ex-T | 09/69 | 09/69 | ? | ? | ? | A Transmission changed (No. 1 convertor breaking up |
| 02/70 | Ex-T | 02/70 | 02/70 | ? | ? | ? | A Engine changed (No. 1 camshaft seized) |
| 03/70 | Ex-T | 03/70 | 03/70 | ? | ? | ? | B Engine changed (final drive torque arm thread stripped) |
| 01/06/70 | LA | 23/06/70 | 08/70 | SW | ? | ? | A Engine changed (throwing oil); B Engine changed (extensive fire damage whilst working 7C11 20.30 Acton to Ponsandane freight on 1 June, and main bearings breaking up) |
| 11/70 | Ex-T | 11/70 | 11/70 | ? | ? | ? | Transmission changed (forward / reverse main bearings defective) |
| 01/71 | Ex-T | 01/71 | 01/71 | ? | ? | ? | B Transmission changed (forward / reverse mechanism to selecting direction) |
| 02/05/71 | Ex-T | | 22/05/71 | NA | | | To store / withdrawn |

D843 SHARPSHOOTER on 17 April 1964 leaving Acton Yard with the 5C30 3.15pm to Hackney Yard, a destination that it was not booked to reach until ten minutes before midnight. (PH Groom)

D843 SHARPSHOOTER on 15 March 1970 approaches the level crossing at Horton Road, Gloucester. The locomotive worked up from Plymouth the previous day on the 1E30 07.40 Plymouth-Newcastle. D843 has the BR symbols under the rail alphabet cab numbers; this livery variation was used by Swindon for all Warships painted blue during 1968. (www.rail-online.co.uk)

# D844 SPARTAN

| Lot no./Works no. | 443/27973 |
|---|---|
| **Significant dates and allocations** | |
| Delivered | 27/02/61 |
| Into traffic - Laira | 16/03/61 |
| Newton Abbot | 03/62 |
| Old Oak Common | 10/67 |
| Newton Abbot | 03/69 |
| Withdrawn (Newton Abbot) | 04/10/71 |
| (Bristol St Philips Marsh Junction) | By 24/10/71 |
| Carriage heating (Worcester) | By 02/11/71 |
| (Swindon) | 26/11/71 |
| Date cut-up | By 26/05/72 |

| **Livery and insignia changes** | |
|---|---|
| Green | 16/03/61 |
| OHLW flashes | By 05/62 |
| Yellow warning panels | 09/07/62 |
| Maroon - yellow warning panels | 02/66 |
| Blue full yellow ends – single insignia, sans serif , no D | 03/01/71 |
| **Recorded mileage** | 726,000 |

**Works visits and depot repairs**

| Stopped | At | On Works | Off Works | At | Type | Days | Work carried out |
|---|---|---|---|---|---|---|---|
| - | - | 27/02/61 | 16/03/61 | SW | D/A | 17 | Delivery inspection and acceptance |
| 07/04/61 | Ex-T | 07/04/61 | 19/05/61 | SW | L/C | 42 | |
| 14/06/62 | NA | 18/06/62 | 09/07/62 | SW | H/C | 25 | |
| 19/07/62 | Ex-T | 23/07/62 | 08/08/62 | NA | Unsch | 20 | A Engine changed (engine sump filled with coolant) |
| 09/08/62 | Ex-T | 09/08/62 | 18/08/62 | SW | H/C | 9 | B Engine Turbo blower damaged by passage of a detached internal exhaust elbow baffle |
| 15/09/62 | Ex-T | 15/09/62 | 05/10/62 | LA | H/C | 20 | |
| 22/10/62 | Ex-T | 23/10/62 | 10/62 | OOC | Unsch | ? | |
| 05/03/63 | Ex-T | 03/63 | 29/03/63 | NA | Unsch | 24 | |
| 22/07/63 | NA | 22/07/63 | 16/08/63 | SW | H/C | 25 | A & B Bogies changed (suspected inner axle flaws and scrap size tyres) |
| 09/09/63 | Ex-T | 09/63 | 23/09/63 | NA | Unsch | 14 | |
| 11/64 | Ex-T | 03/11/64 | 11/64 | LA | H/C | ? | A Engine changed (fractured sump) |
| 03/65 | Ex-T | 11/03/65 | 03/65 | LA | H/C | ? | B Engine changed (low lub. oil pressure) |
| 06/65 | Ex-T | 24/06/65 | 06/65 | NA | Unsch | ? | A Engine Turbo blower changed (short run-down) |
| 11/65 | Ex-T | 11/65 | 02/66 | SW | ? | ? | A Transmission changed (casing fractured); B Transmission changed (forward / reverse gear defects) |
| 04/66 | Ex-T | 04/66 | 04/66 | ? | L/C | ? | |
| 09/66 | Ex-T | 09/66 | 09/66 | ? | H/C | ? | A & B Bogies changed (inner axle flaws) |
| 11/66 | Ex-T | 11/66 | 11/11/66 | LA | L/C | ? | B Engine changed (No. 12 piston crown damaged by a broken exhaust valve) |
| 04/67 | Ex-T | 04/67 | 04/67 | ? | L/C | ? | Engine changed |
| 08/67 | Ex-T | 07/08/67 | 08/67 | NA | Unsch | ? | A Engine Turbo blower changed |
| 12/67 | Ex-T | 12/67 | 68 | SW | ? | ? | A & B Bogies changed (traces on the inner axle) |
| 02/68 | Ex-T | 02/68 | 02/68 | ? | L/C | ? | A Transmission changed (overheating and rotor assembly noisy on turning) |
| 07/68 | Ex-T | 07/68 | 07/68 | ? | L/C | ? | A Engine changed |
| 12/69 | Ex-T | 12/69 | 12/69 | ? | L/C | ? | B Bogie changed |
| 03/70 | Ex-T | 03/70 | 03/70 | ? | L/C | ? | A Engine removed (knocking) |
| 10/70 | Ex-T | 10/70 | 03/ 01/71 | SW | Int | ? | |
| 04/10/71 | Ex-T | | | NA | | | B Transmission defective; Withdrawn |

Just three months old and D844 SPARTAN is at Dawlish Warren with the 1V89 09.05 Liverpool-Plymouth, 24 June 1961. There is some really antique stock in the train, for these were the days when coaches could languish in sidings for months just to be available for peak demand. Old Oak Common actually had a rake of stock which was only used on two weekends per year but as they would not be able to meet the requirements without it, it was kept. (www.rail-online.co.uk)

844 SPARTAN during its last days hauls a class 8 freight out of the sidings at Swindon. It had only gained blue livery at the start of 1971 but it is already looking shabby. Received knowledge would have it that 857 was the last NBL Warship at work, though that distinction was actually owned by 844. Weeks after withdrawal SPARTAN travelled from store at Bristol St Phillips Marsh to Worcester in late October to perform carriage heating duties. Heating duties finished, the locomotive returned light diesel to Swindon for scrapping on 26 November. (www.rail-online.co.uk)

## D845 SPRIGHTLY

| Lot no./Works no. | 443/27974 |
|---|---|
| **Significant dates and allocations** | |
| Delivered | 02/03/61 |
| Into traffic - Laira | 07/04/61 |
| Newton Abbot | 04/62 |
| Old Oak Common | 09/67 |
| Bristol Bath Road (officially stored but used in traffic) | 03/69 |
| Newton Abbot | 06/69 |
| Withdrawn (Laira) | 03/10/71 |
| (Bristol St Philips Marsh Junction) | By 24/10/71 |
| (Swindon) | 30/11/71 |
| Date cut-up | By 19/05/72 |

| **Stored** | **From** | **To** |
|---|---|---|
| Bristol Bath Road (but used on p.way trains and track lifting trains on the old MR route to Bath) | 03/69 | 06/69 |
| Laira | 20/09/71 | 03/10/71 |

| **Livery and insignia changes** | |
|---|---|
| Green | 07/04/61 |
| Experimental warning panel and white cab roof | 30/08/61 |
| OHLW flashes | 09/61 |
| Yellow warning panels | 13/02/64 |
| Maroon | - |
| Blue full yellow ends – single insignia, sans serif , no D | 20/02/70 |
| **Recorded mileage** | 737,000 |

### Works visits and depot repairs

| Stopped | At | On Works | Off Works | At | Type | Days | Work carried out |
|---|---|---|---|---|---|---|---|
| - | - | 02/03/61 | 07/04/61 | SW | D/A | 36 | Delivery inspection and acceptance |
| 07/04/61 | Ex-T | 07/04/61 | 13/04/61 | SW | ? | 6 | |
| 11/08/61 | NA | 16/08/61 | 30/08/61 | SW | L/C | 19 | |
| 11/09/61 | LA | 12/09/61 | 15/09/61 | SW | L/C | 4 | |
| 02/02/62 | BS | 02/02/62 | 05/02/62 | SW | U/C | 3 | |
| 28/02/62 | LA | 13/03/62 | 20/03/62 | SW | L/C | 20 | |
| 30/05/62 | Ex-T | 06/62 | 16/06/62 | LA | L/C | 17 | |
| 09/07/62 | Ex-T | 07/62 | 26/07/62 | NA | Unsch | 17 | |
| 01/11/62 | Ex-T | 03/11/62 | 08/11/62 | LA | H/C | 7 | B Engine changed (high lub. oil consumption and No. 1 cylinder liner fractured) |
| 06/03/63 | Ex-T | 03/63 | 09/03/63 | LA | L/C | 3 | A Engine Turbo blower changed |
| 24/04/63 | Ex-T | 04/63 | 04/05/63 | LA | H/C | 10 | |
| 13/06/63 | Ex-T | 06/63 | 19/06/63 | LA | H/C | 6 | A Engine changed (Nos. 2 and 8 piston and con rods damaged) |
| 10/63 | Ex-T | 17/10/63 | 13/02/64 | SW | U/C | 119 | Modifications; Bogie side control linkage replaced with hydraulic shock absorbers |
| 08/04/64 | Ex-T | 04/64 | 22/04/64 | NA | Unsch | 14 | |
| 05/65 | Ex-T | 05/65 | 05/65 | SW | ? | ? | A & B Engines changed; |
| 07/66 | Ex-T | 07/66 | 07/66 | ? | ? | ? | A Engine changed (No. 5 cylinder liner leaking coolant) |
| 12/66 | Ex-T | 12/66 | 12/66 | ? | ? | ? | B Transmission changed (dynostarter input flange detached) |
| 01/67 | Ex-T | 23/01/67 | 01/67 | NA | L/C | ? | Boiler changed |
| 03/67 | Ex-T | 03/67 | 03/67 | ? | L/C | ? | B Transmission changed (burst diaphragm allowing hot oil onto bearings) |
| 05/67 | Ex-T | 05/67 | 05/67 | ? | L/C | ? | B Engine repaired |
| 06/67 | Ex-T | 06/67 | 06/67 | ? | ? | ? | A Engine changed (No. 7 piston crown damaged) |
| 08/67 | Ex-T | 16/08/67 | 08/67 | ? | ? | ? | Transmission changed (forward / reverse selector ring having broken teeth) |
| 09/68 | Ex-T | 18/09/68 | 09/68 | ? | L/C | ? | A Engine changed (No. 3 or No. 8 con rod fractured) |
| 04/69 | Ex-T | 16/04/69 | 04/69 | ? | L/C | ? | B Engine changed( passing oil) |
| 08/69 | Ex-T | 08/69 | 08/69 | ? | H/C | ? | B Engine changed( passing oil); Boiler changed |
| 07/12/69 | Ex-T | 07/12/69 | 12/69 | LA | Unsch | ? | A & B Engines changed |
| 12/69 | LA | 12/69 | 02/70 | SW | Int | ? | A & B Engines changed( passing oil) |
| 10/70 | Ex-T | 10/70 | 10/70 | ? | ? | ? | A Transmission changed (lift in the output bearings) |
| 10/09/71 | Ex-T | 09/71 | 14/09/71 | LA | L/C | 4 | A Transmission changed (forward / reverse defects) |
| 17/09/71 | Ex-T | 09/71 | 20/09/71 | LA | ? | 3 | A Engines (internal coolant leaks); To store |
| 20/09/71 | Ex-T | | 03/10/71 | LA | | | Withdrawn |

D845 SPRIGHTLY enters Bristol on 26 March 1963 with the 1M99 4pm Plymouth-Liverpool. D845's claim to fame is self evident: the experimental yellow panels which it carried from 30 August 1961 until replaced by the standard pattern in February 1964. SPRIGHTLY also had a white band across the front of the cab roof for this period. An enlarged version of the panel was adopted as standard but the white roof was not taken up. (Alec Swain, www.transporttreasury.co.uk)

845 SPRIGHTLY at Gloucester Horton Road on 18 March 1970. By this time it has long become another anonymous Warship although the new blue livery, applied the previous month, looks bright enough. The photograph illustrates perfectly the final livery that the Warships carried. The locomotive is waiting to take forward the 1V87 12.15 Newcastle-Plymouth from Gloucester Eastgate. (www.rail-online.co.uk)

# D846 STEADFAST

| Lot no./Works no. | 443/27975 |
|---|---|
| **Significant dates and allocations** | |
| Delivered | 04/61 |
| Into traffic - Laira | 12/04/61 |
| Newton Abbot | 05/62 |
| Old Oak Common | 07/67 |
| Tyseley (Temporary) | 08/67 |
| Newton Abbot | 06/70 |
| Withdrawn (Newton Abbot) | 22/05/71 |
| (Bristol St Philips Marsh Junction) | By 30/06/71 |
| (Swindon) | 18/10/71 |
| Date cut-up | By 24/12/71 |

| **Stored** | **From** | **To** |
|---|---|---|
| Newton Abbot | 02/05/71 | 22/05/71 |
| **Livery and insignia changes** | | |
| Green | | 12/04/61 |
| OHLW flashes | | 02/01/62 |
| Yellow warning panels | | 05/09/62 |
| Maroon | | - |
| Blue full yellow ends – double insignia, serif, D-prefix | | 26/04/67 |
| Blue full yellow ends – single insignia, sans serif , no D | | 24/08/70 |
| **Recorded mileage** | | 765,000 |

**Works visits and depot repairs**

| Stopped | At | On Works | Off Works | At | Type | Days | Work carried out |
|---|---|---|---|---|---|---|---|
| - | - | 04/61 | 12/04/61 | SW | D/A | ? | Delivery inspection and acceptance |
| 12/04/62 | Ex-T | 12/04/62 | 13/04/62 | LA | L/C | 1 | |
| 30/07/62 | NA | 17/08/62 | 05/09/62 | SW | H/C | 37 | |
| 16/10/62 | NA | 19/10/62 | 24/10/62 | SW | H/C | 8 | |
| 03/11/62 | Ex-T | 11/62 | 14/11/62 | LA | H/C | 11 | A Engine changed (No. 12 piston and liner damaged); B Engine changed (heavy oil consumption) |
| 31/01/63 | Ex-T | 02/63 | 06/02/63 | LA | H/C | 6 | |
| 03/05/63 | Ex-T | 03/05/63 | 03/05/63 | LA | L/C | 1 | |
| 12/02/64 | NA | 20/02/64 | 24/02/64 | SW | Unsch | 41 | Modifications; Bogie side control linkage replaced with hydraulic shock absorbers |
| 10/04/64 | Ex-T | 13/04/64 | 16/06/64 | SW | Unsch | 67 | B Bogie changed; Repairs to fire damage at A end |
| 15/02/65 | Ex-T | 02/65 | 06/65 | SW | Int | ? | A Engine changed; A & B Bogies changed |
| 08/65 | Ex-T | 19/08/65 | 18/08/65 | LA | L/C | ? | B Bogie changed (final drive defects) |
| 11/65 | Ex-T | 15/11/65 | 11/65 | NA | Unsch | ? | B Engine Turbo blower changed |
| 01/66 | Ex-T | 04/01/66 | 01/66 | ? | Unsch | ? | A Engine changed (No. 3 crank shaft pin damaged); B Engine changed |
| 01/66 | Ex-T | 17/01/66 | 01/66 | ? | Unsch | ? | B end dynostarter changed (earth faults) |
| 02/66 | Ex-T | 16/02/66 | 02/66 | NA | L/C | ? | Boiler changed |
| 03/66 | Ex-T | 03/66 | 03/66 | ? | L/C | ? | A Engine changed (continual governor and flywheel defects since last general repair) |
| 05/66 | Ex-T | 09/05/66 | 05/66 | NA | Unsch | ? | Compressor changed (electrical faults) |
| 05/66 | Ex-T | 20/05/66 | 05/66 | NA | Unsch | ? | A dynostarter changed (burnt out) |
| 20/10/66 | Ex-T | 10/66 | 26/04/67 | SW | Int | 188 | A & B Engines changed; A & B Transmissions changed; A & B Bogies changed; severe collision damage repaired (Nose end crumpled and distorted, buffer beam forced down, co-drivers side buffer ripped off, drivers side buffer pushed inwards and forced up, main frames pushed downwards and forced backwards, both windscreens missing, nose end flattened and dropped approx. 6" with the main tubes and deck plate buckled and pushed downwards) |
| 02/68 | Ex-T | 02/68 | 02/68 | ? | L/C | ? | Boiler changed |
| 09/68 | Ex-T | 09/68 | 09/68 | ? | L/C | ? | A Transmission changed (secondary shaft detached) |
| 10/68 | Ex-T | 10/68 | 10/68 | ? | L/C | ? | A Bogie changed (flats and thin tyres) |
| 11/68 | Ex-T | 11/68 | 11/68 | ? | L/C | ? | B Bogie changed (fractures in the pivot housing) |
| 01/69 | Ex-T | 01/69 | 01/69 | ? | L/C | ? | Transmission changed (control piston seized and metal in filters) |
| 06/69 | Ex-T | 19/06/69 | 23/06/69 | ? | ? | ? | A Transmission changed (overheating and metal in filters); B Transmission changed (rotor knocking when turned, emulsified oil and metal in filters) |
| 08/69 | Ex-T | 08/69 | 08/69 | ? | H/C | ? | A & B Bogies changed (torn side control rubbers) |
| 11/69 | Ex-T | 11/69 | 11/69 | ? | L/C | ? | B Transmission changed (overheating in 2nd convertor) |
| 01/70 | Ex-T | 01/70 | 01/70 | ? | ? | ? | Engine changed |
| 23/05/70 | Ex-T | 05/70 | 24/ 08/70 | SW | Int | 93 | A Engine changed; B Engine changed (hole in the crank case); fire damage repaired |
| 02/71 | Ex-T | 02/71 | 02/71 | ? | L/C | ? | Engine changed |
| 03/71 | Ex-T | 03/71 | 03/71 | ? | L/C | ? | B Transmission changed (forward / reverse gears seized) |
| 02/05/71 | Ex-T | | 22/05/71 | NA | | | To store/withdrawn |

*Left.* Warships were of course not without their mishaps and D846 STEADFAST at Swindon Works on 26 October 1966 demonstrates the result of one such incident. The headcode shows 3A42 so it is possible that the collision occurred while D846 was hauling the 18.00 St Erth-Kensington milk. This photograph is also useful to illustrate the position of the driver's card holder on an NBL Warship, dropped down a couple of inches from the driver's window, unlike the Swindon variant. D846 would emerge from Swindon in the new corporate blue.

*Below.* D846 STEADFAST at Gloucester Horton Road, next to D6995 on 19 November 1969. The livery is a variant carried by only three Warships, D830, D846 and D847. Even then the position of the numerals varied slightly with D847's being further back on the cabside. The small BR symbol above the nameplate was a short-lived digression and did seem to suit the Warships. (www.rail-online.co.uk)

# D847 STRONGBOW

| Lot no./Works no. | 443/27976 |
|---|---|
| **Significant dates and allocations** | |
| Delivered | 13/04/61 |
| Into traffic - Laira | 22/04/61 |
| Newton Abbot | 05/62 |
| Old Oak Common | 08/67 |
| Newton Abbot | 03/69 |
| Withdrawn (Swindon) | 27/03/71 |
| Date cut-up | By 17/03/72 |

| **Livery and insignia changes** | |
|---|---|
| Green | 22/04/61 |
| OHLW flashes | 02/01/62 |
| Yellow warning panels | 26/06/62 |
| Maroon | - |
| Blue full yellow ends – double insignia, serif, D-prefix | 24/02/67 |
| | |
| **Recorded mileage** | 653,000 |

**Works visits and depot repairs**

| Stopped | At | On Works | Off Works | At | Type | Days | Work carried out |
|---|---|---|---|---|---|---|---|
| - | - | 13/04/61 | 22/04/61 | SW | D/A | 9 | Delivery inspection and acceptance |
| 30/11/61 | LA | 12/12/61 | 02/01/62 | SW | L/C | 33 | A Bogie repaired (outer final drive input shaft bearing collapsed) |
| 20/05/62 | LA | 25/05/62 | 26/06/62 | SW | H/C | 37 | B Engine changed (coolant leaks ); B Bogie changed (inner final drive bevel pinion out of mesh and the input bearing collapsed) |
| 30/07/62 | LA | 02/08/62 | 21/08/62 | SW | Unsch | 22 | A Engine repaired; B Engine changed (gases blowing by the pistons and very high lub. oil consumption) |
| 27/10/62 | NA | 28/10/62 | 04/11/62 | LA | H/C | 8 | A Engine changed (exhaust elbows continually glowing white hot, excessive fumes from the crank case breather and high lub. oil consumption) |
| 22/01/63 | LA | 06/02/63 | 13/03/63 | SW | H/C | 50 | A Transmission changed; A Bogie repaired (inner final had broken teeth on gear wheels); B Bogie cardan shafts changed; extensive collision damage to B end nose section repaired, transmission to final drive cardan shafts changed and thrust pads reset |
| 17/04/63 | NA | 23/04/63 | 13/05/63 | SW | H/C | 26 | A Engine changed (broken teeth on the inner final drive bevel pinion gear); Boiler changed |
| 02/06/63 | Ex-T | | 03/06/63 | LA | L/C | 1 | |
| 07/08/63 | Ex-T | | 21/08/63 | NA | Unsch | 14 | |
| 07/09/63 | Ex-T | | 23/09/63 | NA | Unsch | 16 | |
| 03/64 | Ex-T | 16/03/64 | 03/64 | LA | L/C | ? | B Transmission changed (metal in filters) |
| 28/03/64 | Ex-T | | 13/04/64 | NA | Unsch | 16 | |
| 23/05/64 | Ex-T | 26/06/64 | 09/07/64 | SW | Unsch | 47 | A & B Engines changed (high lub. oil consumption and fuming): A & B Bogies changed; Fire damage repaired, B end dynostarter changed; compressor changed, flaking body paint work made good |
| 10/64 | Ex-T | 10/64 | 10/64 | ? | L/C | ? | Boiler changed |
| 17/05/65 | Ex-T | 25/05/65 | 23/07/65 | SW | Unsch | 67 | B Engine changed (cylinder heads leaking coolant ); replacement engine failed on fitting; A Transmission changed; A & B Bogies changed; Modifications; collision damage repairs; plating above A end bogie left hand side damaged and footstep distorted, left hand buffer damaged, skirting and plating holed. A exhauster changed, compressor changed |
| 08/65 | Ex-T | 03/08/65 | 08/65 | NA | Unsch | ? | B end dynostarter changed (burnt out) |
| 10/65 | Ex-T | 13/10/65 | 10/65 | NA | Unsch | ? | B end dynostarter changed (bearings overheating and the commutator throwing solder) |
| 12/65 | Ex-T | 23/12/65 | 12/65 | NA | Unsch | ? | Compressor changed ( bearing suspect) |
| 01/66 | Ex-T | 14/01/66 | 01/66 | LA | L/C | ? | A Engine changed |
| 04/66 | Ex-T | 04/04/66 | 04/66 | NA | Unsch | ? | A end dynostarter changed (burnt out) |
| 04/66 | Ex-T | 23/04/66 | 04/66 | NA | L/C | ? | B Engine Turbo blower changed |
| 07/66 | Ex-T | 20/07/66 | 07/66 | NA | Unsch | ? | A end dynostarter changed (noisy bearings) |
| 11/66 | Ex-T | 23/11/66 | 25/11/66 | NA | Unsch | ? | A Engine fuel pumps changed |
| 01/01/67 | Ex-T | 01/01/67 | 03/01/67 | NA | Unsch | ? | A Engine Turbo blower changed; B end dynostarter changed |
| 01/67 | Ex-T | 06/01/67 | 24/02/67 | SW | Int | 49 | A & B Engines changed (coolant leaks); A & B Transmissions repaired; A & B Bogies changed; Boiler changed; Modifications |
| 11/67 | Ex-T | 09/11/67 | 11/67 | OOC | L/C | ? | B Transmission changed |
| 03/68 | Ex-T | 30/03/68 | 03/68 | OOC | L/C | ? | B Engine changed (heavy fumes from the crank case breather) |
| 07/68 | Ex-T | 02/07/68 | 07/68 | OOC | L/C | ? | B Transmission changed (output flange damaged and teeth stripped from No.7 gear wheel) |
| 11/68 | Ex-T | 07/11/68 | 11/68 | OOC | L/C | ? | B Engine changed (throwing oil) |
| 02/69 | Ex-T | 19/02/69 | 02/69 | LA | L/C | ? | A Engine changed (fumes from the crank case breather) |
| 03/69 | Ex-T | 18/03/69 | 03/69 | LA | L/C | ? | A Engine changed (passing oil) |
| 04/69 | Ex-T | 18/04/69 | 04/69 | NA | Unsch | ? | Compressor changed (noisy) |
| 09/69 | Ex-T | 08/09/69 | 09/69 | LA | L/C | ? | A Transmission changed |
| 17/12/69 | Ex-T | 17/12/69 | 18/12/69 | LA | L/C | 1 | B Engine changed (passing oil) |
| 24/12/69 | Ex-T | 27/12/69 | 29/12/69 | LA | L/C | 5 | B Engine changed (No. 2 con rod parted and the crank case holed) |
| 07/01/70 | Ex-T | 07/01/70 | 13/01/70 | LA | H/C | 6 | B Transmission changed (middle and bottom main casings being fractured and all teeth stripped from the high speed gear on the rotor shaft); A & B Bogies changed |
| 01/70 | Ex-T | 24/01/70 | 01/70 | NA | Unsch | ? | B end dynostarter changed (earth faults) |
| 19/02/70 | Ex-T | 19/02/70 | 20/02/70 | LA | L/C | 1 | B Bogie changed (inner tyre loose, drivers side) |
| 17/03/70 | Ex-T | 17/03/70 | 18/03/70 | LA | L/C | 1 | A Engine changed (passing oil) |
| 05/70 | Ex-T | 09/05/70 | 05/70 | NA | L/C | ? | A Engine Turbo blower changed |
| 29/01/71 | Ex-T | 29/01/71 | 31/01/71 | LA | L/C | 2 | A Bogie changed |
| 15/03/71 | Ex-T | 20/03/71 | 24/03/71 | LA | ? | 9 | A & B Engines changed |
| 15/03/71 | NA | 24/03/71 | ? | SW | Int | ? | B Engine removed |
| 27/03/71 | SW | | | SW | | | Withdrawn |

D847 STRONGBOW at Fowey in the summer of 1961 with a freight from St Blazey. The photograph is a good historical record as the locomotive has gone, as has the signal box, the station and the direct route to Par and St Blazey. The latter has long since been tarmaced over and used as a private road for the lorry transport of china clay to the docks. Fowey's passenger service via Golant to Lostwithiel was withdrawn during the 1964-65 timetable. D847 itself was withdrawn on 27 March 71; it had been sent to Swindon for an intermediate repair but the work was not sanctioned.

On 1 October 1969 D847 STRONGBOW moves through the Up platform road at Totnes with the 7C53 09.45 Tavy Junction-Exeter Riverside. One of the three locomotives with the small BR symbol over the nameplate, the different position of the number, further back on the cabside, can be clearly seen. The air ventilation holes are evidence of its time at Old Oak Common but by the date of this shot STRONGBOW was allocated back to Newton Abbot. (JT Clewley, www.transporttreasury.co.uk)

# D848 SULTAN

| Lot no./Works no. | 443/27977 |
|---|---|
| **Significant dates and allocations** | |
| Delivered | 22/04/61 |
| Into traffic - Laira | 27/04/61 |
| Newton Abbot | 02/62 |
| Old Oak Common | 10/67 |
| Withdrawn (Old Oak Common) | 26/03/69 |
| (Swindon) | 24/04/70 |
| Date cut-up | By 26/05/71 |

| **Stored** | From | To |
|---|---|---|
| Old Oak Common | 28/02/69 | 26/03/69 |

| **Livery and insignia changes** | |
|---|---|
| Green | 27/04/61 |
| OHLW flashes | 31/10/61 |
| Yellow warning panels | 16/03/62 |
| Maroon yellow warning panels | 22/06/66 |
| Blue | - |
| **Recorded mileage** | 537,000 |

### Works visits and depot repairs

| Stopped | At | On Works | Off Works | At | Type | Days | Work carried out |
|---|---|---|---|---|---|---|---|
| - | - | 22/04/61 | 27/04/61 | SW | D/A | 5 | Delivery inspection and acceptance |
| 02/05/61 | Ex-T | 02/05/61 | 04/05/61 | SW | Unsch | 2 | |
| 10/10/61 | Ex-T | 16/10/61 | 31/10/61 | SW | L/C | 21 | A Engine changed (No. 2 cylinder push rods bent, cam follower adrift and camshaft damaged); defective paintwork on nose ends and body sides made good |
| 26/02/62 | Ex-T | 06/03/62 | 16/03/62 | SW | L/C | 18 | A Transmission changed (forward / reverse gear seized and governor jammed) |
| 21/03/62 | Ex-T | 21/03/62 | 06/04/62 | NA | Unsch | 16 | |
| 13/05/62 | Ex-T | 05/62 | 17/05/62 | NA | L/C | 4 | Boiler changed |
| 28/05/62 | NA | 04/06/62 | 04/07/62 | SW | L/C | 37 | B Transmission removed (no filling pressure) |
| 13/09/62 | Ex-T | 09/62 | 22/09/62 | NA | ? | 9 | B Engine changed (low lub. oil pressure) |
| 01/11/62 | NA | 07/11/62 | 23/11/62 | SW | H/C | 22 | B Engine changed (low lub. oil pressure) |
| 28/01/63 | LA | 06/02/63 | 22/02/63 | SW | H/C | 25 | B Transmission changed; B Bogie changed (final drive oil seals leaking) |
| 04/03/63 | Ex-T | 04/03/63 | 19/03/63 | NA | Unsch | 15 | |
| 22/03/63 | Ex-T | 24/03/63 | 12/04/63 | LA | H/C | 21 | B Transmission changed (failing to engage in forward direction); replacement failed; Boiler changed (coils burnt) |
| 09/09/63 | Ex-T | 10/09/63 | 14/09/63 | LA | H/C | 5 | A Engine changed (low lub. oil pressure) |
| 21/09/63 | Ex-T | 09/63 | 30/09/63 | LA | H/C | 9 | B Bogie changed (inner final drive axle shaft fractured) |
| 03/64 | Ex-T | 16/03/64 | 03/64 | LA | Unsch | ? | B Transmission changed (suspect bearings and metal in filters) |
| 10/04/64 | NA | 13/04/64 | 01/05/64 | SW | Unsch | 21 | A & B Bogies changed (axle flaws); Boiler changed; Modifications; Bogie side control linkage replaced with hydraulic shock absorbers |
| 07/64 | Ex-T | 15/07/64 | 07/64 | LA | Unsch | ? | B Engine changed (No. 11 cylinder liner leaking coolant into the sump) |
| 01/65 | Ex-T | 21/01/65 | 01/65 | LA | L/C | ? | B Transmission changed (overheating in No. 1 turbine) |
| 03/05/65 | Ex-T | 03/05/65 | 11/05/65 | LA | H/C | 8 | B Engine changed (internal pipe fractured ); A Bogie changed (outer axle flawed) |
| 07/10/65 | Ex-T | 10/65 | 19/10/65 | LA | H/C | 12 | A Engine changed; Boiler changed |
| 11/65 | Ex-T | 18/11/65 | 11/65 | LA | H/C | ? | A Transmission changed (excessive steel debris in filters); A Bogie changed (inner final drive bolts sheared off) |
| 15/04/66 | NA | 19/04/66 | 22/06/66 | SW | Int | 68 | A & B Engines repaired (fuel leaks); A & B Transmission repaired; Boiler repaired; Modifications; Multiple working jumper cables and sockets removed from buffer beam |
| 01/67 | Ex-T | 24/01/67 | 01/67 | NA | Unsch | ? | B Engine Turbo blower changed |
| 02/67 | Ex-T | 01/02/67 | 02/67 | NA | Unsch | ? | B Engine Turbo blower changed |
| 02/67 | Ex-T | 18/02/67 | 02/67 | NA | Unsch | ? | B end dynostarter changed |
| 06/67 | Ex-T | 26/06/67 | 06/67 | LA | H/C | ? | B Engine changed; B Transmission changed (overheating in 2nd convertor) |
| 11/12/67 | Ex-T | 12/67 | 19/12/67 | OOC | H/C | 8 | A Engine changed; A Transmission changed(overheating in 2nd convertor and fine particles in sump, convertor suspect) |
| 02/68 | Ex-T | 09/02/68 | 02/68 | OOC | L/C | ? | B Transmission changed (overheating in 2nd convertor and thick black oil sludge in sump) |
| 04/68 | Ex-T | 19/04/68 | 04/68 | OOC | L/C | ? | A Bogie changed; B Bogie changed (outer axle flaws) |
| 06/68 | Ex-T | 14/06/68 | 06/68 | OOC | Unsch | ? | B Engine changed |
| 08/68 | Ex-T | 19/08/68 | 08/68 | OOC | Unsch | ? | A Engine changed (crankcase fractures between Nos. 4 and 5 cylinders) |
| 08/68 | Ex-T | 23/08/68 | 08/68 | OOC | Unsch | ? | B Transmission changed (overheating, low speed pinion on rotor shaft worn and seized ) |
| 12/68 | Ex-T | 02/12/68 | 12/68 | OOC | L/C | ? | B Transmission changed (bad ratcheting) |
| 01/69 | Ex-T | 08/01/69 | 01/69 | OOC | H/C | ? | B Engine changed (throwing oil); B Bogie changed (bad vibrations) |
| 01/69 | Ex-T | 20/01/69 | 01/69 | OOC | Unsch | ? | A Engine changed (heavy knocking in the sump) |
| 14/02/69 | Ex-T | 17/02/69 | 17/02/69 | OOC | H/C | 3 | A Engine changed; B Engine changed (partial seizure) |
| 17/02/69 | Ex-T | | 26/03/69 | OOC | | | To store / withdrawn |

**D848 SULTAN is stabled at Old Oak Common on 7 October 1962, the 'Thousand' behind is an early Swindon example carrying the all over maroon livery with yellow bufferbeam. (www.rail-online.co.uk)**

**D848 SULTAN at Newton Abbot on 8 June 1968. It was destined to be one of the first two NBL Warships to be withdrawn, and also the first out of traffic when it was put into store on 28 February 1969; withdrawal followed just under a month later on 26 March. SULTAN was also one of the few to end its days in maroon livery with yellow warning panel.**

# D849 SUPERB

| Lot no./Works no. | 443/27978 |
|---|---|
| **Significant dates and allocations** | |
| Delivered | 28/04/61 |
| Into traffic - Laira | 29/05/61 |
| Newton Abbot | 02/62 |
| Laira | 06/64 |
| Newton Abbot | 06/64 |
| Old Oak Common | 10/67 |
| Newton Abbot | 06/70 |
| Withdrawn (Newton Abbot) | 22/05/71 |
| (Laira) | By 30/06/71 |
| (Newton Abbot) | 16/08/71 |
| (Swindon) | 13/10/71 |
| Date cut-up | By 07/07/72 |

| **Stored** | | |
|---|---|---|
| | **From** | **To** |
| Newton Abbot | 02/05/71 | 22/05/71 |
| **Livery and insignia changes** | | |
| Green | | 29/05/61 |
| OHLW flashes | | 30/6/62 |
| Yellow warning panels | | 14/12/62 |
| Maroon | | - |
| Blue full yellow ends – double insignia, serif, D-prefix | | 06/07/67 |
| Blue full yellow ends – double insignia, sans serif , D-prefix | | 20/06/68 |
| **Recorded mileage** | | 697,000 |

**Works visits and depot repairs**

| Stopped | At | On Works | Off Works | At | Type | Days | Work carried out |
|---|---|---|---|---|---|---|---|
| - | - | 28/04/61 | 29/05/61 | SW | D/A | 31 | Delivery inspection and acceptance |
| 22/04/62 | Ex-T | | 04/05/62 | LA | H/C | 12 | A Transmission changed (convertor seized) |
| 25/05/62 | NA | 27/05/62 | 30/05/62 | LA | H/C | 5 | B Engine changed (No. 3 cylinder bottom end bearing had excessive clearance) |
| 17/11/62 | Ex-T | 19/11/62 | 14/12/62 | SW | H/C | 27 | A Engine changed (low lub, oil pressure, high oil consumption and excessive fumes from the crankcase breather); replacement engine failed; Boiler changed |
| 11/04/63 | OOC | 24/04/63 | 10/05/63 | SW | H/C | 29 | B Transmission changed (output flange damaged by a fractured engine to transmission cardan shaft); A & B Bogies changed |
| 03/06/63 | Ex-T | 06/63 | 07/06/63 | LA | H/C | 4 | B Transmission changed ('double filling', No. 1 control piston seized) |
| 24/07/63 | Ex-T | 24/07/63 | 24/07/63 | LA | Unsch | 1 | A Engine Turbo blower changed (oil leaks) |
| 05/09/63 | Ex-T | 09/63 | 10/09/63 | LA | H/C | 5 | A Engine changed (high oil consumption -1 gallon per 20 miles); B Transmission changed (dynostarter shaft coupling loose); Compressor and motor changed |
| 10/63 | Ex-T | 31/10/63 | 10/63 | LA | Unsch | ? | B Engine changed (No. 4 cylinder liner register leaking profusely and will not seal) |
| 16/11/63 | Ex-T | 16/11/63 | 02/12/63 | LA | Unsch | 16 | |
| 16/01/64 | Ex-T | 01/64 | 24/01/64 | LA | Unsch | 8 | B Engine changed (high oil consumption, defective crankcase breather and loss of power) |
| 18/02/64 | Ex-T | 18/02/64 | 03/03/64 | NA | Unsch | 14 | |
| 22/06/64 | Ex-T | 22/06/64 | 27/06/64 | NA | Unsch | 5 | |
| 29/07/64 | Ex-T | 04/08/64 | 18/11/64 | SW | Int | 112 | A Engine changed (excessive coolant loss from all cylinder heads); B Engine changed (Nos. 4, 8 and 9 pistons passing oil); A & B Transmissions changed; Boiler changed; Modifications; Bogie side control linkage replaced with hydraulic shock absorbers |
| 01/65 | Ex-T | 25/01/65 | 01/65 | NA | Unsch | ? | Boiler changed (not passing 'mid-fire', servo. mechanism suspect) |
| 09/65 | Ex-T | 06/09/65 | 09/65 | NA | Unsch | ? | Compressor changed (fire damage) |
| 09/65 | Ex-T | 15/09/65 | 09/65 | NA | Unsch | ? | A Engine Turbo blower changed |
| 10/65 | Ex-T | 12/10/65 | 10/65 | NA | Unsch | ? | A end dynostarter changed (burnt out) |
| 07/12/65 | NA | 13/12/65 | 17/12/65 | SW | Unsch | 10 | A Engine repaired (drive coupling 'spewing' rubber, several heads leaking, Nos. 1 and 8 cylinder core plugs leaking, turbo blower reported with rapid run-down) ; B Engine repaired (heavy vibrations, rubber coupling breaking away from inside the steel ring, manifold covers adrift, No. 9 cylinder leaking coolant, No. 10 cylinder core plug and 'Telephone' joint leaking coolant) |
| 05/01/66 | Ex-T | 05/01/66 | 08/02/66 | SW | Unsch | 34 | A & B Engines repaired; A Transmission repaired ; B Transmission changed; A bogie changed; B bogie changed (defective inner axle); Modifications |
| 12/09/66 | Ex-T | 21/09/66 | 09/66 | LA | L/C | ? | A Transmission changed (thick black oily sludge and metal debris in sump, No. 2 convertor overheated) |
| 01/67 | Ex-T | 25/01/67 | 30/01/67 | LA | H/C | ? | A & B Engines changed; B Transmission changed (high temperature trips in No. 2 convertor); Boiler changed |
| 04/67 | Ex-T | 26/04/67 | 04/67 | LA | L/C | ? | B Transmission changed (excessive temperatures) |
| 30/05/67 | Ex-T | 30/05/67 | 06/07/67 | SW | Class | 37 | A Engine changed; B Engine repaired (No. 8 cylinder head leaking heavily, No. 3 cylinder core plug leaking fairly heavily and exhaust elbow drain missing); A & B Bogies changed; Bodywork repaired |
| 02/68 | Ex-T | 14/02/68 | 02/68 | OOC | L/C | ? | B Engine changed (fractured crankcase) |
| 25/04/68 | Ex-T | 30/04/68 | 20/06/68 | SW | Int | 56 | A & B Engines repaired (Fractured fuel spill pipe Nos. 7-12 bank repaired in situ, engine downrated from 1,530 rpm to 1,480 rpm); A Bogie (torn side control rubbers, worn buckle bushes on outer laminated springs, loose hand brake cross stay and one damaged life guard); B Bogie changed; Modifications |
| 09/68 | Ex-T | 13/09/68 | 09/68 | LA | L/C | ? | A Engine changed (low compression on No. 7 cylinder) |
| 02/69 | Ex-T | 14/02/69 | 02/69 | OOC | H/C | ? | B Engine changed (end plate and sump joint defects); A Transmission changed (No. 2 convertor breaking up) |
| 07/69 | Ex-T | 07/07/69 | 07/69 | LA | L/C | ? | A Transmission changed (No. 2 convertor overheating) |
| 07/08/69 | Ex-T | 08/08/69 | 09/08/69 | LA | L/C | 2 | A Bogie changed (derailment damage, 'X' member bent) |
| 09/09/69 | Ex-T | 09/69 | 12/09/69 | OOC | L/C | 3 | A Engine changed (throwing oil) |
| 28/05/70 | Ex-T | 06/70 | 05/06/70 | OOC | L/C | 8 | A Bogie changed (damage sustained from a detached cardan shaft) |
| 09/70 | Ex-T | 07/09/70 | 09/70 | LA | L/C | ? | A Bogie changed (lift in the outer final drive input bearing) |
| 08/11/70 | Ex-T | 08/11/70 | 10/11/70 | LA | L/C | 2 | B Engine changed (passing oil) |
| 02/12/70 | Ex-T | 12/70 | 04/12/70 | LA | H/C | 2 | A Transmission changed (metal in filters); B Transmission changed |
| 22/01/71 | Ex-T | 22/01/71 | 23/01/71 | LA | L/C | 1 | B Bogie changed (the torque arm assembly badly worn) |
| 02/05/71 | Ex-T | | 22/05/71 | NA | | | To store / Withdrawn |

D849 SUPERB in July 1962 at West Drayton with the 1A41 6.45am Truro-Paddington 'The Mayflower'; it would receive a yellow warning panel before the year was out. SUPERB was allocated to Newton Abbot at the time of the photograph, one of three periods that it spent allocated to that depot. Most of the coaches in the rake are still in the revived GWR-style chocolate and cream. (www.rail-online.co.uk)

D849 SUPERB on 2 August 1969 comes off Bath Road depot while WESTERN THUNDERER awaits its next turn. The 1V80 headcode would indicate that the locomotive is to take the 10.10 Bradford-Paignton 'Devonian' forward. The records confirm that this was the case and also show that SUPERB developed a fault on one engine and was assisted forward from Taunton by D7037. D849 carried both versions of blue livery with serif and Rail Alphabet numbers. (www.rail-online.co.uk)

# D850 SWIFT

| Lot no./Works no. | 443/27979 |
|---|---|
| **Significant dates and allocations** | |
| Delivered | 25/05/61 |
| Into traffic - Laira | 08/06/61 |
| Newton Abbot | 09/62 |
| Laira | 06/64 |
| Newton Abbot | 06/64 |
| Old Oak Common | 10/67 |
| Newton Abbot | 10/70 |
| Withdrawn (Bristol Bath Road) | 22/05/71 |
| (Bristol St Philips Marsh Junction) | By 01/06/71 |
| (Swindon) | 18/10/71 |
| Date cut-up | By 03/03/72 |

| **Stored** | | |
|---|---|---|
| | **From** | **To** |
| Old Oak Common | 01/03/69 | 01/05/69 |
| Bristol Bath Road | 02/05/71 | 22/05/71 |
| **Livery and insignia changes** | | |
| Green | | 08/06/61 |
| OHLW flashes | | By 04/62 |
| Yellow warning panels | | 21/02/63 |
| Maroon | | - |
| Blue full yellow ends – double insignia, serif, D-prefix | | 14/05/68 |
| **Recorded mileage** | | 654,000 |

**Works visits and depot repairs**

| Stopped | At | On Works | Off Works | At | Type | Days | Work carried out |
|---|---|---|---|---|---|---|---|
| - | - | 25/05/61 | 08/06/61 | SW | D/A | 13 | Delivery inspection and acceptance |
| 30/07/62 | Ex-T | 30/07/62 | 03/08/62 | LA | L/C | 4 | |
| 25/08/62 | Ex-T | 09/62 | 05/09/62 | LA | H/C | 11 | B Engine changed (No. 6 cylinder liner cracked) |
| 22/12/62 | Ex-T | 12/62 | 16/01/63 | LA | H/C | 25 | B Transmission changed (no filling pump pressure) |
| 31/01/63 | LA | 08/02/63 | 21/02/63 | SW | H/C | 21 | A Engine changed; B Transmission changed (no filling pump pressure); Boiler changed; Bodywork repairs (On 30/01/62 a letter requesting D842 and D850 to go to Works was issued, requesting attention be given to the appalling condition of the external paint work. Only D842 arrived, D850 remained in traffic until this visit. On 04/07/62 a further letter regarding the condition of D850 had been issued stating "This locomotive is badly in need of a repaint; the whole of the body work is a mass of blisters where paint is falling off or filler has dropped out. There are a large number of bad patches where the filler has already fallen out") |
| 01/04/63 | NA | 06/04/63 | 09/04/63 | LA | H/C | 8 | A Engine changed (coolant in the No. 9 cylinder and rocker gear damaged) |
| 09/07/63 | Ex-T | 09/07/63 | 10/08/63 | NA | Unsch | 32 | |
| 12/08/63 | Ex-T | 13/08/63 | 19/08/63 | LA | H/C | 7 | B Transmission changed (seized output shaft) |
| 23/09/63 | Ex-T | 25/09/63 | 28/10/63 | SW | H/C | 35 | A Engine changed (high lub. oil consumption); A & B Bogies changed; Boiler changed (overheating); Modifications; Bogie side control linkage replaced with hydraulic shock absorbers |
| 07/02/64 | LA | 21/02/64 | 10/03/64 | SW | Unsch | 32 | A & B Transmissions repaired (output shaft oil seals leaking); A Bogie changed (final drive defects);. B Bogie changed (flawed axles) |
| 04/06/64 | NA | 10/04/64 | 24/04/64 | SW | Unsch | 18 | B Transmission changed (overheating when changing from 2nd to 3rd gear); A & B Bogies changed; Boiler changed |
| 04/06/64 | Ex-T | 15/06/64 | 22/09/64 | SW | Int | 111 | A Engine crank case door seals renewed; B Engine changed (extensive fire damage caused by several fuel leaks); B Transmission changed; A & B Bogies changed |
| 10/64 | Ex-T | 19/10/64 | 10/64 | LA | Unsch | ? | A Engine Turbo blower changed |
| 12/64 | Ex-T | 29/12/64 | 12/64 | LA | Unsch | ? | A Transmission changed (dynostarter input bearing collapsed) |
| 01/65 | Ex-T | 14/01/65 | 01/65 | NA | Unsch | ? | B exhauster changed (earth on the motor) |
| 01/65 | Ex-T | 21/01/65 | 01/65 | NA | Unsch | ? | A end dynostarter changed (field coils burnt) |
| 03/65 | Ex-T | 18/03/65 | 03/65 | NA | Unsch | ? | A Engine Turbo blower changed (exhaust stack stud holes worn) |
| 04/65 | Ex-T | 01/04/65 | 04/65 | NA | Unsch | ? | A Engine Turbo blower changed |
| 04/65 | Ex-T | 10/04/65 | 04/65 | NA | Unsch | ? | A Engine Fuel pumps changed |
| 26/04/65 | NA | 27/04/65 | 04/65 | LA | Unsch | ? | Compressor changed |
| 06/65 | Ex-T | 16/06/65 | 06/65 | NA | Unsch | ? | A Engine Turbo blower changed |
| 10/65 | Ex-T | 06/10/65 | 10/65 | LA | L/C | ? | A Engine changed (coolant leaking from the liners at all cylinder heads) |
| 01/66 | Ex-T | 07/01/66 | 01/66 | NA | Unsch | ? | A end dynostarter changed (burnt out) |
| 03/66 | Ex-T | 22/03/66 | 03/66 | NA | L/C | ? | Boiler changed |
| 22/04/66 | Ex-T | 26/04/66 | 04/66 | NA | Unsch | ? | B Engine Turbo blower changed; B end dynostarter changed |
| 28/06/66 | Ex-T | 28/06/66 | 08/07/66 | SW | Class | 10 | A & B Bogies changed; exterior repaint in green |
| 20/07/66 | Ex-T | 20/07/66 | 21/07/66 | LA | L/C | 1 | B Engine changed |
| 07/66 | Ex-T | 29/07/66 | 07/66 | NA | Unsch | ? | A end dynostarter changed |
| 08/66 | Ex-T | 02/08/66 | 08/66 | NA | Unsch | ? | B end Turbo blower changed (seizure) |
| 11/66 | Ex-T | 15/11/66 | 11/66 | LA | L/C | ? | B Transmission changed (forward / reverse dog clutch seizing) |
| 11/66 | Ex-T | 23/11/66 | 11/66 | NA | Unsch | ? | A Engine Turbo blower changed |
| 12/66 | Ex-T | 19/12/66 | 12/66 | NA | Unsch | ? | B end dynostarter changed |
| 03/67 | Ex-T | 03/03/67 | 03/67 | LA | L/C | ? | A Transmission changed (seizure) |
| 19/06/67 | Ex-T | 19/06/67 | 28/06/67 | LA | H/C | 9 | B Engine changed (low lub oil pressure); replacement failed; A Transmission changed (overheating in 2nd convertor ) |
| 11/67 | Ex-T | 21/11/67 | 11/67 | LA | H/C | ? | A Engine changed (overdue routine overhaul); A Transmission changed (output oil seals leaking) |
| 01/68 | Ex-T | 23/01/68 | 01/68 | OOC | L/C | ? | B Transmission changed (convertor defects) |
| 03/68 | Ex-T | 11/03/68 | 03/68 | OOC | L/C | ? | B Engine change (fractured sump) |
| 03/68 | Ex-T | 02/04/68 | 14/05/68 | SW | Int | 42 | A & B Engines repaired (leaking cylinder heads in situ); A & B Bogies changed; Boiler changed; Modifications; all hoses and cardan shafts changed, exhausters and compressor changed |
| 02/69 | Ex-T | 11/02/69 | 02/69 | OOC | L/C | ? | A Engine changed (throwing oil) |
| 26/02/69 | Ex-T | 26/02/69 | 04/03/69 | OOC | L/C | 6 | B Engine changed (sump fractures) |
| 03/69 | Ex-T | 14/03/69 | 03/69 | OOC | L/C | ? | B Engine changed (passing oil) |
| 01/03/69 | Ex-T | 26/03/69 | 01/05/69 | OOC | | 36 | To store / reinstated to traffic; B Engine changed (passing oil) |
| 06/69 | Ex-T | 26/06/69 | 06/69 | OOC | H/C | ? | B Transmission changed (overheating, control piston seized and metal in filters); B Bogie changed (inner final drive bearings defective) |
| 07/07/69 | Ex-T | 07/07/69 | 07/07/69 | OOC | Unsch | 1 | Compressor changed |
| 08/07/69 | Ex-T | 08/07/69 | 08/07/69 | OOC | L/C | 1 | Boiler changed |
| 09/69 | Ex-T | 22/09/69 | 09/69 | OOC | H/C | ? | A & B Transmissions changed (overheating in 1st convertor) |
| 01/12/69 | OOC | 02/12/69 | 13/03/70 | SW | U/C | 101 | A Engine changed (Nos. 1 and 3 cylinders leaking; B Engine changed; Extensive body repairs |
| 15/09/70 | Ex-T | 09/70 | 06/10/70 | OOC | L/C | 21 | B Transmission changed (temperature trips) |
| 23/11/70 | Ex-T | 23/11/70 | 24/11/70 | LA | L/C | 1 | B Engine changed (sump fractures) |
| 19/02/71 | Ex-T | 19/02/71 | 22/02/71 | LA | L/C | 3 | B Transmission changed (forward / reverse gear suffering intermittent seizures) |
| 02/05/71 | Ex-T | | 22/05/71 | NA | | | Stored / withdrawn |

D850 SWIFT was introduced on 8 June 1961 and it is pictured the following month arriving at Bristol Temple Meads with the Down 'Bristolian'. It carries the ornate style of headboard and certainly looked the part, newly into traffic. However on 30 January 1962 a letter was issued requesting D842 and D850 to go to Works because of the appalling condition of their external paint work. Only D842 arrived, D850 remained in traffic and on 4 July 1962 there was a further letter regarding its condition stating "This locomotive is badly in need of a repaint; the whole of the body work is a mass of blisters where paint is falling off or filler has dropped out. There are a large number of bad patches where the filler has already fallen out". (www.rail-online.co.uk)

D850 SWIFT was one of the NBL Warships which spent some time stored out of traffic during 1969 but it was more fortunate than some and was back working by May that year. On 21 April 1971 and less than two weeks before being stored for the final time, D850 sits on Ranelagh Bridge prior to working the 1C63 15.30 to Paignton. SWIFT had come up from the West the previous day on the 1A32 09.55 off Paignton, and then filled in with a turn to Worcester on the 1B87 17.15 Paddington-Worcester. SWIFT never carried maroon livery, going straight from green into the early blue variant pictured. (PH Groom)

# D851 TEMERAIRE

| Lot no./Works no. | 443/27980 |
|---|---|
| **Significant dates and allocations** | |
| Delivered | 06/07/61 |
| Into traffic - Laira | 10/07/61 |
| Newton Abbot | 09/62 |
| Laira | 06/63 |
| Newton Abbot | 06/64 |
| Old Oak Common | 10/67 |
| Newton Abbot | 02/68 |
| Old Oak Common | 04/68 |
| Newton Abbot | 09/69 |
| Old Oak Common | 06/70 |
| Newton Abbot | 10/70 |
| Withdrawn (Newton Abbot) | 22/05/71 |
| (Laira) | After 25/09/71 |
| (Swindon) | 18/10/71 |
| Date cut-up | By 09/06/72 |

| **Stored** | From | To |
|---|---|---|
| Newton Abbot | 02/05/71 | 22/05/71 |
| **Livery and insignia changes** | | |
| Green | | 10/07/61 |
| OHLW flashes | | 13/10/61 |
| Yellow warning panels | | 01/05/62 |
| Maroon | | - |
| Blue full yellow ends – double insignia, serif, D-prefix | | 07/05/68 |
| **Recorded mileage** | | 714,000 |

**Works visits and depot repairs**

| Stopped | At | On Works | Off Works | At | Type | Days | Work carried out |
|---|---|---|---|---|---|---|---|
| - | - | 06/07/61 | 10/07/61 | SW | D/A | 4 | Delivery inspection and acceptance |
| 18/07/61 | Ex-T | 18/07/61 | 24/07/61 | SW | L/C | 6 | |
| 02/10/61 | LA | 02/10/61 | 13/10/61 | SW | L/C | 11 | B Engine repaired (lub. oil spraying from adjacent to the dip stick when running and exhaust manifold changed during static tests on Nos. 1 - 6 bank) |
| 25/10/61 | LA | 30/10/61 | 09/11/61 | SW | L/C | 15 | B Engine repaired (No. 9 cylinder head changed due to coolant leaks); B Bogie changed (outer final drive input shaft bearing collapsed and final drive seized) |
| 06/04/62 | BS | 12/04/62 | 01/05/62 | SW | H/C | 25 | A Engine changed (No. 2 piston smashed) |
| 07/62 | Ex-T | 17/07/62 | 07/62 | LA | Unsch | ? | B end exhauster changed due to the big end bearing being defective |
| 29/08/62 | Ex-T | 29/08/62 | 06/09/62 | LA | Unsch | 8 | |
| 09/10/62 | NA | 12/10/62 | 07/11/62 | SW | H/C | 29 | A & B Engines repaired; A Bogie changed; B Bogie changed (outer final drive overheating and metal debris in the sump); Boiler changed |
| 11/12/62 | NA | 14/12/62 | 07/01/63 | SW | H/C | 27 | A Engine changed (continual overspeed trips); B Engine changed (defective piston rings) |
| 05/04/63 | Ex-T | 05/04/63 | 11/04/63 | LA | H/C | 6 | B Engine changed (No. 10 cylinder liner leaking coolant and high lub. oil consumption) |
| 10/08/63 | Ex-T | 11/08/63 | 20/08/63 | LA | H/C | 10 | A Engine changed (heavy oil leaks by the flywheel): A & B exhausters changed (earths) |
| 11/63 | Ex-T | 14/11/63 | 11/63 | LA | Unsch | ? | B Engine Turbo blower changed (shaft seizure) |
| 12/63 | Ex-T | 24/12/63 | 12/63 | LA | Unsch | ? | B Engine Turbo blower changed (blade damage) |
| 16/04/64 | Ex-T | 16/04/64 | 21/04/64 | LA | Unsch | 5 | A & B Engine Turbo blowers changed |
| 17/06/64 | LA | 26/06/64 | 20/08/64 | SW | Unsch | 64 | B Transmission changed (metal in filters and in the sump); A Bogie changed (heavy flats); B Bogie changed(weak springs); Modifications; Bogie side control linkage replaced with hydraulic shock absorbers |
| 09/64 | Ex-T | 18/09/64 | 09/64 | LA | L/C | ? | A Transmission changed (no filling pump pressure) |
| 01/65 | Ex-T | 05/01/65 | 01/65 | LA | L/C | ? | B Engine changed (loss of power) |
| 25/02/65 | Ex-T | 01/03/65 | 17/03/65 | SW | Unsch | 20 | A Bogie changed (right hand side platform fractured by the lateral buffing pad and incorrect axle profiles); B Bogie changed (incorrect axle profiles) |
| 09/65 | Ex-T | 26/09/65 | 09/65 | LA | L/C | ? | A Engine changed |
| 04/66 | Ex-T | 26/04/66 | 04/66 | NA | Unsch | ? | B Engine Turbo blower changed |
| 07/66 | Ex-T | 02/07/66 | 07/66 | NA | Unsch | ? | B Engine Fuel pumps changed |
| 07/66 | Ex-T | 18/07/66 | 29/07/66 | SW | Class | ? | A & B Bogies changed; Boiler changed; A & B end dynostarters changed, thrust pads reset, over bogie structure repaired |
| 03/67 | Ex-T | 07/03/67 | 03/67 | LA | L/C | ? | B Engine changed |
| 04/67 | Ex-T | 08/04/67 | 04/67 | LA | L/C | ? | A Bogie changed (traces on the inner axle) |
| 07/67 | Ex-T | 07/07/67 | 07/67 | LA | H/C | ? | B Engine changed (excessive oil mist from the crankcase breather); B Transmission changed (input shaft thrust defective) |
| 08/67 | Ex-T | 01/08/67 | 08/67 | NA | Unsch | ? | A end dynostarter changed |
| 10/67 | Ex-T | 16/10/67 | 10/67 | OOC | H/C | ? | A Engine changed; A Transmission changed (no filling pump pressure) |
| 11/67 | Ex-T | 14/11/67 | 11/67 | NA | Unsch | ? | A end dynostarter changed |
| 01/68 | Ex-T | 10/01/68 | 01/68 | OOC | L/C | ? | B Transmission changed (No. 2 convertor overheated and metal in filters) |
| 02/68 | Ex-T | 19/02/68 | 02/68 | NA | Unsch | ? | B Engine Fuel pumps changed |
| 03/68 | Ex-T | 07/03/68 | 07/05/68 | SW | Int | 60 | A & B Engines changed (coolant leaks in cylinders); A & B Bogies changed (torn side control rubbers); Modifications |
| 06/68 | Ex-T | 17/06/68 | 06/68 | OOC | L/C | ? | Boiler changed |
| 07/68 | Ex-T | 09/07/68 | 07/68 | OOC | L/C | ? | B Transmission changed (excessive vibration) |
| 04/69 | Ex-T | 30/04/69 | 04/69 | OOC | L/C | ? | A Engine changed (throwing oil) |
| 07/69 | Ex-T | 23/07/69 | 07/69 | LA | Unsch | ? | A Engine changed (fire damaged) |
| 08/69 | Ex-T | 20/08/69 | 08/69 | OOC | L/C | ? | B Engine changed (passing oil) |
| 12/09/69 | Ex-T | 09/69 | 18/09/69 | OOC | H/C | 6 | A Engine changed (fractured sump); B Engine changed (no lub. oil pressure) |
| 22/11/69 | Ex-T | 11/69 | 05/12/69 | NA | H/C | 13 | A Engine changed (Nos. 4 and 10 con rods pushed through the crank case); A Transmission changed (no filling pump pressure) |
| 03/03/70 | Ex-T | 03/03/70 | 05/03/70 | LA | L/C | 2 | A Engine changed (throwing oil) |
| 13/03/70 | Ex-T | 13/03/70 | 13/03/70 | NA | Unsch | ? | A end dynostarter changed |
| 16/04/70 | Ex-T | 16/04/70 | 17/04/70 | LA | L/C | 1 | A Engine changed (low lub. oil pressure; internal oil leak suspected) |
| 01/05/70 | Ex-T | 05/70 | 05/05/70 | LA | L/C | 4 | A Engine changed (passing oil) |
| 01/06/70 | Ex-T | 06/70 | 26/06/70 | OOC | H/C | 25 | A Engine changed (throwing oil); B Bogie changed (right trailing tyre loose) |
| 18/08/70 | Ex-T | 08/70 | 30/08/70 | OOC | L/C | 12 | A Bogie changed (4cm trace in groove No. 9 on the outer axle) |
| 27/10/70 | Ex-T | 27/10/70 | 28/10/70 | NA | L/C | 1 | Boiler changed |
| 12/01/71 | Ex-T | 01/71 | 18/01/71 | LA | L/C | 6 | A Transmission changed (metal in filters ) |
| 02/05/71 | Ex-T | | 22/05/71 | NA | | | To store / withdrawn |

**D851 TEMERAIRE** passes a damp Dawlish Warren in September 1967 with a rather short load for the 1V33 07.02 Bradford-Penzance 'Cornishman'. The green livery is looking work stained and D851 would be treated to a fresh coat of blue paint the following Spring during an Intermediate overhaul. (www.rail-online.co.uk)

**D851 TEMERAIRE** exits Exeter Stabling Point on 25 October 1969. **TEMERAIRE** was stored at Newton Abbot in early May 1971 and then officially withdrawn three weeks later on the 22nd. In September 1971 it was moved to Laira before the final trip to Swindon in mid-October in the company of withdrawn classmates D836, D853 and D862. (Great Western)

# D852 TENACIOUS

| Lot no./Works no. | 443/27981 |
|---|---|
| **Significant dates and allocations** | |
| Delivered | 19/07/61 |
| Into traffic – Laira | 24/07/61 |
| Newton Abbot | 09/62 |
| Laira | 06/63 |
| Newton Abbot | 06/64 |
| Old Oak Common | 10/67 |
| Newton Abbot | 04/69 |
| Old Oak Common | 21/11/69 |
| Newton Abbot | 10/70 |
| Withdrawn (Bristol Bath Road) | 03/10/71 |
| (Bristol St Philips Marsh Junction) | 10/71 |
| (Swindon) | 15/10/71 |
| Date cut-up | By 02/06/72 |

| **Stored** | From | To |
|---|---|---|
| Old Oak Common | 03/69 | 04/69 |
| Laira | 25/05/69 | 26/08/69 |
| Newton Abbot | 29/09/71 | 03/10/71 |

| **Livery and insignia changes** | |
|---|---|
| Green | 24/07/61 |
| OHLW flashes | 20/12/61 |
| Yellow warning panels | 19/07/62 |
| Maroon | - |
| Blue full yellow ends – single insignia, sans serif , no D | 21/11/69 |
| **Recorded mileage** | 704,000 |

**Works visits and depot repairs**

| Stopped | At | On Works | Off Works | At | Type | Days | Work carried out |
|---|---|---|---|---|---|---|---|
| - | - | 19/07/61 | 24/07/61 | SW | D/A | 6 | Delivery inspection and acceptance |
| 06/12/61 | OOC | 12/12/61 | 20/12/61 | SW | L/C | 14 | A Engine repaired (heavy oil leaks from the sump joints) |
| 04/07/62 | SW | 04/07/62 | 19/07/62 | SW | H/C | 15 | B Engine changed (overheating) |
| 04/02/63 | Ex-T | 04/02/63 | 12/02/63 | LA | H/C | 8 | A Engine changed (low compression on No. 7 cylinder, 3 p.s.i. only) |
| 12/04/63 | NA | 23/04/63 | 13/05/63 | SW | L/C | 31 | A Bogie changed; B Bogie changed (outer final drive crown wheel damaged); B exhauster changed (earth on motor) |
| 06/10/63 | Ex-T | 08/10/63 | 12/10/63 | LA | H/C | 6 | B Engine changed (low compression on Nos. 7 - 12 bank and overheating) |
| 11/63 | Ex-T | 13/11/63 | 11/63 | LA | Unsch | ? | Compressor changed ( big end bearing failure) |
| 12/12/63 | Ex-T | 12/12/63 | 12/12/63 | LA | Unsch | 1 | |
| 09/03/64 | Ex-T | 09/03/64 | 11/03/64 | LA | Unsch | 2 | B Transmission changed (overheating, centre casing joints leaking oil and bolts missing) |
| 15/04/64 | Ex-T | 15/04/64 | 21/04/64 | LA | H/C | 6 | A Engine changed (overheating and no compression) |
| 07/64 | Ex-T | 21/07/64 | 07/64 | LA | L/C | ? | B Transmission changed (forward / reverse gear defects and the selection ring worn) |
| 08/64 | Ex-T | 17/08/64 | 08/64 | NA | L/C | ? | Boiler changed |
| 09/64 | Ex-T | 30/09/64 | 10/64 | LA | H/C | ? | B Engine changed (high oil consumption); replacement changed (oil leaking from weld lines) |
| 11/64 | Ex-T | 20/11/64 | 11/64 | LA | L/C | ? | A Engine changed (No. 6 con rod broken and pushed through the crank case) |
| 01/65 | Ex-T | 27/01/65 | 01/65 | LA | L/C | ? | A Transmission changed (excessive metal in filters) |
| 05/04/65 | Ex-T | 08/04/65 | 28/07/65 | SW | Int | 114 | A & B Engines changed (coolant leaking from cylinder heads, leaking crank case doors and manifold joints); A & B Transmissions changed (output oil seals leaking); A Bogie changed; B Bogie changed (outer final drive input shaft defective); Boiler repaired; Modifications; all hoses and cardan shafts changed, exhausters and compressor changed |
| 09/66 | Ex-T | 15/09/66 | 09/66 | LA | L/C | ? | A Engine changed (low lub. oil pressure) |
| 10/66 | Ex-T | 24/10/66 | 10/66 | NA | Unsch | ? | B end dynostarter changed (low insulation readings) |
| 11/66 | Ex-T | 21/11/66 | 26/11/66 | NA | H/C | ? | Boiler changed |
| 01/67 | Ex-T | 12/01/67 | 01/67 | LA | L/C | ? | B Engine changed (internal oil leaks, suspect lub. oil return pipe from rocker to sump) |
| 02/67 | Ex-T | 22/02/67 | 02/67 | NA | Unsch | ? | A end dynostarter changed |
| 03/67 | Ex-T | 22/03/67 | 03/67 | NA | Unsch | ? | A end dynostarter changed (burnt out) |
| 07/67 | Ex-T | 12/07/67 | 07/67 | LA | L/C | ? | A Engine changed (No. 4 con rod fractured) |
| 07/67 | Ex-T | 31/07/67 | 07/67 | NA | Unsch | ? | B Engine Fuel pumps changed (overspeed trips) |
| 09/67 | Ex-T | 11/09/67 | 09/67 | LA | H/C | ? | A Bogie changed; B Bogie changed (outer pivot pin upper housing damaged by a detached cardan shaft) |
| 11/01/68 | OOC | 16/01/68 | 18/01/68 | LA | H/C | 2 | A Engine changed (crank case compression and throwing oil); B Engine changed |
| 01/68 | Ex-T | 29/01/68 | 01/68 | OOC | L/C | ? | A Engine changed (internal coolant leaks) |
| 05/68 | Ex-T | 30/05/68 | 05/68 | OOC | L/C | ? | A Transmission changed |
| 26/07/68 | Ex-T | 07/68 | 02/08/68 | LA | H/C | 7 | A Engine changed (oil leaks and throwing oil; B Engine changed (internal knocking; several balance weights loose on the crank shaft); B Transmission changed (reported noisy) |
| 08/68 | Ex-T | 29/08/68 | 08/68 | OOC | L/C | ? | B Engine changed (crank case fractured by No. 1 cylinder) |
| 10/69 | Ex-T | 17/10/68 | 10/68 | OOC | L/C | ? | Boiler changed |
| 04/69 | Ex-T | 30/04/69 | 26/08/69 | LA | ? | 118 | A Engine changed; B Transmission changed; To store on 25/05/69; reinstated |
| 26/08/69 | Ex-T | 10/09/69 | 21/11/69 | SW | Int | 87 | A Engine changed (heavy breathing); B Engine changed (No. 4 cylinder liner damaged); A Transmission changed; B Transmission changed (high temperatures in all converters with No. 3 convertor blackened : A & B Bogies changed; Boiler changed (coil split and burner unit missing); Modifications; all hoses and cardan shafts changed, exhausters and compressor changed |
| 03/02/70 | Ex-T | 03/02/70 | 06/02/70 | OOC | L/C | 3 | B Transmission changed (output casing moved and bolts continually working loose) |
| 25/03/70 | Ex-T | 25/03/70 | 04/04/70 | OOC | L/C | 10 | B Transmission changed (No. 1 turbine broken up and transmission seized) |
| 18/04/70 | Ex-T | 18/04/70 | 22/04/70 | OOC | L/C | 4 | B Bogie changed (heavy vibrations) |
| 28/04/70 | Ex-T | 28/04/70 | 17/05/70 | OOC | H/C | 19 | B Transmission changed (heavy grinding noises above 40 mph); replacement failed on fitting (forward / reverse defects) |
| 15/06/70 | Ex-T | 15/06/70 | 19/06/70 | OOC | L/C | 4 | A Engine changed (passing oil) |
| 09/12/70 | Ex-T | 09/12/70 | 13/12/70 | OOC | L/C | 4 | B Engine changed (passing oil) |
| 04/06/71 | Ex-T | 06/71 | 09/06/71 | OOC | L/C | 5 | A Engine changed (passing oil) |
| 10/08/71 | Ex-T | 08/71 | 18/08/71 | LA | L/C | 8 | B Engine changed (the sump fractured) |
| 22/08/71 | Ex-T | 08/71 | 28/08/71 | LA | L/C | 6 | B Transmission changed (reported internal knocking) |
| 11/09/71 | Ex-T | | 03/10/71 | NA | | | To store / withdrawn |

D852 TENACIOUS on 29 August 1961 comes around the curve at Tavistock Junction with the Western Region's premier named train, the 10.30am Paddington-Penzance 'Cornish Riviera Express'. The lines to the left led to Tavistock South and eventually Launceston and Padstow, all now unfortunately closed. TENACIOUS had the distinction of being the only Warship to have the 'D' prefix removed while still retaining green livery. It did not carry maroon livery and was repainted in the final variant of blue in November 1969. (RC Riley, www.transporttreasury.co.uk)

In September 1969 852 TENACIOUS stood at Laira with most of its windows put out, grills missing, looking derelict and labelled up 'Swindon for scrap', but somehow it survived and was given a full overhaul emerging in November of that year. Here TENACIOUS waits at Exeter Stabling Point with D6343 on 31 July 1971, two months away from its final withdrawal on 3 October 1971, a date which saw a large reduction in the WR hydraulic fleet. (www.rail-online.co.uk)

# D853 THRUSTER

| Lot no./Works no. | 443/27982 |
|---|---|
| **Significant dates and allocations** | |
| Delivered | 17/08/61 |
| Into traffic - Laira | 30/08/61 |
| Newton Abbot | 06/64 |
| Old Oak Common | 10/67 |
| Reinstated (Old Oak Common) | 06/70 |
| Newton Abbot | 10/70 |
| Withdrawn (Taunton) | 03/10/71 |
| (Swindon) | 18/10/71 |
| Date cut-up | By 16/06/72 |

| **Stored** | | |
|---|---|---|
| | **From** | **To** |
| Old Oak Common | 07/07/69 | 03/70 |
| **Livery and insignia changes** | | |
| Green | | 30/08/61 |
| OHLW flashes | | 30/11/61 |
| Yellow warning panels | | After 06/64 |
| Maroon | | - |
| Blue full yellow ends – double insignia, serif, D-prefix | | By 08/67 |
| Blue full yellow ends – single insignia, sans serif, no D | | By 06/70 |
| **Recorded mileage** | | 701,000 |

## Works visits and depot repairs

| Stopped | At | On Works | Off Works | At | Type | Days | Work carried out |
|---|---|---|---|---|---|---|---|
| - | - | 17/08/61 | 30/08/61 | SW | D/A | 13 | Delivery inspection and acceptance |
| 09/11/61 | Ex-T | 11/11/61 | 30/11/61 | SW | ? | 21 | |
| 06/07/62 | Ex-T | 07/62 | 14/07/62 | LA | ? | 8 | |
| 09/10/62 | Ex-T | 17/10/62 | 25/10/62 | LA | ? | 16 | B Transmission changed (input gearing noisy) |
| 21/01/63 | Ex-T | 01/63 | 28/01/63 | ? | ? | 7 | |
| 22/03/63 | Ex-T | 03/63 | 28/03/63 | ? | ? | 6 | |
| 16/05/63 | Ex-T | 05/63 | 17/05/63 | ? | ? | 1 | |
| 10/08/63 | Ex-T | 08/63 | 15/08/63 | ? | ? | 5 | |
| 08/09/63 | Ex-T | 13/09/63 | 18/09/63 | ? | ? | 10 | A Transmission changed (governor drive gear teeth broken) |
| 20/01/64 | Ex-T | 20/01/64 | 21/01/64 | ? | ? | 1 | |
| 02/64 | Ex-T | 08/02/64 | 02/64 | ? | ? | ? | Compressor changed |
| 02/11/64 | Ex-T | 03/11/64 | | SW | ? | ? | A & B Engines changed (leaking coolant); A & B Transmissions changed; A & B Bogies changed (thin tyres); Modifications; Bogie side control linkage replaced with hydraulic shock absorbers; Collision damage to right hand nose section, body paintwork in very poor condition |
| 03/66 | Ex-T | 22/03/66 | 03/66 | LA | ? | ? | B Bogie changed (axle flaws) |
| 04/66 | Ex-T | 04/66 | 04/66 | ? | ? | ? | B Engine changed (low lub. oil pressure, loss through the little end bearings) |
| 08/66 | Ex-T | ? | ? | SW | ? | ? | A Transmission changed (governor drive gear teeth stripped) |
| 10/66 | Ex-T | 10/66 | 29/10/66 | LA | ? | ? | A Engine changed |
| 12/66 | Ex-T | 12/66 | 16/12/66 | LA | ? | ? | B Engine changed (partial seizure) |
| 07/67 | Ex-T | 07/67 | ? | SW | ? | ? | A Engine repaired; A Transmission repaired; A & B Bogies changed; Exterior repaint |
| 27/09/67 | BS | 09/67 | 10/67 | SW | ? | ? | A & B Bogies changed (damage sustained in Didcot incident) |
| 04/68 | Ex-T | 25/04/68 | 04/68 | ? | ? | ? | Transmission changed (No. 2 convertor blackened and overheated and metal in sump ) |
| ? | Ex-T | /68 | ? | ? | ? | ? | A & B Engine changed (high lub. oil consumption) |
| 06/69 | Ex-T | 26/06/69 | 07/07/69 | OOC | ? | ? | Bogie changed; fire damage repairs |
| 07/07/69 | Ex-T | | 03/70 | OOC | ? | ? | Stored, subsequently withdrawn, then called to Swindon for re-instatement in March 1970 |
| 03/70 | OOC | 17/03/70 | 26/06/70 | SW | ? | ? | |
| 02/71 | Ex-T | 02/71 | 02/71 | ? | ? | ? | B Transmission changed (governor drive stripped) |
| 03/10/71 | Ex-T | | | TN | | | Withdrawn |

1 May 1962 and D853 THRUSTER waits at Platform 1 Paddington with the 12.05pm Paddington-Kingswear 'Torbay Express'. This was a regular Warship turn for a number of years and the Class was particularly common on the branch down to Paignton and Kingswear. D853 is seen here in all over green and in fact it wasn't until mid-1964 that THRUSTER finally received a yellow warning panel. It skipped the maroon livery and went into blue by August 1967. (www.rail-online.co.uk)

An excellent illustration of a Warship in the final blue livery variant, the locomotive is less than a month out of Works. 853 THRUSTER stands at Gloucester Horton Road on 23 July 1970. Of all the NBL Warships withdrawn in 1971, THRUSTER was one of only two which wasn't either withdrawn on, or returned to, the West Country depots at Newton Abbot or Laira before despatch to Swindon for scrapping. THRUSTER failed at Taunton on 3 October 1971 and was sent direct to Swindon from there; D861 was the other exception after failing at Worcester, reaching Swindon via Bristol St Philips Marsh. (NE Preedy)

# D854 TIGER

| Lot no./Works no. | 443/27983 |
|---|---|
| **Significant dates and allocations** | |
| Delivered | 19/09/61 |
| Into traffic - Laira | 26/09/61 |
| Newton Abbot | 06/64 |
| Old Oak Common | 01/68 |
| Newton Abbot | 11/68 |
| Old Oak Common | 11/68 |
| Newton Abbot | 04/69 |
| Old Oak Common | 12/69 |
| Newton Abbot | 10/70 |
| Withdrawn (Laira) | 03/10/71 |
| (Bristol St Philips Marsh Junction) | 26/10/71 |
| (Swindon) | 04/01/72 |
| Date cut-up | By 05/05/72 |

| **Stored** | From | To |
|---|---|---|
| Old Oak Common | 03/69 | 04/69 |
| Newton Abbot | 05/69 | 06/69 |
| Newton Abbot | 09/69 | 09/69 |

| **Livery and insignia changes** | |
|---|---|
| Green | 26/09/61 |
| OHLW flashes | By 05/62 |
| Yellow warning panels | 03/04/62 |
| Maroon | - |
| Blue full yellow ends – single insignia, sans serif , no D | 05/12/69 |
| **Recorded mileage** | 688,000 |

**Works visits and depot repairs**

| Stopped | At | On Works | Off Works | At | Type | Days | Work carried out |
|---|---|---|---|---|---|---|---|
| - | - | 19/09/61 | 23/09/61 | SW | D/A | 4 | Delivery inspection and acceptance |
| 12/03/62 | LA | 08/03/62 | 03/04/62 | SW | L/C | 22 | B Bogie changed |
| 09/07/62 | Ex-T | 09/07/62 | 11/07/62 | LA | L/C | 2 | |
| 26/07/62 | LA | 15/08/62 | 18/09/62 | SW | H/C | 54 | B Transmission changed (defective main convertor shaft bearing, heavy vibration at idling, in 'fill' and when under power in all notches ); (D854 was due to arrive at Swindon on 30/07/62 but it was kept at Laira and used as a donor loco) |
| 11/12/62 | Ex-T | 12/62 | 21/12/62 | LA | H/C | 10 | A Engine changed (No. 11 piston damaged, metal debris in air box, and valve heads broken off ) |
| 22/07/63 | Ex-T | 07/63 | 02/08/63 | LA | H/C | 11 | B Engine changed |
| 9/09/63 | Ex-T | 19/09/63 | 21/09/63 | LA | L/C | 2 | B exhauster changed (earth fault on the motor) |
| 19/10/63 | Ex-T | 19/10/63 | 28/10/63 | LA | H/C | 9 | A Engine changed (high oil consumption. 375 fitted) |
| 02/64 | Ex-T | 11/02/64 | 02/64 | LA | L/C | ? | A Transmission changed (not selecting gear and metal in filters) |
| 23/03/64 | Ex-T | 03/64 | 04/04/64 | LA | H/C | 12 | B Engine changed (cylinder heads and liners leaking coolant); B Transmission changed (output bearings and gears defective); B exhauster changed (earth fault on the motor) |
| 27/05/64 | Ex-T | 06/64 | 23/06/64 | LA | L/C | 27 | B Transmission changed (dynostarter drive shaft damaged) |
| 07/64 | Ex-T | 14/07/64 | 07/64 | LA | L/C | ? | B end dynostarter changed (field connecting straps burnt off) |
| 08/64 | Ex-T | 25/08/64 | 08/64 | NA | L/C | ? | Boiler changed |
| 12/64 | Ex-T | 04/12/64 | 12/64 | LA | L/C | ? | A Transmission changed (not changing from 1st convertor and overheating) |
| 16/02/65 | Ex-T | 16/02/65 | 18/02/65 | NA | Unsch | 1 | A exhauster changed |
| 16/02/65 | NA | 18/02/65 | 13/05/65 | SW | Int | 86 | A Engine changed (No. 4 cylinder head joint blowing and Nos. 8 and 10 cylinder heads leaking coolant and Nos. 1-6 bank exhaust manifold joints blowing): B Engine changed (Nos. 9 and 10 cylinder heads leaking coolant and Nos. 1-6 bank exhaust manifold joints blowing); A Transmission changed (No. 2 turbine fractured and impeller damaged); B Transmission changed; A & B Bogies changed; Modifications; Bogie side control linkage replaced with hydraulic shock absorbers |
| 07/65 | Ex-T | 31/07/65 | 08/65 | NA | L/C | ? | A Engine Fuel pumps changed |
| 12/65 | Ex-T | 03/12/65 | 12/65 | NA | L/C | ? | A end dynostarter changed (earthed armature) |
| 02/66 | Ex-T | 17/02/66 | 02/66 | NA | L/C | ? | A & B Engine Turbo blowers changed |
| 03/66 | Ex-T | 16/03/66 | 03/66 | LA | H/C | ? | A Transmission changed (turbine blade suspected to be breaking up) |
| 05/66 | Ex-T | 24/05/65 | 05/66 | NA | L/C | ? | B Engine Turbo blower changed |
| 06/66 | Ex-T | 09/06/66 | 06/66 | LA | H/C | ? | A Engine changed; A Transmission changed (input shaft seized) |
| 06/66 | Ex-T | 23/06/66 | 06/86 | NA | L/C | ? | A end dynostarter changed (throwing solder); B exhauster changed (noisy) |
| 09/66 | Ex-T | 09/09/66 | 09/66 | LA | L/C | ? | A Bogie changed |
| 09/66 | Ex-T | 28/09/66 | 09/66 | NA | L/C | ? | B exhauster changed (motor earth) |
| 11/66 | Ex-T | 18/11/66 | 11/66 | NA | L/C | ? | B exhauster changed (low insulation resistance) |
| 03/67 | Ex-T | 16/03/67 | 03/67 | LA | H/C | ? | B Engine changed; Boiler changed |
| 31/03/67 | LA | 04/04/67 | 23/06/67 | SW | U/C | 84 | A Engine repaired (fire damage); B Engine repaired; A Transmission changed (flexible pipe work melted by fire); B Transmission changed; A Bogie changed (fire damage); B Bogie changed; Modifications; (Extensive fire damage to A end engine room compartment : all coolant flexible hoses burnt, exhauster scorched, lub. oil flexibles and fuel pipes scorched, engine air intake burnt, inner body side skin panels distorted, engine compartment roof section distorted, coolant, transmission temperature, air and lub. oil pressure gauges damaged, underframe under A end engine burnt and slightly distorted, compressor to change) |
| 06/68 | Ex-T | 05/06/68 | 06/68 | OOC | L/C | ? | B Transmission changed (no oil pressure) |
| 06/68 | Ex-T | 27/06/68 | 06/68 | OOC | L/C | ? | A Engine changed |
| 10/68 | Ex-T | 07/10/68 | 10/68 | OOC | H/C | ? | B Engine changed (passing oil); A Bogie changed (worn brake gear) |
| 12/68 | Ex-T | 05/12/68 | 12/68 | NA | L/C | ? | Boiler changed ( fractured coil) |
| 10/09/69 | Ex-T | 29/09/69 | 05/12/69 | SW | Class | 87 | A Engine changed (low oil pressure); B Engine changed (crank case compression); A Transmission changed; B Transmission changed (high temperature trips in no. 2 convertor); A & B Bogies changed; Modifications; all hoses and cardan shafts changed, exhausters and compressor changed (Prior to this works visit, D854 had been 'stored serviceable' between March and April 1969, and again from May to June 1969) |
| 18/12/69 | Ex-T | 18/12/69 | 22/12/69 | LA | L/C | 4 | A Transmission changed (seizure and 5 teeth broken off of No. 1 gear wheel) |
| 05/12/70 | Ex-T | 06/12/70 | 09/12/70 | LA | L/C | 4 | B Engine changed (sump passing oil) |
| 23/03/71 | Ex-T | 23/03/71 | 25/03/71 | LA | H/C | 2 | A Engine changed (passing oil) |
| 24/05/71 | Ex-T | 24/05/71 | 25/05/71 | NA | L/C | 1 | Boiler changed (split coil) |
| 23/07/71 | Ex-T | 23/07/71 | 25/07/71 | LA | L/C | 2 | A Engine changed (fractured sump) |
| 03/10/71 | LA | | | | | | Withdrawn |

854 TIGER with 841 on 28 July 1971 at Exeter. The shedcode is no longer carried on the bufferbeam or the valance but there is now an 83A NEWTON ABBOT sticker behind the driver's door. The sides are oil stained, there is evidence of a light collision on the cabsides and the NBL Worksplate has also disappeared. This was not the only diamond carried by the locomotive as the bogies also had the NBL diamond although these were interchangeable with the Swindon ones. In fact preserved D821 GREYHOUND currently has one of each. (www.rail-online.co.uk)

# D855 TRIUMPH

| Lot no./Works no. | 443/27984 |
|---|---|
| **Significant dates and allocations** | |
| Delivered | 13/10/61 |
| Into traffic - Laira | 25/10/61 |
| Newton Abbot | 06/64 |
| Old Oak Common | 01/68 |
| Newton Abbot | 01/70 |
| Withdrawn (Newton Abbot) | 03/10/71 |
| (Bristol Marsh Junction) | By 22/10/71 |
| (Swindon) | 30/12/71 |
| Date cut-up | By 28/04/72 |

| **Stored** | **From** | **To** |
|---|---|---|
| Old Oak Common | 03/69 | 04/69 |
| Old Oak Common | 13/05/69 | 01/10/69 |
| **Livery and insignia changes** | | |
| Green | | 25/10/61 |
| OHLW flashes | | 25/10/61 |
| Yellow warning panels | | 17/04/62 |
| Maroon yellow warning panels | | 13/05/66 |
| Blue full yellow ends – single insignia, sans serif , no D | | 02/01/70 |
| **Recorded mileage** | | 718,000 |

**Works visits and depot repairs**

| Stopped | At | On Works | Off Works | At | Type | Days | Work carried out |
|---|---|---|---|---|---|---|---|
| - | - | 13/10/61 | 25/10/61 | SW | D/A | 12 | Delivery inspection and acceptance |
| 19/10/61 | Ex-T | 19/10/61 | 26/10/61 | SW | Unsch | 7 | Called back to shops for rectification on 19/10/61 |
| 09/03/62 | NA | 14/03/62 | 17/04/62 | SW | L/C | 39 | A & B Bogies changed; A end collision damage repaired (A end left hand side damaged, underframe damaged, steam heating hose ripped off, leading nose apron and underside air reservoir damaged, driving cab access steps forced back, cab door tight in aperture, bogie coil springs hangers forced back on threaded end, sand pipes and brackets wrenched off, brake gear loose and stays bent upwards, speedo flex torn off, left hand valance scarred and dented, fuel pump drain cocks broken off and train route indicators forced apart) |
| 13/07/62 | Ex-T | 13/07/62 | 20/07/62 | LA | H/C | 7 | A Engine changed (No. 5 cylinder valve broken off) |
| 05/03/63 | Ex-T | 05/03/63 | 06/03/63 | LA | L/C | 1 | |
| 19/06/63 | Ex-T | 19/03/63 | 25/06/63 | LA | H/C | 6 | B Engine changed (heavy oil consumption) |
| 07/63 | Ex-T | 01/07/63 | 07/63 | LA | Unsch | ? | A end dynostarter changed (earth faults); B exhauster changed ( earth faults) |
| 04/08/63 | Ex-T | 04/08/63 | 10/08/63 | LA | H/C | 6 | A Engine changed (heavy oil consumption and sump joints leaking) |
| 09/63 | Ex-T | 13/09/63 | 09/63 | LA | H/C | ? | B Engine Turbo blower changed (noisy on run-down) |
| 26/02/64 | Ex-T | 26/02/64 | 05/03/64 | LA | L/C | 8 | B Engine changed (very bad oil leaks) |
| 22/04/64 | Ex-T | 22/04/64 | 24/04/64 | LA | L/C | 2 | Attention to bogie |
| 04/05/64 | NA | 05/05/64 | 27/05/64 | SW | Unsch | 23 | A & B Bogies changed; Boiler changed; Modifications; Bogie side control linkage replaced with hydraulic shock absorbers; B end frame fracture repaired, A & B end sand boxes repaired, A & B end front aprons repaired |
| 08/64 | Ex-T | 05/08/64 | 10/08/64 | LA | Unsch | ? | A Engine changed (no lub. oil pressure) |
| 08/64 | Ex-T | 17/08/64 | 08/64 | LA | L/C | ? | A Engine changed (low lub. oil pressure when run up) |
| 01/65 | Ex-T | 24/01/65 | 01/65 | LA | Unsch | ? | A Engine changed (5 cylinder liners fractured and the flywheel broken) |
| 11/03/65 | Ex-T | 03/65 | 19/03/65 | NA | H/C | 8 | A Engine repaired (seized valve rocker gear and damaged cam followers rectified in situ); B Engine changed (venting coolant continuously) |
| 11/65 | Ex-T | 26/11/65 | 11/65 | LA | H/C | ? | B Transmission changed (metal in filters; output bearing suspect) |
| 02/03/66 | Ex-T | 05/03/66 | 13/05/66 | SW | Int | 72 | A Engine changed (heavy internal knocking, Nos. 4, 5, 6, 8, and 9 cylinder heads leaking coolant and turbo blower rapid run-down); B Engine repaired (Nos. 4, 7 and 9 cylinder heads leaking coolant and turbo blower rapid run-down); A Transmission changed; B Transmission changed (forward / reverse locking bar stuck); A & B Bogies changed; Boiler changed; Modifications; Multiple working jumper cables and sockets removed from buffer beam; all hoses and cardan shafts changed, exhausters and compressor changed |
| 05/66 | Ex-T | 18/05/66 | 05/66 | LA | Unsch | ? | A Engine changed (heavy knock in the crankcase) |
| 03/67 | Ex-T | 16/03/67 | 03/67 | LA | L/C | ? | B Engine changed |
| 04/67 | Ex-T | 14/04/67 | 04/67 | LA | H/C | ? | B Transmission changed (seized control piston and metal in filters) |
| 05/67 | Ex-T | 03/05/67 | 05/67 | NA | L/C | ? | Boiler changed |
| 10/67 | Ex-T | 14/10/67 | 10/67 | LA | H/C | ? | A Bogie changed; B Bogie changed (inner final drive bearing collapsed) |
| 02/11/67 | Ex-T | 02/11/67 | 02/11/67 | NA | Unsch | 1 | A end dynostarter changed |
| 30/01/68 | Ex-T | 31/01/68 | 16/02/68 | OOC | H/C | 17 | A & B Engines changed |
| 07/68 | Ex-T | 02/07/68 | 07/68 | OOC | L/C | ? | B Bogie changed (inner axle defects) |
| 07/68 | Ex-T | 24/07/68 | 07/68 | OOC | L/C | ? | A Engine changed (fractured sump) |
| 12/68 | Ex-T | 02/12/68 | 12/68 | LA | L/C | ? | A Bogie changed (lift in the input bearing on the outer final drive) |
| 02/69 | Ex-T | 03/02/69 | 02/69 | OOC | Unsch | ? | B Engine changed (heavy internal knocking) |
| 03/69 | Ex-T | 13/05/69 | 01/10/69 | OOC | ? | ? | Several components were exchanged while stored: A & B Engines; A & B Bogies |
| 01/10/69 | Ex-T | 09/10/69 | 24/12/69 | SW | Int | 84 | A & B Engines changed (passing oil); A & B Transmissions changed; A & B Bogies changed; Boiler changed; Modifications; Body repairs; (extensive damage found caused by cannibalisation of pipe work whilst the locomotive was stored) |
| 12/01/70 | Ex-T | 12/01/70 | 14/01/70 | LA | Unsch | 2 | B Bogie changed outer final drive bearing collapsed) |
| 02/02/71 | Ex-T | 02/02/71 | 05/02/71 | LA | H/C | 3 | A & B Engines changed (passing oil) |
| 26/05/71 | Ex-T | 26/05/71 | 27/05/71 | LA | L/C | 1 | B Engine changed (passing oil) |
| 06/07/71 | Ex-T | 06/07/71 | 11/07/71 | LA | H/C | 5 | B Transmission changed (output casing fractured); B Bogie changed (outer final drive input flange damaged) |
| 03/10/71 | Ex-T | | | NA | | | Withdrawn |

D855 TRIUMPH on 9 May 1969 departs from Paddington with the 1B20 18.12 to Weston-super-Mare. TRIUMPH's already well-worn three year old maroon livery would have to last until the end of the year before it was repainted in blue; there is evidence that the paintwork had been touched up but it was a losing battle. Behind the loco is a parcels BRUTE, once a commonplace sight on most railway stations.

The weather looks grim on 15 May 1971 as a very clean 855 TRIUMPH waits at Gloucester Eastgate with the 1B78 12.25 Paignton-Worcester, having worked down that morning on the 1B44 07.20 Worcester-Paignton. TRIUMPH is looking smart because it was spruced up for St Blazey Open Day on the 1st of the month. It was not the only Warship to get the silver buffer treatment for this event and D806 and D854 could also be seen in this unofficial 'livery' during the summer of 1971.It was to be one of the final Class 43 survivors, being withdrawn on 3 October that year. (www.rail-online.co.uk)

# D856 TROJAN

| Lot no./Works no. | 443/27985 |
|---|---|
| **Significant dates and allocations** | |
| Delivered | 06/11/61 |
| Into traffic - Laira | 16/11/61 |
| Newton Abbot | 05/65 |
| Old Oak Common | 01/69 |
| Newton Abbot | 08/69 |
| Withdrawn (Newton Abbot) | 22/05/71 |
| (Laira) | 06/71 |
| (Swindon) | 28/06/71 |
| Date cut-up | By 07/01/72 |

| **Stored** | | |
|---|---|---|
| | **From** | **To** |
| Newton Abbot | 02/05/71 | 22/05/71 |
| **Livery and insignia changes** | | |
| Green | | 16/11/61 |
| OHLW flashes | | 16/11/61 |
| Yellow warning panels | | 18/05/65 |
| Maroon | | - |
| Blue full yellow ends – double insignia, sans serif , no D | | 28/10/68 |
| **Recorded mileage** | | 734,000 |

## Works visits and depot repairs

| Stopped | At | On Works | Off Works | At | Type | Days | Work carried out |
|---|---|---|---|---|---|---|---|
| - | - | 06/11/61 | 16/11/61 | SW | D/A | 10 | Delivery inspection and acceptance; B transmission Forward / reverse defect repaired in conjunction with N.B.L. Co. Engineer. |
| 19/12/61 | Ex-T | 19/12/61 | 19/12/61 | SW | Unsch | 1 | |
| 01/05/62 | Ex-T | 06/05/62 | 11/05/62 | LA | H/C | 10 | A Engine changed |
| 14/07/62 | Ex-T | 17/07/62 | 20/07/62 | LA | H/C | 6 | B Engine changed (No. 12 cylinder liner cracked) |
| 10/11/62 | Ex-T | 10/11/62 | 16/11/62 | LA | L/C | 6 | |
| 12/62 | Ex-T | 02/12/62 | ? | LA | ? | ? | A Engine Turbo blower changed (blade seizure) |
| 22/01/63 | EX-T | 22/01/63 | 05/02/63 | LA | H/C | 14 | |
| 21/03/63 | Ex-T | 21/03/63 | 26/03/63 | LA | L/C | 5 | A Engine Turbo blower changed (no air pressure and short run down); Compressor changed (knocking badly); (It was recorded on 18/01/63 that A end engine No. 365 had excessive oil consumption of 52 miles per gallon and had caught fire on several occasions and B end engine No. 260 had excessive oil consumption of 75 miles per gallon. The locomotive was recommended to Laira for attention) |
| 23/04/63 | Ex-T | 23/04/63 | 03/05/63 | LA | L/C | 10 | A Engine changed (high oil consumption) |
| 02/09/63 | Ex-T | 03/09/63 | 11/09/63 | LA | H/C | 9 | B Engine changed (overheating and excessive oil consumption) |
| 20/10/63 | Ex-T | 20/10/63 | 24/10/63 | LA | L/C | 4 | |
| 17/12/63 | Ex-T | 18/12/63 | 28/12/63 | LA | L/C | 11 | A Engine changed (high oil consumption) |
| 02/64 | Ex-T | 17/02/64 | 02/64 | LA | L/C | ? | B Engine Turbo blower changed (seizure); No. 2 exhauster changed (earth on the motor) |
| 03/64 | Ex-T | 04/03/64 | 03/64 | LA | L/C | ? | A end dynostarter changed (earth) |
| 08/64 | Ex-T | 18/08/64 | 08/64 | LA | Unsch | ? | Boiler changed |
| 10/64 | Ex-T | 08/10/64 | 10/64 | LA | L/C | ? | B Engine changed (cylinder heads blowing) |
| 11/64 | Ex-T | 22/11/64 | 11/64 | LA | H/C | ? | A Engine changed (several liners leaking and lifting) |
| 23/02/65 | Ex-T | 26/02/65 | 03/03/65 | LA | Unsch | ? | B Bogie changed |
| 23/02/65 | Ex-T | 03/03/65 | 18/05/65 | SW | Int | 84 | A & B Engines changed (cylinder liners leaking); A & B Transmissions changed; A Bogie changed (outer torque arm fallen and bogie pivot pin bush worn); B Bogie changed (inner final drive bearing overheated); Boiler changed; Modifications; Bogie side control linkage replaced with hydraulic shock absorbers; all hoses and cardan shafts changed |
| 08/06/65 | Ex-T | 08/06/65 | 11/06/65 | LA | Unsch | 3 | A Transmission changed (Forward / Reverse clutch dogs seized, solder found in sump) |
| 06/65 | Ex-T | 29/06/65 | 06/65 | LA | Unsch | ? | A Transmission changed (input shaft oil seal leaking and overheated) |
| 07/65 | Ex-T | 23/07/65 | 07/65 | LA | Unsch | ? | B Transmission changed (control pistons being seized) |
| 08/65 | Ex-T | 23/08/65 | 08/65 | LA | Unsch | ? | B Transmission repaired (low filling pump pressure) |
| 11/65 | Ex-T | 16/11/65 | 11/65 | LA | Unsch | ? | B Engine Turbo blower changed; B Bogie changed (outer final drive overheating and the input bearing damaged) |
| 12/65 | Ex-T | 04/12/65 | 12/65 | LA | H/C | ? | A Transmission changed (output shaft seizing); B Transmission changed (low filling pump pressure) |
| 04/02/66 | Ex-T | 04/02/66 | 02/66 | LA | L/C | ? | A Engine changed (flywheel oil seals leaking) |
| 03/66 | Ex-T | 18/03/66 | 03/66 | LA | Unsch | ? | B Transmission changed (control piston breaking up, steel and cast iron debris in the sump) |
| 19/04/66 | Ex-T | 20/04/66 | 03/06/66 | SW | U/C | 45 | A & B Engines repaired; A Transmission repaired; B Transmission changed; A & B Bogies changed; Boiler changed; Modifications; Multiple working jumper cables and sockets removed from buffer beam; Collision damage repaired (main frame tube distorted, co/driver's side A end and nose panelling buckled); A & B end preheaters changed, A & B end dynostarter changed, A & B exhausters changed, compressor changed, all hoses and cardan shafts changed |
| 07/66 | Ex-T | 19/07/66 | 07/66 | NA | L/C | ? | B Engine Turbo blower changed |
| 01/67 | Ex-T | 09/01/67 | 01/67 | NA | L/C | ? | A end dynostarter changed |
| 09/02/67 | Ex-T | 10/02/67 | 02/67 | NA | L/C | ? | A Engine Fuel pumps changed (overspeed trips); B end dynostarter changed (defective bearings) |
| 02/67 | Ex-T | 27/02/67 | 02/67 | LA | Unsch | ? | A Transmission changed (overheating) |
| 03/67 | Ex-T | 09/03/67 | 03/67 | NA | Unsch | ? | A end dynostarter changed |
| 03/67 | Ex-T | 20/03/67 | 03/67 | LA | L/C | ? | B Engine changed |
| 04/67 | Ex-T | 19/04/67 | 04/67 | LA | Unsch | ? | B Transmission changed (control piston seizing and metal in filters) |
| 05/67 | Ex-T | 23/05/67 | 05/67 | NA | L/C | ? | A end dynostarter changed |
| 06/67 | Ex-T | 30/06/67 | 06/67 | NA | L/C | ? | Compressor changed |
| 08/67 | Ex-T | 30/08/67 | 08/67 | OOC | Unsch | ? | B Transmission changed (knocking) |
| 10/67 | Ex-T | 27/10/67 | 10/67 | NA | Unsch | ? | Compressor changed |
| 22/04/68 | Ex-T | 23/04/68 | 26/04/68 | LA | H/C | 4 | A Engine changed; A & B Bogies changed |
| 06/68 | Ex-T | 02/06/68 | 06/68 | LA | Unsch | ? | A Bogie changed (A outer final drive input flange damaged) |
| 06/68 | Ex-T | 26/06/68 | 06/68 | NA | L/C | ? | B Engine Fuel pumps changed |
| 07/68 | Ex-T | 16/07/68 | 07/68 | NA | L/C | ? | Boiler changed |
| 21/08/68 | Ex-T | 26/08/68 | 28/10/68 | SW | Class | 68 | A Bogie changed; B Bogie changed (one damaged side control bracket and worn tyres); Modifications; Compressor changed, A &B exhausters changed, all hoses and cardan shafts changed, cab flooring and frame work repaired to modified standard |
| 02/69 | Ex-T | 19/02/69 | 02/69 | NA | Unsch | ? | B Engine Fuel pumps changed |
| 04/69 | Ex-T | 16/04/69 | 04/69 | OOC | Unsch | ? | A Engine changed (fractured sump) |
| 06/69 | Ex-T | 13/06/69 | 06/69 | OOC | Unsch | ? | B Transmission changed (teeth stripped off the output gears) |
| 07/69 | Ex-T | 04/07/69 | 07/69 | OOC | L/C | ? | B Engine changed (fuming and main bearings overheated and scored) |
| 03/02/70 | Ex-T | 03/02/70 | 04/02/70 | NA | Unsch | 1 | Boiler changed (coil splitting and in generally poor condition) |
| 25/06/70 | Ex-T | 26/06/70 | 01/07/70 | NA | L/C | 6 | A Transmission changed |
| 06/10/70 | Ex-T | 07/10/70 | 09/10/70 | LA | L/C | 3 | A Engine changed (fuming) |
| 01/01/71 | Ex-T | 01/01/71 | 03/01/71 | LA | Unsch | 2 | A Engine changed (lub. oil pipe to square 'D' pressure switch broken and passing oil) |
| 22/02/71 | Ex-T | 22/02/71 | 24/02/71 | LA | L/C | 2 | B Engine changed (passing oil) |
| 02/05/71 | Ex-T | | 22/05/71 | NA | | | To store / withdrawn |

D856 TROJAN at Llanvihangel on 18 August 1962 with the 1V88 8.20am Manchester-Penzance. It is an often forgotten piece of Warship history but these locomotives worked the majority of express passenger trains over the North & West line between the South West and Crewe from 1962 until 1964. TROJAN was the last to escape the yellow panel treatment and was in appalling external condition when finally called to Swindon in February 1965 for an Intermediate overhaul. (RC Riley, www.transporttreasury.co.uk)

In its final livery 856 TROJAN waits at Gloucester Central on 9 October 1969; it was the first Warship to be released from Swindon without the 'D' prefix when painted into blue during October 1968 and also it was the only NBL Warship which had its electrification flashes to the fore of the driver's door, similar to D827 KELLY. (www.rail-online.co.uk)

# D857 UNDAUNTED

| Lot no./Works no. | 443/27986 |
|---|---|
| **Significant dates and allocations** | |
| Delivered | 24/11/61 |
| Into traffic - Laira | 11/12/61 |
| Newton Abbot | 05/65 |
| Withdrawn (Newton Abbot) | 04/10/71 |
| (Bristol St Philips Marsh Junction) | By 22/10/71 |
| (Swindon) | 04/01/72 |
| Date cut-up | By 24/08/72 |

| **Stored** | | |
|---|---|---|
| | **From** | **To** |
| Newton Abbot | 04/69 | 12/09/69 |
| **Livery and insignia changes** | | |
| Green | | 11/12/61 |
| OHLW flashes | | 11/12/61 |
| Yellow warning panels | | 20/08/62 |
| Maroon yellow warning panels | | 22/09/65 |
| Blue full yellow ends – double insignia, serif, D-prefix | | 28/04/67 |
| Blue full yellow ends – single insignia, sans serif , no D | | 12/09/69 |
| **Recorded mileage** | | 753,000 |

## Works visits and depot repairs

| Stopped | At | On Works | Off Works | At | Type | Days | Work carried out |
|---|---|---|---|---|---|---|---|
| - | - | 24/11/61 | 11/12/61 | SW | D/A | 19 | Delivery inspection and acceptance; A & B engine exhaust stacks modified to eliminate exhaust fumes |
| 08/08/62 | SHR | 10/08/62 | 20/08/62 | SW | H/C | 12 | A Engine repaired (Lub. oil priming pump and bracket); A Bogie changed (outer final drive overheating) |
| 08/62 | Ex-T | 24/08/62 | 08/62 | LA | Unsch | ? | A Engine Turbo blower changed (shaft seizure) |
| 04/01/63 | Ex-T | 04/01/63 | 22/01/63 | LA | L/C | 18 | |
| 19/02/63 | LA | 25/02/63 | 14/03/63 | SW | H/C | 23 | B Engine changed (connecting rod broken and seized piston); Boiler changed |
| 30/05/63 | Ex-T | 31/05/63 | 05/06/63 | LA | H/C | 6 | A Engine changed |
| 19/06/63 | BS | 21/06/63 | 26/06/63 | SW | L/C | 7 | |
| 06/63 | Ex-T | 28/06/63 | 06/63 | LA | Unsch | ? | A end dynostarter changed (defective armature) |
| 20/10/63 | Ex-T | 20/10/63 | 22/10/63 | LA | ? | 2 | |
| 12/63 | Ex-T | 06/12/63 | 12/63 | LA | Unsch | ? | A Engine Turbo blower changed (partial seizure) |
| 17/01/64 | Ex-T | 17/01/64 | 22/01/64 | LA | L/C | 5 | B Engine changed ( excessive oil consumption and overheating); Boiler changed (inner coil perforated) |
| 03/64 | Ex-T | 05/03/64 | 03/64 | LA | Unsch | ? | B exhauster changed (exhaust valves stuck open) |
| 03/64 | Ex-T | 15/03/64 | 03/64 | LA | L/C | ? | A Engine changed (low lub. oil pressure) |
| 04/64 | Ex-T | 02/04/64 | 04/64 | LA | L/C | ? | B Engine changed (low lub. oil pressure |
| 03/07/64 | Ex-T | 05/07/64 | 06/07/64 | LA | Unsch | 3 | Compressor changed ( bearings knocking) |
| 05/65 | Ex-T | 31/05/65 | 22/09/65 | SW | Int | 114 | A & B Engines changed (several cylinder heads leaking and overheating); A & B Transmissions changed; A & B Bogies changed; Boiler changed; Modifications; Multiple working jumper cables and sockets removed from buffer beam; all hoses and cardan shafts changed, exhausters and compressor changed, intermediate body overhaul |
| 12/65 | Ex-T | 08/12/65 | 12/65 | NA | Unsch | ? | B Engine Fuel pumps changed |
| 08/66 | Ex-T | 15/08/66 | 08/66 | NA | Unsch | ? | B end dynostarter changed |
| 12/66 | Ex-T | 15/12/66 | 12/66 | NA | Unsch | ? | A end dynostarter changed |
| 18/04/67 | Ex-T | 19/04/67 | 28/04/67 | SW | Class | 10 | A & B Bogies changed; Multiple working jumper cables re-fitted |
| 08/67 | Ex-T | 14/08/67 | 08/67 | NA | L/C | ? | Boiler changed |
| 19/08/67 | Ex-T | 19/08/67 | 21/08/67 | LA | H/C | 2 | A Engine changed (coolant leaks); B Engine changed (No. 5 crank pin damaged after No. 11 rod bearing failure) |
| 09/67 | Ex-T | 18/09/67 | 09/67 | LA | L/C | ? | A Engine changed (lub. oil blowing from the filler cap) |
| 12/10/67 | Ex-T | 13/10/67 | 10/67 | LA | L/C | ? | B Engine changed (low lub. oil pressure and No. 1 cylinder little end bearing defective) |
| 04/68 | Ex-T | 10/04/68 | 04/68 | NA | Unsch | ? | A Engine Fuel pumps changed |
| 08/68 | Ex-T | 28/08/68 | 08/68 | LA | L/C | ? | A Transmission changed (reported vibrations, No. 2 convertor oil black and overheated and metal in filters) |
| 01/69 | Ex-T | 09/01/69 | 01/69 | OOC | L/C | ? | A Engine changed (throwing oil) |
| 01/69 | Ex-T | 21/01/69 | 01/69 | LA | L/C | ? | B Transmission changed (internal knocking) |
| 02/69 | Ex-T | 14/02/69 | 02/69 | LA | L/C | ? | B Bogie changed (lift in the input bearing) |
| 23/04/69 | Ex-T | ? | 23/06/69 | NA | ? | 61 | To store / reinstated |
| 23/06/69 | Ex-T | 25/06/69 | 12/09/69 | SW | Class | 81 | A & B Engines repaired; A & B Transmissions repaired; A & B Bogies changed; Boiler changed; Modifications; all hoses and cardan shafts changed, exhausters and compressor changed, A end multiple working jumper plug replaced |
| 25/09/69 | Ex-T | 25/09/69 | 27/09/69 | LA | L/C | 2 | B Bogie changed (outer final drive overheated) |
| 11/69 | Ex-T | 05/11/69 | 11/69 | LA | L/C | ? | B Transmission changed (No. 1 convertor casing split , No. 1 turbine broken up and metal in filters) |
| 15/02/70 | Ex-T | 15/02/70 | 19/02/70 | LA | L/C | 4 | B Transmission changed (secondary casing fractured) |
| 16/04/70 | WES | 21/04/70 | 22/05/70 | SW | U/C | 36 | A Transmission changed (the output casing fractured); A Bogie changed (frame damage); B Bogie changed; A end over bogie structure damage rectified |
| 21/07/70 | Ex-T | 21/07/70 | 23/07/70 | LA | L/C | 2 | B Engine changed (fractures between Nos. 2 and 3 and 8 and 9 crank case doors) |
| 29/12/70 | Ex-T | 29/12/70 | 30/12/70 | LA | L/C | 1 | A Engine changed (passing oil) |
| 23/03/71 | Ex-T | 23/03/71 | 24/03/71 | LA | L/C | 1 | Boiler changed (overheating) |
| 26/06/71 | Ex-T | 26/06/71 | 02/07/71 | LA | H/C | 6 | B Engine changed (No. 1 cylinder liner seal leaking); B Transmission changed (lift in the input shaft) |
| 02/08/71 | Ex-T | 02/08/71 | 03/08/71 | LA | L/C | 2 | A Transmission changed (no drive in 1st convertor) |
| 04/10/71 | Ex-T | | | NA | | | Withdrawn |

D857 UNDAUNTED at Swindon in May 1962, only a few months old and already a victim of light collision damage. D857 was something of a pioneer in the livery field; it was one of the first two Warships into maroon, in September 1965, and one of the first into blue in April 1967. (www.rail-online.co.uk)

857 UNDAUNTED at Gloucester Central on 16 October 1969; it had received the final version of blue livery a few weeks before. It was one of only three Class 43s to regain its multiple working fittings after they were taken off in the mid-1960s. UNDAUNTED was the last NBL Warship to haul a passenger train, on 2 October 1971 when it worked the 1B48 23.25 Paddington-Newton Abbot newspapers, available to passengers as far as Westbury. (N Preedy)

# D858 VALOROUS

| Lot no./Works no. | 443/27987 |
|---|---|
| **Significant dates and allocations** | |
| Delivered | 08/12/61 |
| Into traffic - Laira | 15/12/61 |
| Newton Abbot | 06/65 |
| Withdrawn (Laira) | 19/04/69 |
| Reinstated (Laira) | 24/06/69 |
| Newton Abbot | 14/10/69 |
| Withdrawn (Newton Abbot) | 03/10/71 |
| (Bristol St Philips Marsh Junction) | By 24/10/71 |
| (Swindon) | 30/11/71 |
| Date cut-up | By 09/06/72 |

| **Stored** | | |
|---|---|---|
| | **From** | **To** |
| Stored (Newton Abbot) | 02/03/69 | By 21/03/69 |
| Stored (Laira) | 03/69 | 19/04/69 |
| **Livery and insignia changes** | | |
| Green | | 15/12/61 |
| OHLW flashes | | 15/12/61 |
| Yellow warning panels | | 12/06/63 |
| Maroon yellow warning panels | | 08/10/65 |
| Blue full yellow ends – single insignia, sans serif, no D | | 14/10/69 |
| **Recorded mileage** | | 801,000 |

**Works visits and depot repairs**

| Stopped | At | On Works | Off Works | At | Type | Days | Work carried out |
|---|---|---|---|---|---|---|---|
| - | - | 08/12/61 | 14/12/61 | SW | D/A | 6 | Delivery inspection and acceptance |
| 12/12/62 | Ex-T | 12/12/62 | 13/12/62 | LA | L/C | 1 | |
| 21/12/62 | Ex-T | 21/12/62 | 17/01/63 | LA | H.C | 27 | |
| 19/04/63 | Ex-T | 04/63 | 28/04/63 | LA | H/C | 9 | B Transmission changed (output oil seals leaking) |
| 30/04/63 | LA | 06/05/63 | 12/06/63 | SW | H/C | 43 | A Engine changed (No. 5 cylinder leaking); B Engine changed (exhaust system severely overheating) |
| 14/06/63 | Ex-T | 14/06/63 | 14/06/63 | SW | Unsch | 1 | D858 was shopped for brake testing and tyre exam after B end bogie overheated due to dragging brakes caused by a defective proportional brake valve, which was changed |
| 06/07/63 | Ex-T | 07/63 | 23/07/63 | LA | H/C | 17 | B Transmission changed (overheating) |
| 13/10/63 | Ex-T | 10/63 | 22/10/63 | LA | H/C | 9 | B Transmission changed (the control piston seizing); B end dynostarter changed (riser contacts burning off) |
| 11/63 | Ex-T | 27/11/63 | ? | LA | L/C | ? | B exhauster changed ('earth' on the motor) |
| 12/63 | Ex-T | 28/12/63 | ? | LA | L/C | ? | B Engine Turbo blower changed |
| 26/03/64 | Ex-T | 26/03/64 | 11/04/64 | NA | Unsch | 16 | |
| 06/07/64 | Ex-T | 06/07/64 | 11/07/64 | LA | H/C | 5 | B Transmission changed (control piston seizing and excess metal in filters); Boiler changed (burst coils) |
| 11/11/64 | Ex-T | 11/11/64 | 14/11/64 | LA | L/C | 3 | B Engine Turbo blower changed ( short run-down) |
| 18/05/65 | Ex-T | 05/65 | 04/06/65 | LA | H/C | 17 | A & B Engines changed (cylinder liners leaking); A Transmission changed (3/8" lift in the input shaft); B exhauster changed (defective bearings) |
| 07/65 | Ex-T | 13/07/65 | 07/65 | NA | L/C | ? | A exhauster changed |
| 17/07/65 | NA | 21/07/65 | 08/10/65 | SW | Int | 82 | A Engine changed (15% fuel dilation); B Engine changed; A & B Transmissions changed; A Bogie changed; B Bogie changed (inner final drive torque arm bearing housing bush collapsed); Modifications; all hoses and cardan shafts changed, exhausters changed |
| 11/65 | Ex-T | 01/11/65 | 11/65 | LA | L/C | ? | A Transmission changed (Nos. 1 and 2 converters filling at the same time caused by the complete disintegration of No. 2 labyrinth seal) |
| 12/65 | Ex-T | 02/12/65 | 12/65 | LA | L/C | ? | B Transmission changed (forward / reverse mechanism seizing) |
| 04/66 | Ex-T | 21/04/66 | 04/66 | LA | H/C | ? | A & B Engines changed |
| 05/66 | Ex-T | 20/05/66 | 05/66 | LA | L/C | ? | A Engine changed (No. 1 cylinder head stud hole stripped) |
| 09/66 | Ex-T | 09/06/66 | 06/66 | NA | L/C | ? | B Engine Fuel pumps changed |
| 13/06/66 | Ex-T | 07/07/66 | 07/66 | LA | H/C | ? | A Bogie changed (the bogie frame being distorted by derailment damage) |
| 09/66 | Ex-T | 01/09/66 | 09/66 | NA | L/C | ? | A Engine Fuel pumps changed |
| 10/66 | Ex-T | 17/10/66 | 10/66 | NA | L/C | ? | Boiler changed; A end dynostarter changed ( burnt out) |
| 04/67 | Ex-T | 14/04/67 | 04/67 | LA | L/C | ? | B Transmission changed (not reversing) |
| 05/67 | Ex-T | 22/05/67 | 05/67 | LA | L/C | ? | B Bogie changed |
| 07/67 | Ex-T | 31/07/67 | ? | NA | L/C | ? | Compressor changed |
| 08/67 | Ex-T | 09/08/67 | 08/67 | NA | L/C | ? | Compressor changed (seizure) |
| 08/67 | Ex-T | 31/08/67 | ? | NA | L/C | ? | B Engine Fuel pumps changed (no drive) |
| 12/67 | Ex-T | 29/12/67 | ? | LA | H/C | ? | A Engine changed; B Engine changed (fuel pump bed plate support fractured) |
| 01/68 | Ex-T | 30/01/68 | 01/68 | NA | L/C | ? | Batteries changed |
| 03/68 | Ex-T | 01/03/68 | 03/68 | LA | L/C | ? | A Bogie changed |
| 03/68 | Ex-T | 17/03/68 | ? | NA | L/C | ? | B end dynostarter changed |
| 09/68 | Ex-T | 09/09/68 | | NA | L/C | ? | Boiler changed (going into superheat) |
| 09/68 | Ex-T | 30/09/68 | 68 | LA | L/C | ? | A Engine changed (low lub. oil pressure) |
| 02/03/69 | NA | | 24/06/69 | LA | | 113 | To store; B Engine removed; returned to traffic on 24/06/69 and recommended for Works |
| 24/06/69 | Ex-T | 07/07/69 | 14/10/69 | SW | Int | 111 | A Engine changed; (passing oil); B Engine changed (fractured crank case); A Transmission changed; B Transmission repaired; A & B Bogies changed; Modifications; Bodywork, wiring and piping repaired; all hoses and cardan shafts changed, exhausters and compressor changed |
| 14/01/70 | Ex-T | 14/01/70 | 15/01/70 | LA | L/C | 1 | B Engine changed (low oil pressure and small end bearing defects) |
| 10/10/70 | Ex-T | 10/10/70 | 10/10/70 | NA | L/C | 1 | A Engine Turbo blower changed |
| 24/11/70 | Ex-T | 25/11/70 | 26/11/70 | NA | L/C | 2 | Boiler changed |
| 11/01/71 | Ex-T | 11/01/71 | 15/01/71 | LA | H/C | 4 | B Engine changed (passing oil); B Transmission changed |
| 07/07/71 | Ex-T | 07/07/71 | 09/07/71 | LA | L/C | 2 | A Engine changed (low oil pressure) |
| 28/07/71 | Ex-T | 28/07/71 | 28/07/71 | LA | H/C | 1 | A & B Bogies changed (moved tyres) |
| 03/10/71 | NA | | | | | | Withdrawn |

D858 VALOROUS being painted maroon (the third Warship to be so dealt with) alongside D1006 in Swindon Works 'A' shop in early October 1965. On this occasion D858 was in Swindon for over 80 days for a full Intermediate. Both engines and both transmissions were swapped along with one bogie; the other bogie and the boiler were overhauled and refitted. VALOROUS was a non-runner on arrival at Swindon because Newton Abbot had 'robbed' it of several components to keep D839 running, common and necessary practice in 1960s WR diesel-hydraulic maintenance. (www.transporttreasury.co.uk)

858 VALOROUS on 5 March 1970 sits at Gloucester Horton Road between working 1E30 and 1V87, the up and down Plymouth-Newcastle workings, a regular Class 43 turn at the time. As well as 857, VALOROUS was also on passenger work during the last day of NBL Warship working; it went to Barnstaple and back on the 16.05 off Exeter and 17.55 return. All the Class 43s which lasted into the summer of 1971 were by that time in the final blue livery variant with rail alphabet numbers, no D-prefix and single centrally mounted double arrow symbol. (www.rail-online.co.uk)

# D859 VANQUISHER

| Lot no./Works no. | 443/27988 |
|---|---|
| **Significant dates and allocations** | |
| Delivered | ? |
| Into traffic - Laira | 09/01/62 |
| Newton Abbot | 05/65 |
| Withdrawn (Bristol Bath Road) | 27/03/71 |
| (Newton Abbot) | By 10/04/71 |
| (Laira) | By 04/08/71 |
| (Newton Abbot) | 16/08/71 |
| (Swindon) | 13/10/71 |
| Date cut-up | By 30/06/72 |

| **Livery and insignia changes** | |
|---|---|
| Green | 09/01/62 |
| OHLW flashes | 09/01/62 |
| Yellow warning panels | 09/01/62 |
| Maroon | - |
| Blue full yellow ends – double insignia, serif, D-prefix | 06/67 |
| **Recorded mileage** | 783,000 |

**Works visits and depot repairs**

| Stopped | At | On Works | Off Works | At | Type | Days | Work carried out |
|---|---|---|---|---|---|---|---|
| - | - | ? | 09/01/62 | SW | D/A | ? | Delivery inspection and acceptance |
| 04/07/62 | Ex-T | 10/07/62 | 21/07/62 | SW | L/C | 17 | A end over bogie structure fractured near thrust pads |
| 19/09/62 | Ex-T | 19/09/62 | 21/09/62 | LA | L/C | 2 | |
| 10/12/62 | Ex-T | 12/62 | 17/12/62 | LA | L/C | 7 | A Engine changed |
| 24/03/63 | LA | 25/03/63 | 29/03/63 | SW | H/C | 5 | |
| 23/04/63 | Ex-T | 04/63 | 29/04/63 | LA | H/C | 6 | |
| 09/01/64 | Ex-T | 01/64 | 11/01/64 | LA | L/C | 2 | |
| 30/04/64 | Ex-T | 05/64 | 10/05/64 | LA | L/C | 10 | |
| 22/06/64 | Ex-T | 06/64 | 29/06/64 | LA | L/C | 7 | |
| 18/11/64 | Ex-T | 20/11/64 | ? | SW | ? | ? | A & B Bogies changed |
| 02/03/65 | Ex-T | 03/65 | ? | SW | ? | ? | |
| 06/65 | Ex- | 06/65 | 22/06/65 | ? | L/C | ? | B Engine changed (No. 4 cylinder liner, exhaust valves, inlet valves and piston crown damaged) |
| 09/65 | Ex-T | 28/09/65 | 09/65 | NA | Unsch | ? | B end dynostarter changed |
| 10/6 | Ex-T | 06/10/65 | 10/65 | LA | L/C | ? | B Bogie changed (irregular ride heights) |
| 11/65 | Ex-T | 10/11/65 | 11/65 | NA | Unsch | ? | A end dynostarter changed |
| 04/66 | Ex-T | 28/04/66 | 04/66 | NA | ? | ? | B end dynostarter changed (burnt out) |
| 05/66 | Ex-T | 22/05/66 | 05/66 | LA | ? | ? | A Bogie changed |
| 09/66 | Ex-T | 09/66 | 09/66 | ? | L/C | ? | B Bogie changed (outer final drive defects) |
| 10/66 | Ex-T | 10/66 | 10/66 | ? | Unsch | ? | Boiler changed |
| 02/67 | Ex-T | 08/02/67 | 02/67 | NA | Unsch | ? | B end dynostarter changed (throwing solder) |
| 04/67 | Ex-T | 26/04/67 | 06/67 | SW | 04/67 | ? | Engine changed; A & B Bogies changed |
| 04/68 | Ex-T | 05/04/68 | 04/68 | LA | L/C | ? | A Engine changed |
| 04/68 | Ex-T | 04/68 | 04/68 | ? | L/C | ? | B Engine changed |
| 04/68 | Ex-T | 04/68 | 04/68 | ? | L/C | ? | B Bogie changed (inner final drive oil seals leaking) |
| | | | ? | | SW | ? | D859 was photographed in Swindon Works with collision damage to the front end. The exact date isn't known; however, it was photographed twice, once during September 1968 with the red route availability dot present and again on 24th May 1969 but this time with the newer TOPS Data panel replacing the red dot. |
| 01/69 | Ex-T | 01/69 | 01/69 | ? | L/C | ? | A Bogie changed (lift on a final drive bearing) |
| 08/69 | Ex-T | 08/69 | 08/69 | ? | ? | ? | A Transmission changed (No. 2 convertor overheated and black and metal debris in sump); B Transmission changed (No. 2 rotor knocking when turned and the control piston seized) |
| 02/70 | Ex-T | 24/02/70 | 02/70 | ? | L/C | ? | Transmission changed (metal debris in sump, rotor suspected) |
| 04/70 | Ex-T | 04/70 | 04/70 | ? | L/C | ? | B Bogie changed |
| 04/70 | Ex-T | 20/04/70 | 04/70 | NA | Unsch | ? | A end dynostarter changed (throwing solder) |
| 06/70 | Ex-T | 06/70 | 06/70 | ? | ? | ? | A & B Engines changed (passing oil) |
| 11/70 | Ex-T | 11/70 | 11/70 | ? | ? | ? | A Transmission changed (2nd convertor overheating) |
| 03/71 | Ex-T | 02/03/71 | 03/71 | LA | ? | ? | B Transmission changed (control piston seized) |
| 27/03/71 | BS | | | | | | Withdrawn |

D859 VANQUISHER enters Exeter St David's on 24 May 1969 with a down inter regional working. It is reasonably well-known that D859 was the first Warship to be introduced with yellow warning panels already painted, but a more obscure fact is that VANQUISHER had longer side grab rails on the nose end than the remainder of the Class and I doubt we will ever find out exactly why! It went from green livery into blue with serif numbers and cabside double arrow symbols in June 1967.

# D860 VICTORIOUS

| | |
|---|---|
| Lot no./Works no. | 443/27989 |
| **Significant dates and allocations** | |
| Delivered | 01/62 |
| Into traffic – Laira | 22/01/62 |
| Newton Abbot | 06/65 |
| Withdrawn (Laira) | 28/03/71 |
| (Newton Abbot) | By 31/05/71 |
| (Swindon) | 28/06/71 |
| Date cut-up | By 04/12/71 |

| | |
|---|---|
| **Livery and insignia changes** | |
| Green | 22/01/62 |
| OHLW flashes | 28/08/62 |
| Yellow warning panels | 22/01/62 |
| Maroon | - |
| Blue full yellow ends – double insignia, sans serif, D-prefix | 02/68 |
| **Recorded mileage** | 751,000 |

**Works visits and depot repairs**

| Stopped | At | On Works | Off Works | At | Type | Days | Work carried out |
|---|---|---|---|---|---|---|---|
| - | - | 01/62 | 22/01/62 | SW | D/A | ? | Delivery inspection and acceptance |
| 26/06/62 | Ex-T | 07/62 | 04/07/62 | LA | H/C | 8 | |
| 30/07/62 | LA | 15/08/62 | 28/08/62 | SW | H/C | 29 | |
| 24/12/62 | Ex-T | 24/12/62 | 12/62 | LA | L/C | 6 | B Bogie changed (frame fractures) |
| 02/01/63 | LA | 02/01/63 | 01/02/63 | SW | H/C | 30 | |
| 19/02/63 | Ex-T | 02/63 | 25/02/63 | LA | L/C | 6 | |
| 07/05/63 | Ex-T | 05/63 | 13/05/63 | LA | H/C | 6 | |
| 04/ 06/63 | OOC | 10/06/63 | 25/06/63 | SW | H/C | 30 | A Bogie changed (inner final drive bearing collapsed) |
| 15/01/64 | Ex-T | 01/64 | 18/01/64 | LA | ? | 3 | |
| 03/64 | Ex-T | 02/03/64 | 03/64 | ? | ? | ? | B Engine Turbo blower changed |
| 09/64 | Ex-T | 09/64 | 16/09/64 | ? | ? | ? | B Engine changed |
| 09/64 | Ex-T | 07/10/64 | 24/12/64 | SW | ? | ? | B Bogie changed (frame fractures); Boiler changed |
| 03/66 | Ex-T | 03/66 | 03/66 | ? | ? | ? | B Bogie changed (suspect axles) |
| 06/66 | Ex-T | 06/06/66 | 06/66 | NA | Unsch | ? | Exhauster changed |
| 02/67 | Ex-T | 02/67 | 02/67 | NA | L/C | ? | Boiler changed |
| 04/67 | Ex-T | 21/04/67 | 04/67 | LA | L/C | ? | B Engine changed |
| 08/67 | Ex-T | 13/08/67 | 08/67 | NA | Unsch | ? | B Engine Turbo blower changed ( partial seizure) |
| 08/67 | Ex-T | 28/08/67 | 08/67 | NA | Unsch | ? | A end dynostarter changed |
| 09/67 | Ex-T | 09/67 | 09/67 | ? | Unsch | ? | B Engine changed (excessive oil mist from the crank case breather) |
| 10/67 | Ex-T | 10/67 | 10/67 | ? | Unsch | ? | B Engine changed (suspect piston rings) |
| 16/01/68 | NA | 01/68 | 02/68 | SW | Class | ? | B Engine repaired; A transmission changed (fractured casing); B transmission (leaking output shaft oil seals rectified in situ);A & B Bogies changed; Boiler changed |
| 07/68 | Ex-T | 04/07/68 | 07/68 | LA | L/C | ? | A Engine changed |
| 06/69 | Ex-T | 19/06/69 | 06/69 | ? | L/C | ? | Transmission changed (No. 1 convertor casing fractured, rotor partially seized, overheating and control piston seized) |
| 01/69 | Ex-T | 15/01/69 | 01/69 | ? | L/C | ? | Engine changed (throwing oil) |
| 03/70 | Ex-T | 03/70 | 03/70 | ? | L/C | ? | A Engine changed (throwing oil) |
| 06/70 | Ex-T | 06/70 | 06/70 | ? | L/C | ? | B Bogie changed (the left hand inner tyre loose) |
| 09/70 | Ex-T | 30/09/70 | 09/70 | ? | L/C | ? | A transmission changed (metal in sump) |
| 01/71 | Ex-T | 01/71 | 01/71 | ? | L/C | ? | Engine changed (passing oil) |
| 01/71 | Ex-T | 01/71 | 01/71 | ? | L/C | ? | B transmission changed (overheating) |
| 28/03/71 | Ex-T | | | LA | | | Withdrawn |

D860 at Exeter St David's on 24 September 1967, the first Saturday of the winter timetable. 2C40 was the headcode for the Exeter-Paignton portions which were detached from trains heading further west to Plymouth or Penzance. The portions continued until 1969 when it was decided to run the Paignton, Plymouth and Penzance services as separate trains throughout from Paddington. VICTORIOUS never carried maroon and would enter Swindon a few months later to emerge in blue livery in January 1968. (www.rail-online.co.uk)

D860 VICTORIOUS basks in the spring sunshine at Gloucester Horton Road on 11 April 1970; the following spring would bring its withdrawal. The blue livery is only 15 months old but has worn very badly, almost as poorly as the original NBL paintwork. The headcode, 1V86, relates to a previous day's working of the 13.37 Sheffield-Plymouth. On this particular day VICTORIOUS would work the 1V87 12.15 Newcastle-Plymouth forward from Gloucester, which was a regular Class 43 turn at the time. (N Preedy)

# D861 VIGILANT

| Lot no./Works no. | 443/27990 |
|---|---|
| **Significant dates and allocations** | |
| Delivered | 31/01/62 |
| Into traffic - Laira | 14/02/62 |
| Newton Abbot | 06/65 |
| Old Oak Common | 07/69 |
| Newton Abbot | 08/69 |
| Withdrawn (Bristol Bath Road) | 04/10/71 |
| (Bristol St Philips Marsh Junction) | By 02/11/71 |
| (Swindon) | 04/01/72 |
| Date cut-up | By 29/07/72 |

| **Stored** | From | To |
|---|---|---|
| Old Oak Common | 03/69 | 07/69 |

| **Livery and insignia changes** | |
|---|---|
| Green | 14/02/62 |
| OHLW flashes | 14/02/62 |
| Yellow warning panels | 14/02/62 |
| Maroon yellow warning panels | 23/09/66 |
| Blue full yellow ends – single insignia, sans serif, no D | 08/03/71 |
| **Recorded mileage** | 689,000 |

**Works visits and depot repairs**

| Stopped | At | On Works | Off Works | At | Type | Days | Work carried out |
|---|---|---|---|---|---|---|---|
| - | - | 31/01/62 | 14/02/62 | SW | D/A | | Delivery inspection and acceptance |
| 03/03/63 | Ex-T | 03/63 | 07/03/63 | LA | L/C | 4 | A Engine Turbo blower changed |
| 17/04/63 | Ex-T | 17/04/63 | 21/04/63 | LA | H/C | 6 | A & B Engines changed (high oil consumption -1 gallon per 30 miles) |
| 24/06/63 | Ex-T | 03/07/63 | 20/12/63 | SW | H/C | 179 | B Engine changed (fire damage); A & B Transmissions changed; A & B Bogies changed; Boiler changed; Modifications; Bogie side control linkage replaced with hydraulic shock absorbers |
| 30/01/64 | LA | 04/02/64 | 14/02/64 | SW | Unsch | 15 | A Bogie changed; (inner final drive input flange and cardan shaft damaged) |
| 16/05/64 | Ex-T | 05/64 | 30/05/64 | LA | H/C | 14 | B Transmission changed (overheating) |
| 10/64 | Ex-T | 07/10/64 | 10/64 | LA | L/C | ? | B Engine changed |
| 12/64 | Ex-T | 02/12/64 | 12/64 | LA | L/C | ? | A Transmission changed (control piston seized) |
| 05/65 | Ex-T | 10/05/65 | 05/65 | LA | L/C | ? | A Engine changed (a fractured crankcase) |
| 10/65 | Ex-T | 13/10/65 | 10/65 | LA | L/C | ? | B Transmission changed (overheating in 2nd convertor) |
| 05/66 | Ex-T | 11/05/66 | 25/05/66 | LA | H/C | ? | B Transmission changed (heavy metal debris in filters); replacement failed (primary shaft seized) |
| 04/07/66 | Ex-T | 11/07/66 | 23/09/66 | SW | Int | 82 | A Engine changed (core plugs leaking at Nos. 1, 2 and 4 cylinders, fuel oil leaking from unions, all cylinder flexible lub, oil pipes porous and heavy coolant leak from No. 12 cylinder head); B Engine changed; B Transmission repaired (damaged by a detached cardan shaft); A Bogie changed (outer final drive bearing collapsed); B Bogie changed; Modifications; Multiple working jumper cables and sockets removed from buffer beam; all hoses and cardan shafts changed, exhausters and compressor changed |
| 09/02/67 | Ex-T | 09/02/67 | 10/02/67 | LA | L/C | 1 | B Engine changed (heavy knocking and partially seized) |
| 04/67 | Ex-T | 22/04/67 | 04/67 | LA | L/C | ? | B Bogie changed (right hand inner tyre loose) |
| 05/67 | Ex-T | 05/05/67 | 05/67 | NA | L/C | ? | Boiler changed |
| 11/67 | Ex-T | 06/11/67 | 11/67 | LA | L/C | ? | A Engine changed (cracked weld on the fuel pump flange) |
| 01/68 | Ex-T | 22/01/68 | 01/68 | LA | L/C | ? | B Engine changed (pumping oil past a piston) |
| 08/68 | Ex-T | 16/08/68 | 08/68 | LA | H/C | ? | A Bogie changed; B Bogie changed (frame fracture on the centre box iron) |
| 03/69 | Ex-T | | 26/06/69 | OOC | | ? | To store / reinstated |
| 26/06/69 | Ex-T | 26/06/69 | 07/69 | OOC | L/C | ? | A Engine changed (overheating and fuming); B Engine changed (throwing oil) |
| 08/69 | Ex-T | 20/08/69 | 08/69 | NA | L/C | ? | Boiler removed |
| 23/09/69 | Ex-T | 23/09/69 | 26/09/69 | NA | L/C | 3 | Boiler fitted |
| 18/04/70 | Ex-T | 18/04/70 | 20/04/70 | LA | H/C | 2 | A & B Transmissions changed |
| 06/10/70 | Ex-T | 10/70 | 12/10/70 | LA | Unsch | 6 | A Engine changed (oil leaks) |
| 05/11/70 | Ex-T | 06/11/70 | 08/11/70 | LA | L/C | 3 | A Transmission changed (high convertor temperatures in No. 2 convertor) |
| 09/11/70 | Ex-T | 10/11/70 | 14/11/70 | LA | L/C | 5 | A Transmission changed (metal in filters) |
| 30/12/70 | Ex-T | 30/12/70 | 31/12/70 | LA | Unsch | 1 | A Engine changed |
| 30/12/70 | LA | 04/01/71 | 08/03/71 | SW | Int | 68 | A & B Engines changed; A Transmission changed (forward / reverse defects); B Transmission changed; A Bogie repaired; B Bogie changed; Modifications; all hoses and cardan shafts changed, exhausters and compressor changed, over bogie structure repaired |
| 02/06/71 | Ex-T | 02/06/71 | 05/06/71 | LA | L/C | 3 | B Engine changed (little end bearings defective) |
| 17/08/71 | Ex-T | 17/08/71 | 18/08/71 | LA | H/C | 1 | B Bogie changed (reported bad vibration) |
| 21/09/71 | WOR | 30/09/71 | 04/10/71 | BS | | | Failed due to a pressurised sump and subsequently withdrawn |

**D861 VIGILANT pilots D859 VANQUISHER on the 1C51 10.30am Paddington-Penzance 'Cornish Riviera' at Dawlish Warren on 16 June 1964. It had spent half of the previous year in Swindon Works after fire damage. VIGILANT started life with one NBL style radiator fan cover and one Swindon type, but by the time of this photograph had two flush Swindon style covers. (Millbrook House)**

**861 VIGILANT bringing in ECS from Malago Vale into Bristol Temple Meads on 21 August 1971. The locomotive had only been in its new livery for five months following an Intermediate overhaul but was withdrawn within six weeks. On the day of the photograph 861 worked the 2O52 15.48 Bristol-Weymouth and then the 2V52 19.25 Weymouth-Bristol; the headcode shows that its previous working was the 8B12 02.20 Stoke Gifford-Westbury. VIGILANT was the last Warship in maroon with a small yellow panel and that livery variation on a Warship became extinct in BR service when D861 disappeared into Swindon Works in January 1971. (www.rail-online.co.uk)**

# D862 VIKING

| Lot no./Works no. | 443/27991 |
|---|---|
| **Significant dates and allocations** | |
| Delivered | 03/62 |
| Into traffic - Laira | 13/03/62 |
| Newton Abbot | 06/65 |
| Withdrawn (Laira) | 04/10/71 |
| (Swindon) | 18/10/71 |
| Date cut-up | By 12/05/72 |

| **Stored** | **From** | **To** |
|---|---|---|
| Newton Abbot | 09/69 | 10/69 |
| Newton Abbot | 01/01/70 | 27/04/70 |
| **Livery and insignia changes** | | |
| Green | | 13/03/62 |
| OHLW flashes | | 13/03/62 |
| Yellow warning panels | | 13/03/62 |
| Maroon yellow warning panels | | 26/11/65 |
| Blue full yellow ends – single insignia, sans serif, no D | | 27/04/70 |
| **Recorded mileage** | | 727,000 |

**Works visits and depot repairs**

| Stopped | At | On Works | Off Works | At | Type | Days | Work carried out |
|---|---|---|---|---|---|---|---|
| - | - | 03/62 | 13/03/62 | SW | D/A | | Delivery inspection and acceptance |
| 02/07/62 | Ex-T | 02/07/62 | 07/07/62 | LA | H/C | 5 | |
| 04/09/62 | Ex-T | 05/09/62 | 13/09/62 | LA | H/C | 9 | |
| 09/10/62 | Ex-T | 09/10/62 | 20/10/62 | LA | H/C | 11 | A Transmission changed (fractured sump) |
| 07/02/63 | Ex-T | 07/02/63 | 02/63 | LA | H/C | ? | B end front apron replaced due to minor collision damage |
| 14/04/63 | LA | 15/04/63 | 18/04/63 | SW | L/C | 4 | |
| 03/06/63 | Ex-T | 03/06/63 | 07/06/63 | LA | H/C | 4 | A Transmission changed (no filling pump pressure) |
| 02/08/63 | LA | 12/08/63 | 28/08/63 | SW | H/C | 26 | A & B Bogies changed (excessive thrust pad clearances) |
| 30/01/64 | Ex-T | 30/01/64 | 31/01/64 | LA | ? | 1 | |
| 04/64 | Ex-T | 07/04/64 | 08/04/64 | LA | L/C | ? | B Engine changed (heavy oil leaks) |
| 04/06/64 | Ex-T | 06/64 | 20/06/64 | LA | L/C | 16 | |
| 09/64 | Ex-T | 11/09/64 | 14/09/64 | LA | H/C | ? | B Transmission changed (bronze debris in filters) |
| 14/07/65 | Ex-T | 07/65 | 26/11/65 | SW | Int | 135 | A & B Engines changed; A Transmission changed; B Transmission changed (No. 2 turbine broken apart and metal debris in sump); A & B Bogies changed; Boiler changed; Modifications |
| 05/66 | Ex-T | 05/66 | 05/66 | NA | Unsch | ? | B Engine Fuel pumps changed (overspeeding) |
| 11/66 | Ex-T | 30/11/66 | 11/66 | LA | L/C | ? | B Transmission changed (no oil pressure) |
| 07/67 | Ex-T | 20/07/67 | 07/67 | ? | L/C | ? | B Bogies removed(outer axle labyrinth seal loose) |
| 08/67 | Ex-T | 15/08/67 | 08/67 | LA | L/C | ? | A Engine repaired; A transmission removed (control piston seized) |
| 01/69 | Ex-T | 14/01/69 | 01/69 | ? | H/C | ? | A transmission removed (metal in filters); B Transmission removed (excessive noise) |
| 01/01/70 | Ex-T | ? | 27/04/70 | SW | Int | 116 | In store from 01/01/70 |
| 02/71 | Ex-T | 02/71 | 02/71 | ? | L/C | ? | A Engine changed |
| 04/10/71 | Ex-T | | | LA | | | Withdrawn |

D862 VIKING on the through road at Plymouth North Road in March 1965, with the portion removed from the Down 'Cornish Riviera'; a Hawksworth coach is at the front of this reduced rake. The shedplate is now on the side valance not the bufferbeam; VIKING retains its multiple working fittings but would soon lose them when it went into works for over four months on 14 July, for an Intermediate overhaul. (www.rail-online.co.uk)

D862 VIKING with a van train at Gloucester Eastgate on 19 September 1969. The maroon paintwork is now much worse than the green in the previous photograph. VIKING had worked up to Bristol earlier in the day on 1M95 07.45 Newquay-Manchester. The previous week it had posed at Bath Road Open Day though it would not have been the best possible advertisement for the Western Region. It finally received new paintwork in April 1970 after being restored to traffic following a period in store from the start of that year. (NE Preedy)

# D863 WARRIOR

| Lot no./Works no. | | 443/27992 |
|---|---|---|
| **Significant dates and allocations** | | |
| Delivered | | 03/62 |
| Into traffic - Laira | | 07/04/62 |
| Newton Abbot | | 06/65 |
| Withdrawn (Newton Abbot) | | 26/03/69 |
| (J Cashmore Newport) | | 18/07/69 |
| Date cut-up | | By 13/08/69 |

| **Stored** | **From** | **To** |
|---|---|---|
| Newton Abbot | 05/03/69 | 26/03/69 |
| **Livery and insignia changes** | | |
| Green | | 07/04/62 |
| OHLW flashes | | 07/04/62 |
| Yellow warning panels | | 07/04/62 |
| Maroon yellow warning panels | | 08/65 |
| Blue full yellow ends – double insignia, serif, D-prefix | | 12/67 |
| **Recorded mileage** | | 688,000 |

**Works visits and depot repairs**

| Stopped | At | On Works | Off Works | At | Type | Days | Work carried out |
|---|---|---|---|---|---|---|---|
| - | - | 03/62 | 07/04/62 | SW | D/A | ? | Delivery inspection and acceptance |
| 27/02/63 | Ex-T | 03/63 | 06/03/63 | LA | H/C | 7 | |
| 27/03/63 | Ex-T | 27/03/63 | 29/03/63 | LA | L/C | 2 | |
| 30/05/63 | Ex-T | 30/05/63 | 03/06/63 | LA | H/C | 4 | B Transmission changed (dynostarter output shaft broken) |
| 04/12/63 | Ex-T | 01/63 | 08/12/63 | LA | H/C | 4 | |
| 17/01/64 | Ex-T | 17/01/64 | 18/01/64 | LA | ? | 1 | |
| 02/64 | Ex-T | 05/02/64 | 02/64 | ? | Unsch | ? | A end dynostarter changed |
| 02/64 | Ex-T | 27/02/64 | 02/64 | ? | L/C | ? | B Engine changed (No. 6 con rod uncoupled) |
| 02/05/64 | Ex-T | 03/05/64 | 05/05/64 | ? | L/C | 3 | |
| 02/06/64 | Ex-T | 02/06/64 | 04/06/64 | LA | ? | 2 | A Engine Turbo blower changed (short run-down) |
| 09/64 | Ex-T | 03/09/64 | 09/64 | ? | ? | ? | A Engine changed |
| 14/07/65 | Ex-T | 07/65 | 08/65 | SW | Int | ? | A Engine removed (oil leaks); B Engine (No. 2 cylinder liner leaking); Boiler removed for modification |
| 02/66 | Ex-T | 25/02/66 | 02/66 | NA | Unsch | ? | B end dynostarter changed |
| 05/66 | Ex-T | 16/05/66 | 05/66 | LA | L/C | ? | B Engine changed (No. 11 cylinder liner leaking) |
| 11/66 | Ex-T | 21/11/66 | 11/66 | LA | L/C | ? | B Transmission changed (overheating) |
| 01/67 | Ex-T | 01/67 | 01/67 | ? | L/C | ? | |
| 02/67 | Ex-T | 02/67 | 22/02/67 | LA | L/C | ? | A Engine changed |
| 09/67 | Ex-T | 09/67 | 12/67 | SW | Int | ? | A Engine removed; B Engine removed (low lub. oil pressure) |
| 06/68 | Ex-T | 19/06/68 | 06/68 | NA | Unsch | ? | A Engine Fuel pumps changed |
| 11/68 | Ex-T | 11/11/68 | 11/68 | LA | L/C | ? | B Transmission changed (governor drive sheared; teeth damaged) |
| 01/69 | Ex-T | 01/69 | 01/69 | ? | L/C | ? | Engine removed (oil leaking from the air box) |
| 02/69 | Ex-T | 02/69 | 02/69 | LA | L/C | ? | B Transmission changed (top casing joint leaking oil) |
| 05/03/69 | Ex-T | | 26/03/69 | NA | | | Stored / Withdrawn |

A green Western with a green Warship – D863 next to D1002 WESTERN EXPLORER at Old Oak Common on 28 April 1962. WARRIOR was just three weeks old and the Western had entered service the previous month. (www.rail-online.co.uk)

A delightful period scene in 1967; maroon D863 WARRIOR at Stoke Canon just north of Exeter with the 6C13 15.50 Bristol West Depot to Exeter Riverside freight. D863 had the distinction of being the first Warship to carry maroon livery, in August 1965, but WARRIOR also had the less envious claim to fame of being the shortest lived, having been in traffic two weeks short of seven years when it was withdrawn on 26 March 1969. (www.rail-online.co.uk)

# D864 ZAMBESI

| Lot no./Works no. | 443/27993 |
|---|---|
| **Significant dates and allocations** | |
| Delivered | 06/05/62 |
| Into traffic - Laira | 10/05/62 |
| Newton Abbot | 06/65 |
| Withdrawn (Laira) | 27/03/71 |
| (Newton Abbot) | By 06/71 |
| (Laira) | 06/71 |
| (Swindon) | 28/06/71 |
| Date cut-up | By 19/11/71 |

| **Livery and insignia changes** | |
|---|---|
| Green | 10/05/62 |
| OHLW flashes | 10/05/62 |
| Yellow warning panels | 10/05/62 |
| Maroon | - |
| Blue full yellow ends - double insignia, serif, D-prefix, dark brown underframe and bogies. Numbers below engine room windows | 11/66 |
| Blue full yellow ends - double insignia, serif, D-prefix, dark brown underframe and bogies. Numbers below cab windows | 10/05/67 |
| **Recorded mileage** | 744,000 |

**Works visits and depot repairs**

| Stopped | At | On Works | Off Works | At | Type | Days | Work carried out |
|---|---|---|---|---|---|---|---|
| - | - | 06/05/62 | 10/05/62 | SW | D/A | 4 | Delivery inspection and acceptance |
| 02/11/62 | Ex-T | 11/62 | 11/11/62 | LA | H/C | 9 | |
| 07/04/63 | Ex-T | 07/04/63 | 10/04/63 | LA | L/C | 3 | |
| 15/09/63 | Ex-T | 14/09/63 | 16/09/63 | LA | L/C | 1 | B Engine changed |
| 11/01/64 | Ex-T | 01/64 | 16/01/64 | LA | ? | 5 | |
| 23/07/64 | Ex-T | 07/64 | ? | SW | ? | ? | A Transmission removed (output bearing collapsed); A Bogie removed (inner final drive defective) |
| 03/65 | Ex-T | 03/65 | 03/65 | ? | ? | ? | Engine removed (low lub. oil pressure) |
| 06/65 | Ex-T | 06/65 | 26/06/65 | ? | L/C | ? | B Engine changed |
| 01/66 | Ex-T | 01/66 | 01/66 | ? | L/C | ? | Engine removed |
| 05/66 | Ex-T | 05/66 | 05/66 | ? | L/C | ? | A Engine removed (venting coolant) |
| 08/66 | Ex-T | 04/08/66 | 08/66 | NA | L/C | ? | Boiler removed (split coil) |
| 09/66 | Ex-T | 09/66 | 09/66 | ? | L/C | ? | Transmission removed (not changing gear) |
| ? | Ex-T | ? | 11/66 | SW | Int | ? | A & B Engines changed; A & B Transmissions changed; A & B Bogies changed; Boiler changed |
| 01/67 | Ex-T | 01/67 | 01/67 | ? | L/C | ? | A Transmission changed |
| 09/67 | Ex-T | 09/67 | 09/67 | SW | Unsch | ? | Collision damage to right hand body side panels and nose end damaged. Loco panels repaired, 'stopped up' and repainted. (Collision damage was sustained at St. Anne's, near Bristol, on 11/01/67 running light from Bristol East Depot to Westbury when it ran into the wreckage of a rear end collision between D1067 and D1071. The loco remained in traffic until called to Swindon in May for attention.) |
| 09/67 | Ex-T | 09/67 | 09/67 | ? | ? | ? | A Engine removed |
| 11/67 | Ex-T | 11/67 | 11/67 | ? | ? | ? | B Transmission removed (main lub. oil pump defective) |
| 01/68 | Ex-T | 01/01/68 | 01/68 | ? | ? | ? | B Bogie changed (AWS platform bracket damaged) |
| 05/68 | Ex-T | 05/68 | 05/68 | ? | L/C | ? | A Transmission removed |
| 09/68 | Ex-T | 17/09/68 | 09/68 | NA | L/C | ? | Boiler changed |
| 05/69 | Ex-T | 05/69 | 05/69 | ? | L/C | ? | A Engine removed (No. 5 piston crown damaged) |
| 09/69 | Ex-T | 09/69 | 09/69 | NA | L/C | ? | Boiler changed |
| 10/69 | Ex-T | 10/69 | 10/69 | ? | L/C | ? | A Bogie removed (tyres at maximum tread wear) |
| 31/12/69 | NA | 01/70 | 01/70 | ? | Unsch | | On 31/12/69 D864 was going to Aller Junction to the assistance of the failed 1C16 08.10 Bristol to Plymouth when it struck coaches the rear of 1E37 10.10 Paignton - Bradford 'Devonian'. Considerable damage was caused to the two rear coaches which were later detached at Newton Abbot. It is not known if D864 went to Works for attention. The loco was in traffic by 16/01/70 as it was stopped with a B end engine speed regulator defect. |
| 09/70 | Ex-T | 09/70 | 09/70 | ? | L/C | ? | Engine removed (bearings in poor condition) |
| 01/71 | Ex-T | 01/71 | 01/71 | NA | L/C | ? | Boiler removed (split coil ) |
| 27/03/71 | Ex-T | | | LA | | | Withdrawn |

D864 ZAMBESI at Old Oak on 6 September 1962, in 'as delivered' condition with yellow warning panel. D864 was first into blue livery albeit a unique variation, with dark brown bogies and underframe, with the numbers placed under the engine room windows and the BR double arrows under the cabs. It only ran like this for a few months due to collision damage repairs and it emerged in May 1967 in a more standard blue livery but retaining the dark brown valance which in fact it kept through to withdrawal. (PH Groom)

D864 ZAMBESI in the Bristol area, 20 May 1969; double arrows on the cabsides and serif numbers as applied in May 1967. Unusually ZAMBESI retains its multiple working fittings, although there is no evidence that these were ever used beyond the mid-1960s. D864 was somewhat prone to mishaps and on the last day of 1969 it was involved in a derailment of the 'Devonian' at Newton Abbot which again left the locomotive with collision damage. (www.rail-online.co.uk)

# D865 ZEALOUS

| Lot no./Works no. | 443/27994 |
|---|---|
| **Significant dates and allocations** | |
| Delivered | 17/06/62 |
| Into traffic - Laira | 23/06/62 |
| Newton Abbot | 06/65 |
| Withdrawn (Newton Abbot) | 22/05/71 |
| (Bristol St Philips Marsh Junction) | By 08/71 |
| (Swindon) | 10/12/71 |
| Date cut-up | By 09/06/72 |

| **Stored** | From | To |
|---|---|---|
| Newton Abbot | 04/69 | 31/08/69 |
| Newton Abbot | 02/05/71 | 22/05/71 |
| **Livery and insignia changes** | | |
| Green | | 23/06/62 |
| OHLW flashes | | 23/06/62 |
| Yellow warning panels | | 23/06/62 |
| Maroon yellow warning panels | | 11/11/65 |
| Blue full yellow ends – single insignia, sans serif , no D | | 31/08/69 |
| **Recorded mileage** | | 683,000 |

**Works visits and depot repairs**

| Stopped | At | On Works | Off Works | At | Type | Days | Work carried out |
|---|---|---|---|---|---|---|---|
| - | - | 17/06/62 | 23/06/62 | SW | D/A | 6 | Delivery inspection and acceptance |
| 02/10/62 | Ex-T | 05/10/62 | 25/10/62 | LA | H/C | 23 | B Engine changed (seized and full of coolant) |
| 16/05/63 | Ex-T | 05/63 | 23/05/63 | LA | L/C | 7 | |
| 23/06/63 | Ex-T | 23/06/63 | 26/06/63 | LA | H/C | 3 | |
| 16/10/63 | Ex-T | 10/63 | 20/10/63 | LA | L/C | 4 | |
| 08/01/64 | Ex-T | 01/64 | 16/01/64 | LA | ? | 8 | |
| 03/64 | Ex-T | 09/03/64 | 03/64 | LA | L/C | ? | B Transmission changed (overheating and oil black) |
| 08/06/64 | LA | 10/06/64 | 15/07/64 | SW | Unsch | 37 | A & B Engines removed (cylinder heads leaking); A & B Bogies removed (worn tyres); Boiler removed |
| 06/65 | Ex-T | 02/06/65 | 06/65 | ? | Unsch | ? | A Engine Turbo blower changed (30 second run-down from 1,530 rpm) |
| 06/65 | Ex-T | 02/06/65 | 28/06/65 | ? | Unsch | ? | A Engine changed |
| 13/08/65 | Ex-T | 08/65 | 11/11/65 | SW | Int | 90 | A & B Engines removed ; A & B Transmissions changed |
| 02/66 | Ex-T | 01/02/66 | 02/66 | NA | Unsch | ? | B end dynostarter changed |
| 04/66 | Ex-T | 04/66 | 04/66 | LA | ? | ? | A Transmission removed (standstill coupling defective) |
| 05/66 | Ex-T | 20/05/66 | 05/66 | ? | Unsch | ? | B end dynostarter removed |
| 11/66 | Ex-T | 11/66 | 11/66 | NA | L/C | ? | Boiler removed |
| 12/66 | Ex-T | 12/66 | 12/66 | ? | L/C | ? | A Engine removed (No. 5 cylinder big end bearing suspect) |
| 01/67 | Ex-T | 03/01/67 | 15/01/67 | ? | H/C | ? | A Engine changed (big end knocking); B Engine removed - failed on fitting (fractured crank case); changed |
| 01/68 | Ex-T | 28/01/68 | 01/68 | LA | L/C | ? | B Engine changed |
| 06/68 | Ex-T | 18/06/68 | 06/68 | NA | Unsch | ? | A Engine Turbo blower changed |
| 09/68 | Ex-T | 09/68 | 09/68 | LA | L/C | ? | B Transmission removed (damaged output flange) |
| 12/68 | Ex-T | 12/68 | 12/68 | ? | L/C | ? | A Engine removed, to be scrapped |
| 03/69 | Ex-T | 03/69 | 03/69 | ? | L/C | ? | B Transmission removed (no output in one direction) |
| 06/69 | Ex-T | 06/69 | 09/69 | SW | Class | ? | Engine removed due to No. 5 piston crown damaged) |
| 11/69 | Ex-T | 11/69 | 11/69 | ? | L/C | ? | Engine removed (main bearings in poor condition) |
| 08/70 | Ex-T | 08/70 | 08/70 | ? | L/C | ? | B Engine removed ( passing oil) |
| 09/70 | Ex-T | 09/70 | 09/70 | ? | L/C | ? | B Engine removed |
| 11/70 | Ex-T | 11/70 | 11/70 | ? | L/C | ? | A Engine removed (No. 12 cylinder liner fractured) |
| 02/05/71 | Ex-T | | | NA | | | To store/ withdrawn |

**Maroon-liveried D865 ZEALOUS in 1966 rests at Laira with D816 ECLIPSE sandwiched between it and a Western. The final Warship into service in June 1962, after the collapse of NBL, it was repainted in maroon during an Intermediate overhaul completed in November 1965. (www.rail-online.co.uk)**

**865 ZEALOUS rests at Gloucester Central on 31 October 1969, having been painted into the final blue variant two months previously. 865 was the last D833 to be introduced, on the 28 June 1962 which meant that the whole class had been intact for just over six years when D801 was withdrawn on 3 August 1968. (www.rail-online.co.uk)**

# D866 ZEBRA

| Lot no./Works no. | 437 / - |
|---|---|
| **Significant dates and allocations** | |
| Into traffic - Laira | 24/03/61 |
| Newton Abbot | 05/66 |
| Laira | 08/67 |
| Newton Abbot | 10/71 |
| Withdrawn (Newton Abbot) | 02/01/72 |
| (Bristol St Philips Marsh Junction) | 08/09/72 |
| (Swindon) | 12/09/72 |
| Date cut-up | By 13/10/72 |

| **Livery and insignia changes** | |
|---|---|
| Green | 24/03/61 |
| OHLW flashes | 21/10/61 |
| Yellow warning panels | 27/12/62 |
| Maroon | - |
| Blue full yellow ends – double insignia, sans serif, D-prefix | 17/09/68 |
| **Recorded mileage** | 1,040,000 |

**Works visits and depot repairs**

| Stopped | At | On Works | Off Works | At | Type | Days | Work carried out |
|---|---|---|---|---|---|---|---|
| - | - | - | 24/03/61 | SW | D/A | | A Bogie was ex D839 and had already completed 25,910 miles when fitted |
| 11/10/61 | LA | 11/10/61 | 21/10/61 | SW | ? | 10 | A & B Engines (all cylinder heads changed (old pattern type), cam boxes checked and modification completed);A & B Bogies (brake gear changed and adjusted, all tyres examined and measured at 3") |
| 03/11/61 | Ex-T | 03/11/61 | 03/11/61 | LA | ? | 1 | A Bogie tyres turned (left hand leading tyre pitted) |
| 25/11/61 | LA | 01/12/61 | 11/12/61 | SW | ? | 16 | A Transmission changed (unrecorded defects) |
| 09/62 | Ex-T | 20/09/62 | 09/62 | LA | ? | ? | A Engine Turbo blower changed (collapsed bearing) |
| 08/12/62 | LA | 10/12/62 | 27/12/62 | SW | ? | 19 | A Engine changed; A & B Bogies changed; four transmission to final drive cardan shafts removed, repaired and re-fitted; A end Vapor-Watchman preheater changed |
| 29/01/63 | SW | 30/01/63 | 06/02/63 | LA | ? | 8 | B Engine changed (Nos. 5 and 6 cylinder heads leaking coolant); A Transmission changed (overheating continuously and sluggish in gear changes) |
| 05/04/63 | 999 | 19/04/63 | 09/05/63 | SW | ? | 34 | B Transmission changed (damage sustained by a detached engine to transmission cardan shaft); Modifications |
| 07/63 | Ex-T | 05/07/63 | 07/63 | LA | ? | ? | A end exhauster changed (knocking badly) |
| 07/63 | Ex-T | 25/07/63 | 07/63 | LA | ? | ? | A end exhauster changed (seizure) |
| 16/09/63 | LA | 20/09/63 | 25/10/63 | SW | ? | 39 | A Engine changed; B Transmission changed (bottom casing fractured); A Bogie changed (worn tyres); B Bogie changed (inner final drive cardan shaft broken off at both universal couplings); Boiler changed; Modifications; Bogie side control linkage replaced with hydraulic shock absorbers; B end underframe repaired, bent inner control arm repaired, thrust pads reset, one engine to transmission cardan shaft changed and four engine to transmission cardan shafts changed |
| 28/01/64 | Ex-T | 29/01/64 | 31/01/64 | LA | ? | 2 | B Engine Turbo blower changed (leaking coolant) |
| 03/64 | Ex-T | 19/03/64 | 03/64 | LA | ? | ? | Compressor changed (knocking noise) |
| 09/64 | Ex-T | 10/09/64 | 09/64 | LA | ? | ? | B Engine changed (cylinder heads blowing oil) |
| 10/12/64 | Ex-T | 18/12/64 | 26/02/65 | SW | ? | 77 | A & B Engines changed; A Transmission changed (noisy on trials, four gear wheels found having badly worn teeth); B Transmission removed ( leaking output cardan shaft oil seals); Boiler changed; Modifications; Compressor changed; A and B exhausters changed; over bogie structures repaired, thrust pads reset, nose section repaired, boiler room roof and floor area repaired, buffers changed, various electrical repairs completed, Misc. repairs to batteries, air reservoirs, fire equipment, sanding gear, Serck pump and systems, Vapor-Watchman preheaters, pumps and gauges, part interior repaint completed and exterior repaint |
| 09/65 | Ex-T | 21/09/65 | 09/65 | LA | ? | ? | Boiler changed (hole in the coil) |
| 04/66 | Ex-T | 14/04/66 | 04/66 | LA | ? | ? | A Bogie changed (defective cast on the inner axle) |
| 06/66 | Ex-T | 08/06/66 | 06/66 | LA | ? | ? | B Bogie changed (tyres pitted too deeply to turn) |
| 11/66 | Ex-T | 03/11/66 | 11/66 | NA | ? | ? | A Engine Turbo blower changed |
| 12/66 | Ex-T | 03/12/66 | 12/66 | LA | ? | ? | A Bogie changed |
| 07/01/67 | Ex-T | 07/01/67 | 10/01/67 | LA | ? | 3 | A & B Engines changed; B Transmission changed |
| 04/67 | Ex-T | 09/04/67 | 04/67 | LA | ? | ? | A Transmission changed (output oil seals leaking, No. 6 gear wheel teeth fractured, slipper blocks badly worn and pump wheel gear bearing track badly worn) |
| 07/67 | Ex-T | 07/07/67 | 07/67 | NA | ? | ? | A end dynostarter changed |
| 11/67 | Ex-T | 04/11/67 | 11/67 | LA | ? | ? | Boiler changed |
| 12/67 | Ex-T | 03/12/67 | 12/67 | LA | ? | ? | A Transmission changed (output casing bolts sheared) |
| 01/68 | Ex-T | 05/01/68 | 01/68 | LA | ? | ? | A & B Bogies changed |
| 01/68 | Ex-T | 15/01/68 | 01/68 | LA | ? | ? | A Transmission changed (forward / reverse gear seized - three bearings fitted to the primary shaft had collapsed or were badly damaged and bushes fitted to the No. 7 gear had seized on No. 5 shaft. |
| 27/02/68 | Ex-T | 28/02/68 | 02/68 | LA | ? | ? | A Bogie changed (outer final drive input bearings suspect) |
| 25/04/68 | Ex-T | 27/04/68 | 04/68 | LA | ? | ? | B Transmission changed (coming out of direction) |
| 13/05/68 | Ex-T | 13/05/68 | 05/68 | LA | ? | ? | B Transmission changed (not changing gear) |
| 06/68 | Ex-T | 21/06/68 | 06/68 | LA | ? | ? | A Transmission changed (loss of pressure) |
| 07/68 | Ex-T | 26/07/68 | 17/09/68 | SW | ? | 53 | A & B Engines and A & B Transmissions removed for examination on shop floor; A Bogie changed (torn side controls rubbers and worn bushes); B Bogie changed (torn side controls rubbers); Modifications; all hoses and cardan shafts changed; exhausters and compressor changed, earth faults cleared and multiple working facility re-instated |
| 11/68 | Ex-T | 19/11/68 | 11/68 | LA | ? | ? | B Engine changed (losing coolant) |
| 11/68 | Ex-T | 25/11/68 | 11/68 | LA | ? | ? | A Transmission changed (metal in filters) |
| 03/69 | Ex-T | 04/03/69 | 03/69 | LA | ? | ? | A Engine changed |
| 04/69 | Ex-T | 25/04/69 | 04/69 | LA | ? | ? | A Transmission changed (seized clutches, the bush fitted to No. 8 gear wheel seized on the No. 6 shaft, all gears and bearings blue and overheated suggested a fire had taken place) |
| 07/69 | Ex-T | 04/07/69 | 07/69 | LA | ? | ? | A Transmission changed (output seals and sump joint leaking) |
| 07/69 | Ex-T | 15/07/69 | 07/69 | LA | ? | ? | A Transmission changed (bronze bushes fitted to Nos. 7 and 8 gear wheels had seized on to Nos. 5 and 6 shafts, No. 6 gear wheel overheated, badly worn slipper blocks and metal in filters) |
| 02/09/69 | Ex-T | 02/09/69 | 05/09/69 | LA | ? | 3 | B Engine changed (No. 5 cylinder liner fractured after a hydraulic lock) |
| 10/69 | Ex-T | 23/10/69 | 10/69 | LA | ? | ? | Boiler changed |
| 06/04/70 | Ex-T | 06/04/70 | 10/04/70 | LA | ? | 4 | B Transmission changed |
| 22/05/70 | Ex-T | 22/05/70 | 25/05/70 | LA | ? | 3 | A & B Bogies changed (loose tyres and worn brake gear) |
| 18/11/70 | Ex-T | 18/11/70 | 21/11/70 | LA | ? | 3 | A Transmission changed (metal in filters) |
| 10/02/71 | Ex-T | 10/02/71 | 14/02/71 | LA | ? | 4 | B Engine changed (seized cylinder head studs) |
| 02/06/71 | LA | 02/06/71 | 08/06/71 | LA | ? | 9 | Both transmissions, the transmission to final drives and engine to transmission cardan shafts were removed before the locomotive was hauled to Swindon on 08/06/71 |
| 02/06/71 | LA | 26/07/71 | 27/08/71 | SW | ? | 55 | A & B Engines changed; A & B Transmissions changed; A & B Bogies changed (flats caused during towing); bodywork repaired (A right hand and B left hand buffer flanges damaged, A and B end front aprons damaged, B end frame buckled by body support bracket, B end left hand side fractured, A end body support bracket damaged left hand side and A end cab nose right hand corner badly dented) |
| 16/12/71 | Ex-T | 16/12/71 | 20/12/71 | NA | ? | 4 | B Transmission changed (convertor defect) |
| 02/01/72 | Ex-T | | | NA | - | | Withdrawn |

D866 ZEBRA stands in the down platform at Torquay in the summer of 1962 with the 12.05pm Paddington-Kingswear 'Torbay Express'. An interesting rake of coaches sits in the through road; it may have been a wet summer Saturday and rakes of stock were stored wherever space could be found. Although the buffers on ZEBRA are very work stained there are still signs of the coat of silver paint that they received the previous year. D866 was one of the BR Warships which boasted NBL radiator fan covers. (www.rail-online.co.uk)

D866 ZEBRA on one of the roads of the old GWR shed at Exeter on 22 May 1971; the second Warship is 814 DRAGON. DRAGON had two round trips to Barnstaple that day, at 06.30 and 16.00. ZEBRA had worked into Tiverton Junction in the early hours with the 6V78 22.45 Fawley-Tiverton Junction oil tanks and then travelled light to Exeter for attention to a high water temperature problem on A engine and transmission temperature trips. D866 would work off Exeter that evening on the 1O18 18.00 Exeter-Waterloo. (www.rail-online.co.uk)

# D867 ZENITH

| Lot no./Works no. | 437 / - |
|---|---|
| **Significant dates and allocations** | |
| Into traffic - Laira | 26/04/61 |
| Newton Abbot | 05/66 |
| Laira | 08/67 |
| Withdrawn (Laira) | 18/10/71 |
| (Bristol St Philips Marsh Junction) | 26/10/71 |
| Component recovery (Laira) | 04/07/72 |
| (Bristol St Philips Marsh Junction) | 18/08/72 |
| (Swindon) | 22/08/72 |
| Date cut-up | By 30/09/72 |

| **Livery and insignia changes** | |
|---|---|
| Green | 26/04/61 |
| OHLW flashes | 10/61 |
| Yellow warning panels | 01/08/62 |
| Maroon yellow warning panels | By 09/66 |
| Blue full yellow ends – double insignia, sans serif , no D | 25/09/70 |
| **Recorded mileage** | 991,000 |

**Works visits and depot repairs**

| Stopped | At | On Works | Off Works | At | Type | Days | Work carried out |
|---|---|---|---|---|---|---|---|
| - | - | - | 26/04/61 | SW | D/A | | Delivery inspection and acceptance |
| 10/11/61 | LA | 16/11/61 | 07/12/61 | SW | U/C | 27 | |
| 11/04/62 | Ex-T | 11/04/62 | 12/04/62 | LA | L/C | 1 | |
| 10/07/62 | LA | 18/07/62 | 01/08/62 | SW | L/C | 22 | |
| 13/11/62 | LA | 13/11/62 | 01/12/62 | SW | L/C | 18 | |
| 16/05/63 | LA | 20/05/63 | 13/06/63 | SW | H/C | 28 | |
| 19/07/63 | Ex-T | 23/07/63 | 01/08/63 | BS | H/C | 13 | A Bogie removed (inner final drive input shaft bearing overheated) |
| 07/08/63 | Ex-T | 07/08/63 | 08/08/63 | LA | Unsch | 1 | Turbo blower changed |
| 09/63 | Ex-T | 07/09/63 | 09/63 | LA | H/C | 1 | B Engine changed (No. 3 cylinder liner fractured) |
| 15/01/64 | Ex-T | 15/01/64 | 16/01/64 | LA | U/C | 1 | |
| 09/64 | Ex-T | 10/09/64 | 09/64 | LA | Unsch | ? | Dynostarter changed |
| 11/65 | Ex-T | 11/65 | 11/65 | ? | ? | ? | A Transmission removed (defective convertor) |
| 12/65 | Ex-T | 18/12/65 | 12/65 | LA | ? | ? | A Engine changed |
| ? | Ex-T | 08/66 | 09/66 | SW | Int | ? | A & B Bogies removed for general repair |
| 08/67 | Ex-T | 15/08/67 | 08/67 | ? | ? | ? | A Engine removed (fractured cylinder heads and cams worn) |
| 05/68 | Ex-T | 01/05/68 | 05/68 | LA | H/C | ? | B Engine changed; Boiler changed |
| 07/68 | Ex-T | 07/68 | 07/68 | LA | ? | ? | A Transmission removed (not selecting direction); A & B Bogies removed (flats and tyres too thin to turn) |
| 07/68 | Ex-T | 07/68 | 07/68 | ? | ? | ? | Bogie removed (final drive input bearing overheated) |
| 11/68 | Ex-T | 11/11/68 | 11/68 | ? | ? | ? | A Transmission removed (No. 7 gear bush broken up and debris throughout the transmission) |
| 03/69 | Ex-T | 03/69 | 03/69 | ? | ? | ? | A Transmission removed (knocking) |
| 05/69 | Ex-T | 23/05/69 | 05/69 | ? | ? | ? | A Transmission removed (oil leaking from the convertor) |
| 02/70 | Ex-T | 02/70 | 02/70 | ? | ? | ? | B Engine removed for routine overhaul |
| 08/70 | Ex-T | 08/70 | 08/70 | ? | ? | ? | B Transmission removed (metal in filters) |
| 12/70 | Ex-T | 12/70 | 12/70 | ? | ? | ? | Boiler removed for routine overhaul |
| 01/71 | Ex-T | 01/71 | 01/71 | ? | ? | ? | A Transmission removed (no oil pressure) |
| 03/71 | Ex-T | 03/71 | 03/71 | ? | ? | ? | A Engine removed (No. 3 cylinder head studs seized); A Transmission removed (metal in filters) |
| 04/71 | Ex-T | 04/71 | 04/71 | ? | ? | ? | B Transmission removed (forward / reverse clutch seized) |
| 18/10/71 | Ex-T | | | LA | - | | Withdrawn |

D867 ZENITH is just a couple of months old as it travels light through Bristol Temple Meads in the summer of 1961. D867 was the final Swindon Warship but was inexplicably given NBL radiator fan housings. ZENITH is yet to receive electrification flashes or a yellow panel. It was repainted in maroon in 1966 before going into blue in 1970. (www.rail-online.co.uk)

D867 ZENITH at Gloucester Horton Road shed in August 1963. The headcode denotes that D867 has brought the 9.05am Paddington-Cheltenham into Gloucester Central; a 2-6-2T was at the time still likely to have taken the train forward for the final six miles to Cheltenham St James. The Warships were never the premier motive power over the Golden Valley route through Stroud to Swindon – Hymeks and Westerns were far more usual on this route. (www.rail-online.co.uk)

## D868 ZEPHYR

| Lot no./Works no. | 437 / - |
|---|---|
| **Significant dates and allocations** | |
| Into traffic - Laira | 18/05/61 |
| Newton Abbot | 05/66 |
| Laira | 08/67 |
| Withdrawn (Newton Abbot) | 03/10/71 |
| (Bristol St Philips Marsh Junction) | 20/10/71 |
| (Swindon) | 06/01/72 |
| Date cut-up | By 07/04/72 |

| **Livery and insignia changes** | |
|---|---|
| Green | 18/05/61 |
| OHLW flashes | 01/06/62 |
| Yellow warning panels | 30/05/63 |
| Maroon | - |
| Blue full yellow ends – double insignia, serif, D-prefix | By 12/67 |
| Blue full yellow ends – single insignia, serif , no D (repainted at Laira) | 06/06/71 |
| **Recorded mileage** | 1,008,000 |

**Works visits and depot repairs**

| Stopped | At | On Works | Off Works | At | Type | Days | Work carried out |
|---|---|---|---|---|---|---|---|
| - | - | - | 18/05/61 | SW | D/A | | Delivery inspection and acceptance |
| 05/61 | Ex-T | 05/61 | 31/05/61 | SW | Unsch | ? | D868 was shopped only to fit experiment W/SW/L/190 ("Modified air intake ducting" fitted to A & B Engines) |
| 03/12/61 | Ex-T | 03/12/61 | 06/12/61 | LA | L/C | 3 | |
| 19/01/62 | Ex-T | 19/01/62 | 06/02/62 | LA | U/C | 18 | |
| 22/04/62 | Ex-T | 22/04/62 | 10/05/62 | LA | H/C | 18 | B Transmission changed (output oil seals leaking) |
| 28/05/62 | Ex-T | 29/05/62 | 01/06/62 | SW | L/C | 4 | |
| 17/09/62 | Ex-T | 17/09/62 | 05/10/62 | LA | H/C | 18 | |
| 13/03/63 | Ex-T | 13/03/63 | 19/03/63 | LA | H/C | 6 | |
| 15/05/63 | LA | 15/05/63 | 30/05/63 | SW | H/C | 15 | |
| 23/12/63 | Ex-T | 23/12/63 | 30/12/63 | LA | H/C | 7 | |
| 04/05/64 | Ex-T | 04/05/64 | 07/05/64 | LA | ? | 3 | Component change |
| 03/65 | Ex-T | 23/03/65 | 03/65 | ? | ? | ? | Engine removed (cylinder heads leaking); A & B Transmissions removed for general repair |
| 09/65 | Ex-T | 09/65 | 09/65 | ? | ? | ? | A Engine removed for routine overhaul |
| 03/66 | Ex-T | 03/66 | 03/66 | ? | ? | ? | Boiler removed for routine overhaul |
| 04/66 | Ex-T | 18/04/66 | 04/66 | LA | ? | ? | B Bogie changed (final drive overheating) |
| 07/66 | Ex-T | 26/07/66 | 07/66 | ? | ? | ? | B Transmission changed (coming out of direction); failed on first trip after fitting (forward / reverse faults and metal in filters) |
| 11/66 | Ex-T | 04/11/66 | 11/66 | LA | ? | ? | A Transmission removed (metal in filters); A Bogie changed (derailment damage) |
| 01/67 | Ex-T | 01/67 | 01/67 | ? | ? | ? | Transmission removed (lift in the input shaft bearing) |
| 05/67 | Ex-T | 14/05/67 | 05/67 | LA | ? | ? | A Engine removed (No. 5 cylinder liner fractured) |
| 07/67 | Ex-T | 07/67 | 07/67 | ? | ? | ? | A Transmission removed (stuck in 3rd gear and metal in filters) |
| 09/67 | Ex-T | 05/09/67 | 12/67 | SW | ? | ? | Engine removed; A Transmission removed (stuck in 3rd gear and metal in filters) |
| 03/68 | Ex-T | 03/68 | 03/68 | LA | ? | ? | Boiler changed |
| 04/68 | Ex-T | 04/68 | 04/68 | ? | ? | ? | Boiler removed for routine overhaul |
| 06/68 | Ex-T | 06/68 | 06/68 | ? | ? | ? | A Engine removed for routine overhaul |
| 08/68 | Ex-T | 08/68 | 08/68 | ? | ? | ? | Transmission removed (directional clutch damaged and metal in filters) |
| 06/69 | Ex-T | 06/69 | 06/69 | ? | ? | ? | B Bogie changed |
| 12/69 | Ex-T | ? | ? | ? | ? | ? | B Transmission removed (forward / reverse mechanism seized) |
| 12/70 | Ex-T | 12/70 | 12/70 | ? | ? | ? | Boiler removed for routine overhaul |
| 03/71 | Ex-T | 22/03/71 | 03/71 | ? | ? | ? | B Engine and A Bogie removed for routine overhaul |
| 07/71 | Ex-T | 07/71 | 07/71 | ? | ? | ? | B Transmission removed (overheating) |
| 03/10/71 | Ex-T | | | NA | - | | Withdrawn |

D868 ZEPHYR near Basingstoke working the 1O79 10.25 Exeter-Waterloo in the summer of 1965. The Warships had a long tenure as the principal motive power on this line, for seven years from 1964 to 1971. (RK Blencowe)

D868 ZEPHYR on 30 November 1969 at Bristol Temple Meads in its first version of blue with cabside symbols and serif numbers with the TOPS panel to the right of the number. The multiple working equipment which was refitted in 1968 for the accelerated West of England services is clearly visible. (www.rail-online.co.uk)

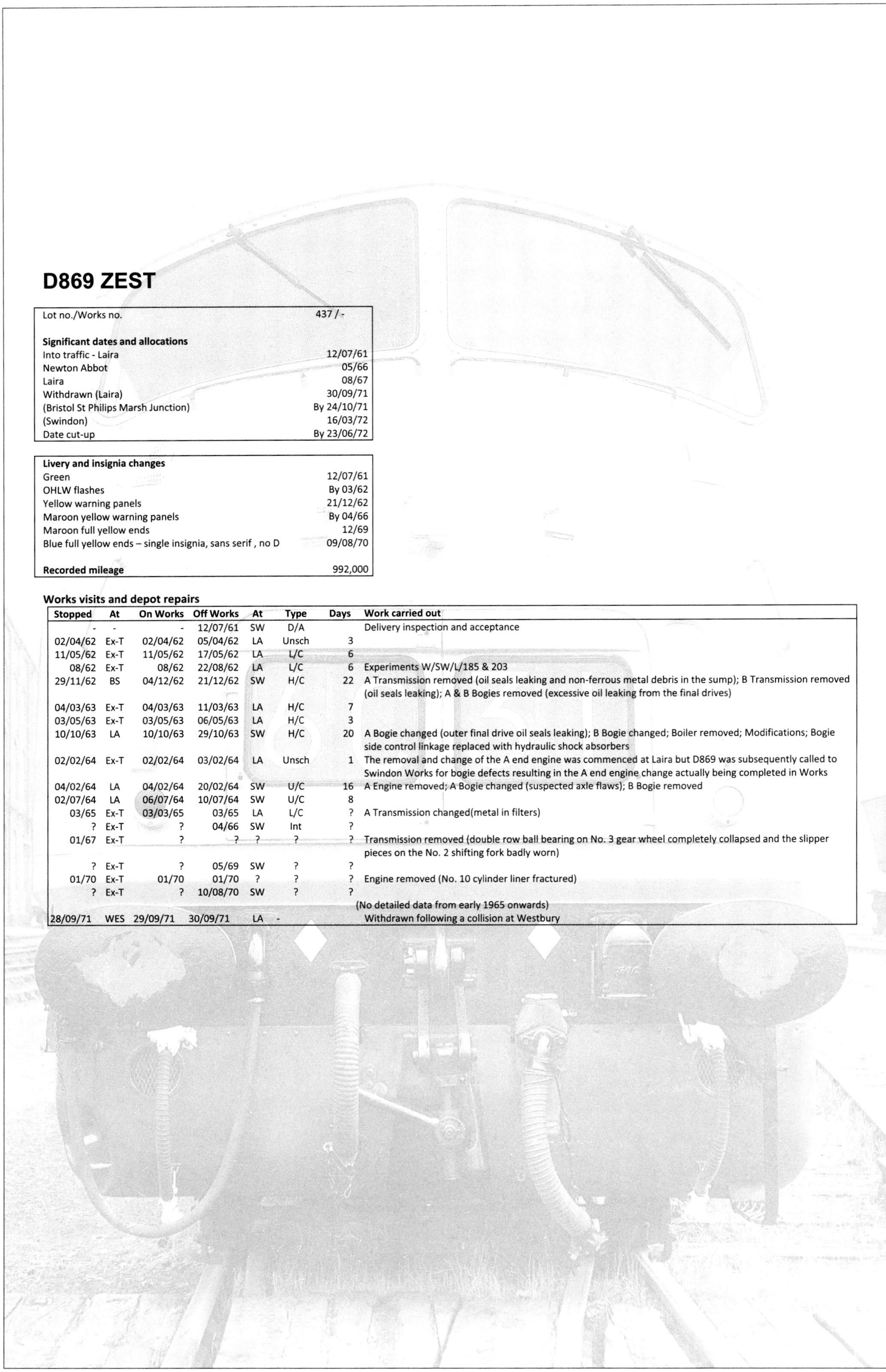

# D869 ZEST

| Lot no./Works no. | 437 / - |
|---|---|
| **Significant dates and allocations** | |
| Into traffic - Laira | 12/07/61 |
| Newton Abbot | 05/66 |
| Laira | 08/67 |
| Withdrawn (Laira) | 30/09/71 |
| (Bristol St Philips Marsh Junction) | By 24/10/71 |
| (Swindon) | 16/03/72 |
| Date cut-up | By 23/06/72 |

| **Livery and insignia changes** | |
|---|---|
| Green | 12/07/61 |
| OHLW flashes | By 03/62 |
| Yellow warning panels | 21/12/62 |
| Maroon yellow warning panels | By 04/66 |
| Maroon full yellow ends | 12/69 |
| Blue full yellow ends – single insignia, sans serif , no D | 09/08/70 |
| **Recorded mileage** | 992,000 |

**Works visits and depot repairs**

| Stopped | At | On Works | Off Works | At | Type | Days | Work carried out |
|---|---|---|---|---|---|---|---|
| - | - | - | 12/07/61 | SW | D/A | | Delivery inspection and acceptance |
| 02/04/62 | Ex-T | 02/04/62 | 05/04/62 | LA | Unsch | 3 | |
| 11/05/62 | Ex-T | 11/05/62 | 17/05/62 | LA | L/C | 6 | |
| 08/62 | Ex-T | 08/62 | 22/08/62 | LA | L/C | 6 | Experiments W/SW/L/185 & 203 |
| 29/11/62 | BS | 04/12/62 | 21/12/62 | SW | H/C | 22 | A Transmission removed (oil seals leaking and non-ferrous metal debris in the sump); B Transmission removed (oil seals leaking); A & B Bogies removed (excessive oil leaking from the final drives) |
| 04/03/63 | Ex-T | 04/03/63 | 11/03/63 | LA | H/C | 7 | |
| 03/05/63 | Ex-T | 03/05/63 | 06/05/63 | LA | H/C | 3 | |
| 10/10/63 | LA | 10/10/63 | 29/10/63 | SW | H/C | 20 | A Bogie changed (outer final drive oil seals leaking); B Bogie changed; Boiler removed; Modifications; Bogie side control linkage replaced with hydraulic shock absorbers |
| 02/02/64 | Ex-T | 02/02/64 | 03/02/64 | LA | Unsch | 1 | The removal and change of the A end engine was commenced at Laira but D869 was subsequently called to Swindon Works for bogie defects resulting in the A end engine change actually being completed in Works |
| 04/02/64 | LA | 04/02/64 | 20/02/64 | SW | U/C | 16 | A Engine removed; A Bogie changed (suspected axle flaws); B Bogie removed |
| 02/07/64 | LA | 06/07/64 | 10/07/64 | SW | U/C | 8 | |
| 03/65 | Ex-T | 03/03/65 | 03/65 | LA | L/C | ? | A Transmission changed(metal in filters) |
| ? | Ex-T | ? | 04/66 | SW | Int | ? | |
| 01/67 | Ex-T | ? | ? | ? | ? | ? | Transmission removed (double row ball bearing on No. 3 gear wheel completely collapsed and the slipper pieces on the No. 2 shifting fork badly worn) |
| ? | Ex-T | ? | 05/69 | SW | ? | ? | |
| 01/70 | Ex-T | 01/70 | 01/70 | ? | ? | ? | Engine removed (No. 10 cylinder liner fractured) |
| ? | Ex-T | ? | 10/08/70 | SW | ? | ? | |
| | | | | | | | (No detailed data from early 1965 onwards) |
| 28/09/71 | WES | 29/09/71 | 30/09/71 | LA | - | | Withdrawn following a collision at Westbury |

D869 ZEST on 16 July 1962 at Newton Abbot with 3A31 12.45pm St Erth-Kensington milk. These trains from the far-flung reaches of the Western Region to London were an integral, and much missed, part of the railway scene. There were creameries at St Erth, Lostwithiel, Totnes, Hemyock and Chard, just to name a few, and all sent their milk by rail to London. ZEST is barely a year old but is already missing one of its headboard clips. The final five locomotives didn't have the ventilation slits in the roof over the nameplate on one side, a feature shared with D800-D812. (www.rail-online.co.uk)

869 ZEST at Bristol Temple Meads on 21 August 1971. It had worked up from Exeter in the early hours on the 6M86 23.20 Plymouth Friary-Carlisle as far as Bristol West Depot. The locomotive is marshalling vans for its next working, the 6A27 12.30 Bristol Malago Vale C.S. to Old Oak Common C.S. Only six weeks before withdrawal, ZEST still has multiple working fittings, the TOPS panel below the number and a stencilled shedcode. (www.rail-online.co.uk)

## D870 ZULU

| Lot no./Works no. | 437 / - |
|---|---|
| **Significant dates and allocations** | |
| Into traffic - Laira | 25/10/61 |
| Newton Abbot | 05/66 |
| Laira | 08/67 |
| Stored (Swindon) | 18/08/71 |
| Withdrawn (Swindon) | 28/08/71 |
| (Derby RTC) | 02/01/72 |
| (Swindon) | By 09/01/72 |
| Date cut-up | By 12/05/72 |

| **Modifications** | |
|---|---|
| **Livery and insignia changes** | |
| Green | 25/10/61 |
| OHLW flashes | 25/10/61 |
| Yellow warning panels | 06/05/63 |
| Maroon yellow warning panels | By 12/65 |
| Maroon full yellow ends | 05/68 |
| Blue full yellow ends – double insignia, sans serif , no D | By 10/69 |
| **Recorded mileage** | 922,000 |

**Works visits and depot repairs**

| Stopped | At | On Works | Off Works | At | Type | Days | Work carried out |
|---|---|---|---|---|---|---|---|
| - | - | - | 25/10/61 | SW | D/A | | Delivery inspection and acceptance |
| 06/09/62 | Ex-T | 06/09/62 | 08/09/62 | LA | L/C | 2 | |
| 03/04/63 | Ex-T | 03/04/63 | 04/04/63 | LA | H/C | 1 | |
| 08/04/63 | LA | 10/04/63 | 06/05/63 | SW | H/C | 28 | A & B Transmissions repaired; A & B Bogies repaired |
| 02/10/63 | Ex-T | 02/10/63 | 11/10/63 | LA | H/C | 9 | |
| 29/11/63 | Ex-T | 29/11/63 | 04/12/63 | LA | H/C | 5 | |
| 25/05/64 | Ex-T | 25/05/64 | 25/05/64 | LA | L/C | 1 | Unscheduled repair and tyres turned |
| 02/65 | Ex-T | 26/02/65 | 02/65 | LA | Unsch | ? | B Bogie changed (inner final drive bearing defects) |
| ? | Ex-T | 09/65 | ? | SW | ? | ? | A & B Bogies removed for intermediate repair |
| | | | | | | | (No other information for 1965-67) |
| 15/07/67 | Ex-T | ? | ? | SW | ? | ? | A & B Engines changed; A Transmission removed due to heavy oil leak from bottom on transmission (unable to detect source with bogie in position); A & B Bogies removed for repair |
| | | | | | | | (No other information for 1967-71) |
| 04/71 | Ex-T | ? | ? | ? | ? | ? | Engine removed (No. 2 liner bottom seal leaking) |
| 08/06/71 | LA | 15/06/71 | ? | SW | Class | | Withdrawn 28/08/71 (severely damaged front end, main tubes bent and deflected downwards. Sent to Derby RTC on 02/01/72 to be used in connection with experiments involving Gas-Turbine-Hydraulic propulsion. Due to collision damage it was deemed unsuitable and returned to Swindon |

*Left.* Last numbered but not the last into service, D870 ZULU trundles along the sea wall at Dawlish with a class 8 freight on 25 March 1963.It is instantly recognisable as the only member of the class with its warning horns roof mounted. This was because there was an intention to experiment with electric train heating and the horns on ZULU were moved to the roof to allow space for the fitting of ETH; the proposal did not come to fruition but D870 remained in this condition. The locomotive was a late recipient of the yellow panels but in the photograph is only two weeks away from the call to Swindon. The paintwork looks in far better condition than most when entering the Works. (www.rail-online.co.uk)

*Below.* 870 ZULU on 5 June 1971 at Exeter St David's; the multiple working equipment has been removed for the second time and blanking plates fitted. The loco has brought in the 1V11 11.00 Waterloo-Exeter, and it would work back on the 1O20 20.07 Exeter-Basingstoke. Just three days later ZULU was running light engine from Newton Abbot to Laira when it collided with the rear of the 861-hauled, 4B45 20.35 Severn Tunnel Junction-Plymouth Friary freight, near Laira Junction. ZULU was sent to Swindon for assessment but was eventually withdrawn unrepaired on 28 August. Like 824 HIGHFLYER, it almost got a reprieve when it was sent to Derby RTC in January 1972 to be used in connection with experiments involving gas turbine-hydraulic propulsion. The collision damage meant was deemed unsuitable and returned to Swindon and cut up in May. (www.rail-online.co.uk)

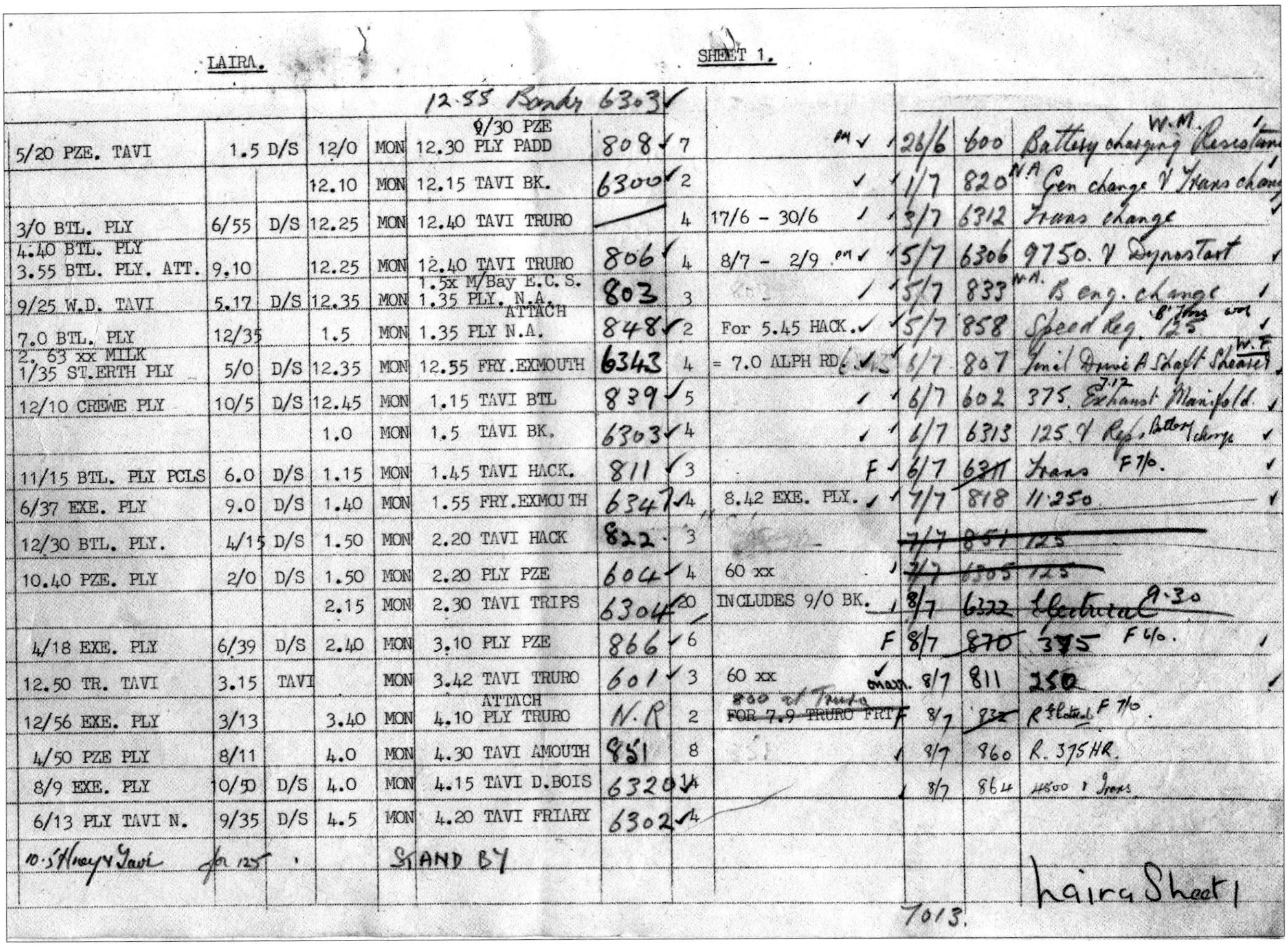

LAIRA. SHEET 1.

12.55 Bondy 6303 ✓

| | | | | | | | | | | | |
|---|---|---|---|---|---|---|---|---|---|---|---|
| 5/20 PZE. TAVI | 1.5 | D/S | 12/0 | MON | 9/30 PZE 12.30 PLY PADD | 808 ✓ | 7 | | 26/6 | 600 | W.M. Battery charging Resistance |
| | | | 12.10 | MON | 12.15 TAVI BK. | 6300 ✓ | 2 | | 1/7 | 820 | N.A. Gen change & Trans change |
| 3/0 BTL. PLY | 6/55 | D/S | 12.25 | MON | 12.40 TAVI TRURO | | 4 | 17/6 - 30/6 | 3/7 | 6312 | Trans change |
| 4.40 BTL. PLY 3.55 BTL. PLY. ATT. | 9.10 | | 12.25 | MON | 12.40 TAVI TRURO | 806 ✓ | 4 | 8/7 - 2/9 | 5/7 | 6306 | 9750. & Dynostart |
| 9/25 W.D. TAVI | 5.17 | D/S | 12.35 | MON | 1.5x M/Bay E.C.S. 1.35 PLY. N.A. | 803 | 3 | | 5/7 | 833 | N.A. B eng. change |
| 7.0 BTL. PLY | 12/35 | | 1.5 | MON | ATTACH 1.35 PLY N.A. | 848 ✓ | 2 | For 5.45 HACK. | 5/7 | 858 | Speed Reg. 125 |
| 2. 63 xx MILK 1/35 ST.ERTH PLY | 5/0 | D/S | 12.35 | MON | 12.55 FRY.EXMOUTH | 6343 | 4 | = 7.0 ALPH RD | 6/7 | 807 | W.F. Final Drive A Shaft Sheared |
| 12/10 CREWE PLY | 10/5 | D/S | 12.45 | MON | 1.15 TAVI BTL | 839 ✓ | 5 | | 6/7 | 602 | 7.12 375. Exhaust Manifold. |
| | | | 1.0 | MON | 1.5 TAVI BK. | 6303 ✓ | 4 | | 6/7 | 6313 | 125 & Rep. Battery charge |
| 11/15 BTL. PLY PCLS | 6.0 | D/S | 1.15 | MON | 1.45 TAVI HACK. | 811 ✓ | 3 | F | 6/7 | ~~6311~~ | Trans F 7/0. |
| 6/37 EXE. PLY | 9.0 | D/S | 1.40 | MON | 1.55 FRY.EXMOUTH | 6347 ✓ | 4 | 8.42 EXE. PLY. | 7/7 | 818 | 11.250 |
| 12/30 BTL. PLY. | 4/15 | D/S | 1.50 | MON | 2.20 TAVI HACK | 822 | 3 | | ~~7/7~~ | ~~851~~ | ~~125~~ |
| 10.40 PZE. PLY | 2/0 | D/S | 1.50 | MON | 2.20 PLY PZE | 604 ✓ | 4 | 60 xx | ~~7/7~~ | ~~6305~~ | ~~125~~ |
| | | | 2.15 | MON | 2.30 TAVI TRIPS | 6304 | 20 | INCLUDES 9/0 BK. | 8/7 | ~~6322~~ | ~~Electrical~~ 9.30 |
| 4/18 EXE. PLY | 6/39 | D/S | 2.40 | MON | 3.10 PLY PZE | 866 ✓ | 6 | F | 8/7 | ~~870~~ | 375 F 4/0. |
| 12.50 TR. TAVI | 3.15 | TAVI | | MON | 3.42 TAVI TRURO | 601 ✓ | 3 | 60 xx | 8/7 | 811 | 250 |
| 12/56 EXE. PLY | 3/13 | | 3.40 | MON | ATTACH 4.10 PLY TRURO | N.R | 2 | ~~FOR 7.9 TRURO FRT~~ F | 8/7 | ~~832~~ | F 7/0. |
| 4/50 PZE PLY | 8/11 | | 4.0 | MON | 4.30 TAVI AMOUTH | 851 | 8 | | 8/7 | 860 | R. 375HR. |
| 8/9 EXE. PLY | 10/50 | D/S | 4.0 | MON | 4.15 TAVI D.BOIS | 6320 ✓ | 4 | | 8/7 | 864 | 4800 & Trans |
| 6/13 PLY TAVI N. | 9/35 | D/S | 4.5 | MON | 4.20 TAVI FRIARY | 6302 ✓ | 4 | | | | |
| 10.5 H'way Tavi | for 125 | | | | STAND BY | | | | | | |

Laira Sheet 1

7013.

One of the Laira 'Day Sheets' for Monday 8 July 1963 showing the trains worked on the left-hand side and details of locomotives under repair on the right.

D603 CONQUEST on 7 April 1963 at Laira. The D600s were confined to the west of Newton Abbot from mid-1962, mainly on freight duties such as those between Fowey and St Blazey, worked by D603 during the period surveyed. (PH Groom)

# Appendices

**Appendix 1 - Workings in July 1963**
Even though the diesels had greater 'pulling ability' than their steam counterparts it could not be guaranteed at that time that steam would not substitute for a diesel, or in fact have booked work over the South Devon gradients on heavy trains. Banking engines were placed at Wellington (headcode 0J20), Aller Junction for Dainton in the down direction (0J00), Totnes for Rattery in the down direction and Dainton in the up (0J11 to 0J14) and Tavistock Junction for Hemerdon in the up direction (0J70 to 0J73). These duties were normally covered by D6300s with Newton Abbot providing locomotives for Aller and Totnes and Laira providing for Hemerdon. The Wellington banker was provided by Taunton shed and was normally the preserve of Hymeks.

Bankers on Monday 8th July 1963
Tavistock Junction: D6300 (12.15am to 2.44am), D6303 (1.05am to 5.22am), D6304 (9.0pm to 2.30am), D6305 (9.25pm to 12.25am) and D6301 (9.25pm to 2.44am).
Totnes: D6327 (1.20am to 1.50pm)
Aller: D6340 (3.05am to 11.0am), D6331 (10.0pm to 12.20am) and D6336 (10.20pm to 1.20am)
Taunton provided D7017 for Wellington (3.45am to 7.45pm).

Bankers on Tuesday 8th July 1963
Tavistock Junction: D6300 (9.25pm to 2.44am) and D6304 (9.0pm to 10.20am).
Totnes: D6336 (7.20am to 1.50pm) and D6327 (10.20pm to 10.20am)
Aller: D6327 (12.06am to 1.10pm), D6330 (1.05am to 5.10am) and D6332 (10.20pm to 1.20am).
Wellington had D7043 (6.30am to 6.30pm).

During the period under review steam stepped in on just a few occasions. In the early hours of Sunday 7th the driver who disposed of D813 at Crewe off Saturday afternoon's 1M96 inadvertently took the locomotive reverser key home with him rendering it undriveable. This was only discovered when the driver booked on to take D813 off shed for the 4.57pm Crewe to Bristol, and Black 5 4-6-0 44675 was turned out in its place.

On Monday 8th D1039 was taken off its booked train, 5C30 the 3.15pm Acton to Hackney Yard, to work the Down *Cornish Riviera Express* from the capital after D852 was failed on its up working, 1A90, with cylinder heads reported as blowing gases. The steam substitute provided by Old Oak Common to work 5C30 was 5914 RIPON HALL. The same day saw the failure of D838 at Harlescott whilst working on the North & West route on 1M68, the 8.0am Bristol-Manchester. It was failed with electrical faults and had to be assisted to Shrewsbury by 6934 BEACHAMWELL HALL. The same engine returned to the Western Region in charge of 1V98, the 3.05pm Manchester to Plymouth, as far as Bristol where D829 took over. The failure of D804 on 1M96, the 11.0am Penzance to Manchester, at Bristol meant that D841 was 'stepped up' to take over from D804 which was booked to work through to Crewe. In turn no locomotive was available for D841's booked train, the 1M99 12.45pm Penzance to Liverpool, which it should have worked forward from Bristol at 7.15pm, taking over from D1057, so Bristol turned out an (unidentified) steam loco. Some Bristol 'Peak' turns were covered by steam on the Monday too; Jubilee 4-6-0s 45690 and 45605 were recorded as covering for unavailable diesel-electrics.

On Tuesday 9th 1021 COUNTY OF MONTGOMERY was turned out to work 1V95, the 12.05pm Liverpool to Plymouth, from Crewe at 12.58pm; Counties were very unusual at Crewe but the locomotive had arrived there with the 8.54am from Shrewsbury. 5943 ELMDON HALL was removed from Monday's 4T12 at Taunton and returned west on 5C56, the 8.50pm Cardiff to Tavistock Junction at 1.55am from Taunton. 4T12 was again steam worked on the Tuesday evening, this time by 5957 HUTTON HALL. The only recorded working of steam in Cornwall on the diesel sheets was 6B77, the 6.40pm Penzance -Tavistock Junction, which enabled D825 to remain 'spare' at Penzance. The steam locomotive was not recorded. Diesel-electrics were again covered by steam with seven turns worked.

The tables which follow record the workings of all the Warships from Sunday 7th to Tuesday 9th July 1963, with additional details for Saturday 6th and Wednesday 10th to complete the picture.

**D814 DRAGON leaves Plymouth on 5 July 1963 with the 1M95 11.00am Plymouth-Manchester which it would work through to Crewe, handing over to an LMR electric for the final leg. After a stay at Crewe North the locomotive returned at 8.32pm with the 1V99 7.25pm Manchester-Bristol.** (RC Riley, www.transporttreasury.co.uk)

**Key**

**> signifies that the locomotive only worked a part of that train's journey, eg / 1C00 12.00 Paddington-Penzance > 4.0pm from Plymouth /**
**If it worked the complete journey it would show / 1C00 12.00 Paddington-Penzance /**
**...... indicates a working continued from the previous day or to the next day**
**??? part of working unknown**
**xxxx part or all of train headcode unknown**
**M/R Maintenance and/or Repairs and it is used commonly on BR record sheets. Maintenance would be planned exams etc; repairs to correct defects.**
**GWO Goods Working Only. Because the loco only had one exhauster it couldn't produce sufficient vacuum to work the brakes on long passenger trains but it could do this successfully on partially fitted or unfitted trains. There could be any number of reasons for GWO. (GWO could also be written FWO Freight Working Only)**
**LWO was Local Work Only; i.e Plymouth-Penzance and back to keep the loco handy for planned M/R;**
**OEO is One Engine Only; HFR was Home For Repair-loco to work to Home Depot for attention.**
**OJO was One Journey Only; the loco was noted as having defects but could work one trip until it could be repaired.**

Saturday 6th

D838 was Ex-Works from Swindon having been released the previous day. D848 was failed at Bristol on 1C08 because it had no boiler; although train heating was not at fault the steam was used to provide hot water to the sleeping cars. D866 was restricted to Goods Working Only because it had an exhauster isolated.

| | |
|---|---|
| D600 | Laira - M/R (*Battery charging and waiting materials; Resistances; stopped since 26 June).* |
| D601 | Truro. |
| D602 | Laira - M/R (*On A.M.; 375 hour exam and exhaust manifold cracked*). |
| D603 | St. Blazey. |
| D604 | ......./ Penzance / 3C74 10.20pm Penzance - Plymouth..... |
| | |
| D800 | / Laira / 1C45 4.30pm Paddington - Truro *'Mayflower'* > 9.11pm from Plymouth (*D1065 off*) / Truro. |
| D801 | Swindon Works (*Heavy casual repair; stopped since 11 June).* |
| D802 | / Bristol Bath Road / 1V95 12.25pm Manchester - Plymouth > 6.0pm from Bristol / 0Z33 9.50pm Plymouth - Newton Abbot / Newton Abbot / 6Z . . 11.0pm Hackney Yard - Tavistock Junction *'Engineers duty'*..... |
| D803 | Bristol Bath Road / 3A32 8.55pm Bristol - West Ealing *'Milk'*..... |
| D804 | Laira - M/R (*375 hour exam and unrecorded repairs; stopped since 5 July).* |
| D805 | ...../ Newton Abbot / 3C46 7.50pm Newton Abbot - Taunton *'Parcels'* / Taunton. |
| D806 | ...Truro / 1M82 7.10pm Penzance - Manchester > 8.31pm from Truro to Plymouth (*D809 forward*) / Laira. |
| D807 | Laira - M/R (*A end final drive shaft sheared; stopped since 6 July).* |
| D808 | ...../ Bristol Bath Road / 3C06 6.30pm Bristol West Depot - Plymouth *'Parcels'* / Laira. |
| D809 | ...../ Bristol Bath Road / 1V93 9.20am Liverpool - Plymouth > 3.0pm from Bristol / Laira / 1M82 7.10pm Penzance - Manchester > 10.32pm from Plymouth (*D806 off*) to Bristol..... |
| D810 | ...../ Old Oak Common / 3C12 10.37pm Paddington - Plymouth *'Parcels'*..... |
| D811 | ...../ Laira / 1A65 7.30am Penzance - Paddington > 10.30am from Plymouth / Old Oak Common. |
| D812 | ...../ 3C09 7.45pm Kensington - Penzance *'Milk Empties & Parcels'* to Plymouth (*D802 forward*)..... |
| D813 | ...../ Laira / 1M96 10.10am Penzance - Manchester > 1.0pm from Plymouth to Crewe / Crewe. |
| D814 | ...../ Penzance / 1M78 4.50pm Penzance - Manchester to Plymouth (*D854 forward*) / Laira / 0B60 LD Laira - Plymouth Millbay / 3M83 10.40pm Plymouth Millbay - Plymouth / 1M83 11.0pm Plymouth - Manchester Victoria to Bristol.... |
| D815 | ...../ Penzance / 1A90 8.55pm Penzance - Paddington *'Sleeper'*..... |
| D816 | ...../ Old Oak Common / 1C86 4.45pm Paddington - Taunton / Taunton. |
| D817 | ...../ Ranelagh Bridge. |
| D818 | Old Oak Common - M/R (*Low lub. oil pressure; stopped since 5 July).* |
| D819 | Newton Abbot / 2C91 10.10am Newton Abbot - Kingswear / 1A66 11.20am Kingswear - Paddington *'Torbay Express'* / Old Oak Common. |
| D820 | Laira - M/R (*Transmission change*). |
| D821 | ...../ Old Oak Common / 1C81 12.05pm Paddington - Kingswear *'Torbay Express'* / 2C76 6.30pm Kingswear - Exeter / Exeter. |
| D822 | ...../ Laira / 5B84 2.30pm Penzance - Bristol West Depot > 8.35pm from Tavistock Junction..... |
| D823 | ...../ 3B25 10.15pm Pontypool Road - Bristol *'Parcels'*..... |
| D824 | ...../ 3C04 2.40pm Wood Lane - Plymouth *'Milk empties'* / Laira. |
| D825 | ...../ Old Oak Common / 1C40 1.30pm Paddington - Penzance / Penzance. |
| D826 | ...../ Laira / 5M44 10.05pm Tavistock Junction - Crewe to Bristol..... |
| D827 | ...../ Laira / 3A42 6.0pm Penzance - Kensington Olympia *'Milk'* > 10.0pm from Plymouth to Southall in tandem from Newton Abbot to Exeter with D864..... |
| D828 | Newton Abbot - M/R (*9,000 hour exam; stopped since 3 July*). |
| D829 | Laira - M/R (*Broken spring; stopped since 6 July*). |
| D830 | Swindon Works (*Heavy casual repair; stopped since 14 May*). |
| D831 | ...../ Crewe / 1V92 9.05am Manchester - Paignton > 10.04am from Crewe / 0Z33 LD Paignton - Newton Abbot / Newton Abbot. |
| D832 | ...../ Laira / 1M99 1.15pm Penzance - Liverpool > 4.0pm from Plymouth to Bristol (*D839 forward*) / Bristol Bath Road / 1A?? (After 7.0pm) Bristol - Paddington / Old Oak Common. |
| D833 | Laira - M/R (*B engine change; stopped since 5 July).* |
| D834 | Newton Abbot - M/R (*8,250 hour exam and 1-6 exhaust joints defective; stopped since 23 June).* |
| D835 | ...../ Old Oak Common / 1B21 3.45pm Paddington - Weston-super-Mare / 0Z26 LD Weston-super-Mare - Bristol Bath Road / Bristol Bath Road. |
| D836 | Newton Abbot - M/R (*Hydrostatic fan defects; stopped since 5 July).* |
| D837 | Swindon Works (*Heavy casual repair; stopped since 3 July).* |
| D838 | Swindon. |
| D839 | ...../ Bristol Bath Road / 1M99 1.45pm Penzance - Liverpool > 7.15pm from Bristol (*D831 off*) to Crewe..... |
| D840 | ...../ Newton Abbot - M/R (*On P.M.; low lub. oil pressure*). |
| D841 | ...../ Laira / 3A31 1.35pm St. Erth - Kensington Olympia *'Milk'* > 4.55pm from Plymouth (*D6307 & D6310 off*)..... |
| D842 | Newton Abbot - M/R (*Serck defects and Fenner coupling defective; stopped since 3 July).* |
| D843 | Newton Abbot - M/R (*Two cylinder heads defective; stopped since 3 July).* |
| D844 | ...../ Old Oak Common / 1C24 7.30am Paddington - Penzance / Penzance. |
| D845 | ...Bristol Bath Road / 1C36 7.55am Carmarthen - Penzance > 12.40pm from Bristol / Penzance. |
| D846 | ...../ Old Oak Common / 1C43 2.30pm Paddington - Penzance / Penzance. |
| D847 | ...../ Penzance / 1A36 9.30pm Penzance - Paddington *'Sleeper'*..... |
| D848 | ...../ Old Oak Common / 1C08 10.30pm Paddington - Penzance *'Sleeper'* to Bristol (*D854 forward*)..... |
| D849 | ...../ Bristol Bath Road / 3C10 8.25pm Cardiff - Plymouth *'Parcels'* > 11.15pm from Bristol..... |
| D850 | Old Oak Common - M/R (*Dynostarter defective; stopped since 3 July).* |
| D851 | Laira - M/R (*On P.M.; Exhaust elbows defective*). |
| D852 | ...../ Penzance - M/R (*On P.M.; exhaust joints blowing gases*). |
| D853 | ...../ 1A11 3.0pm Paignton - Paddington / Old Oak Common. |

| | |
|---|---|
| D854 | ...../ Laira / 1M78 4.50pm Penzance - Manchester > 8.0pm from Plymouth (*D814 off*) to Bristol / Bristol Bath Road. |
| D855 | Bristol Bath Road - M/R (*Engine speed regulator defective*). |
| D856 | ...../ Newton Abbot / 1A32 4.10pm Kingswear - Paddington > 5.12pm from Newton Abbot / Old Oak Common. |
| D857 | ...../ Crewe / 1V98 3.30pm Manchester - Plymouth > 4.27pm from Crewe / Laira. |
| D858 | Laira - M/R (*125 hour exam and engine speed regulator defective; stopped since 5 July*). |
| D859 | ...../ Old Oak Common / 1B31 7.45pm Paddington - Weston-super-Mare / 0Z26 LD Weston-super-Mare - Bristol Bath Road / Bristol Bath Road. |
| D860 | ...../ Penzance / 1A78 8.30pm Penzance - Paddington..... |
| D861 | Swindon Works (*Heavy casual repair; stopped since 3 July*). |
| D862 | ...../ Laira / 1B53 6.0pm Plymouth - Bristol / Bristol Bath Road. |
| D863 | ...../ Newton Abbot - M/R (*On P.M.; Dynostarter holding down bolts loose; bedplate bolt holes worn*). |
| D864 | ...../ 3C48 9.35pm Paignton - Newton Abbot *'Parcels'* / Newton Abbot / 3A42 6.0pm Penzance - Kensington Olympia *'Milk'* > 11.17pm from Newton Abbot to Exeter in tandem with D827 / Exeter. |
| D865 | ...../ Old Oak Common / 5C12 8.30pm Paddington - Penzance to Tavistock Junction (*D804 forward*)..... |
| D866 | ...../ Bristol Bath Road (GWO) / 5C28 9.25pm Bristol West Depot - Tavistock Junction..... |
| D867 | ...../ Old Oak Common / 1C14 11.50pm Paddington - Penzance to Plymouth in tandem from Bristol with D862 (*D851 forward*)..... |
| D868 | ...../ 1A03 12.30pm Newquay - Paddington / Old Oak Common / 0B00 LD Old Oak Common - Kensington Olympia..... |
| D869 | ...../ Crewe / 1V99 7.25pm Manchester - Bristol > 8.32pm from Crewe..... |
| D870 | ...../ Old Oak Common / 1C47 6.30pm Paddington - Plymouth / Laira. |

Sunday 7th
D808 on 1C51 and 1C50 ran via Okehampton; this was so that Laira men kept up route knowledge across North Devon via the 'Southern' route in case of diversion caused by adverse weather on the sea wall. Exmouth Junction men worked the local stopping trains via Dawlish to Newton Abbot and Paignton for the same reasons. D849's train 1C50 ran via Okehampton to Plymouth. D862's train 3A13 formed the 5.15pm to Paddington worked by D856.

| | |
|---|---|
| D600 | Laira - M/R (*Battery charging and waiting materials; Resistances since 26 June*). |
| D601 | Truro. |
| D602 | Laira - M/R (*375 hour exam and exhaust manifold cracked*). |
| D603 | St. Blazey. |
| D604 | .....3C74 to Plymouth / Laira / 1C08 10.30pm Paddington - Penzance *'Sleeper'* > 5.25am from Plymouth (*D854 & D6340 off*) / Penzance / 1A81 9.55am Penzance - Paddington *'Cornish Riviera Express'* to Plymouth (*D1057 forward*) / Laira. |
| | |
| D800 | Truro. |
| D801 | Swindon Works (*Heavy casual repair*). |
| D802 | .....6Z . . Tavistock Junction *'Engineers duty'* / Laira / 3C09 7.45pm Kensington - Penzance *'Milk Empties & Parcels'* > 3.15am from Plymouth (*D812 off*) / Penzance / 1E24 10.40am Penzance - Sheffield *'Cornishman'* to Plymouth (*D835 forward*) / Laira. |
| D803 | 3A32 to West Ealing / 0Z20 LD West Ealing - Old Oak Common / Old Oak Common / 1C29 9.30am Paddington - Plymouth / Laira. |
| D804 | Laira - M/R (*375 hour exam and unrecorded repairs; released for trial run; Off A.M.*) / 5C12 8.30pm Paddington - Penzance > 6.05am from Tavistock Junction (*D865 off*) / Penzance / 1A66 4.50pm Penzance - Paddington to Plymouth assisted from Par by D6348 (*D865 & D829 forward*) / Laira. |
| D805 | Taunton / 2C97 8.40am Taunton - Bridgwater / 2X . . 9.30am Bridgwater - Paignton / 2C40 2.05pm Paignton - Newton Abbot / Newton Abbot / 1A12 11.40am Penzance - Paddington > 3.36pm from Newton Abbot to Exeter in tandem with D870 / 2C91 5.30pm Exeter - Goodrington / 2C77 7.45pm Goodrington - Taunton / Taunton. |
| D806 | Laira / 6C04 2.30am Tavistock Junction - Penzance / Penzance / 1A12 11.40am Penzance - Paddington to Plymouth (*D870 forward*) / Laira. |
| D807 | Laira - M/R (*A end final drive shaft sheared; stopped since 6 July*). |
| D808 | Laira / 1C51 10.10am Plymouth - Waterloo to Exeter / 1C50 9.00am Waterloo - Plymouth > 12.56pm from Exeter / Laira. |
| D809 | .....1M82 to Bristol / Bristol Bath Road / 1V76 9.0pm Manchester - Plymouth > 2.55am from Bristol in tandem with D835 / Laira / 0A90 11.35pm Laira - Plymouth North Road..... |
| D810 | .....3C12 to Plymouth / Laira / 1N68 12.45am Plymouth - Bradford to Bristol (*D19 forward*) / Bristol Bath Road. |
| D811 | Old Oak Common / 1C33 11.30am Paddington - Penzance to Plymouth assisted from Newton Abbot by D6340 (*D854 forward*) / Laira. |
| D812 | Laira / 2C90 9.55am Plymouth - Penzance / Penzance / 1A86 9.30pm Penzance - Paddington to Plymouth (*D808 forward*) / Laira. |
| D813 | Crewe. |
| D814 | .....1M83 to Bristol / Bristol Bath Road / 1V73 1.40am Crewe - Plymouth > 7.0am from Bristol in tandem to Newton Abbot with D822 / Newton Abbot / 3A49 3.30pm Newton Abbot - Kingswear / 2B96 5.15pm Kingswear - Bristol / Bristol Bath Road. |
| D815 | .....1A90 to Paddington / Old Oak Common / 0A58 LD Old Oak Common - Ranelagh Bridge / Ranelagh Bridge / 1C04 10.20pm Paddington - Penzance *'Postal'*...... |
| D816 | Taunton / 1A66 10.35am Taunton - Paddington to Bristol (*D7074 forward*) / 1A74 1.35pm Bristol - Paddington / Old Oak Common. |
| D817 | Ranelagh Bridge / 1C43 4.30pm Paddington - Plymouth / Laira. |
| D818 | Old Oak Common - M/R (*Low lub. oil pressure*) / 0Z36 LD Old Oak Common - Laira / Laira - M/R (*11,250 hour exam*). |
| D819 | Old Oak Common / 1C69 9.15am Paddington - Taunton in tandem from Swindon to Bristol with D856 / Taunton / 1A25 5.20pm Taunton - Paddington / Old Oak Common. |
| D820 | Laira - M/R (*Transmission change*). |
| D821 | Exeter / 3A32 4.30pm Exeter - Kensington Olympia *'Milk'*..... |
| D822 | .....5B84 to Bristol West Depot / Bristol Bath Road / 1V73 1.40am Crewe - Plymouth > 7.0am from Bristol in tandem to Newton Abbot with D814 / Laira. |
| D823 | .....3B25 to Bristol / Bristol Bath Road / 1M91 8.45am Plymouth - Liverpool > 12.45pm from Bristol (*D862 off*) to Crewe / Crewe. |
| D824 | Laira / 0B60 LD Laira - Plymouth Millbay / 3A96 1.55am Plymouth Millbay - Old Oak Common ECS / Old Oak Common / 0C05 6.05pm Old Oak Common - Kensington Olympia / 3C05 7.05pm Kensington Olympia - Plymouth *'Milk Empties & Parcels'*..... |
| D825 | Penzance / 3C18 11.50am Penzance - Paddington *'Perishables'* / Old Oak Common. |
| D826 | .....5M44 to Bristol / Bristol Bath Road / 1V33 8.40am Sheffield - Penzance *'Cornishman'* > 1.30pm from Bristol (*D40 off*) / Penzance. |
| D827 | .....3A42 to Southall / 0Z20 LD Southall - Old Oak Common / Old Oak Common / 1B10 11.15am Paddington - Weston-super-Mare / 1A26 4.40pm Weston-super-Mare - Paddington / Ranelagh Bridge / 1C14 11.50pm Paddington - Penzance to Bristol (*D814 forward*)..... |
| D828 | Newton Abbot - M/R (*9,000 hour exam*). |
| D829 | Laira - M/R (*Broken spring; Off P.M.*) / 1A66 4.50pm Penzance - Paddington > 8.10pm from Plymouth (*D6348 & D804 off*) to Newton Abbot in tandem with D865 / Newton Abbot. |
| D830 | Swindon Works (*Heavy casual repair*). |
| D831 | Newton Abbot / 2C91 9.30am Newton Abbot - Kingswear / 1A62 11.40am Kingswear - Paddington *'Torbay Express'* / Ranelagh Bridge / 1B31 7.30pm Paddington - Weston-super-Mare / 0Z26 LD Weston-super-Mare - Bristol Bath Road / Bristol Bath Road. |
| D832 | Old Oak Common / 3B05 2.20pm Paddington - Swindon *'Parcels'* / Swindon. |
| D833 | Laira - M/R (*B engine change*). |
| D834 | Newton Abbot - M/R (*8,250 hour exam and 1-6 exhaust joints defective*). |
| D835 | Bristol Bath Road / 1V76 9.0pm Manchester - Plymouth > 2.55am from Bristol in tandem with D809 / Laira / 1E24 10.40am Penzance - Sheffield *'Cornishman'* > 1.40pm from Plymouth (*D802 off*) to Bristol (*D83 forward*) / Bristol Bath Road. |

D815 DRUID on 2 March 1963 at Old Oak Common Junction with the 3C05 2.40pm Wood Lane-Plymouth milk empties. Around a fifth of Warship duties at this time were made up of parcels, perishables and milk trains such as this. (A Cottrell, www.transporttreasury.co.uk)

D822 HERCULES in Sonning Cutting on 31 May 1963 with the 4A60 5.30am Plymouth Tavistock Junction-Old Oak Common fitted freight. It returned west on 1B28, the 6.45pm Paddington-Weston-super-Mare, and then took the 2B96 10.45pm Weston-Bristol before retiring to Bristol Bath Road depot. (PH Groom)

| D836 | Newton Abbot - M/R (*Hydrostatic fan defects*). |
|---|---|
| D837 | Swindon Works (*Heavy casual repair*). |
| D838 | Swindon / 0Z26 LD Swindon - Bristol Bath Road / Bristol Bath Road. |
| D839 | .....1M99 to Crewe / Crewe / 1V93 11.00am Liverpool - Plymouth > 12.10pm from Crewe / Laira. |
| D840 | Newton Abbot - M/R (*Low lub. oil pressure; Off A.M.*) / 3C29 7.50am Newton Abbot - Paignton *'Parcels'* / 1N78 10.10am Paignton - Newcastle to Bristol (*D159 forward*) / Bristol Bath Road. |
| D841 | .....3A31 to Kensington Olympia / 0Z20 LD Kensington Olympia - Old Oak Common / Old Oak Common / 1C40 1.30pm Paddington - Penzance / Penzance. |
| D842 | Newton Abbot - M/R (*Serck defects and Fenner coupling defective*). |
| D843 | Newton Abbot - M/R (*Two cylinder heads defective; Off P.M.*). |
| D844 | Penzance / 2C24 6.40pm Penzance - Plymouth / Laira. |
| D845 | Penzance - M/R (*On P.M.; brakes adjusted*). |
| D846 | Penzance / 3A31 2.38pm Penzance - Wood Lane *'Milk'* assisted from Plymouth to Newton Abbot by D6340..... |
| D847 | .....1A36 to Paddington / Old Oak Common. |
| D848 | .....1C08 to Bristol / Bristol Bath Road (*Available N B*) / 3C04 7.20am Bristol - Plymouth *'Fish & Parcels'* / Laira. |
| D849 | .....3C10 to Plymouth / Laira / 3C76 11.50am Plymouth - Exeter / Exeter / 1C50 12.27pm Portsmouth - Plymouth > 4.26pm from Exeter / Laira. |
| D850 | Old Oak Common - M/R (*Dynostarter defective*). |
| D851 | Laira - M/R (*Exhaust elbows defective; Off A.M.*) / 1C14 11.50pm Paddington - Penzance > 7.35am from Plymouth (*D867 & D862 off*) / Penzance / 1A38 1.40pm Penzance - Paddington to Plymouth (*D857 forward*) / Laira. |
| D852 | Penzance - M/R (*Exhaust joints blowing gases; Off P.M.*) / 1A90 8.55pm Penzance - Paddington *'Sleeper'* in tandem from Plymouth to Newton Abbot with D809 ..... |
| D853 | Old Oak Common - M/R (*On A.M.; unrecorded repairs; Off P.M.*). |
| D854 | Bristol Bath Road / 1C08 10.30pm Paddington - Penzance *'Sleeper'* > 1.55am from Bristol (*D848 off*) to Plymouth assisted from Newton Abbot by D6320 (*D604 forward*) / Laira / 1C33 11.30am Paddington - Penzance > 4.40pm from Plymouth (*D811 & D6340 off*) / Penzance. |
| D855 | Bristol Bath Road - M/R (*Engine speed regulator defective*). |
| D856 | Old Oak Common / 3B02 3.30am Paddington - Swindon *'Milk empties & Parcels'* / Swindon / 1C69 9.15am Paddington - Taunton > 11.13am from Swindon to Bristol in tandem with D819 / Bristol Bath Road / 1A13 5.15pm Bristol - Paddington / Ranelagh Bridge / 0Z20 LD Ranelagh Bridge - Old Oak Common / Old Oak Common. |
| D857 | Laira / 1A38 1.40pm Penzance - Paddington > 4.30pm from Plymouth (*D851 off*) / Old Oak Common. |
| D858 | Laira - M/R (*125 hour exam and engine speed regulator defective*). |
| D859 | Bristol Bath Road / 0A20 6.30am Bristol Bath Road - Weston-super-Mare / 1A20 8.0am Weston-super-Mare - Paddington / Old Oak Common / 1C92 5.30pm Paddington - Taunton / Taunton. |
| D860 | .....1A78 to Paddington / Old Oak Common / 1B15 12.15pm Paddington - Weston-super-Mare / 1A47 6.30pm Weston-super-Mare - Paddington / Old Oak Common. |
| D861 | Swindon Works (*Heavy casual repair*). |
| D862 | Bristol Bath Road / 1C14 11.50pm Paddington – Penzance > 3.15am from Bristol to Plymouth in tandem with D867 (*D851 forward*) / Laira / 1M91 8.45am Plymouth Liverpool to Bristol (*D823 forward*) / Bristol Bath Road / 0A13 LD Bristol Bath Road - Malago Vale C.S. / 3A13 4.55pm Malago Vale C.S. - Bristol / 1M99 6.45pm Bristol - Liverpool to Crewe / Crewe. |
| D863 | Newton Abbot - M/R (*Dynostarter holding down bolts loose; bedplate bolt holes worn*). |
| D864 | Exeter / 3C07 4.05am Paddington - Plymouth *'Parcels'* > 12.55am from Exeter (*D7024 off*) / Laira / 2C25 8.30am Penzance - Newton Abbot > 11.30am from Plymouth (*D870 off*) / Newton Abbot / 0A61 LD Newton Abbot - Paignton / 1A32 4.20pm Paignton - Paddington / Ranelagh Bridge / 1C08 10.30pm Paddington - Penzance *'Sleeper'*..... |
| D865 | .....5C12 to Tavistock Junction / Laira - M/R (*On A.M.; oil leaks; Off P.M.*) / 1A66 4.50pm Penzance - Paddington > 8.10pm from Plymouth (*D6348 & D804 off*) in tandem to Newton Abbot with D829..... |
| D866 | .....5C28 to Tavistock Junction / Laira - M/R (*On A.M.; exhauster defect; Off A.M.*) / 8B57 12.15pm Tavistock Junction - Penzance Goods / Penzance / 1A69 7.0pm Penzance - Paddington *'Postal'* to Plymouth (*D1039 forward*) / Laira. |
| D867 | .....1C14 to Plymouth / Laira / 1C30 10.30am Paddington - Penzance *'Cornish Riviera Express'* > 3.30pm from Plymouth (*D1039 & D6315 off*) / Penzance. |
| D868 | .....1B00 12.15am Kensington Olympia - Bristol *'News'* / Bristol Bath Road / 1V23 9.30pm Newcastle - Exeter > 5.50am from Bristol (*D186 off*) / Exeter / 1N36 9.0pm Exeter - Newcastle to Bristol (*D186 forward*) / Bristol Bath Road. |
| D869 | .....1V99 to Bristol / Bristol Bath Road / 1C64 8.30am Cardiff - Paignton > 10.15am from Bristol (*D7017 off*) / 2B46 5.10pm Paignton - Bristol / Bristol Bath Road. |
| D870 | Laira / 1C03 11.15pm Paddington - Penzance *'News'* > 3.43am from Plymouth (*D1057 off*) / 2C25 8.30am Penzance - Newton Abbot to Plymouth (*D864 forward*) / Laira / 1A12 11.40am Penzance - Paddington > 2.30pm from Plymouth (*D806 off*) in tandem from Newton Abbot to Exeter with D805 / Ranelagh Bridge / 1C05 9.45pm Paddington - Plymouth..... |

Monday 8th
D802 worked freight trains in Cornwall on this day covering a D600 diagram. D804 failed passing Laira Signal Box on 1M96 but was able to continue after attention. Although booked to work through to Crewe, it was removed at Bristol in favour of D841. 4C07 became 5C07 from Truro. D808 worked 1C80 after D869 was failed with electrical faults. D813 was failed for 2B96, the 11.0am from Bristol to Weston and Stand-by loco D816 was used to cover the diagram. D826 was ordered to go to Newton Abbot as it was overdue its 375 hour exam. D827's train 4A20 became 5A09 from Taunton. D844's train 3C46 also conveyed vehicles forming 2C76, the 7.35pm Newton Abbot to Exeter. 2C76 should have run from Kingswear at 6.50pm but instead started at Newton Abbot and ran attached to 3C46. D860 was failed for 3A47 and D870 was used instead.

| D600 | Laira - M/R (*Battery charging and waiting materials; Resistances since 26 June*). |
|---|---|
| D601 | Truro / 0Z36 12.50am Truro - Laira / Laira / 4C07 3.42am Tavistock Junction - Penzance to Truro (*D806 forward*) / 5B77 7.25am Truro - Tavistock Junction / 5B81 12.05pm Tavistock Junction - Truro / Truro / 5A17 2.50pm Penzance - Paddington > 6.15pm from Truro (*D6309 off*) to Tavistock Junction (*D866 forward*) / 5B81 9.20pm Tavistock Junction - Truro / Truro. |
| D602 | Laira - M/R (*375 hour exam and exhaust manifold cracked*). |
| D603 | St. Blazey / 5B28 6.45am St. Blazey - Fowey / 5C13 8.10am St Blazey - Burngullow / 5B77 9.40am Burngullow - St Blazey / 5B28 10.35am St. Blazey - Fowey / 5B77 11.10am Fowey - St Blazey / 5B28 11.55am St Blazey - Fowey / 5B77 12.30pm Fowey - St Blazey / 5B78 1.30pm St. Blazey - Tavistock Junction / 5B70 7.30pm Tavistock Junction - St. Blazey / St. Blazey. |
| D604 | Laira / 3C08 2.20am Plymouth - Penzance *'Mails & Milk empties'* / Penzance / 2C74 8.0am Penzance - Plymouth / 3C15 1.55am Swindon - Penzance *'Parcels'* > 11.30am from Plymouth (*D832 off*) / Penzance / 1M78 4.50pm Penzance - Manchester to Plymouth (*D831 & D6340 forward*) / Laira. |
| | |
| D800 | Truro / 1A41 6.45am Truro - Paddington *'Mayflower'* to Plymouth (*D812 forward*) / Laira / 1A81 10.10am Penzance - Paddington *'Cornish Riviera Express'* > 12.30pm from Plymouth (*D1057 off*) / Old Oak Common / 1C04 10.20pm Paddington - Penzance *'Postal'* in tandem from Plymouth with D816 ..... |
| D801 | Swindon Works (*Heavy casual repair*). |
| D802 | Laira / 5B57 8.05am Tavistock Junction - Penzance to Truro (*D6309 forward*) / 5B77 11.45am Truro - Tavistock Junction / 5B81 3.50pm Tavistock Junction - Truro / 5B78 5.0pm Penzance - Bristol West Depot > 8.07pm from Truro (*D6310 off*) to Tavistock Junction (*D7013 forward*) / Laira. |
| D803 | Laira / 0B60 12.40am Laira - Plymouth Millbay / 3C67 1.05am Plymouth Millbay - Plymouth / 3C75 1.35am Plymouth - Newton Abbot in tandem with D848 / Newton Abbot / 6C12 2.05am Bristol West Depot - Tavistock Junction > 7.30am from Hackney Yard (*D7021 off*) / Laira / 1A12 11.30am Penzance - Paddington *'Royal Duchy'* > 2.30pm from Plymouth (*D866 off*) / Old Oak Common / 3C12 10.0pm Paddington - Penzance *'Parcels'* to Plymouth (*D856 forward*)..... |
| D804 | Laira - M/R (*On A.M.; trial run OK; Off A.M.*) / 1M96 11.00am Penzance - Manchester > 2.0pm from Plymouth (*D806 off*) to Bristol (*D841 forward*) / Bristol Bath Road - M/R (*On P.M.; transmission defects; to go to Laira for exams*). |
| D805 | Taunton / 1A30 8.53am Taunton - Paddington to Bristol (*D855 forward*) / Bristol Bath Road / 6C21 1.30pm Bristol West Depot - Exeter Riverside Yard / Exeter / 0V17 LD Exeter - Exmouth Junction / 4V17 9.25pm Exmouth Junction - Avonmouth..... |
| D806 | Laira / 6B57 12.40am Tavistock Junction - Truro / Truro / 5C07 3.42am Tavistock Junction - Penzance > 7.09am from Truro (*D601 off*) / Penzance / 1M96 |

| | |
|---|---|
| | 11.00am Penzance - Manchester to Plymouth (*D804 forward*) / 0C54 2.0pm Plymouth - Par / 2C54 3.50pm Par - Newquay / 2C24 5.55pm Newquay - Plymouth / Laira / 4M44 10.05pm Tavistock Junction - Crewe to Bristol..... |
| D807 | Laira - M/R (*A end final drive shaft sheared*). |
| D808 | Laira / 1A86 9.30pm Penzance - Paddington > 12.30pm from Plymouth (*D812 off*) / Ranelagh Bridge / 1C80 11.45am Paddington - Taunton / 1A33 4.47pm Taunton - Paddington to Swindon / 2B79 7.55pm Swindon - Purton / 3B79 8.30pm Purton - Swindon / 3A27 3.50pm Whitland - Kensington *'Milk'* > 10.05pm from Swindon (*D7035 off*)..... |
| D809 | ..... 1A90 8.55pm Penzance - Paddington *'Sleeper'* > 12.0am from Plymouth to Newton Abbot in tandem with D852 / Newton Abbot / 6Z . . 3.25am Hackney Yard - Tavistock Junction *'Engineers duty'* / 0B60 LD Tavistock Junction - Plymouth Millbay / 3M91 7.30am Plymouth Millbay - Plymouth / 1M91 8.0am Plymouth - Crewe / Crewe / ???? 6.42pm Crewe - Pontypool Road *'Parcels'*..... |
| D810 | Bristol Bath Road / 1M78 12.10am Bristol - Crewe / Crewe / 1V95 12.05pm Manchester - Plymouth > 12.58pm from Crewe / Laira. |
| D811 | Laira / 6B64 1.45am Tavistock Junction - Swindon to Hackney Yard (*D7050 forward*) / Newton Abbot / 5C14 9.10pm Oxley - Tavistock Junction > 10.05am from Hackney Yard / Laira - M/R (*On P.M.; 250 hour exam; Off P.M.*) / 0M63 11.35pm Laira - Tavistock Junction..... |
| D812 | Laira / 1A41 6.45am Truro - Paddington *'Mayflower'* > 8.30am from Plymouth (*D800 off*) / Ranelagh Bridge / 1C43 2.30pm Paddington - Penzance assisted from Newton Abbot to Plymouth by D6340 / Penzance. |
| D813 | Crewe / 1V86 12.45am Manchester - Penzance > 2.0am from Crewe to Bristol (*D831 forward*) / Bristol Bath Road - M/R (*On A.M; A dynostarter cardan shaft bolts defective; Off P.M.*) / 5C33 10.50pm Bristol West Depot - Tavistock Junction..... |
| D814 | Bristol Bath Road / 1C14 11.50pm Paddington - Penzance > 3.12am from Bristol (*D827 off*) to Plymouth (*D817 forward*) / Laira / 1A67 9.20am Falmouth - Paddington > 11.30am from Plymouth (*D6341 off*) / Ranelagh Bridge / 1C47 6.30pm Paddington - Plymouth / Laira. |
| D815 | .....1C04 to Penzance / Penzance / 3A38 2.40pm Penzance - Paddington *'Perishables'*..... |
| D816 | Old Oak Common / 0B17 2.27am Old Oak Common - Acton / 5B17 2.55am Acton - Bristol Kingsland Road / Bristol Bath Road (*Stand-by*) / 2B96 11.00am Bristol - Weston-super-Mare / Weston-super-Mare station Shunts as required / 2B96 5.15pm Weston-super-Mare - Bristol / 0C25 6.13pm Bristol - Avonmouth / 4C25 7.50pm Avonmouth - Tavistock Junction..... |
| D817 | Laira / 1C14 11.50pm Paddington - Penzance > 7.45am from Plymouth (*D814 off*) / Penzance / 1A33 1.50pm Penzance - Paddington to Plymouth (*D868 forward*) / 1B53 6.0pm Plymouth - Bristol / Bristol Bath Road / 3C10 8.25pm Cardiff - Plymouth *'Parcels'* > 11.06pm from Bristol..... |
| D818 | Laira - M/R (*11,250 hour exam*). |
| D819 | Old Oak Common / 1B00 2.15am Paddington - Bristol *'News'* / Bristol Bath Road / 2B96 9.35am Bristol - Weston-super-Mare / 1A50 11.40am Weston-super-Mare - Paddington to Swindon / Swindon / 3C07 1.30pm Paddington - Plymouth *'Parcels'* > 5.30pm from Swindon (*D7025 off*) / Laira. |
| D820 | Laira - M/R (*Transmission change*). |
| D821 | .....3A32 to Kensington Olympia / 0Z20 LD Kensington Olympia - Old Oak Common / Old Oak Common - M/R (*On A.M.; broken spring; Off P.M.*). |
| D822 | Laira / 6T70 2.20am Tavistock Junction - Rogerstone to Hackney Yard (*D7041 forward*) / Newton Abbot / 2C90 12.31pm Newton Abbot - Paignton / 2C90 1.20pm Paignton - Newton Abbot / Newton Abbot / 2C20 4.17pm Newton Abbot - Penzance / 1A86 9.30pm Penzance - Paddington *'Sleeper'*..... |
| D823 | Crewe - M/R (*On A.M.; B engine failed; to go light to Newton Abbot*) / 0V00 LD Crewe - Newton Abbot / Newton Abbot. |
| D824 | .....3C05 to Plymouth / Laira / 2C75 7.20am Plymouth - Newton Abbot / 2C91 7.55am Exeter - Kingswear > 8.48am from Newton Abbot / 1A62 10.50am Kingswear - Paddington *'Torbay Express'* / Ranelagh Bridge / 1C86 4.45pm Paddington - Taunton / 3A47 6.15pm Plymouth - Kensington Olympia *'Perishables'* > 9.25pm from Taunton to Bristol in tandem with D870 / Bristol Bath Road. |
| D825 | Old Oak Common / 1C33 11.30am Paddington - Falmouth to Plymouth (*D6341 forward*) / Laira / 3A42 6.0pm Penzance - Kensington Olympia *'Milk'* > 10.0pm from Plymouth (*D1039 off*) to Southall..... |
| D826 | Penzance / 2C25 7.30am Penzance - Newton Abbot / Newton Abbot - M/R (*On P.M.; 375 hour exam*). |
| D827 | .....1C14 to Bristol / Bristol Bath Road / 3C16 9.0am Bristol - Plymouth *'Parcels'* to Newton Abbot (*Train terminated*) / Newton Abbot / 4A20 6.50pm Newton Abbot - Acton..... |
| D828 | Newton Abbot - M/R (*9,000 hour exam*). |
| D829 | Newton Abbot / 6C10 1.30am Hackney Yard - Tavistock Junction / Laira / 2C70 6.45am Plymouth - Penzance / 1M06 11.35am Penzance - Crewe *'Perishables'* to Bristol / Bristol Bath Road / 1V98 3.05pm Manchester - Plymouth > 9.05pm from Bristol (*6934 off*) / Laira. |
| D830 | Swindon Works (*Heavy casual repair*). |
| D831 | Bristol Bath Road / 1V86 12.45am Manchester - Penzance > 7.15am from Bristol (*D813 off*) / Penzance / 2C24 4.20am Penzance - Plymouth / Laira / 1M78 4.50pm Penzance - Crewe > 8.0pm from Plymouth (*D604 off*) in tandem to Newton Abbot with D6340..... |
| D832 | Swindon / 3C15 1.55am Swindon - Plymouth *'Parcels'* / Laira - M/R (*On A.M.; Exams; Off P.M.*) / 3A36 3.40pm Penzance - Paddington *'Perishables'* > 7.25pm from Plymouth (*D864 off*).... |
| D833 | Laira - M/R (*B engine change*). |
| D834 | Newton Abbot - M/R (*8,250 hour exam and 1-6 exhaust joints defective*). |
| D835 | Bristol Bath Road / 0A20 6.35am Bristol Bath Road - Weston-super-Mare in tandem with D7042 / 1A20 8.30am Weston-super-Mare - Paddington / Ranelagh Bridge / 1B17 1.45pm Paddington - Weston-super-Mare / 2B96 5.55pm Weston-super-Mare - Bristol / Bristol Bath Road / 5C32 9.45pm Bristol West Depot - Penzance to Truro (*D6310 forward*)..... |
| D836 | Newton Abbot - M/R (*Hydrostatic fan defects; Off P.M.*) |
| D837 | Swindon Works (*Heavy casual repair*). |
| D838 | Bristol Bath Road / 1M68 8.0am Bristol - Manchester to Harlescott (*Failed; assisted to Shrewsbury by steam 6934*) / Shrewsbury (*Failed; electrical faults*). |
| D839 | Laira / 4M47 1.15am Tavistock Junction - Crewe to Bristol / Bristol Bath Road / 3A15 11.45am Dr. Days Junction - West Ealing *'Parcels'* / 0Z20 LD West Ealing - Old Oak Common / Old Oak Common / 1C08 10.30pm Paddington - Penzance *'Sleeper'* to Bristol (*D824 forward*)..... |
| D840 | Bristol Bath Road / 2B96 7.20am Bristol - Weston-super-Mare / 1A42 10.35am Weston-super-Mare - Paddington / Ranelagh Bridge / 1B21 3.45pm Paddington - Weston-super-Mare / 0Z26 LD Weston-super-Mare - Bristol Bath Road / Bristol Bath Road / 5A06 9.40pm Bristol - Acton..... |
| D841 | Penzance / 1E24 10.30am Penzance - Sheffield *'Cornishman'* to Bristol (*D30 forward*) / Bristol Bath Road / 1M96 11.0am Penzance - Manchester > 5.25pm from Bristol (*D804 off*) to Crewe / Crewe. |
| D842 | Newton Abbot - M/R (*Serck defects and Fenner coupling defective*). |
| D843 | Newton Abbot / 2C91 6.25am Newton Abbot - Goodrington / 1N37 9.30am Paignton - Bradford *'Devonian'* to Bristol (*D41 forward*) / Bristol Bath Road / 1V39 10.38am Bradford - Paignton *'Devonian'* > 4.05am from Bristol (*D31 off*) / 0Z33 7.35pm Paignton - Newton Abbot / Newton Abbot / 5C26 3.45pm Stoke Gifford Yard - Tavistock Junction > 10.05pm from Hackney Yard (*D7002 off*)..... |
| D844 | Laira / 2C90 9.10am Plymouth - Penzance / 1M99 12.45pm Penzance - Liverpool to Plymouth (*D1057 forward*) / Laira / 3A47 6.15pm Plymouth - Kensington Olympia *'Perishables'* to Newton Abbot in tandem with D870 / 3C46 7.40pm Newton Abbot - Taunton / Taunton / 5A14 11.30pm Taunton - Acton..... |
| D845 | Penzance - M/R (*Brakes adjusted; Off P.M.*) / 1A69 7.0pm Penzance - Paddington *'Postal'*..... |
| D846 | .....3A31 to Wood Lane / 0Z20 LD Wood Lane - Old Oak Common / Old Oak Common / 1B02 7.45am Paddington - Weston-super-Mare / 1A64 12.35pm Weston-super-Mare - Paddington / Old Oak Common / 1B28 6.45pm Paddington - Weston-super-Mare / 2B96 10.45pm Weston-super-Mare - Bristol / Bristol Bath Road. |
| D847 | Old Oak Common / 1C47 4.15pm Paddington - Plymouth / Laira. |
| D848 | Laira / 3C75 1.35am Plymouth - Newton Abbot in tandem with D803 / Newton Abbot / 8C27 5.45am Hackney Yard - Tavistock Junction / Laira / 1M95 11.00am Plymouth - Manchester to Crewe / Crewe / 1V99 7.25pm Manchester - Bristol > 8.32pm from Crewe..... |
| D849 | Laira / 4A60 5.30am Tavistock Junction - Old Oak Common / Old Oak Common - M/R (*On P.M.; unrecorded repairs; Off P.M.*) / 1C45 4.30pm Paddington - Truro *'Mayflower'* / Truro. |
| D850 | Old Oak Common - M/R (*Dynostarter defective; to go light diesel to Newton Abbot*). |
| D851 | Laira / 4B42 4.30am Tavistock Junction - Avonmouth / 0Z26 LD Avonmouth - Bristol Bath Road / Bristol Bath Road / 1A98 4.15pm Bristol - Paddington *'Bristolian'* / Ranelagh Bridge / 1B31 7.45pm Paddington - Weston-super-Mare / 0Z26 LD Weston-super-Mare - Bristol Bath Road / Bristol Bath Road. |
| D852 | .....1A90 to Paddington / Old Oak Common - M/R (*On A.M.; cylinder joints blowing; Off A.M.*) / 0C05 LD Old Oak Common - Wood Lane / 3C05 2.40pm Wood Lane - Plymouth *'Milk empties'* / Laira. |
| D853 | Old Oak Common / 1B04 8.45am Paddington - Bristol *'Bristolian'* / Bristol Bath Road / 1V33 8.10am Sheffield - Penzance *'Cornishman'* > 12.05pm from Bristol (*D40 off*) / 6B77 6.40pm Penzance - Tavistock Junction / Laira. |
| D854 | Penzance / 0B72 LD Penzance - St. Erth / 3A31 12.45pm St. Erth - Wood Lane *'Milk'*..... |

| | |
|---|---|
| D855 | Bristol Bath Road - M/R (*Engine speed regulator defective; Off A.M.*) / 1A30 8.53am Taunton - Paddington > 10.15am from Bristol (*D805 off*) / Ranelagh Bridge / 1B19 2.45pm Paddington - Weston-super-Mare / 1A50 6.58pm Weston-super-Mare - Paddington to Bristol (*D1057 forward*) / Bristol Bath Road / 0Z23 10.30pm Bristol - Swindon / Swindon. |
| D856 | Old Oak Common / 1B08 9.45am Paddington - Weston-super-Mare / 1A74 1.40pm Weston-super-Mare - Paddington / Ranelagh Bridge / 0C09 LD Ranelagh Bridge - Kensington Olympia / 3C09 7.45pm Kensington Olympia - Penzance *'Milk empties & Parcels'* to Plymouth (*D866 forward*)..... |
| D857 | Old Oak Common / 1B10 10.45am Paddington - Weston-super-Mare / 1A14 4.33pm Weston-super-Mare - Paddington / Old Oak Common / 3C15 10.40pm Paddington - Penzance *'Parcels'* to Plymouth (*D604 forward*)..... |
| D858 | Laira - M/R (*125 hour exam and engine speed regulator defective*). |
| D859 | Taunton / 2C26 3.30am Taunton - Newton Abbot *'News & Parcels'* / Newton Abbot / 6C16 12.25pm Hackney Yard - Tavistock Junction / Laira / 2C75 5.30pm Plymouth - Newton Abbot / Newton Abbot. |
| D860 | Old Oak Common / 1C21 5.30am Paddington - Plymouth / Laira - M/R (*On P.M.; 375 hour exam*). |
| D861 | Swindon Works (*Heavy casual repair*). |
| D862 | Crewe / 1V93 9.05am Liverpool - Plymouth > 10.07am from Crewe / Laira - M/R (*On P.M.; unrecorded repairs*). |
| D863 | Newton Abbot - M/R (*Dynostarter holding down bolts loose; bedplate bolt holes worn*). |
| D864 | .....1C08 to Penzance / Penzance / 3A36 3.40pm Penzance - Paddington *'Perishables'* to Plymouth (*D832 forward*) / Laira - M/R (*On P.M.; 4,500 hour exam and transmission defect*). |
| D865 | .....1A66 to Paddington / Old Oak Common / 1C26 8.30am Paddington - Penzance *'Royal Duchy'* / Penzance. |
| D866 | Laira / 3C09 3.10am Plymouth - Penzance *'Milk empties & Parcels'* / Penzance / 1A12 11.30am Penzance - Paddington *'Royal Duchy'* to Plymouth (*D803 forward*) / Laira / 2C70 3.46pm Plymouth - Penzance / 1A90 8.55pm Penzance - Paddington *'Sleeper'* to Plymouth (*D1039 forward*) / Laira. |
| D867 | Penzance / 2C74 1.55pm Penzance - Plymouth / Laira / 4A17 2.50pm Penzance - Paddington > 9.10pm from Tavistock Junction (*D601 off*)..... |
| D868 | Bristol Bath Road / 1C15 6.25am Bristol - Plymouth / Laira - M/R (*On P.M.; unrecorded repairs; Off P.M.*) / 1A33 1.50pm Penzance - Paddington > 4.30pm from Plymouth (*D817 off*) / Ranelagh Bridge / 1C14 11.50pm Paddington - Penzance to Bristol (*D851 forward*)..... |
| D869 | Bristol Bath Road / 0A00 4.20am Bristol Bath Road - Weston-super-Mare / 1A00 6.31am Weston-super-Mare - Paddington / Old Oak Common - M/R (*On A.M.; earth faults; Off P.M.*) / 5C12 8.30pm Paddington - Penzance Goods to Newton Abbot (*Train terminated*)..... |
| D870 | .....1C05 to Plymouth / Laira - M/R (*On A.M.; 375 hour exam; Off P.M.*) / 3A47 6.15pm Plymouth - Kensington Olympia *'Perishables'* in tandem with D844 to Newton Abbot and in tandem from Taunton to Bristol with D824..... |

Tuesday 9th

D601 working 4C07 started at Tavistock Junction today because the train from Paddington was terminated at Newton Abbot, hauled by D869. D821 was used on 1B08 to cover for D867 which, in turn, had been used on 1B10 to cover for D845 which was failed at Old Oak Common. 1E24 forward from Bristol should have been worked by D26 but it had not arrived in time coming in late on the 7.50am Worcester to Bristol. Derby Control were informed of the change and an official 'complaint' was recorded from Derby by the Control Officer at Bristol. D838 was to have gone light engine to Newton Abbot but to save a path, and drivers, the decision was made to work the locomotive home in multiple on a train. D844 failed at Newton Abbot on 1C43 and was replaced by D1008 which was heading light diesel from Old Oak Common. Having previously failed D1008 was already running on one engine so D6340 was added for extra assistance. 2C74 from Penzance also conveyed vehicles for 3A47 from Plymouth. 5A17 became 4A17 from Tavistock Junction. D6322 had failed at Doublebois working 8B21, the 04.15 Tavistock Junction to Doublebois freight trip.

| | |
|---|---|
| D600 | Laira - M/R (*Battery charging and waiting materials; Resistances; Off A.M.*) / 5B57 8.05am Tavistock Junction - Penzance to Truro (*D6309 forward*) / 5B77 11.45am Truro - Tavistock Junction / 5B81 3.50pm Tavistock Junction - Truro / 5B78 5.0pm Penzance - Bristol West Depot > 8.07pm from Truro (*D6310 off*) to Tavistock Junction (*D810 forward*) / Laira. |
| D601 | Truro / 5C05 12.50am Truro - Tavistock Junction / Laira / 4C07 8.30pm Paddington - Penzance > 3.42am starting from Tavistock Junction to Truro (*D849 forward*) / 5B77 7.25am Truro - Tavistock Junction / 5B81 12.05pm Tavistock Junction - Truro / Truro / 5A17 2.50pm Penzance - Paddington > 6.15pm from Truro (*D6309 off*) to Tavistock Junction (*D856 forward*) / 5B81 9.20pm Tavistock Junction - Truro / Truro. |
| D602 | Laira - M/R (*375 hour exam and exhaust manifold cracked*). |
| D603 | St. Blazey / 5B28 6.45am St. Blazey - Fowey / 5C13 8.10am St Blazey - Burngullow / 5B77 9.40am Burngullow - St Blazey / 5B28 10.35am St. Blazey - Fowey / 5B77 11.10am Fowey - St Blazey / 5B28 11.55am St Blazey - Fowey / 5B77 12.30pm Fowey - St Blazey / 5B78 1.30pm St. Blazey - Tavistock Junction / 5B70 7.30pm Tavistock Junction - St. Blazey / St. Blazey. |
| D604 | Laira / 3C08 2.20am Plymouth - Penzance *'Mails & Milk empties'* / Penzance / 2C74 8.0am Penzance - Plymouth / 3C15 10.40pm Paddington - Penzance *'Parcels'* > 11.30am from Plymouth (*D857 off*) / Penzance / 1M78 4.50pm Penzance - Manchester to Plymouth (*D865 forward*) / Laira. |
| | |
| D800 | .....1C04 to Penzance / Penzance / 1A60 3.40pm Penzance - Paddington *'Perishables'*..... |
| D801 | Swindon Works (*Heavy casual repair*). |
| D802 | Laira / 6B64 1.45am Tavistock Junction - Swindon to Hackney Yard (*D7044 forward*) / Newton Abbot / 2C90 12.31pm Newton Abbot - Paignton / 2C90 2.55pm Paignton - Newton Abbot / 2C20 4.17pm Newton Abbot - Penzance / 1A86 9.30pm Penzance – Paddington *'Sleeper'*..... |
| D803 | .....3C12 to Plymouth / Laira / 2C90 9.10am Plymouth - Penzance / 1M99 12.45pm Penzance - Liverpool to Plymouth (*D1057 forward*) / 1M99 12.45pm Penzance - Liverpool > 4.0pm from Plymouth to Newton Abbot in tandem with D1057 / Newton Abbot / 4A20 6.50pm Newton Abbot - Acton..... |
| D804 | Bristol Bath Road - M/R (*Transmission defects; to go to Laira for exams; Off A.M.*) / 3V05 3.30pm Hull - Plymouth *'Fish'* > 2.05am from Bristol / Laira - M/R (*On A.M.; Transmission defects and exams*). |
| D805 | .....4V17 to Avonmouth / 0Z26 LD Avonmouth - Bristol Bath Road / Bristol Bath Road / 0A00 4.20am Bristol Bath Road - Weston-Super-Mare / 1A00 6.31am Weston-super-Mare - Paddington / Ranelagh Bridge / 1C80 11.45am Paddington - Taunton / 1A33 4.47pm Taunton - Paddington to Swindon / 2B79 7.55pm Swindon - Purton / 3B79 8.30pm Purton - Swindon / 3A27 3.50pm Whitland - Kensington *'Milk'* > 10.05pm from Swindon (*D70XX off*)..... |
| D806 | ....4M44 to Bristol / Bristol Bath Road / 1M68 8.0am Bristol - Crewe / Crewe / 1V98 3.05pm Manchester - Plymouth > 3.59pm from Crewe / Laira. |
| D807 | Laira - M/R (*A end final drive shaft sheared*) / 0Z23 11.30am Laira - Swindon Works / Swindon Works. |
| D808 | .....3A27 to Kensington Olympia / 0Z20 LD Kensington Olympia - Old Oak Common / Old Oak Common / 1B00 2.15am Paddington - Bristol *'News'* / Bristol Bath Road / 2B96 9.35am Bristol - Weston-super-Mare / 1A50 11.40am Weston-super-Mare - Paddington to Swindon / Swindon / 3C07 1.30pm Paddington - Plymouth *'Parcels'* > 5.30pm from Swindon (*D7025 off*) / Laira. |
| D809 | .....???? to Pontypool Road / 3B31 2.25am Pontypool Road - Bristol / Bristol Bath Road / 0A20 6.35am Bristol Bath Road - Weston-super-Mare in tandem with D7051 / 1A20 8.30am Weston-super-Mare - Paddington / Ranelagh Bridge / 1B17 1.45pm Paddington - Weston-super-Mare / 2B96 5.55pm Weston-super-Mare - Bristol / Bristol Bath Road / 5C33 10.50pm Bristol West Depot - Tavistock Junction..... |
| D810 | Laira / 4M47 1.15am Tavistock Junction - Crewe to Bristol / Bristol Bath Road / 1V86 12.45am Manchester - Penzance > 7.15am from Bristol (*D841 off*) / Penzance / 2C24 4.20am Penzance - Plymouth / Laira / 5B78 5.0pm Penzance - Bristol West Depot > 11.10pm from Tavistock Junction (*D600 off*)..... |
| D811 | .....4M63 12.05am Tavistock Junction - Woodford to Taunton / Taunton / 1A30 8.53am Taunton - Paddington to Bristol (*D855 forward*) / Bristol Bath Road / 1A98 4.15pm Bristol - Paddington *'Bristolian'* / Ranelagh Bridge / 1B31 7.45pm Paddington - Weston-super-Mare / 0Z26 LD Weston-super-Mare - Bristol Bath Road / Bristol Bath Road. |
| D812 | Penzance / 1E24 10.30am Penzance - Sheffield *'Cornishman'* to Bristol (*D73 forward*) / Bristol Bath Road / 1M99 12.45pm Penzance - Liverpool > 7.15pm from Bristol (*D1057 off*) to Crewe / Crewe. |
| D813 | .....5C33 to Tavistock Junction / 0B60 5.50am Tavistock Junction - Plymouth Millbay / 5M91 7.30am Plymouth Millbay - Plymouth / 1M91 8.0am Plymouth - Crewe / Crewe / |
| D814 | Laira / 1A41 6.45am Truro - Paddington *'Mayflower'* > 8.30am from Plymouth (*D835 off*) / Old Oak Common / 1C45 4.30pm Paddington - Truro *'Mayflower'* / Truro. |
| D815 | .....3A38 to Paddington / Old Oak Common / 3B04 5.05am Paddington - Bristol *'Parcels'* / Bristol Bath Road / 3A15 11.45am Dr. Days Junction - West Ealing *'Parcels'* / 0Z20 LD West Ealing - Old Oak Common / Old Oak Common / 1C08 10.30pm Paddington - Penzance *'Sleeper'*..... |
| D816 | .....4C25 to Tavistock Junction / Laira / 1C04 10.20pm Paddington - Penzance *'Postal'* > 4.10am from Plymouth in tandem with D800 / 2C25 7.30am Penzance - Newton Abbot / Newton Abbot / 6C16 4.35am Stoke Gifford Yard - Tavistock Junction > 12.25pm from Hackney Yard (*D7074 off*) / Laira / 2C75 5.30pm Plymouth - Newton Abbot / 3C04 3.32pm Bristol - Plymouth *'Parcels'* > 8.32pm from Newton Abbot (*D7014 off*) / Laira. |
| D817 | .....3C10 to Plymouth / Laira / 1C14 11.50pm Paddington - Penzance > 7.45am from Plymouth (*D851 off*) / Penzance / 1A33 1.50pm Penzance - Paddington to Plymouth (*D868 forward*) / 1B53 6.0pm Plymouth - Bristol / Bristol Bath Road / 3C10 8.25pm Cardiff - Plymouth *'Parcels'* > 11.06pm from Bristol..... |
| D818 | Laira - M/R (*11,250 hour exam*). |
| D819 | Laira / 2C70 6.45am Plymouth - Penzance / 1M06 11.35am Penzance - Crewe *'Parcels'* to Plymouth (*D857 forward*) / Laira - M/R (*On P.M.; 7,500 hour exam*). |

| | |
|---|---|
| D820 | Laira - M/R (*Transmission change*). |
| D821 | Old Oak Common (*Spare*) / 1B08 9.45am Paddington - Weston-super-Mare / 1A74 1.40pm Weston-super-Mare - Paddington / Ranelagh Bridge / 1C47 6.30pm Paddington - Plymouth / Laira. |
| D822 | ....1A86 to Paddington / Old Oak Common / 1C39 12.30pm Paddington - Kingswear *'Torbay Express'* / 2C76 5.25pm Kingswear - Exeter / 0Z33 7.45pm Exeter - Newton Abbot / Newton Abbot / 5C26 3.45pm Stoke Gifford Yard - Tavistock Junction > 10.20pm from Hackney Yard (*D7002 off*)..... |
| D823 | Newton Abbot - M/R (*On A.M.; B engine and transmission faults*). |
| D824 | Bristol Bath Road / 1C08 10.30pm Paddington - Penzance *'Sleeper'* > 1.55am from Bristol (*D839 off*) / Penzance / 3A38 2.40pm Penzance - Paddington Goods *'Meat'*..... |
| D825 | .....3A42 to Southall / 0Z20 LD Southall - Old Oak Common / Old Oak Common / 1B04 8.45am Paddington - Bristol *'Bristolian'* / Bristol Bath Road / 1V33 8.10am Sheffield - Penzance *'Cornishman'* > 12.05pm from Bristol in tandem with D7028 to Taunton / Penzance (*Spare*). |
| D826 | Newton Abbot - M/R (*375 hour exam; Off A.M.*) / 2C91 7.55am Exeter - Kingswear > 8.48am from Newton Abbot / 1A62 10.50am Kingswear - Paddington *'Torbay Express'* / Ranelagh Bridge / 1C86 4.45pm Paddington - Taunton / 3A47 6.15pm Plymouth - Kensington Olympia *'Perishables'* > 9.25pm from Taunton to Bristol in tandem with D863 / Bristol Bath Road. |
| D827 | .....5A09 to Acton / 0Z20 LD Acton - Old Oak Common / Old Oak Common / 1C26 8.30am Paddington - Penzance *'Royal Duchy'* / Penzance / 1A69 7.0pm Penzance - Paddington *'Postal'*..... |
| D828 | Newton Abbot - M/R (*9,000 hour exam*). |
| D829 | Laira / 4A60 5.30am Tavistock Junction - Old Oak Common / Old Oak Common / 1B28 6.45pm Paddington - Weston-super-Mare / 2B96 10.45pm Weston-super-Mare - Bristol / Bristol Bath Road. |
| D830 | Swindon Works (*Heavy casual*). |
| D831 | .....1M78 to Crewe / Crewe / 1V93 9.05am Liverpool - Plymouth > 10.07am from Crewe in multiple from Shrewsbury to Newton Abbot with D838 / Laira / 3A42 6.0pm Penzance - Kensington Olympia *'Milk'* > 10.0pm from Plymouth (*D1039 off*) to Southall..... |
| D832 | .....3A36 to Paddington / Ranelagh Bridge / 1C21 5.30am Paddington - Plymouth / Laira - M/R (*On P.M.; unrecorded repairs*). |
| D833 | Laira - M/R (*B engine change*). |
| D834 | Newton Abbot - M/R (*8,250 hour exam and 1-6 exhaust joints defective; QCI to ride loco for 6.25am trial run; Off A.M.*) / 2C91 6.25am Newton Abbot - Goodrington / 1N37 9.30am Paignton - Bradford *'Devonian'* to Bristol (*D53 forward*) / Bristol Bath Road / 1V39 10.36am Bradford - Paignton *'Devonian'* > 4.05am from Bristol (*D32 off*) / 0Z33 7.35pm Paignton - Newton Abbot / Newton Abbot. |
| D835 | .....5C32 to Truro / 1A41 6.45am Truro - Paddington *'Mayflower'* to Plymouth (*D814 forward*) / Laira / 1A81 10.10am Penzance - Paddington *'Cornish Riviera Express'* > 12.30pm from Plymouth (*D1057 off*) / Old Oak Common / 1C04 10.20pm Paddington - Penzance *'Postal'* to Plymouth..... |
| D836 | Newton Abbot / 4C11 1.40am Hackney Yard - Tavistock Junction / Laira / 2C75 7.20am Plymouth - Newton Abbot / Newton Abbot - M/R (*On P.M.; 375 hour exam*). |
| D837 | Swindon Works (*Heavy casual repair*). |
| D838 | Shrewsbury (*Failed; available OEO*) / 1V93 9.05am Liverpool - Plymouth from Shrewsbury to Newton Abbot in multiple with D831 / Newton Abbot - M/R (*On P.M.; electrical defects.*). |
| D839 | .....1C08 to Bristol / Bristol Bath Road (*Available OEO*) / 3C16 9.0am Bristol - Plymouth *'Parcels'* to Newton Abbot (*D863 forward*) / Newton Abbot - M/R (*On P.M.; 125 hour exam and unrecorded repairs*). |
| D840 | .....5A06 to Acton / 0Z20 LD Acton - Old Oak Common / Old Oak Common / 1C33 11.30am Paddington - Falmouth to Plymouth (*D6317 forward*) / Laira / 3A47 6.15pm Plymouth - Kensington Olympia *'Perishables'* to Newton Abbot in tandem with D863 / 3C46 7.40pm Newton Abbot - Taunton *'Parcels'* / Taunton / 3H05 11.20pm Taunton - Wolverhampton Low Level *'Parcels'* to Acton..... |
| D841 | Crewe / 1V86 12.45am Manchester - Plymouth > 2.0am from Crewe to Bristol (*D810 forward*) / Bristol Bath Road / 2B96 11.00am Bristol - Weston-super-Mare / Weston-super-Mare station Shunts as required / 2B96 5.15pm Weston-super-Mare - Bristol / 0C25 6.13pm Bristol - Avonmouth / 4C25 7.50pm Avonmouth - Tavistock Junction..... |
| D842 | Newton Abbot - M/R (*Serck defects and Fenner coupling defective*). |
| D843 | .....5C26 to Tavistock Junction / Laira / 6T70 2.20am Tavistock Junction - Rogerstone to Hackney Yard (*D7008 forward*) / Newton Abbot - M/R (*On A.M.; A V R defective; Off P.M.*) / 2C90 10.22pm Newton Abbot - Paignton..... |
| D844 | .....5A14 to Acton / 0Z20 LD Acton - Old Oak Common / Old Oak Common / 1C43 2.30pm Paddington - Penzance to Newton Abbot (*Failed > D1008 & D6340 forward*) / Newton Abbot - M/R (*On P.M.; 125 hour exam and unrecorded repairs*). |
| D845 | .....1A69 to Paddington / Old Oak Common - M/R (*On A.M.; unrecorded repairs*). |
| D846 | Bristol Bath Road / 2B96 7.20am Bristol - Weston-super-Mare / 1A42 10.35am Weston-super-Mare - Paddington / Ranelagh Bridge / 1B21 3.45pm Paddington - Weston-super-Mare / 0Z26 LD Weston-super-Mare - Bristol Bath Road / Bristol Bath Road. |
| D847 | Laira / 1A24 6.30am Plymouth - Paddington / Old Oak Common / 1C39 12.30pm Paddington - Kingswear *'Torbay Express'* to Newton Abbot in tandem with Steam 7011 Banbury Castle (*Steam 7011 forward*) / Newton Abbot - M/R (*On P.M.; 6,750 hour exam and unrecorded repairs*). |
| D848 | .....1V99 to Bristol / Bristol Bath Road / 0C14 3.30am Bristol Bath Road - Stoke Gifford Yard / 5C14 9.10pm Oxley - Tavistock Junction > 4.15am from Stoke Gifford Yard / Laira / 1A12 11.30am Penzance - Paddington *'Royal Duchy'* > 2.30pm from Plymouth (*D866 off*) / Ranelagh Bridge / 3C12 10.0pm Paddington - Penzance *'Parcels'* to Plymouth..... |
| D849 | Truro / 5C07 8.30pm Paddington - Penzance > 7.09am from Truro (*D601 off*) / Penzance / 1M96 11.0am Penzance - Manchester to Plymouth (*D869 forward*) / 0B54 2.0pm Plymouth - Par / 2C54 3.50pm Par - Newquay / 2C24 5.55pm Newquay - Plymouth / Laira / 5M44 10.05pm Tavistock Junction - Crewe to Bristol..... |
| D850 | Old Oak Common / 0Z34 LD Old Oak Common - Taunton / Taunton / 0Z33 11.30pm Taunton - Newton Abbot..... |
| D851 | Bristol Bath Road / 1C14 11.50pm Paddington - Penzance > 3.12am from Bristol (*D868 off*) to Plymouth (*D817 forward*) / Laira / 1M95 11.0am Plymouth - Manchester to Crewe / Crewe / 1V99 7.25pm Manchester - Bristol > 8.32pm from Crewe..... |
| D852 | Laira / 1A24 6.30am Plymouth - Paddington / Old Oak Common / 0C05 LD Old Oak Common - Wood Lane / 3C05 2.40pm Wood Lane - Plymouth *'Milk empties'* / Laira. |
| D853 | Laira / 6B72 1.15am Tavistock Junction - Penzance / 0B72 LD Penzance - St. Erth / 3A31 12.45pm St. Erth - Wood Lane *'Milk'*..... |
| D854 | .....3A31 to Wood Lane / 0Z20 LD Wood Lane - Old Oak Common / Old Oak Common / 1B02 7.45am Paddington - Weston-super-Mare / 1A64 12.35pm Weston-super-Mare - Paddington / Old Oak Common. |
| D855 | Swindon / 3B20 8.20pm Kensington Olympia - Bristol *'Milk empties & Parcels'* > 1.10am from Swindon / Bristol Bath Road / 1A30 8.53am Taunton - Paddington > 10.15am from Bristol (*D811 off*) / Ranelagh Bridge / 1B19 2.45pm Paddington - Weston-super-Mare / 1A50 6.58pm Weston-super-Mare - Paddington to Bristol (*D1057 forward*) / Bristol Bath Road / 0Z23 10.30pm Bristol - Swindon / Swindon. |
| D856 | .....3C09 to Plymouth / Laira / 3C12 10.0pm Paddington - Penzance *'Parcels'* > 8.05am from Plymouth (*D803 off*) / Penzance / 2C74 1.55pm Penzance - Plymouth / Laira / 4A17 2.50pm Penzance - Paddington > 9.10pm from Tavistock Junction (*D601 off*)..... |
| D857 | .....3C15 to Plymouth / Laira / 1M06 11.35am Penzance - Crewe *'Perishables'* > 3.45pm from Plymouth (*D819 off*) to Bristol / Bristol Bath Road / 5C32 9.45pm Bristol West Depot - Penzance to Truro..... |
| D858 | Laira - M/R (*125 hour exam and engine speed regulator defective*). |
| D859 | Newton Abbot / 8C27 5.45am Hackney Yard - Tavistock Junction / Laira / 1A67 9.20am Falmouth - Paddington > 11.30am from Plymouth (*D6341 off*) / Old Oak Common - M/R (*On P.M.; exhaust elbows defective*). |
| D860 | Laira - M/R (*375 hour exam; Off A.M.*) / 1C43 2.30pm Paddington - Penzance > 7.09pm from Plymouth (*D1008 & D6340 off*) / Penzance. |
| D861 | Swindon Works (*Heavy casual repair*). |
| D862 | Laira - M/R (*Unrecorded repairs; Off A.M.*) / 9B86 6.35am Tavistock Junction - Wrangaton *'Engineers duty'* / 0B21 LD Wrangaton - Doublebois / 0Z27 LD Doublebois - Laira hauling D6322 / Laira. |
| D863 | Newton Abbot - M/R (*Dynostarter holding down bolts loose; bedplate bolt holes worn; Off A.M.*) / 3C16 9.0am Bristol - Plymouth *'Parcels'* > 2.0pm from Newton Abbot (*D839 off*) / Laira / 3A47 6.15pm Plymouth - Kensington Olympia *'Perishables'* in tandem with D840 to Newton Abbot and in tandem from Taunton to Bristol with D826..... |
| D864 | Laira - M/R (*4,500 hour exam and transmission defect*). |
| D865 | Penzance (*Stand-by*) / 8B77 8.30am Penzance - Tavistock Junction / 0Z39 LD Tavistock Junction - Penzance / 3M . . ECS Penzance - Tyseley to Plymouth / Laira / 1M78 4.50pm Penzance - Manchester > 8.0pm from Plymouth (*D604 off*) to Crewe..... |
| D866 | Laira / 3C09 7.45pm Kensington Olympia - Penzance *'Milk empties & Parcels'* > 3.10am from Plymouth (*D856 off*) / Penzance / 1A12 11.30am Penzance - Paddington *'Royal Duchy'* to Plymouth (*D848 forward*) / Laira / 2C70 3.46pm Plymouth - Penzance / 1A90 8.55pm Penzance - Paddington *'Sleeper'* to Plymouth (*D1039 forward*) / Laira. |

D829 MAGPIE on 14 September 1963 at Reading with the up 'Mayflower', the 6.45am Truro-Paddington, which it would have taken over at Plymouth from another Warship, departing from there at 8.30am. After visiting Ranelagh Bridge it would have returned with the 1C43 2.30pm Paddington-Penzance. (Alec Swain, www.transporttreasury.co.uk)

D870 on Thursday 19 September 1963, approaching Dawlish Warren. ZULU was on this same working, 1A12 11.40am Penzance-Paddington, on Sunday 9 July leaving Plymouth at 2.30pm. (www.rail-online.co.uk)

| | |
|---|---|
| D867 | .....4A17 to Paddington / Old Oak Common / 1B10 10.45am Paddington - Weston-super-Mare / 1A13 4.33pm Weston-super-Mare - Paddington / Old Oak Common / 3C15 10.40pm Paddington - Penzance *'Parcels'* to Plymouth..... |
| D868 | .....1C14 to Bristol / Bristol Bath Road / 1C15 6.25am Bristol - Plymouth / Laira / 1A33 1.50pm Penzance - Paddington > 4.30pm from Plymouth (*D817 off*) / Ranelagh Bridge / 1C14 11.50pm Paddington - Penzance to Bristol..... |
| D869 | .....5C12 to Newton Abbot / Newton Abbot / 5C60 2.05am Bristol West Depot - Tavistock Junction > 7.30am from Hackney Yard (*D7049 off*) / Laira / 1M96 11.0am Penzance - Manchester > 2.0pm from Plymouth (*D849 off*) to Crewe / Crewe. |
| D870 | .....3A47 to Kensington Olympia / 0Z20 LD Kensington Olympia - Old Oak Common / Old Oak Common / 0C30 LD Old Oak Common - Acton / 5C30 3.15pm Acton - Hackney Yard / Newton Abbot. |

| Wednesday 10th<br>This table shows the end of Tuesday's workings. | |
|---|---|
| D600 | Laira / |
| D601 | Truro / 5C05 12.50am Truro - Tavistock Junction / |
| D602 | Laira - M/R (*375 hour exam and exhaust manifold cracked*). |
| D603 | St. Blazey / |
| D604 | Laira / |
| | |
| D800 | .....1A60 to Paddington / Old Oak Common |
| D801 | Swindon Works (*Heavy casual repair*). |
| D802 | .....1A86 to Paddington / Old Oak Common |
| D803 | .....4A20 to Acton / 0Z20 LD Acton - Old Oak Common / Old Oak Common |
| D804 | Laira - M/R (*On A.M.; Transmission defects and exams; to go to Newton Abbot light diesel at 5.30pm for trial run*). |
| D805 | .....3A27 to Kensington Olympia / 0Z20 LD Kensington Olympia - Old Oak Common / Old Oak Common |
| D806 | Laira / |
| D807 | Laira - M/R (*A end final drive shaft sheared; stopped since 06 July*). |
| D808 | Laira / |
| D809 | .....5C33 to Tavistock Junction / Laira |
| D810 | .....5B78 to Bristol West Depot / Bristol Bath Road |
| D811 | Bristol Bath Road / |
| D812 | Crewe / |
| D813 | Crewe / |
| D814 | Truro / |
| D815 | .....1C08 to Penzance / Penzance |
| D816 | Laira / |
| D817 | .....3C10 to Plymouth / Laira |
| D818 | Laira - M/R (*11,250 hour exam*). |
| D819 | Laira - M/R (*7,500 hour exam*). |
| D820 | Laira - M/R (*Transmission change*). |
| D821 | Laira / |
| D822 | .....5C26 to Tavistock Junction / Laira |
| D823 | Newton Abbot - M/R (*B engine and transmission faults; to go to Laira for repairs and trial run*). |
| D824 | .....3A38 to Paddington Goods / Ranelagh Bridge |
| D825 | Penzance / |
| D826 | Bristol Bath Road / |
| D827 | .....1A69 to Paddington / Old Oak Common |
| D828 | Newton Abbot - M/R (*9,000 hour exam*). |
| D829 | Bristol Bath Road / |
| D830 | Swindon Works (*Heavy casual*). |
| D831 | .....3A42 to Southall / 0Z20 LD Southall - Old Oak Common / Old Oak Common. |
| D832 | Laira - M/R (*Unrecorded repairs*). |
| D833 | Laira - M/R (*B engine change*). |
| D834 | Newton Abbot / |
| D835 | .....1C04 to Plymouth / Laira |
| D836 | Newton Abbot - M/R (*375 hour exam*). |
| D837 | Swindon Works (*Heavy casual repair*). |
| D838 | Newton Abbot - M/R (*Electrical defects*). |
| D839 | Newton Abbot - M/R (*125 hour exam and unrecorded repairs*). |
| D840 | .....3H05 to Acton / 0Z20 LD Acton - Old Oak Common / Old Oak Common. |
| D841 | .....4C25 to Tavistock Junction / Laira. |
| D842 | Newton Abbot - M/R (*Serck defects and Fenner coupling defective*). |
| D843 | .....2C90 12.10am Paignton - Newton Abbot / Newton Abbot |
| D844 | Newton Abbot - M/R (*125 hour exam and unrecorded repairs*). |
| D845 | Old Oak Common - M/R (*Unrecorded repairs*). |
| D846 | Bristol Bath Road / |
| D847 | Newton Abbot - M/R (*6,750 hour exam and unrecorded repairs.*) |
| D848 | .....3C12 to Plymouth / Laira |
| D849 | .....5M44 to Bristol / Bristol Bath Road. |
| D850 | .....0Z33 to Newton Abbot / Newton Abbot - M/R (*On A.M.; 125 hour exam and dynostarter defects*). |
| D851 | .....1V99 to Bristol / Bristol Bath Road |
| D852 | Laira / |
| D853 | .....3A31 to Wood Lane / 0Z20 LD Wood Lane - Old Oak Common / Old Oak Common |
| D854 | Old Oak Common / |
| D855 | Swindon / |
| D856 | ....4A17 to Paddington / Old Oak Common. |

| | |
|---|---|
| D857 | .....5C32 to Truro / |
| D858 | Laira - M/R (*125 hour exam and engine speed regulator defective*). |
| D859 | Old Oak Common - M/R (*Exhaust elbows defective*). |
| D860 | Penzance / |
| D861 | Swindon Works (*Heavy casual repair*). |
| D862 | Laira / |
| D863 | .....3A47 to Kensington Olympia / 0Z20 LD Kensington Olympia - Old Oak Common / Old Oak Common. |
| D864 | Laira - M/R (*4,500 hour exam and transmission defect*). |
| D865 | .....1M78 to Crewe / Crewe |
| D866 | Laira / |
| D867 | .....3C15 to Plymouth / Laira |
| D868 | .....1C14 to Bristol / |
| D869 | Crewe / |
| D870 | Newton Abbot / |

**D856 TROJAN on 11 June 1963 at Swindon with the 11.40am ex-Weston-super-Mare. The Warships were the mainstay of the Paddington-Bristol/Weston services in the early 1960s. (Alec Swain, www.transporttreasury.co.uk)**

*Left.* 3 May 1971 was the first day of the summer timetable and 810 COCKADE spent the day on the Exeter loco yard, what was left of the old Great Western steam shed. 810 is in its final livery style and has no lamp bracket, headboard clips, central marker light or multiple working fittings. (www.rail-online.co.uk)

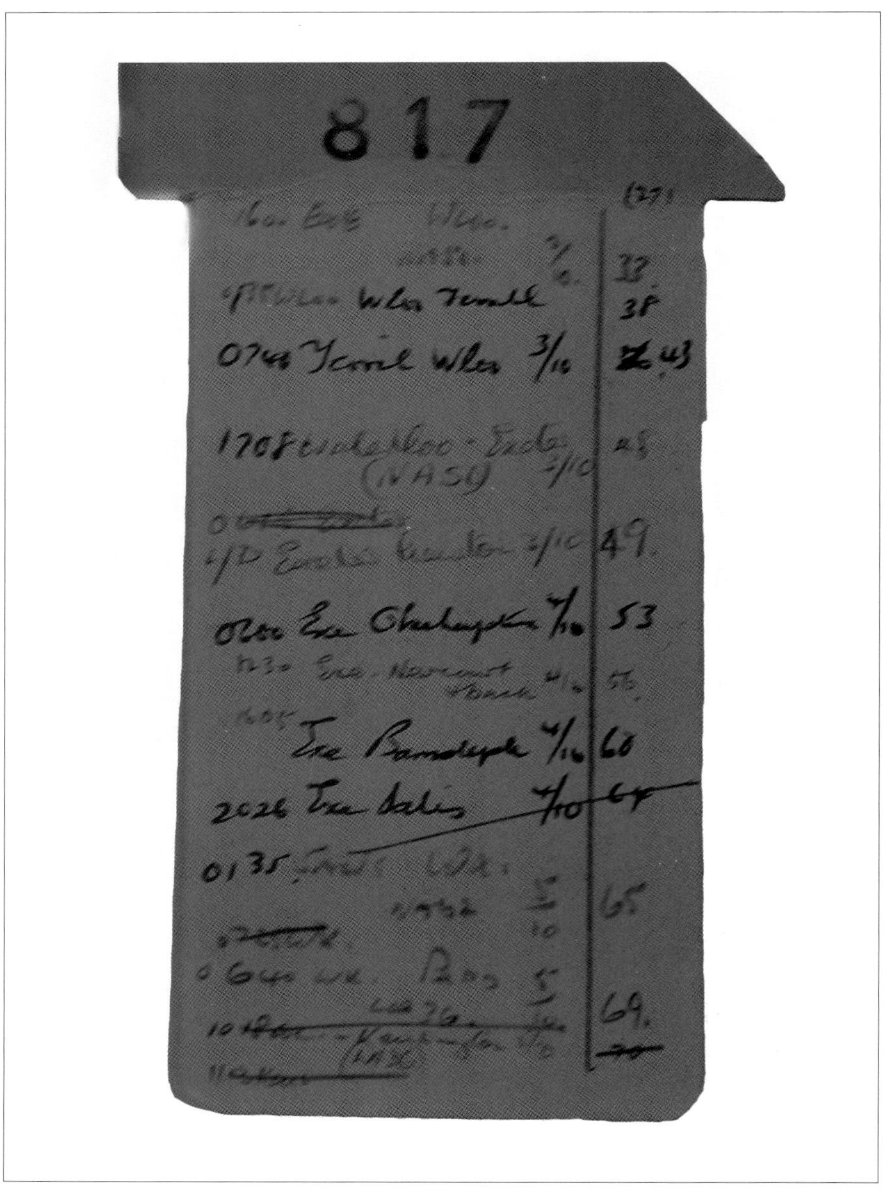


*Left.* The Control 'job card' for 817 for the last part of its working life, in October 1971. Coloured blue for Newton Abbot, the card shows that on 2 October the loco headed for Paddington in charge of 1O16, the 16.00 from Exeter to Waterloo, part of NA 50 diagram. The hours brought over from the previous card (in brackets) show 27 and after completing the workings of NA 50 the hours had risen to 33. Following the card through we see 817 returned to Exeter and then went to Newton Abbot for servicing and fuel before returning light to Exeter on the Monday for 7B65, the 06.00 freight to Okehampton and return, then 7B71 to Newcourt MOD, then 2B99 to Barnstaple and back. Then it was on ballast working 6O81, the 19.00 Meldon Quarry-Salisbury forward from Riverside Yard. 7V18 was the 01.35 to Westbury and then the loco performed its last passenger duty, 1A54, the 06.40 commuter train to Paddington. The next working was actually a Hymek diagram, part of OC 74 turn, 5M07, the 10.18 to Kensington Olympia and return light which shows as crossed out; perhaps the plan to use 817 because of no loco available was scuppered because a Hymek became available at short notice, 817 was not required and was instead withdrawn.

## APPENDIX 2

### Workings for Warships Class 42 and at Newton Abbot and Laira depots from 3rd May 1971

The locomotive diagrams shown operated from 3 May 1971 until further notice. During the operation of the timetable some changes were made which resulted in amended turns being issued. On the original sheets the Reason For Alteration ('RFA') was usually quoted and could be anything from amended workings to being issued on the wrong colour paper.

The Class 42 and 43 turns from Newton Abbot and Laira are detailed below. There were also turns that operated from Severn Tunnel Junction, Old Oak Common and St. Blazey. Mention is made of turn 720 at St. Blazey, which is likely to have been a China Clay trip working to Fowey. Also, it was not unknown for classes to mix with other turns, such as a Class 52 working LA 54 and a Class 42 working LA 123 (Westbury to Merehead stone trips).

Headcodes which are underlined - *8B70* - were conditional services running as required. These trains were not guaranteed to operate and the loco would wait spare until its next duty if the working did not operate.

There are *two* 52, 53 and 69 turns - this is not a typing error - each depot had its own diagrams and used numbers 1 to 199 and higher. Mixed within these numbers were Class 22s, 35s and 52s.

Laira had 17 turns for Class 42; Newton Abbot had 8 turns for Class 42 and 11 turns for Class 43. Of the 34 Class 42s available at the start date, four were in Works (803, 820,821 and 827) with 818 stopped awaiting Works, leaving 29 available in traffic. Of the 25 Class 43s available nine were in store leaving 16 in traffic.

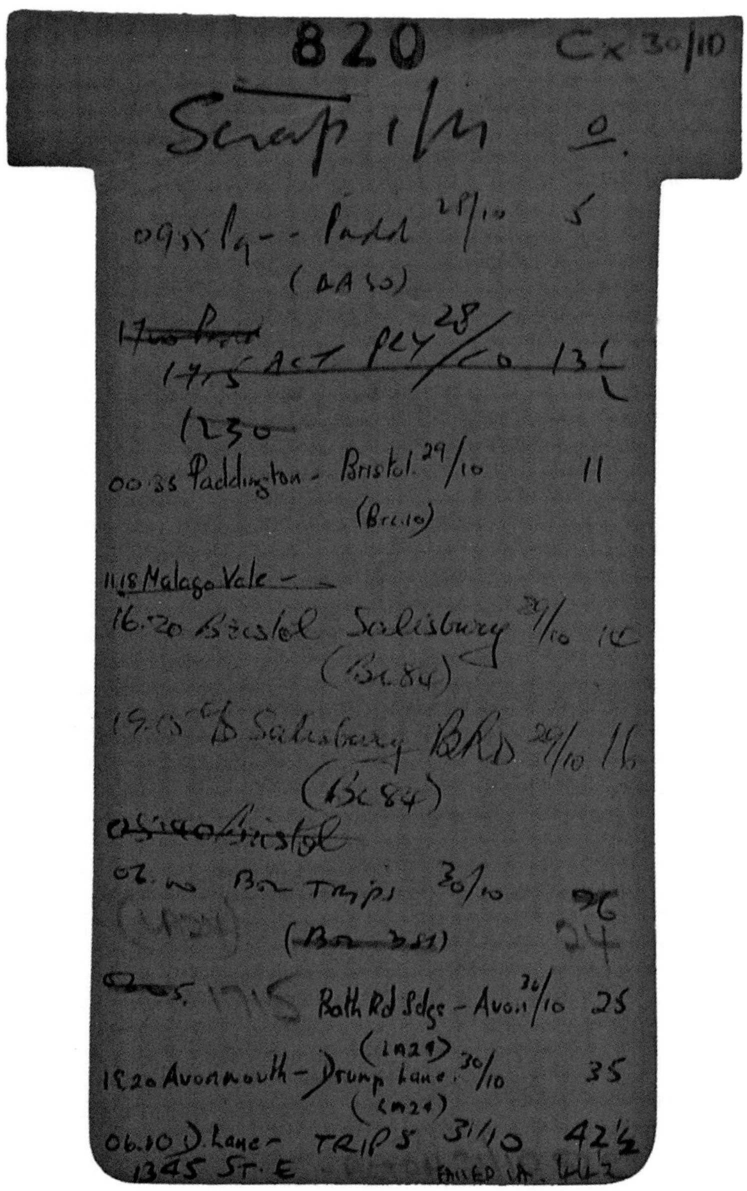


**The orange for 820 denotes Laira and shows workings for GRENVILLE from 28 October 1972. Having just been given an 'A' exam at Newton Abbot already the loco's card is marked SCRAP 1/11. As is common with a lot of the cards only parts of the actual workings were recorded because if every train worked was shown cards would fill up quite quickly. While 1A59, the 09.55 Paignton to Paddington is shown, with five engine hours, the working to Paignton, 2B34 the 08.55 Newton Abbot to Paignton 'stopper' is not. The Diagram (LA 30) was actually for a Class 52 and 17.00 Paddington was 1C07, the 17.00 to Swansea which 820 could not have worked. In the early hours of Sunday morning 820 worked 1B86 (newspapers) to Bristol then an afternoon parcels to Salisbury, returning light to Bath Road. Eight hours working freight trips in the Bristol area was Monday's first duty, then taking empty diesel fuel oil tanks to Avonmouth before heading west on 6B30 to Drump Lane. Freight trips in Cornwall followed on the 31st between Drump Lane and Penzance delivering empty, and collecting full, milk tanks for 6A19 to Acton. Fate dealt its hand here as 820 was failed at Plymouth with transmission defects; 821 took over and 820 retired to Laira and was withdrawn, as predicted, on 1 November.**

| Newton Abbot | | | |
|---|---|---|---|
| Turn | Locos | | |
| 1-49 | | | NOT USED. |
| 50 | Two | | Exeter to Waterloo services. |
| 51 | Two | | Exeter to Waterloo / Waterloo, Clapham Junction, Kensington Olympia and Morden South. |
| 52 | Two | | Exeter to Waterloo / Lapford Milk and Salisbury ballast. |
| 53 | One | | Exeter to Waterloo / Newton Abbot to Paignton. |
| | | | |
| 61 | Two* | Class 43 | Westbury to Paddington / Paddington to Hereford and Worcester. |
| 62 - 63 | | | NOT USED. |
| 64 | Four* | Class 43 | Westbury to Bristol, Salisbury and Exeter / Worcester to Paddington and trips. |
| 65 | Three* | Class 43 | Penzance to Paddington / Paddington to Worcester and Hereford / Paignton to Cardiff. |
| 66 | One | | Newton Abbot to Plymouth and trips / Exeter to Chard Junction and trips. |
| 67 | | | NOT USED. |
| 68 | One* | Class 43 | Paignton to Paddington. |
| 69 | One* | Class 43 | Newton Abbot maintenance turn-over loco. |
| 70 - 149 | | | NOT USED. |
| | | | |
| Laira | | | |
| Turn | Locos | | |
| 52 | Two | | Penzance to Paddington / Cornish milk trips / Plymouth to Cardiff. |
| 53 | One | | Plymouth to Penzance. |
| 54 | Two | | St. Blazey Clay trips / St. Blazey to Paddington. |
| 55 | One | | Plymouth to Penzance |
| 56 | | | NOT USED. |
| 57 | One | | Exeter to Penzance. |
| 58 | One | | Penzance to Plymouth. |
| 59 | | | NOT USED. |
| 60 | One | | Plymouth to Penzance. |
| 61 | One | | Penzance to Plymouth. |
| 62 | Two | | Westbury to Salisbury / Westbury to Swindon and Exeter. |
| 63 - 68 | | | NOT USED. |
| 69 | One | | St. Blazey to Newquay and Plymouth. |
| | | | |
| 151 | One | | Plymouth - Exeter and Chard Junction trips |
| 152 | | | NOT USED. |
| 153 | One | | St. Blazey to Truro and Plymouth Friary. |
| 154 | | | Not used. |
| 155 | One | | Plymouth Friary to Westbury and Fawley. |
| 156 - 157 | | | NOT USED. |
| 158 | One | | Plymouth, Severn Tunnel Junction and Penzance. |
| 158 - 199 | | | NOT USED. |

**Key**

ETS Empty stock

RR Run Round

SH Steam heat

| NEWTON ABBOT - TURN No. 50 - 2 x CLASS 42 ('A' / 'B') - 2200 H.P. | | | | | | | | | | |
|---|---|---|---|---|---|---|---|---|---|---|
| | | | | | | | | | | |
| **From/To** | **Arrive** | **Notes** | **Depart** | **Code** | **Mon** | **Tue** | **Wed** | **Thu** | **Fri** | **Sat** |
| Newton Abbot Depot | | | 4.40 | 0B83 | A | B | A | B | A | -- |
| Newton Abbot C.S. | 4.45 | SH | 5.00 | 5B83 | A | B | A | B | A | -- |
| Exeter St. David's | 5.30 | RR / SH | 6.15 | 1O06 | A | B | A | B | A | -- |
| Waterloo | 10.07 | | 11.12 | 0Y02 | A | B | A | B | A | -- |
| Stewarts Lane | 11.33 | FUEL | 12.15 | 0V13 | A | B | A | B | A | -- |
| Waterloo | 12.36 | SH | 13.08 | 1V13 | A | B | A | B | A | -- |
| Exeter St. David's | 17.00 | RR / SH | 18.00 | 1O18 | A | B | A | B | A | -- |
| Waterloo | 22.02 | | 22.47 | 0Y02 | A | B | A | B | A | -- |
| Stewarts Lane | 23.10 | FUEL | 0.15 | 0V01 | -- | A | B | A | B | A |
| Waterloo (To Yeovil Junction) | 0.36 | SH | 1.45 | 1V01 | B | A | B | A | B | A |
| Salisbury | 3.25 | | 3.27 | LD | B | A | B | A | B | A |
| Salisbury Stabling Point | 3.32 | | 5.45 | 0V58 | B | A | B | A | B | -- |
| Salisbury Bay | 5.50 | SH / # | 6.52 | 2V58 | B | A | B | A | B | -- |
| Exeter Central | 9.05 | SH | 9.21 | 2B58 | B | A | B | A | B | -- |
| Exeter St. David's | 9.24 | RR/SH | 10.15 | 1O10 | B | A | B | A | B | -- |
| Waterloo | 14.02 | | 14.29 | 0Y02 | B | A | B | A | B | -- |
| Stewarts Lane | 14.49 | FUEL | 16.16 | 0V17 | B | A | B | A | B | -- |
| Waterloo | 16.38 | SH | 17.08 | 1V17 | B | A | B | A | B | -- |
| Exeter St. David's | 21.00 | | 21.15 | 0B40 | B | A | B | A | B | -- |
| Exeter Riverside | 21.20 | *Presflo ETS* | 21.55 | 7B40 | B | A | B | A | -- | -- |
| Plymouth Friary | 0.35 | | 0.45 | 0F76 | -- | B | A | B | A | -- |
| Newton Abbot Depot | 2.00 | | | | -- | B | A | B | A | -- |
| | | | | | | | | | | |
| **FUEL** | | | | | | | | | | |
| | | | | | | | | | | |
| **'A' ENGINE** | **Arrive** | **Notes** | **Depart** | **Code** | | | | | | |
| Waterloo (To Yeovil Junction) | | SH | 1.45 | 1V01 | **SO** | | | | | |
| Salisbury | 3.25 | | 3.27 | LD | | | | | | |
| Salisbury Stabling Point | 3.32 | | 5.45 | 0V58 | | | | | | |
| Salisbury | 6.20 | SH | 6.52 | 2V58 | | | | | | |
| Exeter St. David's | 9.06 | SH | 9.23 | 2B99 | | | | | | |
| Barnstaple Junction | 10.34 | | 12.23 | 2B99 | | | | | | |
| Exeter St. David's | 13.33 | | 13.40 | 0F91 | | | | | | |
| Exeter Stabling Point | 13.45 | | 15.30 | 0O16 | | | | | | |
| Exeter St. David's | 15.35 | SH | 16.00 | 1O16 | | | | | | |
| Waterloo | 20.02 | Parcels | 20.33 | 6Y05 | | | | | | |
| Clapham Junction | 20.42 | | 21.15 | 0Y02 | | | | | | |
| Stewarts Lane | 21.25 | | 0.05 | 0V01 | **SUO** | | | | | |
| Waterloo | 0.26 | SH | 1.35 | 1V01 | | | | | | |
| Yeovil Junction | 5.03 | RR / SH | 7.40 | 1O04 | | | | | | |
| Waterloo | 10.02 | | 10.23 | 0Y02 | | | | | | |
| Stewarts Lane | 10.43 | FUEL | 12.12 | 0Y61 | | | | | | |
| Waterloo North Sidings | 12.33 | | 15.50 | 0V17 | | | | | | |
| Waterloo | 15.55 | SH | 17.08 | 1V17 | | | | | | |
| Exeter St. David's | 20.50 | | 21.00 | 5B80 | | | | | | |
| Exeter C.S. | 21.05 | | 21.XX | 0F76 | | | | | | |
| Newton Abbot Depot | 21.XX | | | | | | | | | |
| | | | | | | | | | | |
| To work 'A' Mon | | | | | | | | | | |
| | | | | | | | | | | |
| Notes : When 7B40 did not run the loco was often used on 2B92 21.45 Exeter St. David's to Newton Abbot to get the loco in place. | | | | | | | | | | |
| # : in tandem with Class 35 on Turn BR170 to Yeovil Junction (Cl. 35 for Yeovil stand-by duty). | | | | | | | | | | |
| | | | | | | | | | | |
| To work 'B' Mon | | | | | | | | | | |

| NEWTON ABBOT - TURN No. 50 - 2 x CLASS 42 ('A' / 'B') - 2200 H.P. (continued) | | | | | |
|---|---|---|---|---|---|
| | | | | | |
| **'B' ENGINE** | **Arrive** | **Notes** | **Depart** | **Code** | |
| Exeter St. David's | 21.00 | | 21.05 | 0B40 | **FO (Until 04/06 Only)** |
| Exeter Riverside | 21.15 | *Presflo ETS* | 21.55 | 7B40 | |
| Plymouth Friary | 23.55 | | 0.05 | 0F76 | **SO (Until 05/06 Only)** |
| Newton Abbot Depot | 1.30 | | | | |
| | | | | | |
| **FUEL** | | | | | |
| | | | | | |
| Exeter St. David's | 21.00 | | 21.50 | 0F76 | **FO (From 11/06 - 24/09)** |
| Newton Abbot Depot | 22.20 | | | | |
| | | | | | |
| **FUEL** | | | | | |
| | | | | | |
| Newton Abbot Depot | | | 4.45 | 0B83 | **SO** |
| Newton Abbot C.S. | 4.50 | SH | 5.00 | 5B83 | |
| Exeter St. David's | 5.30 | RR/SH | 6.15 | 1O06 | |
| Waterloo | 10.08 | | 11.10 | 0Y02 | |
| Stewarts Lane | 11.30 | FUEL | 12.15 | 0V13 | |
| Waterloo | 12.36 | SH | 13.00 | 1V13 | |
| Exeter St. David's | 17.05 | RR/SH | 18.10 | 1O18 | |
| Waterloo | 22.02 | | 23.08 | 0Y02 | |
| Stewarts Lane | 23.29 | FUEL | 2.00 | LD | **SUO** |
| Waterloo North Sidings | 2.21 | | 7.27 | 0V09 | |
| Clapham C.S. | 7.40 | | 8.28 | 5V09 | |
| Waterloo | 8.38 | *Vans* | 9.40 | 6W . . | |
| Clapham Junction | 9.49 | | 10.35 | 0V11 | |
| Waterloo | 10.42 | | 11.08 | 1V11 | |
| Exeter St. David's | 14.50 | RR / SH | 16.00 | 1O16 | |
| Waterloo | 20.11 | Off 1O17 | 20.53 | 5W01 | |
| Clapham C.S. | 21.02 | | 22.10 | 0Y02 | |
| Stewarts Lane | 22.20 | FUEL | 23.20 | 0V01 | |
| Waterloo | 23.51 | | 1.45 | 1V01 | **MO** |
| | | | | | |
| To work 'B' Mon | | | | | |

## NEWTON ABBOT - TURN No. 51 - 2 x CLASS 42 ('A' / 'B') - 2200 H.P.

| From/To | Arrive | Notes | Depart | Code | Mon | Tue | Wed | Thu | Fri | Sat |
|---|---|---|---|---|---|---|---|---|---|---|
| Newton Abbot Depot | | | 13.00 | 0O14 | A | B | A | B | A | -- |
| Exeter St. David's | 13.35 | SH | 14.33 | 1O14 | A | B | A | B | A | -- |
| Waterloo | 18.14 | | 19.15 | 0Y02 | A | B | A | B | A | -- |
| Stewarts Lane | 19.35 | FUEL | 20.42 | LD | A | B | A | B | A | -- |
| Clapham Junction | 20.53 | | | | A | B | A | B | A | -- |
| | | | | | | | | | | |
| Clapham Junction | | | 0.20 | 8___ | -- | -- | B | -- | -- | A |
| Waterloo | 0.30 | | 1.00 | 8___ | -- | -- | B | -- | -- | A |
| Clapham Junction | 1.10 | | | | -- | -- | B | -- | -- | A |
| | | | | | | | | | | |
| Clapham Junction | | | 2.10 | 0O13 | -- | A | B | A | B | A |
| Kensington Olympia | 2.20 | Milk | 2.50 | 6O13 | -- | A | B | A | B | A |
| Stewarts Lane | 3.27 | | 3.40 | 0W . . | -- | A | B | A | B | A |
| Clapham Junction | 3.51 | Milk | 4.15 | 6W . . | -- | A | B | A | B | A |
| Morden South | 4.30 | | 4.54 | 0V04 | -- | A | B | A | B | A |
| Clapham Junction | 5.15 | | | | -- | A | B | A | B | A |
| | | | | | | | | | | |
| Clapham C.S. | | | 6.05 | 5V04 | -- | A | B | A | B | -- |
| Waterloo | 6.14 | Vans | 7.17 | 6W . . | -- | A | B | A | B | -- |
| Clapham Junction | 7.27 | | 8.08 | 0Y61 | -- | A | B | A | B | -- |
| Waterloo North Sidings | 8.16 | | 8.35 | 0V09 | -- | A | B | A | B | -- |
| Waterloo | 8.40 | SH / (b) | 9.08 | 1V09 | B | A | B | A | B | -- |
| Exeter St. David's | 12.42 | | 12.50 | 0F91 | B | A | B | A | B | -- |
| Exeter Stabling Point | 12.55 | | 15.40 | 0O16 | B | A | B | A | B | -- |
| Exeter St. David's | 15.45 | SH | 16.00 | 1O16 | B | A | B | A | B | -- |
| Waterloo | 20.02 | Vans | 20.33 | 6W . . | B | A | B | A | B | -- |
| Clapham Junction | 20.42 | | 21.12 | 0Y02 | B | A | B | A | B | -- |
| Stewarts Lane | 21.22 | | | | B | A | B | A | B | -- |
| Stewarts Lane | | | 0.40 | 0K21 | -- | B | A | B | A | B |
| Waterloo (via Kensington) | 1.01 | Vans | 4.05 | 6K21 | -- | B | A | B | A | B |
| Clapham Junction | 5.42 | | 6.17 | 0V04 | -- | B | A | B | A | B |
| Waterloo | 6.25 | (a) | 6.38 | 1V04 | A | B | A | B | A | B |
| Exeter St. David's | 10.25 | ASSIST | 10.42 | 8B70 | A | B | A | B | A | --- |
| Exeter Central | 10.51 | | 11.10 | 0B58 | A | B | A | B | A | --- |
| Exeter St. David's | 11.15 | | 11.25 | 0F76 | A | B | A | B | A | --- |
| Newton Abbot Depot | 11.55 | | | | A | B | A | B | A | --- |
| | | | | | | | | | | |
| **FUEL** | | | | | | | | | | |
| | | | | | | | | | | |

(a) Worked by 'B' (off 02.30 Clapham Junction Mon) (b) worked by 'A' (off 01.25 Kensington)

## NEWTON ABBOT - TURN No. 51 - 2 x CLASS 42 ('A' / 'B') - 2200 H.P. (continued)

| 'A' ENGINE | Arrive | Notes | Depart | Code | |
|---|---|---|---|---|---|
| Clapham Junction | 5.15 | *Vans* | 6.10 | 6M02 | **SO** |
| Kensington Olympia | 6.22 | *Vans* | 7.10 | 6O26 | |
| Clapham Junction | 7.22 | | 8.30 | 0V09 | |
| Waterloo | 8.37 | SH | 9.00 | 1V09 | |
| Exeter St. David's | 12.48 | | 12.55 | 0F91 | |
| Exeter Stabling Point | 13.00 | | 14.00 | 0O14 | |
| Exeter St. David's | 14.05 | | 14.33 | 1O14 | |
| Waterloo | 18.27 | | 19.10 | 0Y02 | |
| Stewarts Lane | 19.30 | FUEL | 20.45 | 0Y61 | |
| Waterloo North Sidings | 21.06 | | | | |
| | | | | | |
| Waterloo North Sidings | | | 8.50 | 0V09 | **SUO** |
| Waterloo | 8.55 | | 9.08 | 1V09 | |
| Exeter St. David's | 12.50 | | 12.55 | 0F91 | |
| Exeter Stabling Point | 13.00 | | 16.35 | 0O17 | |
| Exeter St. David's | 16.40 | | 16.55 | 1O17 | |
| Waterloo | 20.35 | | 21.37 | 0Y02 | |
| Stewarts Lane | 21.57 | FUEL | 23.05 | 0Y62 | |
| Clapham Junction | 23.16 | | | | |
| | | | | | |
| Clapham Junction | | | 2.10 | 0O03 | **MO** |
| Kensington Olympia | 2.20 | *Milk* | 2.50 | 6O03 | |
| Stewarts Lane | 3.08 | | 3.40 | 0V04 | |
| Clapham Junction | 3.51 | | 6.05 | 5V04 | |
| Waterloo | 6.14 | | 6.40 | LD | |
| Waterloo North Sidings | 6.45 | | 8.35 | 0V09 | |
| Waterloo | 8.40 | SH | 9.08 | 1V09 | |
| | | | | | |
| To work 'B' Mon | | | | | |
| **'B' ENGINE** | **Arrive** | **Notes** | **Depart** | **Code** | |
| Waterloo | 5.15 | (b) | 6.38 | 1V04 | **SO** |
| Exeter St. David's | 10.35 | RR | 11.05 | 1O11 | |
| Waterloo | 14.19 | | 15.06 | 0Y02 | |
| Stewarts Lane | 15.29 | FUEL | 18.25 | 0V19 | |
| Waterloo | 18.46 | | 19.00 | 1V19 | |
| Exeter St. David's | 22.55 | | 23.25 | 5B80 | |
| Newton Abbot | 23.55 | | 0.05 | 0F77 | **SUO** |
| Newton Abbot Depot | 0.10 | | | | |
| | | | | | |
| Waterloo | 5.15 | SH / (a) | 6.38 | 1V04 | **SO** |
| Exeter St. David's | 10.35 | | 10.40 | LD | |
| Exeter Stabling Point | 10.45 | | 11.30 | 0O12 | |
| Exeter St. David's | 11.35 | SH | 12.30 | 1O12 | |
| Waterloo | 16.27 | | 17.10 | 0Y02 | |
| Stewarts Lane | 17.30 | FUEL | 18.23 | 0V19 | |
| Waterloo | 18.46 | | 19.00 | 1V19 | |
| Exeter St. David's | 22.55 | | 23.25 | 5B80 | |
| Newton Abbot | 23.55 | | 0.05 | 0F76 | **SUO** |
| Newton Abbot Depot | 0.10 | | | | |
| | | | | | |
| **FUEL** | | | | | |
| | | | | | |
| Newton Abbot Depot | | (c) | 16.15 | 0O18 | **SUO** |
| Newton Abbot | 16.20 | | 16.30 | 5O18 | |
| Exeter St. David's | 17.00 | RR / SH | 18.20 | 1O18 | |
| Waterloo | 22.08 | | 23.17 | 0Y02 | |
| Stewarts Lane | 23.17 | FUEL | 0.15 | 0Y61 | **MO** |
| Waterloo North Sidings | 0.36 | | 6.20 | 0V04 | |
| Waterloo | 6.25 | | 6.38 | 1V04 | |
| | | | | | |
| To work 'A' Mon | | | | | |

(a) NOT 12/06 - 04/09/71 (b) 12/06 - 04/09/71 c) All dates until 03/10/71

| NEWTON ABBOT - TURN No. 52 - 2 x CLASS 42 ('A' / 'B') - 2200 H.P. | | | | | | | | | | |
|---|---|---|---|---|---|---|---|---|---|---|
| | | | | | | | | | | |
| **From/To** | **Arrive** | **Notes** | **Depart** | **Code** | **Mon** | **Tue** | **Wed** | **Thu** | **Fri** | **Sat** |
| Newton Abbot Depot | | | 5.30 | 0B41 | A | B | A | B | A | -- |
| Newton Abbot | 5.35 | SH | 6.10 | 2B41 | A | B | A | B | A | -- |
| Exeter St. David's | 6.46 | | 7.20 | 1O08 | A | B | A | B | A | -- |
| Waterloo | 11.13 | | 13.10 | LD | A | B | A | B | A | -- |
| Waterloo North Sidings | 13.15 | | 14.35 | 0V15 | A | B | A | B | A | -- |
| Waterloo | 14.40 | SH | 15.08 | 1V15 | A | B | A | B | A | -- |
| Exeter St. David's | 19.03 | | 19.15 | 0F91 | A | B | A | B | A | -- |
| Exeter Stabling Point | 19.20 | | 20.05 | 0O81 | A | B | A | B | A | -- |
| Exeter Riverside (19.00 Meldon Quarry) | 20.10 | | 20.26 | 6O81 | A | B | A | B | A | -- |
| Westbury | 22.38 | | 22.40 | 0F90 | -- | A | B | A | B | A |
| Westbury Depot | 22.45 | FUEL | 0.20 | 0O81 | -- | A | B | A | B | A |
| Westbury | 0.25 | | 0.35 | 6O81 | -- | A | B | A | B | A |
| Salisbury East Yard | 1.29 | | 3.20 | LD | -- | A | B | A | B | A |
| Salisbury | 3.25 | | | | -- | A | B | A | B | A |
| | | | | | | | | | | |
| Salisbury Stabling Point | | (b) | 3.20 | 0V01 | B | -- | -- | -- | -- | -- |
| Salisbury | 3.25 | | | | B | -- | -- | -- | -- | -- |
| | | | | | | | | | | |
| Salisbury (01.45 Waterloo) | | | 3.33 | 1V01 | B | A | B | A | B | A |
| | | | | | | | | | | |
| Yeovil Junction | 4.42 | RR / SH | 6.50 | 1O04 | B | A | B | A | B | A |
| Waterloo | 9.32 | | 10.07 | LD | B | A | B | A | B | -- |
| Waterloo North Sidings | 10.12 | | 10.50 | 0V11 | B | A | B | A | B | -- |
| Waterloo | 10.55 | | 11.08 | 1V11 | B | A | B | A | B | -- |
| Exeter St. David's | 14.54 | | 14.57 | 0B21 | B | A | B | A | B | -- |
| Exeter Riverside | 15.00 | *Milk ETS* | 15.14 | 6B21 | B | A | B | A | B | -- |
| Lapford | 15.50 | SHUNT | 17.15 | 6B16 | B | A | B | A | B | -- |
| Exeter St. David's | 17.48 | | 17.58 | 0F91 | B | A | B | A | B | -- |
| Exeter Stabling Point | 18.03 | | 19.45 | 0B84 | B | A | B | A | B | -- |
| Exeter St. David's | 19.50 | SH | 20.10 | 2B84 | B | A | B | A | B | -- |
| Newton Abbot | 20.42 | | 20.50 | 0F76 | B | A | B | A | B | -- |
| Newton Abbot Depot | 20.55 | | | | B | A | B | A | B | -- |
| | | | | | | | | | | |
| **FUEL** | | | | | | | | | | |
| | | | | | | | | | | |
| Exeter Stabling Point | | (a) | 3.35 | 0B38 | A | -- | -- | -- | -- | -- |
| Exeter Riverside | 3.45 | | 3.55 | 7B38 | A | -- | -- | -- | -- | -- |
| Newton Abbot | 4.36 | | 4.40 | 0F76 | A | -- | -- | -- | -- | -- |
| Newton Abbot Depot | 4.45 | | | | A | -- | -- | -- | -- | -- |
| | | | | | | | | | | |
| **FUEL** | | | | | | | | | | |
| | | | | | | | | | | |
| (a) Worked by 'B' Mon | | | | | | | | | | |
| (b) Worked by 'A' Mon (Off 23.50 Basingstoke SO) | | | | | | | | | | |
| | | | | | | | | | | |

| NEWTON ABBOT - TURN No. 52 - 2 x CLASS 42 ('A' / 'B') - 2200 H.P. (continued) | | | | | |
|---|---|---|---|---|---|
| | | | | | |
| **'A' ENGINE** | **Arrive** | **Notes** | **Depart** | **Code** | |
| Waterloo | 9.32 | | 9.46 | LD | **SO** |
| Waterloo North Sidings | 9.51 | | 10.35 | 0V11 | |
| Waterloo | 10.40 | | 11.00 | 1V11 | |
| Exeter St. David's. | 14.55 | | 15.00 | 0F76 | |
| Newton Abbot Depot | 15.30 | | | | |
| | | | | | |
| **FUEL** | | | | | |
| | | | | | |
| Newton Abbot Depot | | | 18.40 | 0B83 | |
| Exeter St. David's. | 19.10 | SH | 20.07 | 1O20 | |
| Basingstoke | 23.00 | RR | 23.50 | 1L02 | |
| Salisbury | 0.31 | | 0.45 | LD | **SUO** |
| Salisbury Stabling Point | 0.50 | | | | |
| | | | | | |
| Work 'B' MO (03.33 Salisbury). | | | | | |
| | | | | | |
| **'B' ENGINE** | **Arrive** | **Notes** | **Depart** | **Code** | |
| Newton Abbot Depot | | | 5.10 | 0B50 | **SO** |
| Newton Abbot (04.00 Friary) | 5.15 | | 5.22 | 8B50 | |
| Exeter Riverside | 6.00 | | 6.10 | 0F91 | |
| Exeter Stabling Point | 6.15 | | 9.50 | 0O10 | |
| Exeter St. David's | 9.55 | | 10.15 | 1O10 | |
| Waterloo | 14.08 | | 15.06 | LD | |
| Waterloo North Siding | 15.11 | | 16.XX | 0V17 | |
| Waterloo | 16.XX | | 17.00 | 1V17 | |
| Exeter St. David's | 21.00 | | 21.05 | 0F91 | |
| Exeter Stabling Point | 21.10 | | | | |
| | | | | | |
| SPARE SUO | | | | | |
| | | | | | |
| Stable for 03.55 Exeter MO | | | | | |
| | | | | | |
| To work 'A' MO | | | | | |

| NEWTON ABBOT - TURN No. 53 - 1 x CLASS 42 - 2200 H.P. | | | | | |
|---|---|---|---|---|---|
| | | | | | |
| **From/To** | **Arrive** | **Notes** | **Depart** | **Code** | |
| Newton Abbot Depot | | | 5.30 | LD | **M-F** |
| Newton Abbot (04.00 Plymouth Friary) | 5.35 | SH 2B22 | 6.50 | 8B50 | |
| Exeter Riverside | 7.36 | | 7.50 | 8B70 | |
| Exmouth Junction | 8.19 | SHUNT | 8.59 | 8B70 | |
| Exeter Riverside | 9.16 | | 9.45 | 8B70 | |
| Exmouth Junction | 10.05 | SHUNT | 10.30 | 0B58 | |
| Exeter Stabling Point | 10.50 | | 11.50 | 0O12 | |
| Exeter St. David's. | 11.55 | SHUNT | 12.30 | 1O12 | |
| Waterloo | 16.10 | | 17.02 | LD | |
| Waterloo North Sidings | 17.07 | | 18.45 | 0V19 | |
| Waterloo | 18.50 | SHUNT | 19.08 | 1V19 | |
| Exeter Central | 22.55 | | 23.05 | 2B58 | |
| Exeter St. David's | 23.09 | RR | 23.25 | 5B80 | |
| Newton Abbot | 23.55 | | 0.05 | 0F76 | **T - S** |
| Newton Abbot Depot | | | | | |
| | | | | | |
| **FUEL** | | | | | |
| | | | | | |
| (2B22 06.35 Newton - Paignton) | | | | | |
| | | | | | |
| Newton Abbot Depot | | | 4.55 | 0B16 | **SO (Until 25/09)** |
| Newton Abbot | 5.00 | | 5.12 | 2B16 | |
| Paignton | 5.32 | RR | 6.00 | 2B43 | |
| Newton Abbot | 6.23 | | 8.00 | 2B45 | |
| Exeter St. David's. | 8.38 | RR | 8.50 | 1O08 | |
| Waterloo | 12.32 | | 13.12 | LD | |
| Waterloo North Sidings | 13.17 | | 14.35 | 0V15 | |
| Waterloo | 14.40 | SHUNT | 15.00 | 1V15 | |
| Exeter St. David's | 19.02 | | 21.43 | 2B92 | |
| Newton Abbot | 22.18 | | 22.25 | 0F76 | |
| Newton Abbot Depot | 22.30 | | | | |
| | | | | | |
| **FUEL** | | | | | |
| | | | | | |
| Newton Abbot Depot | | | 8.45 | 0O10 | **SUO (Until 26/09)** |
| Newton Abbot | 8.50 | | 9.10 | 5O10 | |
| Exeter St. David's. | 9.40 | | 10.15 | 1O10 | |
| Waterloo | 14.02 | | 17.00 | LD | |
| Waterloo North Siding | 17.15 | | 18.10 | 0V19 | |
| Waterloo | 18.15 | | 19.08 | 1V19 | |
| Exeter Central | 22.55 | | 23.05 | 5B58 | |
| Exeter St. David's | 23.09 | | 23.25 | 5B80 | |
| Newton Abbot | 23.55 | | 0.05 | 0F76 | **MO** |
| Newton Abbot Depot | 0.10 | | | | |
| | | | | | |
| **FUEL** | | | | | |

## NEWTON ABBOT - TURN No. 61 - 2 x CLASS 43 ('A' / 'B') - 2200 H.P.

| From/To | Arrive | Notes | Depart | Code | Mon | Tue | Wed | Thu | Fri | Sat |
|---|---|---|---|---|---|---|---|---|---|---|
| Westbury D.S. | | | 6.00 | 0A54 | A | B | A | B | A | -- |
| Westbury | 6.05 | SH | 6.40 | 1A54 | A | B | A | B | A | -- |
| Paddington | 8.42 | | 9.16 | 5A06 | A | B | A | B | A | -- |
| Old Oak Common C.S. | 9.46 | Off 1V02 | 9.51 | 0F05 | A | B | A | B | A | -- |
| Ranelagh Bridge | 10.11 | FUEL | 12.35 | 0C56 | A | B | A | B | A | -- |
| Paddington | 12.40 | SH | 13.15 | 1C56 | A | B | A | B | A | -- |
| Hereford | 16.34 | RR / SH | 18.05 | 1A76 | A | B | A | B | A | -- |
| Paddington | 21.24 | | 21.55 | 0F06 | A | B | A | B | A | -- |
| Old Oak Common C.S. | 22.15 | | 22.30 | 5B65 | A | B | A | B | A | -- |
| Paddington | 22.41 | *News* | 1.10 | 1B01 | -- | A | B | A | B | A |
| Worcester Shrub Hill | 4.15 | | 4.20 | 0F80 | -- | A | B | A | B | A |
| Worcester Depot | 4.30 | | | | -- | A | B | A | B | A |
| | | | | | | | | | | |
| **FUEL** | | | | | | | | | | |
| | | | | | | | | | | |
| Worcester Depot | | | 6.05 | 0A06 | B | A | B | A | B | -- |
| Midland Yard | 6.10 | SH | 6.40 | 5A06 | B | A | B | A | B | -- |
| Worcester Shrub Hill | 6.50 | | 7.00 | 1A06 | B | A | B | A | B | -- |
| Paddington | 9.20 | | 10.46 | 5A06 | B | A | B | A | B | -- |
| Old Oak Common C.S. | 11.16 | Off 1A29 | 11.21 | 0F70 | B | A | B | A | B | -- |
| Old Oak Common Depot | 11.31 | | | | B | A | B | A | B | -- |
| | | | | | | | | | | |
| Old Oak Common Depot | | | 17.10 | 0B84 | B | A | B | A | B | -- |
| Paddington | 17.30 | SH | 17.46 | 1B84 | B | A | B | A | B | -- |
| Westbury | 19.43 | | 19.45 | 0F90 | B | A | B | A | B | -- |
| Westbury D.S. | 19.50 | | | | B | A | B | A | B | -- |
| | | | | | | | | | | |
| **SERVICE AND FUEL** | | | | | | | | | | |
| | | | | | | | | | | |
| Westbury D.S. | | | 22.30 | 0O00 | B | -- | B | -- | B | -- |
| Northam Yard | 0.25 | *Presflos* | 1.00 | 6V76 | -- | B | -- | B | -- | B |
| Westbury A.P.C.M. | 2.45 | | 3.00 | 0F90 | -- | B | -- | B | -- | B |
| Westbury D.S. | 3.05 | | | | -- | B | -- | B | -- | B |
| | | | | | | | | | | |
| **FUEL** | | | | | | | | | | |
| | | | | | | | | | | |
| Westbury D.S. | | | 21.00 | 0O42 | -- | A | -- | A | -- | -- |
| Westbury A.P.C.M. | 21.10 | *Presflos* | 21.55 | 6O42 | -- | A | -- | A | -- | -- |
| Northam Yard | 0.24 | | 1.00 | 0V00 | -- | -- | A | -- | A | -- |
| Westbury D.S. | 2.45 | | | | -- | -- | A | -- | A | -- |
| | | | | | | | | | | |
| **FUEL** | | | | | | | | | | |
| | | | | | | | | | | |
| Spare at Westbury 03.05 SO. 06.35 MO. | | | | | | | | | | |

| NEWTON ABBOT - TURN No. 61 - 2 x CLASS 43 ('A' / 'B') - 2200 H.P. (continued) | | | | | | | | | | |
|---|---|---|---|---|---|---|---|---|---|---|
| | | | | | | | | | | |
| **'A' ENGINE** | **Arrive** | **Notes** | **Depart** | **Code** | | | | | | |
| Worcester Depot | | | 8.25 | 0A46 | **SO** | | | | | |
| Midland Yard | 8.30 | Portion | 8.35 | 5A46 | | | | | | |
| Worcester Shrub Hill (08.05 Hereford) | 8.45 | NA64 off | 9.00 | 1A46 | | | | | | |
| Paddington | 11.25 | | 11.45 | 0F05 | | | | | | |
| Ranelagh Bridge | 11.50 | FUEL | 12.35 | 0C56 | | | | | | |
| Paddington | 12.40 | SH | 13.15 | 1C56 | | | | | | |
| Hereford (To Paddington) | 16.34 | RR / SH | 18.05 | 1A76 | | | | | | |
| Worcester S. H. | 18.52 | | 18.55 | 0F81 | | | | | | |
| Worcester Depot | 19.05 | FUEL | | | | | | | | |
| | | | | | | | | | | |
| Worcester Depot | | | 15.50 | 0C18 | **SUO** | | | | | |
| Worcester Shrub Hill | 16.00 | | 16.20 | 2C18 | | | | | | |
| Hereford | 17.10 | RR / SH | 18.20 | 1A76 | | | | | | |
| Paddington | 21.50 | *News* | 1.10 | 1B01 | **MO** | | | | | |
| Worcester Shrub Hill | 4.15 | | 4.20 | 0F81 | | | | | | |
| Worcester Depot | 4.30 | | | | | | | | | |
| | | | | | | | | | | |
| **FUEL** | | | | | | | | | | |
| | | | | | | | | | | |
| To work 'B' Mon | | | | | | | | | | |
| | | | | | | | | | | |
| | | | | | | | | | | |
| **'B' ENGINE** | | | | | | | | | | |
| | | | | | | | | | | |
| SPARE – WESTBURY | | | | | | | | | | |
| 03.05 SO - 06.00 Mon | | | | | | | | | | |
| | | | | | | | | | | |
| To work 'A' Mon | | | | | | | | | | |
| | | | | | | | | | | |

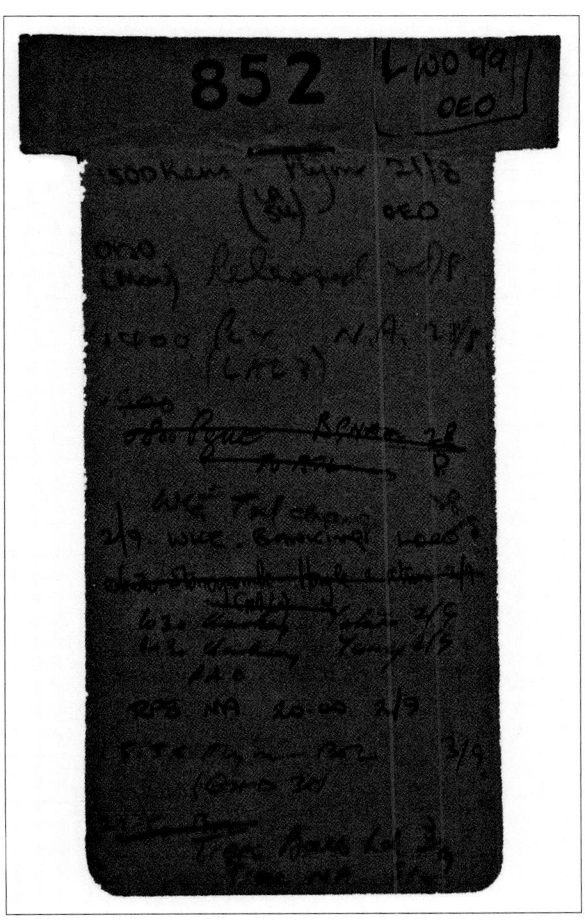


**The green of 852 denotes Newton Abbot; it should have been blue, but several Newton Abbot locos had green cards around August/September 1971. Milk empties are 852's first duties on the card, starting from Saturday 21st August. OEO (One Engine Only) in red indicates the loco was in trouble. In fact it had failed at Paddington on the 20th having arrived on the up postal with a noisy B end transmission. Inspected at Old Oak Common, it was released on OEO to get it to Laira for a transmission change. This was 06.30 on Friday 27th but it did not work until the 28th taking 8B50, the 04.00 from Friary to Exeter as far as Newton Abbot, giving way to 806. Further B transmission troubles kept the loco idle until 2nd September when it performed banking duties to Totnes. Two engineers' trains came next but it was back at Newton by 20.00 hrs. 852 was then failed with flat batteries. On the 3rd it took over 4M05, the 12.50 Penzance-Crewe perishables as far as Bristol. The B transmission was found to be in a 'deplorable condition' and the loco was shown as failed (indicated, oddly, by the word 'TICK') at Bath Road. It was hauled to Newton Abbot on the 4th by D1047, along with 842, and shown again as TICK at Newton Abbot on the 5th. It did work again briefly on freight, getting as far as Westbury, on the 6th and 7th but by the end of the 7th it was back at Newton Abbot with B transmission trouble and 'boiling batteries'. It was stored at Newton Abbot from the 11th but surprisingly hauled to Bristol Bath Road on the 29th with 835 by 815. 852 was eventually withdrawn at Bristol on the 3rd and 835 followed on the 4th, neither locos having worked any trains whilst at Bristol.**

| NEWTON ABBOT - TURN No. 64 - 4 x CLASS 43 ('A' / 'B' / 'C' / 'D') - 2200 H.P. | | | | | | | | | | |
|---|---|---|---|---|---|---|---|---|---|---|
| | | | | | | | | | | |
| **From/To** | **Arrive** | **Notes** | **Depart** | **Code** | **Mon** | **Tue** | **Wed** | **Thu** | **Fri** | **Sat** |
| Westbury D.S. | | | 3.15 | 0B15 | C | D | A | B | C | -- |
| Westbury | 3.20 | | 3.30 | 8B15 | C | D | A | B | C | -- |
| Merehead Quarry | 4.40 | SHUNT | 6.00 | 8B20 | C | D | A | B | C | -- |
| Westbury | 7.45 | | 7.50 | 0F90 | C | D | A | B | C | -- |
| Westbury D.S. | 7.55 | | 9.15 | 0B43 | C | D | A | B | C | -- |
| Westbury | 9.29 | | 9.29 | 8B43 | C | D | A | B | C | -- |
| Yeovil Pen Mill | 10.30 | SHUNT | 12.30 | 8B47 | C | D | A | B | C | -- |
| Westbury | 13.29 | | 13.35 | 0F90 | C | D | A | B | C | -- |
| Westbury D.S. | 13.40 | | 15.15 | 0B68 | C | D | A | B | C | -- |
| Westbury | 15.20 | | 15.38 | 7B68 | C | D | A | B | C | -- |
| Bristol West Depot | 17.45 | | | | C | D | A | B | C | -- |
| | | | | | | | | | | |
| Bristol West Depot | | | 18.00 | 0V95 | C | D | A | B | C* | -- |
| Stoke Gifford Yard | 18.30 | # | 18.40 | 7V95 | C | D | A | B | C* | -- |
| Exeter Riverside | 22.07 | | 22.30 | 0F74 | C | D | A | B | C* | -- |
| Bristol Bath Road Depot | 1.00 | | | | -- | C | D | A | B | C* |
| | | | | | | | | | | |
| Bristol West Depot | 17.45 | (a) | 17.50 | 0F74 | -- | -- | -- | -- | C | -- |
| Bristol Bath Road Depot | 18.00 | | | | -- | -- | -- | -- | C | -- |
| | | | | | | | | | | |
| **FUEL** | | | | | | | | | | |
| | | | | | | | | | | |
| Bristol Bath Road Depot | | | 10.00 | 0B73 | B | C | D | A | B | -- |
| Malago Vale C.S. | 10.10 | *Vans* | 10.30 | 5B73 | B | C | D | A | B | -- |
| Worcester Shrub Hill | 12.52 | | 12.55 | 0F80 | B | C | D | A | B | -- |
| Worcester Depot | 13.05 | | 13.30 | 0A26 | B | C | D | A | B | -- |
| Worcester Shrub Hill | 13.40 | SH | 14.15 | 1A26 | B | C | D | A | B | -- |
| Paddington | 16.40 | | 17.15 | 0F05 | B | C | D | A | B | -- |
| Ranelagh Bridge | 17.20 | FUEL | 18.00 | 0C06 | B | C | D | A | B | -- |
| Paddington | 18.05 | | 18.15 | 1C06 | B | C | D | A | B | -- |
| Hereford | 21.13 | | 21.20 | 0F00 | B | C | D | A | B | -- |
| Hereford Stabling Point | | | | | B | C | D | A | B | -- |
| | | | | | | | | | | |
| * NOT Fridays 07/05 - 24/09 | | | | | | | | | | |
| (a) Fridays from 01/10 | | | | | | | | | | |
| **NOTE** : 7V95 02.09 MO / 04.20 MX Carlisle to Riverside runs as class '6' to Stoke Gifford. | | | | | | | | | | |
| | | | | | | | | | | |

| NEWTON ABBOT - TURN No. 64 - 4 x CLASS 43 ('A' / 'B' / 'C' / 'D') - 2200 H.P. (continued) | | | | | | | | | | |
|---|---|---|---|---|---|---|---|---|---|---|
| | | | | | | | | | | |
| **From/To** | **Arrive** | **Notes** | **Depart** | **Code** | **Mon** | **Tue** | **Wed** | **Thu** | **Fri** | **Sat** |
| Hereford Stabling Point | | | 7.15 | 0A46 | A | B | C | D | A | B |
| Hereford (To Paddington) | 7.20 | SH | 8.05 | 1A46 | A | B | C | D | A | B |
| Worcester Shrub Hill | 8.52 | NA61 on | 8.55 | 0F81 | A | B | C | D | A | B |
| Worcester Depot | 9.05 | FUEL | 10.40 | 0B__ | A | B | C | D | A | B |
| Worcester Yard | 10.45 | | 11.05 | 8B__ | A | B | C | D | A | -- |
| Droitwich Spa | 11.25 | SHUNT | 12.55 | 8B__ | A | B | C | D | A | -- |
| Bromsgrove | 13.20 | SHUNT | 14.35 | 8B__ | A | B | C | D | A | -- |
| Droitwich Spa | 14.55 | SHUNT | 15.30 | 8B__ | A | B | C | D | A | -- |
| Worcester Yard | 15.50 | | 16.00 | 0F81 | A | B | C | D | A | -- |
| Worcester Depot | 16.05 | | 17.10 | 0M20 | A | B | C | D | A | -- |
| Worcester Shrub Hill | 17.20 | *Parcels* | 18.00 | 6M20 | A | B | C | D | A | -- |
| Birmingham New Street | 19.08 | | 19.10 | 0V03 | A | B | C | D | A | -- |
| Birmingham Curzon Street | 19.XX | | 21.30 | 4V03 | A | B | C | D | A | -- |
| Bristol T.M. | 1.44 | SHUNT | 2.30 | 0F74 | -- | A | B | C | D | A |
| Bristol Bath Road | 2.45 | | | | -- | A | B | C | D | A |
| | | | | | | | | | | |
| **FUEL** | | | | | | | | | | |
| | | | | | | | | | | |
| Bristol Bath Road | | (c) | 3.55 | 0O10 | D | A | B | C | D | -- |
| Malago Vale C.S. | 4.10 | | 4.25 | 5O10 | D | A | B | C | D | -- |
| Bristol T.M. | 4.30 | *Parcels* | 5.05 | 4O10 | D | A | B | C | D | -- |
| Westbury | 6.25 | SHUNT | 7.00 | 4O10 | D | A | B | C | D | -- |
| Salisbury | 7.42 | | 8.00 | 0V76 | D | A | B | C | D | -- |
| Salisbury Yard | 8.05 | *Ballast* | 8.20 | 7V76 | D | A | B | C | D | -- |
| Exeter Riverside Yard | 12.09 | RR | 12.35 | 7V76 | D | A | B | C | D | -- |
| Meldon Quarry | 14.00 | | | | D | A | B | C | D | -- |
| | | | | | | | | | | |
| Meldon Quarry | | *Ballast* | 14.50 | 7B60 | D | A | B | C | D | -- |
| Exeter Riverside Yard | 15.37 | | 16.40 | 0O81 | D | A | B | C | D | -- |
| Meldon Quarry | 17.45 | | | | D | A | B | C | D | -- |
| | | | | | | | | | | |
| Meldon Quarry (To Salisbury) | | *Ballast* | 19.00 | 6O81 | D | A | B | C | D | -- |
| Exeter Riverside Yard (Continuation of 14.50 Meldon) | 20.12 | (b) | 21.47 | 7O85 | D | A | B | C | D | -- |
| | | | | | | | | | | |
| Westbury | 0.15 | ~ | 0.20 | 0F90 | -- | D | A | B | C | D |
| Westbury D.S. | 0.25 | | | | -- | D | A | B | C | D |
| | | | | | | | | | | |
| **SERVICE AND FUEL** | | | | | | | | | | |
| | | | | | | | | | | |
| (b) 'Q' T. & Th. (Or as ordered) | | | | | | | | | | |
| (c) 04.45 LD off Depot MO | | | | | | | | | | |
| **NOTE** : ~ 7O85 worked forward from Westbury by Cl. 35 on BR170. | | | | | | | | | | |
| | | | | | | | | | | |

## NEWTON ABBOT - TURN No. 64 - 4 x CLASS 43 ('A' / 'B' / 'C' / 'D') - 2200 H.P. (continued)

| **'A' ENGINE** | **Arrive** | **Notes** | **Depart** | **Code** | |
|---|---|---|---|---|---|
| Bristol Bath Road | | | 4.45 | 0O10 | **SO** |
| Bristol T.M. | 4.45 | Parcels | 4.55 | 4O10 | |
| Westbury | 6.20 | SHUNT | 7.00 | 4O10 | |
| Salisbury | 7.42 | SHUNT | 8.30 | 0V00 | |
| Westbury D.S. | 9.15 | | | | |
| | | | | | |
| Westbury D.S. | | | 14.40 | 0O42 | |
| Westbury | 14.45 | *Prestflos* | 15.00 | 6O42 | |
| Northam | 17.13 | | 18.20 | 0V00 | |
| Westbury D.S. | 19.45 | | | | |
| | | | | | |
| **FUEL** | | | | | |
| | | | | | |
| Westbury D.S. | | | 12.30 | 0M90 | **SUO** |
| Westbury (10.00 Weymouth - Manchester) | 12.35 | *Parcels* | 12.50 | 6M90 | |
| Bristol T.M. | 13.48 | | 13.55 | 0F74 | |
| Bristol Bath Road | 14.05 | | | | |
| | | | | | |
| To work 'D' Mon | | | | | |
| | | | | | |
| **'B' ENGINE** | **Arrive** | **Notes** | **Depart** | **Code** | **Arrive** |
| Worcester Depot | 9.05 | | 13.30 | 0A26 | **SO** |
| Worcester Shrub Hill | 13.40 | SH | 14.15 | 1A26 | |
| Paddington | 16.40 | | 18.15 | 0F05 | |
| Ranelagh Bridge | 18.20 | FUEL | 19.10 | 0B36 | |
| Paddington | 19.15 | | 20.15 | 1B36 | |
| Worcester Shrub Hill | 22.48 | | 22.55 | 0F80 | |
| Worcester Depot | 23.05 | | | | |
| | | | | | |
| **FUEL** | | | | | |
| | | | | | |
| Worcester Depot | | | 9.20 | 0A66 | **SUO** |
| Midland Yard | 9.25 | SH | 9.50 | 5A66 | |
| Worcester Shrub Hill | 10.00 | SH | 10.15 | 1A66 | |
| Paddington | 12.55 | | 13.15 | 0F05 | |
| Ranelagh Bridge | 13.20 | FUEL | 17.50 | 0C06 | |
| Paddington | 17.55 | SH | 18.15 | 1C06 | |
| Hereford | 21.36 | | 21.50 | 0F00 | |
| Hereford Stabling Point | 21.55 | | | | |
| | | | | | |
| To work 'A' Mon | | | | | |
| | | | | | |
| **'C' ENGINE** | **Arrive** | **Notes** | **Depart** | **Code** | |
| Bristol Bath Road | | | 1.35 | 0B12 | **SO (12/06 - 04/09 ONLY)** |
| Stoke Gifford Yard | 2.00 | | 2.20 | 8B12 | |
| Westbury | 3.40 | | 5.30 | 8B02 | |
| Bristol West Depot | 6.45 | | 6.55 | 0F74 | |
| Bristol Bath Road | 7.00 | | | | |
| | | | | | |
| Spare at Bath Road 01.00 SO - 10.00 Mon | | | | | |
| | | | | | |
| To work 'B' Mon | | | | | |
| | | | | | |
| **'D' ENGINE** | | | | | |
| | | | | | |
| Spare Westbury | | | | | |
| SO & SUO | | | | | |
| | | | | | |
| To work 'C' Mon | | | | | |

## NEWTON ABBOT - TURN No. 65 - 3 x CLASS 43 ('A' / 'B' / 'C') - 2200 H.P.

| From/To | Arrive | Notes | Depart | Code | Mon | Tue | Wed | Thu | Fri | Sat |
|---|---|---|---|---|---|---|---|---|---|---|
| **NOT FRIDAYS - UNTIL 24/09** | | | | | | | | | | |
| Newton Abbot Depot | | | 5.30 | 0B10 | A | B | C | A | -- | -- |
| Cowley Loop | 6.00 | | 6.10 | 5B10 | A | B | C | A | -- | -- |
| Exeter St. David's (To Penzance) | 6.15 | SH | 7.10 | 2B10 | A | B | C | A | -- | -- |
| **FRIDAYS ONLY - UNTIL 24/09** | | | | | | | | | | |
| Laira Depot | | | 8.20 | 0B10 | -- | -- | -- | -- | B | -- |
| Plymouth North Road (07.10 Exeter) | 8.35 | | 8.50 | 2B10 | -- | -- | -- | -- | B | -- |
| **ALL DATES** | | | | | | | | | | |
| Penzance (To Paddington) | 11.09 | | 12.25 | 1A45 | A | B | C | A | B | -- |
| Plymouth North Road (07.36 Leeds 'Cornishman') | 14.30 | | 14.55 | 1V70 | A | B | C | A | B | -- |
| Penzance | 17.05 | PROPEL | 17.20 | 5V70 | A | B | C | A | B | -- |
| Slopers Sidings | 17.25 | | 17.30 | 0F79 | A | B | C | A | B | -- |
| Penzance Depot | 17.35 | | | | A | B | C | A | B | -- |
| **FUEL** | | | | | | | | | | |
| Penzance Depot | | | 18.35 | 0A61 | A | B | C | A | B | -- |
| Penzance | 18.40 | *Postal* | 19.00 | 1A61 | A | B | C | A | B | -- |
| Paddington | 3.45 | | 4.45 | 0F70 | -- | A | B | C | A | B |
| Old Oak Common Depot | 5.05 | FUEL | | | -- | A | B | C | A | -- |
| **NOT FRIDAYS 11/06 - 24/09** | | | | | | | | | | |
| Old Oak Common Depot | | | 7.35 | 0B16 | C | A | B | C | A | -- |
| Paddington | 7.55 | | | | C | A | B | C | A | -- |
| **FRIDAYS ONLY 11/06 - 24/09** | | | | | | | | | | |
| Old Oak Common Depot | | | 6.30 | 0F01 | -- | -- | -- | -- | A | -- |
| Old Oak Common C.S. | 6.40 | *Diners* | 6.55 | 5F01 | -- | -- | -- | -- | A | -- |
| Paddington | 7.15 | | | | -- | -- | -- | -- | A | -- |
| **ALL DATES continued** | | | | | | | | | | |
| Paddington | 7.55 | | 8.12 | 1B16 | C | A | B | C | A | -- |
| Worcester Shrub Hill | 10.40 | | 12.15 | 1A86 | C | A | B | C | A | -- |
| Paddington | 14.40 | | 15.15 | 0F05 | C | A | B | C | A | -- |
| Ranelagh Bridge | 15.20 | | | | C | A | B | C | A | -- |
| **FUEL** | | | | | | | | | | |
| Ranelagh Bridge | | | 16.45 | 0B76 | C | A | B | C | A | -- |
| Paddington | 16.50 | | 17.15 | 1B76 | C | A | B | C | A | -- |
| Worcester Shrub Hill | 19.35 | | 19.45 | 0F81 | C | A | B | C | A | -- |
| Worcester Depot | 19.50 | | 19.45 | 0E18 | C | A | B | C | A | -- |
| Worcester Yard (To Temple Mills) | 19.55 | | 20.32 | 7E18 | C | A | B | C | A | -- |
| Swindon | 23.28 | | 23.35 | 0F73 | C | A | B | C | A | -- |
| Swindon Stabling Point | 23.45 | | | | | | | | | |
| Swindon Stabling Point | | | 0.45 | 0A11 | -- | C | A | B | C | A |
| Swindon Cocklebury Yard (22.55 Gloucester Yard) | 0.55 | LA28 off | 1.08 | 7A11 | -- | C | A | B | C | A |

| NEWTON ABBOT - TURN No. 65 - 3 x CLASS 43 ('A' / 'B' / 'C') - 2200 H.P. (continued) | | | | | | | | | | |
|---|---|---|---|---|---|---|---|---|---|---|
| | | | | | | | | | | |
| **From/To** | **Arrive** | **Notes** | **Depart** | **Code** | **Mon** | **Tue** | **Wed** | **Thu** | **Fri** | **Sat** |
| | | | | | | | | | | |
| Paddington Goods | 4.00 | | 4.05 | 0F05 | -- | C | A | B | C | A |
| Ranelagh Bridge | 4.25 | FUEL | 7.05 | 0A06 | B | C | A | B | C | -- |
| Paddington | 7.10 | Off 1A72 | 7.45 | 5A06 | B | C | A | B | C | -- |
| Old Oak Common C.S. | 8.15 | | 8.45 | 5B45 | B | C | A | B | C | -- |
| Paddington | 9.05 | | 9.30 | 0F05 | B | C | A | B | C | -- |
| Ranelagh Bridge | 9.35 | | 9.55 | 0B86 | B | C | A | B | C | -- |
| Paddington | 10.00 | | 11.15 | 1B86 | B | C | A | B | C | -- |
| Worcester Shrub Hill | 13.40 | | 13.45 | 0F81 | B | C | A | B | C | -- |
| Worcester Depot | 13.50 | FUEL | 15.50 | 0A46 | B | C | A | B | C | -- |
| Worcester | 15.55 | SH | 16.15 | 1A46 | B | C | A | B | C | -- |
| Paddington | 18.40 | | 19.30 | 0B07 | B | C | A | B | C | -- |
| Paddington Parcels Line | 19.35 | *BRUTE* | 20.08 | 3B07 | B | C | A | B | C | -- |
| Plymouth North Road | 2.26 | | | | -- | B | C | A | B | C |
| | | | | | | | | | | |
| **NOT FRIDAYS - UNTIL 24/09** | | | | | | | | | | |
| Plymouth North Road | 2.26 | | 2.35 | 0F76 | -- | B | C | A | B | -- |
| Newton Abbot Depot | 3.30 | | | | -- | B | C | A | B | -- |
| | | | | | | | | | | |
| **FUEL** | | | | | | | | | | |
| | | | | | | | | | | |
| **FRIDAYS ONLY UNTIL 24/09** | | | | | | | | | | |
| Plymouth North Road | 2.26 | | 2.35 | 0F77 | -- | -- | -- | -- | B | -- |
| Laira Depot | 2.50 | | | | -- | -- | -- | -- | B | -- |
| | | | | | | | | | | |
| **FUEL** | | | | | | | | | | |
| | | | | | | | | | | |
| **'A' ENGINE** | **Arrive** | **Notes** | **Depart** | **Code** | | | | | | |
| Old Oak Common Depot | 4.05 | FUEL/(a) | 6.20 | 0F01 | **SO** | | | | | |
| Old Oak Common C.S. | 6.30 | *Vans* | 6.40 | 5F01 | | | | | | |
| Paddington (To Barnstaple Junction) | 7.00 | LA62 On | 8.10 | 1B18 | | | | | | |
| Exeter St. David's. | 11.03 | | 11.10 | 0F91 | | | | | | |
| Exeter Stabling Point | 11.15 | | 15.30 | 0A41 | | | | | | |
| Exeter St. David's (14.40 Barnstaple Junction) | 15.35 | LA62 Off | 15.44 | 1A41 | | | | | | |
| Paddington | 18.31 | Off 1A51 / (b) | 19.28 | 5A06 | | | | | | |
| Old Oak Common C.S. | 19.58 | | 20.08 | 0F70 | | | | | | |
| Old Oak Common Depot | 20.18 | | | | | | | | | |
| | | | | | | | | | | |
| **FUEL** | | | | | | | | | | |
| | | | | | | | | | | |
| Paddington | 18.31 | | 18.49 | 0F70 | | | | | | |
| Old Oak Common Depot | 19.09 | | | | | | | | | |
| | | | | | | | | | | |
| **FUEL** | | | | | | | | | | |
| | | | | | | | | | | |
| Old Oak Common Depot | | | 7.40 | 0M11 | **SUO** | | | | | |
| Old Oak Common C.S. | 7.50 | | 8.00 | 5M11 | | | | | | |
| Paddington | 8.20 | | 9.30 | 1B45 | | | | | | |
| Paignton | 13.40 | | 17.05 | 1A74 | | | | | | |
| Paddington | 21.25 | Off 1A75 | 22.04 | 5A06 | | | | | | |
| Old Oak Common C.S. | 22.34 | | 22.44 | LD | | | | | | |
| Old Oak Common Depot | 22.54 | | | | | | | | | |
| | | | | | | | | | | |
| **FUEL** | | | | | | | | | | |
| | | | | | | | | | | |
| To work 'C' Mon | | | | | | | | | | |
| | | | | | | | | | | |

## NEWTON ABBOT - TURN No. 65 - 3 x CLASS 43 ('A' / 'B' / 'C') - 2200 H.P. (continued)

| 'B' ENGINE | Arrive | Notes | Depart | Code | |
|---|---|---|---|---|---|
| Paddington | 3.45 | | 4.45 | 0F05 | **SO** |
| Ranelagh Bridge | 4.50 | FUEL | 5.35 | 0F06 | |
| Old Oak Common C.S. | 5.55 | *Vans* | 6.40 | 5A . . | |
| Paddington | 7.00 | | 7.15 | 0F70 | |
| Old Oak Common C.S. | 7.35 | | 8.30 | 5B36 | |
| Paddington | 8.50 | | 9.15 | 0F06 | |
| Old Oak Common C.S. | 9.45 | | 10.45 | 5B95 | |
| Paddington | 11.05 | | 12.10 | 1B05 | |
| Paignton | 16.02 | | 17.55 | 1B86 | **SO** |
| Bristol T.M. | 20.41 | RR | 21.15 | 1B28 | |
| Plymouth North Road | 0.35 | | 1.00 | 5B75 | **SUO** |
| Laira C.S. | 1.30 | | 1.40 | 0F77 | |
| Laira | 1.45 | | | | |
| | | | | | |
| **FUEL** | | | | | |
| | | | | | |
| Laira | | | 9.30 | 0B28 | |
| Plymouth North Road | 9.45 | | 10.00 | 6B28 | |
| Penzance | 15.15 | SHUNT | 19.00 | 1A61 | |
| Paddington | 3.45 | Off 1A63 | 5.10 | 5A06 | **MO** |
| Old Oak Common C.S. | 5.40 | | 5.45 | 0F05 | |
| Ranelagh Bridge | 6.05 | | | | |
| | | | | | |
| To work 'B' Mon | | | | | |
| | | | | | |
| **'C' ENGINE** | **Arrive** | **Notes** | **Depart** | **Code** | |
| Plymouth North Road | 2.26 | | 2.35 | 0B50 | **SO** |
| Plymouth Friary (To Exeter Riverside) | 2.55 | * | 4.00 | 8B50 | |
| Newton Abbot | 5.13 | | 5.20 | 0F76 | |
| Newton Abbot Depot | 5.25 | | | | |
| | | | | | |
| **FUEL** | | | | | |
| | | | | | |
| Newton Abbot Depot | | (e) | 7.30 | 0B91 | |
| Newton Abbot | 7.35 | | 7.50 | 2B91 | |
| Paignton | 8.09 | | 8.22 | 2B47 | |
| Newton Abbot | 8.47 | | 8.50 | 0F76 | |
| Newton Abbot Depot | 8.55 | | | | |
| | | | | | |
| Newton Abbot Depot | | (a) | 7.30 | 0B91 | |
| Newton Abbot | 7.35 | | 7.50 | 2B91 | |
| Kingswear | 8.30 | RR | 8.45 | 1C36 | |
| Cardiff General | 12.20 | | 12.30 | 5C99 | |
| Cardiff Canton C.S. | 12.35 | | 12.50 | 5B04 | |
| Cardiff General | 12.55 | | 13.10 | 1B04 | |
| Paignton | 16.40 | | 17.10 | 5B80 | |
| Newton Abbot C.S. | 17.25 | | 17.35 | 0F76 | |
| Newton Abbot Depot | 17.40 | | | | |
| | | | | | |
| **FUEL** | | | | | |
| | | | | | |
| SPARE - NEWTON ABBOT SUO | | | | | |
| To work 'A' Mon | | | | | |
| | | | | | |
| (a) SO 12/06 - 25/09 | | | | | |
| (b) SO 12/06 - 04/09 | | | | | |
| (c) SO 11/09 - 25/09 | | | | | |
| (d) SUO Until 26/09 | | | | | |
| (e) SO Until 05/06 | | | | | |
| * ASSIST from 12/06 | | | | | |

## NEWTON ABBOT - TURN No. 66 - SPARE CLASS 42 - 2200 H.P.

| | | | | | | | | | | |
|---|---|---|---|---|---|---|---|---|---|---|
| **From/To** | **Arrive** | **Notes** | **Depart** | **Code** | | | | | | |
| **OFF TURN No. LA 153** | | | | | | | | | | |
| Newton Abbot Depot | | | 23.10 | 0B83 | **FO (Until 24/09)** | | | | | |
| Newton Abbot | 23.15 | | 23.30 | 5B83 | | | | | | |
| Exeter St. David's. | 23.59 | | 0.05 | 0B08 | **SO (Until 24/09)** | | | | | |
| Exeter Riverside Yard | 0.10 | | 0.40 | 7B08 | | | | | | |
| Plymouth Friary | 3.05 | | 3.15 | 0F77 | | | | | | |
| Laira Depot | 3.25 | | | | | | | | | |
| | | | | | | | | | | |
| Laira Depot | | | 4.15 | 0V39 | **SO (12/06 - 25/09)** | | | | | |
| Plymouth North Road (21.27 Manchester) | 4.30 | | 4.45 | 1V39 | | | | | | |
| Newquay (To Nottingham) | 6.40 | | 11.50 | 1M54 | | | | | | |
| Plymouth North Road | 12.41 | | 13.45 | 0F77 | | | | | | |
| Laira Depot | 14.00 | | | | | | | | | |
| | | | | | | | | | | |
| **FUEL** | | | | | | | | | | |
| | | | | | | | | | | |
| Laira Depot | | | 18.45 | 0B__ | **SO** | | | | | |
| Plymouth Friary | 18.55 | | 19.05 | 7B__ | | | | | | |
| Keyham | 19.27 | | 19.40 | 0B65 | | | | | | |
| Plymouth Friary | 20.10 | *Presflos* | 20.30 | 6B65 | | | | | | |
| Exeter Riverside Yard | 22.15 | | 22.25 | LD | | | | | | |
| Exeter Stabling Point | | | | | | | | | | |
| | | | | | | | | | | |
| Exeter Stabling Point | | | 14.25 | 0B18 | **SUO** | | | | | |
| Exeter St. David's | 14.30 | *Milk ETS* | 14.45 | 6B18 | | | | | | |
| Chard Junction | 15.47 | SHUNT | 16.50 | 6B58 | | | | | | |
| Exeter St. David's | 17.57 | | 18.05 | LD | | | | | | |
| Exeter Stabling Point | 18.10 | | | | | | | | | |
| | | | | | | | | | | |
| SPARE - SUO | | | | | | | | | | |
| To work NA 153 Mon | | | | | | | | | | |
| | | | | | | | | | | |

## NEWTON ABBOT - TURN No. 68 - ONE CLASS 43 - 2200 H.P.

| From/To | Arrive | Notes | Depart | Code | |
|---|---|---|---|---|---|
| Work Specials - Newton Abbot | | | | | |
| Except : | | | | | |
| Newton Abbot Depot | | | 17.00 | 0B86 | **FO (09/07 - 10/09)** |
| Paignton | 17.20 | | 17.50 | 1B86 | |
| Bristol T.M. | 20.40 | Attached | 21.15 | 1B28 | |
| Newton Abbot | 23.41 | | 23.45 | 0F76 | |
| Newton Abbot Depot | 23.50 | | | | |
| | | | | | |
| Newton Abbot Depot | | | 8.30 | 0B34 | **SO (Until 24/09)** |
| Newton Abbot | 8.35 | | 8.49 | 2B34 | |
| Paignton | 9.03 | RR | 9.50 | 1A75 | |
| Paddington | 13.48 | Off 1A84 | 14.50 | 5A06 | |
| Old Oak Common C.S. | 15.20 | | 15.25 | 0F70 | |
| Old Oak Common Depot | 15.35 | FUEL | 18.50 | 0C27 | |
| Old Oak Common C.S. | 19.00 | | 19.10 | 5C27 | |
| Paddington | 19.24 | SH | 23.25 | 1B48 | |
| Newton Abbot | 3.20 | | 3.25 | 0F76 | **SUO** |
| Newton Abbot Depot | 3.35 | | | | |
| | | | | | |
| **FUEL** | | | | | |

## NEWTON ABBOT - TURN No. 69 - ONE CLASS 43 - 2200 H.P.

Work Specials - Old Oak Common - Change over with Turn 65 for maintenance as required

**NEWTON ABBOT - TURN No. 153 - 1 x CLASS 43 - 2200 H.P.** ..... *Commencing from 05/07/71*

| From/To | Arrive | Notes | Depart | Code | |
|---|---|---|---|---|---|
| | | | | | |
| **OFF NA 66 SUN** | | | | | |
| Exeter S.P. | | | 01.XX | 0B32 | **MO** |
| Exeter Riverside Yard | 01.XX | | 1.35 | 7B32 | |
| Drump Lane | 6.21 | | 06.XX | 0F79 | |
| Penzance | 07.XX | | | | |
| | | | | | |
| **FUEL** | | | | | |
| | | | | | |
| Exeter S.P. | | | 23.XX | 0B34 | **TUE – FRI** |
| Exeter Riverside Yard (20.03 Bristol T.M. Goods) | 23.XX | | 0.15 | 6B34 | |
| Laira Junction | 1.55 | *AE* | 2.10 | 6B34 | |
| Ponsandane | 6.18 | | 06.XX | 0B10 | |
| Penzance | 06.XX | *Milk ETS* | 6.40 | 6B10 | |
| St. Erth | 6.50 | | | | |
| | | (SHUNT AS REQUIRED) | | | |
| St. Erth | | | 10.15 | 0F79 | |
| Penzance | 10.25 | | | | |
| | | | | | |
| **FUEL** | | | | | |
| | | | | | |
| Penzance | | | 11.XX | 0B . . | **MON – FRI** |
| Ponsandane | 11.XX | | 12.02 | 7B . . | |
| St. Erth | 12.XX | | 12.XX | 7B . . | |
| Hayle Wharf | 13.XX | | 13.34 | 7B . . | |
| Ponsandane | 14.XX | | 14.50 | 6B59 | |
| Plymouth North Road | 18.17 | *AE* | 18.25 | 6B59 | |
| Exeter Riverside Yard | 20.06 | | 20.XX | 0B83 | |
| Exeter S.P. | 20.XX | | 22.10 | 0B65 | |
| Exeter St. Davids Banking Spur | 22.15 | | 22.42 | 6B65 | |
| Exeter Central | 22.50 | | 23.XX | 0B58 | |
| Exeter S.P. | 23.XX | | | | |

| LAIRA - TURN No. 52 - 2 x CLASS 42 ('A' / 'B') - 2200 H.P. | | | | | | | | | | |
|---|---|---|---|---|---|---|---|---|---|---|
| | | | | | | | | | | |
| **From/To** | **Arrive** | **Notes** | **Depart** | **Code** | **Mon** | **Tue** | **Wed** | **Thu** | **Fri** | **Sat** |
| Penzance Depot | | | 13.00 | 0A17 | B | A | B | A | B | -- |
| Penzance | 13.05 | *Perishables* | 15.05 | 6A17 | B | A | B | A | B | -- |
| Paddington | 2.20 | | 5.15 | 4B05 | -- | B | A | B | A | -- |
| Bristol T.M. | 9.31 | | 9.40 | 0F74 | -- | B | A | B | A | -- |
| Bristol Bath Road Depot | 9.45 | | | | -- | B | A | B | A | -- |
| | | | | | | | | | | |
| **FUEL** | | | | | | | | | | |
| | | | | | | | | | | |
| Bristol Bath Road Depot | | | 11.00 | 0A27 | A | B | A | B | A | -- |
| Bristol T.M. (11.00 Malago Vale C.S.) | 11.10 | BR71 off | 11.20 | 6A27 | A | B | A | B | A | -- |
| Old Oak Common C.S. | 17.30 | | 18.10 | 0M07 | A | B | A | B | A | -- |
| Kensington Olympia | 18.25 | SHUNT | 19.00 | 6V07 | A | B | A | B | A | -- |
| Plymouth North Road | 2.40 | SHUNT | 3.35 | 6V07 | -- | A | B | A | B | -- |
| Penzance | 8.20 | SHUNT / (a) | 8.40 | 6B13 | B | A | B | A | B | -- |
| Dolcoath | 9.57 | SHUNT | 10.05 | 0B29 | B | A | B | A | B | -- |
| Drump Lane | 10.15 | SHUNT | 10.40 | 7B29 | B | A | B | A | B | -- |
| Roskear | 10.55 | SHUNT | 11.18 | 0B26 | B | A | B | A | B | -- |
| St. Erth | 11.28 | *Parcels* | 11.35 | 6B28 | B | A | B | A | B | -- |
| Penzance | 11.45 | | 11.55 | 0F79 | B | A | B | A | B | -- |
| Penzance Depot | 11.55 | | | | B | A | B | A | B | -- |
| | | | | | | | | | | |
| **FUEL** | | | | | | | | | | |
| | | | | | | | | | | |
| (a) Off LA 62 'B' Mon | | | | | | | | | | |
| | | | | | | | | | | |

## LAIRA - TURN No. 52 - 2 x CLASS 42 ('A' / 'B') - 2200 H.P. (continued)

| 'A' ENGINE | Arrive | Notes | Depart | Code | |
|---|---|---|---|---|---|
| **SO - Until 05/06 & 11/09 - 25/09** | | | | | |
| Plymouth North Road | 3.52 | | 4.00 | 0F77 | **SO** |
| Laira Depot | 4.15 | FUEL | 7.10 | 0V07 | |
| Plymouth North Road | 7.25 | | 7.40 | 6V07 | |
| Ponsandane | 12.19 | | 12.30 | 0A65 | |
| Penzance (To Paddington) | 12.35 | | 13.45 | 1A65 | |
| Plymouth North Road | 15.55 | | 16.15 | 1C96 | |
| Cardiff General | 20.16 | | 20.26 | 5C99 | |
| Cardiff Canton Sidings | 20.31 | RR | 20.55 | 5B66 | |
| Bristol West Depot | 22.34 | | 22.40 | 0F74 | |
| Bristol Bath Road Depot | 22.50 | | | | |
| | | | | | |
| **FUEL** | | | | | |
| | | | | | |
| SPARE - SUO | | | | | |
| **SO 12/06 - 04/09** | | | | | |
| Plymouth North Road | 3.52 | | 4.00 | 0F77 | **SO** |
| Laira Depot | 4.15 | FUEL | 8.30 | 0B59 | |
| Mount Gould Junction (08.30 Laira C.S.) | 8.35 | | 8.41 | 5B59 | |
| Plymouth North Road | 8.50 | RR | 9.20 | 2B59 | |
| Newton Abbot | 10.09 | | 10.42 | 1A81 | |
| Paddington | 14.04 | | 15.30 | 0F70 | |
| Old Oak Common Depot | 15.50 | FUEL | 20.35 | 0B45 | |
| Old Oak Common C.S. | 20.45 | | 20.55 | 5B45 | |
| Paddington | 21.10 | Attached | 23.45 | 1B58 | |
| Bristol T.M. | 2.35 | | 2.40 | 0F74 | **SUO** |
| Bristol Bath Road Depot | 2.45 | | | | |
| | | | | | |
| SPARE - SUO | | | | | |
| To work 'A' Mon | | | | | |
| **'B' ENGINE** | **Arrive** | **Notes** | **Depart** | **Code** | |
| Paddington | 2.20 | | 3.50 | 0F70 | **SO** |
| Old Oak Common Depot | 4.10 | FUEL | 7.15 | 0B25 | |
| Old Oak Common C.S. | 7.25 | | 7.35 | 5B25 | |
| Paddington | 7.55 | | 8.30 | 0B55 | |
| Old Oak Common C.S. | 8.50 | | 9.05 | 5B55 | |
| Paddington | 9.25 | | 10.15 | 1B58 | |
| Paignton | 13.52 | | | | |
| | | | 14.20 | 0F76 | **(NOT 12/06 - 04/09)** |
| Newton Abbot Depot | 14.36 | | | | |
| | | | | | |
| Paignton | 13.52 | Off 1V62 | 14.20 | 5B80 | **(SO 12/06 - 04/09 ONLY)** |
| Newton Abbot | 14.36 | | 14.45 | 0F76 | |
| Newton Abbot Depot | 14.50 | | | | |
| | | | | | |
| Newton Abbot Depot | | | 16.30 | 0A75 | |
| Paignton | 16.50 | | 17.35 | 1A75 | |
| Paddington | 21.30 | Off 1A85 | 22.40 | 5A06 | |
| Old Oak Common C.S. | 23.10 | | 23.15 | 0F70 | |
| Old Oak Common Depot | 23.25 | | | | |
| | | | | | |
| **FUEL** | | | | | |
| | | | | | |
| Old Oak Common Depot | | | 18.10 | 0M07 | **SUO** |
| Kensington Olympia (To Penzance) | 18.30 | *Milk ETS* | 19.00 | 6V07 | |
| Plymouth North Road | 2.40 | | 2.45 | 0F77 | |
| Laira Depot | 3.00 | FUEL | 4.00 | 0B83 | **MO** |
| Exeter Depot | 5.10 | | 5.40 | 0B65 | |
| Exeter Riverside Yard | 5.45 | | 6.00 | 7B65 | |
| | | | | | |
| To work LA 62/A Mon | | | | | |

## LAIRA - TURN No. 53 - SPARE CLASS 42 - 2200 H.P.

| From/To | Arrive | Notes | Depart | Code | | | | | | |
|---|---|---|---|---|---|---|---|---|---|---|
| | | | | | | | | | | |
| **OFF TURN NO. LA 153** | | | | | | | | | | |
| | | | | | | | | | | |
| Laira Depot | | | 23.55 | 0B25 | **FO (11/06 - 03/09)** | | | | | |
| Plymouth North Road | 0.10 | SH | 2.45 | 1B25 | **SO (12/06 - 04/09)** | | | | | |
| Penzance | 5.08 | PROPEL | 5.30 | 5B79 | | | | | | |
| Ponsandane | 5.35 | RR | 6.55 | 5B72 | | | | | | |
| Par | 8.00 | RR | 8.45 | 2B72 | | | | | | |
| Newquay (To Paddington) | 9.37 | | 13.25 | 1A51 | | | | | | |
| Plymouth North Road | 15.05 | | | | | | | | | |
| | | | | | | | | | | |
| Laira Depot | | | 15.38 | 0V72 | **SO (05/06 - 11 & 18/09 ONLY)** | | | | | |
| Plymouth North Road | 15.53 | | | | | | | | | |
| | | | | | | | | | | |
| Plymouth North Road (08.40 Manchester) | | | 16.00 | 1V72 | **SO (05/06 - 18/09)** | | | | | |
| | | | | | | | | | | |
| Penzance | 18.24 | | 18.45 | 5B79 | | | | | | |
| Ponsandane | 18.50 | | 19.20 | 0F78 | | | | | | |
| St. Blazey Depot | 21.45 | | | | | | | | | |
| | | | | | | | | | | |
| **FUEL** | | | | | | | | | | |
| | | | | | | | | | | |
| To work LA54/A Mon | | | | | | | | | | |
| | | | | | | | | | | |

| LAIRA - TURN No. 54 -2 x CLASS 42 ('A' / 'B') - 2200 H.P. | | | | | | | | | | |
|---|---|---|---|---|---|---|---|---|---|---|
| | | | | | | | | | | |
| **From/To** | **Arrive** | **Notes** | **Depart** | **Code** | **Mon** | **Tue** | **Wed** | **Thu** | **Fri** | **Sat** |
| St. Blazey Depot | | (a) | 4.31 | 0B . . | A | B | A | B | A | -- |
| St. Blazey Yard | 4.36 | *Clay* | 4.51 | 6B . . | A | B | A | B | A | -- |
| Par | 4.56 | | 4.58 | 6B . . | A | B | A | B | A | -- |
| Burngullow | 5.17 | SHUNT | 5.23 | 6B . . | A | B | A | B | A | -- |
| Drinnick Mill | 5.42 | SHUNT | 8.11 | 6B . . | A | B | A | B | A | -- |
| Par | 8.38 | RR | 8.51 | 6B . . | A | B | A | B | A | -- |
| St. Blazey Yard | 8.56 | SHUNT | 9.17 | 6B . . | A | B | A | B | A | -- |
| Par | 9.22 | RR | 9.35 | 7B . . | A | B | A | B | A | -- |
| Drinnick Mill | 10.28 | SHUNT | 10.48 | 7B . . | A | B | A | B | A | -- |
| Par | 11.15 | RR | 11.28 | 7B . . | A | B | A | B | A | -- |
| St. Blazey Yard | 11.33 | | 11.41 | 0F78 | A | B | A | B | A | -- |
| St. Blazey Depot | 11.46 | | 12.45 | 0B . . | A | B | A | B | A | -- |
| St. Blazey Yard | 12.50 | *Clay* | 13.00 | 6B . . | A | B | A | B | A | -- |
| Par | 13.05 | RR | 13.18 | 6B . . | A | B | A | B | A | -- |
| Burngullow | 13.37 | SHUNT | 14.44 | 6B . . | A | B | A | B | A | -- |
| Drinnick Mill | 15.03 | SHUNT | 16.16 | 6B . . | A | B | A | B | A | -- |
| Par | 16.55 | RR | 16.58 | 6B . . | A | B | A | B | A | -- |
| St. Blazey Yard | 17.03 | | 17.10 | 0F78 | A | B | A | B | A | -- |
| St. Blazey Depot | 17.15 | | | | A | B | A | B | A | -- |
| | | | | | | | | | | |
| **FUEL** | | | | | | | | | | |
| | | | | | | | | | | |
| St. Blazey Depot | | | 18.55 | 0A08 | A | B | A | B | A | -- |
| St. Blazey Yard | 19.00 | | 19.10 | 7A08 | A | B | A | B | A | -- |
| Paddington Goods | 6.00 | | 6.05 | 0F70 | -- | A | B | A | B | -- |
| Old Oak Common Depot | 6.25 | | | | -- | A | B | A | B | -- |
| | | | | | | | | | | |
| **FUEL** | | | | | | | | | | |
| | | | | | | | | | | |
| Old Oak Common Depot | | | 9.15 | 0A69 | B | A | B | A | B | -- |
| Acton | 9.35 | | 9.50 | 8A69 | B | A | B | A | B | -- |
| Park Royal | 10.47 | | 11.15 | 8A79 | B | A | B | A | B | -- |
| West Ruislip | 11.35 | SHUNT | 11.55 | 0A69 | B | A | B | A | B | -- |
| South Ruislip | 12.00 | SHUNT | 12.15 | 8A69 | B | A | B | A | B | -- |
| West Ealing | 12.37 | SHUNT | 13.35 | 6M15 | B | A | B | A | B | -- |
| Kensington Olympia | 13.55 | SHUNT | 15.00 | 6V05 | B | A | B | A | B | -- |
| Plymouth North Road | 23.59 | | | | B | A | B | A | B | -- |
| | | | | | | | | | | |
| Plymouth North Road | | | 0.20 | 0F78 | -- | B | A | B | A | -- |
| St. Blazey Depot | 1.30 | | | | -- | B | A | B | A | -- |
| | | | | | | | | | | |
| **FUEL** | | | | | | | | | | |
| | | | | | | | | | | |
| (a) Off Turn LA53 Mon | | | | | | | | | | |
| | | | | | | | | | | |

| LAIRA - TURN No. 54 -2 x CLASS 42 ('A' / 'B') - 2200 H.P. (continued) | | | | | |
|---|---|---|---|---|---|
| | | | | | |
| **'A' ENGINE** | **Arrive** | **Notes** | **Depart** | **Code** | |
| Acton (19.10 St. Blazey) | 5.00 | | 5.10 | 0F70 | **SO** |
| Old Oak Common Depot | 5.30 | FUEL | 8.35 | 0Z00 | |
| West Ealing | 8.50 | SHUNT | 9.50 | 0F70 | |
| Old Oak Common C.S. | 10.00 | | 10.18 | 5M07 | |
| Kensington Olympia | 10.38 | | 10.58 | 0A38 | |
| West Ruislip | 11.28 | | 11.30 | 0A38 | |
| South Ruislip | 11.34 | SHUNT | 11.48 | 6A38 | |
| West Ealing | 12.02 | *Milk ETS* | 13.35 | 6M15 | |
| Kensington Olympia | 14.01 | SHUNT | 15.00 | 6V05 | |
| Plymouth | 23.59 | | 0.10 | OF77 | **SUO** |
| Laira Depot | 0.25 | | | | |
| | | | | | |
| **FUEL** | | | | | |
| | | | | | |
| Laira Depot | | | 0.30 | 0B31 | **MO** |
| Keyham | 1.00 | | 1.20 | 7B31 | |
| Par | 2.40 | | 2.45 | 7B31 | |
| Truro | 3.44 | SHUNT | 5.10 | 8B31 | |
| | | | | | |
| To work Turn LA 153 Mon | | | | | |
| | | | | | |
| **'B' ENGINE** | **Arrive** | **Notes** | **Depart** | **Code** | |
| Plymouth North Road | 1.00 | SHUNT | 1.30 | 6B08 | **SO** |
| Penzance | 4.53 | | 5.10 | 0F79 | |
| Penzance Depot | 5.15 | FUEL | 6.55 | 0A81 | |
| Penzance | 7.00 | | 7.15 | 2B15 | |
| Plymouth North Road (08.15 Bristol) | 9.32 | | 11.08 | 1B04 | |
| Penzance | 13.15 | SHUNT | 15.05 | 6A17 | |
| Paddington | 2.00 | | 3.40 | 0F70 | **SUO** |
| Old Oak Common Canteen Siding | 4.00 | | 7.30 | 0A06 | |
| Paddington | 7.50 | Off 1A71 | 8.00 | 5A06 | |
| Old Oak Common C.S. | 8.30 | | 8.35 | 0A06 | |
| Paddington | 8.55 | Off 1A63 | 9.05 | 5A06 | |
| Old Oak Common C.S. | 9.35 | | 9.40 | 0F70 | |
| Old Oak Common Depot | 9.50 | | | | |
| | | | | | |
| **FUEL** | | | | | |
| | | | | | |
| To work Turn LA 54/B Mon | | | | | |

## LAIRA - TURN No. 55 - ONE CLASS 42 - 2200 H.P.

| From/To | Arrive | Notes | Depart | Code | |
|---|---|---|---|---|---|
| Laira Depot | | | 3.45 | 0B35 | **M-TH** |
| Plymouth North Road (22.25 Paddington) | 4.00 | Postal | 4.15 | 1B35 | |
| Penzance | 6.35 | | 6.50 | 5B79 | |
| Ponsandane | 6.55 | | 7.00 | 0A85 | |
| Penzance (To Paddington) | 7.05 | | 8.05 | 1A85 | |
| Plymouth North Road | 10.19 | | | | |
| | | | | | |
| Plymouth North Road | 10.19 | | 10.22 | 0F77 | **MX** |
| Laira Depot | 10.40 | | | | |
| | | | | | |
| Plymouth North Road | 10.19 | | 10.25 | 0F77 | **MO** |
| Laira Depot | 10.37 | | | | |
| | | | | | |
| Laira Depot | | | 7.35 | 0A31 | **FO** |
| Mount Gould Junction | 7.40 | | 7.46 | 5A31 | |
| Ponsandane | 9.55 | RR / Propel | 10.05 | 5A31 | |
| Penzance (To Paddington) | 10.10 | SH | 11.10 | 1A31 | |
| Plymouth North Road | 13.05 | | 13.10 | 0F77 | |
| Laira Depot | 13.45 | | | | |
| | | | | | |
| Laira Depot | | | 16.25 | 0B24 | **M-F (From 27/09)** |
| Mount Gould Junction | 16.30 | | 16.36 | 5B24 | |
| Plymouth North Road | 16.45 | SH | 17.10 | 2B24 | |
| Penzance | 19.20 | | | | |
| | | | | | |
| Laira Depot | | | 16.40 | 0V76 | **M-F (Until 24/09)** |
| Plymouth North Road (10.25 Manchester) | 16.55 | | 17.10 | 1V76 | |
| Penzance | 19.20 | | | | |
| | | | | | |
| Penzance (To Paddington) | 19.20 | SH | 21.00 | 1A72 | **M-F (ALL DATES)** |
| Plymouth North Road | 23.35 | | | | |
| | | | | | |
| Plymouth North Road | 23.35 | | 23.55 | 0F77 | **M-TH** |
| Laira Depot | 0.10 | | | | |
| | | | | | |
| **FUEL** | | | | | |
| | | | | | |
| Plymouth North Road | 23.38 | Off 1B98 | 23.55 | 5B75 | **FO** |
| Laira C.S. | 0.25 | | 0.30 | 0F77 | **SO** |
| Laira Depot | 0.35 | | 3.35 | 0E99 | |
| Mount Gould Junction (03.35 Laira C.S.) | 3.40 | | 3.46 | 5E99 | |
| Plymouth North Road (22.25 Paddington) | 3.55 | *Postal* | 4.15 | 1B35 | |
| Penzance | 6.35 | PROPEL | 7.00 | 5B79 | |
| Ponsandane | 7.05 | | 7.30 | 0A85 | |
| Penzance (To Paddington) | 7.35 | | 8.15 | 1A85 | |
| Plymouth North Road | 10.30 | | 10.35 | 0F77 | |
| Laira Depot | 10.50 | | | | |
| | | | | | |

## LAIRA - TURN No. 55 - ONE CLASS 42 - 2200 H.P. (continued)

| From/To | Arrive | Notes | Depart | Code | |
|---|---|---|---|---|---|
| Laira Depot | | | 14.20 | OV69 | **SO (Until 04/09)** |
| Plymouth North Road (09.25 Derby) | 14.35 | | 14.55 | 1V69 | |
| Penzance | 17.20 | | 17.45 | 5B79 | |
| Ponsandane | 17.50 | | | | |
| Ponsandane | 17.50 | | 18.25 | 0F77 | **SO (Until 29/05)** |
| Laira Depot | 20.30 | | | | |
| **FUEL** | | | | | |
| Ponsandane (To Derby) | 17.50 | | 18.25 | 5M00 | **SO (05/06 - 04/09)** |
| Plymouth North Road | 20.30 | | 20.35 | 0F77 | |
| Laira Depot | 20.50 | | | | |
| **FUEL** | | | | | |
| Laira Depot | | | 14.40 | 0V70 | **SO (11/09 - 25/09)** |
| Plymouth North Road (07.06 Bradford) | 14.55 | | 15.10 | 1V70 | |
| Penzance | 17.36 | PROPEL | 17.50 | 5V70 | |
| Sea Sidings | 17.55 | | 18.00 | 0F79 | |
| Penzance Depot | 18.05 | | | | |
| Laira Depot | | | 4.05 | 0B09 | **SUO (09/05 - 06/06 Only)** |
| Plymouth North Road | 4.20 | *Milk ETS* | 4.35 | 6B09 | |
| Penzance | 9.39 | | 9.55 | 0F79 | |
| Penzance Depot | 10.00 | | | | |
| Penzance Depot | | | 17.25 | 0A59 | **SUO (NOT 13/06 - 05/09)** |
| Penzance (To Paddington) | 17.30 | | 17.45 | 1A59 | |
| Plymouth North Road | 20.05 | Off 1B15 & 1B35 | 20.15 | 5B75 | |
| Laira C.S. | 20.45 | | 20.50 | 0F77 | |
| Laira Depot | 20.55 | | | | |
| **FUEL** | | | | | |

| LAIRA - TURN No. 57 - SPARE CLASS 42 - 2200 H.P. | | | | | |
|---|---|---|---|---|---|
| | | | | | |
| **From/To** | **Arrive** | **Notes** | **Depart** | **Code** | |
| **OFF TURN LA151** | | | | | |
| Exeter Stabling Point | | | 6.30 | 0B10 | **SO** |
| Exeter St. David's | 6.35 | | 7.10 | 2B10 | |
| Penzance | 11.10 | | 11.35 | 5B10 | |
| Sea Sidings | 11.40 | | 11.45 | 0F79 | |
| Penzance | 11.50 | | | | |
| | | | | | |
| Penzance (To Crewe) | 11.50 | SHUNT | 12.50 | 4M05 | **SO (NOT12/06 - 04/09)** |
| Exeter St. David's | 17.24 | Attached | 18.13 | 4B10 | |
| Plymouth North Road | 19.55 | | 20.00 | 0F77 | |
| Laira Depot | 20.15 | | | | |
| | | | | | |
| **FUEL** | | | | | |
| | | | | | |
| Spare - Laira | | | | | **SUO (Except 13/06 - 05/09)** |
| | | | | | |
| Penzance (To Paddington) | 11.50 | | 12.18 | 1A45 | **SO (12/06 - 04/09)** |
| Plymouth North Road (07.03 Bradford 'Cornishman') | 14.30 | | 15.10 | 1V70 | |
| Penzance | 17.36 | PROPEL | 17.50 | 5V70 | |
| Slopers Sidings | 17.55 | | 18.00 | 0F79 | |
| Penzance Depot | 18.05 | | | | |
| | | | | | |
| **FUEL** | | | | | |
| | | | | | |
| Penzance Depot | | | 17.25 | 0A59 | **SUO (13/06 - 05/09)** |
| Penzance (To Paddington) | 17.30 | | 17.45 | 1A59 | |
| Plymouth North Road | 20.05 | Off 1B15 & 1B35 | 20.15 | 5B75 | |
| Laira C.S. | 20.45 | | 20.50 | 0F77 | |
| Laira Depot | 20.55 | | | | |
| | | | | | |
| To work LA151 Mon | | | | | |
| | | | | | |

## LAIRA - TURN No. 58 - SPARE CLASS 42 - 2200 H.P.

| From/To | Arrive | Notes | Depart | Code | |
|---|---|---|---|---|---|
| | | | | | |
| **OFF TURN LA158** | | | | | |
| Penzance Depot | | | 19.35 | 0B75 | |
| Penzance | 19.40 | | 19.55 | 5B75 | |
| Laira C.S. | 22.33 | | 22.40 | 0F77 | |
| Laira Depot | 22.45 | | | | |
| | | | | | |
| Laira Depot | | | 3.25 | 0V37 | **SO (12/06 - 25/09)** |
| Plymouth North Road (18.20 FO Newcastle) | 3.40 | | 3.55 | 1V37 | |
| Penzance | 6.18 | | 6.28 | 5B79 | |
| Ponsandane | 6.33 | | 6.35 | 0B . . | |
| Penzance | 6.40 | *Milk ETS* | 6.45 | 6B . . | |
| St. Erth | 6.57 | SHUNT | 9.35 | 0B79 | |
| Penzance Depot | 8.45 | | | | |
| | | | | | |
| **FUEL** | | | | | |
| | | | | | |
| Penzance Depot | | | 18.20 | 0B75 | **SO (12/06 - 25/09)** |
| Penzance (To Newcastle) | 18.25 | | 18.40 | 5B75 | |
| Plymouth North Road | 21.00 | | 21.03 | 0F77 | |
| Laira Depot | 21.18 | | | | |
| | | | | | |
| Spare Laira | | | | | **SO (Until 05/06)** |
| | | | | | |
| Laira Depot | | | 10.55 | 0B14 | **SUO (09/05 - 26/09)** |
| Plymouth North Road | 11.10 | | 11.25 | 2B14 | |
| Penzance | 13.45 | | | | |
| | | | | | |
| Run Round & Re-berth stock & Shunt | | | | | |
| | | | | | |
| Penzance | | | 16.00 | 6M19 | |
| Plymouth North Road | 19.22 | | 19.25 | 0F77 | |
| Laira Depot | 19.40 | | | | |
| | | | | | |
| **FUEL** | | | | | |
| | | | | | |
| To work LA158 Mon | | | | | |

## LAIRA - TURN No. 60 - ONE CLASS 42 - 2200 H.P.

| From/To | Arrive | Notes | Depart | Code | |
|---|---|---|---|---|---|
| **WORK SPECIALS AT LAIRA EXCEPT** | | | | | |
| | | | | | |
| Laira Depot | | | 3.45 | 0B35 | **FO** |
| Plymouth North Road (22.25 Paddington) | 4.00 | *Postal* | 4.15 | 1B35 | |
| Penzance (To Paddington) | 6.35 | | 8.05 | 1A85 | |
| Plymouth North Road | 10.19 | | 10.22 | 0F77 | |
| Laira Depot | 10.37 | | | | |
| | | | | | |
| Laira Depot | | | 18.20 | 0B35 | |
| Plymouth North Road (14.30 Paddington) | 18.35 | | 18.50 | 1B35 | |
| Penzance (To Paddington) | 20.55 | *Sleeper* | 22.00 | 1A71 | |
| Plymouth North Road | 0.23 | SHUNT | 0.55 | 0F77 | **SO** |
| Laira Depot | 1.10 | | | | |
| | | | | | |
| Laira Depot | | | 3.05 | 0V47 | **SO (12/06 - 04/09)** |
| Plymouth North Road (22.08 FO Manchester) | 3.20 | | 3.35 | 1V47 | |
| Penzance | 5.55 | | 6.10 | 5B79 | |
| Ponsandane | 6.15 | | 6.20 | 0F79 | |
| Penzance Depot | 6.25 | | 8.25 | 0A01 | |
| Penzance (To Paddington) | 8.30 | | 8.45 | 1A01 | |
| Plymouth North Road | 11.05 | | 11.10 | 0F77 | |
| Laira Depot | 11.25 | FUEL | 13.15 | 0B34 | |
| Plymouth North Road (09.45 Cardiff) | 13.30 | | 13.45 | 1B34 | |
| Penzance | 16.08 | | 16.30 | 0E00 | |
| Penzance Yard (for 18.40 Newcastle) | 16.35 | | 18.00 | 5E00 | |
| Penzance | 18.10 | | 19.00 | 2B37 | |
| Plymouth North Road | 21.23 | | 21.35 | 5B75 | |
| Laira C.S. | 22.12 | | 22.17 | 0F77 | |
| Laira Depot | 22.22 | | | | |
| | | | | | |
| Laira Depot | | | 4.05 | 0B09 | **SUO (13/06 - 05/09 & 26/09)** |
| Plymouth North Road | 4.20 | *Milk ETS* | 4.35 | 6B09 | |
| Penzance | 9.39 | | 9.55 | 0F79 | |
| Penzance Depot | 10.00 | | | | |
| | | | | | |
| Penzance Depot | | Attached | 9.10 | 0M23 | **MO (14/06 - 06/09 & 27/09)** |
| Penzance | 9.15 | Attached | 9.30 | 1M23 | |
| Plymouth North Road | 11.47 | | 11.50 | 0F77 | |
| Laira Depot | 12.05 | | | | |
| | | | | | |
| **FUEL** | | | | | |
| | | | | | |

## LAIRA - TURN No. 61 - ONE CLASS 42 - 2200 H.P.

| From/To | Arrive | Notes | Depart | Code | |
|---|---|---|---|---|---|
| **WORK SPECIALS AT PENZANCE EXCEPT** | | | | | |
| Penzance Depot | | | 15.35 | 0A85 | **FO (11/06 - 03/09)** |
| Penzance (To Paddington) | 15.40 | | 15.55 | 1A85 | |
| Plymouth North Road | 17.55 | | 18.00 | 0B32 | |
| Mount Gould Junction (18.45 Laira C.S.) | 18.15 | | 18.56 | 5B32 | |
| Plymouth North Road | 19.05 | | 19.40 | 2B32 | |
| Penzance | 22.02 | | 22.12 | 5B32 | |
| Sea Sidings | 22.17 | | 22.22 | 0F79 | |
| Penzance Depot | 22.27 | | | | |
| | | | | | |
| Penzance Depot | | | 4.25 | 0M91 | **SO (12/06 - 04/09)** |
| Ponsandane (To Newquay) | 4.30 | *LA24 on* | 4.40 | 5M91 | |
| Truro | 5.12 | | 6.00 | 5A65 | |
| Ponsandane | 6.45 | | 6.50 | 0F79 | |
| Penzance | 7.00 | | | | |
| | | | | | |
| Spare - Penzance SO 07.00 - SUO (12/06 - 04/09) | | | | | |
| | | | | | |
| Penzance Depot | | | 11.10 | 0M19 | **SO (Until 05/06)** |
| Penzance (To Derby) | 11.15 | | 11.30 | 1M19 | |
| Plymouth North Road (07.03 Bradford 'Cornishman') | 14.00 | | 15.10 | 1V70 | |
| Penzance | 17.36 | PROPEL | 17.50 | 5V70 | |
| Sea Sidings | 17.55 | | 18.00 | 0F79 | |
| Penzance Depot | 18.05 | | | | |
| | | | | | |
| Penzance Depot | | | 19.35 | 0B75 | **SO (11/09 & 18/09 ONLY)** |
| Penzance | 19.40 | | 19.55 | 5B75 | |
| Laira C.S. | 22.33 | | 22.40 | 0F77 | |
| Laira Depot | 22.45 | | | | |
| | | | | | |
| **FUEL** | | | | | |
| | | | | | |
| Laira Depot | | | 4.05 | 0B09 | **SUO (12/09 - 19/09 ONLY)** |
| Plymouth North Road | 4.20 | *Milk ETS* | 4.35 | 6B09 | |
| Penzance | 9.39 | | 9.55 | 0F79 | |
| Penzance Depot | 10.00 | | | | |
| | | | | | |
| **FUEL** | | | | | |

| LAIRA - TURN No. 62 - 2 x CLASS 42 ('A' / 'B'- 2200 H.P. | | | | | | | | | | |
|---|---|---|---|---|---|---|---|---|---|---|
| | | | | | | | | | | |
| **From/To** | **Arrive** | **Notes** | **Depart** | **Code** | **Mon** | **Tue** | **Wed** | **Thu** | **Fri** | **Sat** |
| Westbury D.S. | | | 6.30 | 0O52 | B | A | B | A | B | -- |
| Westbury (05.50 Bristol T.M.) | 6.35 | BR71 off | 6.55 | 2O52 | B | A | B | A | B | -- |
| Weymouth | 8.41 | RR / SH | 9.50 | 2V55 | B | A | B | A | B | -- |
| Westbury | 11.23 | | 11.30 | 0F90 | B | A | B | A | B | -- |
| Westbury D.S. | 11.35 | | 11.55 | 0O00 | B | A | B | A | B | -- |
| Warminster | 12.10 | SHUNT | 13.50 | 7V19 | B | A | B | A | B | -- |
| Westbury | 14.04 | | 14.59 | 8B45 | B | A | B | A | B | -- |
| Melksham | 15.27 | SHUNT | 16.15 | 8B45 | B | A | B | A | B | -- |
| Chippenham | 16.32 | SHUNT | 17.25 | 8B45 | B | A | B | A | B | -- |
| Swindon Cocklebury Yard | 18.02 | | | | B | A | B | A | B | -- |
| | | | | | | | | | | |
| Swindon Cocklebury Yard | | | 19.25 | 8B00 | B | A | B | A | B | -- |
| Stoke Gifford Yard | 20.25 | | 22.25 | 7B05 | B | A | B | A | B | -- |
| Exeter Riverside Yard | 2.55 | * | 3.00 | 0F91 | -- | B | A | B | A | B |
| Exeter Stabling Point | 3.05 | | | | -- | B | A | B | A | B |
| | | | | | | | | | | |
| Exeter Stabling Point | | (b) | 5.40 | 0B65 | A | B | -- | B | A | -- |
| Exeter Riverside Yard | 5.45 | | 6.00 | 7B65 | A | B | -- | B | A | -- |
| Okehampton | 7.08 | SHUNT | 9.48 | 7B56 | A | B | -- | B | A | -- |
| Exeter Riverside Yard | 10.42 | | 10.50 | 0F91 | A | B | -- | B | A | -- |
| Exeter Stabling Point | 10.55 | | 12.10 | 0B71 | A | B | A | B | A | -- |
| Exeter Riverside Yard | 12.15 | | 12.30 | 7B71 | A | B | A | B | A | -- |
| Newcourt M. o D. Sidings | 13.12 | SHUNT | 14.28 | 7B71 | A | B | A | B | A | -- |
| Exeter Riverside Yard | 14.50 | | 15.00 | 0B99 | A | B | A | B | A | -- |
| Exeter St. David's. C.S. | 15.05 | SH | 15.30 | 5B99 | A | B | A | B | A | -- |
| Exeter St. David's | 15.35 | SH | 16.05 | 2B99 | A | B | A | B | A | -- |
| Barnstaple Junction | 17.55 | RR / SH | 17.55 | 2B99 | A | B | A | B | A | -- |
| Exeter St. David's. | 19.08 | SH | 20.07 | 1O20 | A | B | A | B | A | -- |
| Basingstoke | 23.00 | RR / SH | 23.52 | 1L02 | A | B | A | B | A | -- |
| Salisbury | 0.31 | | 1.20 | 7V18 | -- | A | B | A | B | A |
| Westbury | 2.09 | | 2.15 | 0F90 | -- | A | B | A | B | A |
| Westbury D.S. | 2.20 | | | | -- | A | B | A | B | A |
| | | | | | | | | | | |
| **Service and FUEL** | | | | | | | | | | |
| | | | | | | | | | | |
| **NOTE :** * 7B05 22.25 Stoke Gifford terminates at Taunton SO mornings 01.05 (12/06 - 04/09) and then 0F91 LD to Exeter. | | | | | | | | | | |
| | | | | | | | | | | |
| (b) Off Laira 52B Mon | | | | | | | | | | |
| | | | | | | | | | | |
| **'A' ENGINE** | **Arrive** | **Notes** | **Depart** | **Code** | | | | | | |
| Westbury D.S. | | | 3.30 | 0B64 | **SO (12/06 - 04/09 ONLY)** | | | | | |
| Bristol Malago Vale C.S. | 5.00 | SH | 5.30 | 5O52 | | | | | | |
| Bristol T.M. | 5.35 | | 5.45 | 2O52 | | | | | | |
| Weymouth | 8.41 | RR / SH | 9.43 | 2V52 | | | | | | |
| Bristol T.M. | 12.05 | | 12.25 | 5B64 | | | | | | |
| Bristol Malago Vale C.S. | 12.42 | RR | 15.22 | 5O52 | | | | | | |
| Bristol T.M. | 15.27 | | 15.48 | 2O52 | | | | | | |
| Weymouth | 18.38 | RR | 19.25 | 2V52 | | | | | | |
| Bristol T.M. | 22.30 | | 23.05 | 5B64 | | | | | | |
| Bristol Malago Vale C.S. | 23.22 | | 23.30 | 0F74 | | | | | | |
| Bristol Bath Road Depot | 23.45 | | | | | | | | | |
| | | | | | | | | | | |
| **FUEL** | | | | | | | | | | |
| | | | | | | | | | | |
| Westbury D.S. | | | 3.30 | 0B64 | **SO (NOT 12/06 - 04/09)** | | | | | |
| Bristol Malago Vale C.S. | 5.00 | SH | 5.30 | 5O52 | | | | | | |
| Bristol T.M. | 5.35 | | 5.45 | 2O52 | | | | | | |
| Weymouth | 8.41 | RR / SH | 9.43 | 2V55 | | | | | | |
| Westbury | 11.08 | | 11.15 | 0F90 | | | | | | |
| Westbury D.S. | 11.25 | | 16.20 | 0O52 | | | | | | |

| | | | | | | | | | | |
|---|---|---|---|---|---|---|---|---|---|---|
| Westbury | 16.25 | SH | 16.47 | 2O52 | | | | | | |
| Weymouth | 18.38 | RR / SH | 19.25 | 2V52 | | | | | | |
| Bristol T.M. | 22.30 | | 23.05 | 5B64 | | | | | | |
| Bristol Malago Vale C.S. | 23.22 | | 23.30 | 0F74 | | | | | | |
| Bristol Bath Road Depot | 23.45 | | | | | | | | | |
| | | | | | | | | | | |
| **FUEL** | | | | | | | | | | |
| | | | | | | | | | | |
| Bristol Bath Road Depot | | | 15.50 | 0O10 | **SUO (ALL dates)** | | | | | |
| Bristol T.M. | 15.55 | *Parcels* | 16.10 | 6O10 | | | | | | |
| Salisbury | 18.40 | | 18.55 | 0O00 | | | | | | |
| Westbury D.S. | 20.00 | | | | | | | | | |
| | | | | | | | | | | |
| To work 'B' Mon | | | | | | | | | | |
| | | | | | | | | | | |
| **'B' ENGINE** | **Arrive** | **Notes** | **Depart** | **Code** | | | | | | |
| Exeter Stabling Point | 3.05 | | 6.00 | 0B99 | **SO (From 12/06 - 25/09)** | | | | | |
| Exeter St. David's. | 6.05 | | 6.30 | 2B99 | | | | | | |
| Barnstaple Junction | 7.33 | RR | 8.50 | 2B99 | | | | | | |
| Exeter St. David's (08.10 Paddington) | 9.51 | NA65 Off | 11.13 | 1B18 | | | | | | |
| Barnstaple Junction (To Paddington) | 12.20 | RR | 14.40 | 1A41 | | | | | | |
| Exeter St. David's | 15.37 | NA65 On | 16.00 | 2B99 | | | | | | |
| Barnstaple Junction | 17.13 | RR | 17.55 | 2B99 | | | | | | |
| Exeter St. David's. | 19.04 | SHUNT | 19.55 | 0F91 | | | | | | |
| Exeter Stabling Point | 20.00 | | | | | | | | | |
| | | | | | | | | | | |
| Exeter Stabling Point | 3.05 | | 6.00 | 0B99 | **SO (Until 05/06)** | | | | | |
| Exeter St. David's. | 6.05 | | 6.30 | 2B99 | | | | | | |
| Barnstaple Junction | 7.33 | RR | 8.50 | 2B99 | | | | | | |
| Exeter St. David's | 9.51 | | 10.00 | 0F91 | | | | | | |
| Exeter Stabling Point | 10.05 | | 15.30 | 0B99 | | | | | | |
| Exeter St. David's | 15.35 | | 16.00 | 2B99 | | | | | | |
| Barnstaple Junction | 17.33 | RR | 17.55 | 2B99 | | | | | | |
| Exeter St. David's. | 19.04 | SHUNT | 19.55 | 0F91 | | | | | | |
| Exeter Stabling Point | 20.00 | | | | | | | | | |
| | | | | | | | | | | |
| Exeter Stabling Point | | | 23.50 | 0B30 | **SUO (ALL dates)** | | | | | |
| Exeter Riverside Yard (To Ponsandane) | 23.55 | | 0.10 | 7B30 | **MO (ALL dates)** | | | | | |
| Laira Junction | 2.00 | | 2.05 | 0F77 | | | | | | |
| Laira | 2.20 | | 2.30 | 0V07 | | | | | | |
| Plymouth North Road (19.00 Kensington Olympia) | 2.45 | SHUNT | 3.35 | 6V07 | | | | | | |
| Penzance | 8.20 | SHUNT | 8.40 | 6B13 | | | | | | |
| | | | | | | | | | | |
| To work LA52/B Mon | | | | | | | | | | |
| | | | | | | | | | | |

## LAIRA - TURN No. 69 - SPARE CLASS 42 - 2200 H.P.

| **From/To** | **Arrive** | **Notes** | **Depart** | **Code** | | | | | | |
|---|---|---|---|---|---|---|---|---|---|---|
| **OFF TURN 720** | | | | | | | | | | |
| St. Blazey Depot | | | 8.30 | 0B72 | **SO (12/06 - 04/09)** | | | | | |
| Par | 8.35 | Attached | 8.45 | 2B72 | | | | | | |
| Newquay | 9.37 | | | | | | | | | |
| | | | | | | | | | | |
| St. Blazey Depot | | | 6.00 | 0M91 | **SO (11/09 - 25/09)** | | | | | |
| Par | 6.05 | Attached | 6.15 | 5M91 | | | | | | |
| Newquay | 7.05 | | | | | | | | | |
| | | | | | | | | | | |
| Newquay (To Paddington) | | | 10.25 | 1A24 | **SO (12/06 - 25/09)** | | | | | |
| Plymouth North Road (09.52 Paddington) | 12.15 | | 14.05 | 1B55 | | | | | | |
| Newquay | 16.00 | | 16.30 | 2B72 | | | | | | |
| Par | 17.26 | | 18.45 | 2B72 | | | | | | |
| Newquay | 19.40 | | 20.15 | 0F78 | | | | | | |
| St. Blazey Depot | 21.05 | | | | | | | | | |
| | | | | | | | | | | |
| To work No. 720 Mon | | | | | | | | | | |

## LAIRA - TURN No. 151 - ONE CLASS 42 - 2200 H.P.

| From/To | Arrive | Notes | Depart | Code | |
|---|---|---|---|---|---|
| | | | | | |
| **OFF TURN LA57 MONDAY** | | | | | |
| Laira Depot | | | 3.20 | 0B80 | **MO (Until 07/06 & from 13/09)** |
| Mount Gould Junction | 3.25 | | 3.31 | 5B80 | |
| Plymouth North Road | 3.40 | RR | 3.50 | 5B80 | |
| Newton Abbot | 4.45 | | 5.00 | 0B06 | |
| Exeter Riverside Yard | 5.45 | | | | |
| | | | | | |
| Laira Depot | | | 3.50 | 0B06 | **MO (14/06 - 06/09)** |
| Exeter Riverside Yard | 5.30 | | | | |
| | | | | | |
| Exeter Riverside Yard | | | 5.55 | 6B06 | **MO (All Dates)** |
| Plymouth Friary | 8.30 | | 9.35 | 7B59 | |
| | | | | | |
| Laira Depot | | | 9.00 | 0B59 | **T-TH** |
| Plymouth Friary | 9.10 | | 9.35 | 7B59 | |
| | | | | | |
| Plymouth Friary | | | 9.35 | 7B59 | **M-TH** |
| Exeter Riverside Yard | 12.38 | | 12.40 | 0F91 | |
| Exeter Stabling Point | 12.45 | | | | |
| | | | | | |
| Laira Depot | | | 8.25 | 0B59 | **FO** |
| Plymouth Friary | 8.35 | | 8.45 | 7B59 | |
| Exeter Riverside Yard | 12.38 | | 12.40 | 0F91 | |
| Exeter Stabling Point | 12.45 | | | | |
| | | | | | |
| Exeter Stabling Point | | | 14.45 | 0B18 | **M-F** |
| Exeter St. David's | 14.50 | *Milk ets* | 15.00 | 6B18 | |
| Chard Junction (To Morden South) | 16.02 | SHUNT | 16.55 | 6O19 | |
| Exeter St. David's. | 18.14 | | 18.30 | 0B36 | |
| Exeter Riverside | 18.35 | | 19.20 | 7B36 | |
| Plymouth Friary | 21.40 | | 21.55 | 0B58 | |
| Plymouth North Road (19.06 Ponsandane - Bristol Kingsland Road) | 22.10 | ASSIST | 23.17 | 7B58 | |
| Newton Abbot | 0.22 | | 0.30 | 0B31 | **T-F** |
| Exeter Riverside Yard | 1.00 | | 2.40 | 7B31 | |
| Keyham | 4.47 | | 4.55 | 0F77 | |
| Laira Depot | 5.20 | | | | |
| | | | | | |
| **FUEL** | | | | | |
| | | | | | |
| Newton Abbot | 0.19 | | 0.25 | 0B83 | **SO** |
| Exeter Stabling Point | 0.55 | | | | |
| | | | | | |
| To work LA 57 Sat | | | | | |
| | | | | | |

## LAIRA - TURN No. 153 - ONE CLASS 42 - 2200 H.P.

| From/To | Arrive | Notes | Depart | Code | |
|---|---|---|---|---|---|
| St. Blazey Depot | | | 2.25 | 0B31 | **T-F** |
| Par (22.55 Plymouth Friary) | 2.30 | | 2.45 | 7B31 | |
| Truro | 3.44 | SHUNT | 5.10 | 8B31 | **M-F** (a) |
| Drump Lane | 5.50 | SHUNT | 6.30 | 7B54 | |
| Truro | 6.45 | SHUNT | 7.25 | 7B54 | |
| St. Blazey Yard (To Bristol West Depot) | 9.30 | | 10.10 | 6B64 | |
| Newton Abbot (11.55 Exeter Riverside Yard) | 13.20 | | 14.17 | 7B33 | |
| Truro | 17.22 | | 19.00 | 7B49 | |
| Plymouth Friary (To Truro) | 22.25 | | 22.55 | 7B31 | **M-TH** |
| Par | 0.43 | | 0.48 | 0F78 | **T-F** |
| St. Blazey Depot | 0.50 | | | | |
| | | | | | |
| **FUEL** | | | | | |
| | | | | | |
| Plymouth Friary | 22.25 | | 22.30 | 0F77 | **FO from 11/06 - 17/09** |
| Laira Depot | 22.40 | | | | |
| | | | | | |
| To work LA53 SO (11/06 - 18/09) from 23.55 | | | | | |
| | | | | | |
| Plymouth Friary | 22.25 | | 22.55 | 7B31 | **FO Until 04/06** |
| Par | 0.43 | | 0.48 | 0F78 | **SO** |
| St. Blazey Depot | 0.53 | | | | |
| | | | | | |
| **FUEL** | | | | | |
| | | | | | |
| St. Blazey Depot | | | 3.24 | 0B31 | |
| Par (02.15 Plymouth Friary) | 3.34 | | 4.04 | 7B31 | |
| Truro | 6.04 | | 6.12 | 7B31 | |
| Drump Lane | 6.37 | SHUNT | 8.05 | 0F78 | |
| Par | 8.50 | | 8.55 | 0F78 | |
| St. Blazey Depot | 9.00 | | | | |
| | | | | | |
| **FUEL** | | | | | |
| | | | | | |
| Plymouth Friary | 22.25 | | 22.30 | 0F78 | **FO 24/09 Only** |
| St. Blazey Depot | 23.40 | | | | |
| | | | | | |
| (a) Off turn 54 Mon | | | | | |

## LAIRA - TURN No. 155- ONE CLASS 42 - 2200 H.P.

| From/To | Arrive | Notes | Depart | Code | |
|---|---|---|---|---|---|
| Exeter Stabling Point | | | 13.45 | 0O55 | **M.WO** |
| Tiverton Junction | 14.07 | | 14.48 | 6O55 | |
| Fawley | 19.59 | | 21.40 | 6V77 | |
| Plymouth Friary | 7.40 | | 7.45 | 0F77 | **T.THO** |
| Laira Depot | 7.55 | FUEL | 10.35 | 0O59 | |
| Plymouth Friary | 10.40 | | 11.15 | 6O59 | |
| Fawley | 19.59 | | | | |
| | | | | | |
| Fawley | 19.59 | | 21.40 | 6V77 | **TO** |
| Westbury | 0.14 | | 0.20 | 0F90 | **WO** |
| Westbury D.S. | 0.25 | FUEL | 5.05 | 0V78 | |
| Westbury | 5.10 | | 5.20 | 6V78 | |
| Tiverton Junction | 9.45 | | 10.00 | 0F91 | |
| Exeter Stabling Point | 10.25 | | | | |
| | | | | | |
| Fawley | 19.59 | | 21.40 | 6V77 | **THO** |
| Westbury | 0.14 | | 0.20 | 0F90 | **FO** |
| Westbury D.S. | 1.25 | | 2.30 | 0V77 | |
| Westbury | 2.35 | | 2.45 | 6V77 | |
| Plymouth Friary | 7.40 | (a) | 7.45 | 0F77 | |
| Laira Depot | 7.55 | FUEL | 10.35 | 0O59 | |
| Plymouth Friary | 10.45 | | 11.15 | 6O59 | |
| Fawley | 19.59 | | 21.40 | 6V65 | |
| Westbury | 0.14 | | 0.20 | 0F90 | **SO** |
| Westbury D.S. | 0.25 | FUEL | 5.05 | 0V65 | |
| Westbury | 5.10 | | 5.20 | 6V65 | |
| Tiverton Junction | 6.30 | | 7.35 | 0F91 | |
| Exeter Stabling Point | 7.55 | | | | |
| | | | | | |
| SPARE EXETER 07.55 SO - 13.50 Mon | | | | | |
| | | | | | |
| (a) Assisted from Newton Abbot by LA158 | | | | | |

## LAIRA - TURN No. 158 - ONE CLASS 42 - 2200 H.P.

| From/To | Arrive | Notes | Depart | Code | |
|---|---|---|---|---|---|
| **OFF TURN 50 MON** | | | | | |
| Laira Depot | | | 8.25 | 0C26 | **M-TH** |
| Plymouth Friary | 8.35 | | 8.45 | 7C26 | |
| Severn Tunnel Junction | 15.22 | | 15.30 | 0F82 | |
| Severn Tunnel Junction Depot | 15.35 | | | | |
| | | | | | |
| **FUEL** | | | | | |
| | | | | | |
| Laira Depot | | | 4.00 | 0F76 | **FO** |
| Newton Abbot (22.45 Fawley) | 5.00 | Assist | 6.10 | 6V78 | |
| Plymouth Friary | 7.40 | | 8.00 | 7C26 | |
| Severn Tunnel Junction | 16.32 | | 16.45 | 0F82 | |
| Severn Tunnel Junction Depot | 16.50 | | | | |
| | | | | | |
| **FUEL** | | | | | |
| | | | | | |
| Severn Tunnel Junction Depot | | | 20.05 | 0B45 | **M-F** |
| Severn Tunnel Junction | 20.15 | | 20.35 | 4B45 | |
| Plymouth Friary | 1.00 | | 1.05 | 0F77 | |
| Laira Depot | 1.15 | | | | |
| | | | | | |
| **FUEL** | | | | | |
| | | | | | |
| Laira Depot | | | 3.30 | 0F76 | **WO** |
| Newton Abbot (18.22 TO Ince & Elton) | 4.30 | Assist | 5.05 | 6V35 | |
| Plymouth Friary | 6.30 | | 6.35 | 0F77 | |
| Laira Depot | 6.45 | | | | |
| | | | | | |
| Laira Depot | | | 4.00 | 0F76 | **T.TH** |
| Newton Abbot (22.45 Fawley) | 5.00 | Assist | 6.10 | 6V77 | |
| Plymouth Friary | 7.40 | | 7.45 | 0F77 | |
| Laira Depot | 7.55 | | | | |
| | | | | | |
| Plymouth Friary | 0.35 | # | 0.50 | 4B45 | **SO (08/05 - 23/05 ONLY)** |
| Plymouth North Road (23.30 Exeter Riverside Yard) | 1.05 | | 1.43 | 7B32 | |
| Ponsandane | 5.23 | | 6.00 | 0F77 | |
| Laira Depot | 8.00 | | | | |
| | | | | | |
| **FUEL** | | | | | |
| | | | | | |
| Plymouth Friary | 0.35 | | 0.50 | 4B45 | **SO (05/06 ONLY)** |
| Plymouth North Road (23.30 Exeter Riverside Yard) | 1.05 | | 1.43 | 7B32 | |
| Ponsandane | 5.23 | | 5.40 | 0F79 | |
| Penzance | 5.45 | | | | |
| | | | | | |
| To work LA58 SO | | | | | |
| | | | | | |
| Plymouth Friary | 0.35 | | 0.50 | 4B45 | **SO (12/06 - 25/09)** |
| Plymouth North Road | 1.05 | | 1.15 | 0F77 | |
| Laira Depot | 1.30 | | | | |
| | | | | | |
| **FUEL** | | | | | |
| | | | | | |
| To work LA58 Sat | | | | | |
| | | | | | |
| NOTE : # Runs with vehicles formed of 4B45 23.35 Severn Tunnel Junction - Plymouth Friary on Fridays ONLY. | | | | | |
| | | | | | |

D823 HERMES departs from Sidmouth on 29 July 1965 in the second year of Warship operation on the ex-LSWR route. The interloper fits in well with the SR infrastructure and green coaching stock. (www.rail-online.co.uk)

803 ALBION at Exeter on a Waterloo service. The fact that the locomotive has headboard clips dates it to the summer of 1971 because when ALBION emerged from Swindon in June it had been fitted with a completely new nose ex-D830 following extensive damage in a derailment at the end of March. 1O04 was the 06.50 to Waterloo; the photographer was up very early! (www.rail-online.co.uk)

816 ECLIPSE at Yeovil Junction on 28 July 1971. It had worked the 1O12 12.30 Exeter-Waterloo the previous day and was shown as having failed in London with the B engine low on coolant. Either the records are incorrect and the loco was removed on the up working at Yeovil or it was repaired and worked back west but failed again at Yeovil. (www.rail-online.co.uk)

## Appendix 3 - Workings in August 1971

Throughout the month 820 GRENVILLE remained in Swindon Works undergoing a Classified repair for fire damage, having been there since April 1st; it was eventually returned to traffic on 6 September. On Sunday 1st 841 ROEBUCK had its B end transmission changed, with No.16877 removed due to the standstill detector shaft being damaged,. It had completed 3,928 hours since its last major repair. No.10851 was fitted, from withdrawn D859 A end; it had completed 2,300 hours and allowed 841 to be released back to traffic on August 6th.

On Monday 2nd there were only two failures. The first was 827 KELLY getting into trouble on 1V13, 13.08 Waterloo-Exeter service. The train arrived at Exeter just three minutes late at 17.04 behind green-liveried D7054 with 827 inside on one engine only. 825 INTREPID on 2B99 17.55 from Barnstaple conveyed eight milk tanks as well as its four Mark 1 coaches and a CCT van and D819 GOLIATH arrived at Exeter on 6B59 assisted by an absolutely ex-works D6319 (released from Swindon 11/06/71). D809 CHAMPION assisted D1040 WESTERN QUEEN on 6A17 from Plymouth to Exeter, went to shed and an hour later was used to replace 826 JUPITER on 1B25, the 19.30 from Paddington after it was failed with its B transmission not changing gear. D6319 was noted as ex-works when it assisted D819 to Riverside on 6B59 but the Type 2 had been released from Swindon on 11th June, indicating it had done little work.

Tuesday 3rd and 808 CENTAUR was at Exeter at 13.40 on an unidentified freight of 19 wagons and one brake van, 825 INTREPID worked 2B14 from Westbury which was formed of loco-hauled stock instead of the booked DMU. D7019 returned to Salisbury in tandem with 811 DARING on 1O14 from Exeter, the former having arrived at Exeter in charge of 1V09. This was almost certainly from Salisbury; 832 ONSLAUGHT had failed at Waterloo with a broken spring and an unidentified loco worked forward. 827 KELLY worked light to Chard Junction for 6O19 instead of working the 6B18 15.00 Exeter to Chard Junction milk empties, 6O19 formed of just four tanks. 855 TRIUMPH took them forward, with the tanks from Lapford. 827 KELLY then worked 7B36 but may have only gone to Newton Abbot where it looks like D809 CHAMPION may have taken over, as it worked the next part of the diagram, assisting 6M55. 814 DRAGON was released from Laira today after an A transmission change, having failed at St. Blazey on 17 July with the sump reported as 'dropped'. Transmission No.10510 was removed, having completed 300 hours and was stored, with No.10492 being fitted. Ironically the replacement transmission already had 1,850 hours in service!

On Wednesday 4th (the maintenance cards held at held at York suggest) 861 VIGILANT was hauled to Newton Abbot from Bristol Bath Road by 853 THRUSTER. However 853 was noted passing through Exeter at 13.35 alone. Although a picture of 853 positioning 861 on the traverser at Newton Abbot appears in *Profile of the Warships*, it seems 861 had already arrived at Newton Abbot before 853. The failure of D815 DRUID with fuel pump faults saw D7019 take over 1V13 at Salisbury, leaving 20 minutes late, then return on 1O18 from Exeter, and just over an hour later 1V15 arrived at Exeter with D7079 in charge! 1V15 should have been hauled by 813 DIADEM but that had failed on the up working of 1O10 at Honiton with a broken cross stay. In fact 1O10 was running so late it terminated at Woking and 1V15 started back from there. When D7079 arrived at Exeter 813 was still on shed, eventually going light to Newton Abbot for repairs at 21.55.

**829 MAGPIE on Saturday 14 August 1971 at Exeter St David's with the 16.00 to Waterloo. Earlier in the day it had worked 1V01 01.45 Waterloo-Yeovil Junction 'news' to Salisbury, handing over to 816. It then took the 2V58 06.52 Salisbury-Exeter. When 829 reached London, it ended the day as 6Y05 20.33 Waterloo-Clapham Junction West London Sidings and 0Y02 21.15 Clapham Junction-Stewarts Lane. (NE Preedy)**

**814 DRAGON began Saturday 14 August 1971 at Newton Abbot, from where it worked the 7B50 04.00 Plymouth Friary-Exeter Riverside Yard forward at 06.50 to Exeter. As shown it headed the 1O10 10.15 Exeter-Waterloo and returned with the 1V17 17.00 Waterloo-Exeter. (NE Preedy)**

803 ALBION was in trouble on the 5th working 1O18 to Waterloo. The train departed seven minutes late due to an A engine fuel pump fault which was attended to at St. David's station by the fitter from the stabling point. 844 took over from 1727 at Exeter on 1A65, departing 24 minutes late, at 10.47. 831 arrived at Exeter on 7B59 no less than 197 minutes late, arriving at 14.17.

On the 6th 827 KELLY worked 5B83 23.30 Newton Abbot- Exeter booked ECS as an additional passenger train.

Alterations to workings on the Newquay branch occurred on the 8th, mainly due to a number of military specials operating. These trains took cadets from all over the country for exercises on Dartmoor. 825 INTREPID worked a train in place of the normal DMU duty of 2B72 12.40 Bodmin Road to Newquay and 2B72 17.50 Newquay to Bodmin Road. Two specials to Newquay were Warship-hauled; 868 ZEPHYR on 1Z40, the 10.00 Gloucester Eastgate to Newquay and 869 ZEST which worked 5Z76 07.05 Laira C.S. to Newquay empties to work 1Z76, the 10.10 Newquay to Peterborough as far as Acton Main Line, returning cadets that had finished their exercises. As 868's train ran from Gloucester Eastgate, and in order to save a run-around movement, the train came into Gloucester via the avoiding line and turned into Gloucester New Yard where it laid over from 08.32 until 09.30. Also on the 8th 805 worked 2B01 hauling a 3 car Swindon Cross-Country DMU set.

On Monday 9th 862 VIKING worked light, making the journey on One Engine Only (OEO) from Bath Road to Exeter on its way to Newton Abbot for attention, having sustained B end Serck oil leaks from the cooling system on its working 1B58, the 23.45 Paddington-Bristol, on Saturday evening. 813 was failed at Waterloo with brake defects, 812 was provided for 1V01 to Salisbury whilst 813 returned to Stewarts Lane for attention.

Tuesday 10th saw 829 MAGPIE working 6B33 which was a booked Class 35 duty. 869 ZEST, with assisting loco D7051, had arrived at Plymouth on 4B10 from Bristol. The failure of 805 for 7B31 saw 803 used as a replacement. 812 was failed for 2B41 with B engine faults and 823 HERMES was used instead. D817 FOXHOUND worked an early morning commuter service to Honiton in place of a DMU, anextra working that was not noted on the 'job' card.

On the 11th 818 GLORY was noted at Exeter showing 9E38 on the 'inside' headcode, the loco having been released earlier that day from Swindon after an Intermediate body and mechanical/ electrical overhaul (18/05/71-11/08/71). It was also photographed earlier in the day at Bath Road in front of the depot signal box with 9E38 in the west end headcode, standing next to 834. Under repair from the 11th to the 20th at Laira D804 AVENGER is thought to have undergone a major exam such as a 'D' or an 'E', although this is not confirmed. Intake sheets from other loco repair folders show that D804 had a B engine change around the time (July/August), removed due to reported knocking. Having come off repairs at Newton Abbot the previous day 841 ROEBUCK was failed again, not having turned a wheel! This time it was B transmission problems which would eventually mean a trip to Laira for a transmission change, its second of the month! Despite being on LWO 806 managed to get to Severn Tunnel Junction. To reiterate that 806 was on restricted workings, the letters LWO were written in capitals across its workings card! 861 conveyed scrap LT 'Q' stock from West Ruislip to Long Marston.

On the 12th withdrawn D837 RAMILLIES was at Laira to surrender its B end bogie to D822. HERCULES was stopped that morning with a fractured Gibson ring and took the B end bogie from D837. The replacement bogie fitted to D837 (No.800/75) had been out of use at Laira for some time and was fitted to D837 to go to Swindon for light attention. 818 GLORY worked an early morning commuter service to Honiton, again substituting for a DMU; this extra working was not noted on the control card. The previous day the duty had been performed by D7010 indicating a short-term shortage of serviceable DMU stock in that week.

On Friday 13th the booked loco for 1O18 was failed at Exeter so Control arranged for 829 MAGPIE working 6O81 to leave Meldon Quarry early, run to Exeter Riverside Yard and work 1O18 from Exeter; 1O18 left Exeter 40 minutes late. 805 BENBOW ran light to Ponsandane for 1A31 which normally was an ECS move, 5A31 07.35 from Laira C.S., which the loco was booked to work from Mount Gould Junction at 07.46.

Saturday 14th was the Swindon Works annual Open Day. Despite still being officially in traffic awaiting a decision as to its fate, 870 was in a line up of condemned locos in the 'Con yard', the crumpled end 'hidden' by coupling the loco to D856. The line was made up of 870, 856, D860, D864, D6307, D6309, D6352 and D6312. In another line were D6332, D847, D6349 and D830. Both 820 and 821 were open for public viewing in A shop. Also on Saturday 14th control cards show 829 MAGPIE as working 1V01 to Salisbury, then spending the day there before picking up 1O16, 16.00 from Exeter at Salisbury. However, evidence from two different sources shows that 829 carried on with the diagram and took 2V58 to Exeter, and actually worked 1O16 throughout. 810 was sent to Swindon for P.W work but was failed before being used. 868 worked the 1B55, 23.45 Paddington-Penzance to Bristol. Normally this train was 1B55 with a 23.45 departure but when heavily loaded it ran in two portions; 1B55 left Paddington at 23.48 and ran to Penzance via Bristol, whilst 1B58 left at 23.45 and ran to Bristol only. It is assumed that on the 14th 1B58 did not run as 1B55 was a pair to Bristol. 833 PANTHER worked 1B86 and 1A46 instead of the booked loco. 862 VIKING was failed at Paignton on 2B34 so Newton Abbot sent 818 GLORY light to Paignton to take up 862's next working of 1A75 whilst 862 returned light 'Home For Repair'. 841 ROEBUCK was in trouble again with its second-hand B transmission. Having completed just 127 operating hours in nine days the transmission failed with leaking oil seals. The replacement transmission's hours exceeded that of the previous one by 1,100 hours but it would last until the locomotive's demise.

On Sunday 15th 825 INTREPID was working 6B28, departing at the retimed 09.40 instead of 10.00; this also conveyed parcels traffic and was due at Penzance at 15.15. However, included in the times was a break at Truro from 12.25-13.50 to shunt and change crew. This still puts an arrival time at Penzance of 13.50 so 1A45 must have left Penzance late and perhaps 825 was used because the booked engine for 1A45 had failed. 2B14 from Plymouth was also retimed today, running five minutes later throughout. 829 MAGPIE, working 1V17, was noted as having an engine room window missing on arrival at Exeter on 1V17. D809 CHAMPION worked a Military Special to Clapham Junction, the stock of which was brought to Exeter by 818 GLORY. On the control card D809 was shown to have worked to London on 1O10 which was then crossed out and 1O10 was worked by 818.

On the 16th 814 DRAGON working 1V17 was piloted from Salisbury by D7014 due to AWS faults. Although the control cards show 831 MONARCH working 1V04 throughout this was not the case. For reasons unknown the loco was removed at Salisbury and 1V04 went forward behind D7043. From Exmouth Junction 807 CARADOC, which was ready to return to Exeter light off a coal trip with no return working, was attached to 1V04 to save a path. 808 CENTAUR hauled withdrawn D837, D849 and D859 as 0F76 08.00 Laira to Newton Abbot. 833 PANTHER worked 1Z90 which was a special running in place of 1V90, 14.30 Leeds to Plymouth. 1V90 was 58 minutes late at Exeter (with D143 in charge).

On the 17th 816 ECLIPSE working 8B43 and 7B47 ran early, and due to the failure of D1008 on 1A65 (due to by-pass Westbury at 11.02) 816 was able to work forward in place of D1008. 806 CAMBRIAN was released from its LWO restriction after engine repairs only to fail before working again due to transmission oil leaks! 867 ZENITH was failed for 1O69, 21.05 Bristol to Eastleigh before leaving Bath Road, the details of which are unknown. 852 TENACIOUS was given a replacement B engine taken from withdrawn D836 (10/08/71-17/08/71). 862 VIKING was reported as failing whilst working 1V70 although the exact details are unknown. Laira shed reported the loco had failed 'somewhere down in the west' whilst Bristol Traction Control reported that they thought the loco had failed at Plymouth. Either way it worked to Penzance with D817 FOXHOUND assisting and was put on temporary restricted workings.

On the 18th 812 ROYAL NAVAL RESERVE 1859-1959 worked 1O13 13.55 Exeter to Brighton to Salisbury after the booked Cl. 33 D6558 was failed at Exeter; however, the card shows Salisbury 'X'ed out and replaced with 'Thro' indicating that 812 did indeed go through to Brighton. Unfortunately there is no record after this on how the locomotive returned to Salisbury if it did indeed go through. The next working was on the 19th at midday from Salisbury to Exeter so there was reasonable time to get back from the coastal resort. 8A04 had a late departure waiting for 825 to arrive from Northam. Freshly ex-works at Swindon after repairs following fire damage, 821 GREYHOUND was noted at 13.00 in the station area and was captured on film standing next to 1200 FALCON which was in charge of 1B02, the 11.45 Paddington to Bristol that 821 followed to Bristol. GREYHOUND had been in Works for a Classified repair (20/04/71-18/08/71) and was later noted on a Keyham to Riverside freight. How the loco got to Plymouth is not recorded. 869 was failed for 0O14 13.00 Newton Abbot-Exeter, at Newton Abbot. No details of the failure are known but 810 worked the diagram instead. 813 was to have gone light to Exeter for 2B10 but was replaced by 853 after transmission faults on 813 meant it had to go to Laira for a transmission change.

On the 19th 869 worked the 1Z15 charter from Paignton (departing at 06.55) to Paddington. Loaded to six vehicles the train was strengthened at Exeter to eleven coaches with stock off 2B32 06.50 Barnstaple to Paignton, normally a DMU duty. In order to get the stock to Barnstaple for 2B32 a special ran from Newton Abbot at 03.00 as 5B99 ECS to Exeter to form 2B99 04.05 Exeter to Barnstaple; again, 2B99 was normally a DMU duty. 2B32 was formed of loco-hauled stock today to convey the extra passengers for 1Z15. In order to get passengers from Barnstaple and local stations on to Paignton, a special DMU service ran as 2B32, starting at Exeter at 08.00. The charter 1Z15 returned from Paddington at 22.00. Delays to services in general occurred due to heavy flooding caused by torrential rain throughout the day. Signal failures at Yeovil Junction forced the cancellation of 1V10 08.52 Brighton-Exeter at Salisbury, passengers being forwarded West on 1V09 with 810 which was being held at Salisbury to form the connection. Later that evening 823 was shown on Bristol control cards as assisting 867 on 6A17; however, this did not happen. 823 was used to work 6B65 in tandem with D1681. 867 on 6A17 was assisted by D6334. 6B18 15.00 Exeter-Chard Junction milk empties did not run either; instead 831 ran light to Chard Junction at 14.30. Notes in the railway press for the 19th record that 812 ROYAL NAVAL RESERVE 1959-1959 covered for a Hymek working the Yeovil stand-by duty. It ran, as booked, in tandem with the loco on 2V58, the 06.52 Salisbury-Exeter Central as far as Yeovil where it was to remain for emergency use, 2V58 had 811 DARING. Later that morning 812 rejoined 811 to get 812 to Salisbury to relieve a Class 33 off 1V11. However, the cards for the locomotive (D812) have no reference to this having taken place, indicating that 'local arrangements' were made. 869 worked 1Z15 to Exeter with six coaches where a further five vehicles

**Maroon liveried D815's day on Saturday 14 August 1971 started with 5B83 05.00 Newton Abbot C.S. to Exeter followed by the 1O06 06.15 Exeter-Waterloo. In the afternoon DRUID returned to Exeter with the 1V13 13.00 Waterloo-Exeter and then went back to London on the 1O18 18.00 Exeter-Waterloo before retiring to Stewarts Lane. (NE Preedy)**

were added, having come from Barnstaple (2B99) at 06.50. Normally 2B99 was a DMU but was formed of loco and coaches today.

On the 20th 857 working 6B45 ran as 7B45 and arrived at Exeter 2 hours 50 minutes late. 807 worked 8O70 and 7V07 instead of the booked Hymek. 852 failed working 6V05 at Reading and was replaced by ex-works D7011, itself being replaced at Newton Abbot by 835, running 60 minutes late. 854 was taken off its freight to work 1C06 from Reading although the train was not booked to stop there.

On Saturday 21st D819 GOLIATH arrived at Exeter on 5B83 loaded to 19 vehicles – imagine a train of that length on today's railway. D817 FOXHOUND got into trouble with its B engine low on coolant whilst working 1O16 16.00 Exeter to Waterloo. The Yeovil Junction stand-by loco D1808 took over from D817 which headed light for Westbury. Unfortunately it wasn't long before D1808 got into trouble too and had to be rescued by 823 which had to come light from Salisbury. At Salisbury 823 shunted off the train to allow D1808 to go on shed, then 823 backed onto 1O16 and continued to London. 808 arrived at Exeter 48 minutes late on 1V11, at 15.43. Due to the confusion Control wrote on the cards for 808 that it had failed at Honiton on 1O16 as that was what it should have worked. The plan was for 808 to have worked 1V01 to Salisbury, go forward to Exeter on 2V58 at 06.52, work 2B99 09.23 Exeter-Barnstaple and back, then onto 1O16. 808 worked through on 1V01, then took 1O04 to London and returned on 1V11; 821 worked 2V58 and 2B99 to Exeter where D817 took over and worked 1O16. 842 worked 8C00 diverted to Exeter Riverside Yard from its normal destination, Severn Tunnel Junction. 862 was booked to spent several hours at Malago Vale Carriage Sidings off 5B64, then work 5O52 15.22 ECS to Bristol for 2O52 15.48 to Weymouth but instead it returned light to Bath Road. 861 took over 862's diagram (LA62), including the following day, both locomotives covering for a Class 42.

On the same date, the 21st, 868's sole duty was to go light from Bristol Bath Road to Swindon for use on engineers' trains the following day. To end the day 806 working 6B65 stalled in St. David's tunnel because the banking engine D1004 failed with coolant faults. 842 ROYAL OAK's headcode workings were 1C06 18.15 Paddington-Hereford/1A46 16.15 Worcester-Paddington. 841 ROEBUCK was failed at Reading on 4A17. 812 was booked to work 7B50 04.00 Plymouth Friary-Exeter Riverside Yard, 05.22 from Newton Abbot but this was cancelled and it ran light from Newton Abbot at 06.40. 835 PEGASUS had its B end transmission No.H200/33 removed due to the forward/reverse mechanism seizing, the transmission having achieved 1,016 hours in service since the loco returned to traffic at Swindon on 8 April 1971. Transmission No.9196 was the replacement.

On Monday 23rd 825 INTREPID's 7B71 working from Newcourt also conveyed a steam crane and tender and 1B28 21.15 Bristol to Plymouth saw one Warship still in maroon with full yellow ends replaced by another in the same livery after D817 replaced D815. It is suspected that 811 DARING worked 1V01 from Waterloo to Salisbury then 2V58 06.52 Salisbury to Exeter before picking up 1O10. 861 VIGILANT working 6O19, started today from Exeter; 6B18 15.00 Exeter-Chard Junction milk empties did not run. After repair at Reading 841 ROEBUCK was available from 11.45, subsequently being allocated to work 8M12, the 16.15 Reading West Junction to Kingsbury diverted to East Usk and running as 8Z12. ROEBUCK was failed again due to being low on fuel. The East Usk special freight was eventually worked by 854 TIGER.

On the 24th D815 DRUID's workings, 6B18 15.00 Exeter-Chard Junction milk empties, followed by 6O19 16.55 Chard Junction-Morden South milk were cancelled, although they were still shown as having run on the control cards. 829 working 6E69 ran as 7E69 forward from Severn Tunnel Junction. 868 arrived at Exeter on 6B59 showing 1A55 in the headcode from its working on the 19th (!). 841 ROEBUCK arrived at Exeter in the late evening on 6B45 only to be declared a failure in Riverside Yard. D1070 took over from 841 which ran to shed at Exeter for examination but then went to Newton Abbot light to be repaired. 844 SPARTAN was failed for its next diagrammed duty, 1A26 14.15 Worcester-Paddington as 'Unfit To Work'. 814 DRAGON worked BR42 diagram covering for a Class 46.

On the 25th 816 ECLIPSE was undergoing a 'B' exam at Newton Abbot when 805 BENBOW and 816 were both failed with transmission pessiflex hoses damaged. In order to return two good locomotives back to traffic the maintenance foreman at Newton Abbot authorised the removal of both of 816's pessiflex hoses, one each to be fitted to 805 and D822 HERCULES respectively. At around the same time as this was being carried out 827 KELLY, stabled at St. Blazey, was used to take over 1B65 00.35 Paddington to Penzance newspaper train from Par after D1040 WESTERN QUEEN ran out of fuel. 854 was required at Newton Abbot for repairs so worked to Newton Abbot on the 20.35 freight for Friary.

On the 26th D822 HERCULES left Exeter on time on 1O06 06.15 to Waterloo but got into trouble at Exeter Central with coolant leaks. The official record cards show the loco returned light to Exeter for attention; however records from the Waterloo foreman's office show D822 *did* arrive at Waterloo on 1O06 and was returned straight away on 1V11. This is confirmed by notes from personal sightings at Exeter which confirm that D822 did in fact arrive at Exeter on time with 1V11. Another Warship in trouble on the Southern that day was D809 CHAMPION which arrived at Exeter on 1V13 with one engine shut down. Although repairs were carried out at Exeter at first it was uncertain that D809 would be ready to return to Waterloo in charge of 1O18, 18.00 from Exeter. As a precaution D822 was prepared for 1O18 but in the event D809 was finished and worked 1O18 as booked; D819 GOLIATH was towed 'dead' to St. David's. Both locos were split in the platform, D819 was then started and coupled to 1O14. 858 was noted on the turntable awaiting repairs for a split coolant hose.

The 27th proved a bad day for services on the Exeter-Waterloo route. D815 DRUID arrived at Waterloo on 1O04 06.50 from Yeovil Junction and was found to have a broken spring hanger; the loco was held at Waterloo and could not return on its booked working of 1V11, the 11.08 departure. 807 CARADOC arrived from Exeter on 1O06 06.15 from Exeter and was shunt released to allow it to take 1V11 back west. 1O08 07.20 from Exeter arrived behind 816 ECLIPSE which was then released to go straight back on 1V13 in place of 807. Just after 14.00 D809 CHAMPION arrived on 1O10 10.15 from Exeter and was found to have sustained a broken spring top plate! The use of 807 on 1V11 at short notice left no loco for 1V15 15.08 to Exeter so D1959 was sent from Old Oak Common. D822 was at Exeter on M/R from 12.30, having been failed for 1012. No details are known and 867 worked the diagram instead. So far so good, until 867 ZENITH failed at the West Crossing outside Waterloo station! This loco was also being 'shunt released' due to the shortage of Warships to work back on the 1V17 17.00 departure. Its booked return from Waterloo off 1O12 should have been the 1V19 19.08 departure. D6580 was hastily summoned to work 1V17 from Waterloo and when

**845 SPRIGHTLY had started Saturday 14th August 1971 with a short run in charge of the 2B91 07.50 Newton Abbot-Kingswear. Here 845 is ready to depart from Exeter with its next working 1C36 08.45 Kingswear-Cardiff which SPRIGHTLY worked throughout, returning on 1B04, the 13.10 Cardiff-Paignton. At no time in their history were Warships particularly common on passenger services to the Welsh capital. The locomotive then returned the stock to Newton Abbot as 5B80 17.10 Paignton-Newton Abbot C.S. SPRIGHTLY hadn't finished though, and left again at 21.00 with an engineers duty to Exeter. (NE Preedy)**

**854 TIGER on Wednesday 18 August emitting clouds of fumes as it runs light to Bath Road depot. It had earlier worked the 7C14 04.30 Acton-East Usk; its next duty was later that evening, taking the 7E12 19.38 Bristol Kingsland Road-Temple Mills as far as Swindon. TIGER had been employed on freight workings for the previous two days and the crews had been remiss in changing the headcode as 8E69 relates to the 13.10 Barry Docks-Temple Mills which it had worked a full two days before. (NE Preedy)**

810 COCKADE arrived at Waterloo on 1O14 14.33 from Exeter that too had to be shunt released to head back on 1V19 instead of staying overnight at Waterloo ready for the next morning 1V09 09.00 departure. This was actually worked by 867 having come off repairs at Stewarts Lane. On that day only D819 GOLIATH managed to work the full diagram! D1959 worked through to Exeter on 1V15 as did D6580 on 1V17. The next part of the diagram, 2B92 21.45 Exeter-Newton Abbot, was picked up by 814 DRAGON and D6580 retired to Exeter stabling point. Despite the problems on the Southern Region the Western Region ran fairly well with numerous reliefs operating over the Bank Holiday period to enable visitors to attend the 'Navy Days' events over the weekend at Plymouth, Paignton and Portsmouth. The release of 866 ZEBRA from Swindon in the morning left the works with one loco under repair, 820 GRENVILLE. 866 headed for Bristol off works and later went to Plymouth in charge of the 21.15 Bristol-Plymouth late evening service. 842 was shown on the control cards to work 1B35 14.30 Paddington-Penzance from Plymouth (relieving D1064), returning to Plymouth in charge of 1A71, the 22.00 Sleeper to London, but instead it was used to work 1Z15 to Paddington, perhaps covering a failure at short notice. 857 was failed for 4B05 at Old Oak Common, being replaced by 841 which later also failed, with oil leaks, becoming available OEO. 866 ZEBRA was released from Swindon Works after an Unscheduled repair and minor collision damage (16/06/71-27/08/71). 857 UNDAUNTED failed for the 05.15 Paddington and 841 wassubstituted.

Saturday 28th saw a couple of Warships in trouble. 813 DIADEM worked 1O20 in tandem with D6580 (off yesterday's 1V17) sustained final drive defects and was removed at Salisbury. The loco later went to Eastleigh for attention. 814 DRAGON was assisted from Yeovil Junction on 1O06 by D7007 after its A transmission became defective; both locos worked to Salisbury where 823 took over. 821 GREYHOUND required a heat exchanger swap after the A end transmission oil became contaminated with coolant water; Laira had the pleasure of this filthy job. 829 MAGPIE failed at Witham on 1A81 and assistance came in the form of D817 FOXHOUND. Both locos worked to Westbury where 829 went on to Westbury shed, D817 continuing forward. 845 SPRIGHTLY just managed to top the Lickey incline whilst working 1M87 when it sustained an engine fault. 845 managed to soldier on to Birmingham New Street where it was left in the station loops. 857 UNDAUNTED, attached at Taunton to an already late 1V86 10.05 Scarborough-Plymouth, caused trouble in Exeter St. David's station due to difficulty in creating vacuum between the two locos. Fitters attended and a 31 minute deficit was turned into a 38 minute deficit, both locos continuing west. 869 ZEST worked 7V70 08.15 Hither Green-Severn Tunnel Junction-Westbury, a booked duty as 7V70 laid over at Westbury until Monday morning at 01.30. In Swindon on Saturday 28th 870 ZULU, which had been 'on decision' since its arrival on 16 June, was withdrawn after sustaining severe collision damage. 828 MAGNIFICENT was also finally withdrawn today, having been stored in early July after sustaining fire damage in the early hours of July 3rd at Nailsea and Backwell while working 6B28 23.35 (02/07) Avonmouth-Plymouth Friary – the 'Nitrogen Liquor' freight. 821 was failed before it could take 1V37 at Plymouth with 844 taking over, en route to Laira from St. Blazey.

Sunday 29th and 821 GREYHOUND was noted standing outside Laira, officially 'on repair' but actually outside the main running shed still awaiting attention. The loco was displaying 1V47/1Z55 in its headcodes; the latter was from its working on the 27th and 1V47 was the 20.20 FO Manchester to Penzance. However 1V47 on the 28th was actually worked by 829 MAGPIE so it is possible that 821 was failed for 1V47 before it left Laira and that 829 took over. 823 HERMES worked a Waterloo-Axminster school charter (1Z34) and at Exeter 823 was used to remove a TSO coach from the rear of 1V11 from Waterloo (which had arrived behind D6509+D6532) to strengthen its return working, again

1Z34. Originally the empty coaches off 1Z34 09.34 from Waterloo had been booked to go to Exeter Central and be stabled there but in order to attach the extra coach 5Z34 actually ran to St. David's and was stabled there instead. 808 CENTUAR worked a train to Portsmouth Harbour but got into difficulties from Salisbury. Due to fuel leaks 808 was OEO from Salisbury and was removed at Eastleigh. There, 813 DIADEM took over, after completion of repairs from its troubles on the 28th, for the remainder of the duty allowing 808 to be repaired. 855 TRIUMPH was booked to work 1Z41 from Bridgwater to Weymouth but failed before the empty coaches left Newton Abbot; 834 PATHFINDER was used instead.

On Monday 30th D815 DRUID hauled a DMU set in the early hours of the morning from Old Oak Common to Reading, whereupon it continued light to Bristol. Had it been a normal Monday morning D815 would have worked 7C21 03.45 Acton-Jersey Marine freight but this did not run on Bank holidays. D822 HERCULES was shown on control records to have worked 6B18 15.00 Exeter-Chard Junction milk empties, returning on 6O19 16.55 Chard Junction-Morden South milk to Exeter. However 6B18 did not run today and D822 spent the day on Exeter shed and 6O19 started from Exeter at 19.50 in the care of D809 CHAMPION.

On August 31st Exeter appeared to have been short of power as Control had shown 824 HIGHFLYER working 7B71 Exeter Riverside Yard to Newcourt MoD trip and then 2B99 16.05 Exeter-Barnstaple and 17.55 return (engine diagram 'LA 62'). 824 was then to have worked light to Tiverton Junction to work 6O55 14.48 oil tank empties to Fawley, running three hours later than booked. However Exeter saved the day and provided D7055 to work 7B71 and 2B99. Unfortunately on its 2B99 17.55 working from Barnstaple, D7055 was failed with loss of coolant and D6334 was taken off 6B67 19.05 Barnstaple-Exeter St. David's freight as a replacement. D7055 was dumped at Barnstaple with 6B67 and 827 KELLY was sent light from Exeter to tow D7055 'dead in train' with 6B67, which arrived at Exeter just after 21.00. The failure of D6548 at Exeter meant no loco for 1O13 13.55 to Brighton, so 831 MONARCH was taken off its booked turn off 6B18, the Chard milk trip, and used for 1O13, which it worked throughout! At Laira 868 ZEPHYR was released at 08.00 for a light engine trial run after which, if all had gone well, it would have worked 2B10 07.10 Exeter-Penzance from Plymouth, but the Inspector riding on the loco failed it and ordered it back on repair and Laira had to find another loco for 2B10. 842 was allocated to work 1Zxx 09.40 Paignton-Paddington relief today (2B59 09.40 Paignton-Newton Abbot DMU extended) but was failed with engine speed regulator faults.

**870 ZULU stored in Swindon Con Yard on 14 August 1971, heading a line up of already withdrawn 856, D860 and D864. It had sustained severe collision damage at Laira Junction on 8 June and was eventually withdrawn because of this on 28 August. ZULU was finally cut up in May 1972. (www.rail-online.co.uk)**

The tables which follow record the workings of all the remaining Warships from Friday 13th to Wednesday 18th August 1971.

**Key**
**> signifies that the locomotive only worked a part of that train's journey, eg / 1C00 12.00 Paddington-Penzance > 4.0pm from Plymouth /**
**If it worked the complete journey it would show / 1C00 12.00 Paddington-Penzance /**
**...... indicates a working continued from the previous day or to the next day**
**??? part of working unknown**
**xxxx part or all of train headcode unknown**
**M/R Maintenance and/or Repairs and it is used commonly on BR record sheets. Maintenance would be planned exams etc; repairs to correct defects.**
**GWO Goods Working Only. Because the loco only had one exhauster it couldn't produce sufficient vacuum to work the brakes on long passenger trains but it could do this successfully on partially fitted or unfitted trains. There could be any number of reasons for GWO. (GWO could also be written FWO Freight Working Only)**
**LWO was Local Work Only; i.e Plymouth-Penzance and back to keep the loco handy for planned M/R;**
**OEO is One Engine Only; HFR was Home For Repair-loco to work to Home Depot for attention.**
**OJO was One Journey Only; the loco was noted as having defects but could work one trip until it could be repaired.**

| Friday 13th | |
|---|---|
| 803 | St. Blazey. |
| D804 | Laira - M/R (*Exams*). |
| 805 | Laira / 5A31 07.35 Laira C.S. – Penzance > 07.46 from Mount Gould Junction / 1A31 11.10 Penzance - Paddington to Plymouth (*D1060 forward*) / Laira. |
| 806 | Newton Abbot (*Res - LWO*) / 0Z66 06.00 Newton Abbot - Stoneycombe / 6Z66 06.30 Stoneycombe - Exeter Riverside Yard *'Ballast'* / Exeter. |
| 807 | Newton Abbot / 0B35 LD Newton Abbot - Dainton / 1B35 22.25 Paddington - Penzance *'Postal'* > 03.XX from Dainton to Plymouth assisting D1647 / 0F76 LD Plymouth - Newton Abbot / Newton Abbot / 0F74 10.00 Newton Abbot - Bristol Bath Road / Bristol Bath Road / 0V95 17.15 Bristol Bath Road - Stoke Gifford Yard / 7V95 02.09 Carlisle - Exeter Riverside Yard > 18.40 from Stoke Gifford / |
| 808 | Exeter / 2B10 07.10 Exeter - Penzance / 1A45 12.25 Penzance - Paddington to Plymouth (*D1044 forward*) / Plymouth North Road / 1V70 07.36 Leeds - Penzance *'Cornishman'* > 14.55 from Plymouth (*D1928 off*) / Penzance / 1A61 19.00 Penzance - Paddington *'Postal'*. |
| D809 | Newton Abbot / 8B50 04.00 Plymouth Friary - Exeter Riverside Yard > 06.50 from Newton Abbot / 7B70 07.50 Exeter Riverside Yard - Exmouth Junction *'Coal'* / 7B70 09.00 Exmouth Junction - Exeter Riverside Yard / Exeter / 1O12 12.30 Exeter - Waterloo / Waterloo / 1V19 19.08 Waterloo - Exeter Central / 2B58 23.05 Exeter Central - Exeter / 5B80 23.25 Exeter - Newton Abbot C.S. |
| 810 | Paddington / 4B05 05.15 Paddington - Bristol / Bristol Bath Road / 6A27 11.00 Malago Vale C.S. - Old Oak Common C.S. > 11.20 from Bristol / Old Oak Common / 0B24 23.00 Old Oak Common - Acton / 7B24 23.35 Acton - Exeter Riverside Yard to Bristol. |
| 811 | Newton Abbot - M/R (*A engine cylinder head defective, Off P.M.*) / 0O14 13.00 Newton Abbot - Exeter C.S. / 5O14 14.15 Exeter C.S. - Exeter / 1O14 14.33 Exeter - Waterloo / 0Y02 19.15 Waterloo - Stewarts Lane / 0W . . 20.42 Stewarts Lane - Clapham Junction / Clapham Junction. |
| 812 | Stewarts Lane / 0Y61 00.40 Stewarts Lane - Waterloo / 6K21 04.05 Waterloo - Clapham Junction *'Vans'* via Kensington / 0V04 06.17 Clapham Junction - Waterloo / 1V04 06.38 Waterloo - Exeter / Exeter / 0O55 13.30 Exeter - Tiverton Junction / 6O55 14.48 Tiverton Junction - Fawley *'Oil tank empties'* / 6V78 21.40 Fawley - Tiverton Junction *'Oil tanks'*. |
| 813 | 6B13 08.40 Penzance - Dolcoath *'Milk empties'* / 0B29 09.50 Dolcoath - Drump Lane / 7B29 10.40 Drump Lane - Roskear / 0B26 LD Roskear - St. Erth / 6B26 11.35 St. Erth - Penzance / Penzance / 6A17 15.05 Penzance - Paddington *'Perishables and milk'*. |
| 814 | Salisbury / 1V01 01.45 Waterloo - Yeovil Junction *'News'* > 03.33 from Salisbury (D*815 off*) / 1O04 06.50 Yeovil Junction - Waterloo / 1V11 11.08 Waterloo - Exeter / 6B21 15.14 Exeter Riverside Yard - Lapford *'Milk empties'* / 6B16 17.15 Lapford - Exeter *'Milk'* / Exeter / 2B84 20.10 Exeter - Newton Abbot / Newton Abbot. |
| D815 | Stewarts Lane / 0V01 00.15 Stewarts Lane - Waterloo / 1V01 01.45 Waterloo - Yeovil Junction *'News'* to Salisbury (8*14 off*) / Salisbury / 2V58 06.52 Salisbury - Exeter Central / 2B58 09.21 Exeter Central - Exeter / 1O10 10.15 Exeter - Waterloo / Waterloo / 1V17 17.00 Waterloo - Exeter / 2B92 21.45 Exeter - Newton Abbot / Newton Abbot. |
| 816 | Newton Abbot / 2B41 06.10 Newton Abbot - Exeter / 1O08 07.20 Exeter - Waterloo / Waterloo / 1V15 15.08 Waterloo - Exeter / Exeter / 6O81 19.00 Meldon Quarry - Salisbury *'Ballast'* > 20.26 from Exeter Riverside Yard (*829 off*). |
| D817 | Salisbury / 7V18 01.20 Salisbury - Westbury / Westbury / 1A54 06.40 Westbury - Paddington / 5A06 09.16 Paddington - Old Oak Common C.S. / Old Oak Common / 1B84 17.46 Paddington - Westbury / Westbury / 7A42 21.00 Westbury - Acton. |
| 818 | Newton Abbot. |
| D819 | Newton Abbot - M/R (*Exams*). |
| 820 | Swindon Works (*Classified repair, fire damage*). |
| 821 | Swindon Works (*Classified repair*). |
| D822 | Laira - M/R (*B bogie change due to right hand Gibson ring fractured, Off P.M.*). |
| 823 | 0B38 LD Acton - Southall / 6B38 01.40 Southall - Exeter City Basin / 6B23 08.20 Exeter City Basin - Westbury / Westbury / 8B45 14.59 Westbury - Swindon Cocklebury Yard / Swindon / 7B00 19.25 Swindon Cocklebury Yard - Stoke Gifford Yard / 0F74 LD Stoke Gifford Yard - Bristol Bath Road / Bristol Bath Road. |
| 824 | 1B65 10.30 Paddington - Penzance *'Cornish Riviera Express'* > 14.07 from Plymouth (*D1018 off*) / 1B16 17.55 Penzance - Bristol / Bristol Bath Road. |
| 825 | Laira / 0F78 00.20 Laira - St. Blazey / St. Blazey / 7A08 19.10 St. Blazey - Paddington Goods. |
| 826 | Newton Abbot / 5B83 05.00 Newton Abbot C.S. - Exeter / 1O06 06.15 Exeter - Waterloo / Waterloo / 1V13 13.08 Waterloo - Exeter to Chard Junction (*Failed, D7058 forward*) / 6O19 16.55 Chard Junction - Morden South *'Milk'* to Exeter (*D7058 off, D1012 forward*) / Exeter (*Failed, B dynostarter cardan shaft fault and engine overspeed trips, available OEO*) / 0F76 22.20 Exeter - Newton Abbot / Newton Abbot- M/R (*On P.M., B dynostarter cardan shaft fault and engine overspeed trips*). |
| 827 | Laira / 2B32 19.10 Plymouth - Penzance / Penzance. |
| 828 | Laira (*In store*). |
| 829 | Bristol Bath Road / 4O10 05.05 Bristol - Salisbury / Salisbury / 7V76 08.20 Salisbury - Meldon Quarry *'Ballast empties'* / 6O81 19.00 Meldon Quarry - Salisbury *'Ballast'* to Exeter Riverside Yard running early (*816 forward*) / Exeter / 1O18 18.00 Exeter - Waterloo / 0Y02 22.47 Waterloo - Stewarts Lane / |
| 831 | Clapham Junction / 0O13 02.10 Clapham Junction - Kensington Olympia / 6O13 02.50 Kensington Olympia - Stewarts Lane *'Milk'* / 0W . . 03.50 Stewarts Lane - Clapham Junction / 6W . . 04.15 Clapham Junction - Morden South *'Milk'* / 0V04 04.54 Morden South - Clapham Junction / 5V04 06.05 Clapham Junction C.S. - Waterloo / 6W . . 07.17 Waterloo - Clapham Junction *'Vans'* / 0V09 08.35 Clapham Junction - Waterloo / Waterloo / 1V09 09.08 Waterloo - Exeter / Exeter / 1O16 16.00 Exeter - Waterloo / 6W . . 20.32 Waterloo - Clapham Junction / 0Y02 21.12 Clapham Junction - Stewarts Lane / Stewarts Lane. |
| 832 | Newton Abbot / 0F77 LD Newton Abbot - Laira / Laira - M/R (*On A.M., turbo blower faults, Off P.M.*). |
| 833 | Paddington / 1B01 01.10 Paddington - Worcester *'News'* / Worcester / 5A06 06.40 Worcester Midland Yard - Worcester / 1A06 07.00 Worcester - Paddington / 5A06 10.46 Paddington - Old Oak Common C.S. / Old Oak Common - M/R (*On A.M., engine faults, released OEO, Off P.M.*) / 0M07 18.10 Old Oak Common - Kensington Olympia / 6V07 19.00 Kensington Olympia - Penzance *'Milk empties'* to Plymouth (*832 forward*). |
| 834 | Newton Abbot - M/R (*On A.M., no details, Off A.M.*) / 6Z66 06.40 Newton Abbot - Liskeard *'Engineers duty'* / 0F76 LD Liskeard - Newton Abbot / Newton Abbot / 1B86 17.50 Paignton – Bristol > 18.16 from Newton Abbot / Bristol Bath Road / 1Z50 22.08 Bristol - Paddington *'Relief'*. |
| 835 | St. Blazey / 7B31 22.55 Plymouth Friary – Truro > 02.05 from Par Yard / 7B31 05.10 Truro - Drump Lane / 7B54 06.40 Drump Lane - Truro / 7B54 07.30 Truro - St. Blazey / St. Blazey / 6B64 10.10 St. Blazey - Bristol West Depot to Newton Abbot (*D1623 forward*) / Newton Abbot / 7B33 11.55 Exeter Riverside Yard – Truro > 14.17 from Newton Abbot (*D1623 off*) / 7B49 19.00 Truro - Plymouth Friary / Laira. |
| 839 | Newton Abbot - M/R (*Transmission faults and turbo blower faults*). |
| 841 | Newton Abbot - M/R (*B transmission fault*). |
| 842 | Hereford / 1A46 08.05 Hereford - Paddington to Worcester / Worcester / 1A86 12.15 Worcester - Paddington / Ranelagh Bridge / 1C06 18.15 Paddington - Hereford / Hereford. |
| 844 | Worcester (*Res - OEO*) / 0F74 LD Worcester - Bristol Bath Road / Bristol Bath Road / 4B10 15.58 Bristol - Plymouth to Newton Abbot (*D1008 forward*) / Newton Abbot. |
| 845 | Westbury / 6V78 21.40 Fawley - Tiverton Junction *'Fuel oil tanks'* > XX.XX from Westbury (*D1914 off*) / 0B83 LD Tiverton Junction - Exeter / Exeter / 0F76 11.15 Exeter - Newton Abbot / Newton Abbot. |
| 852 | Laira - M/R (*B engine change due to high oil consumption and sump fractured*). |
| 853 | Bristol Bath Road (*Failed, loss of power, available OEO*). |
| 854 | Eastleigh / 7V68 00.05 Eastleigh - Severn Tunnel Junction / Severn Tunnel Junction / 8O09 07.50 Severn Tunnel Junction - Hither Green / Hither Green / 7Y71 19.33 Hither Green - Eastleigh / 0Y65 23.25 Eastleigh - Basingstoke. |
| 855 | Exeter / 7B08 00.40 Exeter Riverside Yard - Plymouth Friary extended to Ponsandane / 6B10 06.40 Penzance - St. Erth *'Milk empties'* / Shunt / 0F79 10.15 St. Erth - Penzance / Penzance / 6B59 14.50 Ponsandane - Exeter Riverside Yard assisted from Plymouth to Exeter by D6334 / Exeter. |

| | |
|---|---|
| 857 | 0F76 06.50 Totnes - Newton Abbot / Newton Abbot - M/R (*On A.M., final drive cardan shaft defect*). |
| 858 | Exeter / 7B10 02.40 Exeter Riverside Yard - Liskeard to Keyham / 0F77 04.55 Keyham - Laira / Laira / 2B34 21.17 Plymouth - Truro |
| 861 | Bristol Bath Road / 0F76 10.30 Bristol Bath Road - Newton Abbot / Newton Abbot - M/R (*On P.M., reported vibrations*). |
| 862 | Newton Abbot / 1A25 06.40 Newton Abbot - Paddington to Exeter (*Failed, engine fire*) / Exeter / 0F76 LD Exeter - Newton Abbot / Newton Abbot. |
| 866 | Swindon Works (*Unscheduled repair, collision damage*). |
| 867 | Hither Green / 7V70 09.40 Hither Green - Severn Tunnel Junction / Severn Tunnel Junction / 4B45 20.30 Severn Tunnel Junction - Plymouth Friary. |
| 868 | Bristol Bath Road / 1A61 19.00 Penzance - Paddington *'Postal'* > 00.57 from Bristol (*853 off*) / Old Oak Common / 1B45 09.30 Paddington - Paignton / 1A35 13.55 Paignton - Paddington / Ranelagh Bridge / 1B25 19.30 Paddington - Penzance to Plymouth (*835 forward*). |
| 869 | Old Oak Common / 0A69 09.15 Old Oak Common - Acton / 8A69 09.50 Acton - Park Royal / 8A79 11.15 Park Royal - West Ruislip / 0A69 LD West Ruislip - South Ruislip / 8A69 12.15 South Ruislip - West Ealing *'Milk empties'* / 6M15 13.35 West Ealing - Kensington Olympia *'Milk empties'* / 6V05 15.00 Kensington Olympia - Plymouth *'Milk empties'*. |
| 870 | Swindon Works (*Collision damage*). |

| Saturday 14th | |
|---|---|
| 803 | St. Blazey / 5M91 04.40 Ponsandane – Newquay > 06.15 from Par / 1A24 10.25 Newquay - Paddington to Plymouth / Laira / 1B55 09.52 Paddington – Newquay > 14.05 from Plymouth / 2B72 16.30 Newquay - Par / 2B72 18.45 Par - Newquay / 0F78 20.15 Newquay - St. Blazey / St. Blazey. |
| D804 | Laira - M/R (*Exams*). |
| 805 | Laira / 1V47 20.28 Manchester – Penzance > 03.35 from Plymouth / 1A01 08.45 Penzance - Paddington to Plymouth / Laira. |
| 806 | Exeter (*Res - LWO*) / 0F76 LD Exeter - Newton Abbot / Newton Abbot - M/R (*On P.M., engine faults*). |
| 807 | Exeter / 2B10 07.10 Exeter - Penzance / 1A45 12.18 Penzance - Paddington to Plymouth / Plymouth North Road / 1V70 07.00 Bradford - Penzance *'Cornishman'* > 15.10 from Plymouth / Penzance. |
| 808 | Old Oak Common / 1B05 12.10 Paddington - Paignton / 1B86 17.55 Paignton - Bristol / 1B28 21.15 Bristol - Plymouth. |
| D809 | Newton Abbot / 2B16 05.12 Newton Abbot - Paignton / 2B43 06.00 Paignton - Newton Abbot / 2B45 08.00 Newton Abbot - Exeter / 1O08 08.50 Exeter - Waterloo / Waterloo / 1V15 15.00 Waterloo - Exeter / Exeter / 2B92 21.48 Exeter - Newton Abbot / Newton Abbot. |
| 810 | Bristol Bath Road / 0F73 LD Bristol Bath Road - Swindon / Swindon - M/R (*Failed, No details*). |
| 811 | Clapham Junction / 8W . . 00.20 Clapham Junction - Waterloo / 8W . . 01.00 Waterloo - Clapham Junction / 0O13 02.10 Clapham Junction - Kensington Olympia / 6O13 02.50 Kensington Olympia - Stewarts Lane *'Milk'* / 0W . . 03.50 Stewarts Lane - Clapham Junction / 6W . . 04.15 Clapham Junction - Morden South *'Milk'* / 0V04 04.54 Morden South - Clapham Junction / 5V04 06.05 Clapham Junction C.S. - Waterloo / 6W . . 07.17 Waterloo - Clapham Junction *'Vans'* / 0V09 08.35 Clapham Junction - Waterloo / Waterloo / 1V09 09.00 Waterloo - Exeter / Exeter / 1O14 14.33 Exeter - Waterloo / 0Y02 19.10 Waterloo - Stewarts Lane / Stewarts Lane / 0Y61 20.45 Stewarts Lane - Waterloo North Sidings / Waterloo North Sidings. |
| 812 | 0B83 LD Tiverton Junction - Exeter / 0Z . . 18.30 Exeter - Yeovil Junction / 8Z . . 21.00 Yeovil Junction area *'Engineers duty'*. |
| 813 | 1B88 11.20 Paddington - Penzance to Westbury (*Failed, transmission vibrations*) / Westbury |
| 814 | Newton Abbot / 7B50 04.00 Plymouth Friary - Exeter Riverside Yard > 06.50 from Newton Abbot / Exeter / 1O10 10.15 Exeter - Waterloo / Waterloo / 1V17 17.00 Waterloo - Exeter / Exeter. |
| D815 | Newton Abbot - M/R (*On A.M., investigation of reported rough riding, Off A.M.*) / 5B83 05.00 Newton Abbot C.S. - Exeter / 1O06 06.15 Exeter - Waterloo / Waterloo / 1V13 13.00 Waterloo - Exeter / Exeter / 1O18 18.00 Exeter - Waterloo / 0Y02 23.08 Waterloo - Stewarts Lane / Stewarts Lane. |
| 816 | Salisbury / 1V01 01.45 Waterloo - Yeovil Junction *'News'* > 03.33 from Salisbury (*829 off*) / 1O04 06.50 Yeovil Junction - Waterloo / Waterloo / 1V11 11.00 Waterloo - Exeter / Exeter / 1O20 20.07 Exeter - Basingstoke to Salisbury (*Failed, electrical faults*) / Salisbury (*Failed*). |
| D817 | 0B38 LD Acton - Southall / 6B38 01.40 Southall - Exeter City Basin / 0F76 LD Exeter City Basin - Laira / Laira. |
| 818 | Newton Abbot / 0A75 LD Newton Abbot - Paignton / 1A75 09.50 Paignton - Paddington / Old Oak Common / 1B48 23.25 Paddington - Newton Abbot *'News'*. |
| D819 | Newton Abbot - M/R (*Exams*). |
| 820 | Swindon Works (*Classified repair, fire damage*). |
| 821 | Swindon Works (*Classified repair*). |
| D822 | Laira / 1V37 18.20 Newcastle – Penzance > 03.55 from Plymouth / Penzance / 1E00 18.40 Penzance - Newcastle to Plymouth / Laira. |
| 823 | Bristol Bath Road / 4O10 05.05 Bristol - Salisbury / 0V00 08.20 Salisbury - Westbury / Westbury. |
| 824 | Bristol Bath Road / 1B55 23.45 Paddington – Penzance > 03.00 from Bristol to Plymouth / Laira - M/R (*On A.M., no details*). |
| 825 | Old Oak Common / 0M07 10.18 Old Oak Common - Kensington Olympia / Assist stalled train to North Pole Junction / 0A38 LD North Pole Junction - South Ruislip / 6A38 11.48 South Ruislip - West Ealing / 6M15 13.35 West Ealing - Kensington Olympia *'Milk empties'* / 6V05 15.00 Kensington Olympia - Plymouth *'Milk empties'*. |
| 826 | Newton Abbot - M/R (*B dynostarter cardan shaft fault and engine overspeed trips, Off P.M.*) / 0F77 LD Newton Abbot - Laira / Laira - M/R (*On P.M., B dynostarter cardan shaft fault and engine overspeed trips*). |
| 827 | 2B15 07.15 Penzance - Plymouth / Laira / 1B04 08.15 Bristol – Penzance > 11.08 from Plymouth / Penzance / 6A17 15.05 Penzance - Paddington *'Perishables and milk'*. |
| 828 | Laira (*In store*). |
| 829 | Stewarts Lane / 0V01 00.15 Stewarts Lane - Waterloo / 1V01 01.45 Waterloo - Yeovil Junction *'News'* to Salisbury (*816 forward*) / Salisbury / 2V58 06.52 Salisbury - Exeter / Exeter / 1O16 16.00 Exeter – Waterloo (H) / 6Y05 20.33 Waterloo - Clapham Junction West London Sidings / 0Y02 21.15 Clapham Junction - Stewarts Lane / Stewarts Lane. |
| 831 | Stewarts Lane / 0Y61 00.40 Stewarts Lane - Waterloo / 6K21 04.05 Waterloo - Clapham Junction *'Vans'* via Kensington / 0V04 06.17 Clapham Junction - Waterloo / 1V04 06.38 Waterloo - Exeter / 1O11 11.05 Exeter - Waterloo / Waterloo / 1V19 19.00 Waterloo - Exeter / 5B80 23.25 Exeter– Newton Abbot..... |
| 832 | Laira / 6V07 19.00 Kensington Olympia - Ponsandane *'Milk empties'* > 07.40 from Plymouth (*833 off*) / Penzance (*Failed, B engine fuel pump fault*). |
| 833 | Laira - M/R (*On A.M., exhaust elbow blows, Off A.M.*) / 0F76 LD Laira - Newton Abbot / Newton Abbot. |
| 834 | Ranelagh Bridge / 1M58 02.52 Paddington - Banbury *'News'* / 1V02 07.33 Banbury - Paddington / Old Oak Common / 1B86 11.15 Paddington - Worcester / 1A46 16.15 Worcester - Paddington / Old Oak Common. |
| 835 | Laira / 1B25 19.30 Paddington – Penzance > 02.45 from Plymouth (*868 off*) / 5B72 06.55 Penzance - Par / 2B72 08.45 Par - Newquay / 1A51 13.25 Newquay - Paddington to Plymouth / Laira / 1V72 08.40 Manchester – Penzance > 16.08 from Plymouth / Penzance / 0F78 19.20 Penzance - St. Blazey / St. Blazey. |
| 839 | Newton Abbot - M/R (*Transmission faults and turbo blower faults*). |
| 841 | Newton Abbot - M/R (*B transmission fault, Off P.M.*). |
| 842 | Hereford / 1A46 08.05 Hereford - Paddington to Worcester / Worcester / 1A26 14.15 Worcester - Paddington / Ranelagh Bridge / 1B36 20.15 Paddington - Worcester / Worcester. |
| 844 | Newton Abbot - M/R (*On A.M., A engine exhaust joint blows*). |
| 845 | Newton Abbot / 2B91 07.50 Newton Abbot - Kingswear / 1C36 08.45 Kingswear - Cardiff / 1B04 13.10 Cardiff - Paignton / 5B80 17.10 Paignton - Newton Abbot C.S. / Newton Abbot / 8Z . . 21.00 Newton Abbot - Exeter *'Engineers duty'*. |
| 852 | Laira - M/R (*B engine change due to high oil consumption and sump fractured*). |
| 853 | Bristol Bath Road (*Failed, loss of power, available OEO*) / 0F76 18.00 Bristol Bath Road - Newton Abbot / Newton Abbot - M/R (*On P.M., low lub. oil pressure*). |
| 854 | Basingstoke / 4V14 00.30 Basingstoke - Reading / Reading / 8C00 03.30 Reading West Junction - Severn Tunnel Junction / Severn Tunnel Junction / 8C67 13.45 Severn Tunnel Junction - Ebbw Vale / 8C67 16.35 Ebbw Vale - Severn Tunnel Junction / |
| 855 | Exeter / 7B08 00.40 Exeter Riverside Yard - Plymouth Friary / Laira / 6B65 18.20 Plymouth Friary - Exeter Central *'Presflos'* / 0B58 LD Exeter Central - Exeter / Exeter. |
| 857 | Newton Abbot - M/R (*Final drive cardan shaft defect*). |
| 858 | Truro / 5A65 05.35 Truro - Ponsandane / Penzance / 1A65 13.45 Penzance - Paddington to Plymouth /Laira / 1V83 10.03 Liverpool – Penzance > 17.20 from Plymouth / Penzance. |
| 861 | Newton Abbot - M/R (*Reported vibrations*). |
| 862 | Newton Abbot / 2B34 08.49 Newton Abbot - Paignton / 0F76 LD Paignton - Newton Abbot / Newton Abbot (*Available OEO*). |
| 866 | Swindon Works (*Unscheduled repair, collision damage*). |
| 867 | Laira / 1V39 21.27 Manchester – Newquay > 04.45 from Plymouth / 1M54 11.50 Newquay - Manchester to Plymouth / Laira / 1V69 09.25 Derby – Penzance > 14.55 from Plymouth / 5M00 18.00 Penzance - Derby Chaddesden Sidings to Plymouth / Laira - M/R (*On P.M., reverser defects*). |
| 868 | Laira / 2B59 09.20 Plymouth - Newton Abbot / 1A81 10.42 Newton Abbot - Paddington / Old Oak Common / 1B55 23.45 Paddington - Penzance to Bristol in tandem with train engine. |
| 869 | Laira / 6B08 01.30 Plymouth - Penzance *'Milk empties and parcels'* / Penzance / 0F78 19.20 Penzance - St. Blazey / St. Blazey. |
| 870 | Swindon Works (*Collision damage*). |

| Sunday 15th | |
|---|---|
| 803 | St. Blazey. |
| D804 | Laira - M/R (*Exams*). |
| 805 | Laira. |
| 806 | Newton Abbot - M/R (*Engine faults*). |
| 807 | Penzance / 1A59 17.45 Penzance - Paddington to Plymouth / Laira. |
| 808 | Laira / 2B14 11.30 Plymouth - Penzance / Penzance / 6M19 16.00 Penzance - Kensington Olympia *'Milk'* to Plymouth / Laira. |
| D809 | Newton Abbot / 5O10 09.10 Newton Abbot C.S. - Exeter / Exeter / 1Z40 10.05 Exeter - Clapham Junction *'Military special'* / 5Z40 14.38 Clapham Junction - Newton Abbot C.S. / Newton Abbot. |
| 810 | Swindon - M/R (*Failed, no details*). |
| 811 | Waterloo North Sidings / 1V09 09.08 Waterloo - Exeter / Exeter / 1O17 16.55 Exeter - Waterloo / 0Y02 21.37 Waterloo - Stewarts Lane / Stewarts Lane / 0W . . 23.05 Stewarts Lane - Clapham Junction / |
| 812 | 0B58 09.30 Yeovil Junction - Exeter / Exeter / 1O16 16.00 Exeter - Waterloo / 5W01 20.53 Waterloo - Clapham Junction C.S. / 0Y02 22.10 Clapham Junction C.S. - Stewarts Lane / Stewarts Lane / 0V01 23.20 Stewarts Lane - Waterloo / Waterloo North Sidings. |
| 813 | Westbury (*Failed, transmission vibrations*). |
| 814 | Exeter / 6B18 14.45 Exeter - Chard Junction *'Milk empties'* / 6B58 16.50 Chard Junction - Exeter *'Milk'* / 5Z80 18.55 Exeter C.S. - Exmouth Junction with D1609 attached at rear / Hauled 1Z80 19.35 Exmouth Junction - Swansea to Exeter attached at rear by D1609 / Exeter. |
| D815 | Stewarts Lane / 0Y61 02.00 Stewarts Lane - Waterloo North Sidings / Waterloo North Sidings / 0V09 07.27 Waterloo North Sidings - Clapham Junction C.S. / 5V09 08.28 Clapham Junction C.S. - Waterloo / 5Y02 09.40 Waterloo - Clapham Junction C.S. *'Empty vans'* / 0V11 10.35 Clapham Junction C.S. - Waterloo / 1V11 11.08 Waterloo - Exeter / Exeter - M/R (*On P.M., fuel gauges defective*). |
| 816 | Salisbury (*Failed, electrical faults and batteries burnt out*). |
| D817 | Laira. |
| 818 | Newton Abbot / 5Z40 08.25 Newton Abbot C.S. - Exeter / Exeter / 1O10 10.20 Exeter - Waterloo / Waterloo / 1V19 19.08 Waterloo - Exeter Central to Salisbury (*868 forward*) / Salisbury. |
| D819 | Newton Abbot - M/R (*Exams*). |
| 820 | Swindon Works (*Classified repair, fire damage*). |
| 821 | Swindon Works (*Classified repair*). |
| D822 | Laira / 6B09 04.35 Plymouth - Penzance *'Milk empties and parcels'* / Penzance / 1A72 21.00 Penzance - Paddington to Plymouth / Laira. |
| 823 | Westbury / 7A . . 21.30 Westbury - Theale. |
| 824 | Laira - M/R (*No details*). |
| 825 | Laira / 6B28 09.40 Plymouth - Penzance *'Milk empties and parcels'* / 1A45 12.05 Penzance - Paddington to Plymouth / Laira. |
| 826 | Laira - M/R (*B dynostarter cardan shaft fault and engine overspeed trips*). |
| 827 | Old Oak Common. |
| 828 | Laira (*In store*). |
| 829 | Stewarts Lane / 0V01 00.05 Stewarts Lane - Waterloo / 1V01 01.35 Waterloo - Yeovil Junction *'News'* / 1O04 07.40 Yeovil Junction - Waterloo / Waterloo / 1V17 17.08 Waterloo - Exeter / 5B80 ECS Exeter - Newton Abbot C.S. / Newton Abbot-M/R (*On P.M., engine room window missing*). |
| 831 | Newton Abbot / 5O18 16.30 Newton Abbot C.S. - Exeter / 1O18 18.20 Exeter - Waterloo / 0Y02 23.17 Waterloo - Stewarts Lane / Stewarts Lane. |
| 832 | Penzance (*Failed, B engine fuel pump fault*). |
| 833 | Newton Abbot. |
| 834 | Old Oak Common / 5B45 08.45 Old Oak Common C.S. - Paddington / Ranelagh Bridge / 1B66 10.45 Paddington - Worcester / Worcester / 1A46 16.35 Worcester - Paddington / Ranelagh Bridge - M/R (*On P.M., B transmission fault, Off P.M.*) / 0F06 LD Ranelagh Bridge - Old Oak Common / Old Oak Common - M/R (*On P.M., B transmission fault, Off P.M.*). |
| 835 | St. Blazey. |
| 839 | Newton Abbot - M/R (*Transmission faults and turbo blower faults*). |
| 841 | 0F77 LD Newton Abbot - Laira / Laira - M/R (*On P.M., B transmission change due to oil leaking from convertor casing*). |
| 842 | Worcester / 6E08 20.25 Bristol – Leeds > 00.05 from Worcester to Birmingham / 1V58 02.30 Birmingham - Worcester *'News'* / Worcester / 1A66 10.15 Worcester - Paddington / Ranelagh Bridge / 1C06 18.15 Paddington - Hereford / Hereford. |
| 844 | Newton Abbot - M/R (*A engine exhaust joint blows*). |
| 845 | Newton Abbot. |
| 852 | Laira - M/R (*B engine change due to high oil consumption and sump fractured*). |
| 853 | Newton Abbot - M/R (*Low lub. oil pressure*). |
| 854 | Severn Tunnel Junction. |
| 855 | Exeter. |
| 857 | Newton Abbot - M/R (*Final drive cardan shaft defect*). |
| 858 | Penzance / 1A61 19.10 Penzance - Paddington *'Postal'*. |
| 861 | Newton Abbot - M/R (*Reported vibrations, Off P.M.*). |
| 862 | Newton Abbot (*Res - OEO*) / 8Z . . Newton Abbot area *'Engineers duty'* / Newton Abbot. |
| 866 | Swindon Works (*Unscheduled repair, collision damage*). |
| 867 | Laira / 1B45 23.15 Paddington - Penzance *'News'* > 03.33 from Plymouth / Penzance / 1A85 15.45 Penzance - Paddington to Plymouth / Laira. |
| 868 | Bristol Bath Road / 6O10 16.10 Bristol - Salisbury / Salisbury / 1V19 19.08 Waterloo - Exeter Central > 20.46 from Salisbury (*818 off*) / 5B58 23.05 Exeter Central - Exeter / 5B80 23.25 Exeter - Newton Abbot C.S. |
| 869 | St. Blazey. |
| 870 | Swindon Works (*Collision damage*). |

| Monday 16th | |
|---|---|
| 803 | St. Blazey (*Spare*). |
| D804 | Laira - M/R (*Exams*). |
| 805 | Laira / 0B31 00.30 Laira - Keyham / 7B31 01.20 Keyham - Truro / 0F78 LD Truro - St. Blazey / St. Blazey / 6B64 10.10 St. Blazey - Bristol West Depot to Newton Abbot (*D1662 forward*) / Newton Abbot / 7B33 11.55 Exeter Riverside Yard – Truro > 14.17 from Newton Abbot (*D1662 off*) / 7B49 19.00 Truro - Plymouth Friary / 7B31 22.55 Plymouth Friary - Truro to Par Yard. |
| 806 | Newton Abbot - M/R (*Engine faults*). |
| 807 | Laira / 0B83 02.00 Laira - Exeter / Exeter / 7B65 06.00 Exeter Riverside Yard - Okehampton / 7B56 09.48 Okehampton - Exeter Riverside Yard / 6B70 11.02 Exeter Riverside Yard - Exmouth Junction *'Coal'* / 1V04 06.38 Waterloo – Exeter > 10.16 from Exmouth Junction in tandem with D7043 / 7B71 12.30 Exeter Riverside Yard - Newcourt MoD Sidings / 7B71 14.28 Newcourt MoD Sidings - Exeter Riverside Yard / Exeter / 2B99 16.05 Exeter - Barnstaple / 2B99 17.55 Barnstaple - Exeter / Exeter / 1O20 20.07 Exeter - Basingstoke / 1L02 23.52 Basingstoke - Salisbury. |
| 808 | Laira / 0F76 08.00 Laira - Newton Abbot hauling withdrawn D837, D849 and D859 / Newton Abbot / 0O14 13.00 Newton Abbot - Exeter / Exeter / 1O14 14.33 Exeter - Waterloo / 0Y02 19.15 Waterloo - Stewarts Lane / 0W . . 20.42 Stewarts Lane - Clapham Junction / Clapham Junction. |
| D809 | Newton Abbot / 8B50 04.00 Plymouth Friary - Exeter Riverside Yard > 06.50 from Newton Abbot / 7B70 07.50 Exeter Riverside Yard - Exmouth Junction *'Coal'* / 7B70 09.00 Exmouth Junction - Exeter Riverside Yard / Exeter / 1O12 12.30 Exeter - Waterloo / Waterloo / 1V19 19.08 Waterloo - Exeter Central / 2B58 23.05 Exeter Central - Exeter / 5B80 23.25 Exeter - Newton Abbot C.S. |
| 810 | Swindon - M/R (*Failed, no details*). |
| 811 | Clapham Junction / 0O13 02.10 Clapham Junction - Kensington Olympia / 6O13 02.50 Kensington Olympia - Stewarts Lane *'Milk'* / 0V04 03.40 Stewarts Lane - Clapham Junction C.S. / 5V04 06.05 Clapham Junction C.S. - Waterloo / Waterloo North Sidings / 1V09 09.08 Waterloo - Exeter / Exeter / 1O16 16.00 Exeter – Waterloo (H) / 6W . . 20.32 Waterloo - Clapham Junction / 0Y02 21.12 Clapham Junction - Stewarts Lane / Stewarts Lane. |
| 812 | Waterloo North Sidings / 1V01 01.45 Waterloo - Yeovil Junction *'News'* / 1O04 06.50 Yeovil Junction - Waterloo / Waterloo (*Failed, broken bogie spring top plate*) / 0V00 LD Waterloo - Old Oak Common / Old Oak Common - M/R (*On P.M., broken bogie spring top plate*). |

| | |
|---|---|
| 813 | Westbury / 4O10 05.05 Bristol – Salisbury > 07.00 from Westbury / 7V76 08.20 Salisbury - Meldon Quarry *'Ballast empties'* / 7B60 14.50 Meldon Quarry - Exeter Riverside Yard *'Ballast'* / Exeter / 2B84 20.10 Exeter - Newton Abbot / Newton Abbot. |
| 814 | Exeter / 1O10 10.15 Exeter - Waterloo / Waterloo / 1V17 17.00 Waterloo - Exeter in tandem from Salisbury with D7043 / 2B92 21.45 Exeter - Newton Abbot / Newton Abbot. |
| D815 | Exeter / 2B10 07.10 Exeter - Penzance / 1A45 12.25 Penzance - Paddington to Plymouth (*D1069 forward (H)*) / 1V70 07.36 Leeds - Penzance *'Cornishman* >, 14.55 from Plymouth (*D25 off*) / Penzance / 1A61 19.00 Penzance - Paddington *'Postal'*. |
| 816 | Salisbury (*Failed, electrical faults and batteries burnt out*) / Hauled 0V00 08.00 Salisbury - Westbury by D818 / Westbury - M/R (*On A.M., electrical faults and batteries burnt out*). |
| D817 | Laira / 7C . . 06.45 Plymouth Friary - Tavistock Junction trip / Laira / 1B25 09.30 Paddington - Penzance, 12.50 from Plymouth / 6B14 16.10 Ponsandane - Plymouth *'Perishables and milk'* / Laira. |
| 818 | Salisbury / 0V00 08.00 Salisbury - Westbury hauling D816 / Westbury / 6B . . 18.30 Westbury - Frome / 6B . . 19.00 Frome - Westbury / Westbury / 6A42 21.00 Westbury - Acton. |
| D819 | Newton Abbot - M/R (*Exams, Off P.M.*). |
| 820 | Swindon Works (*Classified repair, fire damage*). |
| 821 | Swindon Works (*Classified repair*). |
| D822 | 7C26 08.45 Plymouth Friary - Severn Tunnel Junction / Severn Tunnel Junction / 8O30 22.20 Severn Tunnel Junction - Hither Green. |
| 823 | 8B . . 02.25 Theale - Westbury / Westbury / 1A54 06.40 Westbury - Paddington / 5A06 09.16 Paddington - Old Oak Common C.S. / 0F05 09.51 Old Oak Common - Ranelagh Bridge / Ranelagh Bridge / 1Z15 12.20 Paddington - Penzance *'Relief'* to Plymouth / Laira. |
| 824 | Laira - M/R (*No details, Off P.M.*). |
| 825 | Laira / 8Z66 02.00 Laira - Exeter Riverside Yard *'Engineers duty'* / 6B35 04.00 Exeter Riverside Yard - Plymouth Friary / Laira / 7B59 09.35 Plymouth Friary - Exeter Riverside Yard / Exeter / 6B21 15.14 Exeter Riverside Yard - Lapford *'Milk empties'* / 6B16 17.15 Lapford - Exeter *'Milk'* / Exeter / 7O85 21.47 Exeter Riverside Yard - Salisbury *'Ballast'*. |
| 826 | Laira - M/R (*B dynostarter cardan shaft fault and engine overspeed trips*). |
| 827 | Old Oak Common / 1B95 11.30 Paddington - Paignton / 1A55 15.55 Paignton - Paddington / Old Oak Common / 6B31 22.20 Paddington Goods - Plymouth Friary *'Sundries'*. |
| 828 | Laira (*In store*). |
| 829 | Newton Abbot / 2B41 06.10 Newton Abbot - Exeter / 1O08 07.20 Exeter - Waterloo / Waterloo / 1V15 15.08 Waterloo - Exeter / Exeter / 6O81 19.00 Meldon Quarry - Salisbury *'Ballast'* > 20.26 from Exeter Riverside Yard. |
| 831 | Stewarts Lane / 0Y61 00.15 Stewarts Lane - Waterloo North Sidings / Waterloo North Sidings / 1V04 06.38 Waterloo - Exeter to Salisbury (*D7043 forward*) / 0V00 LD Salisbury - Westbury / Westbury / 0F76 LD Westbury - Newton Abbot / Newton Abbot. |
| 832 | Penzance (*Failed, B engine fuel pump fault, available OEO*) / 6B14 16.10 Ponsandane - Plymouth *'Perishables and milk'* / Laira. |
| 833 | Newton Abbot / 1Z90 20.XX Newton Abbot - Plymouth / 5B80 ECS Plymouth - Newton Abbot C.S. / Newton Abbot. |
| 834 | Old Oak Common / 0A69 09.15 Old Oak Common - Acton / 8A69 09.50 Acton - Park Royal / 8A79 11.15 Park Royal - West Ruislip / 8A69 12.15 West Ruislip - West Ealing *'Milk empties'* / 6M15 13.35 West Ealing - Kensington Olympia *'Milk empties'* / 6V05 15.00 Kensington Olympia - Plymouth *'Milk empties'* to Newton Abbot / Newton Abbot. |
| 835 | St. Blazey. |
| 839 | Newton Abbot - M/R (*Transmission faults and turbo blower faults*). |
| 841 | Laira - M/R (*B transmission change due to oil leaking from convertor casing*). |
| 842 | 1A46 08.05 Hereford - Paddington to Worcester / Worcester / 1A26 14.15 Worcester - Paddington / Ranelagh Bridge / 1C06 18.15 Paddington - Hereford / Hereford. |
| 844 | Newton Abbot - M/R (*A engine exhaust joint blows, Off P.M.*). |
| 845 | Newton Abbot / 6Z68 08.00 Hackney Yard - Paignton *'Engineers duty'* / Newton Abbot / 6C13 17.50 Newton Abbot - Waterston *'Oil empties'* to Severn Tunnel Junction / Severn Tunnel Junction. |
| 852 | Laira - M/R (*B engine change due to high oil consumption and sump fractured*). |
| 853 | Newton Abbot - M/R (*Low lub. oil pressure*). |
| 854 | Severn Tunnel Junction / 7C20 08.10 Severn Tunnel Junction - Barry Docks / 8E69 13.10 Barry Docks - Temple Mills. |
| 855 | Exeter / 7B32 01.35 Exeter Riverside Yard - Drump Lane / 6B . . 09.05 Drump Lane - Ponsandane / Penzance / 6B59 14.50 Ponsandane - Exeter Riverside Yard assisted from Plymouth by D6337 / Exeter / 6B65 20.20 Plymouth Friary - Exeter Central *'Presflos'* > 22.42 from Exeter (*D1678 and D1675 off*) banked by D1675 / 0B58 23.XX Exeter Central - Exeter / Exeter. |
| 857 | Newton Abbot - M/R (*Final drive cardan shaft defect*). |
| 858 | Old Oak Common - M/R (*On A.M., B engine cylinder heads blowing, released OEO, Off P.M.*). |
| 861 | Newton Abbot / 6Z66 06.00 Hackney Yard - Stoneycombe *'Ballast'* trip / 6Z66 08.00 Stoneycombe - Taunton *'Engineers duty'* / 6Z . . 13.30 Taunton - Hackney Yard *'Engineers duty'* / Newton Abbot. |
| 862 | Newton Abbot - M/R (*On A.M., reverser defects, Off P.M.*). |
| 866 | Swindon Works (*Unscheduled repair, collision damage*). |
| 867 | 6V07 19.00 Kensington Olympia - Penzance *'Milk empties'* > 03.35 from Plymouth / 6B13 08.40 Penzance - Dolcoath *'Milk empties'* / 0B29 09.50 Dolcoath - Drump Lane / 7B29 10.40 Drump Lane - Roskear / 0B26 LD Roskear - St. Erth / 6B26 11.35 St. Erth - Penzance / Penzance / 6A17 15.05 Penzance - Paddington *'Perishables and milk'*. |
| 868 | Newton Abbot / 5B80 05.00 Newton Abbot C.S. - Exeter / 1O06 06.15 Exeter - Waterloo / Waterloo / 1V13 13.08 Waterloo - Exeter / Exeter / 1O18 18.00 Exeter - Waterloo / 0Y02 22.47 Waterloo - Stewarts Lane / Stewarts Lane. |
| 869 | St. Blazey / 7A08 19.10 St. Blazey - Paddington Goods. |
| 870 | Swindon Works (*Collision damage*). |

| Tuesday 17th | |
|---|---|
| 803 | St. Blazey (*Spare*). |
| D804 | Laira - M/R (*Exams*). |
| 805 | St. Blazey / 0B54 LD St. Blazey - Truro / 7B54 07.30 Truro - St. Blazey / St. Blazey / 6B64 10.10 St. Blazey - Bristol West Depot to Newton Abbot (*D1683 forward*) / Newton Abbot / 7B33 11.55 Exeter Riverside Yard – Truro > 14.17 from Newton Abbot (*D1683 off*) / 7B49 19.00 Truro - Plymouth Friary / 7B31 22.55 Plymouth Friary - Truro to Par Yard. |
| 806 | Newton Abbot - M/R (*Engine faults, Off A.M.*) / Newton Abbot - M/R (*On P.M., A transmission leaking oil from convertor casing, Off P.M.*). |
| 807 | Salisbury / 7V18 01.20 Salisbury - Westbury / Westbury / 8B52 05.53 Radstock – Portishead > 06.00 from Westbury / 8B52 10.20 Portishead - Radstock to Frome / 0F91 LD Frome - Westbury / Westbury / 7A42 21.00 Westbury - Acton. |
| 808 | Clapham Junction / 0O13 02.10 Clapham Junction - Kensington Olympia / 6O13 02.50 Kensington Olympia - Stewarts Lane *'Milk'* / 0W . . 03.50 Stewarts Lane - Clapham Junction / 6W . . 04.15 Clapham Junction - Morden South *'Milk'* / 0V04 04.54 Morden South - Clapham Junction / 5V04 06.05 Clapham Junction C.S. - Waterloo / 6W . . 07.17 Waterloo - Clapham Junction *'Vans'* / 0V09 08.35 Clapham Junction - Waterloo / Waterloo / 1V09 09.08 Waterloo - Exeter / Exeter / 1O16 16.00 Exeter - Waterloo / 6W . . 20.32 Waterloo - Clapham Junction / 0Y02 21.12 Clapham Junction - Stewarts Lane / Stewarts Lane. |
| D809 | Newton Abbot / 2B41 06.10 Newton Abbot - Exeter / 1O08 07.20 Exeter - Waterloo / Waterloo / 1V15 15.08 Waterloo - Exeter / Exeter / 6O81 19.00 Meldon Quarry - Salisbury *'Ballast'* > 20.26 from Exeter Riverside Yard. |
| 810 | Swindon - M/R (*Failed, no details, Off A.M.*) / 0F76 LD Swindon - Newton Abbot / Newton Abbot. |
| 811 | Stewarts Lane / 0Y61 00.40 Stewarts Lane - Waterloo / 6K21 04.05 Waterloo - Clapham Junction *'Vans'* via Kensington / 0V04 06.17 Clapham Junction - Waterloo / 1V04 06.38 Waterloo - Exeter / 0F76 11.25 Exeter - Newton Abbot / Newton Abbot. |
| 812 | Old Oak Common - M/R (*Broken bogie spring top plate, Off P.M.*) / 1B98 18.30 Paddington - Plymouth / 5B75 ECS Plymouth - Laira C.S. / Laira. |
| 813 | Newton Abbot - M/R (*On A.M., transmission fault*). |
| 814 | Newton Abbot - M/R (*On A.M., AWS faults and Serck leaks*). |
| D815 | Old Oak Common / 1Z15 08.13 Paddington - Buckfastleigh *'Ian Allan charter'* to Totnes / 0F76 LD Totnes - Newton Abbot / Newton Abbot / 0Z15 LD Newton Abbot - Totnes / 1Z15 16.30 Buckfastleigh - Paddington *'Ian Allan charter'* > 17.30 from Totnes / Old Oak Common. |
| 816 | Westbury / 8B45 09.29 Westbury - Yeovil Pen Mill / 7B47 12.30 Yeovil Pen Mill - Westbury / 1A65 06.35 Penzance – Paddington > 11.10 from Westbury (*D1008 off*) / Ranelagh Bridge / 1B35 14.30 Paddington - Penzance to Plymouth / Laira / 6A17 15.05 Penzance - Paddington *'Perishables and milk'* > 19.20 from Plymouth to Exeter assisting D1048 / Exeter. |
| D817 | Laira / 1V70 07.36 Leeds - Penzance *'Cornishman'* > 14.55 from Plymouth assisting D862 (*D14 off*) / 1A61 19.00 Penzance - Paddington *'Postal'*. |
| 818 | 0B38 LD Acton - Southall / 6B38 01.40 Southall - Exeter City Basin to Westbury / Westbury / 0F76 LD Westbury - Newton Abbot / Newton Abbot - M/R (*On P.M., B transmission faults*). |
| D819 | Newton Abbot / 0O14 13.25 Newton Abbot - Exeter C.S. / 5O14 14.05 Exeter C.S. - Exeter / 1O14 14.33 Exeter - Waterloo / 0Y02 19.15 Waterloo - Stewarts Lane / 0W . . 20.42 Stewarts Lane - Clapham Junction / Clapham Junction. |
| 820 | Swindon Works (*Classified repair, fire damage*). |

| 821 | Swindon Works (*Classified repair*). |
|---|---|
| D822 | 7V70 09.40 Hither Green - Severn Tunnel Junction / Severn Tunnel Junction / 8O30 22.20 Severn Tunnel Junction - Hither Green. |
| 823 | 0F78 00.20 Laira - St. Blazey / St. Blazey / 7A08 19.10 St. Blazey - Paddington Goods assisted from Plymouth to Exeter by D7039. |
| 824 | Laira / 0B83 LD Laira - Exeter / Exeter / 1O12 12.30 Exeter - Waterloo / Waterloo / 1V19 19.08 Waterloo - Exeter Central / 2B58 23.05 Exeter Central - Exeter / 5B80 23.25 Exeter - Newton Abbot C.S. |
| 825 | Salisbury / 0V00 02.30 Salisbury - Westbury / Westbury / 1A54 06.40 Westbury - Paddington / 5A06 09.16 Paddington - Old Oak Common C.S. / Old Oak Common / 1B84 17.46 Paddington - Westbury / 6O42 21.55 Westbury A.P.C.M. - Northam Yard *'Presflos'* > 22.38 from Westbury Yard. |
| 826 | Laira - M/R (*B dynostarter cardan shaft fault and engine overspeed trips, Off P.M.*). |
| 827 | Laira / 7B59 09.35 Plymouth Friary - Exeter Riverside Yard / Exeter / 1O18 18.00 Exeter - Waterloo / 0Y02 22.47 Waterloo - Stewarts Lane / Stewarts Lane. |
| 828 | (*In store*). |
| 829 | Salisbury / 1V01 01.45 Waterloo - Yeovil Junction *'News'* > 03.33 from Salisbury (*868 off*) / 1O04 06.50 Yeovil Junction - Waterloo / Waterloo / 1V11 11.08 Waterloo - Exeter / Exeter - M/R (*On P.M., Emergency Application Brake valve disc punctured, Off P.M.*) / 6B21 15.14 Exeter Riverside Yard - Lapford *'Milk empties'* / 6B16 17.15 Lapford - Exeter *'Milk'* / Exeter / 2B84 20.10 Exeter - Newton Abbot / Newton Abbot. |
| 831 | Newton Abbot / 5B83 05.00 Newton Abbot C.S. - Exeter / 1O06 06.15 Exeter - Waterloo / Waterloo (*Failed on arrival, broken stay rod*) /0V00 13.30 Waterloo - Old Oak Common / Old Oak Common - M/R (*On P.M., broken stay rod*). |
| 832 | Laira - M/R (*On A.M., B engine fuel pump fault, Off P.M.*). |
| 833 | Newton Abbot / 7B50 04.00 Plymouth Friary - Exeter Riverside Yard > 06.50 from Newton Abbot / Exeter / 6B70 07.50 Exeter Riverside Yard - Exmouth Junction *'Coal'* / 6B70 09.00 Exmouth Junction - Exeter Riverside Yard / Exeter / 6B18 15.00 Exeter - Chard Junction *'Milk empties'* / 6O19 16.55 Chard Junction - Morden South *'Milk'* to Exeter / 7B36 19.20 Exeter Riverside Yard - Plymouth Friary / Laira / 0B83 22.25 Laira - Exeter / Exeter. |
| 834 | Newton Abbot - M/R (*On A.M., Serck pump fault*). |
| 835 | St. Blazey / 0F77 09.30 St. Blazey - Laira / Laira - M/R (*On A.M., 'A' exam, Off P.M.*) / 1V76 10.25 Manchester – Penzance > 17.10 from Plymouth (*D183 off*) / 1A72 21.00 Penzance - Paddington to Plymouth / Laira. |
| 839 | Newton Abbot - M/R (*Transmission faults and turbo blower faults*). |
| 841 | Laira - M/R (*B transmission change due to oil leaking from convertor casing*). |
| 842 | Hereford / 1A46 08.05 Hereford - Paddington to Worcester / Worcester / 1A26 14.15 Worcester - Paddington / Ranelagh Bridge / 1C06 18.15 Paddington - Hereford / Hereford. |
| 844 | Newton Abbot / 0F74 00.01 Newton Abbot - Bristol Bath Road / 5B73 10.30 Malago Vale C.S - Worcester / Worcester / 6M20 18.00 Worcester - Birmingham / 0V03 19.10 Birmingham - Birmingham Curzon Street / 4V03 21.30 Birmingham Curzon Street - Bristol. |
| 845 | Severn Tunnel Junction / 8A09 00.55 Severn Tunnel Junction - Taplow / 0F70 LD Taplow - Old Oak Common / Old Oak Common / 1B45 09.30 Paddington - Paignton / 1A35 13.55 Paignton - Paddington to Newton Abbot (*Failed, D857 forward*) / Newton Abbot (*On P.M., A engine speed regulator fault*). |
| 852 | Laira - M/R (*B engine change due to high oil consumption and sump fractured, Off P.M.*). |
| 853 | Newton Abbot - M/R (*Low lub. oil pressure, Off P.M.*). |
| 854 | Temple Mills Yard / 6V59 20.20 Norwich Thorpe - Bristol Kingsland Road > 00.43 from Temple Mills / Bristol Bath Road / 0C22 LD Bristol Bath Road - Avonmouth / 7C22 07.05 Avonmouth - Radyr / 8B41 10.20 Radyr - Filton C.C.D / 0F74 LD Filton - Bristol Bath Road / Bristol Bath Road / 7E12 19.38 Bristol Kingsland Road - Temple Mills to Swindon Cocklebury Yard (*D1959 forward*) / Swindon - M/R (*On P.M., low lub. oil pressure, off P.M.*) / 7E18 20.32 Worcester - Temple Mills > 23.50 from Swindon Cocklebury Yard to West Ealing. |
| 855 | Exeter / 7B34 20.03 Bristol Temple Meads Goods – Ponsandane > 00.15 from Exeter Riverside Yard / Penzance / 6B59 14.50 Ponsandane - Exeter Riverside Yard assisted from Plymouth by D6356 / Exeter |
| 857 | Newton Abbot - M/R (*Final drive cardan shaft defect, Off P.M.*) / 1A35 13.55 Paignton – Paddington > 14.16 from Newton Abbot (*845 off*) / Ranelagh Bridge / 1B25 19.30 Paddington - Plymouth / Laira. |
| 858 | Old Oak Common (*Res - OEO*) / 0A69 09.15 Old Oak Common - Acton / 8A69 09.50 Acton - Park Royal / 8A79 11.15 Park Royal - West Ruislip / 8A69 12.15 West Ruislip - West Ealing *'Milk empties'* / 6M15 13.35 West Ealing - Kensington Olympia *'Milk empties'* / 6V05 15.00 Kensington Olympia - Plymouth *'Milk empties'*. |
| 861 | Newton Abbot / 0Z66 LD Newton Abbot - Stoneycombe / 6Z66 06.30 Stoneycombe *'Ballast'* trips / Laira. |
| 862 | Newton Abbot / 0B83 05.30 Newton Abbot - Exeter / 2B10 07.10 Exeter - Penzance / Penzance / 1A45 12.25 Penzance - Paddington to Plymouth (*D1040 forward*) / 1V70 07.36 Leeds - Penzance *'Cornishman'* > 14.55 from Plymouth assisted by D817 (*D14 off*) / |
| 866 | Swindon Works (*Unscheduled repair, collision damage*). |
| 867 | Paddington / 4B05 05.15 Paddington - Bristol / Bristol Bath Road / 4B15 12.50 Bristol - Yeovil Pen Mill / 4B16 16.10 Yeovil Pen Mill - Bristol / Bristol Bath Road (*Failed for 1O69 21.05 Bristol - Eastleigh, no details*). |
| 868 | Stewarts Lane / 0V01 00.15 Stewarts Lane - Waterloo / 1V01 01.45 Waterloo - Yeovil Junction *'News'* to Salisbury (*829 forward*) / Salisbury / 2V58 06.52 Salisbury - Exeter Central / 2B58 09.21 Exeter Central - Exeter / 1O10 10.15 Exeter - Waterloo / Waterloo / 1V17 17.00 Waterloo - Exeter / 2B92 21.45 Exeter - Newton Abbot / Newton Abbot. |
| 869 | Old Oak Common / 0C41 LD Old Oak Common - Acton / 7C41 10.35 Acton - Severn Tunnel Junction / Severn Tunnel Junction / 7B14 23.24 Severn Tunnel Junction - Totnes. |
| 870 | Swindon Works (*Collision damage*). |

| Wednesday 18th | |
|---|---|
| 803 | St. Blazey (*Spare*). |
| D804 | Laira - M/R (*Exams*). |
| 805 | St. Blazey / 6B64 10.10 St. Blazey - Bristol West Depot to Newton Abbot (*D1630 forward*) / Newton Abbot / 7B33 11.55 Exeter Riverside Yard – Truro > 14.17 from Newton Abbot (*D1630 off*) / 7B49 19.00 Truro - Plymouth Friary / 7B31 22.55 Plymouth Friary - Truro to Par Yard. |
| 806 | Newton Abbot / 5B83 05.00 Newton Abbot C.S. - Exeter / 1O06 06.15 Exeter - Waterloo / 1V13 13.08 Waterloo - Exeter to Salisbury (*Failed, broken spring base plate, D6505 forward*) / Salisbury / 0V00 LD Salisbury - Westbury / Westbury. |
| 807 | 0B38 LD Acton - Southall / 6B38 01.40 Southall - Exeter City Basin to Westbury / Westbury / 1A54 06.40 Westbury - Paddington / 5A06 09.16 Paddington - Old Oak Common C.S. / Old Oak Common - M/R (*On A.M., 'A' exam, Off P.M.*) / 1B84 17.46 Paddington - Westbury / 0B . . LD Westbury - Frome / 6B . . 19.00 Frome - Westbury / Westbury / 7A42 21.00 Westbury - Acton. |
| 808 | Stewarts Lane / 0Y61 00.40 Stewarts Lane - Waterloo / 6K21 04.05 Waterloo - Clapham Junction *'Vans'* via Kensington / 0V04 06.17 Clapham Junction - Waterloo / 1V04 06.38 Waterloo - Exeter / Exeter / 0F76 11.25 LD Exeter-Newton Abbot / Newton Abbot. |
| D809 | Salisbury / 1V01 01.45 Waterloo - Yeovil Junction *'News'* > 03.33 from Salisbury (*827 off*) / 1O04 06.50 Yeovil Junction - Waterloo / Waterloo / 1V11 11.08 Waterloo - Exeter / 6B18 15.00 Exeter - Chard Junction *'Milk empties'* / 6O19 16.55 Chard Junction - Morden South *'Milk'* to Exeter (*D1056 forward*) / 6B36 19.20 Exeter Riverside Yard - Plymouth Friary / 0M55 LD Plymouth Friary - Tavistock Junction / 6M55 20.35 St. Blazey - Stoke-on-Trent *'China clay'* > 22.25 from Tavistock Junction to Exeter assisting train engine. |
| 810 | Newton Abbot - M/R (*On A.M., no details, Off A.M.*) / 0B83 13.00 Newton Abbot - Exeter / 5O14 14.15 Exeter C.S. - Exeter / 1O14 14.33 Exeter - Waterloo / 0Y02 19.15 Waterloo - Stewarts Lane / 0W . . 20.42 Stewarts Lane - Clapham Junction / Clapham Junction. |
| 811 | Newton Abbot / 2B41 06.10 Newton Abbot - Exeter / 1O08 07.20 Exeter - Waterloo / Waterloo / 1V15 15.08 Waterloo - Exeter / Exeter / 6O81 19.00 Meldon Quarry - Salisbury *'Ballast'* > 20.26 from Exeter Riverside Yard. |
| 812 | Laira / 7B59 09.35 Plymouth Friary - Exeter Riverside Yard / Exeter / 1O13 13.55 Exeter - Brighton to Salisbury / Salisbury. |
| 813 | Newton Abbot - M/R (*Transmission fault, Off A.M.*) / 0B83 05.30 Newton Abbot - Exeter / Exeter / Unknown train to Plymouth / Laira - M/R (*On P.M., transmission change*). |
| 814 | Newton Abbot - M/R (*AWS faults and Serck leaks, Off A.M.*) / 8B50 04.00 Plymouth Friary - Exeter Riverside Yard > 06.50 from Newton Abbot / 6B70 07.50 Exeter Riverside Yard - Exmouth Junction *'Coal'* / 6B70 09.00 Exmouth Junction - Exeter Riverside Yard / Exeter / 1O12 12.30 Exeter - Waterloo / Waterloo / 1V19 19.08 Waterloo - Exeter Central / 2B58 23.05 Exeter Central - Exeter / 5B80 23.25 Exeter - Newton Abbot C.S. |
| D815 | Old Oak Common / 4B05 05.15 Paddington - Bristol / Bristol Bath Road / 4B15 12.50 Bristol - Yeovil Pen Mill / 4B16 16.10 Yeovil Pen Mill - Bristol / Bristol Bath Road / 1O69 21.05 Bristol - Eastleigh to Salisbury / Salisbury. |
| 816 | Exeter / 6B34 20.03 Bristol Temple Meads Goods – Ponsandane > 00.15 from Exeter Riverside Yard / Penzance / 6B59 14.50 Ponsandane - Exeter Riverside Yard assisted from Plymouth by D6338 / Exeter / 6B65 20.20 Plymouth Friary - Exeter Central *'Presflos'* > 22.42 from Exeter (*D1073 and D1006 off*) banked by D1006 / 0B58 23.XX Exeter Central - Exeter / Exeter. |
| D817 | Old Oak Common / 0C41 LD Old Oak Common - Acton / 7C41 10.35 Acton - Severn Tunnel Junction / Severn Tunnel Junction / 0Z . . LD Severn Tunnel Junction - Llanwern / 6Z . . 21.25 Llanwern - __________ to Worcester / 0F82 LD Worcester - Severn Tunnel Junction / Severn Tunnel Junction. |
| 818 | Newton Abbot - M/R (*B transmission faults*). |
| D819 | Clapham Junction / 8W . . 00.20 Clapham Junction - Waterloo / 8W . . 01.00 Waterloo - Clapham Junction / 0O13 02.10 Clapham Junction - Kensington Olympia / 6O13 02.50 Kensington Olympia - Stewarts Lane *'Milk'* / 0W . . 03.50 Stewarts Lane - Clapham Junction / 6W . . 04.15 Clapham Junction - Morden South *'Milk'* / 0V04 04.54 Morden South - Clapham Junction / 5V04 06.05 Clapham Junction C.S. - Waterloo / 6W . . 07.17 Waterloo - Clapham Junction *'Vans'* / 0V09 08.35 Clapham Junction - Waterloo / 1V09 09.08 Waterloo - Exeter / Exeter / 1O16 16.00 Exeter – Waterloo (H) / 6W . . 20.32 Waterloo - Clapham Junction / 0Y02 21.12 Clapham Junction - Stewarts Lane / Stewarts Lane. |
| 820 | Swindon Works (*Classified repair, fire damage*). |

| | |
|---|---|
| 821 | Swindon Works (*Classified repair, released to traffic*) / Swindon Works Yard / 0F74 13.XX Swindon - Bristol Bath Road / Bristol Bath Road / Unrecorded train to Plymouth / Laira / 0B44 18.00 Laira - Keyham / 7B44 18.35 Keyham - Exeter Riverside Yard / Exeter. |
| D822 | 7V70 09.40 Hither Green - Severn Tunnel Junction / Severn Tunnel Junction / 8O30 22.20 Severn Tunnel Junction - Hither Green. |
| 823 | 0F70 LD Acton - Old Oak Common / Old Oak Common / 0A69 09.15 Old Oak Common - South Ruislip / 8A69 12.15 South Ruislip - West Ealing *'Milk empties'* / 6M15 13.35 West Ealing - Kensington Olympia *'Milk empties'* / 6V05 15.00 Kensington Olympia - Plymouth *'Milk empties'*. |
| 824 | Newton Abbot - M/R (*On A.M., low transmission oil, released for trial run*) / 5E37 09.20 Newton Abbot - Paignton in tandem with D134 / 1E37 10.10 Paignton - Bradford *'Devonian'* to Taunton in tandem with D134 / 0F76 12.00 Taunton - Newton Abbot / Newton Abbot - M/R (*low transmission oil, Off P.M.*). |
| 825 | 6V76 01.00 Northam Yard - Westbury A.P.C.M. *'Presflo empties'* to Westbury Yard / 8A04 00.45 Westbury - Theale running late / 7B01 03.25 Theale - Westbury running late / Westbury / 8B43 09.29 Westbury - Yeovil Pen Mill / 7B47 12.30 Yeovil Pen Mill - Westbury / Westbury / 8B45 14.59 Westbury - Swindon Cocklebury Yard / Swindon / 7B00 19.25 Swindon Cocklebury Yard - Stoke Gifford Yard / 0F74 LD Stoke Gifford Yard - Bristol Bath Road / Bristol Bath Road. |
| 826 | Laira / 6V07 19.00 Kensington Olympia - Penzance *'Milk empties'* > 03.35 from Plymouth / 6B13 08.40 Penzance - Dolcoath *'Milk empties'* / 0B29 09.50 Dolcoath - Drump Lane / 7B29 10.40 Drump Lane - Roskear / 0B26 LD Roskear - St. Erth / 6B26 11.35 St. Erth - Penzance / Penzance / 6A17 15.05 Penzance - Paddington *'Perishables and milk'*. |
| 827 | Stewarts Lane / 0V01 00.15 Stewarts Lane - Waterloo / 1V01 01.45 Waterloo - Yeovil Junction *'News'* to Salisbury (D809 *forward*) / Salisbury / 2V58 06.52 Salisbury - Exeter Central / 2B58 09.21 Exeter Central – Exeter (H) / 1O10 10.15 Exeter - Waterloo / Waterloo / 1V17 17.00 Waterloo - Exeter / 2B92 21.45 Exeter - Newton Abbot / Newton Abbot. |
| 828 | (*In store*). |
| 829 | Newton Abbot / 6Z68 06.10 Newton Abbot - Stoneycombe *'Ballast'* trips / 6Z68 08.00 Hackney Yard - Tavistock Junction *'Ballast'* / Laira - M/R (*On P.M., A and B engine change and exams*). |
| 831 | Old Oak Common - M/R (*Broken stay rod, Off A.M.*) / 1B95 11.30 Paddington - Paignton / 1A55 15.55 Paignton - Paddington / Old Oak / 6B31 22.20 Paddington Goods - Plymouth Friary *'Sundries'*. |
| 832 | Laira / 1B35 22.25 Paddington - Penzance *'Postal'* > 04.15 from Plymouth / Penzance / 6B14 16.10 Ponsandane - Plymouth *'Perishables and milk'* / Laira. |
| 833 | Exeter / 7B10 02.40 Exeter Riverside Yard - Liskeard to Keyham / 0F77 04.55 Keyham - Laira / Laira / 1E54 14.05 Plymouth - Leeds to Bristol in tandem with D14 / 6Z . . 17.00 Bristol East Depot - Westbury / Westbury / 1B98 18.30 Paddington – Plymouth > 20.13 from Westbury (*D1010 off*) / Laira. |
| 834 | Newton Abbot - M/R (*Serck pump fault, Off P.M.*) / 1B86 17.50 Paignton – Bristol > 18.16 from Newton Abbot / Bristol Bath Road. |
| 835 | Laira / 0F78 00.20 Plymouth - St. Blazey / St. Blazey / 6B . . 04.51 St. Blazey - Drinnick Mill *'China clay empties'* / 6B . . 08.11 Drinnick Mill - St. Blazey *'China clay'* / 6B . . 09.17 St. Blazey - Par *'China clay empties'* / 7B . . 09.35 Par - Drinnick Mill *'China clay empties'* / 7B . . 10.48 Drinnick Mill - St. Blazey *'China clay'* / St. Blazey / 6B . . 13.00 St. Blazey - Burngullow *'China clay empties'* / 6B . . 14.44 Burngullow - Drinnick Mill *'China Clay empties'* / 6B . . 16.16 Drinnick Mill - St. Blazey *'China clay'* / St. Blazey / 7A08 19.10 St. Blazey - Paddington Goods |
| 839 | Newton Abbot - M/R (*Transmission faults and turbo blower faults*). |
| 841 | Laira - M/R (*B transmission change due to oil leaking from convertor casing, Off A.M.*). |
| 842 | Hereford / 1A46 08.05 Hereford - Paddington to Worcester / Worcester / 1A26 14.15 Worcester - Paddington / Ranelagh Bridge / 1C06 18.15 Paddington - Hereford / Hereford. |
| 844 | Bristol Bath Road / 4O10 05.05 Bristol - Salisbury / 7V76 08.20 Salisbury - Meldon Quarry *'Ballast empties'* / 7B60 14.50 Meldon Quarry - Exeter Riverside Yard *'Ballast'* and 6O81 19.00 Meldon Quarry - Salisbury *'Ballast'* combined to Exeter Riverside Yard / 0B83 16.30 Exeter Riverside Yard - Exeter / Exeter / 7O85 21.47 Exeter Riverside Yard - Salisbury *'Ballast'* to Westbury / Westbury. |
| 845 | Newton Abbot (*A engine speed regulator fault, Off P.M.*) / 6Z66 17.20 Hackney Yard - Taunton *'Engineers duty'* / 0F76 LD Taunton - Newton Abbot / Newton Abbot. |
| 852 | Laira / 1V76 10.25 Manchester – Penzance > 17.10 from Plymouth (*D1714 off*) / 1A72 21.00 Penzance - Paddington to Plymouth / Laira. |
| 853 | Newton Abbot / 0B83 05.30 Newton Abbot - Exeter / Exeter / 2B10 07.10 Exeter - Penzance / 1A45 12.25 Penzance - Paddington to Plymouth (*D1008 forward*) / 1V70 07.36 Leeds - Penzance *'Cornishman'* > 14.55 from Plymouth (*D188 off*) / Penzance / 1A61 19.00 Penzance - Paddington *'Postal'*. |
| 854 | 0F70 LD West Ealing - Old Oak Common / Old Oak Common / 0C14 LD Old Oak Common - Acton / 7C14 04.30 Acton - East Usk / 0F74 LD East Usk - Bristol Bath Road / Bristol Bath Road / 7E12 19.38 Bristol Kingsland Road - Temple Mills. |
| 855 | Exeter / 0F76 LD Exeter - Newton Abbot / Newton Abbot - M/R (*On A.M., spring hanger fault, Off P.M.*). |
| 857 | Laira / 0F73 05.40 Laira - Swindon Works hauling D1001 and D1057 / 0F82 LD Swindon - Severn Tunnel Junction / Severn Tunnel Junction / 8A43 16.10 Severn Tunnel Junction - Acton. |
| 858 | 7C26 08.45 Plymouth Friary - Severn Tunnel Junction / Severn Tunnel Junction / 0O67 21.50 Severn Tunnel Junction - Jersey Marine. |
| 861 | Laira / 0F76 LD Laira - Newton Abbot / Newton Abbot / Hackney-Stoneycombe Ballast Workings |
| 862 | Penzance (*Res - LWO*) / 1Z10 08.55 Penzance - Plymouth / 5B75 11.18 Plymouth - Laira C.S. / Laira. |
| 866 | Swindon Works (*Unscheduled repair, collision damage*). |
| 867 | Bristol Bath Road (*Failed, no details*) / 0F77 11.00 Bristol Bath Road - Laira / Laira - M/R (*On P.M., no details, Off P.M.*). |
| 868 | Newton Abbot / 0B83 LD Newton Abbot - Exeter / Exeter (*Stand-by duty 04.45 - 10.00*) / 6B70 11.02 Exeter Riverside Yard - Exmouth Junction *'Coal'* / 6B70 11.50 Exmouth Junction - Exeter Riverside Yard / 7B71 12.30 Exeter Riverside Yard - Newcourt MoD Sidings / 7B71 14.28 Newcourt MoD Sidings - Exeter Riverside Yard / 2B99 16.05 Exeter - Barnstaple / 2B99 17.55 Barnstaple - Exeter / 1O20 20.07 Exeter - Basingstoke / 1L02 23.52 Basingstoke - Salisbury. |
| 869 | 0F76 06.50 Totnes - Newton Abbot / Newton Abbot - M/R (*On P.M., failed, no details, Off P.M.*) / 0B83 14.50 Newton Abbot - Exeter / 6B21 15.14 Exeter Riverside Yard - Lapford *'Milk empties'* / 6B16 17.15 Lapford - Exeter *'Milk'* / Exeter / 2B84 20.10 Exeter - Newton Abbot / Newton Abbot. |
| 870 | Swindon Works (*Collision damage*). |

# Appendix 4 - Experiments and modifications

The surviving details of the Experiments are summarised below.

| Experiment | Authorised | Locos involved |
|---|---|---|
| W/SW/L/162 | 31/03/59 | D801 |
| W/SW/L/165 | 19/10/59 | D802/04 |
| W/SW/L/166 | 12/11/59 | D800/02/13/14 |
| W/SW/L/168 | 23/12/59 | D813 |
| W/SW/L/169 | 23/12/59 | D813 |
| W/SW/L/170 | 23/12/59 | D813/14 |
| W/SW/L/171 | 29/01/60 | D822 |
| W/SW/L/172 | 09/03/60 | D808/17 |
| W/SW/L/173 | 11/02/60 | D818 |
| W/SW/L/175 | 11/04/60 | D800/06/14 |
| W/SW/L/176 | 22/04/60 | D827 |
| W/SW/L/177 | 27/04/60 | D812/28 |
| W/SW/L/178 | 06/05/60 | D802 |
| W/SW/L/181 | 04/08/60 | D826/27 |
| W/SW/L/182 | 14/07/60 | D801/05/06 |
| W/SW/L/185 | 04/01/61 | D868/69 |
| W/SW/L/187 | | Cl 42/43 - Not Authorised |
| W/SW/L/188 | 16/02/61 | D804 |
| W/SW/L/189 | 20/03/61 | D805 |
| W/SW/L/190 | 20/03/61 | D868 |
| W/SW/L/191 | 20/03/61 | D818 |
| W/SW/L/194 | 20/07/61 | D825 |
| W/SW/L/195 | 20/07/61 | D853 |
| W/SW/L/196 | 24/08/61 | D808/11/12 |
| W/SW/L/197 | 12/09/61 | D817/43 |
| W/SW/L/198 | 13/10/61 | D813 |
| W/SW/L/199 | 14/02/62 | D808 |
| W/SW/L/200 | 14/02/62 | D822 |
| W/SW/L/201 | 14/02/62 | D816 |
| W/SW/L/203 | 07/03/62 | D804/08/26/30/32/69 |
| W/SW/L/205 | 20/03/62 | D800/04/11/21/24/25/29/33/37/46/52/69 |
| W/SW/L/208 | 09/08/62 | D813 |
| W/SW/L/210 | 01/10/62 | D827 / D7026 |
| W/SW/L/211 | 01/10/62 | D800 |
| W/SW/L/213 | 18/10/62 | D839 |
| W/SW/L/217 | | D809 - No information |
| W/SW/L/219 | 10/12/62 | D852/51/59 |
| W/SW/L/221 | 08/03/63 | D858 / D1006 / D6311 |
| W/SW/L/223 | 29/04/63 | D838 |
| W/SW/L/224 | 29/04/63 | D834/36/47/49/50/53/55/56/62 D6327 |
| W/SW/L/227 | 08/05/63 | D858 |

| Experiment | Authorised | Locos involved |
|---|---|---|
| W/SW/L/229 | 05/07/63 | D861 |
| W/SW/L/241 | | Cl 42/43 - Not Authorised |
| W/SW/L/242 | 19/11/63 | D833/42 |
| W/SW/L/248 | | Cl 43/22 - Not Authorised |
| W/SW/L/257 | 24/04/64 | D851 / D6305/09/34 |
| W/SW/L/258 | 24/04/64 | D854 |
| W/SW/L/259 | 05/05/64 | D852 |
| W/SW/L/260 | 05/05/64 | Cl 43 - Not Proceeded with |
| W/SW/L/265 | 17/06/64 | D837/49/60 |
| W/SW/L/268 | 08/07/64 | D843/49/60/63 |
| W/SW/L/270 | 17/09/64 | D843/46/52/57 D6314/18 |
| W/SW/L/275 | | D842/51 - No information |
| W/SW/L/279 | | D822 - No information |
| W/SW/L/280 | 09/12/64 | D839/61 D6330/56 |
| W/SW/L/281 | 06/11/64 | D841/43/50/60 D6341 |
| W/SW/L/282 | 17/11/64 | D837/46/48/57/58/59/64/65 |
| W/SW/L/288 | 07/12/64 | D805 |
| W/SW/L/290 | /01/65 | D6333 |
| W/SW/L/291 | 27/01/65 | D833/39/48/62/65 |
| W/SW/L/312 | | Cl 43/22 - No information |
| W/SW/L/318 | | D849 - No information |
| W/SW/L/327 | 24/11/65 | D855 |
| W/SW/L/328 | /11/65 | D834 - No information |
| W/SW/L/329 | 30/11/65 | D808 |
| W/SW/L/330 | 06/12/65 | D839/42/44/46/47/53/55/61/63/65 |
| W/SW/L/331 | | D840 - No information |
| W/SW/L/332 | | Cl 43 - No information |
| W/SW/L/333 | 06/12/65 | D847/65 |
| W/SW/L/334 | 06/12/65 | D823 / D1073 |
| W/SW/L/336 | | Cl 43 - No information |
| W/SW/L/338 | | Cl 42 - No information |
| W/SW/L/344 | | D802 - No information |
| W/SW/L/352 | 18/04/66 | D801/04/09/12/15/21/22/26 |
| W/SW/L/353 | 22/04/66 | D847/49/53/65 D6314/15/35 |
| W/SW/L/354 | 26/04/66 | D842/44/46/53 D6334/37/41/54 |
| W/SW/L/358 | | D855 - No information |
| W/SW/L/370 | | Cl 43/22 - No information |
| W/SW/L/401 | 24/08/67 | Cl 43 |
| W/SW/L/407 | /02/68 | D822 - No information |
| W/SW/L/410 | | Cl 43 - No information |

**W/SW/L/162** **Lubrication of bogie coil spring guides with Molybdenum grease and Black-Moly paste**

**Nature** In an effort to reduce wear in the bogie coil spring guides of hydraulic locomotives, use Molybdenum Disulphide grease as lubricating element to these components on bogies N$^{os}$. 800/20 and 800/21, allocated to locomotive D801, in accordance with the following procedure:-

(1) Spray from 12 approx. the mating parts of the coil spring guides with Black-Moly. Aerosol until a good coverage is given and then allow to stand overnight.
(2) Apply the Black-Moly paste with a sponge.
(3) Pack the guides with Black-Moly M.P. 'Q' grease and assemble.
(4) Subsequent lubrication to be carried out with this grease.

**Fitted to** Loco D801 (A bogie N$^{o}$. 800/20 from 23/03/59 until 18/05/61 and B bogie N$^{o}$. 800/21 from 23/03/59 until 17/03/61).

**Results** The coil spring guides were examined on two occasions when the bogies were removed, once after 117,000 miles service and the other at 136,000 miles service. On both occasions, the guides were found to be in excellent condition, wear and scuffing being much less than normally experienced with guides lubricated in the conventional manner.

In view of this it was considered that this method of bogie coil spring lubrication should be made standard for the D800 class locomotives and the North British built D833 class locomotives.

Full treatment was given to those components on new work and when convenient as bogies were removed for works repairs. Subsequent lubrication was made exclusively with Black-Moly M.P. 'Q' grease, indicated by a small red paint mark on the face of each coil spring guide on the bogies concerned.

The experiment, considered as a success, was made standard on 29/04/60.

**W/SW/L/165** **Modified A.T.C. shoe and shoe switch**

**Nature** Fit two Diesel Hydraulic locomotives of the D800 series with a modified A.T.C. shoe and switch to Drawing N$^{o}$. F. 538.

**Fitted to** Loco D802 from 28/01/60 until 05/04/60.
Loco D804 from 24/10/59 until closed.

**Results** Loco D802 The vertical shoe fitted failed after 11,640 miles in service, due to the actuating cam of the shoe switch seizing at the top pivot. This was caused by compression of the phosphor bronze bush against the fixed spindle by the holding nut. This apparatus was removed after 28,253 miles service and replaced by the arm type as fitted under Experiment Ref. N$^{o}$. W/SW/L/172.

Loco D804 The apparatus fitted has completed approx. 150,000 miles service without any attention required. However, in view of the trouble generally experienced with the vertical type of A.W.S. apparatus it has been decided in conjunction with the Signal Engineer to proceed with the fitting of the new arm type to all D800 Class locomotives under Experiment Ref. N$^{o}$. W/SW/L/172 and to close this experiment as unsuccessful.

This experiment was therefore closed on 16/06/62.

**W/SW/L/166** **Brake cross beam trunions fitted with nylon sleeves**

**Nature** Fit six bogies of Diesel Hydraulic locomotives, D800 series, with nylon sleeves to reduce excessive wear at present being sustained on trunion and brake hanger bushes (the sleeves are turned from solid nylon bar).

**Fitted to**
Loco D800 A bogie N$^{o}$. 800/14 from 30/10/59 until 08/01/60
Loco D800 B bogie N$^{o}$ 800/35 from 30/10/59 until 08/01/60
Loco D813 A bogie N$^{o}$ 800/34 from 09/12/59 until 02/01/61
Loco D813 B bogie N$^{o}$ 800/37 from 09/12/59 until 02/01/61
Loco D814 A bogie N$^{o}$ 800/36 from 01/01/60 until 18/10/60
Loco D814 B bogie N$^{o}$ 800/38 from 01/01/60 until 12/12/61

**Subsequently**
Loco D802 A bogie N$^{o}$ 800/14 from 28/01/60 until 13/04/61
Loco D802 B bogie N$^{o}$ 800/35 from 28/01/60 until 13/04/61

**Results** Loco D800 Bogie N$^{os}$. 800/14 (A) and 800/35 (B) were transferred to D802 during January 1960 after 24,660 miles service, without examination of the nylon sleeves.

Loco D802 At the 1,000 hour exam, after about 46,000 miles service, the nylon sleeves were examined and found to be worn thin at the bottom and on the cross beams. They were considered, however, to have given better service than corresponding steel sleeves and it was decided to fit nylon sleeves in this position to all D800 series class locomotives from that time.

Loco D813 A subsequent R. & M. depot report in respect of bogie N$^{os}$. 800/34 (A) and 800/37 (B) after about 50,000 miles service showed there was an average worn clearance of 0.004 on each sleeve.

Loco D814 No reports were made on bogie N$^{os}$. 800/36 (A) and 800/38 (B). The first of these bogies to be changed was N$^{o}$. 800/36 on 18/10/60, removed due to the inner final drive bevel wheel and pinion teeth pitted (the replacement A bogie allocated to D814 was N$^{o}$. 800/11 and was operating experiment W/SW/L/175). B bogie N$^{o}$. 800/38 was changed on 12/12/61 due to the inner and outer final drive axle seals leaking.

As the design of hangers and cross beams was latter altered to provide a larger bearing area, in conjunction with the elimination of nylon sleeves on the cross beam and the substitution of nylon bushes for steel bushes in the hanger, no further useful information could be obtained on the use of nylon sleeves on the cross beams with the smaller bearing area.

The experiment was therefore regarded as finished and not entirely successful and was closed on 27/09/60.

Further experiments were conducted on the use of self-lubricating bushes of nylatron G.S. and Mintex H5 in the brake hangers with the increased bearing area (experiments W/SW/L/177 and W/SW/L/182).

**W/SW/L/167** **W.R. thick flange tyres with treads turned to German Railways profiles**

**Nature** Fit all wheels of four D800 series locomotives with tyres turned to Drawing N$^{o}$. SK/104, i.e. with treads to German Railways profile.

**Fitted to**
Loco D815 A & B bogies N$^{os}$. 800/39 & 800/40 from 20/01/60
Loco D816 A & B bogies N$^{os}$. 800/41 & 800/13 from 17/02/60 until 13/06/62
Loco D817 A & B bogies N$^{os}$. 800/42 & 800/43 from 09/03/60
Loco D818 A & B bogies N$^{os}$. 800/44 & 800/45 from 30/03/60 until 24/01/61

**Results** The four locomotives ran mileages of 99,760 to 126,760 before the tyres were turned. From wear recorded, it appears that flange wear of the German profiles is more rapid than on the 1 in 20 tyre, but less than the 1 in 50 coned tyre. Treads wear at about the same rate irrespective of the original contour of the tyre.

Definite shelling was noted on the treads of five tyres out of the total of thirty-two tyres involved in the experiment, which is a much lower incidence than is found with the 1 in 20 and 1 in 50 coned treads. Furthermore, the shelling that had occurred, appeared to have developed at a higher mileage than normally experienced with the other types of treads. The reason for this may be that the German treads have a larger area of contact with the rail, thus reducing Hertizan stresses in both tyre and rail.

Running trials have shown that an improvement in the riding qualities of this class of locomotive is effected by the conversion of the tyre treads from 1 in 20 to that conforming with the German profile. However, it became unduly rough at tyre mileages of over 100,000 and it is considered that this tendency could be lessened by a slight modification to the tread.

M.E. Dept., B.R.B. (H.Q.),
SWINDON.

LOCOMOTIVE MODIFICATION ORDER.

MODIFICATION NO: 648

DESCRIPTION:- IMPROVED DRAINING OF WASTE OIL FROM M.A.N. ENGINE. VEE. (FIRE PREVENTION)

CLASS OF LOCOMOTIVE: D833.

LOCOMOTIVE NOS. CONCERNED: D833 - D865.

DRAWING NOS. CONCERNED: SL/SW/1772/A
SL/SW/3648
SL/SW/3649.

DESCRIPTION OF WORK: Remove existing internal drain pipe of MAN engine and replace with with larger bore pipe. Remove strainers over drain pipes. Replace flexible hose with larger diameter hose. Fit overflow pipe from waste oil collecting tank.
Renew or replace waste oil tank drain. Fit notice plate to loco.

NEW ITEMS REQUIRED: All items on SL/SW/3648
" " " SL/SW/3649.
Notice 108/SL/SW/2810.

ITEMS TO BE ALTERED: ~~[illegible]~~

ITEMS DISPLACED:
MAN. Engine Vee drain pipes. and adaptor.
Aeroquip hose 604/8/501/33.
10/SL/SW/1747.

PRIORITY:.

MOD. ORDER NO: ..................../80/40 for Components

" " NO: **** /........../80/41 Fitting to Locomotives.

CHARGE: **** Loco. Number to be quoted.

Signature ...........................
(Authorising Officer)

Date...................

Modification No.648 covered 'Improved draining of waste oil from M.A.N. engine Vee (fire prevention).' The work to be done was specified as 'Remove existing internal drain pipe of MAN engine and replace unit with larger bore pipes. Remove strainers over drain pipes. Replace flexible hose with larger diameter hose. Fit overflow pipe from waste oil collecting tank. Renew and replace waste oil tank drain. Fit notice plate to loco'.

This modified profile is shown on Drawing N°. SL/SW/2751, and tyres of all D800 class locomotives are now being turned to this Drawing when receiving wheel late or ground late attention. The experiment was closed on 06/02/63.

| **W/SW/L/168** | **Fuel tank fillers with 'Zwicky' automatic shut-off valves** |
|---|---|
| **Nature** | Fit an automatic fuel shut-off valve to each fuel tank of one 2,200 H.P. Diesel Hydraulic Locomotive N°. D813 to enable the maximum filling rate to be maintained until the tanks are completely full without an operator being in close control to prevent over filling to waste. |
| **Fitted to** | Loco D813 from 06/01/60 |
| **Results** | It was found that the 'Zwicky' valves fitted to locomotive N°. D813 have been completely successful in automatically shutting off the supply of fuel oil when the tanks are filled, thereby eliminating the spillage to waste which is, at present, often unavoidable. An added advantage of this valve is that the operator need not be in constant attendance during refuelling, making it possible for several locomotives to be refuelled simultaneously by one operator.<br>The Running and Maintenance Officer has made several requests for these valves to be fitted to all Diesel locomotives and the Chief Traction Officer has confirmed his support for a device of this nature which could eliminate fuel spillage.<br>In view of the above, authority has now been granted to fit the 'Zwicky' automatic filling valve retrospectively to all D800 Class locomotives and the experiment was closed.<br>The experiment was made standard from 29/01/62. |

| **W/SW/L/169** | **Suction side of fuel pumps fitted with 'Zwickleen' gas type filter** |
|---|---|
| **Nature** | Fit a 'Zwickleen' Gas Filter to the suction side of the fuel pump at the A end only, in place of the usual Maybach pattern filter on 2,200 H.P. Diesel Hydraulic Locomotive D813 to compare its efficiency with the Maybach pattern filter fitted to the B end. |
| **Fitted to** | Loco D813 from 06/01/60 until made standard. |
| **Results** | Reports submitted over a period of two years have shown the performance of the 'Zwickleen' filter to be highly satisfactory. Running and Maintenance Dept. staff consider that the drain plug removable filter element together with a better cover joint make the 'Zwickleen' filter superior to the Maybach filter in respect of ease of maintenance. Examination has shown that the filtration efficiency of the two filters is approximately equal.<br>It is therefore proposed to make the 'Zwickleen' Gas Filter standard for D800 class locomotives and the experiment was closed.<br>The experiment was made standard from 29/01/62. |

| **W/SW/L/170** | **Laycock exhauster fitted with restrictor valves** |
|---|---|
| **Nature** | Fit a Laycock Exhauster Restrictor Valve to Laycock Eng. C°. drawing N°. 715464A in place of the Westinghouse pattern valve on 2,200 H.P. Diesel Hydraulic locomotives D813 & D814. The valve is simple in design and operation and has successfully undergone bench trials. |
| **Fitted to** | Loco D813 from 06/01/60 until made standard.<br>Loco D814 from 06/01/60 until made standard. |
| **Results** | The Laycock Exhauster Restrictor Valve was found to be completely satisfactory in operation. This valve is now fitted as standard on D.1000 Class, 2,700 H.P. locomotives and as it is interchangeable with the Westinghouse pattern valve without any modifications being required, it can be fitted on D800 class locomotives when renewal is necessary.<br>It is therefore proposed to make the Laycock Exhauster Restrictor Valve standard for D800 class locomotives and the experiment was closed.<br>The experiment was made standard from 29/01/62. |

| **W/SW/L/171** | **Roof panels of translucent Fibreglass / Polyester** |
|---|---|
| **Nature** | During the course on construction of the first available 2,200 H.P. Diesel Hydraulic locomotive of Lot 437 fit two translucent roof panels of Fibreglass / Polyester $^1/_8$ thick at A end engine room bay in accordance with Drawing N°. SL/SW/2182 to provide more light for major examination as requested by the Running and Maintenance Officer. |
| **Fitted to** | Loco D822 — A engine room bay roof section from 15/06/60 until closed. |
| **Results** | Before the release of D822, it was stated by the Swindon Erecting Shop Foreman that the roof panels were very satisfactory in providing necessary light in the engine bay.<br>After five months service the roof panels were reported to be coating over and they were examined at Laira Depot. It was found that the panels were dirty, and cleaning restored them to their original translucency.<br>The Chief Mechanical Foreman pointed out that very little maintenance is carried out directly underneath the panels and that more advantage would be gained if they were situated at the other end of the cover adjacent to the engine room bulkhead. If this were done, the panels would be directly over the Vapor-Watchman preheater and more light diffused over the top of the engine than is at present the case.<br>Subsequent reports submitted by the Running and Maintenance Dept. have reiterated this view, and consequently it is proposed to extend the translucent panels to cover the whole length of the roof cover.<br>Drawings showing this modification are being prepared with a view to extending the trial.<br>Drawing N°. SL/SW/3043 was prepared showing the engine room roof panel in two pieces, each having a translucent section, and this drawing was made standard for renewals only. Consequently the experiment was concluded, and D822 will retain its present roof until renewal becomes necessary.<br>The experiment was therefore closed on 22/07/64. |

| **W/SW/L/172** | **A.T.C. 'Shoe type' arm apparatus** |
|---|---|
| **Nature** | Fit twenty Diesel Hydraulic locomotives of D800 series with an arm type A.W.S. Shoe Apparatus in accordance with the following drawings :-<br>F.542 Arm type A.T.C. Shoe Apparatus.<br>F.543 Carrying bracket extension.<br>F.544 Details of Arm Type A.T.C. Shoe Apparatus.<br>F.545 Arm, pin, rocker and carrying plate bush. |
| **Fitted to** | Loco D808 from 22/03/60 until closed.<br>Loco D817 from 22/03/60 until closed. |
| **Results** | It was originally intended to fit only two D800 class locomotives experimentally with the arm type shoe apparatus but in view of the trouble experienced with the vertical type of A.T.C. apparatus, it was decided, to proceed with the fitting of the new arm type shoe apparatus to the D800 class locomotives running or being built at that date.<br>However, final clearance of the new shoe switch had not been obtained from the Signal Engineer and it was necessary to manufacture and fit this apparatus under experimental procedure.<br>Reports submitted by the Running & Maintenance Dept. in respect of locos. D808 and D817, the first two locomotives fitted, stated that the arm type apparatus was operating satisfactorily. No adverse reports have been received in respect of any of those locomotives fitted with this apparatus to date and only two of the class now remain outstanding.<br>The arm type A.W.S. type shoe apparatus is now virtually standard for D800 class locomotives and this experiment will be closed. However, the final clearance of the 'Dowmic' switch which is used with this apparatus has not yet been obtained and it is understood that design and development of A.W.S. switch gear is to be undertaken by the Signal Engineer as from January 1st 1962, and trials will continue.<br>The experiment was closed on 06/02/63. |

| **W/SW/L/173** | **Laycock drivers brake valves fitted with Dowmic switches** |
|---|---|
| **Nature** | Fit modified Laycock Drivers Vacuum Brake Valves equipped with Dowmic Limit Switches in accordance with Drawing SK/136, to both ends of Diesel Hydraulic Locomotive D818, to determine whether this type of switch is more dependable and positive in action than the present type of switch. |
| **Fitted to** | Loco D818 — A and B end drivers brake valves from 30/04/60 until made standard 07/02/62. |
| **Results** | No faults were reported during the week of Works trials and at the end of this period the valves were tested and found to function correctly.<br>Reports submitted by the Running and Maintenance Dept. in respect of D818 during the period of 12 months and approx. 85,000 miles of service stated that the switches continued to function satisfactorily.<br>In view of the very satisfactory operation in service of these switches they are now being fitted to all D800 Class Locomotives equipped with the Laycock Drivers Vacuum Brake Valve and this experiment will be closed. |

| **W/SW/L/174** | **Bogies fitted with hydraulic dampers** |
|---|---|
| **Nature** | Fit both bogies of one Diesel Hydraulic D800 series locomotive with a modified bogie side control linkage incorporating rubber pad springs and modified thrust bearings to reduce lateral accelerations of the bogie by permitting increased movement between body and bogies. |
| **Fitted to** | Loco D804 — A and B bogies N$^{os}$. 800/22 and 800/23 from 08/03/60 |

**Results** Initial trials showed that improvement in riding qualities had been effected by the modification. Some undesirable resonances remained however and further modifications were made in an effort to reduce them.

Following further trials after the above modifications the locomotive remained in service with a max. permitted speed of 80 mph until shelling necessitated tyre turning.

Examination of the linkage in the factory found one side control link broken and three badly worn. This necessitated the re-design of the link and soft rubbers were fitted at the same time.

Trials were then carried out with softer rubber springs, used in conjunction with hydraulic dampers and tyres turned to a new German Rlys. composite profile. The first trials were carried out at a max. speed of 80 mph, finally this was raised to 90 mph. The riding was considered very satisfactory and it was decided that the locomotive should go into traffic for a trial period.

After a mileage in traffic of 77,530 miles the modified rubber springs were inspected and found to be in reasonably good condition, they were then re-fitted for further service.

It has now been decided as an experiment to dispense with the existing bogie side control linkage as a centring device on both bogies of one D800 class loco. other than D804. This has been initiated under experiment Ref. N°. W/SW/L/204, fitted to locomotive D813 on 31/08/62.

This experiment was therefore closed on 07/01/63.

**W/SW/L/175** **Q 309 'Atlas' brand steel tyres**

**Nature** Fit all wheels on one bogie of three 2,200 H.P. Diesel Hydraulic locomotives with Firth Brown Ltd Q 309 'Atlas' brand high tensile steel tyres to observe whether any improved tyre conditions may be obtained from their use.

**Fitted to**

| | |
|---|---|
| Loco D800 | A bogie N°. 800/64 from 11/12/61 until 09/11/62. |
| Loco D806 | A bogie N°. 800/64 from 04/11/60 until 06/09/61. |
| Loco D814 | A bogie N°. 800/11 from 20/10/60 until 12/12/61. |

**Results**

Loco D814 Severe shelling of the right outer 'Atlas' tyre on A bogie N°. 800/11 occurred after 54,030 miles service. Signs of shelling were found on the other three 'Atlas' tyres. Several small shells had developed on the standard tyres on the B bogie N°. 800/38, which had completed 135,370 miles service.

All tyres of both bogies were turned on the ground lathe during a works visit between 06/04/61 and 19/04/61, due to the A bogie N°. 800/11 having the right hand outer tyre holed. A reduction of $^{25}/_{32}$ in wheel diameter was required to remove the major area of shelling on bogie N°. 800/11, right inner tyre. All tyres of both bogies were examined after completing 49,000 miles service after tyre turning, and no defect was found on any tyre.

However, after the 'Atlas' tyres and standard tyres had completed 68,280 miles service after turning the bogies were removed for attention to the final drives, the loco arriving for the bogie change on 12/12/61. Examination of the tyres found treads to be $^{5}/_{32}$.

All treads had worn $^{1}/_{16}$ full to ½ bore. Slight shelling had occurred on all 'Atlas' tyres but not sufficient to justify turning had the bogie remained under the loco. Because of the tread and flange thickness, the tyres of both bogies were scrapped.

Loco D806 Cracks and shelling were found on the 'Atlas' tyres of the A bogie N°. 800/64 after 61,000 miles service. Several very small shells were found on the standard quality tyres of the B bogie N°. 800/25. After a further 23,000 miles service D806 received tyre attention on 06/09/61, due to the left hand inner tyre of A bogie N°. 800/64 being holed. The 'Atlas' tyres were turned and the standard tyres renewed. Before turning it was noted that the cracking and shelling had considerably increased on all the 'Atlas' tyres.

Turning the 'Atlas' tyres proved to be difficult, the areas of cracking were very hard and metal fell out from between the cracks. The defects were eradicated on the inner wheels with a $^{5}/_{16}$ cut and on the other wheels a ½ cut was required, necessitating a final reduction of 1 $^{1}/_{4}$ in wheel diameter. A fault in the steel of the right inner 'Atlas' tyre was revealed during turning which could not be removed before the last turning size was reached. This tyre was removed and the one spare 'Atlas' tyres was fitted. The bogie was returned to traffic under D800 A.

Loco D800 The tyres on the A bogie N°. 800/64 were examined after about 90,000 miles service, after the bogie had been removed from D800 for repair, the loco arriving on 09/11/62 for a heavy casual repair.

Flange depth was found to have been within $^{1}/_{32}$ of the maximum permissible and severe shelling accompanied by lateral cracking had occurred on the treads of all four tyres. The thickness of the tyres precluded turning and they were replaced with standard quality tyres. The total mileage obtained from the three high tensile steel tyres was about 174,000 miles.

Under the conditions imposed by the nature of the service of locos D800, D806 and D814 it was apparent that no advantage was to be obtained by the use of Q 309 'Atlas' brand tyres in respect of resistance to shelling.

The experiment was therefore considered unsuccessful and was closed on 22/07/64.

**W/SW/L/176** **Combined handle and locking catch for windows**

**Nature** To meet Running and Maintenance Dept. complaints of poor cab ventilation in D800 class locomotives associated with difficulties in operating front cab side sliding windows, fit both side windows in the A end cab only of 2,200 H.P. D.H. locomotive D827 with experimental handles and locking catches in accordance with Beckett, Laycock and Watkinson Drawings N$^{os}$. Y590409X2 and X590409X3.

**Fitted to** Loco D827 A end cab side sliding windows from 04/10/60 until closed.

**Results** The catches were fitted on 17/08/60, during the locomotive construction.

A report after approx. four months service stated that the handle securing screws continually worked loose, and difficulty was experienced in re-tightening the screws. Examination after five months service confirmed the above report, all the securing screws were found to be loose. This tendency of the securing screws to work loose was again noted eight days later although the screws had been tightened before the previous examination.

To overcome this tendency of the securing screws becoming loose the experimental handle and locking catch was slightly modified. This modification has been completely successful over a period of nearly eight months and approx. 80,000 miles service.

Enquiry has shown that footplate staff consider the modified experimental catch a great improvement on the standard pattern.

It is therefore considered that this catch has eliminated the difficulties experienced with the standard fitting and it will be made standard for all D800 class locomotives.

The experiment was made standard from 13/02/62.

**W/SW/L/177** **Brake hangers with 'Mintex' bushes in the bottom holes**

**Nature** Fit Mintex H.5 self lubricating bushes in place of nylon bushes in the bottom hole of brake hangers in accordance with Drawing N°. SL/SW/8110 but without grease lubrication on two bogies of D.H. D800 Class Locomotives. The bogies should be allocated to different locomotives to afford a direct comparison in service with nylon bushes fitted in the hangers of the opposite end bogie.

**Fitted to**

| | |
|---|---|
| Loco D812 | A end bogie N°. 800/62 (Std. nylon) from 08/09/60 until 06/04/62. |
| Loco D812 | B end bogie N°. 800/9 (Mintex) from 08/09/60 until 06/04/62. |
| Loco D828 | A end bogie N°. 800/10 (Std. nylon) from 19/10/60 |
| Loco D828 | B end bogie N°. 800/63 (Mintex) from 19/10/60 |

**Results** D812 ran 72,310 miles, when general wear in the brake gear necessitated its renewal. Wear in the bore of the 'Mintex' and standard nylon bushes was approx. the same and was not considered excessive at this mileage. Examination of the hangers found considerable wear in the bottom bush housings of the eight fitted with 'Mintex' bushes, necessitating repair of the hanger bottom ends before re-bushing for further service. The bottom bush housing of the eight hangers fitted with standard nylon bushes showed no sign of wear.

D828 ran 24,460 miles when two 'Mintex' bushes were lost and two very badly worn, after the loco left the shed without two crossbeam cotters. The four 'Mintex' bushes were replaced by standard nylon.

After 61,400 miles service the four remaining 'Mintex' bushes required to be renewed because of wear, one bush had completely worn through. Examination of the four hangers found between .030 and .040 wear in the bottom bush housings, again necessitating repair before new bushes could be fitted.

This trial has shown that no extension of working life is likely to be obtained from the self lubricated 'Mintex' H.5 bush over that now obtained from the standard nylon bush which is grease lubricated.

The cost of the 'Mintex' bush is 5/5d as against 12/1d for the nylon, this advantage would be nullified by the cost of repair to hanger bottom ends unless he movement of the 'Mintex' bush in the hanger can be prevented.

No further information can be obtained from this experiment as now constituted, it was therefore closed on 05/11/61.

**W/SW/L/178** **Cooler group radiator units with steel inserts welded between the ends of existing water pipes**

**Nature** To obviate the difficulties experienced in replacing flexible connections under the floor of Serck cooling groups on Diesel Hydraulic D800 Class Locomotives replace the flexibles on both cooling units of Locomotive N°. D802 by steel inserts welded between the ends of existing water pipes.

**Fitted to** Loco D802 A and B end cooler group units from 02/06/60 until 13/04/61.

**Results** Reports submitted by the Running and Maintenance Dept. over a period of nine months showed that the steel inserts welded into the inlet and outlet pipe systems of D802 had given trouble free service for approx. 50,000 miles of service.

Visual examination, which was restricted because of the confined space between the cooler and the water tank, was carried out after 48,000 miles of service and no cracks or signs of fatigue could be found on the parts of the system which could be seen.

At this point in the trial after consultation with the Locomotive Works Manager it was agreed that sufficient confidence existed in the result of the experiment to standardize this modification on all Diesel Hydraulic D800 Class Locomotives and to cancel the experiment.

The relevant Drawings have therefore been altered and the experiment closed.

| **W/SW/L/181** | **Cooler group shutter gear rendered inoperative** |
|---|---|

**Nature** To assess the usefulness of hydraulically operated shutter gear fitted to the cooling units of D800 Class Locomotives and its effect on preheating rate, render the shutters inoperative at the A end of two locomotives by removing completely the shutter gear and hydraulic piping to the ram, and blanking off the connections to the ram from the controller.

| **Fitted to** | Loco D826 | A end cooling unit from 07/09/60 until 05/09/61. |
|---|---|---|
| | Loco D827 | A end cooling unit from 04/10/60 |

**Results** Preheating tests were made on both locomotives under shed conditions with an ambient temperature of 55°F.

In the case of D827, a cut-in temperature of 135°F at the A end without shutter gear was reached in 2 hours from a commencing temperature of 60°F, while at the B end with shutters closed, the same temperature was reached in 1 $^{1}/_{2}$ hours from a commencing temperature of 64°F. The ambient temperature remained at 55°F throughout.

The test with D826 occurred during the evening and although the ambient temperature at the commencement was the same as with D827, viz. 55°F, it dropped 12°F during the course of the test. From a cooling water temperature of 56°F at the commencement at the A end, the temperature rose to 135°F in 3 $^{3}/_{4}$ hours, while at the B end with the shutters closed, this temperature was reached in 1 $^{1}/_{2}$ hours.

Cooling out tests were conducted when ambient temperatures ranging from 49°F / 57°F were not as low as been hoped. In general, these tests showed that the critical minimum engine start falling temperature of 98°F was reached in approx. 5 $^{1}/_{2}$ hours with shutters open and about 7 $^{1}/_{2}$ hours with shutters closed.

The tests suggest, however, under extremely cold weather conditions the absence of shutter gear would prove a liability to R. & M. Dept. staff, and in view of the fact that less trouble is now experienced with the operation and maintenance of shutter gear, it is recommended that such gear should be retained.

The experiment was, therefore closed on 02/08/61.

| **W/SW/L/182** | **Brake hangers with Nylatron bushes in bottom holes** |
|---|---|

**Nature** Nylatron self-lubricating bushes impregnated with Molydbenum Disulphide fitted in the bottom hole of the brake hangers in accordance with Drawing Ref. N°. SL/SW/8110, but without grease lubrication, on two bogies of Diesel Hydraulic D800 class locomotives.

| **Fitted to** | Loco D805 | B bogie N°. 800/65 from 14/10/60 until 27/03/61. |
|---|---|---|
| | Loco D806 | A bogie N°. 800/64 from 04/11/60 until 06/09/61. |
| **Subsequently** | Loco D801 | B bogie N°. 800/65 from 11/04/61 until 21/06/62. |

**Results** Bogie N°. 800/64 ran 84,000 miles before being repaired, when the brake gear was found in reasonably good condition for the mileage run; the average wear on the bore diameter being .088 or .009/1,000 miles service. The average wear on the crossbeam ends was .023 or .0003/1,000 miles service. The bogie was removed from D806 A end due to a hole in the left hand inner tyre.

Bogie N°. 800/65 ran a total of 113,900 miles to repair, and again the condition of the brake gear was reasonably good having regard to the mileage run; the average wear on the bore diameter being .129 or .001/1,000 service. The average wear on the crossbeam ends was .048 or .0004/1,000 service. This bogie was removed from D805 B end due to a loose tyre, and removed from D801 B end for a general repair.

Considering no grease lubrication was used, this performance was considered satisfactory.

In view of its much lower cost and satisfactory performance, even without grease lubrication, it was recommended that bushes of Polypenco Nylatron CS. M tube be used, instead of Vulcasacot, in the bottom hole of all D800 class bogie brake hangers, in conjunction with grease lubrication. Considered as successful, the experiment was closed on 03/07/62.

| **W/SW/L/185** | **Demisting deflectors fitted** |
|---|---|

**Nature** Fit de-misting deflectors to two Diesel Hydraulic Locomotives D800 series to Sketch SK/176 as follows :-

A end of one locomotive with Deflector N°. 3 at the L H outer nozzle, N°. 1 at the L H inner nozzle, N°. 2 at the R H inner nozzle and N°. 4 at the R H outer nozzle, the B end of the same locomotive with Deflector N°. 3 at the L H outer nozzle, N°. 2 at the L H inner nozzle, N°. 1 at the R H inner nozzle and N°. 4 at the R H outer nozzle.

A end only of further locomotive with Deflector N°. 3 at the L H outer nozzle, N°. 2 at the L H inner nozzle, N°. 1 at the R H inner nozzle and N°. 4 at the R H outer nozzle.

To determine which type or combination of type is most effective.

| **Fitted to** | Loco D868 | A and B cabs from 18/05/61 |
|---|---|---|
| | Loco D869 | A cab only from 12/07/61 |

**Results** The two locomotives fitted completed 17 and 15 months service covering one complete Winter period in traffic to December 1962.

Periodical reports received to date have stated that the demister deflectors are working satisfactorily, and no adverse reports have been received.

Traffic Headquarters Paddington have been requested to ascertain to opinion of operating staff in respect of the comparative merits of the demisting deflectors and to recommend which of the arrangements, if any, could be considered as suitable for adoption as a standard fitting on D800 Class Locomotives.

In answer to this request it was recommended that an arrangement consisting of N°. 4 Deflectors fitted to the outer nozzles and N°. 1 Deflectors fitted to the inner nozzles should be made standard for D800 Class Locomotives. This is to be the subject of a modification order, and the experiment was closed on 06/02/63.

| **W/SW/L/187** | **Resistance bulb elements** |
|---|---|

**Nature** To obviate the frequent breakage experienced at present with standard 'Hartman Braun' temperature transmitters, fit Ten Diesel Hydraulic Locomotives of D800 series with resistance bulb elements to patterns 'A' and 'B' manufactured by Messrs. Ether L$^{td}$.

Each locomotive to be fitted with four elements, two at each end in the following manner :-

One pattern 'A' to the transmission oil contactor.
One pattern 'B' to the high cooling water temperature contactor.

| **Fitted to** | Class 42 |
|---|---|
| **Results** | No information is available regarding this experiment and the locomotives involved. |

| **W/SW/L/188** | **Voltage regulator circuits** |
|---|---|

**Nature** To reduce or eliminate unstable conditions in voltage regulators on Diesel Hydraulic D803 Class locomotives when selecting a lower engine speed, modify the circuit in accordance with Drawing N°. SK/302 on locomotive D804 to enable both regulators to be held at the same voltage until the speeds at both ends have changed.

| **Fitted to** | Loco D804 | A and B end Automatic Voltage Regulators from 21/03/61 |
|---|---|---|

**Results** Initial trials carried out a Swindon found that where voltage regulators have been accurately calibrated on the locomotive the modification made very little difference but that under out of balance conditions the arcing at the R.C.R. contacts appeared to be reduced.

However, after a short period of service it became apparent that this circuit modification effected no general improvement and the circuit was reverted to its original state.

This experiment was considered as unsuccessful and therefore closed on 21/02/62.

| W/SW/L/189 | Exhaust elbow having baffles of different shapes. |
|---|---|

**Nature** Fit baffle plates of different shapes in the exhaust elbows at both ends of one 2,200 H.P. Diesel Hydraulic locomotive of D800 series in accordance with Drawing Ref. N°. SK/242, with the objective of reducing deposits at the lower end of the ¾ bore drain pipes which cause blockages after approx. 12,000 miles service.

| **Fitted to** | Loco D805 | A engine N°. 112244 from 14/10/60 until 07/11/60. |
|---|---|---|
| | Loco D805 | B engine N°. 112243 from 14/10/60 until 07/11/60. |
| **Subsequently** | Loco D805 | A engine N°. 112247 from 01/12/60 until at 30/10/62 at Laira. |
| | Loco D805 | A engine N°. 112281 from 30/10/62 at Laira until 07/02/64. |
| | Loco D805 | A engine N°. BSM 159 from 31/03/64 until 14/12/64 at Laira. |
| | Loco D805 | A engine N°. BSM 164 from 15/12/64 at Laira until 04/10/65. |
| | Loco D805 | B engine N°. 112239 from 01/12/60 until 23/11/61 at Laira. |
| | Loco D805 | B engine N°. 112272 from 25/11/61 at Laira until 22/05/63 at Laira. |
| | Loco D805 | B engine N°. 112592 from 25/05/63 at Laira until 18/10/63 at Laira. |
| | Loco D805 | B engine N°. 112266 from 18/10/63 at Laira until 07/02/64. |
| | Loco D805 | B engine N°. 112268 from 31/03/64 until 04/10/65. |

**Results** D805 was found to be fitted with the experimental baffle plates during repair 18/07/61. It was subsequently learnt that the baffles were fitted when the loco. went to traffic 19/04/61*

Unfortunately no notification of this fitting was sent to the C. M. & E. E. or to the Running & Maintenance Dept. Officer. Consequently it has not been possible to follow the progress of the experiment in service. The mileage since fitting to repair was 25,710.

When the drain pipes were removed 18/07/61 they were found to be almost blocked with about $^3/_{16}$ orifice left. Enquiry revealed that Laira are apparently working to the old M.P. 11 which stipulated drain pipes should be cleaned at 500 hour examinations instead of weekly, as laid down in M.P. 11 dated January 1961. It is possible therefore that the drain pipes had not been cleaned out since fitting and the build up had been over a period of three months.

The build up in both drain pipes was about the same, suggesting that a varied shape of baffles as between A and B engines makes little difference.

Some drain pipes however, are known to have been blocked after between 11,000 and 14,000 miles service. The mileage of D805 to date since the baffles were fitted is approx. 162,000 and reports submitted, state examinations have found that the baffles were in a satisfactory condition.

The experiment was allowed to continue during which time satisfactory reports were received, but meanwhile it was found that by reducing the length of the drain pipes below deck plate to a minimum the problem of deposits occurring ceased to exist thus rendering the baffle plates valueless.

The experiment was therefore closed on 27/09/65.

* Evidence in the locomotive maintenance folder suggests that Experiment W/SW/L/189 was actually fitted from 14/10/60.

**W/SW/L/190** **Modified air intake ducting**

**Nature** Fit modified air intake ducting for both engines during the course of construction of one 2,200 H.P. Diesel Hydraulic Locomotive of Lot 448 in accordance with Drawing Ref. N°. SL/SW/2431/C to facilitate the fitting of rubber seals with a view to improve air filtration.

**Fitted to** Loco D868 from 31/05/61

**Results** Examination after Loco. N°. D868 had completed 836 hours running with the modification fitted, found the air intake ducting to be in a satisfactory condition.

Since the locomotive has completed over 5,000 hours with the modification fitted and no adverse reports have been received in respect of this modification.

On 10/01/63 the C. M. & E. E.'s Dept., in answering a request for information, reported that the modified air intake trunking was mostly effective. The air filter made a good face on the engine side of the filter and no evidence was present which would suggest air had been by-passing the filter. The A end engine had almost completed 6,000 hours service and the B end engine had been changed several times. Report Form 'C' dated 23/12/62 showed everything was satisfactory.

The modified air intake ducting continued to prove satisfactory and a favourable report was submitted by Laira Depot on 17/02/65. By this time the acceptance of the modification was recommended and arrangements put in hand for the issue of Modification Orders N$^{os}$. MB.414/64 (D803-D870) and MB.414/65 (D800-D802) to cover all D800 Class Locomotives.

The experiment was therefore closed on 13/07/65.

**W/SW/L/191** **Spanner MK. III boiler in place of Stone-Vapor generator**

**Nature** To obtain experience with and to assess the potentialities of this type of boiler before being installed in the new 2,700 H.P. D H locomotives fit a MK. III Spanner boiler in place of an existing Stone-Vapor type generator in one Swindon built D800 Class locomotive.

**Fitted to** Loco D818 Boiler from 14/06/61 until closed on 21/11/62.

**Results** Progress report 09/11/62; The MK. III Spanner boiler installed in loco N°. D818 has now completed 16 months service in traffic and similar units have been installed and are now in service in 2,700 H.P. D.1000 Class locomotives.

The unit has been generally well received by Operating and Running and Maintenance staff. Minor modifications have been suggested which have now been carried out on the MK. III boilers now in service and on new boilers for 2,700 H.P. D.1000 Class locomotives.

As the MK. III Spanner boiler is now being fitted as standard in the D.1000 Class locomotives it is not intended to proceed further with this experiment and it will be concluded.

Difficulty has been experienced with the Alfloc water treatment of this boiler because of the failure of brickets to completely dissolve. Investigation into the use of a liquid softening agent has been initiated under Experiment Ref. N°. W/SW/L/210.

Experiment W/SW/L/210 was fitted to D827 (20/12/62) and D7026 (05/05/67).

**W/SW/L/194** **Westinghouse drivers brake valve**

**Nature** Fit one 2,200 H.P. diesel hydraulic locomotive of D800 class numbered between D819 and D832 (except D830) at present fitted with Laycock Drivers Vac. brake valves, with Drivers Vac. brake valves, Part No. D.74515/2 and Rectifiers Part No. 14A6, supplied on loan by Westinghouse Brake & Signal Co., to compare their efficiency and dependability in service with that of the Laycock valves.

**Fitted to** Loco D825 A & B cabs (fitted 07/12/61) from 11/12/61 until closed.

**Results** The Westinghouse Drivers Vacuum Brake Valves and Rectifiers were reported satisfactory after 31,550 miles service.

The experiment continued with no defects, or complaints against the valves being reported during approx. 220,000 miles service. At this time it was considered that the valves had proved very reliable but that the cost of converting other D800 class locomotives would not be justified in view of the reasonably satisfactory performance of the standard Laycock valves.

Loco. D825 would retain the Westinghouse valves until life expired.

The experiment was closed on 15/12/64.

**W/SW/L/195** **Cass and Phillips engine hour counters**

**Nature** Fit the first available new D.H. Locomotive of D833 Class with Cass & Phillips Engine Hour counters in accordance with SK/358 to afford a comparison in accuracy and dependability with the Smiths hour counter already fitted which should be retained on selected locomotives.

Of the three instruments supplied ('A', 'B', and 'C') on loan two are standard and are to be fitted one each end of the locomotive. The third instrument incorporates voltage stabilising and is to be connected in parallel with one of the standard instruments.

**Fitted to** Loco D853 A and B engines. from 30/08/61

**Results** During the period of 30/08/61 to the loco. being stopped for shopping on 09/11/61 agreement was fairly consistent between the readings of instruments 'A' and 'B' at the A end but instrument 'C' at the B end read consistently low. This instrument was replaced in November 1961 during shopping.

The subsequent performance of these instruments was unsatisfactory and after examination by Messrs. Cass & Phillips they were replaced by three new instruments on 17/05/62. The new instruments incorporate stiffer flexible mountings and a new flexible connection in an effort to reduce the vibration to which the instruments are subjected.

Examinations on 30/05/62 and 08/06/62 found that the instrument 'B' at the B end of the locomotive had ceased to record because of a broken electrical lead. This fault was repaired and examination on 22/06/62 found the three instruments were keeping in step, however, subsequent reports dated 24/08/62 and 10/10/62 indicate that the 'A' instrument at the A end had ceased to record.

Although the performance of the Cass & Phillips instruments has been far from satisfactory to date they have proved to be more reliable than the Smiths counters fitted to the same locomotive which appear to be valueless on this locomotive.

The experiment was closed on 28/11/62.

**W/SW/L/196** **Brake shoes incorporating double blocks**

**Nature** Fit both bogies, having newly turned tyres, on one 2,200 H.P. Diesel Hydraulic of D800 Class with double brake blocks in accordance with Drawing Ref. N°. SL/SW/2882 to determine whether such fittings will reduce tyre temperatures and therefore reduce tendency of tyre movement on wheel centres and shelling or spalling on treads due to thermal effects.

| | | |
|---|---|---|
| **Fitted to** | Loco D808 | A and B bogies N$^{os}$. 800/48 and 800/49 from 09/03/62 until 09/10/62 |
| **Subsequently** | Loco D808 | A and B bogies N$^{os}$. 800/48 and 800/63 from 26/10/62 until 31/07/63. |
| | Loco D811 | A and B bogies N$^{os}$. 800/63 and 800/48 from 23/09/63 until 20/01/64. |
| | Loco D812 | A and B bogies N$^{os}$. 800/87 and 800/63 from 07/05/64 until 28/09/65. |

**Results** Examination on 08/06/62 found that with the exception of A bogie left outer all tyres had moved, these were found tight, remarked and dated 08/06/62. The double brake blocks on B bogie $N^{o}$. 800/49 had a minimum thickness of 1, i.e. 1 ½ of wear and were replaced by new blocks. The double brake blocks on A bogie $N^{o}$. 800/48 had a minimum thickness of 1 ½ and were left for further service. Mileage of the experimental blocks on 08/06/62 since fitting was 32,000 run over a period of 13 weeks.

The double brake blocks on A bogie $N^{o}$. 800/48 were renewed on 29/07/62, being approx. 1 thick after 46,750 miles service run over a period of approx. 19 weeks.

Examination on 23/08/62 and again on 10/10/62 when D808 was in the factory for attention to final drives, found no further movement of tyres had occurred since 08/06/62 and both bogies were still fitted with the second set of double brake blocks. The minimum thickness of the double brake blocks on 10/10/62 was 1 $^{5}/_{8}$ on A bogie $N^{o}$. 800/48 after 25,250 miles service and 1 $^{3}/_{16}$ on B bogie $N^{o}$. 800/49 after 40,000 miles service, run over periods of 10 and 16 weeks respectively.

The general condition of the gear was considered satisfactory having regard to the mileage run. No shelling or spalling of tyre treads could be found. Tread wear was approx. $^{3}/_{32}$ on all tyres which is normal for a tyre mileage of 72,000.

Bogie $N^{o}$. 800/49 was removed from D808 on 17/10/62 during shopping for attention to a final drive defect, and the experimental brake gear from the bogie, after replacement of hanger bottom bushes and brake blocks, was fitted to bogie $N^{o}$. 800/63 which was returned to service under the B end of loco. D808, fitted with new tyres.

Further examination of the brake blocks and tyres was made at Laira on 15/01/63. A bogie $N^{o}$. 800/48 brake blocks were still in use at a mileage of 42,350 after 21 weeks service and B bogie $N^{o}$. 800/63 brake blocks had recently been renewed when their mileage was 57,100 after 28 weeks service. The figures obtained for tyre wear were satisfactory for the mileage, 89,100, for A bogie and 17,740 for B bogie, and no signs of shelling or movement were detected.

On 05/03/63 the tyres on A bogie $N^{o}$. 800/48 were turned and the brake blocks were changed. Tyre profiles were taken at Laira on 10/04/63 and on 01/08/63, and on each occasion the wear was not excessive for the miles run and the treads were in good condition. The visit to Swindon was for a bogie repair and during this the brake gear, which was in poor condition, was overhauled and re-blocked. Under D808 the brake gear had completed 144,030 miles in 73 weeks and three sets of blocks had been worn out thus giving an average life of 24 weeks per set. The stated figure for the life of single blocks was 10 ½ weeks per set.

Bogies $N^{os}$. 800/48 and 800/63, rebuilt with the experimental brake gear and new tyres, were fitted to B and A ends respectively of D811, to traffic on 23/09/63. On 24/01/64 loco. D811 came to Swindon for axle examination and the bogies were stripped. It appeared that the blocks had not been changed since previously and as their condition was good they would be put back into service. The brake gear, having some new keys, was rebuilt on bogies $N^{os}$. 800/63 and 800/87 having newly turned tyres and fitted to the B and A ends of loco D812 respectively, to traffic on 08/05/64.

On 14/08/64 the tyres of D812 were examined and found satisfactory for the mileage of 28,030. They continued to be in a satisfactory condition but the extra time required for changing brake blocks proved to be inconvenient to the depots. As the incidence of tyre defects were much reduced in any case it was decided to revert to standard brake blocks.

The experiment was therefore closed on 23/03/65.

**W/SW/L/197** **Brake slack adjusters of 'Weslak' type**

**Nature** Fit both bogies, having new tyres, on one D.H. Locomotive of D800 series with a full set of 'Weslak' slack adjusters in accordance with Drawing Ref. $N^{o}$. 8621/4 to obviate seizures of existing adjusters and the necessity of daily brake adjustments to maintain an efficient brake.

| | | |
|---|---|---|
| **Fitted to** | Loco D817 | A and B Bogies $N^{os}$. 800/69 and 800/23 from 08/03/63 until 07/01/64. |
| **Subsequently** | Loco D843 | A and B Bogies $N^{os}$. 800/69 and 800/23 from 07/02/64 until 10/08/64. |
| | Loco D817 | A and B Bogies $N^{os}$. 800/69 and 800/23 from 23/10/64 |

**Results** On 20/03/63 after 3,200 miles Laira reported a failure of the fixed toggle arm on B bogie $N^{o}$. 800/23 L H inner adjuster and had the broken arm removed. Later examination of the adjusters revealed that the failure had been due to the pin connecting the operating link to the sliding portion fracturing, possibly due to a shock overload. Arrangements were put in hand for W. A and B Bogies $N^{os}$. 800/69 and 800/23B. & S. $C^{o}$. to replace the damaged parts and these were re-fitted to D817 during mid April 1963. At this time the adjusters were left in good working order although the behaviour of the brake return springs was not considered 100%.

A routine check on 23/04/63 showed all was well, and on 03/05/63 the R H inner sliding pawl lever, which was missing, was replaced.

On 11/12/63 Laira reported that A and B bogie L H inner actuating arms had failed, and on 19/12/63 an examination revealed a failure to a third one. The remaining slack adjusters were in good condition but the inner ones were isolated pending repair to the defective ones.

D817 returned to Swindon for a bogie change immediately afterwards, mileage since fitting was 96,850, and opportunity was taken to make good all the damage to the brake adjusters. Bogie $N^{os}$. 800/23 and 800/69, with the adjusters overhauled, were re-fitted to Loco. D843 B and A ends respectively on 08/02/64.

During August 1964 Loco. D843 entered Swindon Works and Bogies $N^{os}$. 800/23 and 800/69 were removed for overhaul. The adjusters were in working order but the set bolt retaining the outer sleeve in position needed replacing, and the pin securing the dog paw was loose. After repair the adjusters were considered in satisfactory condition and the bogies were to be allocated to another loco.

Bogie $N^{os}$. 800/23 and 800/69 were returned to service under D817 B and A ends respectively, to traffic on 23/10/64.

On 19/02/65 Laira depot reported that the 'Weslak' brake adjusters were in good condition and functioning correctly, and that their acceptance as standard was recommended. M. E. (Design) would make the final investigation.

Satisfactory reports of the slack adjusters continued to be received but a final decision on whether or not to adopt them as standard was deferred while careful consideration was given to the economic aspect of fitting.

A detailed economic comparison between 'Weslak' adjusters and 'pin in hole' method based on annual return over the remaining 14 years life expectancy of the locomotive class, showed that the adoption of the 'Weslak' adjuster to the fleet could not be justified financially.

The experiment was therefore closed on 08/07/66.

**W/SW/L/198** **Rolvisor type sun visors**

**Nature** Fit two 'Rolvisor' sun visors in both cabs of one Diesel Hydraulic Loco. of D800 series in accordance with Sketch Ref. $N^{o}$. SK/400, to determine whether this type will prove as efficient as and more robust than the extendable arm type at present in use, which has a high defect rate.

| | | |
|---|---|---|
| **Fitted to** | Loco D813 | A and B cabs from 01/02/62 |

**Results** The experimental sun visor became the subject of considerable criticism by foot plate staff immediately after Locomotive $N^{o}$. D813 went into traffic.

Drivers interviewed have expressed strong disapproval of this sun visor for the following reasons :-

(1) That it obstructs the driver's line of vision when standing in the cab.

(2) That it restricts freedom of movement on the top of the circuit breaker housing, being cumbersome and generally in the way whilst serving no useful purpose.

It is considered that these views are justified and that this arrangement of sun visor is unsatisfactory.

D813 was involved in further 'Rolvisor' sun visor experiments with experiment W/SW/L/208 in August 1962.

The experiment was there closed, considered as unsuccessful, on 26/03/62.

**W/SW/L/199** **Sanding gear bowls**

**Nature** Fit four experimental sanding bowls incorporating renewable rubber pads in accordance with Laycock Eng. $L^{td}$. Drawing Ref. $N^{o}$. $89825^{A}$ on the R H side and four new standard bowls on the L H side of one D. H. D800 Class Locomotive to afford a direct comparison in service, with the object of obviating frequent renewals of whole sanding bowls due to erosion penetrating the wall of existing bowls.

| | | |
|---|---|---|
| **Fitted to** | Loco D808 | A and B end sanding bowls from 09/03/62 |

**Results** The rubber pads have been examined after 32,600, 54,410 and 72,000 miles service. Negligible wear has taken place to date at the centre of the rubber pads but at the four edges the pads are worn to a thickness of ¼, a reduction of $^{1}/_{16}$. This pattern of wear has made the surface of the pad convex.

A further examination on 15/01/63 after 89,100 miles service revealed the condition of the rubber pads was much as before, i.e. the average thickness being from $^{5}/_{16}$ - $^{9}/_{32}$ in the centre to ¼ on the outer edge. However, one rubber pad (that from the A end outer bowl) was missing and arrangements were made for its replacement with a new pad from Swindon Locomotive Works stock. The four standard sanding bowls were externally examined for wear in the vicinity of the air blast impingement, but no signs of the metal having perforated were visible.

Periodic examinations continued up to a mileage of 230,000 and on each occasion the condition of both experimental and the standard bowls was good. However, a modification made by Messrs. Laycock to their stand bowls incorporating an angled air inlet pipe has proved very satisfactory, and it was considered that little purpose could be achieved in keeping the experiment open.

The experiment was therefore closed as successful but would not be adopted.

**W/SW/L/200** **Smiths body mounted True engine hour counter**

**Nature** To overcome trouble experienced with the Smiths True Hours Counter when mounted on engines, fit one D800 Class Locomotive with one counter of this type mounted at each end in accordance with Drawing Ref. $N^{o}$. $SK/377^{A}$ which shows an arrangement whereby the instruments are mounted on the locomotive structure and driven from the engine by a flexible drive.

| | | |
|---|---|---|
| **Fitted to** | Loco D822 | A and B engines $N^{os}$. BSM 108 and 112258 from 26/01/62 until 06/03/62 |
| **Subsequently** | Loco D822 | A and B engines $N^{os}$. 112257 and 112258 from 20/03/62 until 26/04/62 |
| | Loco D822 | A and B engines $N^{os}$. 112257 and 112287 from 07/05/62 until 10/06/63 at Laira. |
| | Loco D822 | A and B engines $N^{os}$. 112257 and 112263 from 14/06/63 at Laira until 05/06/64. |
| | Loco D822 | A and B engines $N^{os}$. 112269 and 112263 from 29/06/64 until 23/02/65 at Laira. |
| | Loco D822 | A and B engines $N^{os}$. 112269 and 112252 from 23/02/65 at Laira until 23/07/65. |

**Results** A and B engines required to be changed on 06/03/62 and 26/04/62 respectively. The true hour counters at the A and B ends of Loco. D822 were retained and coupled to the new engines to enable continuance of this experiment.

Figures of engine hours recorded taken from consecutive periodical reports show the following difference between the recorded and assessed engine hours of A and B engines :-

A engine hours - 62, 31, 32, 43, 28, 51, 62, 111
B engine hours - 58, 26, 22, 30, 39, 67, 82, 112

The figures above cover a period of eight months and show a great improvement in consistency and accuracy of similar instruments fitted directly on the engine.

It has been suggested that the addition of two clips spaced at equal distance between the engine end of the flexible drive and the existing clip would assist in the prevention of flexing at both ends.

Further examination of the counters on 18/12/62 in Works showed that they were working satisfactorily and the mechanism appeared to be on good order. Readings were noted as A engine - 2,940 and B engine - 2,926.

Having regard to the large numbers of failures which have occurred with other arrangements of engine hour counters, it has been decided to extend this experiment by fitting the fitting of a further locomotive so that a more accurate assumption can be made of the merits of this arrangement.

On 22/06/63 Locomotive D822 was seen at Newton Abbot and the readings for the counters were noted as A engine - 3,267 and B engine - 3,216. At this time Shopping Control assessed hours were 3,054, giving a difference of $213^{+}$ for the A engine and $162^{+}$ for the B engine. It is considered, however, that the difference between recorded hours and assessed hours based on the locomotives diagrammed workings, will inevitably increase as the trial period increases, due to varying factors such as engines running in depots and journey times exceeding diagrammed times through delays and late running, the assessed hours are likely to be low.

Examination on 08/10/63 at Laira, 05/11/63 and 09/06/64 Works showed the counters of D822 to be functioning but the A end continued to creep ahead of the B end. The last of the three examinations showed A end hours as 8,221 and B end hours as 6,921.

The fitting of a further five locomotives has been delayed pending investigation into the whole question of engine hour counters.

On 05/08/64 readings were taken at Newton Abbot. They were noted as A engine - 8,535 hours and B engine - 6,921 hours, the assed hours being 7,884. The B end counter was not functioning and on 10/10/64 examination was made of the mechanism. The counter was in good working order, and so was the drive except that this lacked lubrication. The accessory drive gearbox was found at fault and this was repaired. Newton Abbot depot recommended that the experiment be adopted.

Following further satisfactory reports up to 10,000 hours the question of engine hour records was again raised with the C. M. & E. E. (W.R.), but it was felt that the system of assessing hours must be retained so there would be little point in duplicating this.

The experiment was therefore concluded and closed, as satisfactory but not to be adopted, on 07/05/65.

**W/SW/L/201 Hole type brake adjustment rods**

**Nature** Fit both bogies of one D800 class locomotive with new brake pull rods having simple hole adjustment in lieu of screwed brake adjusters, together with modified cross-beams in accordance with Drawing Ref. No. SL/SW/2993, to obviate the frequent trouble with the existing type of adjuster which reduces locomotive availability and causes difficulties with meeting replacement demands.

**Fitted to** Loco D816 A and B bogie $N^{os}$. 800/62 and 800/9. from 21/06/62 until 27/02/64.

**Results** Bogie $N^{os}$. 800/9 and 800/62 were inspected immediately after fitting to Locomotive D816. The wheel size on both bogies was recorded as 3'-3$^{3}/_{8}$ i.e. $^{1}/_{8}$ below standard size. When pulling back the brake rigging to the fullest extent with the pull rods pinned in the first hole position the measurement between the free brake block and the wheel rim was recorded. These were as follows :-

| | | | |
|---|---|---|---|
| A bogie | 800/62 | Inner axle $^{5}/_{8}$ | Outer axle $^{5}/_{8}$ |
| B bogie | 800/9 | Inner axle $^{3}/_{4}$ | Outer axle $^{5}/_{8}$ |

The brake rigging was again examined after 12,610 miles service on the occasion of the second pull rod adjustment which was a total make up on the pull rod of 3. The measurement from brake block to wheel with the rigging pulled one way averaged one inch throughout the locomotive, before adjustment. Brake beam pins and bushes showed no sign of wear.

After adjustment the measurements from brake block to wheel were again taken with the brake rigging pulled one way, these were as follows :-

| | | | |
|---|---|---|---|
| A bogie | 800/62 | Inner axle RHS $^{1}/_{8}$ | Outer axle RHS $^{1}/_{8}$ |
| | | Inner axle LHS $^{1}/_{4}$ | Outer axle LHS $^{1}/_{8}$ |
| B bogie | 800/9 | Inner axle RHS $^{5}/_{16}$ | Outer axle RHS $^{3}/_{16}$ |
| | | Inner axle LHS $^{3}/_{16}$ | Outer axle LHS $^{3}/_{16}$ |

The experiment was made standard, and closed, on 11/04/63.

**W/SW/L/203 Layrub $N^{o}$. 90 type 2/4 cardan shafts**

**Nature** To obviate frequent failures of existing dynostarter cardan shafts on D800 class locomotives, fit both ends of locomotive D830 (Paxman engines) as soon as possible and four other locomotives numbered between D800-D832 and D866-D870 when failure necessitate replacements, with Laycock Eng. $C^{o}$. Layrub $N^{o}$. 90 type 2/4 series propeller shafts in accordance with Drawing Ref. No. SL/SW/L/959.

The fitting of replacement shafts should be carried out at R. & M. Depots as failures of existing shafts occur.

| | | |
|---|---|---|
| **Fitted to** | Loco D804 | A and B end dynostarters. from 09/07/62 I |
| | Loco D808 | A and B end dynostarters. from 18/07/62 at Laira |
| | Loco D826 | A and B end dynostarters. from 10/09/62 at Laira |
| | Loco D830 | A and B end dynostarters. from 16/08/62 at Newton Abbot |
| | Loco D869 | A and B end dynostarters. from 22/08/62 at Laira |
| **Subsequently** | Loco D832 | A and B end dynostarters. from 10/12/62 at Laira |

**Results** The Laycock propeller shafts fitted to the A end of D808 failed on 28/08/62 after approx. 6 weeks service. Failure was attributed to the loosening of the dynostarter holding down bolts and breakage of the dynostarter foot. Examination found that contact with the safety bow had worn a groove in the tube which made the shaft unfit for repair and a conventional type of shaft was re-fitted at the A end.

The failure of the two Laycock shafts and damage to another was reported on 19/09/62. The Layrub rubbers had pulled out of the shaft at the B end of locomotive D830 and damage had occurred at A end. However, at the time of the report this shaft was still in service. These two shafts had each given five weeks service.

The Layrub rubbers have also pulled out of the Laycock shaft on the B end of loco $N^{o}$. D869 after three weeks service.

Examination of the Laycock shafts and Layrub couplings on locomotive $N^{o}$. D826, after 13,670 miles service, revealed no outward defects and no reports have been made of loose attachments.

The experimental shafts from A and B ends of locomotive $N^{o}$. D830 have been repaired and re-fitted to the same locomotive.

The experimental shaft from the B end of Loco $N^{o}$. D869 has been replaced by a conventional shaft.

At the request of Laycock representatives another locomotive was fitted with experimental shafts but with the safety bows omitted. For this purpose the repaired shaft from the B end of locomotive $N^{o}$. D869 and the replacement shaft for the A end of locomotive $N^{o}$. D808 were fitted to locomotive $N^{o}$. D832 thus still keeping the number of experimental shafts in service at 10.

The experiment continued throughout 1963 and a summary of the reports received is given below :-

| | | |
|---|---|---|
| 23/02/63 | D826 and D830 | Condition satisfactory. |
| 04/03/63 | D832 | Condition satisfactory. |
| 21/03/63 | D830 | B shaft failed; rubber block torn from bonding. |
| 22/04/63 | D808 | Bolts broken in coupling flange. |
| 30/04/63 | D869 | A end condition satisfactory. |
| 10/05/63 | D804 | A end condition satisfactory. |
| 10/05/63 | D804 | B end condition; slight fraying around edge of rubber mouldings. |
| 18/05/63 | D826 | A end condition; spigot pulled out of rubber block, shaft contacted safety bow and broke. |
| 27/05/63 | D826 | B end condition satisfactory and shaft removed for fitting to D830 B end. |
| 16/08/63 | D832 | A end condition; splits occurring in rubber after 2,025 hours service - shaft renewed. |
| 16/08/63 | D832 | B end condition; Failed with split rubbers after 2,025 hours service - shaft renewed. |
| 23/10/63 | D830 | Both shafts renewed due to circumferential splits in rubber blocks. |
| 11/11/63 | D832 | Examination at 1,080 hours; Replacement shafts operating satisfactorily. |

While the experiment was progressing a shaft having double Layrubs and a locking spline was introduced on a number of locomotives. This proved more successful than the standard shafts or the shafts with double Layrubs only, and at a liaison meeting between the C.M. & E.E.'s Dept. and the M.E. (Design) Dept. held on 30th July 1964, a decision was made to fit the shaft with double Layrubs and locking spline as standard.

The experiment was therefore closed on 27/08/64.

**W/SW/L/204 Bogies fitted with hydraulic dampers**

**Nature** Dispense with the existing bogie side control linkage as a centring device on both bogies of one D800 Class Locomotive, other than D804, having an approximate tyre mileage since last turning of between 55,000 and 60,000 miles.

The bogies must be fitted with brackets etc. to Drawing Ref. $N^{os}$. SL/SW/3046 and SL/SW/3080 and side stops to Drawing Ref. $N^{o}$. SK/398.

**Fitted to** Loco D813 A and B bogie $N^{os}$. 800/XX and 800/XX from 31/08/62

| | |
|---|---|
| **Results** | Initial trials were carried out in three stages as follows at speeds of up to 90 mph :- |

1) A controlled test run under the supervision of the Research Dept. with both hydraulic dampers in position on one bogie with none on the other bogie.
2) As stage 1, but with one hydraulic damper in position on each bogie.
3) As stage 1, but with both hydraulic dampers in position on each bogie.

The riding of the locomotive was satisfactory during all three tests and it is now in traffic with the two hydraulic dampers in position on each bogie. It is now intended to observe the effect of tyre wear on the riding qualities of the locomotive and the rate of wear on the rubber bogie side stops.

On 22/10/62 a track test was conducted by the Research and Development staff and the locomotive was found to be riding satisfactorily. At this time the bogies had a mileage of 78,840 since the previous tyre attention, but flats were observed on the tyres of B bogie and after the run the tyres on this bogie received attention at Laira. The locomotive re-entered service on 23/10/62.

Due to the initial success of the experiment approval was granted in October by the W.R. General Manager for the conversion of a further 12 D800 Class Locomotives.

On 02/01/63 Locomotive D813 was involved in a collision and returned to Swindon Works for attention to body and bogies. Tyre mileage for A bogie was then 104,450 and due to shelling of three tyres re-turning was found necessary. The tyres on B bogie were in good condition having run only 24,000 miles since turning at Laira in October 1962.

Back in service D813 continued to prove satisfactory, and the additional locomotives fitted also showed good results.

The experiment was adopted as standard and became the subject of Modification N°. 621. It was therefore closed on 07/08/64.

| **W/SW/L/205** | **Class 'E' steel tyres** |
|---|---|

**Nature** To reduce the incidents of tread defects fit six bogies of D800 class locomotives with special 'Steel, Peech and Tozer' produced tyres in quenched and tempered vacuum cast steel generally with B.S.S. class 'E' tensile range, with carbon and manganese content of about 0.062% and 0.85% respectively, i.e. slightly lower in carbon and slightly higher in manganese than is normal for this class of steel.

Three of the chosen bogies would have fine grain (F) steel tyres and three would have coarse grain (C).

**Notes** The routine swapping of wheel sets within bogies carried out meant that thirteen individual bogies were included in this experiment.

The condition of the treads was to be reported on every four weeks.

| | | |
|---|---|---|
| **Fitted to** | Loco D811 | A bogie N°. 800/16 (F) from 26/09/62 until 02/09/63. |
| | Loco D811 | B bogie N°. 800/51 (F) from 26/09/62 until 02/09/63. |
| | Loco D825 | A bogie N°. 800/39 (C) from 31/08/62 until 03/05/63. |
| | Loco D829 | A bogie N°. 800/53 (C) from 13/09/62 |
| | Loco D829 | B bogie N°. 800/41 (C) from 13/09/62 |
| | Loco D837 | B bogie N°. 800/44 (F) from 07/09/62 until 26/06/64. |
| **Subsequently** | Loco D800 | B bogie N°. 800/112 (C) from 06/08/65 until 30/12/66. |
| | Loco D804 | B bogie N°. 800/75 (F) from 04/05/65 |
| | Loco D811 | B bogie N°. 800/132 (F) from 07/09/64 until 31/08/65. |
| | Loco D821 | B bogie N°. 800/144 (C) from 07/02/64 until 09/03/66. |
| | Loco D824 | B bogie N°. 800/57 (C) from 17/01/64 until 20/04/65 at Laira. |
| | Loco D824 | A bogie N°. 800/14 (F) from 16/08/65 until 20/07/67 at Laira. |
| | Loco D833 | B bogie N°. 800/16 (F) from 11/11/63 until 26/05/64. |
| | Loco D846 | B bogie N°. 800/16 (F) from 16/06/64 until 15/02/65. |
| | Loco D852 | A bogie N°. 800/39 (C) from 13/05/63 until 08/04/65. |
| | Loco D869 | A bogie N°. 800/48 (F) from 20/02/64 |

**Results** Locos D825 / D8xx During the first year of the tyres being in service checks were made at regular intervals on the conditions of Loco D837 the treads and wear rate. In the case of D825 and D837 a direct comparison was possible between the class 'E' steel tyres at the one end and the standard tyres at the other end. The wear rate was favourable with both fine and coarse graded tyres. Movement of the tyres was noted from time to time but shelling was almost non-existent, being confined to occasional cases of pits less than ½" diameter and of no appreciable depth.

Loco D829 Flats developed on the bogies of this loco during September 1963 and the tyres were re-profiled on the wheel lathe at Laira without reference of the experiment to Swindon. This was unfortunate as on 24/09/63 the loco was shopped for bogie change and the tyres were again reprofiled, thus wasting metal.

All of the tyres were now becoming due for reprofiling and to some extent this coincided with the discovery of faulty stress relieving grooves on axles and many of the wheel sets with the experimental tyres were transferred to different bogies.

All of the tyres were successfully reprofiled and during February 1964 the allocations of the tyres and bogies were as follows :-

D821, B bogie N°. 800/144 (C); D824, B bogie N°. 800/57 (C); D833, B bogie N°. 800/16 (F);
D837, B bogie N°. 800/44 (F); D852, A bogie N°. 800/39 (C); D869, A bogie N°. 800/48 (F).

Taking tyres profiles continued at regular intervals on the six bogies concerned and these showed the wear to be satisfactory and in some cases very good. A little movement was recorded but practically no shelling.

In February 1965 bogie N°. 800/16 from D846 B was in Swindon and the tyres were reprofiled. During the operation some scaling developed but not to a serious extent and the tyres and wheel sets were returned to service in bogie N°. 800/75, under D804 B from 04/05/65 from Swindon. However, on 17/06/65 this bogie was in trouble and the tyres were again back.

Locos D852 / D8xx On 08/04/65 bogie N°. 800/39 from D852 A came to Swindon for attention and the tyres were reprofiled

Loco D824 27/04/65 bogie N°. 800/57 from D824 B also came to Swindon, having been removed at Laira on 20/04/65 due to suspected axle flaws. These tyres were also due for turning, but the thickness did not permit further turning and these tyres were scrapped at a total mileage of 203,930 miles service (these tyres were one of the original sets under D829).

Loco D811 On 11/06/65 bogie N°. 800/132 under D811 B became due for reprofiling at Laira and some shells were noted on the treads. These shells were the biggest so far experienced with class 'E' steel tyres, but they did not prevent turning. The bogie remained under D811 until the loco was shopped on 31/08/65, B bogie N°. 800/132 being removed for general repair.

Other tyres remained satisfactory and following further changes and turnings the allocations of the tyres and bogies was as follows :-

D800, B bogie N°. 800/112 (C); D821, B bogie N°. 800/144 (C);
D824, A bogie N°. 800/14 (F); D869, A bogie N°. 800/48 (F).

During 1966 four of the bogie sets of tyres became due for scrapping, having attained mileages of 257,270, 304,410, 346,630 and 355,530 respectively. Results throughout had showed the tyres to have been satisfactory with no difference between the fine and coarse grades in respect of wear, machining and shelling. However, with the standardisation of class 'D' steel for all main line locomotives, and the fact that the incidence of tread defects on the D800 class locos had greatly diminished with the reduction in brake cylinder pressure, the special class 'E' steel tyres were not adopted.

Bogie N°. 800/112 was removed from D800 B on 30/12/66 for general repair, bogie N°. 800/144 was removed from D821 B on 09/03/66 for intermediate repair, bogie N°. 800/14 was removed from D824 A at Laira on 20/07/67 for a routine change, the bogie details for 800/48 from D869 A are not recorded.

In view of the above the experiment was closed on 20/03/67.

| **W/SW/L/208** | **Rolvisor type sun visors** |
|---|---|

**Nature** Re-fit the existing 'Rolvisor' sun visors in both cabs of locomotive D813 in accordance with Drawing Ref. N°. SK/525 to determine whether the position is satisfactory and the sun visors more robust than the extendable arm type at present in use which has a high defect rate on this class of locomotive.

| | | |
|---|---|---|
| **Fitted to** | Loco D813 | A and B cabs from 31/08/62 |

**Results** The 'Rolvisor' sun visors have been examined by Traffic Headquarters Inspectors and found satisfactory. Further reports are to be submitted in due course.

Meanwhile, the whole question of sun visors under consideration and some Perspex Visors were experimented with on D.1000 2,200 H.P. Locomotives. Their advantages soon became apparent and the C. M. & E. E. (W.R.) requested that they be made standard.

Modification Orders were issued for Swindon sponsored locomotives, and that for the D800 class, Mod. N°. 655, superseded this experiment.

D813 was involved in previous 'Rolvisor' sun visor experiments with experiment W/SW/L/198 in February 1962.

The experiment was therefore closed on 10/12/64.

| **W/SW/L/210** | **Liquid form of 'Alfloc 300' water treatment** |
|---|---|

**Nature** Fit one D800 Class and one D.7000 Class Locomotive, each having a Stone-Vapor steam generator, with a liquid form of 'Alfloc' water treatment using a solution of 104X/7 powder instead of the existing briquette treatment, in an endeavour to extend the acid wash-out period.

| | | |
|---|---|---|
| **Fitted to** | Loco D827 | Boiler 20345 from 20/12/62 until 23/09/64 at Laira. |
| | Loco D827 | Boiler 20946 from 23/09/64 at Laira until 31/01/67 at Laira. |
| | Loco D827 | Boiler 20359 from 31/01/67 at Laira until closed. |
| **Subsequently** | Loco D.7026 | Boiler from 05/05/67 until 12/67 |
| | Loco D.7026 | Boiler from 12/67 at Laira until closed. |

**Results** Loco. D827 During the first twelve months it only became necessary to acid wash the generator once, this being when the increase in coil pressure reached 340 p.s.i. However, the chemical tank was not robust enough and was replaced by a steel tank.

In September 1964, concentrated instead of diluted solution was inadvertently used in the tank and this caused a blockage in the coil. It was necessary to change the generator but the equipment was retained in the locomotive.

On 13/04/65 the locomotive was examined at Laira and it was discovered that the delivery from the chemical pump was connected into the pressure side of the water feed pipe to the boiler instead of into the suction side, and that the water connection to the solenoid had been broken off the suction side of the water pump. Prior to the examination the loco. had been Works for a lengthy repair (19/11/64 - 12/02/65) and it was assumed that the mistake occurred there at that time. The defects were rectified and the system put in order.

On 29/06/65 a satisfactory report of the liquid treatment was submitted by Laira depot. The liquid form of treatment was by this time being fitted as a modification to some D.6306 Class Locomotives and the success of these would be considered with the results of the experiment.

Twice during 1966 the generator was reported as having been acid washed, and the experiment continued satisfactorily apart from one case of the suction filter and pipe work becoming blocked due to the chemical coming out of solution. Early in 1967, a similar blockage occurred and Depots were reminded of the importance of keeping the system flushed. At this time a change to a solution of 104X/7 powder in place of the '304' liquid was advocated so arrangements were made for its introduction. The experiment was extended to include D.7000 Class Locomotive D7026 which was previously fitted with Experiment W/SW/L/239 (I.C.I. water treatment for Stone-Vapor generator).

At the end of 1967 the generator of D7026 was changed for routine overhaul. Works the coil was found to be in poor condition requiring four times as much acid and over twice the time to clear the coil as compared with the average for a generator having standard treatment. This result was quite disappointing but was not conclusive as the generator in question had been in service for over a year before the experiment was tried.

Meanwhile Loco D827 continued with the treatment but once again, in December 1967, a pipe blockage occurred, and the opinion was expressed that 104X/7 powder had a tendency to crystallize in the pipe work and was therefore no improvement on the '304' liquid.

Based on the results the treatment appeared to be satisfactory provided adequate maintenance could be assured. However, with the introduction of soft water plants throughout the Western Region the cost of introducing the treatment could not be justified.

The experiment was therefore closed on 02/03/68.

| **W/SW/L/211** | **Heat exchanger to transmission pipe with Metalflex tubing connection** | |
|---|---|---|
| **Nature** | To obviate the failures of existing flexible connections between transmission and heat exchanger, fit the A end of one D800 Class Locomotive numbered between D800 and D802 with Power Flex Tubing C°. L$^{td}$. Metalflex tubing in accordance with Drawing Ref. N°. SK/558. | |
| **Note** | Also fit new hoses of existing type items 1 and 2/SL/SW/1454 in accordance with the original arrangement shown on Drawing Ref. N°. SL/SW/1287 at the B end to afford a direct comparison of performance of the two types. | |
| **Fitted to** | Loco D800 | A heat exchanger from 13/02/63 until withdrawn. |

**Results** When D800 entered traffic there was some doubt whether in fact the experimental hoses had been fitted and for some time the experiment was considered to have been lost.

However, on 05/02/65 D800 entered Swindon for an intermediate repair and it was discovered that one of the experimental hoses was indeed fitted to the A. The hose was removed and examined, and found to be in good condition and was re-fitted. The standard hose was also in apparent good condition and so it too was re-fitted.

Enquiries showed that the two spare experimental hoses held in stock had been issued to unidentified locomotives and their whereabouts were unknown.

Investigations of failure rates of the hoses involved showed that the rate of failure of the existing original type hose was not as great as originally supposed and that the failure rate of the experimental hose was comparable.

In consequence, there appeared no justification at all for authorising the cost of fitting D800 B, D801 and D802 with the experimental hose as standard, or for reverting D800 A to its original condition.

The experiment was deemed to have been neither a failure or success and was therefore closed on 01/09/66.

| **W/SW/L/212** | **B.R Standard profile 'A' tyres** | |
|---|---|---|
| **Nature** | Fit both bogies of four D800 class locomotives, having the bogie side control linkage removed and hydraulic dampers connected directly from bogie to body, with tyres to B.R. Standard Profile 'A' in an effort to establish whether the modified connection between bogies and underframe or the W.R. Composite tyre profiles has made the greater improvement to riding qualities. | |
| **Fitted to** | Loco D819 | A and B bogies N$^{os}$. 800/5 and 800/36 from 23/05/63 |
| **Subsequently** | Loco D806 | A and B bogies N$^{os}$. 800/5 and 800/72 from 30/10/64 until 15/04/66. |
| | Loco D811 | A and B bogies N$^{os}$. 800/5 and 800/72 from 11/03/64 until 17/08/64. |
| | Loco D815 | A and B bogies N$^{os}$. 800/24 and 800/10 from 29/10/64 |
| | Loco D832 | A and B bogies N$^{os}$. 800/125 and 800/47 from 16/10/64 |
| | Loco D843 | A and B bogies N$^{os}$. 800/96 and 800/45 from 16/11/64 |
| | Loco D849 | B bogie N°. 800/45 from 08/02/66 until 30/05/67. |

**Results** Within a year of fitting it became apparent that restricting the experiment to one locomotive was undesirable as due to failures the feasibility of attaining high tyre mileage was limited. In consequence the experiment was extended in August 1964 to cover both bogies of four locomotives, and the experiment recommended fitting as shown subsequently.

Riding trials were conducted at regular intervals on the four locomotives thus accumulating records at many different tyre mileages up to a maximum of 100,000 miles. Comparison of these records against those for locomotives with W.R. Composite Profiles, at similar tyre mileages and on similar routes, showed that the profile made little difference to the riding qualities.

Regular examination of the tyres showed the tread wear to be slightly heavier than with the W.R. Composite Profile, but the difference was considered to be insufficient as far as tyre life was concerned. To aid standardisation of the tyre profiles therefore, the B.R. Profile 'A' was adopted for the D800, D833 and D.1000 class locomotives.

The experiment was therefore closed on 06/03/67.

| **W/SW/L/213** | **Temperature protection of oil and water temperatures using 'De Haviland' equipment** | |
|---|---|---|
| **Nature** | Fit Locomotive D839 with 'De Haviland' temperature protection equipment in place of the Teddington capillary and bellows switch for cooling water and transmission oil at B end only, to test the reliability of this transistorised system on a locomotive in service. | |
| **Fitted to** | Loco D839 | B end from 23/10/62 until closed. |

**Results** During the five years of service no adverse reports were received although the equipment was regularly checked. A proving test was carried out in November, 1965, and this confirmed the transmission temperature 'pre-warning' light and 'trip' to operate sat 218$^0$F and 249$^0$F respectively.

The cooling water temperature 'pre-warning' light operated at 191$^0$F, but the temperature for cooling water 'trip' could not be obtained. A peculiarity was however witnessed on temperature fall, i.e., after the light extinguished at 240$^0$F, the light re-lit at 225$^0$F and extinguished again at 218$^0$F. This was considered due to possible interference between the two channels in the common sensing unit and not due to any mal-function.

From experience gained with the equipment coupled with progress in the electronics field a revised system was developed. This incorporated simplified circuitry, which also omitted pre-warning lights, and the equipment was manufactured using tolerances closer to the requirements for locomotive operation.

The cost was substantially reduced, and the equipment was introduced on D.1000 2,700 D. H. Locomotives as experiment W/SW/L/367, and later as Modification MB.408/16.

The experiment was therefore closed on 10/10/67.

| **W/SW/L/217** | **Laycock-Knorr air compressor fitted with oil bath filter** | |
|---|---|---|
| **Nature** | Fit five 2,200 HP D800 Class Locomotives with Laycock Eng. C°. Oil Bath Filters to new or reconditioned Laycock Knorr Air Compressors Type V.V.100/100, in place of the existing suction strainers in accordance with Drawing SK/568A, to prevent ingress of dirt to the compressor and extend the period between re-boring. The compressors concerned should be fitted with sump breather filters in accordance with Modification N°. 63, and they should have new compressor oil when the bath filters are fitted. | |
| **Fitted to** | Loco D809 | from 04/03/66 |
| **Results** | No information is available regarding this experiment. | |

| **W/SW/L/219** | **M.A.N. engine fitted with 'Wallisec' compressed asbestos fibre sump joints** | |
|---|---|---|
| **Nature** | Fit two M.A.N. engines, N$^{os}$. 345 and 357, with sump joints $^1/_{16}$ thick made from compressed asbestos fibre of 'Wallisec' brand supplied by Messrs. James Walker & C°. Ltd. in lieu of 'Gaskoid' joints which tend to seep oil during service. The sump bolts on both engines are of the hexagon headed type and have been locked with tab washers. | |
| **Fitted to** | Loco D851 | A engine N°. 345 from 07/01/63 until 10/08/63 at Laira. |
| | Loco D859 | A engine N°. 357 from 17/12/62 at Laira |
| **Subsequently** | Loco D852 | B engine N°. 345 from 12/10/63 at Laira until 30/09/64 at Laira. |

**Results** After 1,800 hours in service engine N°. 345 failed with a suspected faulty sump joint, but on examination the joint was found to be sound. Actually, another joint higher on the engine was found to have been leaking oil which had trickled around the sump joint and this had given a false impression. The engine returned to service in D852 B end and, to 22/02/64, had completed another 1,775 hours. The joint on engine N°. 357 has not been disturbed since fitting and has given 3,425 hours service. No adverse reports have been received of the joints on either engine.

In view of the obvious improvement of 'Wallisec' jointing over that previously used, it has been adopted as standard for M.A.N. engine sump joints and the experiment is concluded.

The experiment was therefore closed on 23/04/64.

### W/SW/L/221 Engine air intake bellows of 'Tico' type

**Nature** Fit Tico Engine Air Intake Bellows to James Walker & C°. Drawing N°. 93234 to one side of the engine or engines of one D.H. locomotive of each of D833, D.6300 and D.1000 class and also fit new standard leather bellows to Drawing SL/SW/889 to the other side of the same engine or engines on the same locomotives, to afford a direct comparison of service obtained from each type of bellows.

The present standard leather bellows tend to deteriorate and break, thereby creating the possibility of foreign bodies being drawn into the turbo charger.

| | | |
|---|---|---|
| **Fitted to** | Loco D858 | A engine N°. 290. from 12/06/63 until 18/05/65 at Laira. |
| | Loco D.1006 | B engine N°. 655186 from 24/05/63 until 17/02/64 |
| | Loco D.6311 | Engine N°. 295. from 02/07/63 until 03/12/65 at Laira. |
| **Subsequently** | Loco D.1006 | B engine N°. 655253 from 17/02/64 until 07/04/65 |

**Results** On 05/11/63 Loco D.1006 was in Swindon Works and the air intake bellows all appeared to be in good condition, although the leather bellows were stretched much tighter than the 'Tico' one. During December 1963 D.1006 entered Swindon Works for an engine change but the bellows, still being in good condition, were retained.

On 16/03/64 the 'Tico' bellows on D858 and D.6311 were reported in good condition after 2,220 and 2,398 hours in service respectively. Further, on 20/07/64 the 'Tico' bellows on D858 and D.6311 were reported in good condition after 3,332 and 3,316 hours in service respectively.

Loco D.1006 was in Swindon Works on 14/09/64 and the opportunity was taken to examine the 'Tico' bellows and the leather bellow on the same engine. Both were in good condition.

The bellows on D858 were reported to be in good condition after 4,080 hours (examination at Laira on 13/11/64). Loco mileage at this time was approx. 100,820. After 5,178 hours service (124,060 miles) the 'Tico' bellows on D858 were reported to be in condition. On 06/04/65 the 'Tico' bellows on D858 were again reported to be in good condition, the hours service then being 6,019 (162,910 miles). At 6,700 hours D858 was reported on by Newton Abbot depot which stated that little difference could be observed between the condition of the 'Tico' and standard leather bellows. Shortly after this the locomotive was shopped Works for an Intermediate repair and the bellows were changed in accordance with standard procedure for such repairs.

During August 1965 it was discovered that the 'Tico' bellows had been removed from D.1006 without any record being made of the reason. At this time D.6311 was still in service and both air intake bellows were reported to be in good condition.

All bellows had by now been fitted for a period of 2 or more years but the experiment had proved inconclusive in showing that the 'Tico' bellows were more durable than the standard leather bellows.

In view of this, and the extra cost involved in using 'Tico' bellows, they would not be adopted to replace the standard leather type.

The experiment was therefore closed on 28/09/65.

### W/SW/L/223 C.A.V. fuel pumps fitted with vent valves

**Nature** In accordance with Drawing Ref. N°. SK/692, fit both C.A.V. fuel pumps in one M.A.N. engine on one D833 Class Locomotive with C.A.V. Fuel Pump vent valves, Part N°. 7010/617$^{A}$, in place of the existing vent plugs, and to the Vent Valves fit drain pipes leading to the drain in the Vee of the engine. The object of the experiment is to reduce the fire risk which at present is increased by the existing vent plugs ejecting oil when loose.

| | | |
|---|---|---|
| **Fitted to** | Loco D838 | B engine N°. 396 from 05/07/63 until 10/11/63 at Laira. |
| | Loco D838 | B engine N°. 234 from 11/10/63 at Laira |

**Results** On 10/11/63 engine N°. 396 failed and was replaced at Laira by engine N° 234. The experimental apparatus was transferred from engine N°. 396 to engine N°. 394 in order to keep the experiment on D838 B engine, and at the same time the clipping of the pipe ends over the drain in the vee of the engine was modified by the depot staff. The clipping was still not considered entirely satisfactory and a modification to the Drawing was put in hand.

Newton Abbot Depot reported on 25/10/63 that the vent drain valves were an improvement but maintained that the chief fire risk was the engine vee not draining properly. This became the subject of a separate investigation, and in this respect it was suggested that if the draining was improved then the pipes from the vent valves could be shortened, thus eliminating the need for clipping.

After 3,200 hours (31/10/64) the experiment was still satisfactory on D838 B engine N°. 234 and schemes were in hand for making the vent valves a standard modification.

The vent valves were again reported satisfactory after 3,728 and 3,950 hours, and on 25/02/65 Modification Order N°. SW/3902 was issued to standardise a slightly modified version of the experiment.

The experiment was therefore closed on 02/03/65.

### W/SW/L/224 M.A.N. engine - clipping arrangement of fuel pipes

**Nature** In accordance with Drawing Ref. N°. SL/SW/3324, improve the clipping of the fuel pipes from the C.A.V. fuel pumps to the M.A.N. engine on one end of a D833 Class Locomotive to reduce the incidence of broken pipe joints and leaking fuel oil.

| | | |
|---|---|---|
| **Fitted to** | Loco D838 | A engine N°. 249 from 05/07/63 until 07/63 |
| **Subsequently** | Loco D850 | A engine N°. 249 from 28/10/63 until 06/10/65 at Laira. |

**Results** Shortly after fitting to D838 engine N°. 249 failed and was returned to Swindon Works for repair at the end of July 1963. Opportunity was taken to examine the pipe joints and clipping and these were found in good condition. After repair engine N°. 249 was fitted to Loco. D850 A end in Swindon Works during October 1963.

On 03/09/63 agreement was made to extend the trial to cover six other engines and the necessary arrangements were made. The engines and locos. fitted were as follows :-

| | |
|---|---|
| Loco D.6327 | Engine N°. 141 from 20/03/64 until 09/66. |
| Loco D855 | B engine N°. 265 from 05/03/64 at Laira until 11/03/65 at Newton Abbot. |
| Loco D836 | A engine N°. 287 from 13/03/64 until 17/02/65. |
| Loco D849 | B engine N°. 310 from 24/01/64 at Laira until 04/08/64. |
| Loco D862 | B engine N°. 343 from 07/04/64 until 08/65 at |
| Loco D834 | B engine N°. 352 from 26/03/64 until 23/03/66. |

On 09/09/64 two clip bolts and rubbers were reported missing from 1-6 bank of engine N°. 343 (D862 B end). These were replaced and at this time the engine hours were 1,261.

On 31/10/64, after 2,000 hours in service, the clips on D850 A end were reported as satisfactory.

The clips on D862 B end were reported to be satisfactory after 1,121 hours in service (38,660 miles) and as far as was known no fractures to pipes had occurred.

Satisfactory reports continued to be received from depots and during March 1965 the question of making the clips standard was raised. However, it was agreed to let the experiment run further until the result of a full investigation into oil pipes was made known.

Engine N°. 310 was transferred from D849 B end to D853 B end in early 1965 and later engine N°. 287 was transferred from D836 A end to D856 A end. Engine N°. 265 was transferred from D855 B end to D847 B end after attention in Swindon Works but was immediately failed on fitting and removed.

| | |
|---|---|
| Loco D847 | B engine N°. 265 from 07/65 until 07/65 (failed). |
| Loco D853 | B engine N°. 310 from 1965 |
| Loco D856 | A engine N°. 287 from 18/05/65 until 04/02/66 at Laira. |

As these engines passed through Swindon Works 'BD' shops for repair satisfaction with the clipping arrangement was expressed by staff.

Engine N°. 310 (D853 B end) was reported on after 1,237 hours, clipping examined and found satisfactory, but when engine N°. 343 (D862 B end) was removed for return to Swindon Works at the beginning of August 1965, five of the eight clips were found to be missing. Engines N$^{os}$. 287 (D856 A end) and 352 (D834 B end) were reported as satisfactory after 563 and 4,452 hours respectively.

The reports generally tended to comment on the satisfactory state of the clips rather than on the effectiveness at preventing fuel pipe fractures, and in consequence the results were not entirely conclusive but it became the considered opinion that the small cost involved of fitting the improve clips would be justified in view of the continuing fracturing of pipes. Modification N°. MB.420/12 was therefore issued to adopt the experiment in all M.A.N. engines.

The experiment was therefore closed on 25/08/66.

### W/SW/L/227 Modified type 'Ardleigh' engine governor

**Nature** Fit one end of a D833 Class Locomotive having an overhauled M.A.N. engine and new piston rings, with a modified Ardleigh governor to reduce starting fuel from 100% to 75% full rack, in an effort to reduce the incidence of broken piston rings on M.A.N. engines. For comparison purposes, also if possible, install and overhauled M.A.N. engine with new piston rings and a standard Ardleigh governor at the other end of the same locomotive. Drawing Ref. N°. SK/703 shows the alteration to the wiring on the Ardleigh Governor for this purpose.

| | | |
|---|---|---|
| **Fitted to** | Loco D858 | A engine N°. 290 (Modified governor) from 12/06/63 until 18/05/65 at Laira. |
| | Loco D858 | B engine N°. 461 (Standard governor) from 12/06/63 until 18/05/65 at Laira. |

**Results** An examination of the modified governor at the end of March 1964 (approx. 2,500 hors service) revealed that it was not functioning, and steps were taken by Inspector Davey, M.E. (Design), Swindon, to rectify the fault which was due to incorrect resistances. On 08/04/64 the modified governor was again working satisfactorily.

On 13/11/64 (examination at Laira) the Ardleigh governor was reported to be working satisfactorily after 4,080 hours service, approx. 100,820 miles.

During June 1965 the modified governor was examined while in Swindon Works and the condition was satisfactory. Prior to this some trouble had been experienced but this was due to worn bushes and was in no way connected with this modification. The modified governor was re-fitted to an engine which was supplied to B.I.C.E.R.I.

The engines N$^{os}$. 290 and 461 were stripped for overhaul and a close examination was made of the pistons, rings, etc. but no conclusive results could be drawn. Further investigation of the history of these two engines was necessary.

As no positive results were forthcoming the experiment was concluded, further tests to be conducted by B.I.C.E.R.I.

The experiment was therefore closed on 20/12/66.

**W/SW/L/229** **Route indicator screens made of 'Vita-Film plastic**

**Nature** In order to reduce the incidence of train route indicator failures caused by the standard fabric screens becoming badly torn and the screen edges doubling over, fit the indicator boxes at the A end of one D800 Class Locomotive, numbered D813 onwards, with a set of four Reeves Eng. L$^{td}$. plastic 'Vita-Film' screens. Also fit a new set of standard fabric screens in the indicator boxes at the B end of the same locomotive, to afford a direct comparison in service of the reliability and durability of the two types of screens.

**Fitted to** Loco D861 A and B end headcode boxes from 20/12/63 until closed.

**Results** Before fitting the 'Vita-Film' screens into D861 they were vigorously tested in the Drawing Office and were found to be strong and resisted any tendency to roll over on the edges.

After 6 months in service, during which time no reports were received, D861 was examined at Laira. Both boxes at the A end and one at the B end contained standard fabric screens, the condition of which were not good, and the remaining box contained 'Vita-Film' screens in good condition.

A report from Laira dated 10/11/64 stated that the indicator screens at the A end were in good condition and that the screen at the B end had failed and been replaced on 20/10/64. From this report and the previous examination the position was not clear and further investigation was necessary.

On 03/07/65 a report from Newton Abbot Depot confirmed that no 'Vita-Film' screens were fitted. The repair card history had been thoroughly checked in an attempt to establish where and when these screens were removed but to no avail.

The results were therefore inconclusive but as 'Vita-Film' screens in Reeves boxes are standard equipment on D.9500 Class Locomotives it was considered that ample opportunity existed for gaining service experience and the experiment was concluded on 05/08/65.

**W/SW/L/241** **Greasing method of axle bearings**

**Nature** Both bogies of one overhauled D800 Class Locomotive fitted with standard SKF axle bearings to be allowed to run for a period extended from 1,500 to 3,000 hours between axle bearing greasing attention, to determine if such an arrangement is practical.

**Fitted to** Class 42

**Results** No information is available on this experiment.

**W/SW/L/242** **M.A.N. engine fitted with 'Aeroquip' hose assemblies**

**Nature** Fit two M.A.N. engines for D833 Class Locomotives with 'Aeroquip' N°. 2807 High Temperature Polymer Hose Assemblies in place of the existing 1525 hoses for fuel and lubrication oil, in an effort to reduce the incidence of hose failures which are thought to be a contributory factor in locomotive fires.

| | | |
|---|---|---|
| **Fitted to** | Loco D833 | A engine N°. 373 from 05/05/64 at Laira until 06/65. |
| | Loco D833 | A engine N°. 373 from 22/09/65 |
| | Loco D842 | A engine N°. 473 from 12/05/64 at Laira until 14/11/65 at Laira. |
| **Subsequently** | Loco D833 | A engine N°. 373 from 22/09/65 at Laira until 15/04/66. |

**Results** Engine N°. 473 (D842 A end) failed at Newton Abbot on 15/09/64 due to no pressure on the 7-12 bank fuel line caused by a leaking hose. This was removed and returned to Messrs. Super Oil Seals with a request for a replacement hose, and their comments on the failure.

This failure, which occurred at 1,060 hours, was apparently due to a severe blow causing the inner lining to deform and perforate. A replacement hose was delivered to Newton Abbot Depot during the week ending 08/11/64.

On 17/02/65 a satisfactory report was made of the hoses on engine N°. 473 which had then completed 2,572 hours.

Engine N°. 373 (D833 A end) was reported satisfactory at 2,575 hours (26/02/65) and at 2,760 hours (22/03/65) except that one hose, the Balance Vessel to N°. 1-6 fuel pump, had been replaced by a standard hose under circumstances unknown. This hose was later traced and found in a damaged condition on another engine. The damage had apparently occurred through miss-use of spanners, and it was necessary to withdraw it from service.

During May 1965, engine N°. 373 was removed from D833 A end for overhaul and an examination of the hoses found two further defective ones. One, a lub. oil rail to cylinder head, hose had been maltreated on the end connections and the other, a fuel filter to rail hose, was leaking. These two hoses together with the balance vessel to N$^{os}$. 1-6 fuel pump hose were returned to Messrs. Super Oil Seals for examination and replacement. The fuel filter to rail hose was found to have a punctured lining due to electrostatic discharge and this was replaced by a hose having a conductive lining. All three replacement hoses would be fitted to engine N°. 473 before it re-entry to service.

Engine N°. 473 (D842 A end) was reported satisfactory at 3,200, 3,450 and 4,011 hours service.

When engine N°. 373 re-entered service in D833 A end (on 22/09/65) it had not been possible to replace all of the experimental hoses as was hoped but arrangements were made for this to be done at a depot when the hoses were available.

At the request of the C. M. & E. E. (W.R.) the fitting of the lub. oil pipe from the rail to N°. 7 cylinder with 'Aeroquip' N°. 2807 hose was made standard as this flexible was in a vulnerable position on the engine, and was subject to external heat thus accounting for approx. 50% of the failures which occurred to all the 20 hoses per engine together. The adoption only of the experimental hose on that position would therefore eliminate many failures and the risk of damage due to maltreatment of hoses would be kept to a minimum. The full cost of re-fitting engines with the more expensive experimental hoses and the problem of electrostatic discharges on the fuel hoses would not have to be faced.

The experiment was therefore closed on 16/12/66.

**W/SW/L/248** **M.A.N. engine fitted with fuel pipe grips**

**Nature** Fit thicker pipe holders in accordance with M.A.N. Drawings N$^{os}$. 5D23580, 5D23581 and 5D23582 and alloy grips in accordance with Drawing N°. 5D23583 to complete new sets of fuel pressure pipes in the 'Vee' of six M.A.N. engines, to reduce the incidence of fractured end connections on these pipes. The new sets of pipes should be made identifiable by means of one red and one white band of paint approximately 2 wide to the pipes adjacent the connections to the fuel pump.

**Fitted to** Class 43

**Results** Investigation in the 'BD' shop on 28/01/64 revealed that the pipe grips were already being fitted in accordance with Drawing N°. 5D23583, i.e. with a gap between the two halves, so nothing could be gained by following this experimentally. With regard to the thicker retaining plates this was obviously required as the existing plates, which varied in thickness of between $^1/_{16}$ and $^1/_8$, were bending under the strain of the bolts. In view of this the experiment was not proceeded with but was covered as a modification.

**W/SW/L/257** **M.A.N. engine fitted with 'O' ring oil seals to inlet valve stems**

**Nature** Fit four M.A.N. engines with 'O' ring oil seals to the inlet valve stems in an attempt to reduce the carbon deposit occurring in the inlet valve port. This 'O' ring is the same type as that made standard on the exhaust stem.

| | | |
|---|---|---|
| **Fitted to** | Loco D851 | A end engine N°. 449 from 20/08/63 at Laira until 26/09/65 at Laira. |
| | Loco D.6305 | Engine N°. 334 from 30/08/63 |
| | Loco D.6309 | Engine N°. 285 from 26/09/63 at Laira |
| | Loco D.6334 | Engine N°. 261 from 02/09/63 at Laira |

**Results** During March 1965 engine N°. 285, fitted to loco D.6309, with approx. 4,000 hours service was returned to Swindon Works for an overhaul and an examination was made. However, no conclusive results could be obtained due to the bad state of the engine. A report was submitted to this effect, and during its overhaul engine N°. 285 was reverted to standard.

With regard to the other engines these were allowed to continue in service until their Works overhauls when the following was noted -

Engine N°. 261 (9,745 hours); The 'O' ring seals had hardened and the carbon build up at the inlet ports and valves was no improvement on the standard after a comparable period of service.

Engine N°. 334 (8,000 hours); Two cylinder heads were removed at 7,004 hours and their inlet ports and valves were heavily carbonised and the 'O' ring seals had hardened. When the remaining heads were removed at engine overhaul, the experiment was over-looked and no record of its condition was made.

Engine N°. 449 (6,450 hours); The experiment was over-looked and no record of its condition was made.

The experiment was therefore inconclusive but was not considered to be worthy of further trial, and was closed on 01/02/67.

**W/SW/L/258** **M.A.N. engine fitted with metallic exhaust bellows**

**Nature** To overcome trouble experienced with the exhaust systems of M.A.N. engines, fit engine N°. 297, for a D833 class locomotive, with a modified exhaust arrangement incorporating metallic bellows in the exhaust elbows generally in accordance with Swindon Locomotive Works Jig and Tool section Drawings as follows :-

JTS. 2243A - Arrangement of proposed alteration to exhaust bellows.
JTS. 2244 - Details of exhaust elbows.

| | |
|---|---|
| **Notes** | This experiment to be reported on at each engine change to another locomotive, or in the event of a failure. |
| **Fitted to** | Loco D854 A engine N°. 297 from 04/04/64 at Laira until 16/10/64 |

**Results** Engine N°. 297 was originally fitted with this experiment as W/SW/L/221 in March 1963 and was installed in loco D857 B from 14/06/63 until January 1964 when it was removed at Laira due to overheating and excessive oil consumption. On 16/01/64 engine N°. 297 was returned to the Swindon 'BD' workshop where the bellows were found to be in poor condition (report by Inspector Raven, 14/02/64). The bellows were repaired and a decision to follow them under standard procedure was made.

On 10/08/64, at 774 hours service, the ring joint between the manifold and the elbow of N^os^. 7-12 bank, needed renewing, and on 15/09/64, at 1,154 hours service, it was noticed that the covers over the bellows were loose and some set bolts had sheared. This was rectified, but on 16/10/64, at 1,570 hours service, investigation showed that N^os^. 1-6 bank bellows to be fractured. The experimental apparatus was removed for return to Swindon and the standard exhaust system was re-fitted to engine N°. 297.

Examination of the apparatus was made, and it was considered that nothing could be gained by keeping the experiment open, in view of the institution of experiment W/SW/L/275 Twin exhaust system.

The experiment was therefore closed on 25/11/64 as considered unsuccessful.

**W/SW/L/259 M.A.N. engine fitted with pistons having anodised ring grooves**

**Nature** In an attempt to reduce excessive piston top ring groove wear which is occurring on M.A.N. engines, one overhauled engine, preferably with new liners, for a D833 Class Locomotive to be fitted with a new set of S.132 alloy pistons having anodised crown and ring grooves. The piston assemblies will be as Voith offer Reference G.336/A, and the two spare assemblies will be retained for replacement purposes.

**Fitted to** Loco D852 B end engine N°. 448 from 28/07/65 until 01/67 at Laira.

**Results** The engine remained in service without relevant failure until January 1967, when it entered Swindon Works for overhaul after 5,575 hours.

Thorough examination revealed that in comparison with the standard piston and ring arrangement, there was no improvement in the rate of wear at the top groove. It was noted that the majority of wear had taken place at the bottom land of the groove, where on the standard piston wear is normally found on the top land. When measuring the thickness of the top ring the rate of wear had increased compared with the standard arrangement

The experiment was therefore closed, considered as unsuccessful, on 16/03/67.

**W/SW/L/260 M.A.N. engine fitted with unbonded piston inserts**

**Nature** In an attempt to reduce the excessive piston top ring groove wear which is occurring on M.A.N. engines, fit one overhauled engine, preferably with new liners, for a D833 Class Locomotive to be fitted with a new set of S.132 alloy pistons having unbonded iron top ring carrier inserts. The piston assemblies will be as Voith Offer Reference G.336/B and two spare assemblies will be retained for replacement purposes.

**Fitted to** Class 43

**Results** At the time of the initiation, an order was placed for the piston assemblies on Messrs. Voith but they were unable to supply. However, during the time that the order was outstanding research into piston troubles indicated that pistons having bonded inserts would be favourable to pistons having unbonded inserts and consequently agreement was reached not to proceed with the experiment.

The experiment was therefore closed on 22/07/66.

**W/SW/L/265 Exhaust elbow and roof cover fitted with a flexible connection**

**Nature** In order to prevent exhaust fumes circulating in engine room and cab, and also to reduce the incidence of fractures to turbo blower exhaust outlet flange studs, fit a flexible connection between the turbo blower exhaust elbow and roof cover of both ends of three D833 Class locomotives in accordance with Drawing SK/828.

Modification N°. 601 Extended M.A.N. engine exhaust uptake for D833 class which is related to the same problem, is now formally cancelled.

| **Fitted to** | | |
|---|---|---|
| | Loco D837 | A and B end engine N^os^. 470 and 158. from 13/10/64 until experiment closed. |
| | Loco D849 | A and B end engine N^os^. 447 and 309. from 18/11/64 until experiment closed. |
| | Loco D860 | A and B end engine N^os^. from 24/12/64 |

**Results** On 30/10/64, after 150 hours service, the bellows on B ends engine N°. 158 became detached from the roof exhaust pipe and were re-fitted. The A end was reported as satisfactory but a recommendation was made that a flange or bead should be added to the end of the pipe on D837.

Loco D849 was examined during its works trial run and again during November 1964 and on 17/12/64, and the equipment was found to have been fitted satisfactorily. On 17/12/64 loco D837 was also examined and whilst the A end was found to be in good order the clips were not fitted correctly at the B end. On 01/01/65 these clips were still not fitted correctly but this was rectified by 11/01/65 (560 hours) and examination on that day, and later that month in traffic, showed the bellows to be satisfactory.

Examination of the bellows on D860 on 08/01/65, and D849 on 10/01/65 (852 hours) showed them to be in good order.

The bellows on D837 and D849 were found satisfactory after 945 and 881 hours respectively.

On 12/03/65 the bellows on D849 had completed approx. 1000 hours service and those on the B end engine were replaced with new bellows. The removed bellows were thoroughly examined and passed as being in good condition, and were returned to stores for further use. Mod. N°. M.B.414/59 was authorised to cover the fitting of the remaining D833 Class locomotives, but the experiment would be kept open to follow the three locomotives originally fitted.

The bellows continued to be reported in satisfactory condition and it was agreed that the experiment should be concluded.

The experiment was therefore closed on 20/05/65 and considered as successful.

**W/SW/L/268 M.A.N. engines fitted with clips on the exhaust pipes**

**Nature** On ten M.A.N. 12V18/21 engines for D833 Class Locomotives, fit clips attached to three of the six bolts in each expansion sleeve flange at both ends of the exhaust elbows. The clips are to extend to the edge of the sleeve to prevent the end piston ring in the expansion joint protruding beyond the edge of the sleeve, thus allowing the splitters joints to part.

| **Fitted to** | | |
|---|---|---|
| | Loco D843 | A end engine N°. 307 from 16/11/64 |
| | Loco D849 | B end engine N°. 309 from 18/11/64 until 25/01/67 at Laira. |
| | Loco D860 | B end engine N°. 220 from 16/09/64 |
| | Loco D863 | A end engine N°. 361 from 03/09/64 at Laira until 14/07/65. |

**Results** During the fitting and trial runs of these first engines it became apparent that the clips should afford an improvement, and Modification Order N°. 3903 that they should be made standard was submitted and approved.

The experiment was therefore closed, as made standard, on 20/11/64.

**W/SW/L/270 M.A.N. engine fitted with lubricating pipes to the crank case**

**Nature** On ten M.A.N. engines, eliminate the loss of oil pressure at the seal of the lubricating oil pump delivery pipe passing through the sump and improve the accessibility of the joint connections for both this pipe and the priming pump suction pipe, by passing both pipes through the crank case in accordance with Drawings SL/SW/3667 and SL/SW/3668.

Eight of the engines should be fitted into four D833 class locomotives, the connecting pipe work to be to Drawing SK/836, and the remaining two engines should be for D.6306 class locomotives, the connecting pipe work to be to Drawing SL/SW/3664.

| **Fitted to** | | |
|---|---|---|
| | Loco D843 | B end engine N°. 285 from 07/10/66 |
| | Loco D846 | B end engine N°. 386 from 26/04/67 |
| | Loco D852 | A end engine N°. 264 from 16/01/68 at Laira |
| | Loco D857 | B end engine N°. 390 from 21/08/67 at Laira until 13/10/67 at Laira |
| | Loco D857 | B end engine N°. 344 from 13/10/67 at Laira until 25/06/69. |
| | Loco D.6314 | Engine N°. 307 from 16/01/67 at Laira until 05/67 at Laira. |
| | Loco D.6318 | Engine N°. 141 from 14/04/67 |

**Results** Work on the remaining engines to complete the experimental order was cancelled as it became apparent that, due to the proposed limited life of these engines, benefits to be gained from the alteration could not be economically justified.

The engines which had been fitted however were satisfactory as far as could be assessed over the comparatively short period in which they were in service.

The experiment was therefore closed on 20/05/68.

**W/SW/L/275 Twin exhaust systems**

**Nature** Fit 6 M.A.N. L12V18/215 engines with twin exhaust systems for installation in three D833 Class Locomotives in accordance with the following Drawings :-

| | |
|---|---|
| SL/SW/3687 | Arrangement of twin exhaust. |
| SL/SW/3688 | Arrangement of twin exhaust Manifold to Turbocharger. |
| SL/SW/3689 | Details of twin exhaust Manifold to Turbocharger. |
| SL/SW/3690 | Arrangement of lagging for twin exhaust. |

| | | |
|---|---|---|
| **Fitted to** | Loco D842 | A end engine N°. 385 from 19/11/65 at Laira until 19/11/67 at Laira. |
| **Subsequently** | Loco D851 | A end engine N°. 240 from 07/05/68 until 04/69 at Old Oak Common. |
| | Loco D851 | B end engine N°. 478 from 07/05/68 until 08/69 at Old Oak Common. |

**Results** No information is available regarding this experiment.

**W/SW/L/279** **Wellman Biddy cardan shafts**

**Nature**

**Fitted to** Loco D822 A end transmission to dynostarter from 08/09/65 until 24/01/68.

**Results** No information is available regarding this experiment and the locomotives involved.

**W/SW/L/280** **Voith LT.306r transmission with re-designed side output shaft**

**Nature** Five new Voith LT.306r transmissions ordered as spares from Messrs. Voith Engineering L$^{td}$., Glasgow, and incorporating all agreed modifications to date plus a new design side output shaft, which should eliminate vibration troubles coupled with gear tooth wear, to be carefully watched and controlled in traffic in order to determine their reliability.

Four of the transmissions should be fitted to two D833 class locomotives, both ends of one locomotive being fitted at the same time, and the remaining transmission to be fitted into a D.6306 class locomotive.

| | | |
|---|---|---|
| **Fitted to** | Loco D839 | A end transmission N°. 16880 from 24/02/66 |
| | Loco D839 | B end transmission N°. 16877 from 17/01/66 |
| | Loco D861 | B end transmission N°. 16876 from 25/05/66 at Laira until 18/04/70 at Laira. |

**Results** Within a month of fitting, 175 hours service, transmission N°. 16876, fitted to loco D861 B end, was damaged by a dynostarter cardan shaft fracturing and distorting its connecting flange. To rectify the damage partial stripping of the transmission was necessary, and several bearings in the rotor assembly were renewed for corrosion. Because of the damage the primary shaft was also renewed. Subsequently the transmission was satisfactory in further service.

Of the other four transmissions only one required special attention. That was transmission N°. 16878 which, after 3,275 hours service, had metal particles in the filters. Examination revealed that the selector ring had broken into two and that the clutch coupling was slightly worn on the forward side. In the governor two bearings, the control piston, balance weights and levers were all in need of attention. After a total of 5,380 hours service the transmission again had a broken selector ring.

The experiment was closed, as inconclusive, on 29/05/68.

**W/SW/L/281** **M.A.N. engine with bonded inserts of pistons**

**Nature** In an attempt to reduce the excessive piston top ring groove wear which is occurring on M.A.N. engines, fit five overhauled engines having new liners with S.132 alloy pistons with bonded iron top ring carrier inserts. The piston assemblies will be as Voith Offer Reference G630/A and two spare assemblies will be retained for replacement purposes.

The five engines should be fitted into D833 class locomotives.

| | | |
|---|---|---|
| **Fitted to** | Loco D841 | B end engine N°. 394 from 21/06/66 at Laira until 16/04/67 at Laira. |
| | Loco D843 | B end engine N°. 285 from 07/10/66 |
| | Loco D850 | B end engine N°. 343 from 21/07/66 at Laira until 28/06/67 at Laira. |
| | Loco D860 | B end engine N°. 373 from 28/07/66 |
| | Loco D.6341 | Engine N°. 480 from 28/09/66 |

**Results** After 2,600 hours in service engine N°. 394 failed due to high oil consumption and heavy crank case breathing. In stripping, the bonded inserts in the pistons were found to have completely failed, all pistons being affected either by the bonding failing or by the inserts and/or the pistons developing fractures.

At the same time engine N°. 373 in loco D860 was also suspect and this, and the other three engines fitted with the experiment were withdrawn from service. Examination of the pistons in all of the engines revealed the same pattern of failure in varying degrees on that reported for engine N°. 394.

In consequence the engines were converted to standard, and samples of the pistons were returned to Messrs. Voith and in turn Messrs. Specialloid for their analysis.

The experiment was therefore closed, considered as unsuccessful, on 30/11/67.

**W/SW/L/282** **Additional oil thrower ring fitted to M.A.N. engine**

**Nature** To six M.A.N. engines which, during overhaul, have had their crankshaft white metal oil seals machined in situ in accordance with the latest Swindon Works practice, fit an additional oil thrower ring to the crankshaft as detailed on M.A.N. Drawings N$^{os}$. 1D15693 and 4D21010. The six engines should be fitted into D833 Class locomotives.

| | | |
|---|---|---|
| **Fitted to** | Loco D837 | A end engine N°. 265 from 11/01/66 at Laira until 10/08/67 at Laira. |
| | Loco D846 | A end engine N°. 474 from 06/65 |
| | Loco D858 | A end engine N°. 286 from 04/06/65 at Laira until 21/07/65. |
| | Loco D859 | B end engine N°. 280 from 22/06/65 at Laira until 04/67. |
| | Loco D864 | B end engine N°. 393 from 06/65 until 09/67 |
| | Loco D865 | A end engine N°. 247 from 28/06/65 |
| **Subsequently** | Loco D857 | B end engine N°. 286 from 22/09/65 until 19/08/67 at Laira. |
| | Loco D848 | A end engine N°. 247 from 19/10/65 at Laira until 11/12/67 at Old Oak |

**Results** Due to minor defects, in no way associated with the experiment, engine N$^{os}$. 286 and 247 were removed from their locomotives within two months of fitting and re-entered service in locos D857 B end from 22/09/65 and D848 A end from 19/10/65.

Throughout 1966 similar instances of engine changes in locos occurred but no conclusive results of the experiment were possible.

As the engines concerned became due for overhauls examination of the additional oil thrower rings showed them to remain in good condition. Excessive oil leakage was not apparent but it was not possible to establish a method of accurately recording quantities of lubricating oil used by the engines. No positive results were there obtained, but a gradual improvement in Works fitting techniques for the standard seal arrangement had reduced the seriousness of the problem.

The experiment was therefore closed, considered as unsuccessful, on 01/03/68.

**W/SW/L/288** **MD 650 engine fitted with roughened chrome liners**

**Nature** Fit Bristol Siddeley Maybach MD 650 engine N°. BSM 159, having a crank case which is in good condition, with a set of roughened chrome liners. The liners have already had 5,500 hours service and remain in good condition. At future shops overhauls, examination of the liners and crank case should be made with a view of detecting cavitations caused by erosion.

**Fitted to** Loco D805 A end engine N°. BSM 159 from 15/12/64 at Laira until 26/07/65 at Laira.

**Results** During servicing of the engine prior to the initiation of the experiment it was discovered that one of the liners, that of N°. 1 cylinder, was faulty and it was replaced with an Alfin dipped liner. Cylinders N$^{os}$. 2-12 retained their roughened chrome liners.

Late in July 1965 the engine was removed from the Loco. for return to Swindon with suspected cylinder heads and liners leaking. Examination showed the N°. 1 cylinder Alfin dipped liner needed replacing and this was done with a semi-roughened chrome liner.

The engine then continued in service for a further 3,118 hours before receiving a major overhaul at which time a thorough examination of the liners was made. The results showed that they were satisfactory but there was no improvement over the Alfin dipped liners so they would not be adopted.

The experiment was therefore closed on 30/11/66.

**W/SW/L/290** **Mechanical forward / reverse mechanism fitted to Voith transmission**

**Nature** During repair of ten LT306r transmissions for installation in both ends of five D833 Class locomotives during normal transmission change fit mechanical forward / reverse mechanism, Voith DRWG. Z00455, in conjunction with Becker Control switch 2015 A.

**Fitted to** Loco D.6333 Transmission N°. H300/96 from 21/07/67 until 07/68 at Laira.

**Results** No information is available regarding this experiment.

**W/SW/L/291** **Transmission LT.306r fitted with 'Becker' control switch**

**Nature** Fit 'Becker' Control Switches 2015A, suitable to contend with Auto-Fill settings, supplied by Messrs. Voith Engineering L$^{td}$., Glasgow, under their reference 30.510, in place of Sharps Switches to ten LT.306r transmissions with the existing type of forward / reverse mechanism on locomotives of either or both D833 and D.6306 class.

| | | |
|---|---|---|
| **Fitted to** | Loco D833 | A end transmission N°. H230/65 from 18/11/65 until 01/67 at Laira. |
| | Loco D833 | B end transmission N°. H220/52 from 18/11/65 |
| | Loco D839 | A end transmission N°. 16880 from 24/02/66 until 06/68 at Laira. |
| | Loco D839 | B end transmission N°. 16877 from 24/02/66 until 01/70 at Laira. |
| | Loco D848 | A end transmission N°. H310/101 from 16/11/65 at Laira until 11/12/67 at Old Oak. |
| | Loco D848 | B end transmission N°. 10848 from 16/11/65 at Laira until 06/67 at Laira. |
| | Loco D862 | A end transmission N°. H210/41 from 26/11/65 until 08/67 at Laira. |
| | Loco D862 | B end transmission N°. 10985 from 26/11/65 |
| | Loco D865 | A end transmission N°. H210/38 from 11/11/65 until 04/66 at Laira. |
| | Loco D865 | B end transmission N°. 9194 from 11/11/65 until 09/68 at Laira. |

**Results** Initial reports submitted on the transmissions indicated that the 'Becker' switches were very satisfactory in service whereas difficulties continued to be experienced with the Sharps switches.

However, after the experiment had been proceeded with for only a short while replacement parts for Sharps switches became unobtainable from the supplier and the adoption of an alternative switch became a priority. Accordingly, agreement was reached to make 'Becker' switches standard.

The experiment was therefore closed on 25/08/66.

**W/SW/L/327 Engine exhaust uptake with an adjustable flange**

**Nature** In order to provide for correct alignment of the exhaust stack with the engine exhaust elbow on D833 Class Locomotives, and thereby ensure that the Walker's Twilstele Bellows are correctly positioned on assembly and re-assembly, convert both exhaust stacks of one locomotive so that they each comprise of two sections, being bolted together through flanges having slotted holes.

**Fitted to** Loco D855 from 13/05/66 until closed.

**Results** Inspection of the exhaust stacks during the Swindon Works trial run showed there to be a reasonable amount of adjustment which would be enough to prevent internal chaffing of the bellows by the baffle sleeve.

Reports from depots were not forthcoming but the experiment was kept under observation by Swindon Drawing Office Staff and its adoption proved to be desirable. Mod. M.B.414/81 (Alteration to provide adjustment to exhaust stack) was authorised for the fitting of the remaining D833 class locomotives.

The experiment was therefore closed on 21/12/66.

**W/SW/L/329 MD 650 engine fitted with a metal water pump coupling**

**Nature** Fit new type water pump flexible metal couplings to 6 over-hauled MD 650 B.S.E./Maybach engines to overcome hardening and premature failures of existing rubber type couplings.

**Fitted to** Loco D808 A end engine N°. 112166 from 07/02/66

**Results** After 100 hours in service, the water pump coupling failed due to the flexible metal section fracturing and in consequence the fitting of the five remaining couplings was suspended. Following an examination of the failed coupling by Messrs. B.S.E., it was returned to the manufacturer for their comment and meanwhile the experiment was superseded by Experiment W/SW/L/352 MD 650 engine 'Goetze' rubber water pump coupling.

The experiment was therefore closed on 07/10/66.

**W/SW/L/330 M.A.N. engine fitted with copper coated cylinder head joints**

**Nature** Fit 13 overhauled M.A.N. engines with liners having 3 grooves each 0.2mm deep on the top face, and 1.5mm thick copper coated ferrous cylinder head joints, to prevent cylinder heads blowing.

**Fitted to**

| | |
|---|---|
| Loco D839 | A end engine N°. 336 from 13/03/67 |
| Loco D842 | B end engine N°. 344 from 03/12/66 at Laira until 05/02/67 at Laira. |
| Loco D844 | B end engine N°. 469 from 11/11/66 at Laira |
| Loco D846 | A end engine N°. 306 from 26/04/67 |
| Loco D846 | B end engine N°. 386 from 26/04/67 |
| Loco D847 | A end engine N°. 381 from 24/02/67 until 19/02/69 at Laira. |
| Loco D847 | B end engine N°. 223 from 24/02/67 until 30/03/68 at Old Oak Common. |
| Loco D853 | A end engine N°. 220 from 29/10/66 at Laira until 1968 |
| Loco D855 | B end engine N°. 240 from 16/03/67 at Laira until 30/01/68 at Old Oak |
| Loco D861 | A end engine N°. 146 from 23/09/66 until 11/67 at Laira. |
| Loco D861 | B end engine N°. 449 from 10/02/67 at Laira until 01/68 at Laira. |
| Loco D863 | A end engine N°. 341 from 22/02/67 at Laira until 14/07/65. |
| Loco D865 | A end engine N°. 261 from 15/01/67 |

**Results** Following success at B.I.C.E.R.I. with an engine having copper coated ferrous joints but without grooves in the liner top faces, it was agreed that the last six engines fitted under the experiment should also not have the grooves machined. These engines were N$^{os}$. 223 (D847 B end); 306 (D846 A end); 336 (D839 A end); 341 (D863 A end); 381 (D847 A end) and 449 (D861 B end).

After 450 hours service engine N°. 344 was in Swindon Works for attention and the joints were noted to be in good condition.

Experience with the rings in service over the first 12 months proved that in themselves they were satisfactory, but unfortunate cases of fractures did occur. Investigations at the time of such failures showed that the use of an older type of air box joint had started the troubles by not allowing the cylinder heads to be pulled down correctly. In consequences gas blows resulted which in turn caused a fracture to the ring at the point of the blow.

This type of failure occurred to seven rings, six of these being on engines without the grooves in the liner top face, and one being to an engine with grooves. One case also occurred of a ring fractured and a metallurgical examination indicated that the fracture occurred at a point where the ring had been filed. This was against workshop practise for this type of ring.

Experience gained from the experiment together with that from B.I.C.E.R.I. showed that with normal care in fitting and with the use of a softer silicone rubber air box joint the copper coated ferrous joint should be satisfactory and its adoption as standard was very desirable. The cost of machining grooves in the liner top face could not however be justified and therefore the rings should be fitted against a plain face.

The experiment was therefore closed on 17/04/68.

**W/SW/L/331 Powdered valve seats fitted to M.A.N. engines**

**Nature** Fit six cylinder heads having powder welded cylinder head valve seats to one bank of an overhauled M.A.N., to determine efficiency of reclamation of worn seats by powder welding as carried out by Messrs. Deloro Stellie.

**Fitted to** Loco D840 B engine N°. 397 1-6 bank cylinder heads. from 20/10/66 until 05/04/68 at Old Oak Common.

**Note** Cylinder head N$^{os}$. fitted were 255, 2260, 635, 1587, 752 and 415, previously fitted to engine N°. 141 (D6327).

**Results** No information is available regarding this experiment and the locomotives involved.

**W/SW/L/333 M.A.N. engine fitted with 'Wellworthy' piston rings**

**Nature** Fit three overhauled M.A.N. engines with one set of special Piston rings supplied by Messrs. Wellworthy.

**Fitted to**

| | |
|---|---|
| Loco D847 | A end engine N°. 381 From 24/02/67 until 02/69 at Laira. |
| Loco D847 | B end engine N°. 223 From 24/02/67 until 03/68 at Old Oak Common. |
| Loco D865 | A end engine N°. 261 From 15/01/67 at Laira until 12/68 at Laira. |

**Results** At the time of fitting the question of piston rings on M.A.N. engines was receiving considerable attention because of the troubles caused by relatively excessive piston ring and liner wear due to the effect of high temperatures on the standard rings.

In consequence this was not the only experiment to be initiated on the subject, and the successful results since obtained from Experiment W/SW/L/358, Messrs. Specialloid D.T.D. 485 rings, have indicated that those rings are most likely to meet with the desired requirements, and there is now little to be gained from pursuing any other trials.

The experiment was therefore closed on 24/04/68.

**W/SW/L/334 Turbo blower fitted with loose blade nozzle rings**

**Nature** Fit seven overhauled turbo blowers with loose blade nozzle rings to one MD 650, four MD 655 and one MD 870 engines, to test the durability of loose nozzle blades which can be replaced if damaged.

**Fitted to** Loco D823 A end turbo blower N°. B.S. 448 from 30/08/66

**Results** The turbo blower, being an interchangeable component between engines, records of service were difficult to maintain and an examination of the loose blade rings could only be conducted during stripping, reports were restricted to those submitted by Swindon Works at turbo blower overhaul.

These reports, whilst not entirely conclusive, indicated that the loose blade rings were satisfactory.

However, concurrent with the experiment the introduction of fixed blade rings of a more equal thickness throughout the material, resulted in a general improvement to life and performance and there appeared to be little need for further change.

The experiment was therefore closed, considered as inconclusive, on 24/04/68.

**W/SW/L/338 Crankcase breather re-routed to cooler group compartment**

**Nature** On 10 overhauled Bristol Siddeley Maybach MD 650 engines remove the existing crank case breather pipes to the turbo blower and, with new pipes and hoses, re-route the crank case breathers to the cooler groups.

The vapour from the crank case will thus be prevented from causing excess oil to collect in the turbo blowers and any effects on valve seat wear may also be checked.

**Fitted to**

| | |
|---|---|
| Loco D808 | from 12/67 |
| Loco D821 | B end turbo blower N°. 465 from 11/01/68 until 03/10/68 at Newton Abbot. |

**Results** No information is available regarding this experiment.

**W/SW/L/352 MD 650 engine 'Goetze' rubber water pump coupling**

**Nature** Fit one overhauled MD 650 B.S.E. / Maybach engine with a new type 'Goetze' water pump rubber coupling and covers to overcome hardening and premature failures of existing type couplings.

**Fitted to** Loco D826 — A engine N$^{o}$. 112288 from 04/08/66 until 08/04/68 at Laira.
**Subsequently** Loco D801 — B engine N$^{o}$. 112594 from 24/11/67 at Laira until loco withdrawn.
Loco D804 — A engine N$^{o}$. 112279 until 09/69 at Laira.
Loco D809 — B engine N$^{o}$. 112240 from 30/11/67 at Laira until 01/11/69 at Laira.
Loco D812 — A engine N$^{o}$. 112271 from 11/11/67 at Laira until 26/08/69 at Laira.
Loco D815 — B engine N$^{o}$. 112268 from 29/01/68 until 03/08/68 at Laira.
Loco D821 — B engine N$^{o}$. 112267 from 11/01/68 until 06/03/70 at Laira.
Loco D822 — A engine N$^{o}$. BSM 110 from 29/11/67 at Laira until 15/06/70 at Laira.
Loco D869 — B engine N$^{o}$. 112166 from 12/02/68 at Laira

**Results** Following one month's satisfactory service with engine N$^{o}$. 112288, fitted to D826 A, the continuing high failure rate of the standard couplings enforced the experiment to cover a further ten engines in ten locomotives. Promising results obtained, while not over a long period, influenced the decision to adopt the 'Goetze' coupling in place of the unreliable standard coupling as modification Ref. N$^{o}$. MB. 417/20.

The reasons for removal of the engines from the locomotives was as follows :-

Loco D801 Remained with locomotive until withdrawn.
Loco D804 Routine overhaul.
Loco D809 Venting coolant.
Loco D812 N$^{os}$. 1 and 7 bottom registers eroded.
Loco D815 N$^{o}$. 11 cylinder liner fractured.
Loco D821 Blowing oil.
Loco D822 Routine overhaul.
Loco D826 Loosing coolant.
Loco D869 Not known

No information is available on engine N$^{os.}$ 112287 and 112595.

**W/SW/L/353** **M.A.N. engine fitted with 'Walker' rocker cover joints**

**Nature** Fit $^{1}/_{8}$ thick Walker's 'Nebar' joints in place of these existing $^{1}/_{16}$ thick joints under all rocker covers of eight overhauled N.B.L. L12V18/21s engines, to prevent oil leakage past the joints.

**Fitted to** Loco D847 — A end engine N$^{o}$. 381 From 24/02/67 until 02/69 at Laira
Loco D847 — B end engine N$^{o}$. 223 From 24/02/67 until 03/68 at Old Oak Common
Loco D849 — B end engine N$^{o}$. 476 From 30/01/67 at Laira until 02/68 at Old Oak Common
Loco D853 — B end engine N$^{o}$. 495 From 16/12/66 at Laira until 1968
Loco D865 — A end engine N$^{o}$. 261 From 15/01/67 at Laira until 12/68 at Laira.

**Results** After only a short while in service cases began to arise where joints were damage by over-tightening of the rocker covers. The covers tended to guillotine the joints into strips and oil seepage occurred where this had taken place. The first joint to fail in this way was on engine N$^{o.}$ 476 (D849 B end) after 125 hours service, but this was followed by a similar failure on engine N$^{o}$. 223 (D847 B end) after 140 hours service.

On engine N$^{o}$ 495 (D853 B end) after 800 hours service all of the joints were damaged during removal of the rocker covers owing to the joints sticking partly to the rocker covers and partly to the cylinder heads. The engine was reverted to standard. This problem of the joints being damaged on removal of the rocker covers, together with the guillotining action, also caused engine N$^{o}$. 307 (D6314) to be reverted to standard at an early date, and of the six remaining engines further cases arose where one or more joints on an engine required replacement at depots.

It was apparent that the $^{1}/_{8}$ thick 'Nebar' joints were no improvement on the existing standard joint and that further research into the question of what would be a suitable joint was required.

The experiment was therefore closed on 22/05/68.

**W/SW/L/354** **M.A.N engine fitted with 'Klinger' rocker cover joints**

**Nature** Fit $^{1}/_{8}$ thick Klingers Neoprene Bonded Cork joints in place of the existing $^{1}/_{16}$ thick joints under all rocker covers of eight overhauled N.B.L. L12V18/21s engines, to prevent oil leakage past the joints.

**Fitted to** Loco D842 — B end engine N$^{o}$. 344 from 03/12/66
Loco D844 — B end engine N$^{o}$. 469 from 11/11/66
Loco D846 — B end engine N$^{o}$. 386 from 26/04/67
Loco D853 — A end engine N$^{o}$. 220 from 29/10/66

**Results** Initial reports received indicated that the joints were satisfactory.

On 16/02/67, whilst removing rocker covers from engine N$^{o}$. 469 (D844 B end) at Newton Abbot, two joints were damaged beyond further use due to them sticking partly to the rocker cover and partly to the cylinder head. Replacement Klinger joints were supplied for fitting.

Of the Klinger joints that remained in service periodic examination showed that there was a tendency for the rockers covers to be pulled down sufficiently tight to guillotine the edges, but where this had happened there was no oil seepage past the joint at first. However, the clean edge of the joint having been lost the rate of deterioration increased so that sooner or later replacement became necessary.

It was apparent that further research into the question of what would be a suitable joint was required but meanwhile the $^{1}/_{8}$ thick Klinger joints had been as satisfactory as the standard.

The experiment was therefore closed on 22/05/68.

**W/SW/L/401** **M.A.N. engine fitted with stainless steel lined fuel injection pipes**

**Nature** To one overhauled M.A.N. L12V18/21 engine for a D833 Class Locomotive fit a set of fuel injection pipes having a stainless steel lining in place of the existing all steel pipes which are prone to failure due to cavitation erosion.

**Fitted to** Class 43

**Results** The special pipes were ordered on Messrs. Voith Engineering (Glasgow) L$^{td}$. but prior to delivery a change of circumstance affecting the future service life of the M.A.N. engines resulted in the order being cancelled.

## Modifications

The Modifications applied to the D800s and D833s are listed below:

| Mod. No. / details |
|---|
| 601 - Extended M.A.N. engine exhaust uptake for D833 class |
| 602 - Replacement of W.C. (locos fitted with Stones steam generators) |
| 603 - Serck pump bracket strengthened |
| 604 - Strengthened side plate doors and stops for Cooler Group compartment |
| 605 - Additional warning notices fitted |
| 606 - Dynostarter cardan shaft safety bow modified |
| 607 – No details |
| 608 - Improved cab window locking catch fitted |
| 609 - Primary and secondary filters replaced with one large filter for boiler filling system |
| 610 - Dynostarter support modified |
| 611 - Addition of governor motor chain guard |
| 612 - Re-arrangement of air inlet for Stones Vapor generator |
| 613 - 1 drain cocks fitted to fuel tanks |
| 614 - Replacement of W.C. (locos fitted with Spanner boilers) |
| 615 - Modified brake adjusters fitted to obviate fractures |
| 616 - 20 modified dynostarter cardan shaft (double Layrub with spline) fitted |
| 617 - Grease nipples changed on G W B cardan shafts to facilitate compressed air apparatus |
| 618 - Hand brake 'Off' indicator added |
| 619 - No details |
| 620 - Fan pump support bracket stiffened |
| 621 - Bogie side control linkage replaced with hydraulic shock absorbers |
| 622 - CANCELLED (replaced with Mods. 631 & 637). |
| 623 - Engine lubrication oil heat exchanger drain fitted |
| 624 - Transmission gearbox switch fitted with Nyloc nuts |
| 625 - CANCELLED (Mr. Ridgeways letter dated 02/12/64) |
| 626 - Securing of gong on fire bell |
| 627 - Improved retaining devices for brake block pins fitted |
| 628 - Revised method of locking retaining rings on cab door locks |
| 629 - Steam separators fitted to carriage warming slide valves |
| 630 - Removal of hot air cab heaters and fitting electric cab heaters |
| 631 - Hot air demisters replaced by Therglass |
| 632 - Tapped hole added in body spring pivot pin for extraction purposes |
| 633 - Loco pipe work altered to suit modified position of safety valve and separator blow down flanges (interchangability of Stones generators) |
| 634 - Alteration to underframe to allow fitting of Hardy-Spicer cardan shafts |
| 635 - No details |
| 636 - Transmission heat exchanger drain cock repositioned as a precaution against freezing |
| 637 - Hot air demisting replaced by Therglass |
| 638 - Replacement of vitromant urinal by fibreglass urinal |
| 639 - Replacement of W.C. by glass fibre urinal |
| 640 - Provision of guard over Cooler Group unit fan |
| 641 - Insulation of CO.2 fire bottle cabinet |
| 642 - Sight glasses fitted to hydrostatic tank |
| 643 - Modified governor motor chain guard (superseding Mod. 611) |
| 644 - Zwicky 'Full stop' bulk loading valve fitted |
| 645 - Deadman's isolating cock in cab repositioned |
| 646 - Side pieces fitted to top cab steps to prevent foot slipping off |
| 647 - Extra lifting points for jacking purposes |
| 648 - Improved draining of waste oil from M.A.N. engine 'vee' – Fire Prevention (with SW/3901) |
| 649 - Fuel pump repositioned |
| 650 - Provision of cock wrench and notice plate in fuel system |
| 651 - Provision of cock wrenches and chains in water supply system |
| 652 - Laycock-Knorr air suction strainer modified |
| 653 - Main CO.2 bottle piercing head tip angle altered to 300. |
| 654 - Mowbray sequencing valve blow down pipe discharge redirected |
| 655 - Perspex sun visors fitted in cabs |
| 656 - Additional doorstop fitted to drivers desks |
| 657 - Vent pipe added to Cooler Group compartment |
| 658 - Rubber hose in Cooler Group replaced with steel pipe |
| 659 - Crank case breather pipes moved to Cooler Group (D800-D832/66-D870) |
| 660 - Grab fitted between cooker and door in cab |
| 661 - Standardisation of markings on air double pressure gauges |
| 662 - Torque arm support assembly modified |
| 663 - Air filter fitted to crank case of Laycock-Knorr compressor |
| 664 - Provision of lubrication for thrust bearing |
| 665 - Bolt replacement of carriage warming flexible connections |
| 666 - No details |
| 667 - Vapor-watchman preheater pump welded to base plate |
| 668 - Interchangability of Laycock-Knorr compressors |
| 669 - Modification of engine speed setting circuits |
| 670 - No details |

| Mod. No. / details |
|---|
| M.B.414/1-6 No details |
| M.B.414/7 - Improved cab window locking catch fitted |
| M.B.414/8 -11 No details |
| M.B.414/12 - 1 drain cocks fitted to fuel tanks |
| M.B.414/13 -17 No details |
| M.B.414/18 - Securing of gong on fire bell |
| M.B.414/19 - Revised method of locking retaining rings on cab door locks |
| M.B.414/20 - No details |
| M.B.414/21 - Loco pipe work altered to suit modified position of safety valve and separator blow down flanges (interchangability of Stones generators) |
| M.B.414/22 – 33 No details |
| M.B.414/34 - Improved draining of waste oil from M.A.N. engine 'vee' (with SW/3901) |
| M.B.414/35 -40 No details |
| M.B.414/41 - Perspex sun visors fitted in cabs |
| M.B.414/42 – 46 No details |
| M.B.414/47 - Standardisation of markings on air double pressure gauges |
| M.B.414/48 – 51 No details |
| M.B.414/52 - Tapped hole added in body spring pivot pin for extraction purposes |
| M.B.414/53 - Alteration of Vacuum governor from E16 to E2 type |
| M.B.414/54 - Alteration of Vacuum relief valves and proportional valves |
| M.B.414/55 - 'Full stop' bulk loading valve and pilot valve seat redesigned |
| M.B.414/56 - Liquid water treatment for Stones steam generator |
| M.B.414/57 - Modified dial for existing coolant capacity gauge fitted |
| M.B.414/58 - Angled piercing head and tapered safety pin fitted to CO.2 bottle |
| M.B.414/59 - Modified arrangement of engine exhaust uptake fitted |
| M.B.414/60 - Modified arrangement of engine exhaust uptake fitted |
| M.B.414/61 - Alteration to steam pipe joints |
| M.B.414/62 - Modified bracket assembly for coolant capacity gauges fitted |
| M.B.414/63 - Installation of modified type vapor-watchman preheater |
| M.B.414/64 - Modified engine air intake (D803-D870) |
| M.B.414/65 - Modified engine air intake (D800-D802) |
| M.B.414/66 - New striking plate fitted for cab doors |
| M.B.414/67 - 21/2 instantaneous boiler water connection (D800-D802) |
| M.B.414/68 - Transmission trunion mounting |
| M.B.414/69 - Magnetic filler plug fitted |
| M.B.414/70 - Bonding of torque arm rubbers to inter. plate |
| M.B.414/71 – No details |
| M.B.414/72 - Multiple working jumper cables and sockets removed from buffer beam |
| M.B.414/73 - Alteration to carriage warming securing bolts |
| M.B.414/74 - Deck plate below dynostarter safety bow bracket strengthened |
| M.B.414/75 - Cab side access flaps fitted with hinges |
| M.B.414/76 - No details |
| M.B.414/77 - Amendment of existing lub. oil pipe work |
| M.B.414/78 - Turbo charger cleaned in situ |
| M.B.414/79 - Modified floor construction and covering |
| M.B.414/80 - Supplementary valve fitted to W.R. A.W.S. cab apparatus |
| M.B.414/81 - Alteration to provide adjustment to exhaust stack |
| M.B.414/82 - Mechanical stop for drivers speed control handle |
| M.B.414/83 - Existing grill boilers replaced with hot plate unit |
| M.B.414/84 - Track circuit shorting bonds repositioned |
| M.B.414/85 - No details |
| M.B.414/86 - Dual fitting of BR / WR A.W.S. |
| M.B.414/87 - Fire equipment master cylinder operation by wire rope |
| M.B.414/88 - Alteration of dynostarter mounting feet |
| M.B.414/89 - No details |
| M.B.414/90 - Provision of standard detonators case in cabs |
| M.B.414/91 - Additional sealing of cab floor fitted |
| M.B.414/92 - Improved cab ventilation fitted |
| M.B.414/93 - No details |
| M.B.414/94 - Securing of S.R. short circuiting bar and paddle (D803-D821) |
| M.B.414/95 - Fitting of data panels |
| M.B.414/96 - B.R. A.W.S. fitted with castle nuts |
| |
| C.M.33 - Fitting of A.W.S. (1968 programme) |
| |
| M.B.415/1 - Transmission gearbox switch fitted with Nyloc nuts |
| M.B.415/2 - Removal of hot air cab heaters and fitting electric cab heaters |
| M.B.415/3 - Hot air demisting replaced by Therglass (D803-D870) |
| M.B.415/4 - Hot air demisting replaced by Therglass (D800-D802) |
| M.B.415/5 - Auxiliaries repositioned to allow Ultrasonic testing |
| M.B.415/6 - Engine speed motor setting modified |
| M.B.415/7 - Conversion of engine start timing relay to engine start contactor relay |
| M.B.415/8 - Addition of excess temperature relay |
| M.B.415/9 - No details |
| M.B.415/10 - Re-routing conduit and cables to boiler control panel |
| M.B.415/11 - Fitting of K D G temperature switches and revised circuitry (to be carried out at depots) |